The Best Book of

Microsoft Word 5

RELATED TITLES

The First Book of WordPerfect® 5.1
Kate Barnes

The First Book of Quicken
Gordon McComb
(forthcoming)

The First Book of PC Tools® Deluxe
Gordon McComb

The First Book of Microsoft® Word 5
Brent D. Heslop and David Angell
(forthcoming)

The First Book of Lotus® 1-2-3® Release 2.2
Alan Simpson and Paul Lichtman

The First Book of Paradox® 3
Jonathan Kamin

The Best Book of: Lotus® 1-2-3®, Third Edition, Release 2.2
Alan Simpson

The Best Book of: dBASE II®/III®
Ken Knecht

The Best Book of: Microsoft® Works for the PC
Ruth Witkin

The Best Book of: Paradox 3
Celeste Robinson

The Best Book of: WordPerfect® 5.1, Second Edition
Vincent Alfieri,
Revised by Ralph Blodgett

The Best Book of: WordStar® (Features Release 5)
Vincent Alfieri

The Best Book of: DOS
Alan Simpson

The Waite Group's MS-DOS® Bible, Third Edition
Steven Simrin

The Waite Group's Using PC DOS™
The Waite Group

For the retailer nearest you, or to order directly from the publisher, call
800-257-5755. International orders telephone 609-461-6500.

The Best Book of

of

Microsoft

Word 5

Kate Barnes

HAYDEN BOOKS

A Division of Howard W. Sams & Company
11711 North College, Suite 141, Carmel, IN 46032 USA

International Standard Book Number: 0-672-48459-5
Library of Congress Catalog Card Number: 89-62990

Acquisitions Editor: *Richard Swadley*
Development Editor: *C. Herbert Feltner*
Manuscript Editor: *Online Press*
Production Editor: *Marj Hopper*
Production Coordinator: *Becky Imel*
Illustrator: *T. R. Emrick*
Indexer: *Ted Laux*
Production: *Jennifer Matthews, Dennis Sheehan,
Louise Shinault, Sally Copenhaver, Bill Hurley,
Wm. D. Basham, Don Clemons, Larry Lynch,
Mary Beth Wakefield, Jodi Jensen, and Lori Lyons*
Cover Art: *DGS&D Advertising, Inc.*
Cover Photography: *Cassell Productions, Inc.*

Printed in the United States of America

Trademarks

Overview

Contents

Preface

Good news for beginners . . . with the right guidance, you'll find Microsoft Word an easy word processor to learn. Even better news for beginners . . . Word has all the features you've come to expect from a sophisticated and powerful word processor. As your word-processing needs grow, Word will grow with you. And this book will be there to guide you as your knowledge and skill level increases.

Written in simple, straightforward language, *The Best Book of Microsoft Word 5* is for beginning users. Going beyond the manual that accompanies the Word program, *The Best Book of Microsoft Word 5* is rich in step-by-step instructions, examples, hands-on exercises, useful hints, and marginal notes describing tricks and traps.

The book is organized to explain new terms and concepts as you are likely to need them, giving you the tools to master the program. Early chapters cover the basic features you'll use most often, and later chapters describe the powerful features that set Word apart from other programs.

Features of the Book

Step-by-Step Instructions

The numbered, step-by-step instructions are designed to lead you keystroke by keystroke (or button press by button press) through each procedure. Within the instructions, the following conventions are used:

- Word command and field names appear exactly as they do on the command menus.

- An instruction such as:

  Select Transfer Load

  means that you can make the selection using either the keyboard or the mouse.

- If you are working from the keyboard, the keys you press to select a particular command always appear in bold captial letters; for example, **P**rint pre**V**iew and **F**ormat s**E**arch.

- Field names always appear in italics. The options you can select within a particular field appear in regular type with an initial capital letter, just as they do in the command menus. The capital letter is bold if you are being told to select that option.

- Key names appear as they do on a normal keyboard; for example, Enter, Ctrl, PgDn, F3. The arrow keys appear as Up Arrow, Down Arrow, Right Arrow, and Left Arrow. Keys to be pressed are bold; keys that are to be pressed simultaneously are separated by a hyphen; for example, **Alt-F1** and **Ctrl-Shift-Esc**.

Hints, Notes, and Cautions

Throughout the book your attention is drawn to useful tidbits of information that will make working with Word easier or more efficient. Short notes appear in the margin. Longer comments appear in the text but are easy to spot because they are set off with an icon:

 Hint

 Note

 Caution

When a comment appears in the middle of an explanation or a set of instructions, you might want to simply glance through it and then continue reading. The icon will guide you back to the comment at a later time.

Exercises

The discussion of each feature is accompanied by an exercise that walks you through the step-by-step instructions with a real example. The exercises in some chapters use documents created in previous chapters, so always be sure to save the files you create with the names suggested.

Acknowledgments

Thanks to Richard Swadley, Herb Feltner, and the other staff at Howard W. Sams & Company for turning ideas and manuscripts into useful books.

Introduction to Microsoft Word

Microsoft Word is one of the most popular word-processing programs for IBM Personal Computers and compatible computers. Word is a comfortable word processor for beginners. It features an easy-to-use menu system from which even the most inexperienced user can select desired functions. Simple word-processing tasks can be performed with minimum effort. For the more advanced user, Word offers the most sophisticated array of word-processing features available.

Word "grows with you." As you become more familiar with its features, you'll find that you will master, step by step, more and more complex word-processing tasks. Microsoft, the manufacturer of Word, is constantly upgrading Word's features to keep up with new technologies and to meet users' word-processing needs. For example, recent releases have included more graphics capabilities to take advantage of laser printers and provide "electronic-publishing" duties. Microsoft's commitment to Word means that the time you invest in learning to use Word will be well spent. The skills you learn now will serve you for years to come. And if you decide to upgrade your computer or printer, Word will be able to fully utilize the capabilities of your new equipment.

Microsoft Word and Your Personal Computer

Your personal-computer system is made up of hardware and software. *Hardware* refers to the components that you can see and touch (see Figure 1-1). *Software* refers to the programs you run, all of which are sets of instructions to the hardware. Word is a program—actually a whole group of interdependent programs—that allows you to use your computer hardware to perform word-processing tasks.

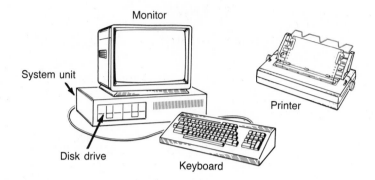

Figure 1-1. The hardware components of a personal computer

To run Word, you need a personal computer that meets certain minimum requirements. You need:

- An IBM Personal Computer (PC, XT, AT, or PS/2) or a computer that is compatible
- 384 kilobytes, or KB, of memory (that's 384,000 bytes)
- Two floppy-disk drives (either 3½-inch or 5¼-inch), or a hard-disk drive and one floppy-disk drive
- A monitor and video adapter
- A keyboard
- A mouse (optional)
- A printer (optional)
- Operating-system software (DOS or OS/2)
- The Word software
- Extra disks for storing the documents you will create (if you are using a system with two floppy-disk drives, you will need at least 10 blank disks; if you are using a hard-disk system, you will still need a few blank disks on which to store backup copies of your documents)

"Compatible" Computers

If you are using an IBM computer, Word's features will work exactly as described in this book. Many "IBM compatible" computers work just as well as those manufactured by IBM and typically cost less. Common compatible computers include Compaq, Zenith, Toshiba, and Sharp. Although hundreds of computer manufacturers claim their equipment is IBM compatible, the degree of compatibility varies somewhat. Therefore, if you are using a compatible computer and find that some of Word's functions don't work as described in this book, the degree of compatibility may be the culprit.

Memory

Your computer has two types of memory: ROM (Read-Only Memory) and RAM (Random-Access Memory). ROM is where basic information necessary for running the computer is stored. Ordinarily, you don't have to be concerned about ROM. You do, however, need to understand a bit about RAM.

RAM is located in the system unit and is where your documents are temporarily stored while you work. When you turn off your computer (or if the electrical supply is accidently interrupted), everything that is stored in RAM is lost. Because RAM is only active while the computer is turned on, it is important to always transfer, or save, your work to disk storage before you turn off your computer. You should also periodically save your documents while you are working on them.

Disk Drives

Your computer's disk drives "read" information from disks and "write" information on disks. You can use Word on a two-disk-drive system but not a one-disk-drive system. You must have two floppy-disk drives or one floppy-disk drive and one hard-disk drive.

Floppy-disk drives can be built to work with either 3½-inch or 5¼-inch disks. The Word program is available on both disk sizes, and when you buy Word, you need to know which size drives your computer has so that you can be sure to get the right version of the program.

Benefits of using a hard disk

A hard-disk system with one floppy-disk drive provides faster processing and more convenient storage than a two-floppy-disk system. If you have a hard disk, you can store Word programs and other files permanently in your computer. That way, you don't have to use disks to store your Word and document files for everyday use. The benefits to you are:

- Faster access to your work
- More space for documents
- Less time spent "disk swapping"

Hard-disk drives are getting less and less expensive. If you do not have a hard disk, you might want to consider upgrading your system by installing one.

Disks

The 3½-inch disks are sturdier than the 5¼-inch size. However, it is important to be careful when handling either type of disk. Here are the rules to follow:

- Don't touch the recording surface of the disk.
- Keep disks in their jackets to protect them from dust.
- Write on labels and then place them on the disk. If you must write on a label that is already on a disk, use a felt-tip pen.
- Don't bend disks.
- Don't leave disks in an environment of intense heat or cold. Keep them in places that are over 50 degrees and under 125 degrees Fahrenheit. A car is not a good storage location for a disk.
- Don't get disks wet.
- Don't place disks near magnetic fields (such as magnetic paper-clip holders or small motors).
- Pass disks through airport security rather than risk damage by an X-ray device.
- Keep disks away from fluorescent lights. At close range (1 foot or closer), these lights can damage disks.
- Carefully insert disks into the disk drive. Forcing a disk into a drive can cause damage to the drive, the disk, or both.

Monitors and Adapters

A computer monitor resembles a television screen. It is through this monitor that Word communicates with you and you with Word.

Your computer's central processing unit (CPU) contains a video adapter that translates the signals sent from your CPU to your monitor. Not all video adapters are the same. The most common distinction between adapters is whether the adapter creates a monochrome display (two shades) or handles several colors or graphics. Make sure you know which kind of video adapter you have. When you run the Word Setup utility (which we'll discuss in Chapter 2, "Starting Microsoft Word"), you will be asked to identify the type of adapter you have. A video-driver file, called SCREEN.VID, is then created to store the information Word needs to work with your adapter.

Popular video displays

Word works with all the most popular monitors and video adapters, including the following:

- Color/graphics adapter or Enhanced Graphics Adapter, and 80 column monochrome, color monitor, or Enhanced Color Display
- Hercules Graphics Card (GB101 or GB102) and IBM Personal Computer Display (monochrome—IBM only)
- Hercules Plus Card (GB112) or InColor Card (GB222) and Enhanced Color Display
- Printer adapter and 80-column monochrome monitor or mono-chrome display
- IBM Personal Computer or compatible with a built-in monitor
- Any IBM PS/2 graphics adapter and monitor
- IBM VGA adapter or compatible and PS/2 monitor or compatible
- IBM 8514/A graphics adapter and 8514 monitor
- HP Vectra standard adapter and monitor
- AT&T 6300 standard adapter and monitor; may include Display Enhancement Board (DEB)
- Genius Adapter and full-page monitor

This list is not comprehensive. If your monitor or adapter is not included, contact Microsoft Product Support to inquire about your particular brand.

The Keyboard

Though it is possible in science fiction movies to communicate with a computer by simply saying "Hello computer," the technology has not yet taken us that far. Instead, the keyboard is your primary way of communicating with Word. The keys on a typical IBM-compatible computer are shown in Figure 1-2.

Take the time to familiarize yourself with the keys on your key-board. The keys fall into three main groupings:

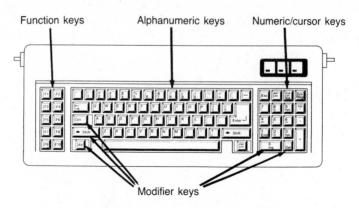

Figure 1-2. The keyboard for IBM-compatible computers

- **Alphanumeric keys:** These are the letter and number keys that are typically found on a typewriter. You use these keys to enter text in documents.

- **Modifier Keys:** The Alt, Control (Ctrl), Shift, Insert (Ins), and Delete (Del) keys are called modifier keys because you can use them in combination with other keys to perform certain functions. For example, in Word, pressing the Alt key and the H key at the same time brings up Help information. You use the Ins and Del keys to insert and delete text.

- **Numeric/cursor keys:** These are usually on the right side of the keyboard. On smaller lap-top computers, the numeric keys might be combined with some letter keys. You use the numeric/cursor keys to move your place marker or cursor (which is called the *highlight* in Word). When you press the key marked Num Lock, you can use the same keys to enter numbers. Pressing the Num Lock key again switches the function of the keys back to moving the highlight.

- **Function keys:** These are located across the top of the keyboard (or on the left side on some keyboards). They are usually numbered F1 through F10. You use them in Word to perform specific functions. For example, pressing the F4 key repeats your last editing action. If you type in the phrase *and so on* and then press F4, the phrase is automatically repeated, with this result:

and so on and so on

Word's keyboard template can speed up learning.

The Word package includes a template that you can lay on your keyboard for quick reference. This piece of plastic lists the actions possible with each key or key combination. A quick-reference summary of keyboard actions, similar to the information on the template, is included in Appendix A of this book. Templates and quick references can be a valuable aid in learning Word quickly and in refreshing your memory about how to perform various functions. For people familiar with another word processor, templates and quick references are valuable aids for finding out which keys to press in Word to perform common word-processing activities.

The Mouse

Microsoft Word is designed to work with a mouse. A mouse is a device used to point at text or make selections on the screen. Figure 1-3 and Figure 1-4 are illustrations of the top and bottom of a typical mouse.

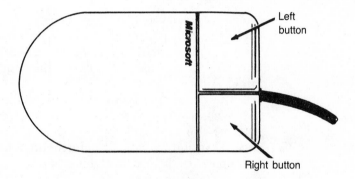

Figure 1-3. The mouse viewed from the top

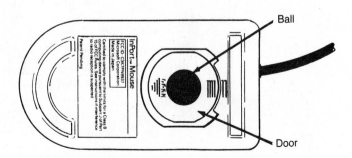

Figure 1-4. The mouse viewed from the bottom

The top of the mouse has a left and a right button. (Some brands have three buttons; the instructions in this book are for the common

Microsoft mouse design, which features two buttons.) For easy handling, place the mouse on your desk with the cord away from you. Use your hand to move the mouse and your index and middle fingers to press the buttons.

The bottom of the mouse has a rubber coated ball that rolls when you slide the mouse across your desk. This ball controls the movement of the highlight on the screen. When you slide the mouse on your desk, the ball rolls and the highlight on the screen follows right along. You don't need much desk space to have control of your screen. Roughly, a 5-inch or 6-inch square is adequate. If you do run out of space, just pick up the mouse and reposition it on your desk. The highlight stays in its current position until you put down the mouse and start sliding it again.

Mouse Actions

You've seen that moving the mouse across a desk moves the highlight that marks your place on the screen. The mouse highlight in Word is a light box the size of one character. In Word's special graphics mode (available with some computers), the mouse highlight may be an arrow.

The distinction between the highlight and the mouse highlight may be confusing at first, but you'll soon learn to distinguish between the two. The highlight that you move around the screen with the Arrow keys and the mouse highlight are two separate things and both can appear on the screen at the same time. (To perform some operations, you may need to use both the Arrow keys and the mouse.)

You use the mouse to perform three basic actions:

- **Pointing:** Pointing refers to sliding the mouse across your desk so that the highlight is positioned over, or pointing at, the desired element on the screen—for example, a word, a character, or a menu selection. Just pointing does not communicate anything to Word, however. You need to click one of the mouse buttons to tell Word what you want to do with the selection.

- **Clicking (and double clicking):** Clicking is a quick pressing and releasing of a button. In Word, you will click some selections to choose them. Clicking a single button twice is sometimes referred to as *double clicking*. In Word, as in many programs, clicking both buttons at the same time is often used to cancel a command.

- **Dragging:** Dragging refers to pointing at a place on the screen and then pressing and holding down a mouse button while you move the mouse across your desk. The highlight expands to follow the mouse's movement. Once the highlight is positioned as you want, you release the mouse button. For example, in Figure 1-5 the highlight was placed on the first character of a paragraph. Then, the right button was pressed and the highlight was dragged down the screen and to the right with the mouse. Starting where the button was pressed, the text was highlighted as the mouse was dragged. Figure 1-6 shows the result. Using Word, the highlighted text can now be manipulated (such as copied or deleted). Or, you could press the left button to remove the highlight.

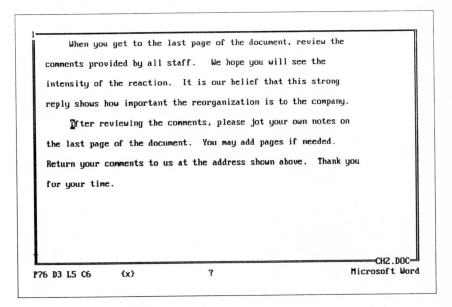

When you get to the last page of the document, review the comments provided by all staff. We hope you will see the intensity of the reaction. It is our belief that this strong reply shows how important the reorganization is to the company.

After reviewing the comments, please jot your own notes on the last page of the document. You may add pages if needed. Return your comments to us at the address shown above. Thank you for your time.

P76 D3 L5 C6   {x}   ?   CH2.DOC
                                                              Microsoft Word

Figure 1-5. The screen before dragging

Choosing and Using a Mouse

Some people prefer using the mouse rather than the keyboard. If you are very "keyboard literate," the mouse can seem slow and cumbersome at first. After all, you have to remove your hands from the keyboard to perform a task that is less familiar and less accurate than pressing a key. People who are slow on the keyboard like the mouse for its "point-and-select" simplicity. No alphanumeric keys to search out! Whatever your background, if you have a mouse, it is worthwhile spending some time experimenting with a mouse and Word. That way, you can experience Word's mouse capabilities and judge for yourself when it's best to use the keyboard and when it's best to use the mouse.

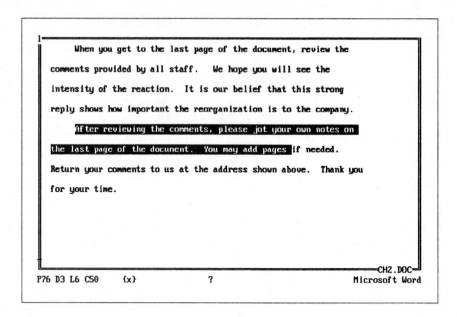

```
|
        When you get to the last page of the document, review the

  comments provided by all staff.   We hope you will see the

  intensity of the reaction.  It is our belief that this strong

  reply shows how important the reorganization is to the company.

        After reviewing the comments, please jot your own notes on

  the last page of the document.  You may add pages if needed.

  Return your comments to us at the address shown above.  Thank you

  for your time.




                                                      CH2.DOC
  P76 D3 L6 C50        {x}              ?            Microsoft Word
```

Figure 1-6. The screen after dragging

Talk to your computer dealer about the type of mouse that will work with both your computer and Microsoft Word. A mouse can be attached to either a serial port, a parallel port, or a bus interface. Follow the instructions that come with your mouse when installing the device. The instructions in this book assume that the mouse is already installed and describe how to use the mouse to perform specific Word functions.

How to control the sensitivity of your mouse

If you have a Microsoft mouse and you have installed the software that came with the device, you can control the sensitivity of the pointer on the screen to the mouse's movement on your desk. To adjust the sensitivity, you can press Ctrl-Alt to display the control panel shown in Figure 1-7. (If the control panel is not set up to be loaded each time you start your machine, you can enter *CPANEL* at the system prompt to display the control panel.) You can then press either mouse button to change the sensitivity of the mouse. (If you install the mouse software using Word's Setup utility, which we discuss in Chapter 2, "Starting Microsoft Word," the CPANEL command may not be available to you.)

Keep the desk surface where you use the mouse clean of dust and crumbs. If you have trouble moving the mouse, you may want to clean the ball. Make sure the cable between the mouse and your computer is disconnected. On most mice, you just open the door that holds in the ball and the ball drops out. Don't try and force it out or

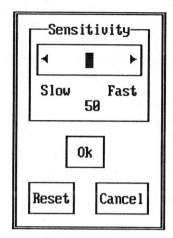

Figure 1-7. The mouse-sensitivity control panel

you can damage the housing. Once you have removed the ball, clean it with a soft cloth or sticky tape. Also wipe out the inside of the housing, using a cotton swab moistened with alcohol to loosen any dirt. Replace the ball without forcing it and then replace the door. Reconnect the cable, and you're ready to resume work.

Printers

The printer is the component of your computer on which you produce a paper copy of your work. Your printer may be one of several general types of printers.

Regardless of the type of printer you have, Word probably has a printer driver you can use. A printer driver is a file containing the information Word needs to print a document on a particular kind of printer. The Word package includes drivers for most common printers and quite a few not-so-common ones. If it doesn't include the driver you need, you can adapt a printer driver for your printer (see the Word manual for more information).

The Operating System

To use Word you need either DOS 2.0 (or later) or the OS/2 operating system. You can think of the operating system as the "traffic cop" of your computer. The operating system controls the interface between the software (such as Word) and your computer's hardware. Word is designed so that you don't have to understand the commands for your operating system to run the program. However, a few commands do come in handy (such as the CD and CHKDSK commands, which we'll experiment with in Chapter 2, "Starting Microsoft Word"). Other useful operating-system commands are explained in this book in the context of the specific operation to which they relate.

The advantages of learning DOS

Though Word lets you get by with knowing only a few operating-system commands, you may want to learn more. Some commands allow you to perform an operation faster or easier. For example, the COPY command comes in handy when you want to manage files and disk space outside of Word. When you are using Word, you must load a document into memory to copy it to a disk. There is no quick way to mark several documents to be copied and then copy them one after the other. From DOS, you can copy several files at once by using wildcard characters. By way of illustration, the following command copies all the documents with the .DOC extension, no matter what their file name, from the hard disk (C>) to a disk in drive A (A:).

```
C>COPY *.DOC A:
```

Consult your operating-system manual for more information about COPY and other commands.

The Word Package

The Word package comes with several manuals, a few disks, and a keyboard template. The disks include these parts of the Word system:

- The Program
- A set of Utilities
- The Spell program
- The Thesaurus program
- A set of printer drivers
- The Learning Word tutorials

The number of disks you receive depends on whether you have 3½-inch disk drives or 5¼-inch disk drives. If you have the wrong size disks for your disk drives, take the entire software package back to the store where you bought it and ask to exchange it for the correct size. You can also contact Microsoft Customer Service if the correct disks are not available from your dealer.

How Microsoft Word Works

Microsoft Word is a menu-driven program. Its menus provide options, or commands, from which you can choose. Menus are one of the reasons Word is an excellent word-processor choice for the beginning user, because the user is never faced with a "blank" screen with no options. Figure 1-8 shows Word's command menu. Notice that the selections are clearly labeled.

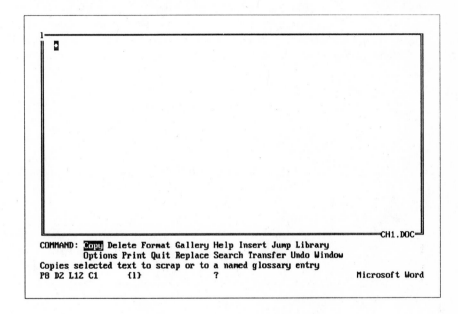

Figure 1-8. Word's command menu

Keyboard or mouse?

With Word, you simply use your keyboard or mouse to select the command you want. Word follows your instructions. When you become more familiar with Word, you might want to use Word's speed keys—key combinations that bypass the menu and can speed up your work. You might also want to "turn off" the menu to create more work space on your screen. Using speed keys and turning off the menu display are covered in detail in later chapters.

Document Basics

With Word, you organize your work into documents (also called files). You assign each document a name so that you can easily recognize its contents. Then you store the document on a hard disk or on a floppy disk. A single 5¼-inch disk can hold a minimum of one hundred pages of information; a 3½-inch disk and a hard disk can hold much more. When you want to use the document, you load it back into Word and view it on your screen.

If necessary, you can print copies of your documents. If you are a new computer user, you might at first find that you feel more comfortable having both a paper and a disk copy of your work. However, as you become more experienced and gain more confidence, you will find that often a disk copy is all you need. Unless you need to share your documents with others, you can save paper and storage space by keeping your documents on disk. Paper copies have a way of becoming less and less important as you use word processing more and more.

Tasks Word Can Perform

Word processors automate many tasks that are very time consuming to perform on a typewriter or by hand. However, not all word processors are created equal, and Word is more flexible and more powerful than most.

With Word, it is very easy to copy, delete, insert, and move text. When you perform any of these tasks, your document realigns immediately to fit within the margins you have set. Word automatically determines where lines and pages should break and does all the necessary calculations for formats such as centered text. You can easily move around a page and between pages. You can search for and replace characters, create running heads at the top or bottom of every page, sort text, and create little "programs," called macros, for further automating tasks you perform frequently.

In addition to making everyday word-processing tasks more efficient, Word has many features for adding organization to your documents, such as indexes, annotations, bookmarks, tables of contents, numbered paragraphs, outlines, and footnotes. And you can use Word's graphics capabilities to enhance any document. Finally, no matter how well you write, spell, or proofread, Word's spell checking and thesaurus capabilities can assist in creating a first rate document every time. Increased clarity and professionalism is the result.

Don't forget the Undo command.

One feature not to be overlooked is Word's capability of undoing your last action. In this book, we cover the Undo command early. You'll be more confident knowing that if you make a mistake, you can say "oops" and not suffer undue consequences.

How Word Differs from Other Word Processors

If you are familiar with another word processor, Word may take a little getting used to. Your first job will be to identify which keys to press and how to position your cursor to perform the basic functions that have become standard with most word processors, such as insert, delete, move, copy, spell, and search. This book makes that job easy by identifying typical word-processing tasks and presenting a step by step approach for completing them. You will also need to learn how Word is organized in terms of its menu functions.

When migrating from another word processor to Word, you will want to pay special attention to Chapter 6, "Formatting Documents." This chapter covers Word's somewhat different approach to formatting information by document, by division, by paragraph, and by character. You will also want to explore the use of stylesheets for handling formatting functions. Proficiency with stylesheets will enable you to quickly "try on" different formatting options so that you can select the look that's most appropriate for your documents.

As you will learn in the following chapters, Word is a powerful and full-featured word processor. You can use it to perform simple tasks with plain documents or very complex tasks with very sophisticated documents. All it takes is some time, study, and practice. The benefits of mastering Word's features will pay back in high-quality documents and time saved.

Starting Microsoft Word

Before you can use Microsoft Word, you need to take a few steps in preparation. These steps include:

- Checking your computer's memory
- Preparing storage disks
- Installing Word on your computer

This chapter covers the hardware and software required and actions you need to carry out to get up and running on Word.

Checking Memory

As mentioned in Chapter 1, your computer needs a minimum of 384 KB of memory to run Word. To identify how much memory your computer has, you can use the CHECK DISK (CHKDSK) command provided by your operating system. Follow these steps:

1. If you have a two-floppy-disk system, place the operating-system disk (DOS or OS/2) in drive A. This is usually the drive on the top or the left, depending on whether your drives are arranged vertically or horizontally.

2. Turn on your computer.

3. If you have a hard-disk system, you may need to go to the location where the operating system is stored. This is referred to as "changing directories." For example, if you are using DOS, you

may need to change to the DOS directory, by using the CHANGE DIRECTORY (CD) command. Type in the following command after the system prompt (C>) and press **Enter**:

```
CD DOS
```

4. With either a hard-disk system or two-floppy-disk system, you can now check the memory on the disk. Make sure you are at the system prompt. On a two-floppy-disk system, this prompt is usually A>. On a hard-disk system, the system prompt is usually C>. Enter the following command and press **Enter** to check the available memory on the disk:

```
CHKDSK
```

Information about your computer's memory appears on the screen. The following example shows what you might see if your computer has a 20-megabyte (MB) hard disk with more than ample memory for Word. Here, the total memory is over 650 KB.

```
21204992 bytes total disk space
   73728 bytes in 6 hidden files
   67584 bytes in 18 directories
19515392 bytes in 1035 user files
 1548288 bytes available on disk

  655360 bytes total memory
  601808 bytes free
```

As you can see, the CHKDSK command gives you a lot of information. In addition to the amount of total memory and available memory in your computer, the total space on the disk is shown, along with the space used by stored files and directories. The two most important pieces of information when it comes to word processing are the amount of storage space available on the disk and the amount free for use. Don't allow your disks to become completely full, or errors may result.

Preparing Extra Disks

If you have a two-floppy-disk system, you will need enough blank disks to store a copy of the contents of each Word disk. The goal is to create working disks that you will use on a daily basis so that you can store your original Word disks in a safe place. That way, if your working disks become damaged, you can pull out the original Word disks and make new working disks.

Whether you have a two-floppy-disk system or a hard-disk system, you will also need several blank disks for storing copies of your documents. Make sure you buy the size and type of disks that will work with your computer. See your computer dealer or computer manual for information about the type of disks to buy.

Format blank disks before you start.

Before you start using Word, you will need to format the blank disks so that they work with the type of operating system you are using. You can format disks by using Word's Setup utility (described later in this chapter) or by using your operating system's FORMAT command. See your operating-system manual for information on how to use FORMAT.

Installing Word on Your Computer

You use a program called Setup on the Word Utilities disk to install the Word program on your computer. You use the Setup utility whether you have a two-floppy-disk system or a hard-disk system, and whether or not you are using Word on a network, where several computers are linked together.

What You Need to Use Setup

Setup is used to copy the Word files from their original disks to your working floppy disks or hard disk. During the setup procedure, you also give the program information about the type of hardware you are using, including information about your printer, mouse, video adapter, and monitor.

Setup can also be used to format the blank disks on which you will store your documents. This formatting process makes the disks readable by your computer.

When you first use Setup, step through all the options one by one. Later, if you change printers, for example, or want to format more disks, you can run Setup and proceed directly to the option you need, skipping the other options.

Before using Word's Setup program, make sure you have this information at hand:

- The brand of your computer
- The brand of your video adapter
- The brand of your monitor
- The brand and model of your printer
- The port your printer is connected to (such as LPT1 or LPT2 for parallel printers; COM1 or COM2 for serial printers)
- The name of the directory in which you will place Word

Also make sure you have these disks readily available:

- If you have a two-floppy-disk system, a DOS disk with version 2.0 or later of the operating system
- The Word disks
- Blank, unformatted disks onto which you will copy the Word program files (for a two-floppy-disk system)
- Blank, unformatted disks for document storage (if you have a hard disk, you will still need these disks for backups)

Setup Steps

Whether you have a two-floppy-disk or a hard-disk system, follow these instructions for using Setup:

1. Place the Word Utilities disk in drive A.
2. At the A> prompt on a two-floppy-disk system, type in:

   SETUP

   At the C> prompt on a hard-disk system, type in:

   A:SETUP

3. Press **Enter**.
4. See Figure 2-1. The Setup screen appears. Make sure you have the information listed on the screen handy and press Enter.
5. See Figure 2-2. Here, Word has detected that the system has a hard disk. Select **H** if you have a hard disk. If you have a two-floppy-disk system, select that option.
6. See Figure 2-3. Setup suggests the drive and directory it should use for storing Word based on the default or an existing drive and directory. If you want to use a different drive or directory,

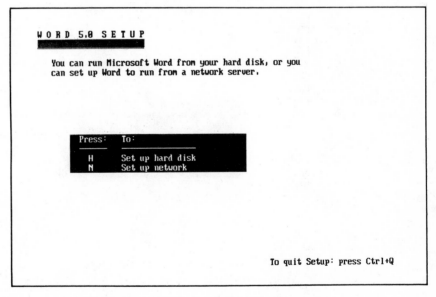

Figure 2-1. The Setup screen

```
W O R D  5.0  S E T U P

You can run Microsoft Word from your hard disk, or you
can set up Word to run from a network server,

              Press:  To:

                H     Set up hard disk
                N     Set up network


                                   To quit Setup: press Ctrl+Q
```

Figure 2-2. The hard-disk selection screen

enter the new drive and directory here and press **Enter**, or just press **Enter** to use the suggested drive and directory.

7. See Figure 2-4. Word gives you a chance to change the directory you entered. Press **C** to continue or **D** to enter a different directory. If you press D, Setup takes you back to step 6.

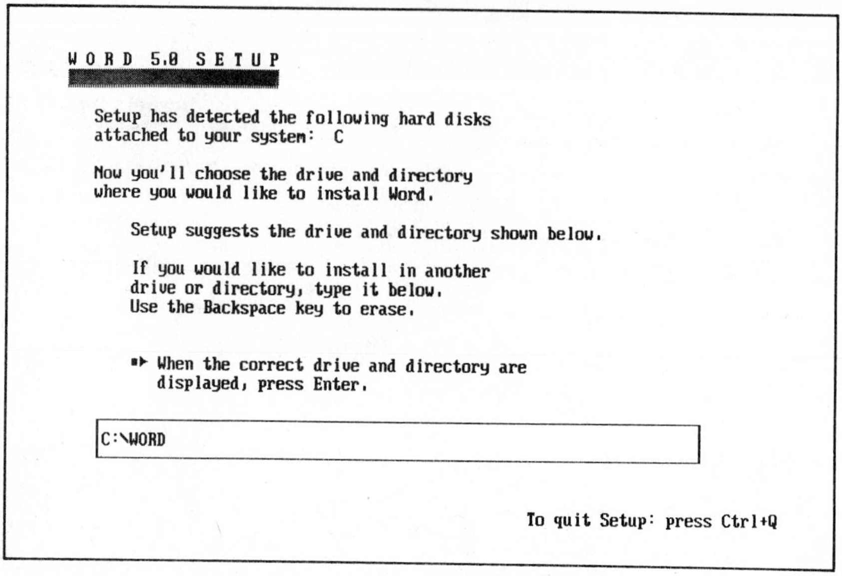

```
WORD 5.0 SETUP
████████████████

  Setup has detected the following hard disks
  attached to your system:  C

  Now you'll choose the drive and directory
  where you would like to install Word.

    Setup suggests the drive and directory shown below.

    If you would like to install in another
    drive or directory, type it below.
    Use the Backspace key to erase.


  ▪▸ When the correct drive and directory are
     displayed, press Enter.

 ┌─────────────────────────────────────────────────────────┐
 │ C:\WORD                                                  │
 └─────────────────────────────────────────────────────────┘


                               To quit Setup: press Ctrl+Q
```

Figure 2-3. The directory selection screen

```
WORD 5.0 SETUP
████████████████

  You've chosen the following directory.

    C:\WORD

  If this is OK, press C to continue.
  If not, press D to go back and change the directory.


       ┌────────────────────────────────────────┐
       │ Press:   To:                            │
       │ ──────────                              │
       │   C      Continue Setup                 │
       │   D      Go back to change directory    │
       └────────────────────────────────────────┘




                               To quit Setup: press Ctrl+Q
```

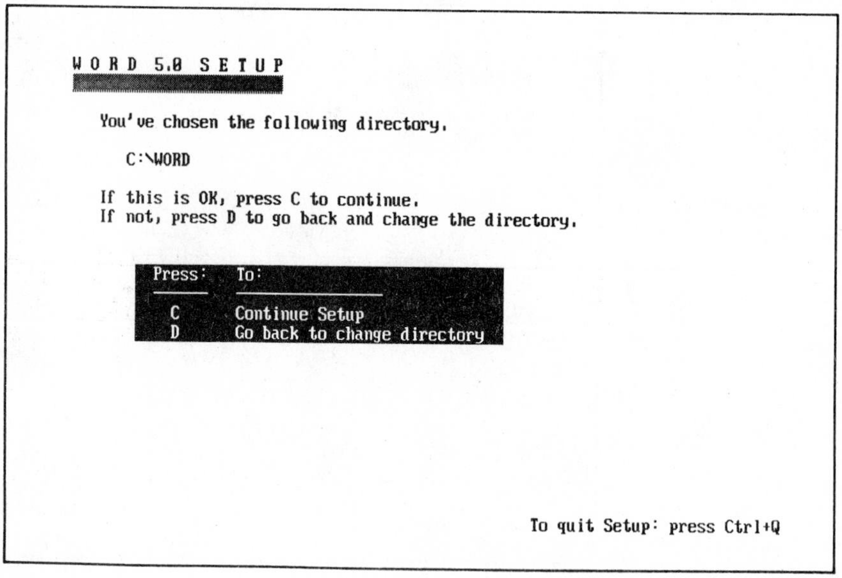

Figure 2-4. The directory selection screen: second chance

8. See Figure 2-5. Assuming you pressed C to continue, the Setup menu appears. This menu gives you setup options from which to choose. If this is the first time you have used Setup, work through each option in order. When you complete an option in

this session, Word marks the option with an asterisk (*). Later, you can change certain items of information (such as the printer setup) by selecting only that option. To begin, select **W** to copy the Word program.

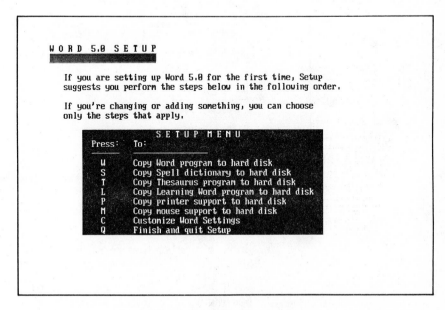

Figure 2-5. The setup menu

9. See Figure 2-6. Place the first Word disk in drive A and press **Enter**. Follow the prompts, inserting the program disks one by one so that Setup can copy them. These messages appear:

```
Setup is now copying the Word Program 1 disk.
Number of files copied: 1
```

If you place the wrong disk in the drive, this message alerts you to try another disk:

```
The wrong disk is in the drive.
```

If you are using 3½-inch disks, more than one "disk" can be contained on one physical disk. For example, the Program 1 disk and Program 2 disk are contained on one 3½-inch disk.

Setup configures Word to match your system.

Also during the Setup process you need to:

   a. Enter a number that corresponds with your type of computer.

W O R D 5.8 S E T U P
▬▬▬▬▬▬▬▬▬

When you copy the Word program to your hard
disk, you'll copy the Word Program 1 and 2
disks, the Utilities 1, 2, and 3 disks,
and the Spell disk.
You'll also confirm the type of computer and
video adapter you're using.
First, you'll copy the Word Program 1 disk.

    Insert the Word Program 1 disk in
    drive A.

    Program 1 disk

■▶ Press Enter to continue.

    To return to Setup menu: press Ctrl+R

Figure 2-6. The program-disk insertion prompt

b. Enter a number that corresponds with your type of video adapter.

c. Enter a number that corresponds with your type of printer. See Figure 2-7. If your printer is not displayed, select one of these from the bottom of the list:

    Standard printer

    Standard printer with support for backspace

    Standard printer with support for form feeds

    Standard daisywheel printer

    Other

See Chapter 5, "Printing Documents," for more information on selecting printers. As mentioned, you can rerun Setup at any time and select another printer.

    d. If the printer you select has font options, enter numbers corresponding to the fonts you want to use.

    e. If necessary, select options that change the printer support or finish installation of the printer.

    f. Enter the number corresponding to the port to which your printer is attached.

10. From the Setup menu, select **S** to copy the Spell dictionary. Follow the prompts, carrying out the instructions on the screen. You will eventually return to the Setup menu.

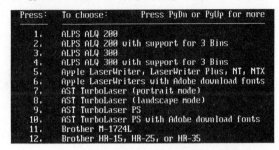

Figure 2-7. The printer-installation screen

11. From the Setup menu, select **T** to copy the Thesaurus program. Follow the prompts, carrying out the instructions on the screen. You will eventually return to the Setup menu.

12. From the Setup menu, select **L** to copy the Learning Word program. Follow the prompts, carrying out the instructions on the screen. You will eventually return to the Setup menu.

13. From the Setup menu, select **P** to install any additional printers you may need to use with Word.

14. From the Setup menu, select **M** if you have a mouse. The screen shown in Figure 2-8 appears. Press **M** to copy the mouse-driver program.

15. From the Setup menu, select **C** to customize Word settings.

16. See Figure 2-9. You are given a chance to change your mind. Press **S** to see details about the Word settings that can be customized.

Customizing your screen   17. See Figure 2-10. On this screen you can set the default display mode that Word will use. You must have a graphics adapter to set Word to graphics mode which displays formatted characters. Text mode is faster. You can change the default mode once you are in Word by choosing Options from Word's menu and setting the display mode option. For now, press **T** to set the initial default to text mode or **G** to set the initial default to graphics mode.

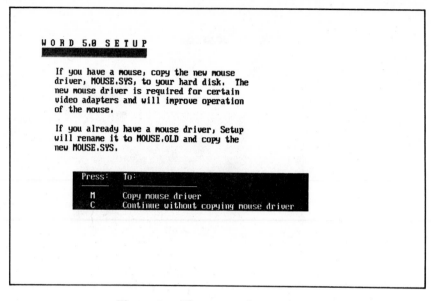

Figure 2-8. The mouse-driver screen

18. Word's command menu is shown in Figure 2-11. On the Setup screen shown in Figure 2-12, enter **D** to display the Word menu or **H** to hide the menu. If you hide the menu, pressing the **Esc**

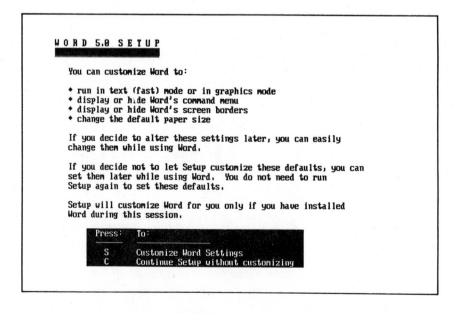

Figure 2-9. The customization screen

```
WORD 5.8 SETUP
███████████████

    You can display Word in text mode or graphics mode.

    Word is very fast in text mode.  This is the default mode.

    Graphics mode lets you see special formats like italics
    and boldface on the screen much as they will appear when you print.
    You must have a graphics display adapter to use graphics mode.

    You can run Word in text mode so it's fast, and quickly
    switch to graphics mode to see special formats as you
    work by pressing Alt+F9.

    For more information on Text and Graphics modes see page 15 in
    the Using Microsoft Word Manual.

        ┌─────────────────────────────────────────┐
        │ Press:  To:                              │
        │ ─────────────────────────────────────    │
        │   T     Run Word in text mode            │
        │   G     Run Word in graphics mode        │
        └─────────────────────────────────────────┘

                          To return to Setup menu: press Ctrl+R
```

Figure 2-10. The default graphics-mode or text-mode screen

(Escape) key makes it visible. You can also reset this default from within the Word program by choosing Options and resetting the *show menu* field.

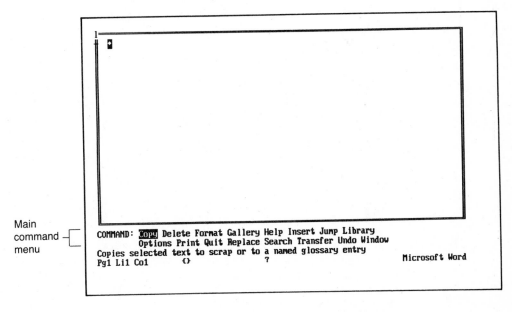

Main command menu

```
COMMAND: Copy Delete Format Gallery Help Insert Jump Library
         Options Print Quit Replace Search Transfer Undo Window
Copies selected text to scrap or to a named glossary entry
Pg1 Li1 Co1        {}              ?                        Microsoft Word
```

Figure 2-11. Word's command menu

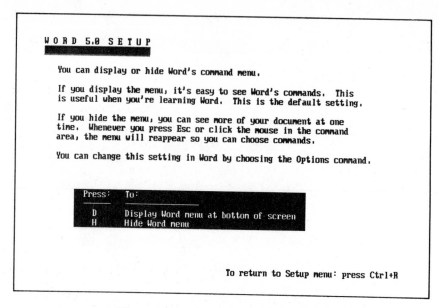

Figure 2-12. The default menu screen

19. The Word screen has a border around the text area, as shown in Figure 2-13. You can choose to hide or display the border as a default. This default can be reset from within Word by choosing

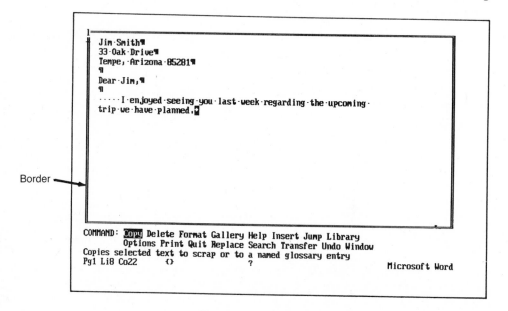

Figure 2-13. Word's border

Options and resetting the *borders* field. If you are using a mouse, you will want to use the border. On the Setup screen (see Figure 2-14) press **D** to display the border or **H** to hide the border.

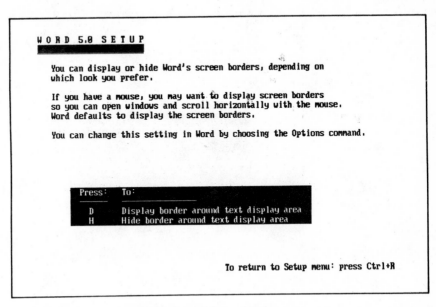

Figure 2-14. The default border screen

20. See Figure 2-15. Set the default paper setting. The default can be changed from within Word by choosing the Format Division Margins command.

21. From the Setup menu, select **Q** to quit Setup. You are given the option of changing the AUTOEXEC.BAT and CONFIG.SYS file. (These files are briefly discussed in Appendix D.) Select the option you want. Then view any suggested documents. Finally, quit setup.

Making a DOS Startup Disk

Typically, if you have a two-floppy-disk drive system, you will start your computer with a DOS disk and then switch to the Word disk for word processing. You can create a Word disk with the necessary DOS files on it so that you can start your computer directly from the Word disk.

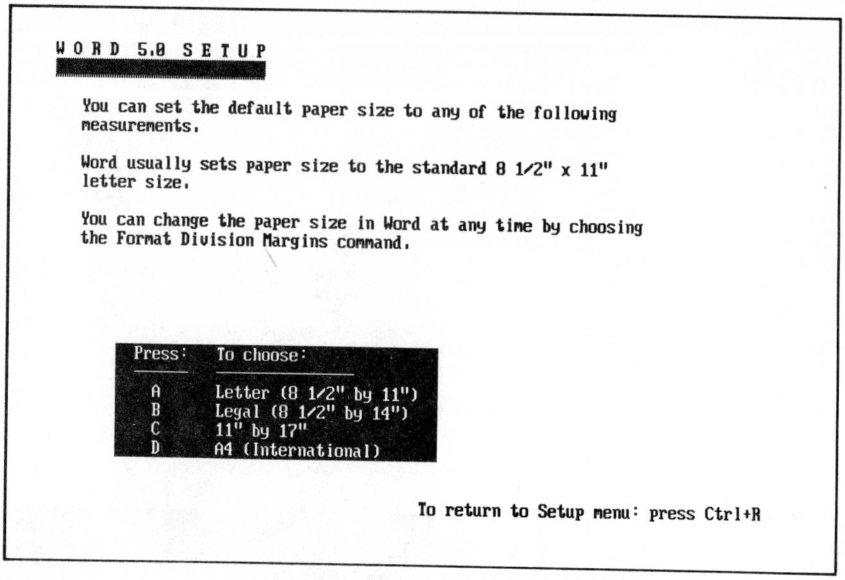

```
WORD 5.0 SETUP
▓▓▓▓▓▓▓▓▓▓▓▓▓▓▓

    You can set the default paper size to any of the following
    measurements.

    Word usually sets paper size to the standard 8 1/2" x 11"
    letter size.

    You can change the paper size in Word at any time by choosing
    the Format Division Margins command.




        Press:    To choose:
        ────────────────────────────
          A       Letter (8 1/2" by 11")
          B       Legal (8 1/2" by 14")
          C       11" by 17"
          D       A4 (International)


                        To return to Setup menu: press Ctrl+R
```

Figure 2-15. The default paper-setting screen

This procedure requires a 720-KB, 1.2-MB, or 1.4-MB disk. (A 360-KB disk will not hold all the required DOS and Word files.) Follow these instructions for creating a DOS startup disk:

1. Place a blank, unformatted disk in drive B.
2. With the DOS disk in drive A, format the disk in drive B by typing in this command at the A> system prompt:

   FORMAT B: /S

3. Press **Enter**.
4. When the disk is formatted, place in drive A the Word disk you created when you ran Setup.
5. After the A> system prompt, copy the files from the Word disk in drive A to the DOS startup disk in drive B by typing in this command:

   COPY *.* B:

6. Press **Enter**.

Using Word on a Network

On a network, a single copy of Word resides on the network server. All the workstations attached to the server use that copy of Word. It is recommended that each workstation have 512 KB of RAM available for Word.

Figure 2-16 shows a small network layout. In the figure, the server has three workstations attached to it along with a server printer. Word resides on the server's hard disk. Each workstation has access to the server printer. One workstation has its own printer.

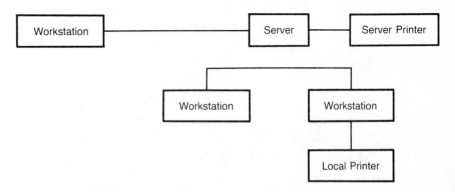

Figure 2-16. An example of a small network layout

Word's network safeguards

With several workstations using one server, opportunity is ripe for collisions. However, Word protects against one user writing over another user's files. Word also allows you to make files "read only" (meaning the file can be viewed but cannot be changed) versus "read/write" (meaning the file can be both viewed and changed). See "Creating Read-Only Files" in Appendix D for more information.

What You Need to Use Setup on a Network

Before using Word's Setup program on a network, make sure you have this information at hand:

- The brand of your computer
- The brand of your video adapter
- The brand of your monitor

- The brand and model of your printer
- The port your printer is connected to (such as LPT1 or LPT2 for parallel printers; COM1 or COM2 for serial printers)
- The name of the directory in which you will place Word (you can create the directory or have Word's Setup program create it for you; see "Creating a Directory" earlier in this chapter for more information)

You also need these disks:

- If you have a two-floppy-disk system, a DOS disk, with version 2.0 or later of the operating system
- The Word disks
- Blank, unformatted disks for document storage

Setup should be run on the network server first and then a special Setup program for network workstations should be run on each workstation.

Where to Put Files

"Where to put what?" is a common question users ask when first setting up a network workstation. The server disk should contain the following files in its Word directory (which, in the following discussion, we assume is called WORD):

- The Word program
- System-wide documents, style sheets, spelling dictionaries, and downloadable fonts
- NORMAL.STY (Word's default style sheet; you learn about style sheets in Chapter 9, "Style Sheets")
- NORMAL.GLY (Word's default glossary; glossaries are discussed in Chapter 16, "Glossaries")
- Files with the extensions .PRD, .INI, and .DAT for driving printers and using fonts
- DOWN_DOS.EXE or DOWN_OS2.EXE (Word's utility for downloading fonts)

All downloadable fonts, printer drivers, and font data files (the latter have the .DAT extension) must be placed in the same directory. This directory does not have to be the directory that contains the Word program files. However, it is best to keep the utility for downloading fonts (DOWN_DOS.EXE for DOS or DOWN_OS2.EXE for OS2) in the directory that contains the Word program files.

Protecting NORMAL.STY and NORMAL.GLY from changes

You may want to make NORMAL.STY and NORMAL.GLY read only. This prevents a user from changing these files, which are available for use by all users.

The workstation's WORD directory can contain the following individual user files:

- MW.INI (which stores the changes you have made to Word's default settings)
- The documents, style sheets, dictionaries, and glossaries created by the user of the workstation

Any NORMAL.STY and NORMAL.GLY files that are stored in workstation WORD directories will not be shared by other users on the network.

A workstation with a hard disk should have in its directory an AUTOEXEC.BAT file that executes automatically every time the workstation is turned on. The AUTOEXEC.BAT file must contain the path to the server's WORD directory, such as:

```
PATH E:\WORD
```

The file must also contain a command to identify the location of the WORD directory on the workstation. Here is an example:

```
SET MSWNET=C:\WORD
```

If you have a workstation with two floppy-disk drives (no hard disk), when starting your system, you should use a DOS disk with an AUTOEXEC.BAT containing these lines (substitute the appropriate path information):

```
PATH E:\WORD
SET MSWNET=B:\
```

The first line identifies the path to the server's WORD directory, and the second line identifies the location of the workstation's WORD directory.

Setup Steps for a Network Server

To set up Word on a network server, follow the instructions given for hard-disk systems in "Setup Steps" earlier in this chapter. In step 5, instead of selecting H to indicate you want to set up Word on a hard disk, select N for network at the appropriate prompt.

Setup Steps for a Network Workstation

After you have set up Word on the network server, run Setup on each workstation that will use Word. Follow these steps:

1. After the system prompt, enter the server path, followed by the command SETUP USER. For example:

   ```
   E:\WORD\SETUP USER
   ```

2. Press **Enter**.

3. Follow the screen instructions. The setup procedure is similar to the procedure for the server.

Setup results

When you have run Setup for each workstation, these are the results:

- The WORD directory on the workstation has been identified; it contains the MW.INI file (the changes you have made to Word's default settings), along with Spell dictionary files.
- The correct video driver has been copied to a file called SCREEN.VID in the workstation's WORD directory.

Network Notes

Take these tips into consideration when you are working in a network environment:

- You should start Word from your workstation (not from the network).
- Your style sheets and glossary files should be stored in your workstation WORD directory unless you want all users to share your files. Word searches for style-sheet and glossary files in this order:
  - On the workstation's current directory
  - On the workstation's WORD directory
  - On the server's WORD directory

- When you run the Spell program, Word uses the dictionary in the server's WORD directory. Then, it checks the workstation's WORD directory for words you have added to the dictionary.

- When you load a read/write file (including a style sheet or glossary) from the server, it is locked to prevent other users from simultaneously loading and editing it. If another user tries to load the file, a message appears on his or her screen. To make a file accessible by other users while you are working with it, make the file read only (see "Creating Read-Only Files" in Appendix D).

- You should use Word's Print Printer command to print documents. To see whether other documents are ahead of yours in the print queue, use the appropriate network-operating-system command. These are the steps for giving this command without leaving Word:

  1. From within Word, select **L**ibrary **R**un.

  2. Type in the network command.

  3. Press **Enter**.

  For more information about printing on a network, see Chapter 5, "Printing Documents."

- Temporary files with the .TMP extension are occasionally stored by Word on the server's hard disk for purposes such as automatic backup. To free the space, .TMP files can be deleted when no one is using Word.

Using Word with Windows

You can use Word with Microsoft's Windows product. If you have a hard-disk system, the necessary WORD.PIF file is copied from the Word Program 1 disk to your hard disk when you use the Setup program. If you have a two-floppy-disk system, you will have to copy the WORD.PIF file from the Word Utilities disk to your Word program disk. Follow these instructions to copy the file:

1. Place the Word Utilities disk in drive A and the Word program disk you created with Setup in drive B.

2. Enter the following command after the A> prompt and press Enter after each command:

```
COPY WORD.PIF B:
```

Starting Word is the topic of the next section. While you are reading that section, keep in mind that to start Word under Microsoft Windows, you need to run WORD.PIF instead of WORD.EXE. Trying to run the .EXE file will result in an error message.

Starting Word

When you start Word, you can specify that you want to start the Word session with one or more of the following options set:

Word's startup options

- Type in *WORD* to go to a new, "blank" document screen (shown in Figure 2-17). You can load an existing file from this screen or begin a new document. If you want to work with an existing file, you should start from that file's subdirectory or list the path with the file name. Chapter 3, "Creating Documents," discusses directories and paths in detail.

- Type in *WORD* followed by a space and then a file name to start the program and load an existing document or create a new document with that name. If the named document exists, it is displayed. If it does not exist, Word asks whether you want to create a new document. If you respond **Yes**, the document is created and you are taken to a blank document screen. When you

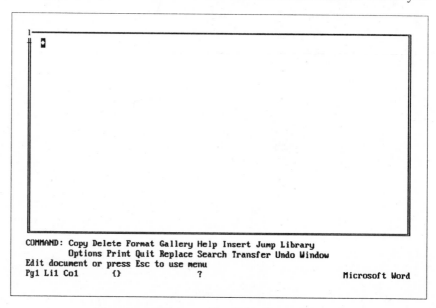

Figure 2-17. A new, blank document screen

save your work, Word already knows the name you are likely to want to use.

- Type in *WORD* followed by a space and the letter *L* (for *last*) to load the last document you worked on when you left Word and position the highlight where it was when you selected Quit.

- Type in *WORD* followed by a space and the letter *Y* to tell Word to scroll up half a screen when displaying the end of a document (Word 4.0 default).

- If you have used the *Y* switch and want to return to the Word default, type in *WORD* followed by the letter *Z* to tell Word to show a complete screenful of information when displaying the end of a document (Word 5.0 default).

- Type in *WORD* followed by a space and the letter *X* to tell Word not to use expanded memory.

- Type in *WORD* followed by a space and *Bnn* substituting for *nn* the number of buffers, or storage spaces in memory, you want Word to use. You can specify a minimum of 4 and a maximum of 1500. The more buffers you specify, the more of the document can be loaded into memory, reducing Word's need to access the disk where the document is stored and speeding operations. Obviously, you shouldn't specify more buffers than your memory can handle.

- Type in *WORD* followed by a space and the /K to use an enhanced keyboard.

- Type in *WORD* followed by a space and the /N for Novell network support.

How you start Word depends on the type of system you have: a two-floppy-disk system; a hard-disk system running DOS; a hard-disk system running just OS/2, or a hard-disk system running DOS under OS/2. Specific instructions for each type of system follow.

Starting Word with a Two-Floppy-Disk System

Whether or not your computer is a network workstation, to start Word on a two-floppy-disk system, follow these steps:

1. Make sure the system A> prompt is on your screen. If it is not, enter the following command and press **Enter** to get the prompt to appear:

   A:

2. Place the Word program disk you created with Setup in drive A.

3. Place a blank, formatted disk in drive B. This is where the documents you create will be stored.

4. Start Word by typing in *WORD*. You may want to follow the command with one of the options discussed in the previous section. Then press **Enter**.

Starting Word with a Hard-Disk System and DOS

Whether or not your computer is a network workstation, follow these steps to start Word using a hard-disk system and the DOS operating system:

1. Make sure the system prompt is on your screen (usually C>). If it is not, enter the following command and press **Enter** to get the prompt to appear:

   ```
   C:
   ```

2. Use the CHANGE DIRECTORY command to go to the directory that contains your Word program files. Or, if you want to load an existing file, go to the subdirectory that contains your document files. For example, type in this command after the operating-system prompt and press **Enter** to change to the directory called WORD:

   ```
   CD WORD
   ```

   We discuss directories in more detail in Chapter 3, "Creating Documents."

3. Start Word by typing in *WORD*. You may want to follow the command with one of the options discussed in the previous section. Then press **Enter**.

Starting Word with a Hard-Disk System and OS/2

Whether or not your computer is a network workstation, follow these steps to start Word using a hard-disk system and the OS/2 operating system:

1. From the OS/2 Program Selector screen, select Word (from the Start A Program menu).

2. Press **Enter** to go to a blank, unnamed document screen. (With OS/2, you do not have the option of going to an existing file, a new file, or the last edited file.)

Starting Word as a DOS Application under OS/2

You can run Word as a DOS application in OS/2's DOS-compatibility mode. Follow these steps:

1. Select the DOS Command Prompt option on the Switch To A Running Program menu of the Program Selector screen.

2. At the operating-system prompt, type in *CD* (for *change directory*) and the name of the directory where the Word programs are stored, and then press **Enter**. For example:

```
CD DIRECTORYNAME
```

3. Start Word by typing in *WORD*. You may want to follow the command with one of the options discussed in the previous section. Then press **Enter**.

The /K Option for Keyboard Functioning

If you use an enhanced keyboard or terminate-and-stay-resident program, you will want to know about the /K option. If after starting Word the keys on your keyboard do not work as they should, try starting Word with the /K option. When you set this option, the F11 and F12 function keys are turned off, and pressing the extended-keypad keys with Num Lock activated has no effect.

To use the /K option when starting Word, type in the following at the operating-system prompt:

```
WORD /K
```

Use Ctrl-Shift-\ to redraw the screen.

Once Word is loaded, you may need to press Ctrl-Shift-\ to redraw the screen if you are using a terminate-and-stay resident program in graphics mode.

The Word Screen

When you start Word, the Word screen appears. Figure 2-18 shows the Word screen without a document loaded. The window, which is currently blank, is where Word will display the text of the document on which you are working. The command area at the bottom of the screen includes the command menu, the message line, and the status line which is the last line of the screen.

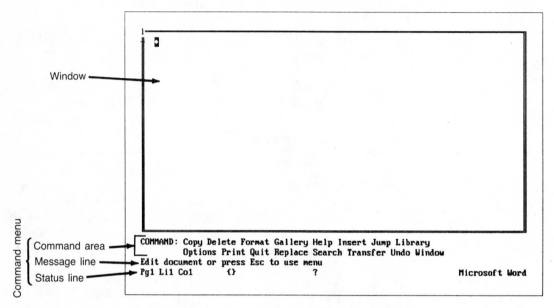

Figure 2-18. The Word screen

Word Windows

Word windows have these elements (see Figure 2-19):

- The window number
- The document name
- The end mark
- Scroll bars and a scroll mark
- The window split bar
- The selection bar

This section covers each part of the window. Chapter 11, "Windows," covers the use of Word's windows in detail.

Window Elements

The window number is identified in the upper-left corner of the window. The window that appears on your monitor when you start Word

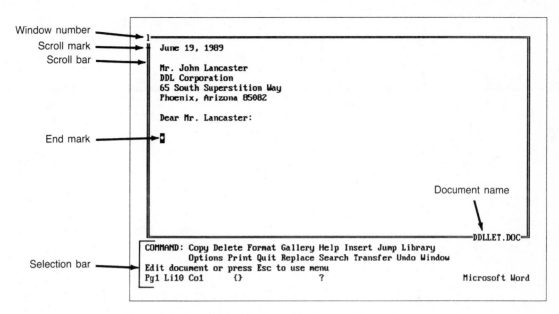

Window number

Scroll mark

Scroll bar

End mark

Document name

Selection bar

Figure 2-19. The parts of a window

is window 1. You can have as many as eight windows on your monitor at one time. You can use windows to view different documents or to view different sections of the same document. Figure 2-20 shows

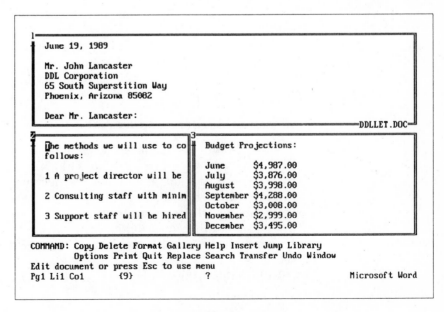

Figure 2-20. Multiple windows

multiple windows on the screen. The number of the "active" window (window 2) is highlighted.

The document name is shown in the lower-right corner of the window. No name is displayed if you have not yet assigned a name to the document. If an asterisk appears before the name of the document, the document is read only; it cannot be edited and then saved under the same name. See "Creating Read-Only Files" in Appendix D for more information.

The end mark is a diamond-shaped character that marks the end of the document.

The scroll bars are the left and bottom borders of a window. Clicking the scroll bars with a mouse allows you to move quickly through a document.

The thumb marks your place in a document.

The scroll mark (also called the **thumb**) is the small horizontal line that crosses the left scroll bar. When the scroll mark is near the top of the left scroll bar, you are near the top of the document. When the scroll mark is near the bottom of the scroll bar, you are near the bottom of the document. For example, assume you have a document that is 40 pages long. When you are on page 1, the scroll mark is at the top of the left border. When you are on page 20, the scroll mark is near the middle of the left border. When you are on page 40, the scroll mark is at the bottom of the left border.

The remaining two window elements are used only with a mouse:

The window split bars are the top and right borders of the window. With a mouse, you can use the window split bars to create new windows.

The selection bar is the far-left column of the window. The selection bar is used with a mouse to select a line, a paragraph, or a whole document for editing. You can also use the Window Split command to split windows.

Controlling Border Display

If only one window is displayed, you can turn off the display of the borders. You gain two lines and two columns in the text area. The scroll mark still appears, along with the document file name. When you turn off the border display, you can't perform some mouse functions that require the window borders (such as splitting a window).

When more than one window appears on the screen, or if you add a new window to the display, the borders are automatically turned back on.

To turn the display of borders on and off, follow these steps:

1. Select **O**ptions.

2. Move to the *show borders* field and select **Yes** to show the borders or **No** to hide the borders.

3. Press **Enter**.

The *show borders* setting is saved when you quit Word.

The Ruler

The top window border is sometimes replaced with a ruler. The ruler shows tab and indent settings for paragraphs. You can set an option that causes the ruler to be displayed all the time. Otherwise, Word displays the ruler only when you set tabs or paragraph formats (such as indents). Figure 2-21 shows a window with a ruler.

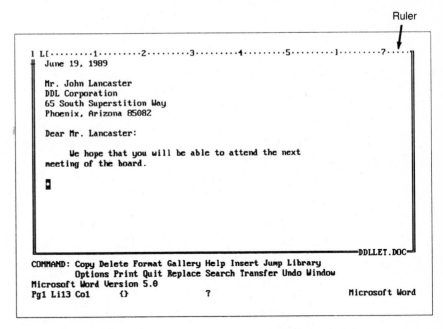

Figure 2-21. A window with the ruler displayed

As mentioned, you can have Word display the ruler at all times. Follow these steps if you are using the keyboard:

1. Select **O**ptions.

2. Go to the *show ruler* field and select **Yes** to show the ruler or **No** to turn the ruler off.

3. Press **Enter**.

Follow these steps if you are using a mouse:

1. Point to the upper-right corner of the window.
2. Click either:

The left button	to turn the ruler on
Both buttons	to turn the ruler off

The *show ruler* setting is saved when you quit Word.

The Command Area

As you saw in Figure 2-18, the command area comprises two lines of commands (the command menu), one message line, and one line for status information.

Selecting a Command

Here's how to select a command:

1. Press **Esc** to activate the command area. (If the command area is hidden and you are using a mouse, place the mouse highlight in the status line and click the left or right button.) The first command, Copy, is highlighted.
2. Select a command by using one of these options:
   - Press the capital letter displayed in the command name and then press **Enter**.
   - Press the **Spacebar**, the **Tab** key, or the **Arrow** keys to highlight the command you want and then press **Enter**.
   - Point to the command you want and click the left mouse button.

If Word needs more information before it can carry out the command, you are taken to a submenu. Otherwise, Word carries out the command.

Submenus

Many selections in the command area lead you to other menus. These submenus allow you to select more specific commands or make settings in fields. Here is how submenus work with different types of fields:

To move between fields

- Use the Arrow keys or the Tab key.
- Use the PgDn (page down) or End key to go to the last field.
- Use the PgUp (page up) or Home key to go to the first field.
- Point to the field you want with the mouse and click the left button.

To enter text in a field:

- Type in the text and press Enter.
- Press F1 to see a list of possible options; highlight the option you want and press Enter.
- Point to the field and press the right mouse button to see a list of possible options; point to the option you want and then press the left mouse button to select the option.

To make a selection in a field (such as Yes or No):

- Use the Spacebar to highlight the selection and press Enter.
- Press the capital letter in the desired option name and press Enter.
- Point to the option you want and press the left mouse button.

Submenu example

The Print Options menu (see Figure 2-22) includes examples of all the different ways you can enter information in a field. Depend-

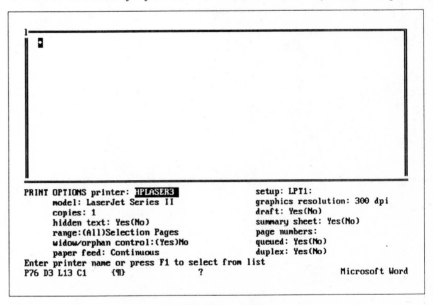

Figure 2-22. The Print Options menu

ing on what information is required, you can type in text, select an option from a list, or move to the field and choose one of the options presented.

For example, in the *printer* field, you can type in the name of the printer (shown in Figure 2-22 as HPLASER3). Or, as the message on the next to last line of the screen indicates, you can press F1 to select from a list of printer names. (If you are using a mouse you can click the right button in the *printer* field to select a printer name.)

Now look at the *setup* field in the first line of the right column. To move the highlight to this field, you use the Arrow keys, the Tab key, or the mouse. Don't use the Spacebar; it won't move you to the next field. Instead, the current *printer* field contents will be deleted and replaced by a space character.

The PgDn or End key moves you to *duplex*, the last field on the menu. The PgUp or Home key moves you to *printer*, the first field on the menu.

When you are in a field that presents options (such as the *draft* field), you have several alternatives. You can press the Spacebar to highlight your selection; press the capital letter in the option name (in the case of the *draft* field, press Y for Yes or N for No); or point to the desired option with the mouse and click either button. Whichever way you choose to make your selection, Word encloses your selection in parentheses to indicate which option is active.

When you have made your selections from a given menu, press Enter or click the left mouse button to carry out your command.

Cancelling a Command

Everyone changes his or her mind from time to time. If you decide not to go through with a command, you can cancel it and return to your work. You have several options:

- Press Esc to return to your document. (If you are in the Gallery or Library Document-retrieval menus, select Exit.)

- If you are using a mouse, point to the command area and click both buttons to return to the document. (If you are in the Gallery, Library Document-retrieval, or Print Preview menus, click on the Exit command with either button.)

- Press Ctrl-Esc to return to the main command menu. There is no way to use the mouse to return to the main command menu.

The settings that were active before you started to choose the command remain in effect.

Repeating a Command

Commands can be repeated by pressing the F4 function key. If you are familiar with the concept of macros in word processing, think of this "repeat key" as a "quick-and-dirty" temporary macro. When you press F4, the last action you completed is repeated. If you entered text, the text is entered a second time. Or, if your last action was selecting a command sequence, the command sequence is repeated.

Using the F4 key

Here's an example. Suppose you want to underline several words in a document. The steps for underlining are:

1. Highlight the text to be underlined.
2. Select **F**ormat **C**haracter and then select **Y**es in the *underline* field.
3. Press **Enter**.
4. Repeat steps 1 through 3 for each word or group of words to be underlined.

By using the F4 key, this process can be streamlined to:

1. Highlight the text to be underlined
2. Select **F**ormat **C**haracter and then select **Y**es in the *underline* field.
3. Press **Enter**.
4. Highlight the next piece of text to be underlined and press **F4**.

As soon as you type in more text or select another command, that action becomes the action that will be repeated when you press F4.

The following commands can be repeated:

Copy

Delete

Format-menu commands

Insert

Library Autosort

Library Hyphenate

Library Index

Library Table

Name (on the Gallery menu)

Replace (see special instructions in Chapter 12, "Search and Replace")

Search (again, see special instructions in Chapter 12, "Search and Replace")

Transfer Merge

Undo

To repeat your previous command using a mouse, point to the word COMMAND in the command menu and click either mouse button. (You must have the Options command's *show menu* field set to Yes to repeat a command using a mouse. This is the only way to access the word COMMAND in the proper sequence.)

Command-Menu Operation Summary

Here is a summary of how to operate the command menus:

Function	Action
Enter or leave the command area	Press Esc
Move in and select from the command menu	Press the capital letter in the command name and then Enter; press the Spacebar, Tab key, or Arrow keys and then Enter; or point with a mouse and click either button
Move in a submenu	Press the Tab key or Arrow keys, or point with a mouse
Last field in a submenu	Press the PgDn or End key
First field in a submenu	PgUp or Home key
Enter text in a field	Type in text from the keyboard; press F1, highlight one of the options listed, and then press Enter; or click the right mouse button with the highlight in the desired field, point to one of the options listed, and then press the left mouse button
Make a selection among choices	Press the Spacebar to highlight the desired option and press Enter; press the capital letter in the option name and then Enter; or point to the desired selection and press the left mouse button
Carry out the command	Press Enter; or click the right mouse button in the menu area

Leave menu "as was" when entered and return to document	Press Esc; or click both mouse buttons in the command area
Return to command menu	Press Ctrl-Esc
Repeat a command	Press F4; or click COMMAND in the main command menu

As you become familiar with Word, you will discover keyboard shortcuts, or speed keys, that you can use to avoid the use of the menus. Speed keys allow you to press a couple of keys instead of walking through the menus to complete often-used tasks. These speed keys are summarized in Appendix A and are included in instructions throughout this book.

Special Mouse Notes

Usually, you use the left mouse button when working in the command menu. However, by using the right button, you can take some shortcuts. You can select a command from the main command menu, select a menu option from a submenu, or select an option in a field. Here is a comparison of the results of using the left and right buttons, along with some special button activities:

- When pointing to a command, clicking the left button chooses the command only; clicking the right button chooses the command and the first choice in the submenu (except in the Help menu).
- When pointing to an option in a field, clicking the left button chooses the option only; clicking the right button chooses the option and carries out the command.

Use the right mouse button to see options.

- When pointing to a field, clicking the right button displays a list of options (equivalent to pressing the F1 key).
- When Word wants you to press Yes in response to a prompt, click either button in the command area (the mouse cannot be used to respond No).
- Whenever you can press the Esc key, clicking both buttons in the command area achieves the same result.

Hiding the Command Area

The command menu and message line can be hidden until you press Esc. (The status line is always visible). The benefit of hiding the command area is the gain in window space. If you might want to repeat a command with the mouse, however, do not hide the command area because then COMMAND will not be available to carry out the repeat function.

Figure 2-23 shows the appearance of the screen without the command menu and message line. Notice that only the status line appears at the bottom of the screen. When Word needs to display a message, it replaces the status line with the message. After reading the message, simply continue working. The message disappears and the status line reappears when you press a key or click the mouse button.

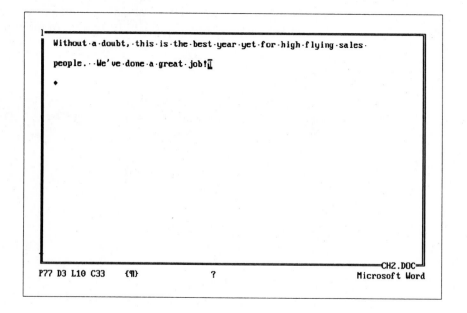

Figure 2-23. The Word screen with the command menu and message line hidden

To hide the command area, complete these steps:

1. Select **O**ptions.
2. In the *show menu* field, select **N**o.
3. Press **Enter** or click the command area.

The setting in the *show menu* field is saved when you quit Word. To display the command area so that you can select a command, simply press Esc.

The Message Line

As you work, pay special attention to the message line. It provides prompts and gives important information. For example, a message you saw earlier when we were discussing the Print Options menu is:

`Enter printer name or press F1 to select from a list`

This message indicates that you can either enter the name of the driver for the printer you will use or you can press the F1 key to make a selection from a list of available drivers.

Here's another example. When you try to quit Word or close a document without saving it, Word displays this important message:

`Enter Y to save changes to document, N to lose changes, or Esc to cancel`

The message presents you with the three options you have for proceeding.

Word has over 100 messages. Most are self-explanatory when considered in the context of what you are trying to do. If you see a message you do not understand, think carefully about what action you are trying to perform. Consider how the terms are used in Word. And, if all else fails, consult the chapter on messages in the *Reference to Microsoft Word*, which came in your Word package.

The Status Line

Word's status line gives you valuable information about your work. Specifically, you might see:

- The number of the page your highlight is on
- The number of the division you are working on
- The number of the line where your highlight is positioned
- The number of the column where your highlight is positioned
- The scrap area, showing the text you last copied or deleted
- The key status, indicating which toggle keys are currently turned on
- A help mark, for getting help (only available if you have a mouse)
- On occasion, a SAVE message, reminding you to save your work

The status line in Figure 2-24 shows some of these items of information.

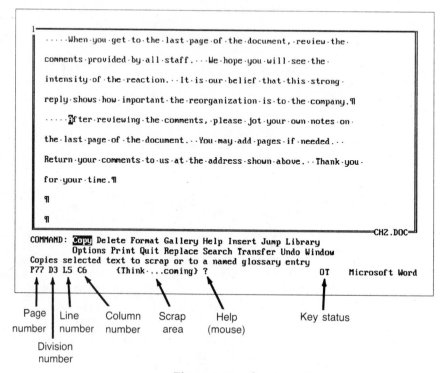

Figure 2-24. The status line

Starting from the left of the status line shown in the illustration, you can see that the highlight is on page 77, in division 3, line 5, and column 6. (The highlight marks the first letter of the second paragraph on the screen.)

Knowing the page number can help you judge the length of your document. It is also helpful when you want to quickly jump from page to page. Because formats are assigned to divisions, knowing the division number is helpful for identifying what division formats are governing the text. (You learn more about divisions and division formats in Chapter 6, "Formatting Documents.")

The line number is counted from the last page or division break. The column number is counted from the first character of the line. The line and column numbers are useful for identifying how close you are to the end of a page, for setting up tabs and columns, and for splitting windows.

The page number, division number, and column number always appear on the Word status line and cannot be "turned off." However, you can control whether or not the line number appears.

Hiding the Line Number

You can turn the line-number display on and off. When the line-number display is turned on, you may notice that Word runs slightly slower during editing (especially when inserting text).

If you choose to display line numbers, you can specify whether or not to count blank lines. For example, if you double space the text, you may have 25 lines on a typical page. If you count the blank lines, the count includes nonstandard spaces. For example, on a typical double-spaced page, the first line might be 9.8 (to account for the top margin), the second line 11.8, and the last line 57.8.

To control the line-number display:

1. Select **O**ptions.
2. In the *line numbers* field, select **Y**es to show the line number or **N**o to cause line numbers to disappear.
3. In the *count blank spaces* field, enter **Y**es to have Word count blank lines or **N**o to count lines of text only.
4. Press **Enter** or click the command area.

The setting of the *line numbers* field is saved when you quit Word.

The Scrap Area

The scrap area shows the text you last deleted or copied. The entire text appears if you deleted or copied only a few characters. The beginning and end of the text appear if the text is too large to display in its entirety. For example, this scrap area shows that the word *time* was the last text copied or deleted:

{Time}

The following scrap area shows how the sentence you are now reading would look if it were copied:

{The fo...opied:}

Notice that the first six characters of the sentence are in the scrap area followed by three dots followed by the last six characters in the sentence.

The Key Status

Word has several toggle keys that can be pressed to turn a function either on or off. A two-letter code representing the toggle keys that are turned on is displayed in the status line. You use this key status to identify why Word is operating as it is. For example, a change in your screen display may be accompanied by the appearance of LY in the status line. If you don't know that the LY key status means the *show layout* field of the Options command has been set to Yes, you might get nervous about the "health" of your system. Another example: When OT appears in the status line, you will overtype characters when you type rather than inserting characters at the highlight.

Refer to the following chart for key-status information. Information about each key or command is given in the appropriate section in this book.

Key status code	Key pressed or command selected	Meaning
CS	Shift-F6	Column-selection mode turned on
EX	F6	Selection-extension mode turned on
NL	Num Lock	Numeric keypad enters numbers
SL	Scroll Lock	Arrow keys scroll text rather than moving the highlight
CL	Caps Lock	Letters typed in are capital
OT	F5	Typing overtypes existing text rather than inserting characters in front of existing text
LD	Ctrl-F5	Line-draw mode turned on
RM	Shift-F3	Record-macro mode turned on
ST	Ctrl-F3	Macro-step mode turned on
ZM	Ctrl-F1	Zoom-window mode turned on
MR	Format revision-Marks Options	Mark-revisions mode turned on
LY	Options *show layout* field	Layout mode is turned on

If several toggle keys are turned on, several codes may be displayed. Some codes share the same "spot" in the status line. The following table shows which key-status codes appear in the same position and, of those, which have precedence:

Code with precedence	Spot shared with
LD	NL
ZM	SL
OT	MR
CS/EX (only one can be on at once)	

The Help Mark

How to get help quickly using a mouse

If you are working with a mouse, Word's help mark (?) appears in the status line. If you click the help mark, you are given information about the task you are trying to perform. More information about Word's help function is given in this chapter under the section entitled "Getting Help."

The Save Message

Many Word users have been rescued from losing a document by the SAVE message. SAVE appears in the status line when you are running out of space in memory or on the Word disk. If SAVE appears, immediately save all your work (including your documents, glossaries, and style sheets). Then determine how you might free up space in memory or on the Word disk so that you can continue working.

Memory can be freed up to some extent by quitting Word, since leaving the program erases Word's temporary files. Disk space requirements are best handled by moving files to other disks for storage, deleting unnecessary files, or getting another (or a bigger) disk.

Text and Graphics Mode

As already mentioned, Word has two display modes: text and graphics. Word's default is text mode. Figure 2-25 shows character styles in text mode. This screen illustration was taken from a color monitor, so the different character styles actually appear in different colors. Figure 2-26 shows the same screen in graphics mode. Notice that the displayed character styles are close to the way they will be when printed. Also notice that the mouse pointer is an arrow (in the figure, it is pointing to the window number in the upper-left corner of the screen).

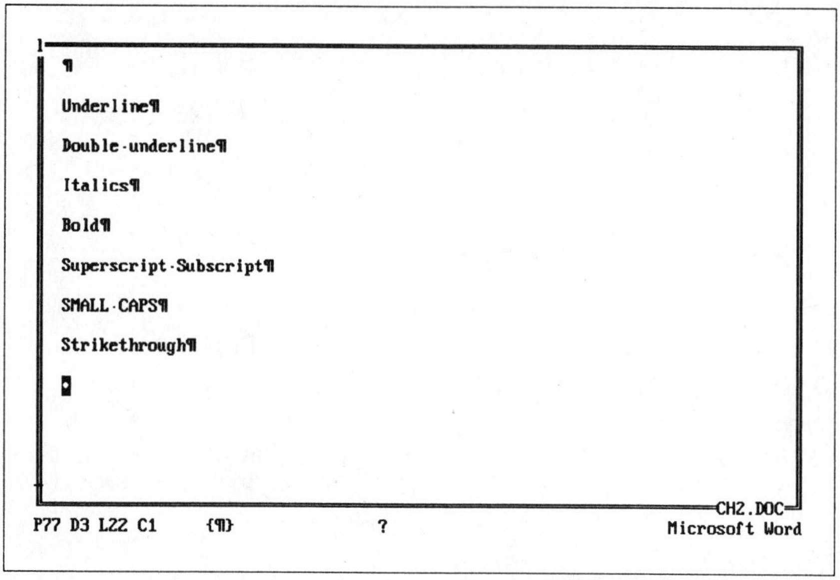

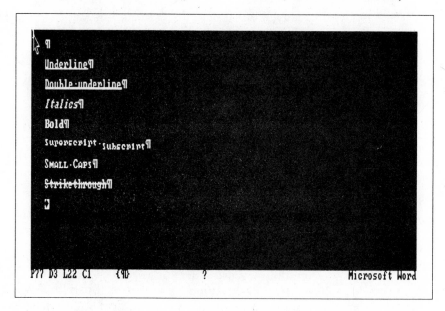

Figure 2-25. Character styles in text mode (with a color monitor)

Figure 2-26. Character styles in graphics mode (with the same monitor)

Choosing the best mode for you

    In text mode, Word runs faster. Characters with different styles appear in different shades. For example, on most monochrome systems, bold appears as intense characters and all other characters with special formatting (such as italics or underline) appear underlined. If your system handles colors, characters with special formatting appear in different colors. (See "Screen Colors" in this chapter for information about how to change the colors used for backgrounds and different styles of text.)

Graphics mode causes the text on the screen to be displayed more as it will be printed than text mode does. For example, in graphics mode, italics, bold, small capitals, underline, double underline, superscript, subscript, and strikethrough are all shown on the screen. To use graphics mode, you must have a video adapter that handles graphics.

Some mouse users prefer to work in graphics mode because they find it easier to make precise mouse selections in that mode than in text mode. This is because in text mode, the mouse highlight is a box, whereas in graphics mode, it is an arrow.

Even if your system handles graphics mode, you may still want to use text mode to take advantage of Word's speed when you are editing or performing functions such as spell checking. Then you may want to change to graphics mode to view the document before printing.

Changing Modes Through the Menu

To change the mode using the menu, follow these instructions:

1. Select **O**ptions.
2. Move to the *display mode* field.
3. Press **F1** to see the display modes supported by your video adapter (text mode or text and graphics modes).
4. Select the mode you want.
5. Press **Enter**.

The display immediately changes to reflect the option you selected. The *display mode* setting is saved when you quit Word.

Changing Modes from the Keyboard

To change the mode using a speed key, follow these instructions:

1. Press **Alt-F9**. If the display is in text mode, it immediately switches to graphics mode and vice versa (assuming your computer supports both modes).
2. Press **Alt-F9** to switch back.

Screen Colors

If your system handles colors, you can alter the colors used for your display. You can specify the background color, the border color, the colors used in the command area, and the colors for font sizes and special character formats (such as italics).

You use the top part of the Options-command menu, shown in Figure 2-27, to alter colors. Each setting includes sample text so that you can see what a particular character color looks like on a particular on the background color. The letters across the top of the screen (A through P) show the colors that are available, displayed on the color selected in the *background for window 1* field. To select a color, you highlight the field whose color you want to alter and press the letter of the color (A through P).

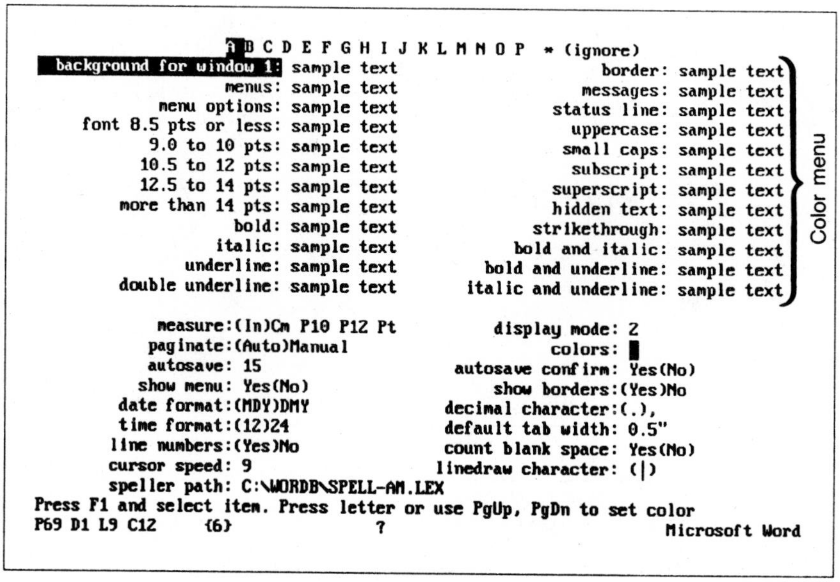

```
              A B C D E F G H I J K L M N O P  * (ignore)
background for window 1: sample text              border: sample text
               menus: sample text              messages: sample text
        menu options: sample text           status line: sample text
 font 8.5 pts or less: sample text             uppercase: sample text
       9.0 to 10 pts: sample text            small caps: sample text
      10.5 to 12 pts: sample text             subscript: sample text
      12.5 to 14 pts: sample text           superscript: sample text
    more than 14 pts: sample text           hidden text: sample text
                bold: sample text         strikethrough: sample text
              italic: sample text        bold and italic: sample text
           underline: sample text     bold and underline: sample text
    double underline: sample text    italic and underline: sample text

         measure:(In)Cm P10 P12 Pt          display mode: 2
        paginate:(Auto)Manual                     colors: █
         autosave: 15                    autosave confirm: Yes(No)
        show menu: Yes(No)                  show borders:(Yes)No
     date format:(MDY)DMY               decimal character:(.),
     time format:(12)24                default tab width: 0.5"
    line numbers:(Yes)No                count blank space: Yes(No)
    cursor speed: 9                    linedraw character: (|)
    speller path: C:\WORDB\SPELL-AM.LEX
Press F1 and select item. Press letter or use PgUp, PgDn to set color
P69 D1 L9 C12      {6}                    ?                    Microsoft Word
```

Figure 2-27. The color menu

On the menu, elements and styles are listed by priority. The item with highest priority is at the top of the left column and the item with lowest priority is at the bottom of the right column. When characters have more than one style (such as bold, underlined text), the text appears in the color of the highest-priority style. To give a field a lower priority than those below it, type in an asterisk (*) instead of a color letter.

As you can see in Figure 2-27, these are the elements for which colors can be changed:

- Background for windows (inside the window borders)
- Menus (menu title and menu field names)
- Menu options (options and field contents)
- Font sizes (five sizes from 8.5 points or less to 14 points or more; see Chapter 6, "Formatting Documents," for more information)
- Border (of the window)
- Messages (on the message line)
- Status line (the entire bottom line of the screen)
- Character styles (bold, italic, underline, double underline, uppercase, small caps, subscript, superscript, hidden text, strikethrough, bold and italic, bold and underline, and italic and underline)

When you choose colors, first identify the elements of the screen that you think are most important to distinguish. For example, you may want to have the message line appear in red on a black background to draw your attention to messages. Also consider which text styles you will use most often. If, for example, you rarely use superscripts and subscripts but often use italic and bold italic, make sure the colors for italic and bold italic are easily distinguishable. Since there are limited color choices, you might want superscripts and subscripts to be displayed in the same color.

Pay special attention to the selection of colors that are easily readable. If you are setting colors for use on a network, remember that some people are color blind and may have difficulty telling the difference between certain color combinations.

Finally, choose colors that are pleasing to you. Colors can add interest and enjoyment to working with Word.

To change the default colors, follow these steps:

1. Select **O**ptions.
2. Move to the *colors* field and press **F1**; the color options appear.
3. Place the cursor in the field you want to alter.
4. Change the color of the sample text using one of these methods:

    - Press the letter (A through P) that appears at the top of the screen in the color you want.
    - Identify the letter of the current color and press **PgUp** to select the color to the right of that letter or **PgDn** to select the color to the left of the letter. Continue pressing **PgUp** or **PgDn** to see all the color choices.

- Type in an asterisk (*) to give the field a lower priority than the fields below it on the menu.

5. Press **Enter** when the colors are set or press **Esc** to return to the colors that were set when you entered the menu.

The color changes you make are saved when you quit Word.

If you are using a CGA card, you must be in text mode to change colors. If you are in graphics mode and press F1 to see the color menu, the menu appears in monochrome. Use Alt-F9 to switch between text and graphics mode.

Controlling Highlight Speed

You can control how fast the highlight moves on the screen when you hold down a key. For example, if the highlight moves too slowly as you press the Down Arrow, Backspace, or Del key, you can tell Word to move the highlight faster.

If you use Word for some time and then reset the speed, you may find that you need some practice to get used to the new speed. For example, you will probably have grown accustomed to how long you need to hold down an Arrow key to move halfway across a line. Increasing the highlight speed will get you to the same place quicker, but don't be surprised if you overshoot your destination a few times at first. With time, you will grow accustomed to the new speed.

Controlling the highlight speed does not affect the speed of any functions that are not related to moving the highlight on the screen, such as saving text or paging through a document).

To control the highlight speed:

1. Select **O**ptions.

2. Under GENERAL OPTIONS, go to the *cursor speed* field. (Word also calls the highlight the *cursor.*)

3. Enter a number from 0 (slow) to 9 (fast).

4. Press **Enter** or click the command area.

The new highlight speed takes effect immediately. When you leave Word, the *cursor speed* setting is saved and will remain in effect during future Word sessions, unless you change it again.

Controlling Sound

How to get rid of the beep

Word beeps when you try to do something that it can't handle. For example, if you try to move the highlight beyond the beginning or end of a document, Word beeps a warning. Some people find this beep helpful; others find it annoying. If you are a member of the latter group, you can turn the beep off. A beepless Word is called *mute*. Follow these steps to turn off the beep:

1. Select **O**ptions.
2. Under GENERAL OPTIONS, go to the *mute* field.
3. Select **Y**es to mute (suppress) the beep. Select **N**o to have Word continue beeping.
4. Press **Enter** or click the command area.

The mute setting is effective immediately. It is saved by Word when you quit.

Getting Help

Word provides help at the press of a key. A typical Help screen is shown in Figure 2-28, where Word is giving instructions for deleting

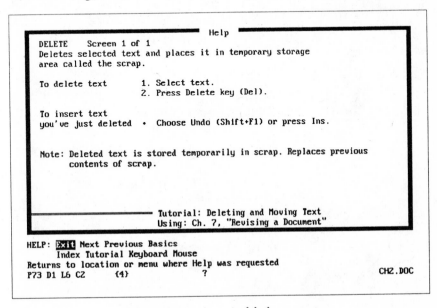

Figure 2-28. A typical help screen

text. Notice that the Learning Word tutorial section and the page in the Word manual are referenced at the bottom of the Help screen.

If you just need to jog your memory about how to perform a task, you can access Quick Help to check commands and command fields. Or, you can select from a list of other Quick Help topics. For more in-depth coverage, you can request Tutorial Help, which covers word-processing activities.

Quick Help

When you ask for Quick Help, the information you receive depends on what you are doing. For example, if you are editing text, you receive information about how to perform editing tasks. If you are using a command, you receive information about that particular command.

To use Quick Help, follow these steps:

1. Place your highlight on a command name or field or on the text you are editing.

2. If you are using the keyboard, press **Alt-H** (or **Alt-X-H** if a style sheet is attached to your document). If you are using a mouse, point to the help mark on the status line and click the left button.

3. A Help screen appears. Press **Next** or **PgDn** to go to the next screen, or press **Previous** or **PgUp** to go to the previous screen.

4. Select one of these options:

Index	to see an index of topics
Basics	to view information on how to use help
Tutorial	to use lessons (see "Tutorial Help" later in this chapter)
Keyboard	to learn about speed keys and other keyboard information
Mouse	to learn about using the mouse

5. Press Exit when you are done using the help information.

Word even provides instructions about how to use the Help facility. To get help on help:

1. Select **H**elp.

2. A Help screen appears. Press **N**ext or **PgDn** to go to the next screen, or press **P**revious or **PgUp** to go to the previous screen.

3. Select any of the options listed for the previous procedure.

4. Press **E**xit when you are done using the help information.

Tutorial Help

Using the tutorial within Word

If you want to learn how to perform a task without quitting Word, you can view the relevant lesson from the Learning Word tutorial through the Tutorial Help facility. Note that if are running Word under DOS and you want to use Tutorial Help, you need a minimum of 384 KB of memory. You don't need to be concerned about memory requirements if you are running Word under OS/2.

To access Tutorial Help:

1. Select **H**elp and then choose **T**utorial, or press **Alt-H** (or **Alt-X-H** if a style sheet is attached to your document) and then choose **T**utorial.

2. Select **L**esson or **I**ndex.

3. If you are not using a hard disk with Learning Word installed, a message appears asking you to insert the Word Essentials disk. If you see this message, select **Y**es.

4. Press **Ctrl** to move into the Tutorial lesson. Press the first letter of the option you want. Or, if you are using a mouse, click Course Controls and then click the option you want.

5. When you are done using Tutorial Help, press **Ctrl-Q** to return to Quick Help. Or, if you are using a mouse, point to *To return to Quick Help* and click the left button.)

6. To return to your document, select **E**xit.

Creating Documents

What should you do with a new word-processing program? Write a letter or make a list! This chapter covers the basics of how to create a simple document to get you up and running quickly. Once you've created a document, you'll have all kinds of questions about how to add or delete text, print the document, and perform other word-processing tasks like adding running heads. The skills and know-how needed to carry out these tasks are covered in later chapters.

A Word document can be any type of written material—for example, a report, a memo, an agenda, an outline, or a chapter of a book.

Length and Size Guidelines

Word puts some limits on the size and length of a document. However, a document that reached these limits would be much larger than most people would ever dream of creating.

Kilobytes and Megabytes

Document size and length is often referred to in terms of kilobytes (KB) and megabytes (MB). A byte is roughly one character. A kilobyte represents roughly one thousand characters, and a megabyte represents roughly one million characters.

Document Maximums

The maximum document size is 8.3 MB. Typical hard disks hold 10 or 20 MB of information or more. However, if you make backup copies of your documents on disks, remember that floppy disks hold considerably less than 8.3 MB of text. For example, a 3 1/2-inch disk holds about 720 KB of information.

It is important to limit your documents to a size that can be saved on whatever kind of disk you are using, whether a hard disk or floppy disks. A double-spaced page of text (25 lines) with a line length of 65 characters contains about 1625 characters. A 100-page double-spaced document will be 162,500 bytes or 162 KB long.

In addition to making sure you create documents that will fit on your storage medium, consider that the longer the document, the more cumbersome it can be to manipulate. The longer the document, the more time it takes to load, save, and move between pages. It makes sense to break long documents into sections or chapters to make them easier to handle. You can always combine separate documents later if you need to.

For example, this book was written using Microsoft Word. Each chapter was developed as a separate document. That way, backup copies of each chapter could be easily saved from hard disk to floppy disks for safe keeping. If necessary, the chapters could have been combined at the end of the writing process so that common formatting features could be applied to the entire manuscript.

Word sets other limits on documents. The maximum page length and width is 22 inches. The 22-inch maximum means Word can be used to print on different sizes of paper up to this size, which is the largest standard paper size. If you try to set a bigger page length or width, you will see this message:

```
Not a valid number
```

The maximum number of characters in a line is 255. The number of characters in a line is unrelated to the printed length of the line. With the typical 10 or 12 characters-per-inch type size and depending on how you have set your margins, Word allows you to see approximately 75 characters on a line at a time. Lines that are longer than 75 characters can be viewed by scrolling your highlight to the right on the screen.

The maximum size of a paragraph is 32 KB, or about 19 double-spaced pages. Who would want a 19-page paragraph? In Word, the word *paragraph* has a different meaning than the standard English definition. A paragraph is simply a block of text that ends with a paragraph mark. The block can be formatted as a unit, and Word attaches the formatting information to the paragraph mark. The following formatting characteristics can be set for a paragraph:

- Alignment (left, centered, right, and justified)
- Indents
- Line spacing (such as single or double spaced)
- The way one paragraph behaves in relationship to other paragraphs

Use the newline character to format several paragraphs at once

In Word, you have two ways to end what you typically think of as a paragraph: by inserting a paragraph mark (press Enter); and by inserting a newline character (press Shift-Enter). If you use the second way to create several "paragraphs," you can format all the paragraphs as a group and the formatting will be contained in the paragraph mark at the end of the group. Figure 3-1 illustrates this sometimes-confusing concept.

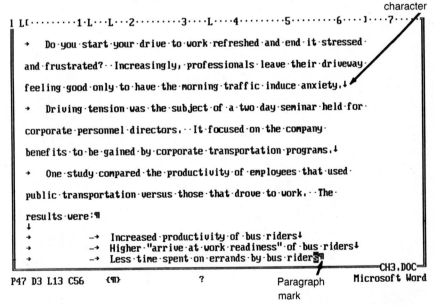

Figure 3-1. One paragraph that consists of three newline "paragraphs"

In Figure 3-1, the first two "paragraphs" end with the newline character (displayed on the screen as a downward-pointing arrow). The entire group of three paragraphs ends with the paragraph mark. The components of the group all have the same tab settings and are double spaced. This formatting is contained in the single paragraph mark that ends the group. As you can see, by using newline characters instead of paragraph marks, you can develop a paragraph that extends over several pages and then format the paragraph as a whole, rather than one component at a time.

Notice that the last paragraph in Figure 3-1 has different tab settings from the first three "paragraphs" and is single spaced. This formatting is contained in the paragraph mark after the word *riders*.

The following table summarizes the Word document size limits:

Maximum	Size
Size of a document	8.3 MB
Page length	22 inches
Page width	22 inches
Number of characters in a line	255
Paragraph size	32 KB (about 19 double-spaced pages)

Entering Text and Moving the Highlight

When you start Word with its default settings, you see the screen shown in Figure 3-2.

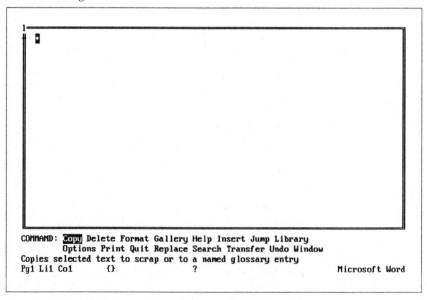

```
1
  ▓


















COMMAND: Copy Delete Format Gallery Help Insert Jump Library
         Options Print Quit Replace Search Transfer Undo Window
Copies selected text to scrap or to a named glossary entry
Pg1 Li1 Co1      {}                  ?                    Microsoft Word
```

Figure 3-2. An empty Word document screen

The screen has one window open and ready for you to enter text. The diamond symbol marks the end of the document. Your location on the screen is marked by a small box, which, as you already know, is called the highlight (or cursor). To begin writing a document, simply enter text. Significant keys for entering text and moving around the Word screen are shown in Figure 3-3.

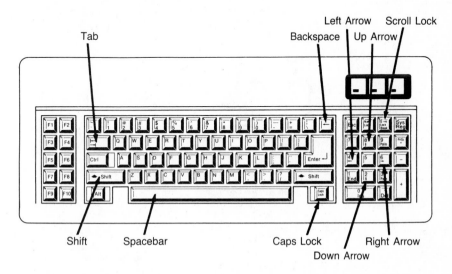

Figure 3-3. The keys used to enter text and move around the screen

Press the Spacebar to enter a blank space between words. If you press the Spacebar with your highlight in existing text, a space is inserted to the left of the highlight because, by default, Word is in *insert mode*. You can also set Word to *overtype mode*, in which case the character you type in replaces the character under the highlight. See Chapter 4, "Editing Documents," for information about insert and overtype modes.

Capital Letters, Numbers, and Symbols

To type in capital letters, hold down the Shift key when you press a letter key. Holding down the Shift key while pressing one of the number keys across the top of the keyboard enters the punctuation mark or symbol that appears on the key above the number.

If you want to type in all capital letters, press the Caps Lock (Capitals Lock) key. While Caps Lock is "on," you can type in a small letter by pressing Shift and that letter. Press Caps Lock again to turn capital letters off and go back to typing in small letters.

Wordwrap

In Word, as in most word processors, the text you type in wraps around when it reaches the right margin of your document. This is commonly referred to as *wordwrap*. Always allow Word to wrap the lines instead of pressing Enter when you reach the right margin, unless you want the line to end before reaching the right margin. That way, when you later insert or delete text, Word automatically realigns the text between the margins. Figure 3-4 illustrates this concept.

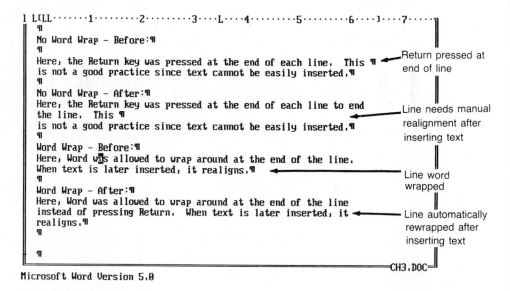

Microsoft Word Version 5.0

Figure 3-4. Inserting text in lines ended by pressing Enter versus inserting text in lines that Word had wordwrapped

As you enter text, remember to press the Enter key (or press Shift-Enter to insert a newline character) only when you end a paragraph or want to end a line before you reach the right margin.

Moving in All Directions

The letter, number, and symbol keys and the Spacebar all move the highlight forward on your screen by inserting characters to the left of the highlight. Other keys allow you to move in other directions. These keys are described in the following sections.

The Tab Key

To indent your text, you can use the Tab key. When you press Tab, the highlight moves to the next tab stop. You'll learn all about tab stops and how to set them in Chapter 6, "Formatting Documents."

The Backspace Key

To backup the highlight by deleting the character to its left, use the Backspace key. Do not use the Backspace key unless you want to delete characters. The Backspace key is used to delete characters in insert mode. In overtype mode, only the characters typed in since entering that mode can be deleted with the Backspace key.

The Arrow Keys

To move the highlight without changing existing text, use the Arrow keys. The Up Arrow key moves the highlight up one line. The Down Arrow key moves the highlight down one line. The Left Arrow and Right Arrow keys move the highlight one character left and right, respectively. At the end of a line, pressing the Right Arrow key moves your highlight to the beginning of the next line. At the beginning of a line, pressing the Left Arrow key moves your highlight to the end of the previous line.

You can use the Arrow keys to move the highlight only in the areas where you have entered text. The highlight will not move past the diamond mark at the end of your document. Nor will it move into areas beyond your margins or past a paragraph or newline symbol on a line.

Using Scroll Lock with the Arrow Keys

You can use the Scroll Lock key to change the effect of pressing the Arrow keys. When you press Scroll Lock, the letters SL appear in the status line at the bottom of the Word screen to remind you that you have turned on Scroll Lock.

Use Scroll Lock to scroll one screen at a time

Turning on Scroll Lock causes the screen to scroll when you press the Up Arrow or Down Arrow key. For example, if your highlight is in the middle of the screen, holding down the Down Arrow key with Scroll Lock turned off causes the highlight to move down toward the bottom of the window. Holding down the Down Arrow key with Scroll Lock turned on causes the highlight to remain in the same place while the text scrolls under it.

A drawback to working with Scroll Lock turned on is that the Right Arrow and Left Arrow keys are then more cumbersome to use. When Scroll Lock is turned on, pressing the Left Arrow key shifts the text one-third of a window (or less, depending on the amount of text

Caution

there is to shift) to the left. Pressing the Right Arrow key with Scroll Lock turned on shifts text one-third of a window (or less) to the right. This means that you essentially "lose" the use of the Left Arrow and Right Arrow keys for many word-processing tasks.

Moving Around with a Mouse

You can also scroll text using a mouse. You can scroll in all directions: up and down or left and right. You position the mouse pointer on the left screen border to scroll up or down and on the bottom border to scroll left or right (see Figure 3-5). Notice the up-and-down-pointing arrow on the left border. In graphics mode, the mouse highlight takes on this shape when it is on the left border, to remind you that you can scroll up or down. In text mode, the mouse highlight retains its usual shape.

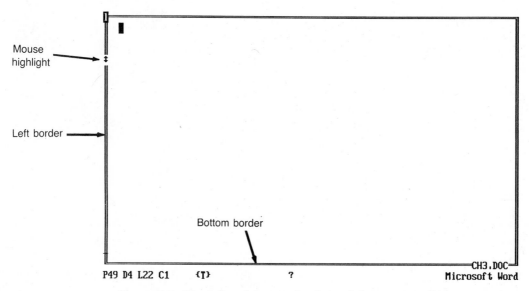

Figure 3-5. The left and bottom borders of the screen, which are used for scrolling with the mouse

With the mouse highlight on the left border, pressing the right mouse button causes the text to scroll up. Pressing the left button causes the text to scroll down. If you place the mouse highlight at the top of the left border and click a button, the text scrolls a line at a time. If you place the mouse highlight at the bottom of the left border, the text scrolls a screenful at a time. Placing the highlight anywhere between those two points causes larger or smaller chunks of text to scroll. For example, placing the highlight in the center of the border causes half a screenful to scroll.

To scroll up and down with the mouse:

1. Position the mouse highlight on the left window border, according to the amount you want to scroll.
2. Click the right button to cause the text to scroll up or the left button to cause the text to scroll down.

If your document is wider than the document window, you can use the mouse to scroll from left to right. Here are the steps:

1. Position the mouse highlight on the bottom window border, according to the amount you want to scroll.
2. Click the left button to cause the text to scroll left or the right button to cause the text to scroll right.

Using a mouse to quickly move around a document

You can also use the mouse to move to a different part of the document. If you place the mouse at the top of the left border and click both buttons at once, you are taken to the first page of the document. If you place the mouse at the bottom of the left border and click both buttons at once, you are taken to the last page of the document. If you place the mouse between those two points on the left border and click both buttons, you are taken to that relative position in the document. For example, if you have a 40-page document, placing the mouse highlight in the middle of the left border and pressing both buttons at the same time takes you to the middle of the document (page 20).

When you move around in a document by using the mouse in the left border, your highlight stays in the same place in your document. After you scroll (by clicking one button) or move to another page (by clicking both buttons), you can press any letter, number, or symbol key to return to your original spot. Be aware, however, that the key you press will be inserted in the text. Remember to delete it once you are back at the highlight. To avoid this problem, you might want to use an Arrow key to return to your spot. Then the only effect is that your highlight will be one line or character away from its original location.

Quick Highlight Movements

Moving a character or line at a time can be time consuming. With Word, you have many options for moving the highlight quickly on the screen. Though memorizing all the options can seem a little over-whelming at first, once you begin using the options, you will soon get the hang of things. At first, you may want to use the summary table shown later in this chapter as a quick reference to moving around a document. With time, you will find yourself referring to this table less and less frequently.

The following sections describe the quick highlight-movement options in detail.

Ctrl with Up Arrow and Down Arrow

Pressing the Ctrl key with the Up Arrow key causes the highlight to move to the first character of the paragraph (remember, "paragraphs" ending with newline symbols are considered to be only part of a para-graph). If you continue pressing Ctrl with the Up Arrow key, the high-light skips from the beginning of one paragraph to the beginning of the next.

Pressing Ctrl with the Down Arrow key causes your highlight to go to the first character of the next paragraph.

Ctrl with Left Arrow and Right Arrow

The Ctrl key can also be combined with the Left Arrow and Right Arrow keys to move the highlight. When you press Ctrl with the Left Arrow key, the highlight moves to the first letter of the word in which your highlight resides. If you continue to press Ctrl with the Left Arrow key, the highlight moves to the first character in the next word to the left. Press Ctrl with the Right Arrow key and the highlight moves to the first letter of the word to the right.

The Function Keys

You can use several of the function keys to highlight blocks of text. These keys are typically used to identify text for manipulation (such as text to be copied or deleted). However, these keys can also be viewed as quick ways to move your highlight.

Press F7 and the entire word to the left of your highlight is high-lighted. (If the word is followed by a punctuation mark, the punctua-tion is highlighted separately, not as part of the word.) If you enter text while the word is highlighted, the text is inserted to the left of the highlighted word. This is a speedy way to move to the left.

Press Shift-F7 and the sentence to the left of your highlight is highlighted. Begin typing and the new text is inserted to the left of the highlighted sentence. This is a quick way to move to the begin-ning of a previous sentence.

Press F9 and the paragraph you are in is highlighted. Begin typ-ing and the new text is inserted at the beginning of the paragraph. If you press F9 repeatedly, the next previous paragraph is highlighted. Using F9 is a quick way to move to the beginning of the current paragraph or a previous paragraph.

Press Shift-F9 to highlight the current line. Any text you type in is then inserted at the beginning of the line. (Actually, a better way to move to the beginning of the line is to use the Home key (see below), because you can move to the same place by pressing a single key instead of a key combination.)

Press F10 to highlight the paragraph in which your highlight currently resides. Press F10 again and the following paragraph is highlighted. If you type in text, the text is inserted at the beginning of the highlighted paragraph.

The Home and End Keys

The Home and End keys can be used alone and in combination with the Ctrl key to quickly move the highlight.

Pressing Home moves the highlight to the first character in the current line. (If you are already at the beginning of the line, pressing Home has no effect.) Pressing End moves the highlight to the last character in the line (assuming the highlight is not already there).

Holding down Ctrl and pressing Home moves your highlight to the first character of the first line of the window. The text remains where it is. Holding down Ctrl and pressing End moves the highlight to the first character of the last line of the window. Again, the text remains where it is.

The PgUp and PgDn Keys

The PgUp (page up) key moves the text one screenful backward in the document. The highlight stays on the same line of the window (not the same place in the text). The PgDn (page down) key moves the text one screenful forward in the document. Again, the highlight stays on the same line of the window.

Press Ctrl and PgUp simultaneously and your highlight is placed on the first character of the first line in the document. Press Ctrl and PgDn and your highlight is placed on the diamond mark at the end of your document.

The Jump Page Command

When you have more then one page in a document, you can use the Jump Page command to move quickly to any page. Pages are usually separated by dotted lines like this one:

....

Breaking a document into pages is described in detail in Chapter 4, "Editing Documents." As you'll learn in later chapters, division breaks can also cause page breaks.

To jump to another page in your document, you have to enter the number of the page to which you want to move. This page number must be a number assigned by Word, not a number in a running head. If the document has more than one division, you identify the page you want to jump to by entering the page number followed by the division number. For example, entering 10D2 will take you to page 10, division 2. (You'll learn more about divisions in Chapter 6, "Formatting Documents.")

Using Jump Page to quickly move around a document

If you enter a number that is greater than the last page number in the document, you are taken to the first character of the first line of the last page of the document. Contrast this action with that of Ctrl-PgDn, which takes you to the diamond mark at the very end of the document.

Jump Page can also be used to move quickly to the first character and first line of the page on which you are working. When you select Jump Page, the current page number is displayed in the *number* field. Simply press Enter to move to the top of the page.

To use Jump Page:

1. From the command menu, select **J**ump. In the *to* field, Page is highlighted. The message line tells you what the Jump Page command does:

   `Moves to specified page`

2. Select **P**age. This message appears on the message line:

   `Enter page number`

3. Enter the number of the page to which you want to jump and press **Enter**.

The text at the beginning of the page appears on your screen. The highlight is on the first character of the page.

A quick way to jump to a new page is to use the Alt key in combination with the F5 key. This approach involves pressing fewer keys and skips one menu level. Here are the steps:

1. Hold down **Alt** and press **F5**. You are taken straight to the Jump Page menu with the current page number shown in the *number* field. The message line instructs you to:

   ```
   Enter page number
   ```

2. Type in the number of the page you want to display and press **Enter**.

The text at the beginning of the page appears on your screen. The highlight is on the first character of the page.

If Jump Page doesn't seem to work, it will probably be because Word has not yet broken your document into pages. You need to print or paginate your document, by using the Print Printer or Print Repaginate command. Both commands calculate new page breaks, giving Jump Page the information it needs to be able to find a specified page.

Exercise: Entering Text

To get a bit of practice in performing the tasks just covered, try this exercise. Start Word (see Chapter 2, "Starting Microsoft Word," for instructions for your type of computer). Word displays a blank document window on your screen.

Notice that the highlight is on the diamond symbol that marks the end of the document. Begin your document by pressing the Tab key and then enter the following text (that's right, just type it in):

```
The committee charged with reorganizing the product
development group met on January 12th. All ten members were
present.
```

The Tab key moved your highlight to the first default tab stop set by Word. When you entered *January 12th*, you used the Shift key with the J key to capitalize the first letter of *January* and you used the number keys across the top of the keyboard to enter the number *12*.

Oops. We want to add a few words to the last sentence. With your highlight still on the diamond mark, press the Backspace key to delete the period and then press the Spacebar. Now enter:

```
in person or through a representative.
```

Now we need to end the paragraph, so press the Enter key at the end of the sentence. Notice that the highlight moves to a new line. The document looks like this:

```
     The committee charged with reorganizing the product
development group met on January 12th. All ten members were
present in person or through a representative.
```

Move to the beginning of the paragraph by pressing Ctrl-Up Arrow. Use the Right Arrow key to move the highlight to the *T* in *The*. Type in this sentence, followed by a space:

```
     Last fall, the board directed that our product group be
reorganized to reduce redundant efforts.
```

The text you type is inserted at the beginning of the paragraph. As you type, notice that Word rewraps the text to fit in the margins.

Press Home to move to the beginning of the line. Assuming you are using Word's default margins, the first character on the line is the *r* in *reorganized*. Enter this word followed by a space:

```
completely
```

Here is the result:

```
     Last fall, the board directed that our product group be
completely reorganized to reduce redundant efforts. The
committee charged with reorganizing the product development
group met on January 12th. All ten members were present in
person or through a representative.
```

This example gives you just a taste of how it feels to work in Word. You may want to try out other keys. If so, refer to the summary table that follows. This paragraph will be used in later examples, so when you've finished experimenting, return it to the state it is in now.

Quick-Reference Summary

The following table is a quick reference to the keys to press and methods to use to enter text and move around a Word document. You may need to refer to this table often when you first begin using Word. Once you become more familiar with Word, you will probably refer to the summary table less frequently.

Action	Result
Press the Spacebar	Enters a blank space between words

Action	Result
Press Shift and a letter (Caps Lock off)	Enters a capital letter
Press Shift and a number across the top of the keyboard	Enters the symbol shown above the number on the key
Press Caps Lock (toggle)	Switches between typing in all capital letters and small letters
Press Enter	Ends a paragraph
Press Tab	Moves the highlight to the next tab stop
Press Backspace	Moves the highlight backward by deleting the character to its left
Press Up Arrow (Scroll Lock off)	Moves the highlight up one line without disturbing the existing text display (unless the highlight is in the top line)
Press Up Arrow (Scroll Lock on)	The text (not the highlight) moves up one line on the screen
Press Down Arrow (Scroll Lock off)	Moves the highlight down one line without disturbing the existing text display (unless the highlight is in the bottom line)
Press Down Arrow (Scroll Lock on)	The text (not the highlight) moves down one line on the screen
Press Left Arrow (Scroll Lock off)	Moves the highlight one character to the left without disturbing the existing text display
Press Left Arrow (Scroll Lock on)	Shifts the text one-third of a window or less to the left
Press Right Arrow (Scroll Lock off)	Moves the highlight one character to the right without disturbing the existing text display
Press Right Arrow (Scroll Lock on)	Shifts the text one-third of a window or less to the right
Press Ctrl-Up Arrow	Moves the highlight to the first character of the paragraph
Press Ctrl-Down Arrow	Moves the highlight to the first character of the next paragraph
Press Ctrl-Left Arrow	Moves the highlight to the first letter of the word to the left

Action	Result
Press Ctrl-Right Arrow	Moves the highlight to the first letter of the word to the right
Press F7	Highlights the word to the left; text will be inserted to the left of the highlighted word
Press Shift-F7	Highlights the sentence to the left; text will be inserted to the left of the highlighted sentence
Press F9	Highlights the paragraph; text will be inserted at the beginning of the paragraph
Press Shift-F9	Highlights the line; text will be inserted at the beginning of the line
Press F10	Highlights the paragraph; text will be inserted at the beginning of the paragraph
Press Shift-F10	Highlights the whole document; text will be inserted at the beginning of the document
Press Home	Moves the highlight to the first character in the line
Press End	Moves the highlight to the last character in the line
Press Ctrl-Home	Moves the highlight to the upper-left corner of the window
Press Ctrl-End	Moves the highlight to the lower-left corner of the window
Press PgUp	Moves the highlight backward one screenful of text in the document
Press PgDn	Moves the highlight forward one screenful of text in the document
Press Ctrl-PgUp	Moves the highlight to the first character in the first line of the document
Press Ctrl-PgDn	Moves the highlight to the diamond mark at the end of the document

Action	Result
Select **J**ump **P**age command; enter page number	Moves the highlight to the beginning of the page indicated
Press Alt-F5; enter page number	Moves the highlight to the beginning of the page indicated
Place mouse highlight on left border; click right button	Text scrolls up according to highlight placement (close to top: fewer lines scroll up; close to bottom: more lines scroll up)
Place mouse highlight on left border; click left button	Text scrolls down according to highlight placement (close to top: fewer lines scroll up; close to bottom: more lines scroll up)
Place mouse highlight on bottom border; click left button	Text scrolls left
Place mouse highlight on bottom border; click right button	Text scrolls right
Place mouse highlight on left border; click both buttons	Displays the page that is in the same relative position in the document as the highlight placement on the border (close to top: closer to beginning of document; close to bottom: closer to end of document)

Printing the Screen

Most computers have the capability of printing the screen. This capability comes in handy when you want a printed copy of part of your text. It is especially useful if you have a problem that you want to discuss with Microsoft's technical-support department or a more knowledgeable friend. Using the print-screen capability, you can make a record of the problem situation and of the messages associated with the problem.

To test the print-screen feature, you need to make sure that your printer is set up, connected to your computer, and turned on, and that it has an adequate supply of paper. For information about setting up your computer, see Chapter 2, "Starting Microsoft Word." For information about printing with Word, see Chapter 5, "Printing Documents."

To test whether your computer can print the screen:

1. Hold down **Shift** and press the key marked **PrtSc** (for print screen). You may see a small highlight flash down the screen.

That's all there is to it: The screen is printed.
If the screen does not print:

- Check your computer manual to make sure the computer has print-screen capability.
- Check the cable between your computer and your printer to make sure it is secure.
- Make sure your printer is turned on and the "on line" light is lit.
- Make sure paper is available and the ribbon (if your computer has one) is operational.

Undoing Mistakes

You'll be happy to know that editing changes and formatting work can be undone in Word. If you make a mistake, you can often reverse your previous action as long as you do it immediately. The Undo command is especially useful when you have deleted text and want to get it back.

Undoing the Undo command

You can also undo the Undo command. That way, you can check what effects a change will have on your text and can then go back to the text as it was before the change. Having seen both versions, you can make a decision about which is best.

Unless you use the Undo command immediately after performing the action you want to undo, the action will not be easy to reverse. Word keeps track of the previous state of your document but doesn't maintain a record of all your actions.

How much does Undo undo? If you enter text and use Undo, the text you entered is deleted. If you delete text and use Undo, the text is restored. For example, suppose you enter the following line:

```
January March
```

Then you move your highlight between the two words and insert the word *February*:

```
January February March
```

If you use Undo, only the word *February* is deleted. To get *February* back, you can use Undo again.

You can also reverse commands with Undo. The following commands, most of which are covered in later chapters, can be reversed:

Copy
Delete
Format
Insert
Name
Transfer Merge
Undo

You cannot reverse these commands:

Exit
Help
Print
Transfer (except Transfer Merge)

If you try to use Undo when you haven't carried out an action that Word can reverse, Word tells you:

No edit to undo

Using Undo

To undo your last action by using the command menu:

1. Select Undo.
2. Your last action is undone. To replay the action, select Undo again.

To undo your last action by using a speed key:

1. Hold down **Shift** and press **F1**.
2. Your last action is undone. To replay the action, select Undo again.

Exercise: Undoing an Action

Try using the Undo command with this text, which you entered earlier:

```
    Last fall, the board directed that our product group be
completely reorganized to reduce redundant efforts. The
committee charged with reorganizing the product development
group met on January 12th. All ten members were present in
person or through a representative.
```

Press Ctrl-PgDn to move to the diamond mark at the end of the document. Press the Tab key and add this text:

```
The meeting started with opening remarks
```

In mid-sentence, you decide to kill the line. Press Shift-F1 to undo your typing. The line disappears. You change your mind. Press Shift-F1 again. The line is restored exactly as you entered it. Press the Left Arrow key to move your highlight to the end of the line. Complete the sentence:

```
The meeting started with opening remarks by Jim Tailor,
the newly appointed Director of Product Development.
```

Non-Printing Symbols

Word displays the text on the screen approximately the way it will look when printed. Some people want to see non-printing symbols, such as paragraph marks and the spaces inserted by pressing the Spacebar. You can set three levels of display for non-printing symbols:

- None
- Partial
- All

Figure 3-6 shows a screen with no non-printing symbols, Figure 3-7 shows the same screen with a partial display of non-printing symbols, and Figure 3-8 shows the screen with all non-printing symbols displayed.

When the option that controls the level of display is set to None, symbols that will not be printed are hidden on the screen. The exceptions are page breaks and hidden text. In the example, the hidden text *.c.* appears, marking a heading for inclusion in a table of contents. (The display of hidden text is controlled separately through the

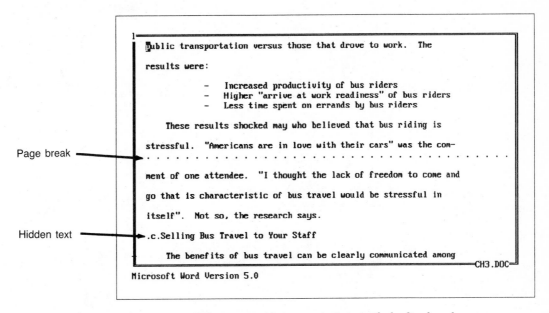

Figure 3-6. No non-printing symbols displayed

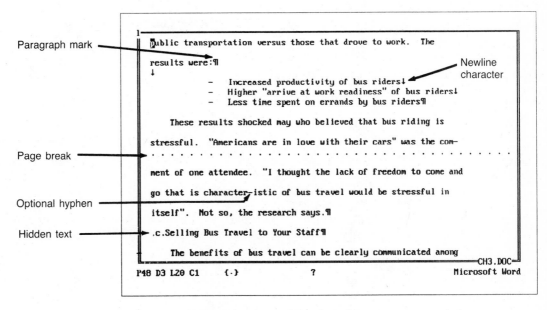

Figure 3-7. Partial display of non-printing symbols

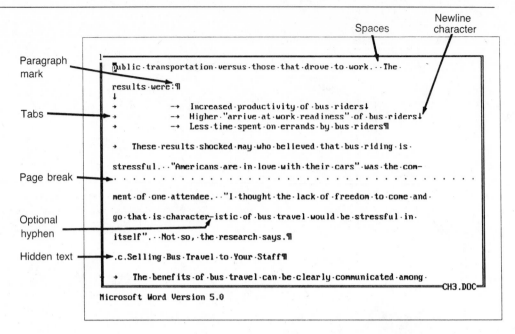

Figure 3-8. All non-printing symbols displayed

Options menu and through the Print Options menu. See "Hidden Text" in this chapter.)

When the option is set to Partial, these symbols appear:

- Paragraph marks
- Newline characters
- Optional hyphens

When the option is set to All, the symbols that appear at the Partial level appear, as well as spaces, which are represented by dots, and tab marks, which are represented by right-pointing arrows.

Show non-printing symbols to catch errors

Which setting you use depends on your preference. Some people like to see all the non-printing symbols. That way, if there is a problem, such as an extra tab mark where there should be a space, they can usually discover and correct it immediately. Other people find the non-printing symbols a distraction and prefer to see text only. A good use of this option is to work with the display set to All to catch errors and then change the setting to display the document with no symbols before you print, to check the appearance of the document.

When you set the status of non-printing symbols, Word maintains that setting until you set it again, even if you quit the program. To set the status of non-printing symbols, follow these steps:

1. Select **O**ptions.

2. Under Window Options, move the highlight to the *show non-printing symbols* field.

3. Use one of two methods to complete the selection:

   - If you are using the keyboard, select **N**one, **P**artial, or **A**ll and press **Enter**.

   - If you have a mouse, point to None, Partial, or All and click the right button.

The screen changes immediately to reflect your choice.

Hidden Text

Some of the work you do in Word will involve adding hidden text. For example, when this book was written in Word, each heading had a hidden-text entry that marked it for the table of contents. This is a sample of one of those entries:

`.c.Hidden Text`

The hidden .c. tells Word that the heading following the .c. and ending with a paragraph mark is to be placed in the table of contents. On a color monitor, hidden text appears in a different color. In text mode, hidden text typically appears with a dotted underline.

The uses of hidden text   Hidden text is used to:

- Mark index entries
- Identify table-of-contents entries
- Set off notes and comments
- Generate field labels
- Handle other functions that require special marks that do not print

Once you have entered hidden text, it doesn't have to actually stay hidden. You can determine whether it is displayed on the screen, and you can decide whether it is printed with the rest of the document.

Displaying Hidden Text

When you are entering hidden text, you will find it easier if you can see what you enter. That way, you are less likely to inadvertently move the hidden text to another spot or to insert other text around it inappropriately. It is simple to turn the display of hidden text on and off. The display setting is maintained in Word until you change it.

To turn the display of hidden text on or off:

1. Select **O**ptions.
2. Under Window Options, go to the *show hidden text* field.
3. Do one of the following to complete the selection:
   - If you are using the keyboard, press **Y**es or **N**o and then press **Enter**.
   - If you have a mouse, point to Yes or No and click the right button.

The screen display immediately puts your selection into effect.

Entering Hidden Text

A few specific hidden-text codes are defined by Word for such functions as creating indexes and tables of contents. These codes are discussed in this book along with those functions. Here, we'll take a look at hidden text you might want to enter for your own purposes.

To use a command to format personal notes as hidden text, follow these steps:

1. Select the text you want to hide by highlighting it. For example, you might position your highlight on the first character of the sentence you want to select, press **F6**, and then press the **Right Arrow** key until the whole sentence is highlighted. You can press **F6** again to get rid of the highlight if you change your mind. (Using F6 and other options for selecting text is discussed in Chapter 4, "Editing Documents.")
2. Select **F**ormat **C**haracter.
3. In the *hidden* field, select **Y**es to mark the text as hidden or **N**o to remove hidden-text status.
4. Press **Enter**.

The text is now marked as hidden.

To use the keyboard to format your notes as hidden text, do the following:

1. Select the text (see step 1 above).
2. Press **Alt-E** (or **Alt-X-E** if you have a style sheet attached to your document).

That's all there is to it! The text is now marked as hidden.

To use the keyboard to remove hidden-text status, follow these steps:

1. Select the text.
2. Press **Alt-Spacebar** (or **Alt-X-Spacebar**).

The on-screen formatting for hidden text is removed. The selection has reverted to "normal" text.

Printing Hidden Text

Using the Print Options menu, you can control whether or not hidden text is printed with the rest of your document.

1. Select **P**rint **O**ptions.
2. In the *hidden text* field, select **Y**es to print the hidden text with the document or **N**o to suppress printing of the hidden text.
3. Press **Enter**.

Exercise: Formatting Hidden Text

Use the paragraphs you have already entered to practice formatting hidden text. Select Options and make sure the *show hidden text* field is set to Yes. Then press Enter to return to the document screen. Position your highlight at the end of the last paragraph, press the Spacebar, and add this sentence:

NOTE: Check his title.

so that the document looks like this:

Last fall, the board directed that our product group be completely reorganized to reduce redundant efforts. The

```
committee charged with reorganizing the product development
group met on January 12th. All ten members were present in
person or through a representative.
     The meeting started with opening remarks by Jim Tailor,
the newly appointed Director of Product Development. NOTE:
Check his title.
```

With your highlight on the diamond mark after the period, press Shift-F7. The sentence you just typed in is highlighted. Press Alt-E to format the text as hidden. Depending on the kind of monitor you have, the text is now distinguished from other paragraphs by a dotted underline or a different color.

To check that you have indeed applied the hidden-text format to the text, place the highlight anywhere in the sentence and select For-mat Character. You will see that the *hidden* field is now set to Yes.

Document Storage

Once you have developed your document, you will want to save it on your hard disk or on a floppy disk. *Transfer* is the term Word uses for moving documents between storage in RAM and storage on disk. Word sets a default location for document storage. If you have a two-floppy-disk system, drive B is used as the default. If you have a hard-disk system, the current directory (usually the WORD direc-tory) is used as the default. Before we can discuss how you change the storage location, you need to understand the basics of directories and paths.

Directories

You create directories to organize your files. You might, for example, want to store the files for different software programs in discrete loca-tions. You can also use directories to separate your document files.

Understanding directories   Directories are most useful for organizing the files on hard disks. Figure 3-9 shows an example of how a hard disk might be organized. This example illustrates why directories are usually described as upside-down trees. The top level is called the *root* and is identified with a slash (\) by most operating systems. In the example, the level below the root includes a directory for the operating-system files (DOS, in this case), a directory for the Word program files (WORD), and a directory for the program files for a popular spreadsheet pro-gram called EXCEL, which was also developed by Microsoft. The

DOS directory has no subdirectories. The WORD directory has two subdirectories. One is called DOC and includes miscellaneous documents, and the other is called PROP (for *proposals*). Three document files (such as KIMLET.DOC) are stored in the DOC subdirectory. The EXCEL directory includes only one subdirectory, XLS, which could be used to store all the spreadsheets created with Microsoft Excel.

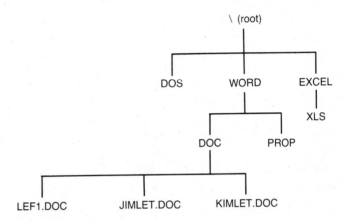

Figure 3-9. An example of how a hard disk might be organized

You can create any number of directories and subdirectories and give them any names that make sense to you in your work. Operating-system commands, like MAKE DIRECTORY (MD), allow you to set up directories.

Creating a Directory

To create a directory, first make sure you are in the directory immediately above the one you want to create. Then follow these steps:

1. Type in the following, substituting the name you want to give your directory for DOC:

   `MD DOC`

2. Press **Enter**.

To go to the directory you've just created, you use the CHANGE DIRECTORY (CD) command. Follow these steps:

1. Type in the following, substituting the full path of the directory for DOC:

CD *DOC*

2. Press **Enter**.

See your operating-system manual for more information about the commands related to directories.

Paths

As you will see later, you can tell Word where to look for the documents you need by entering a *path* that leads to the document. The path specifies the route from the root to the directory containing the file you want. In Figure 3-9, the path from the root to KIMLET.DOC is:

\WORD\DOC\KIMLET.DOC

When you change the document storage location, you need to enter both the drive and the path of the new storage location. For example, this drive and path instructs Word to locate documents on drive C, in the directory called WORD, and in the subdirectory named DOC:

C:\WORD\DOC

Changing the Document Storage Location

To change the default storage location, you use the Transfer Options command. The drive and path you specify for the storage location can be saved as the new storage-location default, meaning that Word will use this drive and path even if you leave and reenter the program. You can also set a drive and path for Word to use during the current session of Word but have the old default restored if you leave and reenter the program. It is obviously most efficient to save the drive and path that will be used most often as the default.

Select Transfer Options to change your active directory

As you work, you can change the location at any time by using the Transfer Options command. You can also change the location to save or load specific documents.

To change the document storage location:

1. Select Transfer **O**ptions.

2. In the *save between sessions* field, select **Y**es to retain the location between Word sessions or **N**o to use the location for this session of Word only.

3. In the *setup* field, enter the drive and path of the new storage location. To see the options you have, you can press **F1**. A screen like the one shown in Figure 3-10 appears. As you can see, other available drives and directories are shown in brackets. In this example, selecting [..] takes you to the next higher directory, selecting [DOC] sets the path to the DOC directory, and selecting [A:] sets the path to the A drive. Highlight your selection and press **Enter**.

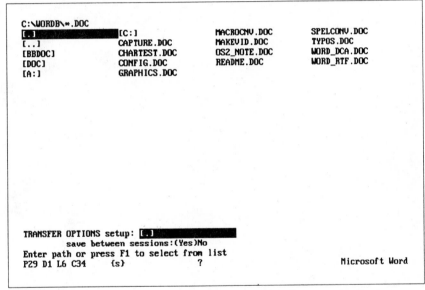

```
C:\WORDB\*.DOC
[.]                  [C:]          MACROCNV.DOC      SPELCONV.DOC
[..]                 CAPTURE.DOC   MAKEVID.DOC       TYPOS.DOC
[BBDOC]              CHARTEST.DOC  OS2_NOTE.DOC      WORD_DCA.DOC
[DOC]                CONFIG.DOC    README.DOC        WORD_RTF.DOC
[A:]                 GRAPHICS.DOC




TRANSFER OPTIONS setup: [.]
          save between sessions:(Yes)No
Enter path or press F1 to select from list
P29 D1 L6 C34       {s}              ?              Microsoft Word
```

Figure 3-10. The options available for use in the Transfer Options setup field

You are returned to your document with the new storage location set. You can select Transfer Options again to check that the setting is correct.

Exercise: Using Transfer Options

If you haven't already done so, check that Word will save your documents on the drive and in the directory you want. Select Transfer Options. In the *setup* field, enter the correct drive and directory path. Press Enter when you are done. You will save your document soon. The default you have set here will appear at that time.

Saving Documents

Saving your documents regularly is probably the most important task to remember to perform as you use Word. While you are working on a document, it is held in RAM. This type of computer memory is temporary; it lasts only as long as your computer is turned on and as long as you have not quit Word. If there is a power cut in the middle of your Word session or if you quit Word without saving your document, any changes you have made to your document are lost.

A common way to lose your work is by accident. Accidents do and will happen. Someone trips over the power cord and pulls out the plug; the electricity fails; the computer malfunctions. When an accident happens, you'll avoid frustration and loss of time if you have recently saved your work.

You can use Word's autosave feature to make sure changes to a document are saved regularly. Only the edits are automatically saved, however. After the first autosave, Word cannot automatically save your document in its entirety. (See "Autosave" later in this chapter for more information.)

Word takes the precaution of displaying a SAVE message in the status line when the storage space in RAM that Word needs for keeping track of your changes is starting to get low. Word will also remind you to save your work before quitting the program. When you quit, Word detects whether you have made any changes since you last saved the document. If you have, the following message appears:

```
Enter Y to save changes to document, N to lose changes, or
Esc to cancel
```

Unless you intend to discard your changes, always press Y to save the document.

Backup Copies

When you save a document in Word, the previous version of your document is retained on the same disk as the new version. Word gives the previous version the file extension .BAK (for backup).

Because Word's .BAK version is not the most recent version of your document and because it is stored on the same disk as the latest version, you may want to make backup copies of your documents on a separate disk. Backup copies are important in case your original disk becomes damaged, you accidentally delete the document, or you incorrectly edit the document and want to go back to the earlier version.

Many people store backup copies of important documents "off site." For example, suppose you keep the original copies in the office and the copies are lost, stolen, or damaged by fire. As long as you have kept a backup at another location—at home, perhaps—you will be able to start again without too much trouble. A safe deposit box at a bank is a good place to keep backup copies of critical work.

Rotate backup disks for extra file protection

Another precautionary measure is to rotate the disks on which you make backup copies and to have a regular schedule for backing up documents. That way, if somehow both the original disk and the disk containing the backup copy are destroyed, you still have a recent version of the disk available. For example, you might have two sets of disks for backup copies. You would back up documents on set 1 on Fridays, and you would back up documents on set 2 on Wednesdays. The "oldest" backup set would be used to make the new backup copies each time.

With Word, you must save document by document to create backup copies. Each document must be in RAM and on your screen so that you can save it with the Transfer Save command. If you have many documents to back up, you may want to use your operating system's BACKUP command or use its COPY command with wildcard characters. See your DOS or OS/2 manual for more information.

There are also backup programs on the market that speed the process of backing up many documents.

If you have many documents to backup, you may want to consider using a storage medium other than floppy disks. For example, tape storage devices can hold many more files than disks and can cut down the time it takes to perform backups.

Using the Transfer Save Command

To save a document, you use the Transfer Save command. When you save a document for the first time, you will be asked to:

- Name the document
- Complete a summary information sheet

Naming Documents

To save a document, you must give it a name. A document name can be up to eight characters long. You can use numbers, letters, and some symbols. The following symbols are not valid:

$$* \ + \ = \ [\ ]: " : < > , . ? |$$

Do not use spaces in document names. If you enter characters that Word does not accept, Word highlights the unacceptable character and those that follow it. This message is displayed:

`Not a valid file name`

Simply type in the name again, this time choosing valid characters.

When you enter a name, make sure that the name is not already in use. Otherwise, you run the risk of accidently "saving over," or replacing, the existing document. If you enter a name that is already being used for another document, Word provides this warning:

`The file already exists. Enter Y to replace or Esc to Cancel`

To lose the existing document, you can enter Y for Yes. The old document is given the extension .BAK and the new document is saved with the name you entered. If you don't want to lose the existing document, press Esc to cancel the save operation and start over.

When you name a new document and save it, Word automatically appends the .DOC extension to the name you specify. You can enter another extension if you want. However, it is usually best to stick with the .DOC extension. That way, when you perform operations such as loading documents, you can easily display a list of documents with the .DOC extension to select from. Figure 3-11 shows such a list.

Regardless of the extension you use, Word keeps the previous version of the document when you save a new version, by replacing the extension with the .BAK extension.

When you name files, use a name that reminds you of the document's contents. For example, the following document contains a letter to a company called CromoCo:

DOC1

This is a better name:

LETCROMC

You may want to use naming conventions that are based on the types of documents you typically create. For example, all documents containing letters could begin with *let*:

```
C:\WORDB\BBDOC\*.DOC
APPA.DOC          CH2.DOC        CH8.DOC          TOWLB.DOC
APPB.DOC          CH3.DOC        DDLLET.DOC       WORDTO.DOC
APPC.DOC          CH4.DOC        JUNK.DOC         [..]
BBOOKOUT.DOC      CH5.DOC        JUNK5.DOC        [A:]
BBTODO.DOC        CH6.DOC        RTF.DOC          [C:]
CH1.DOC           CH7.DOC        SAVETO.DOC




TRANSFER LOAD filename: APPA.DOC            read only: Yes(No)

Enter filename or press F1 to select from list (3868672 bytes free)
P33 D1 L8 C9      {t}                   ?              Microsoft Word
```

Figure 3-11. The list of .DOC files from which you can select a document for loading

> LETJOHN
>
> LETSTATS
>
> LETCLUB

All documents containing reports could begin with *r* for *report* followed by the month, year, and work group:

> R0189PRD
>
> R0289MKT
>
> R1289SAL

File names are not etched in stone. Files can be renamed at any time. See Chapter 14, "Handling Files and Running DOS Commands," for more information.

Summary Information Sheets

When you save a document for the first time, you have the option of entering information about the document on what is called a summary sheet. Later, you can search, edit, or print this information. Figure 3-12 shows a summary sheet that has been filled in for the document displayed on the screen. Notice that the summary sheet includes information about who worked on the document, keywords to search, comments, and dates. Figure 3-13 shows a printed version of the same summary sheet. The character count (number of characters in the document) is added to the printed information.

```
┌─┬────────────────────────────────────────────────────────────────┐
│1│                                                                  │
│ │  ▓▓One·study·compared·the·productivity·of·employees·that·used·   │
│ │                                                                  │
│ │  public·transportation·versus·those·that·drove·to·work.··The·    │
│ │                                                                  │
│ │  results·were:¶                                                  │
│ │  ↓                                                               │
│ │  →          →   Increased·productivity·of·bus·riders↓            │
│ │  →          →   Higher·"arrive·at·work·readiness"·of·bus·riders↓ │
│ │  →          →   Less·time·spent·on·errands·by·bus·riders¶        │
│ │                                                                  │
│ │  →  These·results·shocked·may·who·believed·that·bus·riding·is·   │
│ │                                                                  │
│ │  stressful.··"Americans·are·in·love·with·their·cars"·was·the·com─│
│ │  ·  ·  ·  ·  ·  ·  ·  ·  ·  ·  ·  ·  ·  ·  ·  ·  ·  ·  ·  ·  ·  · │
```

```
SUMMARY INFORMATION
   title: reptbus                         version number:
   author: j. jackson                     creation date: 05/11/89
   operator: k. smitty                    revision date: 06/12/89
   keywords: report bus productivity car employees
   comments: report on how commuting alternatives increase productivity▮
Enter text
P5Z D3 L19 C1      {x}              ?                    Microsoft Word
```

Figure 3-12. The summary sheet as it appears on the screen

```
     filename: C:\WORDB\BBDOC\REPTBUS.DOC
     title: reptbus
     author: j. jackson
     operator: k. smitty
     keywords: report bus productivity car employees
     comments: report on how commuting alternatives increase
        productivity
     version number:
     creation date: 05/11/89
     revision date: 06/12/89
     char count: 62882
```

Figure 3-13. The printed summary sheet

In this chapter, we will cover filling in summary sheets. For more information on searching or editing summary sheets, see the discussion of the Library Document-retrieval command in Chapter 14, "Handling Files and Running DOS Commands." To learn how to print summary sheets, see Chapter 5, "Printing Documents."

Be consistent when filling out summary sheets

To search summary sheet information, you enter the text or date ranges you want to find. Word matches the characters you enter exactly. You can choose whether Word should take case (capital letters are uppercase and small letters are lowercase) into consideration while searching. Because of the need to match characters, it is important to be consistent in how you enter text in the summary sheet.

For example, if your name is James Thomas Rundy, you should be consistent when entering your name in the *author* field. You could enter JTR, JT Rundy, Jim Rundy, or Jimmy R. However, unless you pick one version of your name and stick to it, your summary sheets will be difficult and time consuming to search because you will have to perform a separate search on each version of your name.

To move between fields on the summary sheet, you use the Tab or Arrow keys. Don't use Enter; Word will assume you are done with the summary sheet and will finish saving the document.

These are the fields you can fill in on the summary sheet when you first save a document:

Field	Input
title	A descriptive title for the document; 40 characters or less
author	The author's name (be consistent); 40 characters or less
operator	The name of the person who worked on the document (again, be consistent); 40 characters or less
keywords	Descriptive words that categorize the document; up to 80 characters (including spaces)
comments	Notes about the document; up to 220 characters
version number	The version number of the document (any number or identifier you desire that is meaningful to help organize your work); up to 10 characters
creation date	Word enters this date automatically when you create the document. Though you can edit this field on the screen, Word will change it back to reflect your computer's system date when the summary sheet is saved.

revision date   Word enters this date each time you update the document. Though you can edit this field on the screen, Word will change it back to reflect your computer's system date when the summary sheet is saved.

If you don't want to fill out a summary sheet, you can leave it blank and simply press Enter.

The Summary Sheet Option

You can specify whether you want to create summary sheets with your documents by using the Options command.

To turn summary-sheet display on and off:

1. Select **O**ptions.
2. Under General Options, go to the *summary sheet* field.
3. Select **Y**es to create summary sheets or **N**o to skip the creation of summary sheets for new documents.
4. Press **Enter**.

The setting takes effect immediately and is saved even after you leave Word. You can, of course, change the setting at any time.

Saving New Documents

Now that we have covered how to name documents and complete a summary sheet, it is time to proceed with the steps for saving a document.

To save a document for the first time:

1. Select **T**ransfer **S**ave.
2. The Transfer Save menu appears. In the *filename* field, enter the drive and path (if you want the document to be stored in a location other than the default) and a unique document name of eight characters or less. If you don't specify another extension, Word will add the .DOC extension.
3. In the *format* field, make sure the Word format is selected.
4. Press **Enter**.

A message like this one appears while Word saves the document:

```
Saving C:\WORD\DOC\MYDOC.DOC
```

When Word is done, the number of characters saved appears briefly and you are returned to the document.

Saving Existing Documents

Ways to save a document

There are several ways to save a document:

- Use the Transfer Save command to manually save the document. You can set the drive, path, and file name during the process.
- Use a speed key to manually save the document. Word assumes you want to use the default drive, path, and file name.
- Save the document in a different location.

Saving Existing Documents with Transfer Save

Remember to save your documents every 15 minutes or whenever you have entered text or made changes that you would hate to lose. Many users like to save their documents regualarly even if they are using Word's autosave feature, because autosave saves recent edits only, not the whole document.

When you save an existing document, Word knows the document's name because the name was used to load the document. As a result, the process is a little more streamlined than saving a document for the first time. You do not have to name the document or deal with the summary sheet. Here are the steps:

1. Select **T**ransfer **S**ave.
2. The Transfer Save *filename* and *format* fields appear. Make sure the Word format is selected. Also check to make sure the drive, path, and file name are correct. You can change any of the information if required.
3. Press **Enter**.

A message like this one appears while Word saves the document:

```
Saving C:\WORD\DOC\MYDOC.DOC
```

When Word is done, the number of characters saved appears briefly and you are returned to the document.

Saving Existing Documents with a Speed Key

The quickest way to save a document is to press Ctrl-F10. When you do this, the document is saved with the drive, path, file name, and format that is specified when you select Transfer Save. If you have any doubt that this information is correct, select the Transfer Save command and check the document storage location before pressing Enter to save the document.

To save an existing document:

1. Hold down **Ctrl** and press **F10**.

2. If the document has no name, Word presents the Transfer Save menu so that you can enter a name in the *filename* field and press **Enter**.

   As Word begins the save process, it displays the document storage location and format. You cannot change the location or format at this time or press Esc to stop the process. Once Word begins saving the document, a message like this appears:

   ```
   Saving C:\WORD\DOC\MYDOC.DOC
   ```

3. If this is the first time you have saved the document, a blank summary sheet appears. Complete the fields and press **Enter** when you are finished.

When Word is done, the number of characters saved appears briefly and you are returned to the document.

Saving in a Different Storage Location

As you know, the default drive and path that appear when you save a document is set through the Transfer Options command. If you have a hard-disk system, you can save a backup copy of your document by simply changing the drive and/or path designation and saving on a floppy disk. If you have a two-floppy-disk system, you can save a backup copy simply by saving first on one disk, swapping disks, and then saving again.

Here's the procedure to follow:

1. Select Transfer **S**ave.

2. The Transfer Save menu appears. Make sure the Word format is selected in the *format* field.

3. In the *filename* field, enter the drive and path (if required) and a unique file name of eight characters or less. If you don't enter an extension, Word automatically adds the .DOC extension.

4. Press **Enter**.

5. If a document with the specified name already exists on the disk, a message like this one appears:

`File already exists. Enter Y to replace or Esc to cancel.`

Press **Y**, and Word immediately begins to save the file. A message like this one appears:

`Saving A:MYDOC.DOC`

6. If the Options *summary sheet* field is set to Yes, Word displays the document's summary sheet so that you can update it. (This only happens when you change the drive and/or path designation.) Update the summary sheet and press **Enter** or just press **Enter** to save the document without updating the summary sheet.

When Word is done, the number of characters saved appears briefly and you are returned to the document.

The drive and path designation you set remains in effect until you leave Word. The next time you start Word, the defaults set through Transfer Options will again be in effect.

Exercise: Saving a Document

If you haven't already done so, save your document now. Press Ctrl-F10. In the Transfer Save *filename* field, enter this name and press Enter:

PDREORG

Since this is the first time you've saved the document, the summary sheet appears. Fill in the fields with the appropriate entries, using Tab to move from field to field. (You don't have to fill in all the information now. You can always update the summary sheet by using the Library Document-retrieval command, which is discussed in detail in Chapter 14, "Handling Files and Running DOS Commands.") Press Enter when you are done. The document is saved in the document storage location you entered earlier using the Transfer Options command. Word automatically adds the .DOC extension to the file name.

Autosave

You can set up Word to periodically save the edits you have made to your document. That way, changes can be retrieved from backup files in case an accident (such as a power loss) occurs. When Word saves your document edits, it saves style sheets and changes to the glossary as well. (You'll learn about Word's style-sheet and glossary features in later chapters.)

You determine how often Word should automatically save your changes. And you decide whether Word should carry out autosave automatically or only when you indicate. In addition, Word saves your changes whenever the SAVE message appears in the status line.

Often, Word users decide not to use autosave because the process takes some time. While Word is autosaving, you cannot edit your document. The first autosave saves the entire document and can be bothersome if the document is long. Subsequent autosaves only save new edits and are usually performed quickly. Even though autosave can be a bit annoying, it is a useful precaution against loss of work. It is worthwhile turning it on and getting used to how it functions.

Don't rely on Autosave alone

Even when you use autosave, you will want to periodically save your whole document—not just the edits—using Transfer Save (or Transfer Allsave, which is covered later in this chapter). When you use Transfer Save or Transfer Allsave, the autosave backup file is deleted. The next autosave backup file contains only the edits made since you last used Transfer Save. The backup files are also deleted when you quit Word.

When Word autosaves, it gives the backup files it creates the same name as the document file (or with the name Untitled if you have not yet assigned a name to the document). These extensions are added:

.SVD   for the document backup file

.SVS   for the style-sheet backup file

.SVG   for the glossary backup file

Setting Autosave

To turn autosave on and off:

1. Select **O**ptions.
2. In the *autosave* field, enter the number of minutes between each autosave. (For example, enter *20* if you want Word to save every 20 minutes.) Or, if you do not want Word to autosave, press the **Backspace** key to delete the number in the field.

3. In the *autosave confirm* field, select **Yes** if you want to be prompted before each autosave with this message:

```
About to backup changes with autosave. Enter Y to backup
or Esc to cancel.
```

Or, select **No** for Word to interrupt your work to autosave.

4. Press **Enter**.

So what happens if your system fails when you are using autosave? The next time you start Word, a message appears inquiring whether you want to recover the backup files or ignore them:

- If you select Recover, each backup file is restored with the appropriate extension (.DOC, .STY, or .GLY). The files are saved on the Word program disk or in the WORD directory.
- If you select Ignore, the backup files are left as is. You can recover them later. If you want to load the document, rename the autosave files first. Otherwise, the autosave files will be deleted when you save the document or quit Word. As long as you rename the autosave files, they will remain intact.

Exercise: Autosaving

If you have not used autosave before, turn it on now. Select Options and enter *15* in the *autosave* field. In the *autosave confirm* field, select No. Every 15 minutes, you will see a message that Word is automatically saving the edits you have made since the last time you saved the full document.

Saving in Different Formats

You can save documents in formats other than the regular Word format. The most popular alternate format is ASCII (American Standard Code for Information Interchange). ASCII is the "universal language" of computers. Many personal-computer programs accept ASCII-formatted files. ASCII is also a useful file format to use if you are transferring text over a modem and telephone lines. Another alternate format, RTF (Rich Text Format), can be useful in transferring files over 7-bit communication lines.

Word saves documents in four different formats

Through Transfer Save, you can save a document in:

- **Word format:** The file is saved as a regular Word document with all formatting intact.

- **Text-only format:** The file is saved as an unformatted ASCII file, without the line breaks created by Word wordwrapping. The file retains tabs and carriage returns.

- **Text-only-with-line-breaks format:** The file is saved as an unformatted ASCII file, but with the line breaks created by Word wordwrapping. ASCII carriage returns are added at the end of every line. Spaces replace tabs. Use this option if you want lines to be a particular length.

- **RTF format:** RTF is sometimes called *Interchange Format*. This text format was created by Microsoft to facilitate the communication of Word documents. Word's formatting is encoded in ASCII so that it can be read by other programs. If a style sheet is attached to the document, the style sheet is transferred as well. When you save a document in RTF format, the document is first saved as a Word document with the .DOC extension. Then the document is converted to an RTF file.

Note to DOS/Macintosh users: RTF is not the same as RFT.

You can also use Word to convert documents to and from other word-processing formats. See Appendix D in the *Reference to Microsoft Word* for information about converting Word documents to other word-processing formats.

Saving Documents in ASCII Format

To save a document in ASCII format:

1. Select **T**ransfer **S**ave.

2. The Transfer Save menu appears. In the *format* field, highlight the ASCII format you want:
   - Text-only
   - Text-only-with-line-breaks

3. In the *filename* field, enter the drive, path, and file name, including the file name extension (if necessary).

4. Press **Enter**.

5. This message may appear:

   `Enter Y to confirm loss of formatting`

   Press **Y**.

Word immediately saves the file to the designated storage location. A message like this one appears while Word is saving the file:

`Saving: C:\TEXTTO.ASC`

Once the file is saved, the number of characters appears. You can then continue working in Word.

Saving Documents in RTF Format

To save a document in RTF format:

1. Select **Transfer S**ave.
2. The Transfer Save menu appears. In the *format* field, highlight **R**TF as the format you want.
3. In the *filename* field, enter the drive, path, and file name. Do not add an extension.
4. Press **Enter.**

Word saves the document with a .DOC extension. A message like this one appears:

`Saving as C:\WORD\DOC\NEWLET.DOC`

Next, the document is converted to an RTF file with a .RTF extension. A message like this one appears:

`Converting to: C:\WORD\DOC\NEWLET.RTF`

Once the file is saved, the number of characters appears. You can then continue working in Word.

Viewing ASCII and RTF Files

Once you have saved an ASCII or RTF file, you can view the file by loading it back into Word. However, the file may be changed when you do this. (See Chapter 4, "Editing Documents," for information on loading ASCII and RTF files.)

Use DOS to view ASCII files

Another way to view the file is to have your operating system display it. This method is useful for determining whether the file you saved is free of unanticipated characters and line breaks. You can also use this method to compare documents saved in text-only format and those saved in text-only-with-line-breaks format, to see which format best suits your requirements.

To view a file from DOS:

1. At the system prompt, enter the following (substituting the appropriate file name and extension):

   TYPE *FILENAME.EXT*

2. Press **Enter**.

The contents of the file you specified scroll on your screen. If the file was not saved in text format, additional "odd" characters representing formatting may be displayed.

 When you save a Word document in another file format, always keep a backup copy of the original document saved in Word format. That way, you can always go back to the original document and save it in another format if necessary. For example, suppose you have saved a document in text-only or text-only-with-line-breaks format. If later you need to load it back into Word, the document will have a paragraph mark at the end of each line instead of at the end of each paragraph. To use the document, you may need to delete the paragraph marks at the end of most lines. If you have kept a backup of the original Word document, editing will be unnecessary.

Using the Transfer Allsave Command

If you work with windows, you may want to save all the documents in all the windows at one time. To do this, you use the Transfer Allsave command. Not only does Word save all open documents, but it saves all active style sheets and the current glossary file as well.

Each document is saved with the drive, path, file name, and format that appears when you select Transfer Save from that document's window. If you are unsure whether the correct drive, path, file name, and format is set, use Transfer Save to check the destination. If you have not yet saved a document, you are given an opportunity to enter the drive, path, and file name for that particular document.

To save all files:

1. Select **Transfer Allsave**. This message appears:

   Saving all files...

2. As the first file is being saved, a message like this one appears:

   Saving C:\WORD\DOC\MYFILE.DOC

A similar message appears for each file. If you have not yet saved a file, the Transfer Save menu appears. Enter the drive, path, and file name. Make sure the *format* field is set to Word. Press **Enter**.

3. If the Options *summary sheet* field is set to Yes, a summary sheet appears. Complete the summary sheet if desired. Press **Enter** to continue on to the next document.

When Word is done, all the files in all the windows have been saved.

Quit

When you have finished working in Word, leave Word by using the Quit command. Never reset your system or turn off your computer while the Word window is on your screen. Doing so can damage your documents or your Word program files. Always remember to save your work before you quit. When you quit Word, temporary backup files created with autosave are deleted.

Using the Quit Command

To quit Word:

1. Select **Quit**.
2. If you have not saved your work, this message appears for each document, glossary, and/or style sheet:

   Enter Y to save changes to document, N to lose changes, or
   Esc to cancel

   Select one of these options by pressing:

   Y   to save the changes you have made since your last full save (with Transfer Save or Transfer Allsave) and quit.

   N   to lose any changes you have made since your last full save (with Transfer Save or Transfer Allsave) and quit.

   Esc   to cancel the Quit command and continue working in Word.

   If you press Y or N to quit, you are returned to the system prompt.

Default Options and Print Options

When you quit, these Options and Print Options settings are saved and will be in effect the next time you use Word (the settings become the new defaults):

Options:

autosave

background colors

cursor speed

date format

decimal character

default tab width

display mode

foreground colors

linedraw character

line numbers

measurement unit

mute

paginate

show borders

show hidden text

show layout

show line breaks

show menu

show non-printing symbols

show ruler

show style bar

speller path

summary sheet

time format

Print Options:

draft

duplex

graphics resolution

hidden text

model

paper feed

printer

setup

widow/orphan control

In addition, these settings are maintained:

- The Transfer Options *setup* field (if *save between sessions* is set to Yes)
- The name of the document in window 1
- The name of the current glossary
- The drive/directory path for Library Document-retrieval
- The last selection in the document
- The document's read-only status
- The status of overtype mode (on or off)
- The Spell Options settings
- The Print preView Options settings
- The Format Division Margins settings (if the *save as default* field is set to Yes)
- The last annotation mark

Exercise: Quitting

You can quit Word now. Select Quit. If you have changes to save and this prompt appears:

```
Enter Y to save changes to document, N to lose changes, or Esc
to cancel
```

enter Y. You will then be taken back to the operating system.

Editing Documents

The beauty of word processing really doesn't emerge until you edit your documents. Instead of time-consuming rewriting and retyping, you'll find you can easily change the documents you create in Word. In this chapter, you will learn how to load a document into Word and perform numerous editing tasks, including deleting, inserting, over-typing, moving, and copying text. You'll also learn how to clear the screen to start a new document.

Loading Word Documents

Displaying a Word document in a window is referred to as "loading" the document. In effect, the document is copied from storage on disk into RAM. Unless you delete the original copy of the document, it remains on the storage disk until you replace it with an edited version.

You can start Word and load a document at the same time. Chapter 2, "Starting Microsoft Word," describes how to load:

- A new, unnamed document
- A new, named document
- The last document you used in the previous Word session

If you start Word and then want to load an existing document, you usually use the Transfer Load command. You can use a speed key instead of selecting from the menu.

Selecting a Document to Load

After you select Transfer Load, Word displays the Transfer Load menu so that you can identify the document you want to load. In the *filename* field, you can:

- Type in the document's name. Word will look for the document on the drive and path specified in the Transfer Options *setup* field.
- Enter the document's drive, path, and name. Word will look for the document on the drive and path you enter.
- Press F1 or click the *filename* field with the mouse to see a list of documents. You can specify which list you want Word to display by doing the following:

Action	**List displayed**
Leave *filename* field blank	The files with the .DOC extension on the drive and in the directory specified in Transfer Options
Enter drive (such as A:)	The .DOC files on the disk in the drive specified
Enter drive and *.* (such as A:*.*)	All the files on the disk in the drive (not just the .DOC files)
Enter *.*	All the files on the drive and in the directory specified in Transfer Options
Enter drive, path, and *.* (such as C:\WORD\DOC*.*)	All the files on the drive and path
Enter *. and extension (such as *.LET)	All the files ending with the specified extension
Enter drive, path, *., and extension (such as *.LET)	All the files on the drive and path ending with the specified extension

Figure 4-1 shows a typical selection screen. In this example, the *filename* field was left blank and F1 was pressed. Only files with the .DOC extension are displayed. You can select any document shown.

If the document you want is not on the list, you can change the drive and directory without leaving the list. Other available drives and directories are shown in brackets. For example, in Figure 4-1, the following is a subdirectory of the current directory:

[DOC]

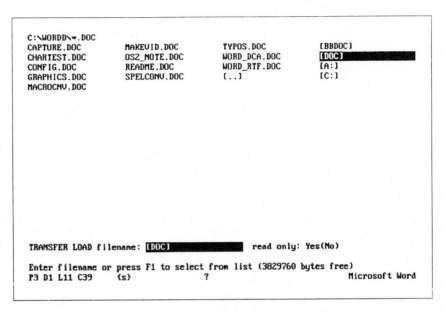

Figure 4-1. A list of the documents available for loading

If you want to view a list of the documents stored in the DOC subdirectory, you simply highlight [DOC] and press F1. Word "refreshes" the screen and displays the documents in the DOC subdirectory (see Figure 4-2).

You can also "step back" one directory level by selecting the parent directory of the directory you are in. The parent directory is represented by two periods in brackets like this:

[..]

You can find and load a document from anywhere on your hard disk.

You can change drives from the list. For example, if you want to view a list of documents stored on the disk in drive A, you highlight [A:] and press F1. Each time you select a directory, subdirectory, or drive, Word refreshes the screen and displays the documents, directories, and drives available from that location. If you have a hard disk, this feature is especially useful because you can view all the files anywhere on your system.

You may have noticed the *read only* field on the Transfer Load menu. By default, this field is set to No, which means that you will be able to both view and change (read and write to) the document after Word has loaded it. If you just want to view the document rather than edit it, select Yes in the *read only* field. See Appendix D for more information about creating and using read-only files.

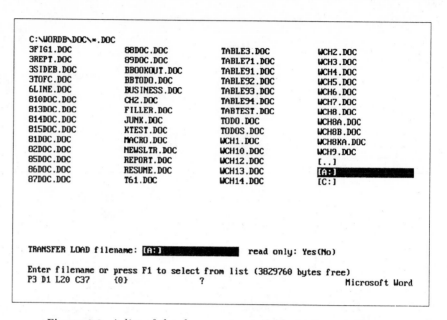

Figure 4-2. A list of the documents available in the subdirectory

Using the Transfer Load Command

You can load a document into a blank document window or into a window that contains another document. If a document is already displayed in the window, Word gives you the option of saving any changes to the document before it is replaced by the new document. For example, suppose you have been editing DOC1.DOC in window 1. If you use Transfer Load to load an existing document called DOC2.DOC into the window, Word gives you the opportunity to save the changes you have made to DOC1.DOC. Then Word replaces DOC1.DOC with DOC2.DOC. Unlike some word processors, Word does not insert DOC2.DOC into DOC1.DOC or add it onto the end of the document already in the window.

You can also use Transfer Load to clear a document from the window and create a new named document. For example, suppose you have just completed a document called JACLET.DOC in window 1. Now you want to create a new document called BILRPT.DOC in the same window. Even though BILRPT.DOC doesn't yet exist, you can use Transfer Load to save any unsaved edits to JACLET.DOC and then create a blank document called BILRPT.DOC. After selecting Transfer Load, you type in BILRPT.DOC as the document name. When you press Enter, Word asks whether you first want to save any changes you have made to JACLET.DOC. After you respond to this prompt, Word clears the window and loads a new blank document called BILRPT.DOC.

Loading Existing Documents

Here is the process for loading a document into a blank document window or a window that currently displays a document:

1. Activate the window into which you want Word to load the document. If necessary, use **F1** to move between windows. (The window number in the upper-left corner of the window is highlighted when that window is active.)

2. Select **T**ransfer **O**ptions. Check the *setup* field to see which drive and path Word will use as the default when loading the document. Change the drive and path if necessary. Press **Enter** when you are done with this menu.

3. Select **T**ransfer **L**oad.

4. The Transfer Load menu appears. In the *filename* field, identify the document you want Word to load. You have these options:

   • Enter a file name of up to eight characters (preceding the name with a drive and path if necessary). Press **Tab** if you want to go to the *read only* field.

   • Use the keyboard to select from a list. If necessary, enter any specific information (such as the path or extension) about the documents you want Word to include in the list and then press **F1** to see the list. Use the **Arrow** keys or the mouse to highlight the name of the document you want. Press **Tab** if you want to go to the *read only* field.

   • Use the mouse to select from a list. If necessary, enter any specific information (such as the path or extension) about the documents you want Word to include in the list and then point to the *filename* field and click the right button to see the list. Point to the desired document and click the right button to load the document. Or, click the left button to highlight the document's name and then click the right button to move to the *read only* field.

5. In the *read only* field, select **N**o if you want to be able to read, edit, and save the document under the same name. Select **Y**es if you want to be able to read the file only, or if you want to be able to edit it but save it only under a different name.

6. Press **Enter**.

7. If a document is already displayed in the window and you have made changes to it that you have not saved, this message appears:

```
Enter Y to save changes to document, N to lose changes, or Esc
to cancel
```

If you select **Y**, Word saves the existing document with the path and file name that would appear in the Transfer Save *filename* field. Word then clears the existing document from the window and loads the new document. If you select **N**, Word proceeds with loading the new document without saving the existing document.

When the document is loaded, Word displays its name in the lower-right corner of the window.

Change the drive and path in the Transfer Options *setup* field only if you will use the new drive and path for some time. Word saves whatever drive and path you enter in the Transfer Option *setup* field when you quit and uses them as the default until you change them. To temporarily access other drives and paths, just type in the drive and path when you use Transfer Load.

Loading Blank, Named Documents

Whether or not you have a document in the window, you can load a new, blank document and assign it a name. If a document is already displayed in the window, before clearing the window, Word gives you the opportunity to save any changes you have made since you last saved the document.

Loading a blank document saves time later.

Clearing the window and naming a new document comes in handy if you like to use Ctrl-F10 to save existing documents quickly. Using Ctrl-F10 involves fewer keystrokes than using Transfer Save. Once the document is saved, you can use Transfer Load (or Ctrl-F7) and enter the file name to load the blank, named document. And, if you are using autosave, Word will give the temporary files the same name as the document instead of calling the files Untitled.

To clear the window and load a new blank, named document:

1. Activate the window into which you want Word to load the document.

2. Select **T**ransfer **O**ptions to check which drive and path are set as Word's default. You can change the field if necessary. Press **Enter** when you are done with this menu.

3. Select **T**ransfer **L**oad.

4. The Transfer Load menu appears. In the *filename* field, identify the document to be loaded. Enter a file name of up to eight characters (preceding the name with the drive and path, if necessary).

5. The *read only* field is usually set at No, meaning that you will be able to read or write to (edit) the document. If you want to load a read-only file that cannot be edited and then saved under the same name, select **Yes** in this field. Press **Enter**.

6. If a document is already in the window (and is not displayed in another window), the newly loaded document replaces the existing document. If you have changed the document in the window since the last time you saved it, this message appears:

`Enter Y to save changes to document, N to lose changes, or Esc`
`to cancel`

If you select **Y**, Word saves the existing document.

7. After Word has saved the document, it displays this message regarding the new file you want to create:

`File does not exist. Enter Y to create or Esc to cancel`

Press **Y** to create the new document. Word clears the window and displays the new document's name in the lower-right corner of the blank window. (If you press Esc, Word does not clear the window but instead returns you to the exisitng document.)

 If you are using multiple windows, before using the Transfer Load command, always carefully check which window is active. Many document updates have been lost when users failed to check the highlighted window number and responded No to the message:

`Enter Y to save changes to document, N to lose changes, or Esc`
`to cancel`

Responding No to this message with your highlight in the wrong window can cost you the time it takes to reconstruct valuable edits you have lost.

Loading with a Speed Key

You can use a speed key to quickly display a list of the documents available for loading. From this list, you can also select a different drive or directory. Or, you can simply enter the path and name of the document you want to load in the *filename* field. For example, in Figure 4-3, Word will load the document that has been specified in the *filename* field:

`C:\WORDB\DOC\MTGSEPT.DOC`

even though this document is not in the displayed selection list because it is stored in a directory other than the one displayed.

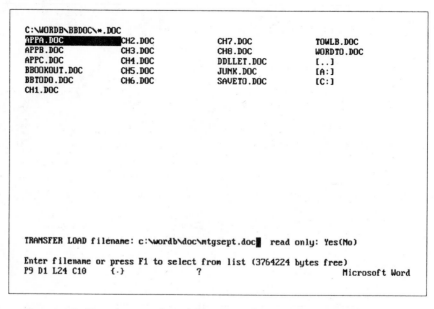

```
C:\WORDB\BBDOC\*.DOC
APPA.DOC        CH2.DOC        CH7.DOC        TOWLB.DOC
APPB.DOC        CH3.DOC        CH8.DOC        WORDTO.DOC
APPC.DOC        CH4.DOC        DDLLET.DOC     [..]
BBOOKOUT.DOC    CH5.DOC        JUNK.DOC       [A:]
BBTODO.DOC      CH6.DOC        SAVETO.DOC     [C:]
CH1.DOC




TRANSFER LOAD filename: c:\wordb\doc\mtgsept.doc█  read only: Yes(No)

Enter filename or press F1 to select from list (3764224 bytes free)
P9 D1 L24 C10     {.}                    ?                    Microsoft Word
```

Figure 4-3. Entering a path and file name that is not in the selection list

Press Ctrl-F7 to speed up document loading

Using the speed key makes the loading process faster because you don't need to select Transfer Load and press F1 or click with the mouse. Here are the steps:

1. Activate the window into which the document should be loaded.

2. Press **Ctrl-F7**.

3. In the *filename* field, identify the document you want Word to load. You have these options:

   • If you are using the keyboard, use the **Arrow** keys to highlight the name of the document you want, switch to a different drive or directory and highlight the document name, or enter a path and document name in the *filename* field. If you want to change the read-only status of the file, use the **Tab** key to move to that field.

- If you are using a mouse, make sure you are in the drive and directory desired. Then point to the desired document and click the right button to both make your selection and carry out the command. Or, if you want to change the read-only status of the file, click the left button to highlight the file and then click the right button to move to the *read only* field. You can also click LOAD with either button to carry out the command with the current settings.

4. In the *read only* field, select **N**o to be able to edit the document and save it with the same name or select **Y**es to make the document read only.

5. Finally, press **Enter** to complete the selection.

6. The file is loaded. If an existing document is already displayed in the window and you have made changes to the document since you last saved it, this message appears:

```
Enter Y to save changes to document, N to lose changes, or Esc
to cancel
```

If you select **Y**, Word saves the existing document before replacing it with the new document.

When the file is loaded, Word displays the document name in the lower-right corner of the window.

Exercise: Loading a File

Try loading a file. Start Word, and when the blank document window is on your screen, select Transfer Options. The *setup* default should be the same setting you entered for the exercises in the last chapter. Press Esc to cancel the Transfer Options command and return to the document window. Press Ctrl-F7. In the selection list, highlight or point to the document you created and saved in the exercises in the last chapter:

```
PDREORG.DOC
```

Press Enter. Word displays the document in the window.

Loading ASCII and RTF Files

You can load ASCII files into Word like any Word-format file. Simply enter the drive, path, and name of the document. Depending on how the ASCII file was created, each line in the ASCII file may end with a paragraph mark. If you want to remove the paragraph marks, you can use the Replace command to get rid of them. (See Chapter 12, "Search and Replace," for more information.) Another alternative is to use a program supplied by Microsoft to automatically remove the paragraph marks.

You can load RTF files into Word as a Word-format document or as an RTF-format file. Figure 4-4 shows an RTF file that has been loaded as a Word-format document. As you can see, the file appears as typical Word text.

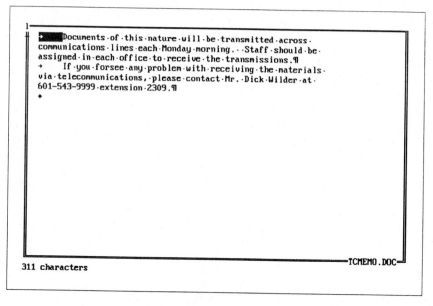

Figure 4-4. An RTF-format file that has been loaded in Word format

What you see in Rich Text Format

When you load the file as an RTF-format file, the embedded RTF formatting codes are displayed. Figures 4-5 through 4-7 show the same file loaded as an RTF-format file, complete with the RTF codes. Screen One (Figure 4-5) starts with identifying information, such as the month, day, and year of creation and revision. The file then describes the fonts that are available (Word's Normal style sheet was used to create the original Word file). These fonts are also shown in

Screen Two (Figure 4-6). In Screen Three (Figure 4-7), more identifying information appears. In the text of the document, paragraphs and tabs are also indicated.

```
\rtf1\pc
{\info{\revtim\mo06\dy12\yr1989}{\creatim\mo06\dy12\yr1989}¶
{\nofchars311}}\deff0{\fonttbl{\f0\fmodern·pica;}¶
{\f1\fmodern·Courier;}{\f2\fmodern·elite;}{\f3\fmodern·
prestige;}¶
{\f4\fmodern·lettergothic;}{\f5\fmodern·gothicPS;}¶
{\f6\fmodern·cubicPS;}{\f7\fmodern·lineprinter;}¶
{\f8\fswiss·Helvetica;}{\f9\fmodern·avantegarde;}¶
{\f10\fmodern·spartan;}{\f11\fmodern·metro;}¶
{\f12\fmodern·presentation;}{\f13\fmodern·APL;}{\f14\fmodern·
OCRA;}¶
{\f15\fmodern·OCRB;}{\f16\froman·boldPS;}{\f17\froman·
emperorPS;}¶
{\f18\froman·madaleine;}{\f19\froman·zapf·humanist;}¶
{\f20\froman·classic;}{\f21\froman·roman·f;}{\f22\froman·
roman·g;}¶
{\f23\froman·roman·h;}{\f24\froman·timesroman;}{\f25\froman·
century;}¶
{\f26\froman·palantino;}{\f27\froman·souvenir;}{\f28\froman·
garamond;}¶
{\f29\froman·caledonia;}{\f30\froman·bodini;}{\f31\froman·
university;}¶
```
```
Pg1 Li1 Co1        {d}              ?              Microsoft Word
```

Figure 4-5. The same RTF file, loaded as an RTF-format file—
Screen One

```
{\f29\froman·caledonia;}{\f30\froman·bodini;}{\f31\froman·
university;}¶
{\f32\fscript·script;}{\f33\fscript·scriptPS;}{\f34\fscript·
script·c;}¶
{\f35\fscript·script·d;}{\f36\fscript·commercial·script;}¶
{\f37\fscript·park·avenue;}{\f38\fscript·coronet;}¶
{\f39\fscript·script·h;}{\f40\fscript·greek;}{\f41\froman·
kana;}¶
{\f42\froman·hebrew;}{\f43\froman·roman·s;}{\f44\froman·
russian;}¶
{\f45\froman·roman·u;}{\f46\froman·roman·v;}{\f47\froman·
roman·w;}¶
{\f48\fdecor·narrator;}{\f49\fdecor·emphasis;}¶
{\f50\fdecor·zapf·chancery;}{\f51\fdecor·decor·d;}¶
{\f52\fdecor·old·english;}{\f53\fdecor·decor·f;}{\f54\fdecor·
decor·g;}¶
{\f55\fdecor·cooper·black;}{\f56\ftech·Symbol;}{\f57\ftech·
linedraw;}¶
{\f58\ftech·math7;}{\f59\ftech·math8;}{\f60\ftech·bar3of9;}¶
{\f61\ftech·EAN;}{\f62\ftech·pcline;}{\f63\ftech·tech·h;}}¶
\ftnbj\ftnrestart\widowctrl·\sectd·\linex576\endnhere·\pard·
\sl-240·¶
```
```
Pg1 Li21 Co1       {d}              ?              Microsoft Word
```

Figure 4-6. The RTF file loaded as an RTF-format file—Screen Two

```
| ═══════════════════════════════════════════════════
|
 ¶ftnbj\ftnrestart\widowctrl·\sectd·\linex576\endnhere·\pard·
 \sl-240·¶
 \plain·\tab·Documents·of·this·nature·will·be·transmitted·
 across·communications·lines·each·Monday·morning.··Staff·
 should·be·assigned·in·each·office·to·receive·the·
 transmissions.\par·¶
 \tab·If·you·forsee·any·problem·with·receiving·the·materials·
 via·telecommunications,·please·contact·Mr.·Dick·Wilder·at·
 601-543-9999·extension·2309.\par·¶
 }◆



 ╺TCMEMO.RTF╸
 Pg1 Li41 Co1        {d}            ?              Microsoft Word
```

Figure 4-7. The RTF file loaded as an RTF-format file—Screen Three

Remember that when Word saves RTF files, it creates a .DOC file as well as an .RTF file. When you load the RTF file, make sure you specify the .RTF extension. Otherwise you may load the .DOC file by mistake.

Here is the procedure for loading an RTF file:

1. Select **T**ransfer **L**oad.

2. Select the RTF file using one of these methods:

   - Enter the drive, path, and document name (ending in .RTF) to load the document. Press **Enter**.

   - Enter the drive, path, and *.RTF and then press **F1** or click the right mouse button in the *filename* field to see a list of .RTF files. Highlight the file you want and press **Enter** or click the right mouse button.

3. This message appears:

   ```
   File is RTF format. Enter Y to convert to Word format, or
   N to load text-only
   ```

   Perform one of these options:

   - Enter **Y** to convert to Word format. A .DOC document was created when the file was saved in RTF format. If that file exists in the drive and path, this message appears:

DRIVE/PATH/DOCUMENTNAME.DOC already exists. Enter Y to replace.

If you enter **Y**, Word replaces the .RTF file with the .DOC file. If you enter **N**, the operation stops. If Word did not find a .DOC file in the drive and path, it saves the .RTF file with the .DOC extension and loads the file. In either case, the original file with the .RTF extension is not changed.

- Enter **N** to load the RTF file into Word. The text and RTF codes are displayed.
- Press **Esc** to abort the procedure and return to your document.

Clearing the Screen

What if you want to save the changes you have made to the document or documents you are currently working on and clear the screen without loading an existing document or naming a new document? As we saw earlier, the Transfer Load command can be used to clear a window and name a new document; the Transfer Save command saves the current document but doesn't clear the window; and the Quit command clears the window but takes you out of Word. To simply clear one or more windows, you need to use the Transfer Clear command. The following table gives you a quick guide to the actions of these four commands when a document is displayed in the window:

Command	Action
Transfer Clear	Saves changes to existing document if desired; clears document from window
Transfer Load	Saves changes to existing document if desired; loads "new" document
Transfer Save	Saves changes to document if desired; returns to same document
Quit	Saves changes to document if desired; leaves Word

With Transfer Clear, you are given a choice of saving any changes you have made to the document since the last full save or of losing the changes. After you respond to the option to save your work, Word clears the document from the window.

When to use
Transfer Clear

Transfer Clear is useful if you are working on one document and want to clear the window to begin work on a brand new document but don't want to name the document yet. It is also useful if you have changed your mind about the edits you have made since the last time you saved the document with Transfer Save or Ctrl-F10. Once you have cleared the window with Transfer Clear, you can decide whether to load the previous saved version of the same document or work on something else.

Using the Transfer Clear Command

To clear the current document from a window:

1. If you want to clear only one window, make that window active by pressing **F1** until the number of the window you want to clear is highlighted.

2. If you have more than one document loaded in more than one window and you want to save them all before clearing their windows, you may want to check the Transfer Save *filename* field in each window to make sure the file will be saved to the path and file name desired. If the Transfer Save *filename* field is not correct, change it and save the document. You can then clear the window using **Transfer Clear Window**.

3. Select **Transfer Clear**.

4. The Transfer Clear menu appears with two options. Select:

All to clear all documents, unsaved style-sheet entries, unsaved glossary entries, and the scrap area. This selection takes a while to implement because Word has several tasks to perform.

Window to clear only the active window. The scrap area, unsaved style-sheet entries, and glossary entries are left "as is." This selection is faster than choosing All because Word has fewer items to clear.

5. If you are clearing more than one window, this message appears for each window:

```
Enter Y to save changes to document, N to lose changes, or
Esc to cancel
```

Respond to the message by pressing:

Y to save the document in the window with the drive, path, and file name that appears in the Transfer Save *filename* field for the document.

N to lose all the changes you have made since the last time you saved the document using Transfer Save or Ctrl-F10. Note that edits that have been saved by Word's autosave feature are not saved as part of the document if you press N at this point.

Esc to abort the Transfer Clear operation and return to your document.

Assuming you chose to complete the operation, Word saves your document or documents and displays one clear window.

When you have multiple windows open and start the process to clear one of them, always make sure that the window you want to clear is active. Quickly choosing Transfer Clear Window with the wrong window activated is a common and potentially problematic mistake.

Exercise: Using Transfer Clear

Try using Transfer Clear now. With the PDREORG.DOC document in your window, clear the window. Select Transfer Clear. When you see the Transfer Clear menu, select Window. If you have changed the document in any way, enter Y to save the changes or N to lose the changes. Word then clears the window.

To get ready for the next exercise, load the document again, using the Transfer Load command. Select Transfer Load. In the *filename* field, enter this file name:

`PDREORG.DOC`

Make sure the *read only* field is set at No and then press Enter. The document reappears in the window.

Basic Editing Techniques

Word is designed to allow you to easily insert, delete, move, or copy text.

As you have seen, when you add text to an existing document, the new text is inserted in the existing text. The existing text is moved to the right to make room for the insertion, and Word rewraps the lines within the document's margins. When you delete text, the remaining text is moved to the left to take the place of the deleted text, and Word again rewraps the lines within the margins.

Moving and copying text

When you delete or copy text, that text is saved in the scrap area until you delete or copy another piece of text. If you delete the text, it is removed from the document. However, because the text is saved in the scrap area, you can put it back in the document. Thus, moving text involves deleting it from one place and putting it back somewhere else. If you copy the text, Word leaves the original text in place and saves a copy in the scrap area, allowing you to repeat the text in a second spot in the document.

You can delete, move, or copy a whole block of text at one time. First you highlight, or select, the text and then you carry out the desired operation.

Inserting vs. Overtyping

As you know, you can insert text or overtype it. Recall that inserting text means that anything you type in is added to the existing text, causing existing text to move to make room for it. Overtyping means that anything you type in replaces the existing text.

Insert Mode

When you start Word, the program is in what is referred to as insert mode. When you enter text, whatever you type in is inserted to the left of the highlight within the existing text. For example, suppose you have already entered this sentence:

`The counter staff looks beautiful today.`

You decide you want to insert a word in this sentence. Place the highlight on the letter *b* in *beautiful* (see Figure 4-8 for highlight placement). Enter the word *unusually*, followed by a space. Figure 4-9 shows the result. Notice that when you insert text, the character or space on which the highlight rests moves to the right, and the characters and spaces you type are inserted to its left.

In summary, to use insert mode:

1. Position the highlight on the character or space before which you want to insert text.

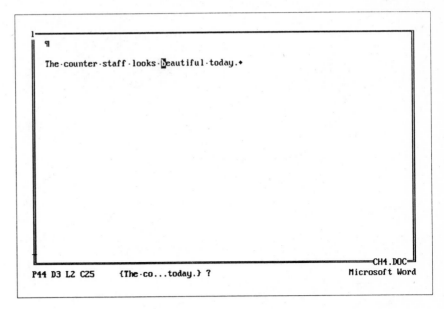

Figure 4-8. The sentence with the highlight on the *b* of *beautiful*

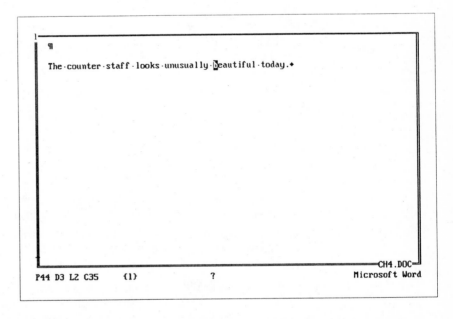

Figure 4-9. The sentence after inserting a word; the highlight is still on the *b* of *beautiful*

2. Begin typing. Word moves the highlighted character or space and all following text to the right and realigns the text between the margins.

If you see OT in the status line, you are in overtype mode and cannot insert text. See "Overtype Mode" in this chapter for more information.

Overtype Mode

You may want to overtype text instead of insert it. You do this in overtype mode. When you overtype, the text you type in replaces the existing text. Consider this sentence as an example:

```
The counter staff looks beautiful today.
```

Suppose you want to replace the word *beautiful* with *wonderful*. If you type the word *wonderful* while in insert mode, this is the result:

```
The counter staff looks wonderful beautiful today.
```

Then you would need to delete the word *beautiful*. A faster way is to overtype *beautiful* with *wonderful* for this immediate result:

```
The counter staff looks wonderful today.
```

In this case, both words contain the same number of letters so no deletion is required.

To overtype text:

1. Press **F5**. OT (for OverType) appears in the status line.
2. Place your highlight on the first character or space you want to overtype.
3. Begin typing. Existing characters and spaces are replaced with whatever you enter, rather than moving to make room for it.
4. To leave overtype mode and return to insert mode, press **F5**. OT disappears from the status line.

When you are in overtype mode, you cannot use the Backspace key to delete the character to the left of the highlight unless you have typed in that character since entering overtype mode.

Exercise: Inserting and Overtyping

Try your hand at inserting and overtyping. The PDREORG.DOC document should be loaded and this text should be on your screen:

```
Last fall, the board directed that our product group be
completely reorganized to reduce redundant efforts. The
committee charged with reorganizing the product development
group met on January 12th. All ten members were present in
person or through a representative.
    The meeting started with opening remarks by Jim Tailor,
the newly appointed Director of Product Development. NOTE:
Check his title.
```

Press F5 to put Word in overtype mode. The OT symbol appears in the status line. Now, place your highlight on the first *r* in *reduce redundant efforts*. Enter this line:

```
streamline operations
```

We will see more efficient ways to delete text later in this chapter. For now, place your highlight on the period at the end of this sentence. Press F5 to go back to insert mode so that you can use the Backspace key. Press Backspace three times. The period now follows the word *operations*.

Next, place your highlight on the *T* in *The committee charged*. Make sure OT is not displayed in the status line. If it is displayed, toggle the F5 key to go to insert mode. Enter this line, followed by a space:

```
This important effort is underway.
```

Notice that Word rewrapped the lines as you inserted the text. This is the final outcome:

```
Last fall, the board directed that our product group be
completely reorganized to streamline operations. This
important effort is underway. The committee charged with
reorganizing the product development group met on January
12th. All ten members were present in person or through a
representative.
    The meeting started with opening remarks by Jim Tailor,
the newly appointed Director of Product Development. NOTE:
Check his title.
```

Selecting Text

When you want to delete, move, or copy text, you must first identify the text you want to manipulate. Then you can tell Word exactly what you want it to do. Identifying the text is called selecting the text. When you select text, the text appears highlighted (with dark or colored text on a lighter background). For example, Figure 4-10 shows a selected sentence.

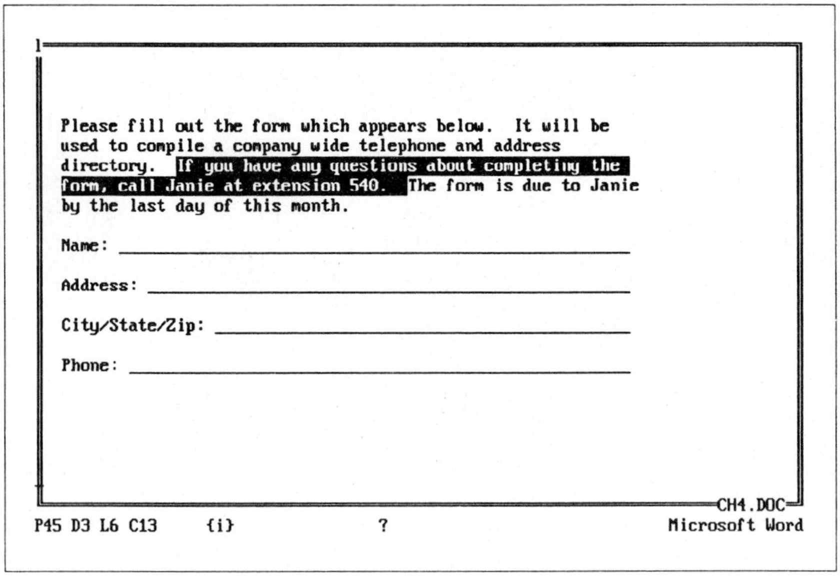

```
┌─────────────────────────────────────────────────────────┐
│ ╔═══════════════════════════════════════════════════╗    │
│ ║                                                    ║    │
│                                                           │
│     Please fill out the form which appears below.  It will be  │
│     used to compile a company wide telephone and address  │
│     directory.  ▓If you have any questions about completing the▓  │
│     ▓form, call Janie at extension 540.▓  The form is due to Janie  │
│     by the last day of this month.                        │
│                                                           │
│     Name: _____          │
│                                                           │
│     Address: _____          │
│                                                           │
│     City/State/Zip: _____          │
│                                                           │
│     Phone: _____          │
│                                                           │
│                                              ═CH4.DOC═     │
│ P45 D3 L6 C13      {i}              ?         Microsoft Word   │
└─────────────────────────────────────────────────────────┘
```

Figure 4-10. A selected sentence

To select text, place your highlight on the text you want to manipulate. Word allows you to select text either to the left or right of the highlight, using either the keyboard or a mouse. When you select text, any hidden text or non-printing symbols in the highlighted area are included in the selection.

You can choose to select by character, word, sentence, paragraph, line, or column, or you can select the whole document. Figures 4-11 through 4-17 show a one-page document with different selection units highlighted. Notice that many selections include trailing spaces. How Word defines each of the selection options is discussed next.

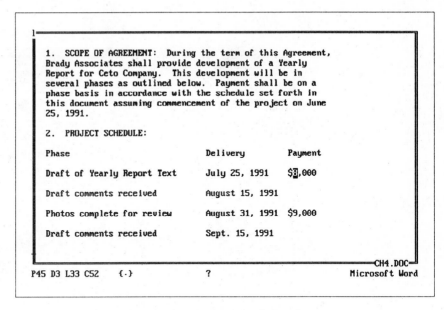

Figure 4-11. A selected character

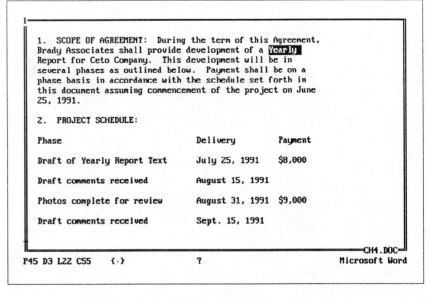

Figure 4-12. A selected word (and trailing spaces)

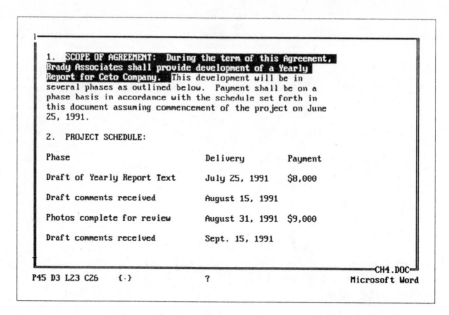

Figure 4-13. A selected sentence (and trailing spaces)

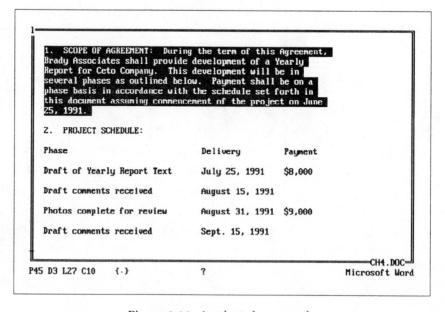

Figure 4-14. A selected paragraph

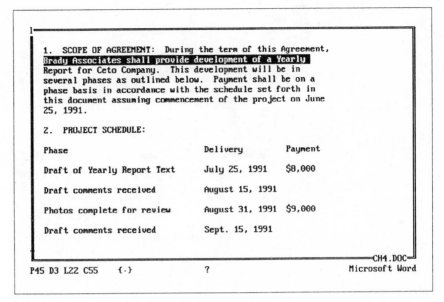

Figure 4-15. A selected line

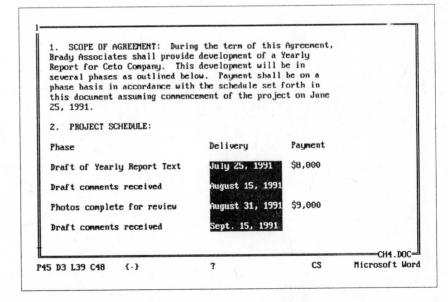

Figure 4-16. A selected column

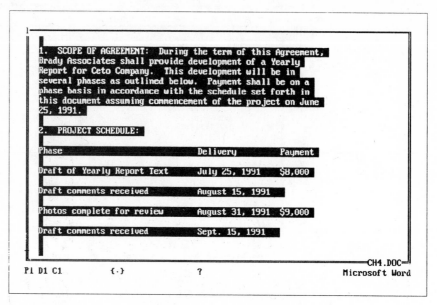

Figure 4-17. A selected document

A Character

A character is selected when it is marked with the highlight. A character can be a letter, number, symbol, or punctuation symbol. You can also select a single space.

A Word

How Word defines a word

A word is recognized as a string of characters with one or more spaces before and after the characters. A word can also be set off by tabs, hyphens, or punctuation symbols. The following table illustrates this definition of a word as it relates to punctuation and spaces. The examples assume you press the F8 key several times to select the text.

Example	Effect of pressing F8
dog. The	First, *dog* (not the period) is selected. Next, the period and space is selected as one "word." Then, *The* is selected.
ding-a-ling	There are five "words": First, *ding* is selected, then the hyphen as one "word," then *a*, then the next hyphen, and finally *ling*. (If optional hyphens were inserted with Ctrl-hyphen, *ding-a-ling* is considered to be one word.)
^tStop	First, the tab before *Stop* is selected, then *Stop*.

A Sentence

When you select a sentence, Word highlights all the characters in the sentence, together with the ending punctuation (the period, question mark, or exclamation point) and trailing spaces. Other punctuation in the sentence is ignored. If the sentence contains a period, question mark, or exclamation point with no space before or after it, Word does not treat that punctuation as ending the sentence.

For example, Word treats the following sentence as just one sentence because the punctuation within the sentence is not a period, question mark, or exclamation point:

The man said, "I never quit."

However, Word recognizes the following sentence as two "sentences" because there is a period within the sentence:

Word uses the .DOC extension.

According to Word, *Word uses the .* is one sentence and *DOC extension.* is another.

Word considers the following sentence to be just one sentence because the period in the document name is surrounded by characters, not spaces:

My file is called KITLET.DOC.

A Paragraph

Word defines a paragraph as the characters from the beginning of a document or following a paragraph mark up to and including the next paragraph mark. The paragraph mark is considered part of the paragraph because that is where Word stores all the formatting information for the paragraph.

A paragraph can be any length: a single word, a line, several lines, or even several pages. In fact, as you'll learn later, a paragraph can consist of just a paragraph mark.

A Line

A line is considered by Word to be the text between the left and right document indents. If you highlight a line that includes a paragraph mark or a newline character, those symbols are highlighted as well.

A Column

A column can be any block of characters, whether it is in column format or not. For example, Figures 4-18 through 4-21 show different column-selection options. Notice that you can select part of a column, all of a column, several columns, or even text that is not in column format.

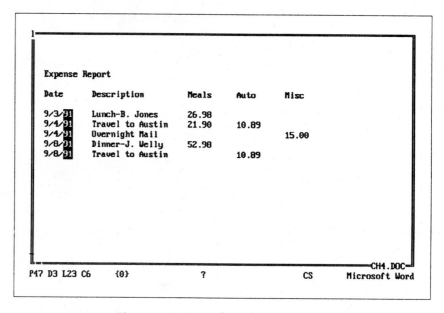

Figure 4-18. Part of a column selected

A Document

You can select an entire document in a single operation. When you select a document, the footnotes, running heads, and page numbers are also selected. For example, if you select a document that contains footnotes and copy it to another window, the footnotes are copied, too.

Extending the Selection

When selecting text, you are not limited to Word's standard selection units. When you want to select text that is not exactly a word, sentence, line, paragraph, or document, you can extend the selection. The text in Figure 4-22 was selected using Word's extend select feature. Notice that the letters EX appear in the status line, indicating that extend select has been turned on.

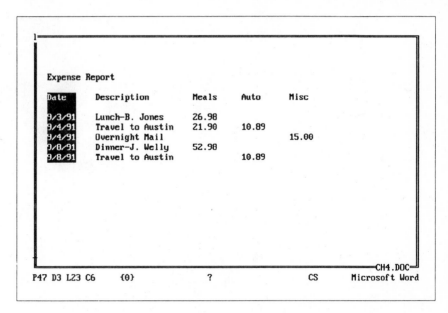

Figure 4-19. All of a column selected

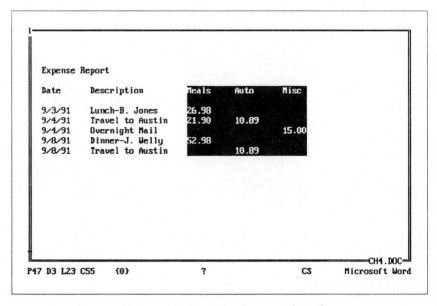

Figure 4-20. Several columns selected

Extend a selection with F6

You turn on extend select by pressing the F6 key. When extend select is active, you can move the highlight to select as much text as desired from the current highlight position. Many Word users never take the time to learn which keys select which units, knowing they

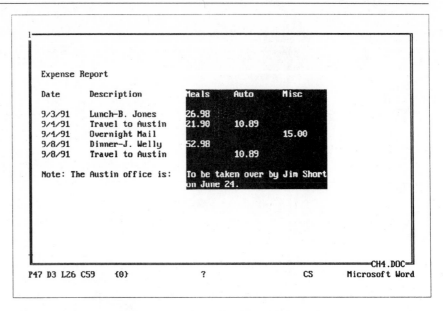

Figure 4-21. Text outside the columns selected

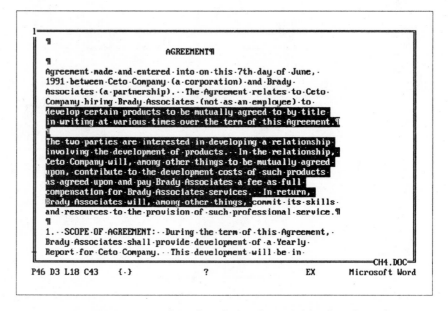

Figure 4-22. Text selected with Word's extend select feature

can always use extend select to highlight the text they want to manipulate. However, the best use of extend select is in conjunction with
the selection keys. For example, you could turn on extend select and
then press End to extend the selection from the character under your
highlight to the end of the line. Or, you could select a word by press-

ing F8, turn on extend select, and then press Shift-F8 to extend the selection through the next sentence.

If you decide you don't want to extend the selection after all, you can stop it. With the keyboard, you turn extend select off simply by pressing F6 a second time. With a mouse, you click one of the buttons. See "Selecting with the Keyboard" and "Selecting with a Mouse" in this chapter for more detailed information.

Selecting with the Keyboard

You have many options for quickly selecting text with the keyboard. To begin, position the highlight at one end of the text you want to manipulate and then use one of the keys or key combinations listed in the following table:

Key(s) pressed	Result
Up Arrow, Down Arrow, Left Arrow, Right Arrow	A character (or space) is selected.
F7	If your highlight is after the first character of the word, the word is selected. In any other position, the previous word is selected. If you continue to press F7, each preceding word is individually selected.
F8	If your highlight is in a word, the word is selected. If you continue to press F8, each following word is individually selected.
Shift-F7	The sentence your highlight is in is selected. If you continue to press Shift-F7, each previous sentence is individually selected.
Shift-F8	The sentence your highlight is in is selected. If you continue to press Shift-F8, each following sentence is individually selected.
F9	The paragraph your highlight is in is selected (including the paragraph mark). If you continue to press F9, each previous paragraph is individually selected.

F10	The paragraph your highlight is in is selected (including the paragraph mark). If you continue to press F10, each following paragraph is individually selected.
Shift-F9	The line your highlight is in is selected (margin to margin).
Shift-Up Arrow	Characters are selected from your highlight upward. The number of characters selected is equivalent to one line (from margin to margin) plus one character.
Shift-Down Arrow	Characters are selected from your highlight downward. The number of characters selected is equivalent to one line (from margin to margin) plus one character.
Shift-Right Arrow	Characters are selected to the right of your highlight, character by character.
Shift-Left Arrow	Characters are selected to the left of your highlight, character by character.
Shift-F10	The complete document is selected (including footnotes, running heads, and page numbers).
Alt-F5 (enter page number)	The first character of the page entered is selected.
F6 (then move the highlight)	Extend select is turned on. EX appears in the status line. The selection is extended from your highlight position. Most key combinations can be used to extend to the selection. These include: Up Arrow Down Arrow Left Arrow Right Arrow Home End

	PgUp PgDn Ctrl-Up Arrow Ctrl-Down Arrow Ctrl-Left Arrow Ctrl-Right Arrow Ctrl-PgUp Ctrl-PgDn Alt-F5 (page number)
	Press F6 again to stop extend select.
Shift-F6 (then move the highlight)	Column select is turned on. CS appears in the status line. The position of your highlight becomes any corner of a rectangular selection. Press Shift-F6 again to stop column select.

If you select text with any key combination other than extend select and decide you don't want it selected after all, simply press an Arrow key to go back to regular editing.

Two other ways to extend a selection

In addition to the selection methods listed above, there are two ways to use your keyboard to extend the selection across several pages in a document. First, you can use the Jump Page command, and second, you can use the Search command. Both commands are useful to quickly select large portions of text.

To use the Jump Page command to extend the selection:

1. Place your highlight on either the first or last character to be selected.
2. Press **F6**.
3. Select **J**ump **P**age or press **Alt-F5**.
4. Enter the page number and press **Enter**.

The highlight is extended to the first character of the page number you entered.

To use the Search command to extend the selection:

1. Place your highlight on either the first or last character to be selected.
2. Press **F6**.
3. Select **S**earch.

4. Complete the following steps:

   a. Enter the text Word should search for.

   b. In the *direction* field, select **U**p or **D**own.

   c. In the *case* field, select **Y**es to exactly match capital and small letters or **N**o to match characters regardless of case.

   d. In the *whole word* field, select **Y**es to search out only whole words (surrounded by spaces, tabs, or punctuation marks) or **N**o to simply match the characters specified regardless of whether they constitute a whole word or part of a word.

5. Press **Enter**. The selection is extended to include the first occurrence of the text you searched for.

6. Press **Shift-F4** if you want to extend the selection to the next occurrence of the text.

Selecting with a Mouse

Many Word users prefer to select text with a mouse rather than the keyboard. Experienced Word users often combine use of the keyboard and a mouse to quickly select exactly the text required. With practice, you will find the methods that work best for you.

Sometimes, selecting text with a mouse involves pointing to the desired text and clicking. At other times, selecting text involves pointing to the selection bar and clicking. (The selection bar is the area between the left border and the text.) The various ways to select text with a mouse are summarized in the following table:

Mouse action	Result
Point to a character or space; click left button	The character or space is selected.
Point to a word; click right button	The word is selected.
Point to a space; click right button	The preceding word is selected
Point in a sentence; click both buttons	The sentence and trailing spaces are selected.
Point to the spaces following a sentence; click both buttons	The preceding sentence and trailing spaces are selected.
Point in the selection bar to the left of a line; click left button	The line (between the margins) is selected.
Point in the selection bar adjacent to a paragraph; click right button	The paragraph (including the paragraph mark) is selected.

Point in the selection bar; click both buttons	The document is selected (including footnotes, running heads, and page numbers).
Point to one corner of a column; click left button. Press Shift-F6; CS appears in the status line. Point to the opposite corner of the column; click left button. Press Shift-F6 to remove CS from the status line and turn off column select	The column of text is selected.
Point to the beginning or ending of an extended selection, hold down one or both buttons, move the pointer to the other end of the selection, release the button(s)	The text which is selected according to the button(s) chosen is selected first. Then from that point to the final point is selected.
Point to where the selection should begin; press one or both buttons. Press F6 and point to where the selection should end; press one or both buttons. Press F6 again to turn off extend select	The text from the first point and click to the second point and click is selected. EX appears in the status line. The button(s) you click determine how much text is highlighted: left button for a character, right button for a word, and both buttons for a sentence.

 You can also drag with the mouse to create a custom selection. There are two ways to use the mouse to highlight text across pages: The first way is to use the Jump Page command; the second way is to use the Search command. Use these commands when you want to select a large amount of text that extends across several pages.

Follow these steps to use Jump Page with the mouse to select text:

1. Point on or near the first or last character you want to select.
2. Click the left button to select the character, the right button to select the word, or both buttons to select the sentence.
3. Press **F6**.
4. Select **J**ump **P**age or press **Alt-F5**.
5. Enter the page number and press **Enter**.

The highlight is extended to the first character of the page number you entered.

To use the Search command with the mouse to extend a selection, follow these steps:

1. Point on or near the first or last character you want to select.

2. Click the left button to select the character, the right button to select the word, or both buttons to select the sentence.

3. Press **F6**.

4. Select **S**earch.

5. Complete the following steps:

   a. Enter the text Word should search for.

   b. In the *direction* field, select **U**p or **D**own.

   c. In the *case* field, select **Y**es to exactly match capital and small letters or **N**o to match characters regardless of case.

   d. In the *whole word* field, select **Y**es to search out only whole words (surrounded by spaces, tabs, or punctuation marks) or **N**o to simply match the characters specified regardless of whether they constitute a whole word or part of a word.

6. Press **Enter**. The selection is extended to include the first occurrence of the text.

7. Press **Shift-F4** if you want to extend the selection to the next occurrence of the text.

Using the Scrap Area

As you know, the scrap area is a temporary storage location used to hold the most recently deleted or copied text. Word represents the scrap area in the status line by curly braces. The most recently deleted or copied text is displayed between these braces. If the text in the scrap area is too large to appear in the space allocated to the scrap area in the status line, only the beginning and ending characters are displayed, separated by an ellipsis. For example, consider this sentence:

```
Mr. Johnson will arrive Friday, June 28th.
```

When this sentence is deleted, the representation of the sentence in the scrap area looks like this:

```
{MR. Jo...28TH.}
```

How the scrap area works

Word has only one scrap area, and the scrap area can hold only one piece of text at a time. When you delete or copy a piece of text, Word gets rid of anything that is already in the scrap area and replaces it with the deleted or copied text. You can copy the text from the scrap area back into your document (or into another document) as long as you don't delete or copy anything else, and as long as you don't quit Word. When you leave Word, the text in the scrap area is lost.

If you accidently delete or copy text over the contents of the scrap area and want to recover the former contents, you can use the Undo command to undo the delete or copy and restore the lost text to the scrap area. In effect, if you deleted the text to the scrap area from your document, Word puts the text back in the document; if you copied the text to the scrap area, Word discards the copy. It is important to use Undo immediately, however. If you perform any other significant editing tasks or select editing commands before you discover your mistake, you may not be able to undo the delete or copy operation that overwrote the text you need.

To use Undo to recover the text that was most recently stored in the scrap area, follow these steps:

1. Copy or delete text to the scrap area.

2. Before completing commands or performing other significant edits, press **Shift-F1** to undo the previous step. Word puts the copied or deleted text back in the document at its original location and restores the text that was overwritten in the scrap area.

Exercise: Selecting Text and Experimenting with the Scrap Area

To see how the scrap area works (and get some practice selecting text), you are going to delete a piece of text from PDREORG.DOC and then undo the deletion. Follow the instructions exactly. If you delete another piece of text during the process, you will lose the contents of the scrap area and will not be able to undo the deletion.

With your highlight on the *L* of *Last fall* at the beginning the document, press Shift-F8 to highlight the sentence. Press the Del key to delete the text into the scrap area.

Now undo this edit by pressing Shift-F1 (the speed key for the Undo command). Word puts the sentence back in the document. Press the Down Arrow key to remove the highlight.

Deleting Text

In order to delete text, you first have to select it. (See "Selecting Text" in this chapter.) Then, you can delete the text to the scrap. Another option is to delete the text without affecting the current contents of the scrap area.

Deleting Text to the Scrap Area

Getting in the habit of deleting to the scrap is good insurance. That way, if you decide you want to restore the deletion, you can use the Undo command (Shift-F1).

There are two ways to delete text to the scrap. You can:

- Select the text and press the Del key (on some computers, this key may be called Delete). The text you have deleted is represented between the curly braces of the scrap area in the status line.

- Select the text. Select the Delete command and press Enter. Again, the deleted text is represented between the curly braces of the scrap area.

Deleting Text Without Affecting the Scrap

You can delete text without placing the deleted text in the scrap area. This is helpful if you want to preserve the text that is currently in the scrap for another use. For example, suppose you have deleted some text to scrap that you know you need to insert at another location. After deleting the text, you notice three other deletions you want to make before scrolling the document to the place where you will insert the deleted text. Making even one of these deletions to the scrap area would wipe out the text you want to put back in the document. Scrolling to the place where you want to make the insertion and then coming back to make the other deletions is inefficient because you will pass by the deletions on the way. If you don't need to save the other deletions, a good alternative is to delete that text in a way that leaves the scrap area untouched. That way, you save the current contents of the scrap area until you can insert the text in its final destination.

Use Shift-Del to delete text without placing it in scrap

As you know, to delete text character by character without affecting the contents of the scrap, you can use the Backspace key. The text you delete this way is not placed in the scrap. To use the Backspace key, you must be in insert mode, not overtype mode. (A Backspace key that deletes characters, instead of simply passing over them as the backspace key on a typewriter does, is sometimes called a destructive backspace.)

To delete more than a character of text at a time, without affecting the scrap area, follow these steps:

1. Select the text you want to delete.
2. Press **Shift-Del**. The text is deleted and not placed in the scrap area.

 When you use the Backspace key or press Shift-Del to delete text without putting it in the scrap area, the text is permanently gone. That is, you cannot use the Undo command to restore the deleted text.

Exercise: Deleting Text

The PDREORG.DOC should still be on your screen, and the text should look like this:

```
Last fall, the board directed that our product group be
completely reorganized to streamline operations. This
important effort is underway. The committee charged with
reorganizing the product development group met on January
12th. All ten members were present in person or through a
representative.
    The meeting started with opening remarks by Jim Tailor,
the newly appointed Director of Product Development. NOTE:
Check his title.
```

To delete text to the scrap area, place your highlight on the word *important* in the third line. Press F8 to highlight the word. Notice the contents of the scrap area. Press Del to delete the selected word to the scrap area. Now notice that the scrap area looks like this:

```
{Important }
```

Place your highlight on the *ly* of *newly* in the next-to-the-last line. Press F6 to turn on extend select. Notice that EX appears in your status line. Move your highlight to extend the selection to the *d* in *appointed*. Again, notice the contents of the scrap area. Press Shift-Del to delete the selected text without affecting the scrap area. Notice that the text is deleted but the scrap area is unchanged. Your text now looks like this:

```
Last fall, the board directed that our product group be
completely reorganized to streamline operations. This
```

effort is underway. The committee charged with reorganizing
the product development group met on January 12th. All ten
members were present in person or through a representative.

The meeting started with opening remarks by Jim Tailor,
the new Director of Product Development. NOTE: Check his
title.

Moving Text

You can move text using the keyboard or using the mouse. When you
use the keyboard, deleting and moving text are closely related. You
delete the text you want to move to the scrap area, position the highlight in the new location, and then insert the text from the scrap area
into the document at that new location. Though the outcome is that
the text is moved, you really use a combination of Word's delete and
insert functions to make the move.

*Use a mouse to
move text*

As you'll soon learn, when you use a mouse to move text, you
can carry out the task without disturbing the scrap or using the Del
and Ins keys or commands.

Consider exactly what text you have deleted when you are identifying where to place your highlight before inserting. For example, if
you delete text that ends with a period and trailing spaces, you will
want to place the cursor on the first letter of a sentence when you
insert the text. That way, the spacing will be correct after you insert
the new text. Suppose you have deleted this sentence and a trailing
space:

Staff morale is high.

and you want to insert the text between these two sentences:

The stock is strong. We can't lose.

You would place your highlight on the *W* of *We* when you insert, to
get this result:

The stock is strong. Staff morale is high. We can't lose.

When you move text, consider what you don't see as well as
what you do. When you delete hidden text and non-printing symbols,
they are placed in the scrap area and are inserted along with the text.
Because paragraph marks include the formatting for the paragraph,
you should move them with the paragraph to maintain the formatting.

Similarly, because division marks include the formatting for the division, you should move them with the division if you want to keep the formatting. It is a good idea to set the Options *show hidden text* field to Yes and the Options *show non-printing symbols* field to All so that you can see exactly what you are manipulating.

To move text using the keyboard:

1. Select the text you want to move.

2. Press the **Del** key or select **Delete** and press **Enter**. The text is placed in the scrap.

3. Place the highlight at the location where you want to insert the text. You can use any highlight-moving speed keys (such as **Alt-F5** for Jump Page) to get to the new location. The text will be inserted immediately to the left of your highlight.

4. Press the **Ins** key or select **Insert** and press **Enter**. Word inserts the contents of the scrap right before the highlight.

To move text with the mouse:

1. Select the text you want to move.

2. Hold down the **Ctrl** key, point, and click one of these buttons:

   In a window:

Left button	to insert before the character to which you are pointing
Right button	to insert before the word to which you are pointing
Both buttons	to insert before the sentence to which you are pointing

   In the selection bar:

Left button	to insert before the line adjacent to where you are pointing
Right button	to insert before the paragraph adjacent to where you are pointing
Both buttons	to insert before the start of the document

Assuming you held down the Ctrl key, Word inserts the text according to where you pointed and the button(s) you clicked. The scrap area is unaffected.

H

You can move text from one window to another. Just delete the text to the scrap area, press F1 to move to the desired window, and then insert the text in the new location.

You can use the mouse (but not the keyboard) to transpose (switch the positions of) two characters, two words, or two sentences. The two pieces of text you want to transpose must be adjacent. These examples illustrate common applications.

Characters:

See yuo then.   See you then.

Words:

The plan is good looking.   The plan is looking good.

Sentences:

Call Bob. Set a date.   Set a date. Call Bob.

To transpose two characters using the mouse:

1. Point to the second character and click the left button to select the character.
2. Point to the first character.
3. Hold down the **Ctrl** key and click the left button. The first and second characters are transposed.

To transpose two words using the mouse:

1. Point to the second word and click the right button to select the word.
2. Point to the first word.
3. Hold down the **Ctrl** key and click the right button. The words are transposed.

To transpose two sentences using the mouse:

1. Point to the second sentence and click both buttons to select the sentence.
2. Point to the first sentence.
3. Hold down the **Ctrl** key and click both buttons. The sentences are transposed.

As you can see, when you transpose characters, words, and sentences, you follow the same steps. It is easy to remember which button to click because you use the same button(s) to select a character, word, or sentence that you use to transpose those text units.

Exercise: Moving Text

This example gives you practice in moving text. The PDREORG.DOC should be on your screen:

```
    Last fall, the board directed that our product group be
completely reorganized to streamline operations. This
effort is underway. The committee charged with reorganizing
the product development group met on January 12th. All ten
members were present in person or through a representative.
    The meeting started with opening remarks by Jim Tailor,
the new Director of Product Development. NOTE: Check his
title.
```

You are going to delete and then insert a word in order to move it.

Inserting text from scrap
Place your highlight on the word *completely* in the second line. Press F8 to highlight the word and the trailing space. Notice the contents of the scrap area. Press Del to delete the text to the scrap area. Place your highlight on the *t* in the word *to*. Press Ins. Notice that the text is inserted along with the space so that the correct spacing is maintained. Also notice the scrap area. You could insert the word *completely* again at another location if you wanted to.

Copying Text

Copying text is different from moving it because you leave the original text in place rather than delete it. The result of copying is that the same text appears in two locations. To copy, you first select the text. You then use the keyboard to copy the text to the scrap area, position your highlight in the new location, and insert the text.

It is important to consider what you want to copy when you make your selection. Think about the results you want. Make sure you copy leading or trailing spaces if necessary. Include hidden text and non-printing symbols as needed. You may also need to include paragraph marks and division marks that include formatting.

Just as you can move text from one window to another, so you can copy text from one window to another. Copy the text to the scrap area, press F1 to move to the appropriate window, and then insert the text.

You can copy text using the keyboard or the mouse. Instructions for both follow.

To copy text using the keyboard:

1. Select the text you want to copy.
2. Press **Alt-F3** or select **C**opy and press **Enter**. The selected text is copied to the scrap area.
3. Place the highlight in the location where you want the new copy of the text to appear. Word will insert the text immediately before your highlight.
4. Press the **Ins** key or select **I**nsert and press **Enter**.

To copy text with the mouse, bypassing the scrap area:

1. Select the text you want to copy.
2. Hold down the **Shift** key, point, and click one of these buttons:

In a window:

Left button	to insert before the character to which you are pointing
Right button	to insert before the word to which you are pointing
Both buttons	to insert before the sentence to which you are pointing

In the selection bar:

Left button	to insert before the line adjacent to where you are pointing
Right button	to insert before the paragraph adjacent to where you are pointing
Both buttons	to insert before the start of the document

Assuming you held down the Shift key, Word inserts the text according to where you pointed and the button(s) you clicked. The scrap area is unaffected.

Exercise: Copying Text

In this exercise, you are going to copy text to a new part of the PDREORG.DOC document. To set off the text, add a series of dashes across the top line of your document. This is how the text looks after you have added the dashes

---

```
    Last fall, the board directed that our product group be
reorganized completely to streamline operations. This
effort is underway. The committee charged with reorganizing
```

the product development group met on January 12th. All ten
members were present in person or through a representative.

The meeting started with opening remarks by Jim Tailor,
the new Director of Product Development. NOTE: Check his
title.

Place your highlight in the line of dashes and press Shift-F9
to highlight the whole line. Notice what is in the scrap area. Press
Alt-F3 (the speed key for the Copy command) to copy the line. Take a
look at the scrap area now. The dashes have been saved there. Move
your highlight to the line after the last paragraph. (Don't delete anything to the scrap area in the mean time.) Press Ins. The dashed line
is copied after the last line of the document.

Printing Documents

A printed document is the desired final result of most word-processing tasks. If you don't get exactly what you want on the first printing, take heart. Typically, new users don't get correct printed results the first time they try. This chapter helps you identify the steps to take to ensure that Word will print your documents the way you want them and, with practice, on the first try.

If you are a beginning Word user and you are working through this book from front to back, you will print your first document using many of Word's default settings. As you learn more about Word in later chapters, you will identify ways to control the appearance of your printed documents through the use of page numbers, margins, and other formatting options.

Figure 5-1 shows a letter developed with Word using only the features covered in the book thus far. Figure 5-2 shows the printed letter. In this chapter, you will learn how to achieve this printed result.

Types of Printers

There are many types of printers. The generic categories are:

- **Dot matrix:** Letters are built with dots.
- **Daisywheel:** Letters are created by a metal or plastic form of the letter.
- **Laser:** Letters are produced photographically in much the same way as those produced by a copy machine.

```
|■
  January·31,·1990¶
  ¶
  Ms.·Jennifer·G.·Young↓
  The·Weldon·Company↓
  430·Black·Canyon·Highway↓
  Mail·Stop·33↓
  Phoenix,·Arizona·85082¶
  ¶
  Dear·Jennifer:¶
  ¶
  →    Jim·and·I·enjoyed·talking·with·you·yesterday·about·the·
  services·Oberfeld·and·Company·can·offer.···It·appears·that·
  your·needs·and·our·strengths·are·a·good·match.··¶
  ¶
  →    I'll·call·you·in·the·next·few·days·to·discuss·when·we·
  might·meet·to·finalize·plans.¶
  ¶
  Sincerely,¶
  ¶
  ¶
  Katie·Magill↓
  President¶
                                                  ═CH5.DOC═
  P62 D3 L23 C10    {¶}              ?            Microsoft Word
```

Figure 5-1. A letter as it appears on the screen

```
January 31, 1990

Ms. Jennifer G. Young
The Weldon Company
430 Black Canyon Highway
Mail Stop 33
Phoenix, Arizona 85082

Dear Jennifer:

     Jim and I enjoyed talking with you yesterday about the
services Oberfeld and Company can offer.  It appears that
your needs and our strengths are a good match.

     I'll call you in the next few days to discuss when we
might meet to finalize plans.

Sincerely,


Katie Magill
President
```

Figure 5-2. The same letter after printing

Paper Feed

Printers are also distinguished by the type of paper feeder they use. It may be possible to use more than one of the following types with your printer:

- **Continuous form:** Pages feed into the printer in one long strip that usually has pin feed holes along both sides. Pages are separated by perforations.
- **Single sheet:** Pages feed into the printer one at a time.
- **Sheet feeder:** Pages feed into the printer one at a time from an add-on feeder. The feeder is not required for the printer to operate.

Portrait and Landscape Printing

Printers may accommodate single-direction or two-direction printing. The typical orientation is called *portrait*. Figure 5-3 shows portrait printing. The other orientation is called *landscape*. Figure 5-4 shows landscape printing. Landscape printing is often used on laser printers to print addresses on envelopes that are fed into the printer "short side" first.

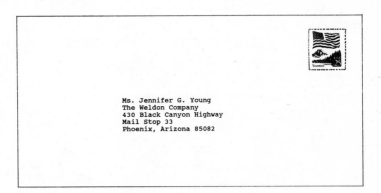

Figure 5-3. Portrait printing

Fonts

Some printers provide the option of using different character styles, referred to as fonts. Fonts are often identified by type face (such as

Figure 5-4. Landscape printing

Courier), pitch and point size, and character weight. Figure 5-5 shows several fonts.

Different printers access fonts in different ways:

- The fonts may be built into the hardware and software of the machine, in which case they are called *internal fonts*.
- The fonts may be stored in removable hardware devices called *cartridges*.
- The fonts may exist as software on disks, in which case they are called *downloadable fonts*. You transfer them from storage on your computer into the memory of the printer when you need them. Some downloadable fonts are scalable, meaning that you can change their size.

Chapter 2, "Starting Microsoft Word," covers how to set up the files necessary for Word to use fonts. This chapter describes how to identify additional files that you may need if you want to use certain types of fonts. Chapter 6, "Formatting Documents," covers how to change the look of a document by changing the font.

Helvetica Bold 14.4 point

Times Roman Medium 10 point

Times Roman Bold 10 point

Times Roman Medium Italic 10 point

Times Roman Light 8 point

Line Printer Light 8.5 point

PRESENTATION BOLD 18 POINT

PRESENTATION BOLD 16 POINT

PRESENTATION BOLD 14 POINT

Letter Gothic Medium 14 point

`Courier 10 point`

`Courier Bold 10 point`

Figure 5-5. Font examples

Printer Ports and Communication Parameters

The printer port is where the printer cable is attached to your computer. Ports are either serial or parallel. Serial ports are typically male ports (the pins stick out) with 25 or 9 pins. Parallel ports are typically female ports with 25 holes. Make sure you have the correct cable for your printer. See your dealer or printer manual if you are uncertain about the cable. The cable should fit securely in the back of your computer and in the printer.

When the printer and computer initially "talk" or communicate with each other, the communication is referred to as a *handshake*. Certain parameters must be set in your operating system to ensure that the handshake takes place correctly. You use the MODE command and/or the SETCOM command to set these parameters. (See Chapter 2, "Starting Microsoft Word," and your operating system manual for more information.) Most personal computer users like to put the MODE and SETCOM commands in an AUTOEXEC.BAT file. That way, the commands are automatically entered every time you start up your computer.

Printer-Driver Setup

In order to print, your computer needs access to the printer-driver file that enables it to send Word documents to your printer. The printer drivers for most printers are supplied with Word. (The .PRD files are printer drivers; the .DAT files with the same names as the .PRD files are necessary only if you are using downloadable fonts). Consult Appendix B of this book or the *Printer Information for Microsoft Word* manual that comes with Word to identify the .PRD files for your printer. The Word manual includes the following information (some of which is not included in Appendix B of this book):

- Information specific to the printer
- A list of the .PRD file(s)
- Model names, line-drawing fonts, IBM graphics characters, graphics resolution, bin support, and unprintable regions
- Printer features (availability of bold, italic, small caps, strikethrough, super/subscript, underline, double underline, microspace justify, and graphics)
- Fonts, font sizes, and notes

Most dot-matrix printers emulate both IBM and Epson printers. If you can't find a printer driver for your printer, check the manual to see whether your printer supports IBM and/or Epson emulation. These drivers will give you a wider selection of features than TTY drivers.

If you cannot find a .PRD file for your printer, read the PRINTERS.DOC file on the Word Printers disk. This file identifies the .PRD files that may have been added recently. Another alternative is to check your printer manual to see whether your printer emulates another popular printer. If it does, try the .PRD file for that printer. Ask your printer dealer or call the manufacturer to see if either can suggest an appropriate .PRD file. Microsoft Product Support can also provide the information. You can also try the generic .PRD files that come with Word. Use the generic file that matches the type of printer you have. These are the options:

Generic .PRD file	Type of printer
TTY.PRD	Dot matrix or teletype-like
TTYBS.PRD	Dot matrix or teletype-like with backspace
TTYFF.PRD	Dot matrix or teletype-like, but recognizes form-feed characters at page ends instead of carriage-return characters
TTYWHEEL.PRD	Daisywheel

A final alternative for technically oriented users is to create your own .PRD file. To make a printer driver or customize an existing one, use the MakePRD program (see "MakePRD" in this chapter for general information).

To tell Word which printers and special fonts you'll be using, use Word's Setup utility. When you use the Setup utility, Word copies the appropriate .PRD file(s) to your Word program disk or WORD directory (along with the appropriate .DAT files if you are using downloadable fonts).

You can use the Setup utility as often as you need to change printer information. Setup is described in detail in Chapter 2, "Starting Microsoft Word." Or you can copy the appropriate .PRD and .DAT files to your Word program disk or WORD directory using operating-system commands.

Nearly all of Word's .PRD files assume the following:

- The switch settings in your printer are the factory defaults. (See Appendix B for exceptions.) If you have trouble printing, check the switch settings against those defaults shown in the printer manual.

- The carriage-return switch delivers only a carriage return and not a line feed.

- Control panels (such as those on laser printers) are set to draft mode and 10 characters per inch. (See Appendix B for exceptions.) If you have set other options through the control panel, Word typically, but not necessarily always, overrides them.

Copying .PRD and .DAT Files Using DOS

To copy the .PRD and .DAT files to your disk or directory (not using the Setup utility), follow these steps:

1. Identify the appropriate .PRD and .DAT file(s) for your printer. The .DAT files are needed if you are using downloadable fonts. The .DAT files have the same name as the .PRD files for the printer except that the .DAT extension is substituted for the .PRD extension.

2. Find the appropriate printer driver and .DAT files on one of the Word Printers disks. To do this:

   a. Type in the drive containing the Printers disk and press **Enter**. For example, if the disk is in drive A, type in:

   A:

b. View the contents of the disk by entering the following and pressing **Enter**:

DIR/P

c. If necessary, change directories by entering the following and pressing **Enter** (substitute the subdirectory name):

CD*SUBDIRECTORY*

d. To search for the printer driver you need, type in the DIR command and printer-driver file name (or .DAT file name) and press **Enter**:

DIR *DRIVERFILE*.PRD

e. Look in each of the subdirectories supplied by Word until you find the printer driver you need.

3. Copy the necessary printer driver and .DAT files to your Word program disk or WORD directory. From the prompt for the drive containing the Printers disk, type in a command like the following and press **Enter** (make sure you enter the correct drive and path to the Word program disk or WORD directory):

COPY *DRIVERFILE*.PRD *C:*\WORD

You can now access the .PRD file from the *printer* field of Word's Printer Options menu.

Printing a Reminder List

Before you print, consider the issues discussed in this section. If you are a beginning Word user and have not entered special formatting into your document, you can omit some or all of these considerations as you prepare to print. If you are more advanced and have used Word's more sophisticated features in your document, carefully read through this reminder list:

- **Check content and formatting:** One factor determining the result of your print is whether your document has been entered properly. Carefully proofread the document and check the accuracy of how you have handled special formatting, such as bold text or the inclusion of index marks. For example, if you want certain characters to appear underlined but haven't used the Format Character command to underline the text, the underline won't appear.

- **Check margins and page numbers:** Make sure margins and page numbers are correctly set. Default margins are 1-inch top and bottom margins and 1.25-inch side margins for 8.5-by-11-inch paper. (To change margins or page number settings, see the "Formatting Divisions" section in Chapter 6, "Formatting Documents.")

- **Check running heads:** Running heads are text paragraphs that appear on each page. Check to make sure any running heads you've entered are marked correctly. (To add or check a running head, see Chapter 7, "Running Heads, Footnotes, and Annotations.")

- **Check the style sheet:** Style sheets contain formatting information. Word's default style sheet is called NORMAL.STY. Make sure the style sheet you intend to use is attached to the document you are printing. (To check the current style sheet, see the "Attaching Style Sheets" section in Chapter 9, "Style Sheets.")

- **Check your spelling:** If desired, check the spelling of the document as a final step before printing. (See Chapter 8, "Checking Your Spelling and Using the Thesaurus," for more information.)

You perform these quality controls outside the Print command. The following Word print features are controlled with the Print command and are covered in detail this chapter. Before you print, skim this list as a reminder:

If you have more than one document to print, set up a print queue using the Library Document-retrieval Print command. See Chapter 14, "Handling Files and Running DOS Commands," for details.

- **Check the Print Options settings:** Make sure they are set as you want them (including identification of the correct .PRD file).

- **Preview the printed result:** To see what your printed document will look like, use Print preView.

- **Select Print Printer:** When everything is ready, print your document.

- **Use Print Queue:** This feature is especially useful if it is necessary to pause or stop the print.

The Print Options Command

The Print Options command allows you to control many printer functions. Figure 5-6 shows the Print Options menu. Before you print, check the print options to make sure they are set according to your requirements. In this section, each print option is covered.

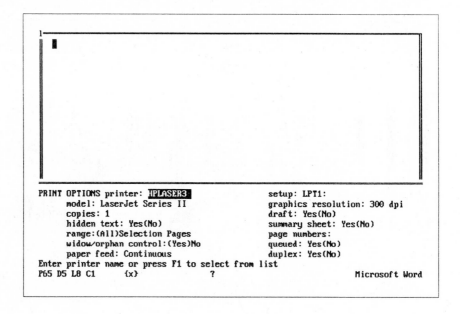

```
PRINT OPTIONS printer: IPLASER3           setup: LPT1:
        model: LaserJet Series II          graphics resolution: 300 dpi
        copies: 1                          draft: Yes(No)
        hidden text: Yes(No)               summary sheet: Yes(No)
        range:(All)Selection Pages         page numbers:
        widow/orphan control:(Yes)No       queued: Yes(No)
        paper feed: Continuous             duplex: Yes(No)
Enter printer name or press F1 to select from list
P65 D5 L8 C1        {x}                 ?                      Microsoft Word
```

Figure 5-6. The Print Options menu

Printer

In the *printer* field of the Print Options menu, you enter the name of the printer driver you want to use. Include the path and the file name if the .PRD file is not in the same directory as Word. If you do not know the name of the printer driver, you can see those on your Word program disk or WORD directory by pressing F1 (or clicking the field with the right mouse button). The drivers are made available through the Setup utility (see the "Printer-Driver Setup" section in this chapter and Chapter 2, "Starting Microsoft Word"). Or, you can copy them (see "Copying .PRD and .DAT Files Using DOS" in this chapter).

 Word retains the *printer* field setting when you quit the program. If you use only one printer driver, you can easily remember its name. However, if you have a sophisticated printer (such as a laser printer), you may use different printer drivers for different documents because of their font requirements. Because the *printer* field is maintained with Word (and not with your document), you may want to jot down the printer driver used by each document if you are using more than one printer driver. That way, you can easily remember which printer driver to use with each document. For example, if you use several downloadable fonts or font cartridges, you may have several printer drivers loaded to use with different documents, even though you have only one printer. A cross reference of documents and printer drivers will help you and others remember which driver to use.

Setup

You enter the port to which your printer is connected in the *setup* field of the Print Options menu. Here are the options typically available:

Parallel ports	Serial ports
LPT1	COM1
LPT2	COM2
LPT3	

Word retains the *setup* field setting when you quit the program.

Model

Enter the model name of your printer in the *model* field of the Print Options menu. The model is associated with the printer-driver file name you entered in the *printer* field. You can press F1 or click the right mouse button in the field to see a list of printer model names. Word retains this setting when you quit the program.

Graphics Resolution

The *graphics resolution* field in the Print Options menu determines the quality of the printed result. Resolution is expressed in dots per inch (dpi). The larger the number, the better the result. For example, laser printers typically use 150 dpi or 300 dpi. A printer that uses 300 dpi will produce a more professional-looking result than one that uses 150 dpi. Though resolution is important when printing text, it can be critical when printing detailed graphics.

If your printer has limited memory, you may want to select a lower graphics resolution. The higher the graphics resolution, the more memory required.

To enter the graphics resolution, you can press F1 or click the right mouse button in the field to select from a list. Word retains this setting when you quit the program.

Copies

You can print a single copy or more than one copy. In the *copies* field of the Print Options menu, enter the number of copies you want. If the document has multiple pages, the entire first copy of the document is printed, then the second, and so forth. You can enter a number as large as 99999 in this field. However, if you are printing anything even close to that many copies, you may want to use a professional printing or copying service to save money.

After you print multiple copies, you may want to get in the habit of resetting the *copies* field to 1. That way, you won't accidentally start multiple-copy printing when you print future documents.

Draft

The absence of microspace justification in draft mode can cause justified text to print incorrectly. If you are justifying text, always set the draft field to No.

The *draft* field of the Print Options menu allows you to identify whether you want to print in draft mode or regular mode. Enter Yes for draft mode or No for regular mode.

Draft mode saves printing time and, on some printers, saves ink or ribbons. In draft mode, however, the document is printed without microspace justification or graphics. (You can see where graphics should appear because Word leaves a blank space for them.)

Word retains this setting when you quit the program.

Hidden Text

Hidden text is a character format (see Chapter 3, "Creating Documents"). If you have entered hidden notes in the document or want Word to print hidden codes, you can tell Word to print hidden text. In the *hidden text* field of the Print Options menu, enter Yes to print the hidden text or No to omit hidden text. Word retains this setting when you quit the program.

Figure 5-7 shows a document with hidden codes printed and the same document with hidden codes not printed.

```
January 31, 1990

Ms. Jennifer G. Young
The Weldon Company
430 Black Canyon Highway
Mail Stop 33
Phoenix, Arizona 85082

Dear Jennifer:

     Jim and I enjoyed talking with you yesterday about the
services Oberfeld and Company can offer.  It appears that
your needs and our strengths are a good match.  Jim: should
we list the main benefits here?

     I'll call you in the next few days to discuss when we
might meet to finalize plans.  Jim: is this too strong?  Are
we at the "finalize plans" point?

Sincerely,


Katie Magill
President
```

Hidden
text

```
January 31, 1990

Ms. Jennifer G. Young
The Weldon Company
430 Black Canyon Highway
Mail Stop 33
Phoenix, Arizona 85082

Dear Jennifer:

     Jim and I enjoyed talking with you yesterday about the
services Oberfeld and Company can offer.  It appears that
your needs and our strengths are a good match.

     I'll call you in the next few days to discuss when we
might meet to finalize plans.

Sincerely,


Katie Magill
President
```

Figure 5-7. Hidden codes printed and not printed

 Hidden text may not be visible if the *show hidden text* field on the Options menu is set to No. You can print hidden text whether or not they are visible on your screen. The codes print in their entirety.

Summary Sheets

Summary sheets are used to record information about your documents. When you save a new document, you have the option of creat-

```
1
 ^Chapter·5·Printing·a·Document· · · · · · · · · · · · · · · · · · · · · ·5-(page)¶

  .c.Chapter·5·Printing·a·Document¶

  · · · · ·A·printed·document·is·the·desired·final·result·of·most·word·

  processing·tasks.· · ·If·you·don't·get·the·exact·result·you·desire·

  on·the·first·print,·take·heart.· · ·Typically,·new·users·don't·get·

  the·correct·printed·results·first·time,·every·time.· · ·This·chapter·

  helps·you·identify·the·steps·to·take·to·insure·that·you·have·a·

 ────────────────────────────────────────────────────────
 SUMMARY INFORMATION
     title: Chapter 5 Printing a Document        version number: beta
     author: K. Barnes                           creation date: 05/18/89
     operator: K. Barnes                         revision date: 06/13/89
     keywords: print .PRD .DAT
     comments: review use of .prd files in final version
 Enter text
 P1 D1 C1              {n}              ?                    Microsoft Word
```

Figure 5-8. A summary sheet as it appears on the screen

ing a summary sheet. (This option is controlled through the Options command *summary sheet* field.)

You can choose whether or not to print a summary sheet when you print your document. In the *summary sheet* field of the Print Options menu, enter Yes to print the summary sheet or No to omit the summary sheet from the printing process. (For information about filling out a summary sheet, see Chapter 3, "Creating Documents." For information about searching or editing summary sheets, see Chapter 14, "Handling Files and Running DOS Commands.")

The summary sheet that appears on the screen is a little different than the printed summary sheet. Figure 5-8 shows the screen appearance of the summary sheet used during development of this chapter. Figure 5-9 shows the same summary sheet when printed. The file name is added to the printed summary sheet, along with the character count.

```
filename: C:\WORDB\BBDOC\CH5.DOC
title: Chapter 5 Printing a Document
author: K. Barnes
operator: K. Barnes
keywords: print .PRD .DAT
comments: review use of .prd files in final version
version number: beta
creation date: 05/18/89
revision date: 06/13/89
char count: 76148
```

Figure 5-9. The printed summary sheet

Range

You can print a range of pages by completing the *range* field in the Print Options menu. Select one of these alternatives:

Option	Action
All	Prints all the pages in the document.
Selection	Prints only a portion of a long document. For example, you may want to print only the first page of a 15-page document. If the selection includes footnote references, the footnotes are printed. If a running head appears on a page selected, it prints. Selection works differently on different printers. Test this option on your printer. If the result is not what you want, use the Pages option.
Pages	Prints a range of pages according to what you enter in the *page numbers* field on this menu.

Page Numbers

If you enter Pages in the *range* field of the Print Options menu, you must enter the numbers of the pages you want to print. You can enter a single page, a range, or a combination of pages and ranges. These are the combinations you can enter:

Option	Example	Result
Single pages separated by commas	i, 5, 19, 34	Prints pages 1, 5, 19, and 34 only
Groups of pages with a colon or hyphen between the first and last pages	9:13	Prints from page 9 through and including page 13
	14–18	Prints from page 14 through and including page 18
Groups of pages and single pages together	4, 8–17, 19:22, 34	Prints page 4, pages 8 through 17, pages 19 through 22, and page 34
Single pages in a division	5D1, 12d2	Prints page 5 in division 1 and page 12 in division 2

Option	Example	Result
Groups of division numbers	2D3-24D4, 2d5:3d6	Prints page 2 in division 3 through page 24 in division 4 and then prints page 2 in division 5 through page 3 in division 6

Widow/Orphan Control

To Word, a widow is a single line of a paragraph printed at the top of a page; an orphan is a single line of a paragraph at the bottom of the page. Figure 5-10 shows a widow and an orphan.

```
the story without the background to interpret it. ◄──────────── Widow

        Without a strong background in the subject area, most

reporters on this paper lose sight of the important issues.

As a result, the reporter relies on superficial

understandings which lead to bland reporting at best and

incorrect interpretations at worst.  It is the job of every

staff person to be as informed as possible.  Only with

information can we have a strong basis for reporting.

        With this goal in mind, we are instituting a regular ◄──── Orphan
```

Figure 5-10. Widow and orphan

You can prevent Word from automatically making page breaks in a way that creates widows and orphans. In the *widow/orphan control* field of the Print Options menu, enter Yes to have Word prevent widows and orphans. Word moves the line of text before a widow to the next page or moves an orphan to the next page. Enter No to allow widows and orphans to occur when Word repaginates. Whatever you set, Word retains the setting when you quit the program.

Queued

If you are using a network, there is no need to set the Print Options queued field to Yes. The network operating system manages the printer queue.

While you print a document, you cannot continue working in Word. Your computer is tied up until the printing process is complete. If you need to send several documents to the printer, you may find the interruption inefficient and frustrating.

To print one or more documents and continue editing, you can set the *queued* field to Yes on the Print Options menu. This technique has its price, however. Setting *queued* to Yes may slow the speed of Word and consumes disk space because Word creates a temporary print file for storing your documents.

If you are using a hard disk with plenty of space, you can queue many documents to print and continue working. If you are using a two-floppy-disk system with document disks that are quite full, you will be limited in the number of documents (and the length of documents) you can queue.

If you queue documents to print and Word does not have enough space to create the temporary file, Word sends you a message to that effect. If you are using a floppy disk, you may be able to switch disks and continue (depending on how many files you are printing and where Word is storing the temporary files).

If after you set *queued* to Yes you encounter major speed or space problems, you can set the *queued* field back to No at any time.

If you do a lot of word processing, experimenting with the print queue is a good idea. If successful, you can save considerable time that would otherwise be spent waiting for documents to print.

Paper Feed

You can change how paper feeds through the printer and where the paper originates. Use the *paper feed* option on the Print Options menu for this purpose. You can enter one of the following options (if it is valid for the printer selected in the *printer* field). Or, you can press F1 (or click the right mouse button in the field) to see the valid options and select from the list. The possible *paper feed* options are listed here:

Option	Action
Manual	The printer will stop at the end of each page. A message appears reminding you to insert paper and press Y to continue.
Continuous	The document is printed in its entirety through the end without halting.
Bin 1	The paper the document is printed on is fed from bin 1 of a sheet feeder.
Bin 2	The paper the document is printed on is fed from bin 2 of a sheet feeder.
Bin 3	The paper the document is printed on is fed from bin 3 of a sheet feeder.
Mixed	The paper from bin 1 is used for the first page. The remainder of the document is printed on paper from bin 2.

Envelope   Envelopes from an envelope feeder are printed.

Whatever you set in this field is retained when you quit Word.

Duplex

If your printer is capable of printing on both sides of a page, you can set the *duplex* field on the Print Options menu to Yes. Experiment with your printer to see how it handles this option when set. Word retains this setting when you quit the program.

Print Preview

If you have a video adapter and graphics capabilities, you can use the Print preView command to look at the layout of your document before printing. For most simple documents, the use of Print preView may be unnecessary since the printed results look very similar to the screen appearance. For more complex documents involving columns, graphics, and different font styles, Print preView is invaluable. You can save a lot of time by viewing the document before taking the time to s-l-o-w-l-y print graphics and text.

Figure 5-11 shows an example of a print-preview screen. Two pages can appear on your screen at a time. The first page is the one

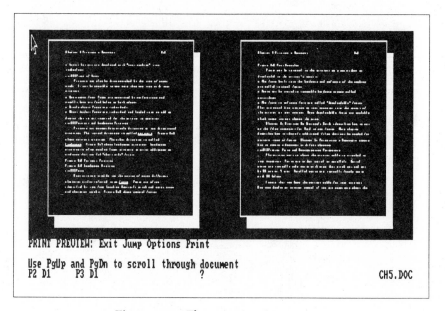

Figure 5-11. The print-preview screen

where your highlight rested when you selected Print preView. Print preView menu options appear, along with a reminder to use PgUp and PgDn to move through the document. Notice that the page and division numbers of each of the two pages appears at the bottom of the screen.

The following elements of your document appear in print-preview mode but not in regular document mode:

- Paragraph and character formatting
- Fonts scaled to size
- Margins
- Running heads in position
- Footnotes in position
- Page and line numbers
- Side-by-side paragraphs
- Multiple text columns
- Graphics scaled to fit the frames (the Print Options *draft* field must be set to No for the graphic to appear)
- Borders and revision marks
- Paragraphs positioned with the Format pOsition command
- Proportionally spaced text

Your screen may be able to display formats that your printer cannot print and vice versa. For example, you may be able to identify some text as italic (set through Format Character) even though your printer will not print the text in italics. If you enter a smaller font than 10 pitch (fixed pitch), the font may not appear on your screen but may print just fine (assuming your printer handles that font). Paragraphs formatted with proportional fonts may look incorrect on the screen even though they will print properly.

Previewing Pages

Word defaults to previewing two document pages, beginning with the page your highlight rests on. You can change the option to preview a single page or facing pages.

To preview pages of a document:

1. Place your highlight on the page that you want to preview first.

2. Select **P**rint pre**V**iew or press **Ctrl-F9**.

If you use the Word default, the page your highlight was on appears on the left and the following page appears on the right. The page number and division for each page appears in the status line.

3. If you want to change to another page-display setting, select **O**ptions. Select from the following:

1-page	to display one page at a time. The page is the same size as when two pages are displayed. The page is centered on the screen.
2-page	to display two pages at once. As you move through the document, one page is replaced at a time. For example, if pages 16 and 17 appear and you press PgDn, your screen displays pages 17 and 18.
Facing pages	to display facing pages together. Page 1 is shown alone (just like in a bound book). After that, even pages are shown on the right and odd pages on the left. When you scroll through the document, the screen refreshes with two new pages at a time. For example, if pages 16 and 17 are on the screen and you press PgDn, pages 18 and 19 appear.

Scrolling the Preview Document

You can scroll through a preview document using the keyboard or a mouse. The following table lists the methods:

Action	Result
Press PgUp	Moves backward through document page by page
Press PgDn	Moves forward through document page by page
Press Ctrl-PgUp	First page of document
Press Ctrl-PgDn	Last page of document
Point to left border; click left button	Move backward through document page by page
Point to left border; click right button	Move forward through document page by page

Point at top of left border; click both buttons	First page of document
Point at bottom of left border; click both buttons	Last page of document

Using Jump

Before previewing your document, assign bookmarks to the passages of particular concern. Then use the Print preView Jump command to quickly move from one passage to the next.

You can jump to a page or a bookmark while in page-preview mode. This is a quicker way of moving about your document than using PgUp and PgDn or the mouse. If you are working in a document with more than one division, you must identify both the page number and division. For example, if you want to go to page 6 in division 2, you would enter 6D2 or 6d2. Check the status line to identify the page number on which your highlight is resting.

To jump to a page or bookmark:

1. Select **P**rint pre**V**iew or press **Ctrl-F9**.
2. The print-preview screen appears. The screen displays the page your highlight rests on (and possibly a second page).
3. Select **J**ump.
4. In the Jump *to* field, select **P**age or bookmar**K**.
5. According to your selection:
   - Enter the page number (and division if necessary).
   - Enter the name of the bookmark or press **F1** to select from a list.
6. Press **Enter** or click the command name.

Word takes you to the page or bookmark entered.

Printing from Print Preview

You can print from print-preview mode. The Print preView Options menu is equivalent to the Print Options menu and the options work identically. The settings you enter on either menu affect both methods of printing.

Here are the steps for printing from print-preview mode (for more details on the options you can select, see "The Print Options Command," "The Print Printer Command," and "The Print File Command" in this chapter):

1. Select **P**rint pre**V**iew or press **Ctrl-F9**. The print-preview screen appears.
2. Select **P**rint.
3. Select one of the following:

   Printer   to print to the printer set up through Options
   File   to print to a file
   Options   to change printer options

4. Enter any additional information that may be required.

Exiting Print Preview

To exit from print-preview mode, select Exit. Word returns you to your document.

The Print Printer Command

Word allows you to print the document in the active window. A window is active when the number in the upper left corner is highlighted. Use F1 to change windows. With the Print Printer command, you cannot print a file from disk without first bringing the document in a window and making the window active.

To print a document:

1. Make sure the window in which the document appears is active. The window number in the upper-left corner should be highlighted.
2. Use the **P**rint **O**ptions command if necessary to check the settings.
3. Check that your printer is turned on, attached to your computer, and ready to print.
4. Select **P**rint **P**rinter or press **Ctrl-F8**.
5. If you are using a .PRD file (named in the Print Options *printer* field) that uses downloadable fonts, Word presents you with these options:

```
Enter Y to download new fonts, A to download all fonts,
N to skip
```

Press one of the following:

Y   to download fonts that haven't already been downloaded in this Word session.

A   to erase all downloaded fonts in the printer's memory and to download all fonts for which the document is formatted.

N   to print the document without downloading any additional fonts. If the fonts are available in memory, the document is printed using them. If the fonts required by the document are not available, Word substitutes fonts.

Word then prints your document.

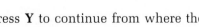

If you are using downloadable fonts and you see this message:

```
Font file not found
```

check the following:

- Make sure that the printer-driver (.PRD) files, font files, and data (.DAT) files are stored in the same directory. The directory may or may not be the Word Program directory.
- Make sure the path to the directory is entered in the Print Options *printer* field.
- If the directory and path is set up properly and you are using a Hewlett-Packard LaserJet printer, make sure all fonts larger than 14 points are formatted as bold.

To stop printing completely, you can use Print Queue (see this chapter) or simply press Esc. This is the process for using Esc:

1. Press **Esc**
2. The printer pauses and this message appears:

```
Enter Y to continue or Esc to cancel
```

Press **Y** to continue from where the print was paused. Press **Esc** to stop the print entirely.

Exercise: Printing

You can print the PDREORG.DOC with Print Printer. Make sure your printer is attached and ready to print. From the document window, select the Print Options screen to make sure the options are set as you need them for your printer. Then, select Print Printer to print the document.

The Print Queue Command

The Print Options *queued* field can be set to Yes to allow you to print one or more documents while continuing your work in Word. When you do this, you can use the Print Queue command to:

- Pause the document printing
- Stop the document printing
- Continue the document printing at the point printing was paused
- Restart the document printing at the beginning

Each of the Print Queue options affects the document currently printing from the queue. You cannot affect documents that may be waiting in the queue to be printed.

If you do not use the Print Options *queued* field, you cannot use Print Queue because the main command menu is not available during the print. Simply use Esc to pause, stop, or continue printing. There is no way to reprint a document from the beginning when you use Esc.

A good reason to pause printing is to realign paper that may be off track, change a ribbon, or change paper. If part of the document has been printed incorrectly (for example, on the wrong paper), you can restart the print from the beginning after making the necessary correction.

Follow these steps:

1. Make sure the Print Options *queued* field is set to **Yes**.

2. Select **P**rint **P**rinter as often as you like to send documents to print (see "The Print Printer Command" in this chapter).

3. To affect a document currently printing, select one of these options:

Print **Q**ueue **C**ontinue   to continue printing a document that is paused (with Print Queue Pause) from where it was paused.

Print **Q**ueue **P**ause   to pause printing. Use Print Queue Continue to continue printing, Print Queue Stop to stop printing, or Print Queue Restart to begin from the first page selected.

Print **Q**ueue **R**estart   to restart printing from the beginning of the document (or the first page selected if you have entered a value in the *page numbers* field of the Print Options menu).

Print **Q**ueue **S**top   to stop printing. You must use Print Printer to begin the print again. You can stop the print or pause first and then stop the print.

Your document is handled according to the Print Queue option selected.

The Print Direct Command

Use Print Direct for printing addresses on envelopes using a dot-matrix printer. Just make sure your printer's paper feed can handle the thickness of the envelopes.

Creating a document and then printing it is not always the most efficient way to complete your work in Word. Instead, you may want to enter text from your computer and have it immediately print on your printer in the manner of a typewriter. This approach is especially helpful when printing forms. Rather than word processing the entire form on your computer and then experimenting with where the text falls, you can position the print head and the blank of the form and then type. Print Direct is the command you use.

To print direct, follow these steps:

1. Select **P**rint **D**irect.

2. Enter the text. You may need to press **Enter** to get the printer to print.

3. After the text is printed, press **Esc** to go back to document editing.

The Print File Command

Use the Print File command to print a document in an active window to a file. The result is a document containing codes that another program can use to implement the formatting. Running heads appear on each page.

A print file can be used for transferring the document to other programs. The result, however, is not an ASCII file. Figures 5-12 through 5-15 show the result of saving a document using several different methods. The illustrations were made by using the DOS TYPE command and they show the different formatting codes introduced into the file with different approaches. Figure 5-12 shows the document produced by Print File. Figure 5-13 shows the same document after saving with Transfer Save in Word's document mode. Figure 5-14 shows the same document after saving with Transfer Save in Text-only mode. Figure 5-15 shows the document after saving with Transfer Save in Text-only-with-line-breaks mode. If you are transferring documents, you may want to experiment with Print File and Transfer Save to see which result is closest to what you need.

To use Print File:

1. Check that the document is in the active window. (Use **F1** to highlight the window number in the upper-left corner of the screen.)

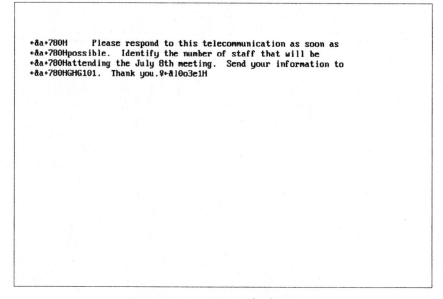

Figure 5-12. A Print File document

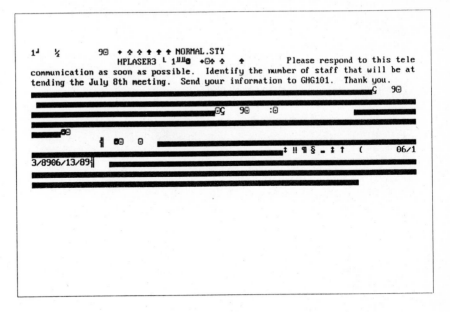

Figure 5-13. The same document saved with Transfer Save
and Word format

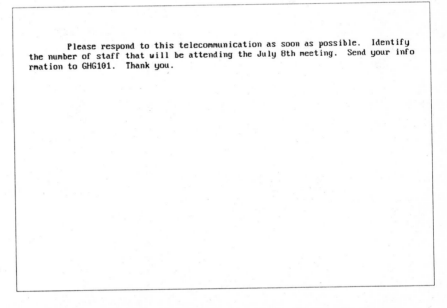

Figure 5-14. The same document saved with Transfer Save
and Text-only format

```
        Please respond to this telecommunication as soon as
possible.  Identify the number of staff that will be
attending the July 8th meeting.  Send your information to
GHG101.  Thank you.
```

Figure 5-15. The same document saved with Transfer Save
and Text-only-with-line-breaks format

2. Select **Print File**.

3. Enter a name for the document. You will probably want to give
   the document a name other than the original name. Otherwise,
   the result from Print File will replace the original document.
   Some users like to put *pf* (for *print file*) in the document name.
   For example:

   JIMLET.DOC   could be JIMLETPF.DOC

   WILLYCOM.DOC   could be WILLYCPF.DOC

4. Press **Enter**.

   Word displays a message like this one while it is printing the
   document to a file:

   ```
   Printing page 12 of ch5.doc
   ```

   When the document is printed, a message identifying the number of lines and words appears briefly. Word then returns you to
   document editing.

The Extended Character Set

Your printer may be able to print the extended character set. It includes 256 characters with capital letters, small letters, symbols, foreign characters, mathematical, and graphic characters. Appendix C of this book and Appendix A of *The Reference to Microsoft Word* illustrate these characters. Even if your printer does not handle these characters on its own, you may be able to print them. Word includes the characters in some of the .PRD files.

Displaying Characters on Your Screen

You can display extended-character-set characters on the screen. See the next section for an easy way to test which characters will print on your printer.

To enter a single character, follow these steps:

1. Hold down the **Alt** key and enter the code for the character (0 to 255) using the numeric keypad (not the numbers across the top of your keyboard).
2. Release the **Alt** key.

The character should appear on your screen.

To enter a long hyphen (em dash), press Ctrl-Alt-Hyphen. This will appear as a regular hyphen on the screen but will print out as an em dash.

If you use a character often (such as a bullet ■) you may want to create a macro to store the keystrokes involved. See Chapter 21, "Macros," for information on creating and running macros.

Some characters are reserved for use in Word and you cannot print them on the screen. For example, the character code 13 produces no result when entered. Other character codes are used for actions. To illustrate, code 10 results in a paragraph code on your screen and moves your highlight to the next line.

Testing Your Printer

You will have to experiment with your printer to see how many of the characters in the extended character set will print. Word supplies a macro to use in testing your printer. This macro is called

CHARACTER_TEST.MAC and comes on a Word Utility disk in a glossary file called MACRO.GLY. The CHARTEST.DOC is used along with the macro. This macro relieves you from having to enter each character code 0 through 255 to see which ones will print with your printer.

To use this macro:

1. Make sure the CHARTEST.DOC and MACRO.GLY files are in your directory or disk.

2. Work from an empty Word window. If you are editing a document, you may want to open a new window just to use the macro. If you start this macro from a window with a document, you will be asked whether you want to save your work before continuing or whether you want to lose your edits.

3. Select the .PRD file you want to test by selecting **Print Options** and entering the .PRD file name in the *printer* field. If more than one font is supported by the .PRD file, you will be able to select some or all of the fonts for the test. Press **Enter** when you are done.

4. Select **Transfer Glossary Load**.

5. In the *filename* field, enter the path (if necessary), MACRO.GLY, and press **Enter**. Or, press **F1** then select MACRO.GLY.

6. From the main command menu, select **Insert** and press **F1** to see the list of glossary entries. Highlight CHARACTER_TEST.MAC and press **Enter**.

7. Word begins running the macro and looks for the CHARTEST.DOC file. If Word cannot find the file, a message like this appears:

```
CHARTEST.DOC not found. Enter full pathname, or press Esc
twice to abort macro
```

Enter the drive and path of the directory containing CHARTEST.DOC and press **Enter**. For example:

```
C:\WORD\CHARTEST.DOC
```

8. If several fonts are supported by the selected .PRD file, the macro asks if you want to print every font available with the following message. Enter **Y** or **N** and press **Enter**.

```
Do you want to print a sample of every font (y/n)?
```

9. If you pressed Y, Word prints each font supported by the .PRD file. If you pressed N, Word presents a screen like that shown in Figure 5-16. Select the font you want and press **Enter**. That font is printed. Then, this message appears:

```
Print another sample font (y/n)?
```

Press **Y** to select another font or enter **N** to complete the printing.

```
Courier (modern a)              CourierPC (modern b)
Prestige[J] (modern c)          LetterGothic[R] (modern e)
LetterGothicLegal[R] (modern f) LinePrinter (modern h)
HELV[Z] (modern i)              Presentation[R] (modern m)
PresentationLegal[R] (modern n) TMSRMN[Z] (roman a)
PiFont[J] (symbol a)            LineDraw[R] (symbol b)
Math7[J] (symbol c)             Math8[J] (symbol d)
PCLine[R] (symbol g)



FORMAT CHARACTER bold: Yes(No)     italic: Yes(No)       underline: Yes(No)
        strikethrough: Yes(No)     uppercase: Yes(No)    small caps: Yes(No)
        double underline: Yes(No)  position:(Normal)Superscript Subscript
        font name: Courier         font size: 12         font color: Black
        hidden: Yes(No)
Select the font you want and press Enter
                {x}                     ?                    Microsoft Word
```

Figure 5-16. The font-selection screen

Once the printing is completed, the macro stops running. If you opened a special window in which to run the macro, that window closes. Word returns you to document-editing mode.

Printer Control Codes

Most .PRD files include all the instructions necessary to take full advantage of your printer. However, you may have some codes suggested in your printer manual to control the printing differently from Word's .PRD file. You can enter the printer control code. To enter an escape character, hold down Alt and type in 27 (using the numeric keypad). Then type the rest of the command. For control codes below ASCII 32, use Alt and the decimal number.

Some printers require that each printer command be entered on a separate line. Check your printer manual for more information. Do not enter font-selection, line-spacing, or page-formatting control codes unless you are using a plain TTY.PRD file. These codes will cause Word to print pages incorrectly.

Envelopes

Most Word users want to know how to perform the common, but sometimes difficult, task of printing envelopes. For example, when you use a Hewlett-Packard LaserJet Series II printer, you feed the envelope sideways into the printer. The address must have the correct top and left margins and must be printed in landscape mode.

Check your printer manual to see whether you will feed envelopes in top to bottom (portrait printing) or on the side (landscape printing). As indicated in Appendix B, many printers have special .PRD files for landscape printing.

Also check your printer manual to see if the printer requires that the Print Options *paper feed* field be set to manual or envelope feed. Generally speaking, you will use envelope feed only if your printer has an envelope feeder attached. If you cannot identify this information, you can go to the Print Options *paper feed* field, press F1, and see what options are available for the .PRD file you are using. If manual and envelope are both available, experiment with both to see which works best for you.

When you print envelopes, you may want to test the function and placement of the text on paper first. That way, if the function doesn't work or the margins aren't right, you have not wasted an envelope.

For portrait-printed envelopes, you can set the left margin on the screen by using the Tab or Spacebar key. The top margin can be controlled by positioning the envelope in the proper spot under the print head and using no top margin. Or, you can use the Format Division Margins command to set the top and left margin. (See Chapter 6, "Formatting Documents," for more information on setting margins from within Word.) The approach you use depends on whether you prefer to reset margins through Format Division Margins or whether it is easier to use spaces on the screen and position the envelope in the printer. Do whichever seems easiest to you.

Envelopes: Letter-Quality or Serial Printer

Most printers make hard work of printing envelopes. You may want to hang on to your typewriter for no other reason than to address envelopes.

To print an envelope, first set the Print Options and then print the envelope:

1. Select **P**rint **O**ptions.
2. In the *paper feed* field, type in or select **M**anual. If your printer has an envelope feeder, enter **E**nvelope. Press **Enter**. The option is set until you change it.
3. Print the envelope by selecting **P**rint **P**rinter.

Word prints the envelope.

Envelopes: Laser Printer

Laser printers generally require that you feed envelopes into the printer sideways through the manual feed slot. For the address information to come out correctly, use landscape mode. Appendix B lists the .PRD files for the most popular laser printers. Note that there are separate .PRD files for landscape versus portrait printing. For specific information about printing in landscape mode with Apple LaserWriter or Hewlett-Packard LaserJet printers, see those sections in this chapter and in Appendix B.

To print an envelope:

1. Identify the .PRD file for your printer that will result in landscape mode. (See Appendix B for this information.)
2. Copy the .PRD file to your Word program disk or WORD directory. (See "Copying .PRD and .DAT Files Using DOS" in this chapter for instructions on copying the file.) Or use the Setup utility (Chapter 2, "Starting Microsoft Word," covers how to use Setup). Set the printer to landscape mode.
3. Select **P**rint **O**ptions.
4. Type in the name of the .PRD file in the *printer* field or press **F1** and select the name from a list.
5. On the Print Options menu, fill in the *paper feed* field with the appropriate entry. Select **M**anual to feed the envelope manually if your printer does not have an envelope feeder. If your printer has an envelope feeder, enter **E**nvelope. You can press **F1** to see the options to select for the .PRD file entered.
6. Select **D**ivision **M**argins and enter the exact dimensions of the envelope in the *page length* and *width* fields.

7. Press **Enter** or click the command name.

8. Select **P**rint **P**rinter to print the address on the envelope.

When you print envelopes with most laser printers, you have to position return addresses awkwardly because of the unprintable region. This area is usually about 0.5 inch on all sides of the page.

Using Laser Printers

Laser printers allow you to use a variety of font styles; however, some special considerations apply when you use them. This section discusses some things to note regarding the three most popular laser printer types: PostScript-type printers, the Apple LaserWriter series, and the Hewlett-Packard LaserJet series.

PostScript Printers

PostScript printers can read the Adobe PostScript page-description language. They allow you to print PostScript files created by desktop-publishing software and, in Word, to change the size of (scale) fonts and print imported PostScript graphics. There are a number of brands of PostScript printers on the market.

Setup Instructions

Place the POSTSCRP.PRD file, the POSTSCRP.DAT file, and an .INI file in the same directory. Usually, POSTSCRPT.INI should be used. If you have a DEC LN03R, use the DECLNO3R.INI file.

If you use Adobe downloadable fonts, use PSDOWN.PRD and the related files. You can use MergePRD to merge the PSDOWN.PRD file with the POSTSCRP.PRD file.

Word's Setup utility automatically copies the appropriate .PRD, .DAT, and .INI files to your directory or disk.

Use Instructions

PostScript fonts don't take up a great deal of memory. However, the PostScript .INI file does. If you have 512 KB of memory in your printer, you probably shouldn't use more than three downloadable fonts at once. If you have 1 MB of memory in the printer, you can probably have up to ten downloadable fonts in memory at a time.

Most PostScript printers have unprintable regions, meaning you will not be able to print right to the edge of the paper.

Apple LaserWriter Printers

The Apple LaserWriter is a widely used brand of PostScript printer. Word supports three Apple LaserWriter models, including Laser-Writer, LaserWriter Plus, and LaserWriter NT/NTX. You need a special serial cable to connect a PC to a LaserWriter.

Setup Instructions

The two .PRD files used are POSTSCRP.PRD (for internal fonts) and PSDOWN.PRD (for downloadable Adobe fonts). If you use downloadable fonts, you also need PSDOWN.DAT. The directory or drive with the .PRD and .DAT files must also contain: POSTSCRP.INI and PSDOWN.INI.

The switch on the side of the LaserWriter must be set to 9600 baud. The MODE command should be set to:

```
9600 baud, no parity, 8 data bits, and 1 stop bit
```

If you are using COM1, this is the command to use (substitute COM2 if that is the port you'll use):

```
MODE COM1:9600,N,8,1,p
```

Use Instructions

Because LaserWriter printers rotate text for landscape printing, you do not need a special .PRD file for landscape. However, you do need to use Format Division Margins to switch the settings in the *page length* and *width* fields. For example, to print in landscape on a regular 8.5-by-11-inch paper, enter the *page length* as 8.5″ and the *width* as 11″. The *page length* and *width* fields are set by division, allowing you to print a document with landscape pages intermixed with portrait pages.

If you are using POSTSCRP.PRD in the Print Options *model* field, use the PostScript Single Bin model. If you are using PSDOWN.PRD for downloadable fonts, select Adobe Download Fonts in the *model* field.

Hewlett-Packard LaserJet Printers

Hewlett-Packard LaserJet printers allow you to use built-in, cartridge, and downloadable fonts. There are two types of downloadable fonts: permanent and temporary. Permanent fonts stay in the printer's memory until the printer is turned off. Temporary fonts stay in the printer's memory until the memory is reset or the printer is turned off.

Word's .DAT files create temporary fonts. When you use the Print Printer command with a .PRD file including downloadable fonts, this message appears:

```
Enter Y to download new fonts, A to download all fonts, N to skip
```

Pressing Y adds new fonts to those in memory, pressing A erases temporary fonts and downloads new fonts, and pressing N doesn't change the fonts in memory. Since Word creates temporary fonts, selecting A helps you keep the memory clear by loading only those fonts you desire for the particular document.

You can opt to download fonts as permanent fonts to keep them in memory until the printer is shut off. Permanent fonts are useful for network situations where all the users want to take advantage of the same fonts. Downloading fonts once saves repeated downloading. To download fonts as permanent, use the utility program that comes with the fonts prior to starting up Word. That way, you don't have to download any fonts through Word.

Setup Instructions

To use downloadable fonts, these files must be in the directory or on the disk.

- The .PRD file(s)
- The .DAT file with the same name as the .PRD file
- The font files

Word's Setup utility automatically copies the .PRD and .DAT files. You only need to add the font files to the directory or disk.

If you want to print in landscape mode, copy only the .PRD files identified specifically for that mode. The exceptions to this are the LaserJet IID and LaserJet 2000 models, which do not need a special landscape .PRD file since they perform autorotation.

Use Instructions

In the Print Options *printer* field, enter the name of the .PRD file for the cartridge or downloadable font you'll use. If want to create documents that use both cartridges and downloadable fonts, you can use MergePRD to merge the .PRD files used. (See "MergePRD" in this chapter for more information.) The Hewlett-Packard line has several models. Use the appropriate model name in the Print Options *model* field.

The LaserJet printers have memory built in. If you overload the memory, your results will be incorrect. To reduce the memory requirements when using graphics, reduce the Print Options *graphics resolution* field setting or reduce the amount or size of the graphics.

You can reduce memory requirements by substituting cartridge fonts (stored on cartridge) for downloadable fonts (stored in memory). Using fewer or smaller downloadable fonts will also reduce memory requirements.

Most LaserJet printers have a maximum number of fonts allowed per page (usually 16 or 32). For example, Times Roman 10, Times Roman Bold 10, Times Roman Italic 10 are considered three fonts. If you try to exceed the printer's font limit, the formatting of the page may be affected. An exception is the LaserJet IID which can print an unlimited number of fonts on a page. Mixing too many fonts on a page can create a downright ugly and confusing document. Some LaserJet printers also have maximums on the size of the fonts. Check your printer manual to see what restrictions exist.

LaserJet printers support symbol sets (character sets). To access the symbol set, choose a .PRD file that not only supports the cartridge or font set, but that also supports the specific symbol set. If you want to use a symbol that is not supported by Word, you can modify the .PRD file (see "MakePRD" in this chapter).

To use line draw, you should use CourierPC or Linedraw fonts. Otherwise, Word's line-draw feature may not give you the results expected. For margins, set the exact number of inches from the edge of the paper desired. You cannot print to the edge of the paper since the LaserJet series (like most laser printers) has an unprintable region next to the edge.

If you have a LaserJet IID or LaserJet 2000 model, you do not need a special .PRD file or switch the Format Division Margins page length or page width settings.

To print in landscape mode, you need the special .PRD file for landscape. You must reverse the Format Division Margins *page length* and *width* settings. A standard 8.5-by-11-inch page will have a length of 8.5 inches and a width of 11 inches for landscape mode. The *page length* and *width* settings are assigned to the division. A document can contain both portrait and landscape pages.

Network Considerations

If you are using a network, there are some special considerations both for setting up to print and for printing.

Setting Up to Print

When you setup Word on a network, you will copy the printer drivers to the server. With downloadable fonts, the .PRD files, the font files, and the .DAT files must be in the same directory. This does not necessarily have to be the Word Program directory; however, it is a good practice to keep them in the Word Program directory until the workstations are setup. If you decide to move the files to a separate directory, you will need to change the path name in the Print Options *printer* field.

See Chapter 2, "Starting Microsoft Word," for more information about the setup process for networks.

Network Solutions

Most networks are set up to share a printer with a print spooler (memory to hold documents to be printed). To change to another printer, select Print Options and set the *printer, model, setup* (port), and other options before printing. When *paper field* is set to Continuous, the print job is sent to the printer as one job. When *paper field* is set to Manual, the job is sent page by page. Use Manual when the paper must be changed in between pages. The workstations maintain the printer settings in the MW.INI file. These settings remain unchanged until you reset them.

The Print Printer command should be used to print. When you send a job via the Print Printer command, that job goes to the print queue of the network operating system. If you are using downloadable fonts, the file to print and the fonts or .INI file are sent with the document as a print job. You may be asked whether fonts should be downloaded. If the downloadable fonts are already downloaded for system-wide use, enter N. If the fonts are not downloaded, enter Y.

Do not use the Print Options *queue* field with a network. Instead, use the network operating system's print queue command. You may see the print queue of the network operating system using the commands for that network.

To enter network operating system commands from Word:

1. Select **Library Run**.

2. Enter the network commands.

3. Press **Enter**

Troubleshooting

Avoid unexpected printing problems by using Word's show layout and Print preView features to make sure your document formatting is correct before you print.

The result you get when you print may not be the one expected. Some users have trouble getting the printer to print at all. Others, though the printer prints, cannot get the visual result desired. Check these troubleshooting tips to give you some ideas about what to consider in achieving the desired outcome. When you walk through problems, always make one change then test the outcome. That way, you will know what change corrected the problem.

If the printer is not printing your document, try printing from the operating system level. In DOS, go to the system prompt and type in a command like the following then press Enter:

```
PRINT \WORD\MY.DOC
```

Make sure you have the valid path and file name. If you see a message like the following, enter the port or press Enter:

```
Name of list device
```

The operating system will identify that you are printing. If you cannot print from the operating system, the handshake between your computer, operating system, and printer has not been established. Check all the print requirements between the hardware and at the operating system level.

If you cannot print from the operating system or if Word displays the message *Printer is not ready*:

- Check the MODE command (and the SETCOM command in OS/2).
- Make sure the baud rate is set correctly if connection is serial.
- If your printer manual identifies that the printer uses more than one handshaking protocol, make sure the printer is using either ETX/ACK or XON/XOFF. Word expects XON/XOFF for most printers except Diablo. For Diablo printers, Word uses ETX/ACK.
- Check the printer switch and Ctrl panel settings against the defaults in the manual. (Most of Word's .PRD files anticipate the factory settings.)
- Check your printer cable to make sure it is the correct cable and that it is securely fastened to both the computer and printer.
- Make sure the computer is plugged in and is turned on.

- Check to see that the printer is on line. Usually there is an on line button and a light appears when the printer is on line and ready to print.
- Identify that there are not ribbon or paper jams preventing printing.
- Various printers signal problems by means of operational lights or messages. Look up the meaning of these signals in the printer manual and make any corrections needed.
- Turn off your computer or reset it to try to establish the handshake again.

If you can print from DOS but are not getting the desired printed results from Word:

- Check to see where the print head is placed when you start to print.
- If you have a laser printer, the printer may not be capable of printing off the edge of the paper.
- Check the Print Options fields to make sure they are set as you desire.
- If you are using Print Merge, make sure the DATA statement is at the start of the main document. Ensure that the instructions in the document are correct. Look at the Transfer Options *setup* field to make sure the drive and path are entered to find the data document.
- Check Format Character to make sure the settings are as desired.
- Check Format Paragraph to make sure *line spacing* is Auto or large enough for the font size you want.
- If you are using a running head, make sure it is identifying only the running head and not the entire document. The caret (^) marks each running-head line.
- See that the text isn't all hidden text (with dotted lines or in a different color).
- If you are using a font cartridge, make sure it is pushed all the way into the printer receptacle.
- If you are using downloadable fonts and see this message:

`Font download unsuccessful`

check the printer connection, the Print Options *setup* field, and the MODE command. If your printer shows an error, you may have attempted to load more fonts into memory than it will hold. Pay special attention to the messages in the status line.

MergePRD

Word has a utility program called MergePRD that you can use to change fonts, feeders, and symbol settings in .PRD files. More specifically, MergePRD is used to:

- Combine fonts from various .PRD files. For example, you can have a laser printer with limited memory. You can select precisely the mix of downloadable, cartridge, and built-in fonts that are supported in the .PRD file. Another application is to create several .PRD files for downloadable fonts, each designed to meet the needs of particular sets of documents. You can also add support for fonts that Word does not support.
- Delete undesired fonts. This saves memory and prevents accidental formatting in an unwanted font style.
- Update drivers from Word 4 to Word 5. Customized .PRD files in Word 4 can be updated to be used with Word 5 with MergePRD.
- Change the font for line drawing. The .PRD file determines the fonts used in line drawing. You can change these settings to better accommodate the fonts available to you.
- Add support for sheet or envelope feeder support. If you add a sheet or envelope feeder and the .PRD file does not support it, you can customize the .PRD file to accommodate the feeder.
- Change the symbol set of fixed-pitch fonts for LaserJet printers. Some LaserJet options include a selection of character sets in a font. You can access a different character set than accessed through the .PRD file with MergePRD.

The Main Menu

Caution: Don't use MergePRD to merge .PRD files for different printers. And don't merge landscape and portrait .PRD files unless your printer supports autorotation.

When using MergePRD, you will often use the Main Menu shown in Figure 5-17. The following table lists the options available:

Option	Action
Enter input .PRD file list	Enters the .PRD path and file names.

Display the list of available fonts and font sizes	Shows the fonts for the .PRD files entered through selection 1.
Print the list of available fonts and font sizes	Prints (or saves to a file) the fonts entered through selection 1. When you print, enter the port (such as LPT1 or COM1). Don't put a colon after the port name.
Select fonts and font sizes	Accesses the Select Fonts and Font Sizes menu to add or delete fonts and font sizes. (See "Select Fonts and Font Sizes Menu" in this chapter.)
Display selected fonts and font size entries	Used to view the fonts and sizes added to the .PRD file created.
Change bin support	To add bin support.
Create the output .PRD file with the fonts you have selected	Creates the new .PRD file.
Quit program	Returns you to the operating system.

```
        MergePRD - Microsoft Word .PRD Merging Utility


                         Main Menu

        1) Enter input .PRD list
        2) Display the list of available fonts and font sizes
        3) Print the list of available fonts and font sizes
        4) Select fonts and font sizes
        5) Display selected fonts and font size entries
        6) Change bin support
        7) Create the output .PRD file with the fonts you have selected
        8) Quit program

        Enter selection:
```

Figure 5-17. The MergePRD Main Menu

Select Fonts and Font Sizes Menu

The Select Fonts and Font Sizes menu is shown in Figure 5-18. The options on this menu vary depending on the type of printer you are using. These are the menu choices that may be available:

Option	Use to
Add font/size from .PRDs already entered	Add fonts to the .PRD file created.
Change symbol set for font	Select alternate LaserJet symbol set (if available).
Add a new download font using an Adobe Font Metrics File	For PostScript printers, used to add support for Adobe PostScript fonts with Adobe Font Metrics (supplied by Adobe).
Delete existing font/size entry	Delete fonts.
Display current font/size entries	See the fonts added to the new .PRD file.
Change linedraw font	Identify the font used for the line-draw feature (not available if you are using a PostScript printer).
Enter to Main Menu	Go back to the MergePRD Main Menu.

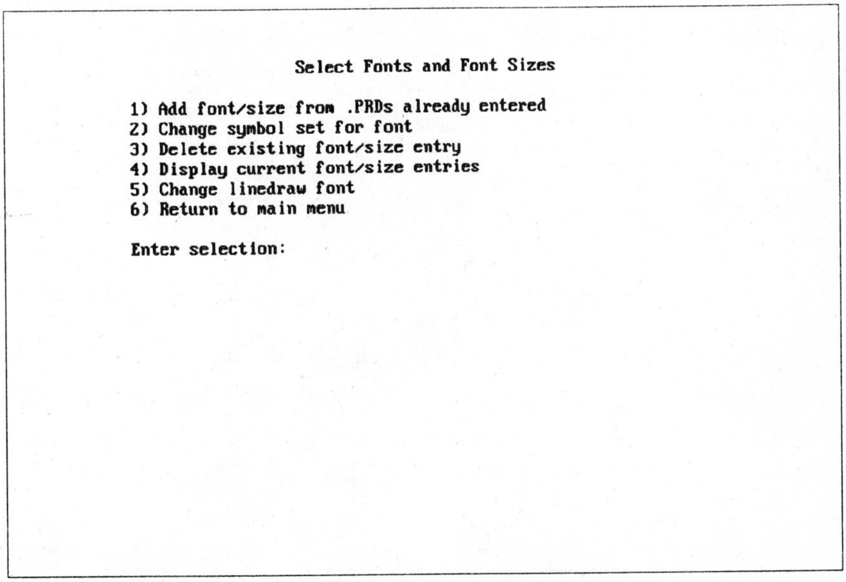

```
                    Select Fonts and Font Sizes

      1) Add font/size from .PRDs already entered
      2) Change symbol set for font
      3) Delete existing font/size entry
      4) Display current font/size entries
      5) Change linedraw font
      6) Return to main menu

   Enter selection:
```

Figure 5-18. The Select Fonts and Font Sizes menu

Combining Fonts from .PRD Files

Follow these steps to combine fonts from .PRD files:

1. Make a backup copy of the original .PRD files.
2. If there are any .DAT and .INI files related to the .PRD file, make sure they are in the same directory as the .PRD file.
3. If you are using OS/2, use DOS compatibility mode.
4. At the operating system prompt, type in the following and press **Enter**:

   MERGEPRD

   (You could also enter the .PRD files with which you want to work: MERGEPRD FILENAME1.PRD FILENAME2.PRD.)
5. The MergePRD screen shown in Figure 5-19 appears.

```
MergePRD 2.00 - Microsoft Word Printer Description (.PRD) Merging Utility

Copyright (C) James E. Walsh, 1987, 1988, 1989. All Rights Reserved.
Portions Copyright (C) Intuition Systems Corporation, 1987, 1988, 1989.
All Rights Reserved.


        Welcome to MergePRD.  This utility will help you customize your
        printer driver for the fonts you are using with Microsoft Word.


                    What type of printer are you using?

        1) A Hewlett-Packard LaserJet Series printer or compatible.  (For
             example, HP LaserJet, HP LaserJet+, HP Series II, HP 2000, etc.)
        2) A PostScript printer.  (For example, an Apple LaserWriter)
        3) Other.  (For example, an Epson Printer)

        Enter selection:
```

Figure 5-19. The MergePRD screen

Enter the number of the type of printer you use and press **Enter**. A Main Menu like the one already shown in Figure 5-17 appears.

The selections, which relate to the type of printer you have, are placed in the order to follow when completing the tasks.

6. From the Main Menu, type in 1 then the .PRD path (if necessary) and file name(s) you wish to merge. You may be required to select from a list of models. Then, type in another file name to merge or press **Enter** when you have entered all the file names and are ready to go back to the Main Menu.

7. An optional step is to type in **2** to see the list of fonts and font sizes and/or type in **3** to print the list. Figure 5-20 shows a sample printed list.

```
Font   PRD File   Generic    Font Name      Sizes
#
0      HPLASTAX   Modern a   Courier        12
1      HPLASTAX   Modern b   CourierPC      12
2      HPLASTAX   Modern h   LinePrinter    8.5
3      HPLASTAX   Modern i   HELV           6  8 10 12 14
4      HPLASTAX   Symbol b   LineDraw       12
```

Figure 5-20. A sample printed list of fonts and font sizes

8. At the Main Menu, type in **4** to select fonts and font sizes. The Select Fonts and Font Sizes menu like the one already shown in Figure 5-18 appears.

9. In the Select Fonts and Font Sizes menu, type in **1** to add font/size from .PRDs already entered.

A list of fonts supported by the .PRD files appears (see Figure 5-21).

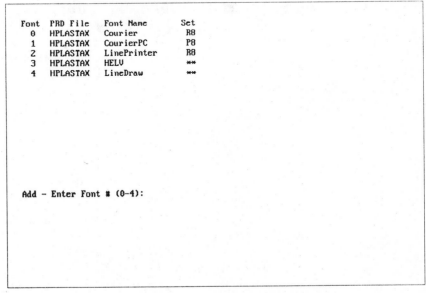

Figure 5-21. The list of supported fonts

10. Enter the number of the font support you want to add to the .PRD file. Then, enter the size. (Type in **All** for all sizes if desired.) Continue adding font support until all are added. Press **Enter** to go to the Select Fonts and Font Sizes menu. (MergePRD stops you from unnecessarily adding the same font support twice. If a font name is the same between two or more .PRD files but the sizes are different, you can rename the .PRD files through MakePRD before using MergePRD.)

11. From the Select Fonts and Font Sizes menu, type in **6** to go back to the Main Menu.

12. Enter **5** from the Main Menu to check the fonts and font sizes selected. If the list is incorrect, repeat steps 8 through 12 to add or delete font support.

13. Once the list is correct, enter **7** from the Main Menu to create the new .PRD file. Give the .PRD file a unique name. A message like the following appears:

```
Reading data from .PRD file HPLASTAX.PRD
Creating output .PRD file MYLAS1.PRD
End of program execution
```

You are returned to the operating system. You can use the new .PRD file.

Adding Support for Downloadable Adobe PostScript Fonts

You can add font support to the PSDOWN.PRD for PostScript fonts. These are the steps:

1. Make sure the PSDOWN.PRD, .INI, and .DAT files along with the Adobe Font Metrics (AFM) files are on the same directory or disk. (Use DECDOWN.INI for DEC LN03R files.)

2. Ensure that each font file has a corresponding AFM file.

3. Make a backup copy of the original .PRD files.

4. If you are using OS/2, use DOS compatibility mode.

5. At the operating system prompt, type in the following and press **Enter**:

```
MERGEPRD
```

6. The MergePRD screen appears. Enter the number of the type of printer you use and press **Enter**.

7. The Main Menu appears. Enter **1** and then the path and PSDOWN as the input file. Select the model of the printer.

8. From the Main Menu, enter **4** to select fonts.

9. At the Select Fonts and Font Sizes menu, enter **1** to add fonts from PSDOWN.PRD to the new .PRD file. Press **Enter** when you are done.

10. On the Select Fonts and Font Sizes menu, enter **2** to add downloadable font support with an Adobe Font Metrics file. Enter the file name for the base font, then the file names for italic, bold, and bold italic. Enter the name of the Word font family. Enter a number for the font. Press **Enter** to go back to the Select Fonts and Font Sizes menu.

11. Enter **5** to go back to the Main Menu.

12. Once the list is correct, enter **7** from the Main Menu to create the new .PRD file. Give the .PRD file a unique name.

You are returned to the operating system. You can now use the new .PRD file.

Updating a Word 4 .PRD File

You can update Word 4 .PRD files to use with Word 5. Use the same steps as outlined earlier in this chapter. Make sure you have the Word 5 .PRD file that supports the printer and the Word 4 .PRD files you want. Merge the fonts desired.

Adding Sheet- or Envelope-Feeder Support

If support is not already present, you can add sheet- or envelope-feeder support to your .PRD file with the steps identified earlier in this chapter. These are the special considerations:

- Use your printer manual to identify the control sequences that are used to start and stop the sheet feeder.
- After adding the fonts, return to the Main Menu and enter 6 to change bin support. These options appear:

0 = Manual feed
1 = Bin 1
2 = Bin 2
3 = Bin 3
4 = Envelope feed

Enter the number of the support desired then enter the beginning and ending control sequences. You can enter the control sequences in decimal or hexadecimal (hexadecimal codes end with h). ESC can be used for the escape code.

When you've finished, select 7 from the Main Menu to create the new .PRD file.

Changing the Line-Drawing Font

You can only change the line-drawing font if you have a LaserJet printer. You cannot change the line-drawing font if you use a Post-Script printer. To change the font, complete the steps described earlier in this chapter. After adding fonts and font sizes, select *Change line drawing font.* Enter the font number of the new line drawing font. Press Enter to go back to the Select Fonts and Font Sizes menu. Go back to the Main Menu to create the new .PRD file.

Changing the LaserJet Fixed-Pitch Font Character Set

You can change the fixed-pitch font character set for LaserJet printer .PRD files. Use the steps covered earlier in this chapter. Once you have selected the fonts and font sizes, enter 2 to change the symbol set. Select the symbol set desired. Go back to the Main Menu to create the new .PRD file.

MakePRD

If you are a very experienced computer user and have a technical bent, you can make a .PRD file. Making a .PRD file is useful if you have a printer that Microsoft does not support. It also can be helpful to get special effects or characters from your printer that the .PRD file available from Word does not allow.

The process involves taking a binary .PRD file, turning it into a text file, modifying it, then creating a new, binary .PRD file. You will need the technical guide for your printer and you will need technical expertise to make a .PRD file. The *Printer Information for Microsoft Word* manual contains the Word information needed to make a .PRD file. What follows here are the general steps for using MakePRD:

1. Read the technical manual from the printer manufacturer.
2. Read the section in the *Printer Information for Microsoft Word* manual that pertains to MakePRD.
3. Identify the .PRD files that are closest to the end result desired.
4. Make backup copies of those .PRD files.
5. Run MakePRD to make a binary .PRD file into a text file:
   a. Insert the Word Utilities/Printers disk in drive A.
   b. At that operating system prompt, enter:

      MAKEPRD

   c. Type in the .PRD file name of the file to alter.
   d. Type in the name for the text file to create.
   e. Type in **T** to make a text file.

      A message appears indicating that the conversion is complete.
6. Select **T**ransfer **L**oad to load the text file into Word.
7. Change the text file.
8. Select **T**ransfer **S**ave and in the *format* field, select **T**ext-only.
9. Run MakePRD to make the text file into a binary .PRD file:
   a. Make sure the Word Utilities Disk 2 is in drive A.
   b. At that operating system prompt, enter:

      MAKEPRD

   c. Type in the .PRD file name of the file to create.
   d. Type in the name for the text file just edited.
   e. Press **P** to create a new .PRD file.

      A message appears indicating that the conversion is complete.
10. Copy the new .PRD file to your Word program disk or WORD directory.
11. Go to the **P**rint **O**ptions *printer* field to enter the name of the new .PRD file to use.
12. Test out your new .PRD file to ensure it works as desired.

Formatting Documents

With Word's text formatting capabilities, you can create professional-quality documents by applying sophisticated formatting to a division, a paragraph, or even a single character.

The concept of a division may be familiar if you have used other word processors. All Word documents are divided into one or more divisions. Within the division, you can control margins, page numbers, columns, line numbers, running heads, and page size. At the paragraph level, you can control text alignment, indents, tabs, borders, and line spacing. At the character level, you can control the appearance of text—for example, by making it bold or italic.

To look at your document's formatting before printing, you can use the Print preView command (see Chapter 5, "Printing Documents" for more information).

Units of Measurement

As you choose from among Word 5's numerous format options, you will often need to enter measurements. When formatting characters, for example, you may need to enter the font size. When formatting paragraphs, you may need to indicate indents and line spacing. When formatting divisions, you may need to tell Word the size of paper you are using and how wide to set the margins. Word recognizes several units of measurement including inches, centimeters, picas, point, and pitch.

When you first load Word 5, all measurements except line spacing and font size are expressed in inches, which works just fine for most users most of the time. If you are preparing documents for publication, you may want to use picas and points—the standard units of measure in typography. Otherwise, you can stick with inches.

To change Word's default unit of measurement, follow these steps:

1. Select **O**ptions.

2. In the *measure* field, select the unit of measurement you prefer.

3. Press **Enter** or click the command name.

This new unit of measurement will remain Word's default until you change it, even if you quit Word.

Regardless of what unit of measurement is the current default, you can use other units simply by entering the appropriate abbreviation after the amount. Word automatically converts whatever you enter to the default measurement. Word recognizes the following abbreviations for units of measurement:

Measurement	Indicator	Inch equivalence
Inches	in or "	
Centimeters	cm	2.54
10 pitch (pica)	p10	10
12 pitch (elite)	p12	12
Points	pt	72
Lines	li	6 (vertical)

Although the abbreviation for lines (li) is most often used for indicating line spacing in paragraphs, it can also be used to indicate picas even when the measurement called for is horizontal rather than vertical. In other words, whenever you want to enter a measurement in picas, type in the number of picas followed by the abbreviation li.

Formatting Divisions

For purposes of specifying margins, page layout, pagination, and the assignment of line numbers, Word divides documents into one or more parts called divisions. Within each division, formatting with regard to page size, margins, number of columns, page numbers, running heads, and line numbers is consistent. To change the formatting of these elements within the space of a single document, you must create and format a new division. You can add as many new divisions as you need to make your document look the way you want.

When you start a new document, it consists of a single division formatted according to Word's default values. To change these values, select the Format Division command and enter new ones. (This chapter covers all Format Division options except the position of running heads. For information on running heads, see Chapter 7, "Running Heads, Footnotes, and Annotations.") When you execute the command, Word inserts a division mark—a double row of dots that extends horizontally across the screen—just above the end mark of the document. The division mark contains all the formatting instructions for the text that precedes it. If you delete the division mark, the division formatting reverts to Word's defaults.

To create a new division, follow these steps:

1. Highlight the first character in the new division or the last character in the old division.

2. Press **Ctrl-Enter**.

Word inserts a division mark as shown in Figure 6-1. This mark governs the formatting of the pages above it, up to any previous division mark that may occur in the document.

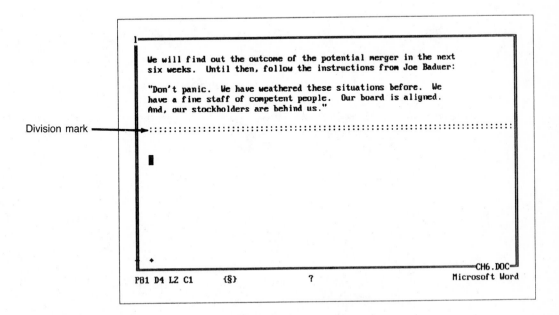

Figure 6-1. Division mark

When you choose the Library Table or Library Index command (see Chapter 18, "Indexes, Outlines, and Tables of Contents"), Word automatically inserts division marks to separate the table of contents or index from the rest of the document.

To format a new division:

1. Place your highlight in the division (above the division mark).
2. Select **F**ormat **D**ivision and choose the appropriate command (**M**argins, **P**age numbers, **L**ayout, line-**N**umbers) from the menu.
3. Change the field values as you like and press **Enter** to carry out the command.
4. To continue division formatting, repeat steps 2 and 3 as necessary.

The new formatting takes effect immediately. You can change division formatting as often as you like. If you delete the division mark, the formatting for that division changes to that of the following division. If there is no subsequent division mark, the division formatting reverts to Word's default settings.

If you don't like the formatting, you can either change it or simply delete the new division mark altogether.

Deleting Division Marks

To delete a division mark, follow these steps:

1. Highlight the division mark.
2. Press **Del**.

Using the Division Break Option

If you accidentally delete a division mark, you can use Undo (or Ins) to restore it.

A division mark normally causes Word to break the text and begin a new page. If you prefer a different break, use the Format Layout command to select other options. These are the available division break options:

Option	Effect
Page	The division mark serves as a page break. The next page begins a new division. This is the default setting.
Continuous	The division mark does not create a new page. The text in the new division continues on the same page as the previous division. If the specified page size is different, the new page size starts on the first whole page of the new division.

Column   The text of the new division starts in a new
                  column (see "Creating Columns," later in this
                  chapter).

Even or Odd   The text in the division is printed on the next even
                  or odd page (a blank page may be left). Use this
                  option to have first pages of sections or columns
                  print on a consistent side. For example, many
                  books have the first page of each chapter on the
                  right-hand (odd) page.

Figure 6-2 shows the four division break options. Divisions 4
and 5 are set up as page breaks. Division 6 is continuous and prints
on the previous page. Division 7 is set to print on the even page (so a
page will be skipped between divisions 6 and 7). Figure 6-3 shows
how the pages would actually break.

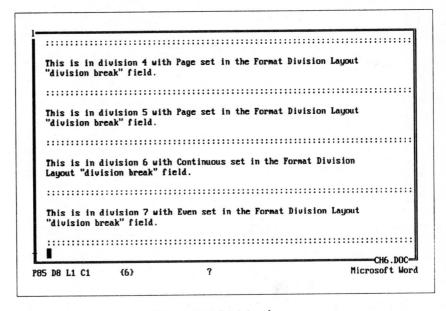

Figure 6-2. Division layout

To change how divisions break, follow these steps:

1. Select **F**ormat **D**ivision **L**ayout
2. In the *division break* field, select one of the following:

   Page

   Continuous

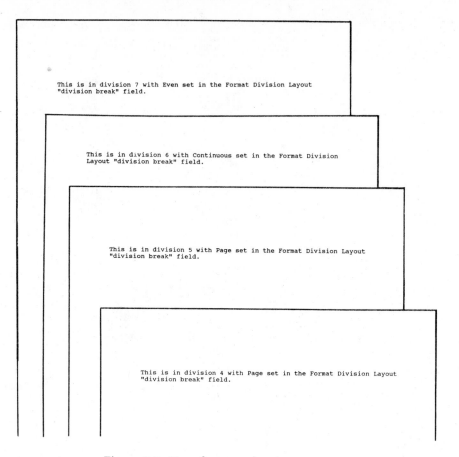

Figure 6-3. How the pages break

    Column

    Even or **O**dd

3. Press **Enter** or click the command name.

Setting Margins

Margins extend from the edges of the text to the edges of the page. Usually, Word does not print in the margins. Word's defaults are 1.25 inches for the left and right margins, and 1 inch for the top and bottom margins.

You can change Word's default margins as needed, and a single document can have two or more divisions, each with its own margin settings. For example, Figure 6-4 shows a document with two divisions and different margin settings; the left and right margins are 1 inch in the first division and 3 inches in the second. Notice, in Figure

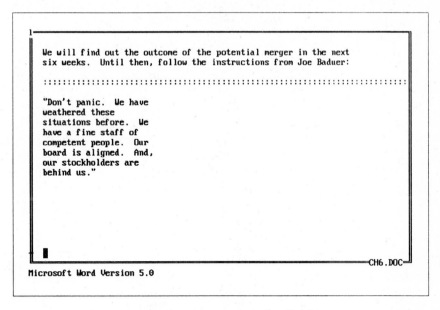

We will find out the outcome of the potential merger in the next
six weeks. Until then, follow the instructions from Joe Baduer:

:::

"Don't panic. We have
weathered these
situations before. We
have a fine staff of
competent people. Our
board is aligned. And,
our stockholders are
behind us."

CH6.DOC

Microsoft Word Version 5.0

Figure 6-4. Margin settings for divisions

We will find out the outcome of the potential merger in the next
six weeks. Until then, follow the instructions from Joe Baduer:

        "Don't panic. We have
        weathered these
        situations before. We
        have a fine staff of
        competent people. Our
        board is aligned. And,
        our stockholders are
        behind us."

Figure 6-5. The printed result

6-5, that the 3-inch margins line up correctly when printed. Because
the first division was set to Format Division Layout Page and the second division was set to Format Division Layout Continuous, the two
divisions print on one page.

To change margins, follow these steps:

1. Select **F**ormat **D**ivision **M**argins.

2. Enter the *top*, *bottom*, *left*, and *right* margin measurements in
    inches. Enter the actual inches from the edge of the page. The
    measurements can be in decimals (such as 1.25 inches).

3. Press **Enter** or click the command name.

Using the Gutter Margin Option

You may want your document to be printed on both sides of the page with enough room on the inside margin, or gutter, to be bound or inserted in a binder. If so, use the *gutter margin* field of the Format Division Margin menu.

When you print a document, the gutter margin is added to the left side of odd-numbered pages and the right side of even-numbered pages. That way, when the pages are printed on both sides, the gutter margin always ends up in the center. Typically, you want to keep left and right margins the same when you use a gutter margin (see Figure 6-6).

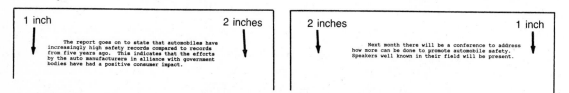

Figure 6-6. Pages with gutter margins

If you are printing a double-sided document and your layout specifies unequal left and right margins in addition to gutter margins, set mirror margins to Yes. For more information, see "Using the Mirror Margin Option," later in this chapter.

To specify a gutter margin, follow these steps:

1. Select **Format Division Margins**.

2. Enter the *gutter margin* measurement in inches. The measurements can be in decimals (such as 1.25 inches) and will be added to the *right* and *left* margin settings on the same menu.

3. Press **Enter** or click the command name.

Using the Mirror Margin Option

Mirror margins allow you to enter unequal left and right margins and reverse them for every other page. This is useful for bound documents in which the layout is asymmetrical. Figure 6-7 shows a document with a left margin of 1 inch, a right margin of 2 inches, a gutter margin of 0, and No selected in the *mirror margins* field. Figure 6-8 shows the same document with Yes selected.

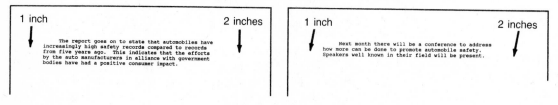

Figure 6-7. Pages without mirror margins

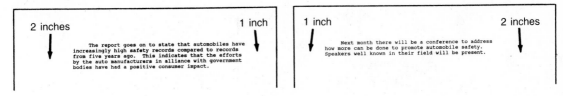

Figure 6-8. Pages with mirror margins

In Figure 6-7 the left margin is 1 inch and the right margin is 2 inches, regardless of the page number or position. In Figure 6-8, however, the margins on page 2 are the reverse of those on page 1, and they will alternate in this way for the entire length of the division.

Using gutter margins with mirror margins is useful when you want left and right margins of unequal values, plus additional space on the inside margin of each page for binding. Figure 6-9 shows a document with a left margin of 2 inches, a right margin of 1 inch, a gutter margin of 0.5 inch, and No selected in the *mirror margins* field.

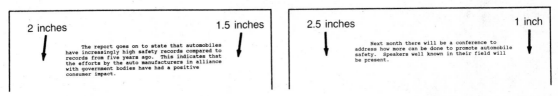

Figure 6-9. Pages with unequal margins and gutter margins and without mirror margins

As you can see, because the left and right margins are not reversed every other page, the page on the left has a 2-inch left margin and a 1.5-inch right margin, while the page on the right has a 2.5-inch left margin and a 1-inch right margin. The gutter effect is lost because the margins making up the "center" of the pages are uneven.

Figure 6-10 shows the same pages with Yes selected in *mirror margins*.

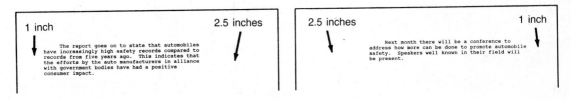

Figure 6-10. Pages with unequal margins, gutter margins, and mirror margins

Because the left and right margins are switched on every other page, the "outside" margins of both pages are 2.5 inches and the "inside" margins of both pages are 1 inch. This creates a balanced appearance.

To use mirror margins, follow these steps:

1. Select **Format Division Margins**.
2. Enter the margins you want to appear on odd pages in the *left* and *right* fields.
3. Select **Yes** in the *mirror margins* field.
4. Press **Enter** or click the command name.

Setting Margin Defaults

Your Format Division Margins settings will revert to Word's defaults when you quit the program, unless you set them as new defaults. You can do so with the following settings:

- Margins
- Page size
- Running-head position

To make your settings Word's new defaults:

1. Select **Format Division Margins**.
2. Enter the values for the margin, page size, and running-head position.
3. In the *use as default* field, select **Yes** to make the values you have just entered the defaults for future Word sessions.
4. Press **Enter** or click the command name.

 If you are using style sheets to format your divisions, remember that division style settings override the defaults entered through the Format Division Margins menu.

Specifying Page Size

Word assumes your printed output will be on 8.5-by-11-inch paper. If you plan to use another size—legal paper, for example, or an envelope —you need to tell Word in order to make sure your document prints out correctly.

To change the size of the page, follow these steps:

1. Select Format Division Margins.

2. Enter the *page length* and *width* fields in inches (22″ is the maximum allowed).

3. Press **Enter** or click the command name.

Specifying Page Breaks

A page break appears as a single dotted line across your screen as shown in Figure 6-11.

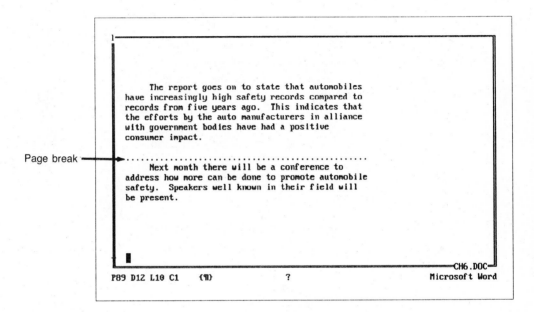

Figure 6-11. A page break

Word 5 lets you choose between entering page breaks manually or having the program automatically enter them for you. You make this choice by choosing Auto or Manual from the General Options section of the Options command menu. The default is Auto. The value set in the *paginate* field when you leave Word becomes the default for the next session.

Auto pagination means that Word will periodically calculate page breaks and display them on the screen. *Manual pagination* means that Word will calculate page breaks only when you select Print Repaginate or Print Printer. (The only advantage of manual pagination is speed and memory usage.) Regardless of whether auto pagination is turned on or off, you can enter manual page breaks at any time.

Selecting Automatic Page Breaks

When you choose Auto, Word automatically inserts page breaks as you work. In determining where those breaks should occur, the program takes a variety of factors into consideration, including page size, margins, font and font size, the number of spaces between lines and paragraphs, and special character formatting.

To have Word enter page breaks automatically, follow these steps:

1. Select **O**ptions.
2. In the *paginate* field, select **A**uto.
3. Press **Enter** or click the command.

Sometimes you need to control where page breaks fall. For example, if you have a table, you may want it to occupy a single page regardless of whether it fills up that page or not. If Auto is selected in the *paginate* field, Word will fill the contents page with text that you want to begin on the following page. To prevent this, simply turn off Word's automatic page breaks:

1. Select **O**ptions.
2. In the *paginate* field, select **M**anual.
3. Press **Enter** or click the command.

Now Word will enter page breaks only when and where you instruct it to do so.

Selecting Manual (Hard) Page Breaks

Whether the *paginate* field of the Options command is set to Auto or Manual, you can enter manual page breaks by pressing Ctrl-Shift-Enter. Manual page breaks are represented by a denser dotted line than automatic page breaks (see Figure 6-12 for a comparison). Manual page breaks—also called hard breaks—stay in place until you delete or move them. Even the Print Repaginate command (see the following section) does not display them.

To enter a manual page break, follow these steps:

1. Place the highlight on the character above which you want the page break to fall.

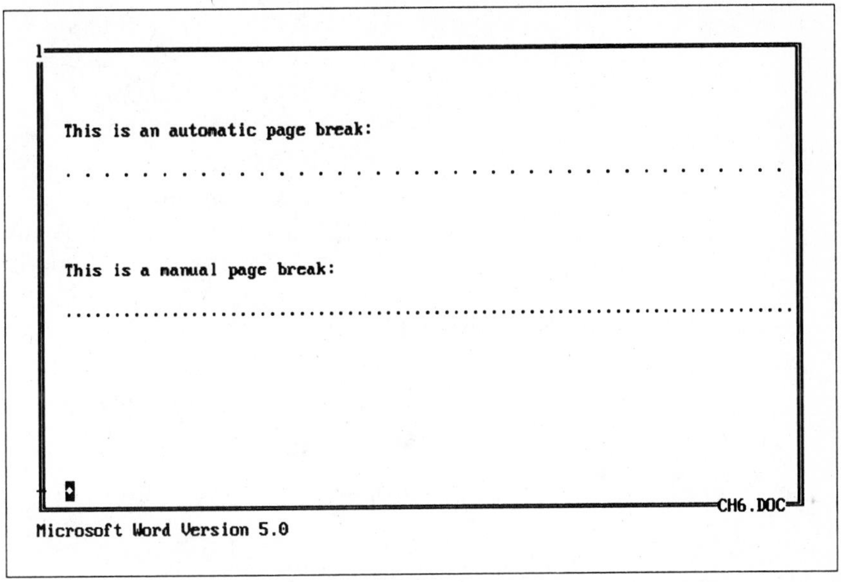

Figure 6-12. A manual page break and an automatic page break

2. Press **Ctrl-Shift-Enter**.

3. A dense dotted line appears across the screen.

Using the Print Repaginate Command

You can use Print Repaginate in two ways:

- To paginate a document all at once, regardless of whether Auto or Manual is selected in the Options *paginate* field.
- To reset automatic page breaks.

When you repaginate, you can choose to confirm page breaks or not. Choose the latter if your page breaks are routine or you are in a hurry. Choose the former if you are concerned that one or more page breaks may fall in a bad place (such as the middle of a table).

To repaginate a document, follow these steps:

1. Select **P**rint **R**epaginate.

2. In the *confirm page breaks* field, select one of these:

No   to allow Word to enter all page breaks automatically.

Yes   for Word to ask for confirmation of every proposed page break.

3. Press **Enter** or click the command name.

4. If you select No in the *confirm page breaks* field, Word will quickly paginate the entire document. If you select Yes, Word will pause at each and every proposed page break to ask you for confirmation.

   • If the page break to be confirmed is one proposed by Word, press **Y** to keep it or use the **Up Arrow** key to move it to a new location. Then press **Y** to confirm the new location. (When you move a page break proposed by Word, the program enters it in its new location as a hard break.)

   • If the page break to be confirmed was entered manually, press **Y** to keep it or **R** to remove it. (You cannot relocate manual page breaks with the arrow keys.)

You can stop repagination at any point by pressing Esc.

Adding Page Numbers

You can add page numbers through Format Division Page-numbers. Or, you can enter page numbers through a running head (see Chapter 7, "Running Heads, Footnotes, and Annotations," for more information).

Unless instructed otherwise, the Format Division Page-numbers command starts numbering on the first page of the division and prints numbers in the same position on every subsequent page of the division.

When you select Format Division Page-numbers, Word lets you choose the format (arabic numerals, roman numerals, or letters) for the page numbers. Additional formatting of page numbers—whether, for example, they are to be bold or italic—requires using the style sheet reserved style for page numbers. (For information on using style sheets, see Chapter 9, "Style Sheets.")

Adding Page Numbers

To add page numbers to a division, follow these steps:

1. Place the highlight in the division where the page numbers are to be located.

2. Select Format **D**ivision **P**age-numbers.

3. Select **Y**es to include page numbers in the division.

4. In the *from top* field, enter a measurement to identify how far from the top of the page the number should be printed. (Entering

a number like 10.5 will print the page number at the bottom of the page.)

When you position page numbers with the from top *and* from left *fields, do not place the page numbers where document text will be printing.*

5. In the *from left* field, enter a measurement to identify how far from the left of the page the number should be printed.

6. In the *numbering* field, select **C**ontinuous to start at page 1 and continue on each page thereafter. If you want to start with some other number, select **S**tart and enter the page number to be used for the first page in the division. Subsequent pages are numbered consecutively.

7. In the *number format* field, enter one of these options:

Option	Example	Format
1	1, 2, 3	Arabic
I	I, II, III	Roman uppercase
i	i, ii, iii	Roman lowercase
A	A, B, C	Alphabetic uppercase
a	a, b, c	Alphabetic lowercase

8. After choosing a number format, press **Enter** or click the command name.

Page numbers do not appear on the document screen, but you can see how they will appear on the printed page by using Word's Print pre**V**iew command. (For more information, see "Print Preview" in Chapter 5, "Printing Documents.")

If you are using a laser printer, do not try to position the page numbers in the unprintable area.

Specifying Odd or Even First Pages

If you want to specify whether the first page numbered is odd or even, use the Format Division Layout command and the *division break* field. Word sets the first page to be numbered as odd or even and, if necessary to fill gaps thus created in the pagination, "prints" a blank page ahead of the first numbered page.

For example, if the highlight is on the start of a new division that begins on page 10, and you set the Format Division Page-number *numbering* field to Continuous and the Format Division Layout *division break* field to Odd, the page number changes to page 11 and Word "prints" a blank page 10 to fill the gap. That is, Word sends a form-feed command to the printer before printing page 11.

Though blank pages created in this way do not appear on the screen, the page numbers shown in the status line for the pages on either side reveal their existence. You can verify the presence of a blank page before printing by using the Print preView command. (For more information, see "Print Preview" in Chapter 5, "Printing Documents.")

Numbering Lines

It is common in legal documents to have line numbers printed down the left column as shown in Figure 6-13. Line numbers can also be used in other documents.

```
1        The report goes on to state that automobiles have
2    increasingly high safety records compared to records from five
3    years ago.  This indicates that the efforts by the auto
4    manufacturers in alliance with government bodies have had a
5    positive consumer impact.
6
```

Figure 6-13. Line numbers

When you choose the Format line-Numbers command, Word inserts Arabic numerals (1,2,3) in the left margin at an interval of your choice. Even though the numbers do not appear on the text-entry screen, they do print. You can confirm this by using the Print preView command. (For more information, see "Print Preview" in Chapter 5, "Printing Documents.") Numbers appear only alongside the lines in the main body of the document; they do not appear beside running heads or footnotes.

In side-by-side paragraphs, Word does not number lines. When you use columns, each column is numbered.

Printing Line Numbers

To print line numbers, follow these steps:

1. Select **F**ormat **D**ivision line-**N**umbers.

2. Select **Y**es for line numbers.

3. In the *from text* field, enter the distance from the left margin of your document at which the numbers should print. The numbers are right aligned.

4. In the *restart at* field, select one of the following options:

Page   to restart each page with
                    line 1

Division	to restart each division with line 1
Continuous	to have line numbers consecutive throughout the document for each division where line numbers are selected

If line numbers do not print, make sure that there is enough room in the margin to accommodate the numbers.

5. In the *increments* field, enter the number of the interval at which you wish line numbers to appear. For example, choose 2 if you want every other line to be numbered, 5 if you want every 5 lines to be numbered, and so on.

6. Press **Enter** or click the command name.

If you use the Print Options command to print only a selected portion of a document, Word considers the first line of the selected text to be line 1, regardless of the line numbering of the document as a whole.

Matching Line Count and Printed Numbers

Some users want printed line numbers and the line count shown in the status line to match.

To match printed line numbers and the line count:

1. Select **O**ptions.

2. In the *line numbers* field, select **Y**es to have the line count appear in the status line. This value is maintained after you leave Word.

3. In the *count blank space* field, select **N**o. Lines created with the Format Paragraph *space before* and *space after* fields will not be counted.

4. In the *show line breaks* field, select **Y**es. The lines on the screen will break where they will be printed on the specified printer.

5. Press **Enter** or click the command name.

Creating Columns

Using multiple columns can add a professional touch to newsletters and reports, as well as enhance their readability. With Word, you can print pages in newspaper-style columns. That is, when the text reaches the bottom of one column, it wraps up to the start of the next column. Figure 6-14 shows a document created with Word's column function.

The report goes on to state that automobiles have increasingly high safety records compared to records from five years ago. This indicates that the efforts by the auto manufacturers in alliance with government bodies have had a positive consumer impact. This idea is echoed in many states. Next month a conference will address how more can be done to promote automobile safety. Speakers well known in their field will be present. To get tickets for the event, call Shari-Lynn Chambers at 876-9988. The cost for the conference is $30 for adults.

Figure 6-14. A document created with the column function to print newspaper-style columns

The present discussion deals only with newspaper-style columns. If you want the effect of side-by-side columns, where paragraphs in the left column line up with corresponding paragraphs in the right column, see "Aligning Paragraphs Side by Side" in this chapter.

Displaying Columns

Word 5 offers three modes in which to display columns:

- **Document (text entry):** This is the normal screen mode. It displays all text in a single column of the same width as it will appear in print (see Figure 6-15). This mode is faster for text

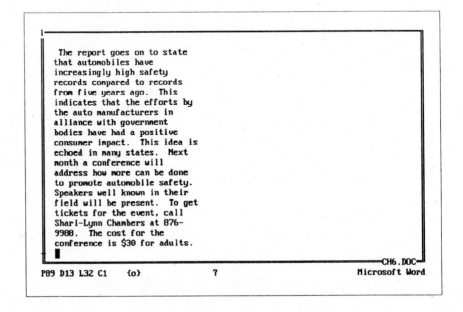

Figure 6-15. Columns in text-entry mode

entry, but does not show how columns will actually appear on the printed page.

- **Show layout:** This mode displays columns next to each other on the screen as they will appear on the printed page (see Figure 6-16). Text entry is appreciably slower because the screen is redrawn continuously to accommodate changes.

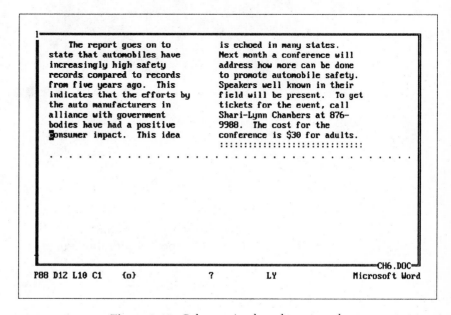

Figure 6-16. Columns in show-layout mode

- **Print Preview:** The columns appear on a special preview screen as they will be printed (see Figure 6-17). Select Print pre-View to use this mode. You can only view (not edit) your document in this mode. (For more information, see "Print Preview" in Chapter 5, "Printing Documents.")

Using the Show-Layout Mode

Use the show-layout mode to see and edit columns as they will appear when printed.

The text-entry mode is one in which you usually work, but you can switch to the show-layout mode whenever you like and work there as well. Word provides two ways of switching between the text-entry and show-layout modes.

The quickest way is to press Alt-F4 (hold down the Alt key and press the F4 key). If you are in text-entry mode, you will switch to the

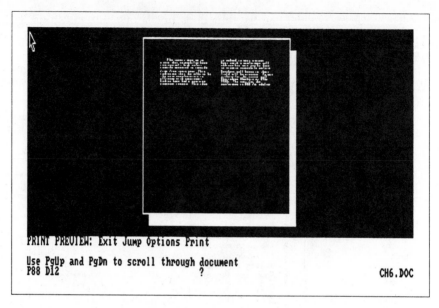

PRINT PREVIEW: Exit Jump Options Print

Use PgUp and PgDn to scroll through document
P88 D12   ?   CH6.DOC

Figure 6-17. Columns in print-preview mode

show-layout mode and vice-versa. When you are in show-layout mode, LY appears in the status line.

To switch to the show-layout mode using the menu, follow these steps:

1. Select **O**ptions.
2. Select **Y**es in the Window Options *show layout* field.

The appearance of LY in the status line indicates that the show-layout mode is active. In this mode, the ruler along the top screen border starts at zero for each column. In show-layout mode, Word provides the following special key combinations for moving between columns (the number 5 is the one on the numeric keypad):

Key combinations	Action
Ctrl-5-Right Arrow	Jumps to the next column
Ctrl-5-Left Arrow	Jumps to the previous column
Ctrl-Up Arrow	Moves to the first character of the paragraph above
Ctrl-Down Arrow	Moves to the first character of the paragraph below

Working in text-entry mode is generally faster and the results are usually more predictable. To switch from show-layout mode to text-entry mode using the menu, follow these steps:

1. Select **O**ptions.
2. Select **N**o in the Window Options *show layout* field.

The LY code disappears from the status line, and the columns appear as a single column.

Creating Multiple Columns

You can enter multiple columns in either show-layout or text-entry mode. You can enter a single set of columns on a page, or, by continuing the division on the page, you can enter more than one set of columns.

To enter multiple columns, follow these steps:

1. Press **Alt-F4** to switch to show-layout (LY) or text-entry mode as desired.
2. Select **F**ormat **D**ivision **L**ayout.
3. In the *number of columns* field, enter the number of columns.
4. In the *space between columns* field, enter the amount of space you want between columns according to the measurement entered through the Options *measure* field (usually inches).
5. To place other columns on the same page, select **C**ontinuous in the *division break* field. To have this be the only column setting on the page, select **P**age in the *division break* field.
6. Press **Enter** or click the command name.
7. If you are in text-entry mode, the text you enter becomes a single column of the appropriate width. If you are in show-layout mode, you can enter multiple columns of text on your screen. Use **Ctrl-5-Right Arrow** and **Ctrl-5-Left Arrow** to move between columns. Use **Ctrl-Up Arrow** and **Ctrl-Down Arrow** to move to the first character of the paragraph above and below.
8. You can let Word size columns automatically according to the dimensions specified through the Format Division Margins command. Or, you can end columns with a page break or a division break (use the division break if you wish to specify special division formatting for the new column):
    a. Place the highlight in the position where the column will break. Use the beginning of the line to insert the break

above the highlight or the end of a line to insert the break below the highlight.

b. Press **Ctrl-Alt-Enter** for a page break or **Ctrl-Enter** for a division break.

A page break (single dotted line) or division break (double dotted line) appears the length of the column. Word leaves the space from the column's end to the end of the page blank. The text following the break will print at the top of the next column.

If you enter more columns than can be accommodated by the width of the page, the margins, and the space between columns, Word ignores your entry. To calculate how many columns you can have on a page, review these settings:

- Format Division Margins: *width*, *left* margin, and *right* margin
- Format Division Layout: *space between columns*

Take the width of the page, subtract the left and right margin settings, then subtract the total space taken up by the *space between columns*. This gives you the total amount left for columns. To calculate the width of each column, divide the total amount by the number of columns you want. Make adjustments as necessary.

For example, if the page width is 8.5 inches with a left and right margin of 1 inch each, 6.5 inches are left for columns and the spaces between them. If you want four columns, there will be three spaces between them. If the *space between columns* is set at 0.5 inch, you need to subtract 1.5 inches from the total of 6.5 inches, leaving 5 inches for columns. Each of the four columns will be 1.25 inches wide.

Exercise: Using Format Division

In this exercise, you will have an opportunity to try many of the division functions. In a blank window, select Format Division Margins. Type 1 in the *left* and *right* fields. Type 3 in the *page length* field. Then, set Format Division Page-numbers to Yes. Type .5 in the *from top* field and 4.25 in the *from left* field. Select Continuous in the *numbering* field. Now, select Format Division Layout and type 2 in the *number of columns* field. Finally, type .5 in the *space between columns* field and enter this text:

```
The Harris Manufacturing Company has been taking a hard look
at incentive rates. The goal of such efforts is greater
```

productivity. However, some programs seem to have had negative
rather than positive results.

To get a clear view of the problems, a consultant was
brought in to consider the situation.

The consultant organized group sessions of two days with
selected work groups. The program was unstructured at the front
end. By the afternoon of the first day, issues began to arise.

The text aligns in a single column. Select Options and then Yes
in the *show layout* field. The text aligns in the two-column mode.
You can print the document with Print Printer. Notice that the page
number prints in the center of the page. Save the document under the
name COLUMNS and then clear the window with Transfer Clear.

Formatting Paragraphs

The definition of a paragraph in Word is the text that extends after a
paragraph mark up to, and including, the next paragraph mark. The
maximum paragraph size is 32 KB. This is equivalent to approximately 32,000 characters or about 20 double-spaced pages.

The formatting for a paragraph is stored in the paragraph mark
that ends the paragraph. Paragraph marks can be displayed or hidden
by changing the selection in the Options *show non-printing symbols*
field.

Paragraph formatting includes the following elements:

- **Alignment:** Controls the positioning of paragraphs between left
  and right indents (such as centered paragraphs)
- **Indents:** Controls the placement of paragraphs and portions of
  paragraphs between left and right margins (such as hanging
  indents)
- **Line spacing:** Controls the amount of space between lines
  (such as double spacing)

*One way to quickly
format paragraphs: Copy
formatted paragraph
marks as glossary entries
with distinctive codes.
When you want to insert
a paragraph mark with a
particular format, type the
corresponding code and
press F3. (see Chapter
17, "Glossaries.")*

When you format paragraphs, you select the text first, then
apply the formatting. You can also format individual paragraph marks
and add the text afterwards. To select a single paragraph, or paragraph mark, simply place your highlight in the paragraph or on the
mark. To affect more text, select several paragraphs or the entire document (with Shift-F10). When you select Format Paragraph, you
always activate the ruler.

To duplicate paragraph formatting, you can split a paragraph
into two paragraphs. To do this, place the highlight on the character

you want to be the first character of the new paragraph and then press Enter. The formatting of the new paragraph is identical to the formatting of the original paragraph. You can also recreate paragraph formatting by copying the paragraph mark.

Copying, moving, or deleting paragraph marks is especially helpful if you need to affect a larger section of text or to change the formatting of a paragraph. For example, you can join paragraphs by placing the highlight on the paragraph mark and pressing Del. (You may need to add spaces for form.) The paragraph mark that ends the paragraph holds the formatting for the new paragraph.

When a paragraph mark is deleted, the paragraph merges with and assumes the formatting of the one that follows. If the deleted paragraph mark is followed by the end mark, the paragraph formatting reverts to the default for that document. For example, Figure 6-18 shows a paragraph formatted for centered alignment. Figure 6-19 shows what the paragraph looks like when the paragraph mark is deleted and the default of left alignment is restored.

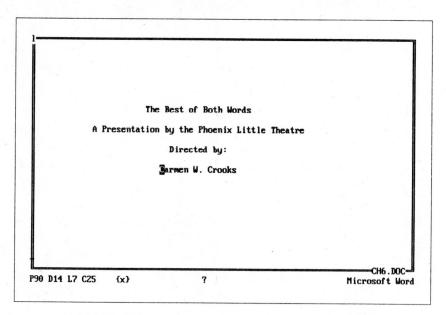

Figure 6-18. Centered-alignment formatting, stored in the paragraph mark

Paragraph marks that have been deleted with the Del key can be restored immediately with the Undo or Insert commands.

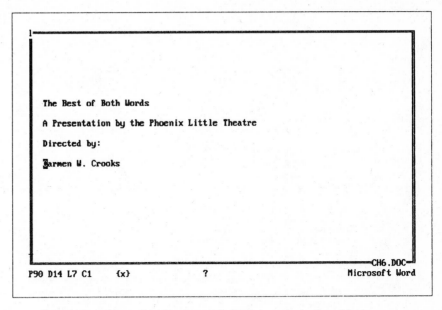

Figure 6-19. Left-alignment default, restored after deleting
paragraph mark

Controlling Paragraph Alignment

You can control the placement, or alignment, of each line of a paragraph relative to the left and right indents. Word provides several alignment options:

- **Center:** Text is centered between the left and right indents.
- **Left:** Text is aligned flush left with a ragged right margin.
- **Right:** Text is aligned flush right with a ragged left margin.
- **Justified:** Text is distributed evenly between indents, creating even right and left margins.

Figure 6-20 shows a letter where each type of alignment is used. The letterhead is centered, the date is right aligned, and the address is left aligned. The body of the letter is justified between margins.

To align a paragraph, follow these steps:

1. Select the paragraph(s) you want to format.
2. Select **Format P**aragraph, select an option in the *alignment* field, and press **Enter**. Or, hold down **Alt** (or **Alt-X** if you are using a style sheet) and press one of these letters:

C	for centered alignment
L	for left alignment
R	for right alignment
J	for justified alignment

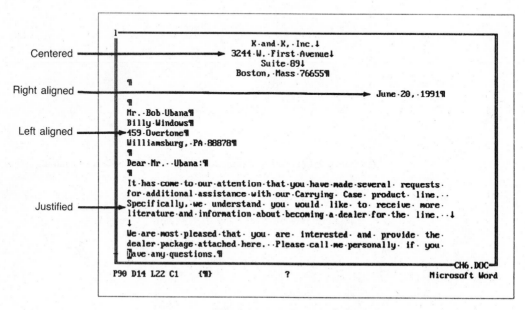

Figure 6-20. Types of alignment

Creating Indents

Indents are measured from the margins. For example, if you have a 1-inch margin and then indent the first line of the paragraph 1 inch, the line will start 2 inches from the left edge of the paper.

These are the types of indents Word supports:

- **Hanging indent:** The first line of the paragraph is flush with the left margin and the rest of the paragraph is indented.
- **First-line indent:** The first line of the paragraph is indented and the rest of the paragraph is flush with the left margin.
- **Right indent:** All lines of the paragraph are flush with the left margin and are indented from the right margin.
- **Left indent:** All lines of the paragraph are indented from the left margin and are flush with the right margin.

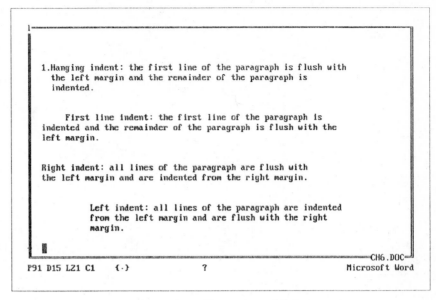

Figure 6-21. Four types of indents

Creating Hanging Indents

A second quick way to format paragraphs: Format one or more paragraph marks and copy them into a second window, identifying each with a brief description. Then copy them back into your document as needed. (See Chapter 11, "Windows.")

Hanging indents are useful for making bulleted lists or for numbering paragraphs. The first line is flush with the left margin and the rest of the paragraph is indented to the first tab stop. You can create a hanging indent with the Format Paragraph command or with speed formatting keys. When you use the Format Paragraph command, you can control the size of the indent. If you use the speed formatting keys, the current default tab stops are used.

When you create a hanging indent with the Format Paragraph command, you type in a left-indent measurement for the entire paragraph (from the left margin) and a negative first-line indent measurement (from the edge of the indented paragraph). Figure 6-22 illustrates the screen appearance of these two measurements. The left indent for the entire paragraph is 0.5 inch, but the first line indent is -0.5 inch. (Note that the first-line measurement is always entered as a negative number for a hanging paragraph, to extend it past the rest of the paragraph.) Figure 6-23 shows the final printed result.

To use the Format Paragraph command to create a hanging indent, follow these steps:

```
1 L¦LL··[····1·········2·········3···L··4·········5·········6····]····7····¶
      ¶
  Anderson, ·Carol·Anne, ·"Grant·Writing", ·Small·Business·
        Administration, ·1979.¶
      ¶
  Raule, ·Brian·Anderson, ·"Request·for·Proposals·for·Government", ·
        Federal·Weekly·News, ·June·1989¶
      ¶
  Wilson, ·Karen, ·"Methods·to·Raise·Public·Funds:█Essay·Today", ·
        Government·Free·Press, ·July·1989.¶
      ¶
      ¶
      ¶
      ¶
      ¶
      ¶
      ¶
      ¶

FORMAT PARAGRAPH alignment:(Left)Centered Right Justified
      left indent: 0.5"        first line: -0.5"     right indent: 0"
      line spacing: 1 li       space before: 0 li    space after: 0 li
      keep together: Yes(No)   keep follow: Yes(No)  side by side: Yes(No)
Enter measurement
P92 D16 L8 C47    {s}                 ?                 Microsoft Word
```

Figure 6-22. Left indent and first-line measurements for a
hanging indent

```
                                                                      92




Anderson, Carol Anne, "Grant Writing", Small Business
      Administration, 1979.

Raule, Brian Anderson, "Request for Proposals for Government",
      Federal Weekly News, June 1989

—.5" first line ──►  Wilson, Karen, "Methods to Raise Public Funds: Essay Today",
.5" left indent    ──►Government Free Press, July 1989.
```

Figure 6-23. A hanging indent, after printing

1. Select the paragraph(s) you want to indent.

2. Select **F**ormat **P**aragraph.

3. In the *left indent* field, type in a measurement.

4. In the *first line* field, type in a negative number. This number represents the amount you want to extend the first line past the rest of the paragraph. If you want the first-line indent to align

with the left margin, make it the negative amount of the left indent.

5. Press **Enter** or click the command name.

To use the speed formatting keys to create a hanging indent, follow these steps:

1. If necessary, check and reset the tab stops. (See "Tabs" later in this chapter for information.)
2. Select the paragraph(s) you want to indent.
3. Press **Alt-T** (or **Alt-X-T** if you are using a style sheet). The first line is aligned with the left margin and the rest of the paragraph is aligned to the first tab stop. To indent the paragraph further, continue to press **Alt-T** or **Alt-X-T**.

Creating First-Line Indents

To create a first line indent with the tab key, follow these steps:

1. Select the paragraph(s) you want to indent.
2. Select **F**ormat **P**aragraph.
3. In the *first line* field, type in the indent measurement.
4. Press **Enter** or click the command name.

Creating Right Indents

When you right-justify a paragraph, all lines are set flush right. When you right-indent a paragraph, all lines remain flush left, but the right margin moves from its default position.

When you right-indent a paragraph, the lines of the paragraph are aligned flush left and indented from the right margin. To right-indent a paragraph using the Format Paragraph command, follow these steps:

1. Select the paragraphs you want to indent.
2. Select **F**ormat **P**aragraph.
3. In the *right indent* field, type in a measurement.
4. Press **Enter** or click the command name.

There is no speed formatting key to create a right indent.

Creating Left Indents

When you left-indent the paragraph, the entire paragraph is indented from the left margin. The right side of the paragraph is flush with the right margin. To left-indent using the Format Paragraph command, follow these steps:

1. Select the paragraph(s) you want to indent.
2. Select **F**ormat **P**aragraph.
3. In the *left indent* field, type in a measurement for the indent.
4. Press **Enter** or click the command name.

You can use speed formatting keys to left-indent the paragraph. It is indented to the first tab stop to the right. If you keep pressing the speed keys, the paragraph will continue to indent, one tab stop at a time. You can use speed formatting keys to reduce the left indent as well.

To left-indent a paragraph using speed keys, follow these steps:

1. Select the paragraphs you want to indent.
2. Press **Alt-N** or **Alt-X-N** to left-indent. To indent further, continue to press **Alt-N** or **Alt-X-N**. To decrease the left indent, press **Alt-M** or **Alt-X-M**.

Creating Left and Right Indents Together

You may want to indent a paragraph from both the left and right margins. For example, Figure 6-24 shows a paragraph that has been formatted with a 2-inch left indent and a 1-inch right indent.

```
1 L0LL·······1··········[·········3····L····4········5····]····6·········7·····
        Specifically, we understand you would like to receive more
        literature and information about becoming a dealer for the line.

        We are most pleased that you are interested and provide the
        dealer package attached here.  Please call me personally if you
        have any questions.

        Our company is committed to its dealer program.  Business News
        quoted our President, Carly Young:

                        Our dealers are the life and blood
                        of our organization.  Without them,
                        we would not have a business.  We
                        put them first█

        Thank you for your interest.


FORMAT PARAGRAPH alignment: Left Centered Right Justified
        left indent: 2"           first line: 0"         right indent: 1"
        line spacing: 1 li        space before: 0 li     space after: 0 li
        keep together: Yes(No)    keep follow: Yes(No)   side by side: Yes(No)
Select option
P90 D14 L30 C35    {n}                 ?                      Microsoft Word
```

Figure 6-24. Left and right indents combined

Using left and right indents is different than centering a paragraph. With right and left indents, the last line of the paragraph is flush left. Figure 6-25 shows the same paragraph with identical left and right indents. Centered is selected in the Format Paragraph *alignment* field. Notice that when *alignment* is set to centered, each line in the paragraph is centered. This is an inappropriate appearance for most purposes. It is useful, however, when you want to center a paragraph for title pages or flyers.

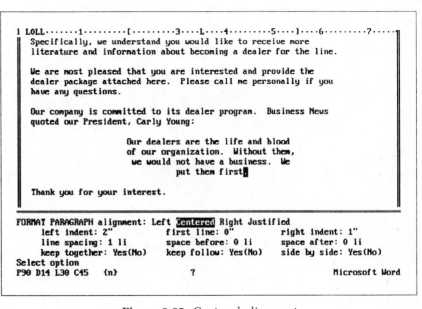

Figure 6-25. Centered alignment

As we've seen, when you use the Format Paragraph command, the right- and left-indent measurements can be equal or different. Follow these steps to center a paragraph using the Format Paragraph command:

1. Select the paragraphs you want to indent.
2. Select Format **P**aragraph.
3. In the *left indent field*, type in a measurement.
4. In the *right indent* field, type in a measurement.
5. Press **Enter** or click the command name.

The paragraph is formatted with the left and right indents you've identified.

You can use speed formatting keys to create left and right indents. The left side of the paragraph is indented to the first tab stop, and the right side is indented an equal amount (regardless of where tab stops appear on the far right of the ruler).

To create left and right indents using speed keys, follow these steps:

1. Select the paragraphs you want to indent.
2. Press **Alt-Q** or **Alt-X-Q** to left-indent and right-indent the paragraph(s). To indent further, continue to press **Alt-Q** or **Alt-X-Q**.

Changing Indents With the Mouse

You can use the following symbols to change the paragraph indents with a mouse:

Symbol	Identifies and controls
|	First-line indent
[	Left indent
]	Right indent

To change the indents with the mouse, follow these steps:

1. To activate the ruler, point to the upper-right border of the window and click the right button. Or use the **O**ptions *show ruler* field.
2. Select the paragraphs whose indents you want to change.
3. Point to the symbol to be moved.
4. Hold down the right button.
5. Drag to the new position and release the button.

Controlling Line Spacing

The third and quickest way to format a paragraph: Press Enter to create a new paragraph mark, then apply a paragraph style that you have defined earlier. (See Chapter 9, "Style Sheets.")

Line spacing governs how much space is placed between the lines in a paragraph. You can also control the line spacing between paragraphs.

Controlling Spacing Within Paragraphs

When you use Format Paragraph, you can control the line spacing precisely.

To control line spacing, follow these steps:

1. Select the paragraph(s) whose spacing you want to change.
2. Select **F**ormat **P**aragraph.
3. In the *line spacing* field, enter the space that will be placed between printed lines:
   - The number of lines (li); 2 indicates double-spaced lines
   - The measurement in inches (in or ″)
   - The measurement in points (pt); one line equals 12 points (make the line spacing larger then the point size of the largest font)
   - Auto to handle the largest font in each line
4. Press **Enter** or click the command name.
5. The line spacing is immediately reflected in the paragraph.

You can use speed formatting keys to double space text.

1. Select the paragraph(s) you want to change.
2. Press **Alt-2** (or **Alt-X-2** if you are using a style sheet).

Controlling Spacing Between Paragraphs

You can use the Format Paragraph command to specify the amount of space between paragraphs.

To adjust space between paragraphs, follow these steps:

1. Select the paragraph(s) you want to work with.
2. Select **F**ormat **P**aragraph.
3. In the *space before* and *space after* fields, enter the space which will be placed before and after the paragraph:
   - The number of lines (li); 2 indicates double-spaced lines
   - The measurement in inches (in or″)
   - The measurement in points (pt); one line equals 12 points
4. Press **Enter** or click the command name.

You can use speed formatting keys to add one blank line above a paragraph. The space added is the same line spacing as contained in the paragraph. Figure 6-26 shows a line added above a single-spaced paragraph and a line added above a double-spaced paragraph. Notice that the lines are part of the paragraph; they are not followed by a paragraph mark.

To add a blank line, using speed formatting keys, follow these steps:

```
1 L[LL········1·········2·········3···L···4·········5·········]·········7····┐
  ¶
  Warning:··This·product·is·sold·as·is·without·warranties.··
  Any·use·of·the·product·is·at·your·own·risk.··There·are·no·
  stated·or·implied·guarantees.¶

  ▌e·hope·you·enjoy·using·your·new·power·lawn·mower.··

  Carefully·read·the·instructions·for·use.··By·following·the·

  instructions,·you·will·enjoy·years·of·problem·free·

  operation.¶

  ¶
```
```
FORMAT PARAGRAPH alignment: Left Centered Right Justified
      left indent: 0"        first line: 0"         right indent: 0"
      line spacing: 2 li      space before: 1 li     space after: 0 li
      keep together: Yes(No)  keep follow: Yes(No)   side by side: Yes(No)
Select option
P38 D1 L15 C1      {¶}               ?                    Microsoft Word
```

Figure 6-26. Lines above paragraphs

1. Select the paragraph(s) you want to work with.
2. Press **Alt-O** (or **Alt-X-O** if you are using a style sheet).

Restoring Default Paragraph Formatting

After you've entered new paragraph formatting, you can restore the defaults set in Word (or the style-sheet defaults).

To revert to Word's defaults, follow these steps:

1. Select the paragraph(s) you want to work with.
2. Press **Alt-P** (or **Alt-X-P** if you are using a style sheet).

It is easy to use the Alt-P function; just remember that *P* means *normal paragraph* (Word's default).

Summary of Paragraph Speed Formatting Keys

The following table summarizes the speed keys you can use to format paragraphs. These functions were described in detail earlier in this chapter. The speed keys are useful as shortcuts for simple formatting functions, but you can perform more complex formatting with the Format Paragraph command.

Format	Press Alt (or Alt-X) and
Center alignment	C
Left alignment	L
Right alignment	R
Justified alignment	J
First-line indent (each press adds one tab stop)	F
Increase indent (each press adds one tab stop)	N
Decrease indent (each press removes one tab stop)	M
Hanging indent (each press adds one tab stop)	T
Double space	2
Blank line before paragraph	O (letter O)
Normal paragraph	P
Left and right indent (each press adds one tab stop)	Q

Keeping Paragraphs Together

With Word, you can prevent page breaks from occurring within a paragraph. Use this feature to prevent important tables or text from being broken between pages.

To prevent page breaks from occurring within paragraphs, follow these steps:

1. Select the paragraph(s) you want to work with.
2. Select **F**ormat **P**aragraph.
3. In the *keep together* field, select **Yes**.
4. Press **Enter** or click the command name.

When Word prints the paragraph, it moves the paragraph to the next page if it does not completely fit at the end of a page.

At times, you may want to prevent a page break from occurring between paragraphs. This is necessary if you have a title followed by a paragraph, for example.

To prevent page breaks from occurring between paragraphs, follow these steps:

1. Select the paragraph(s) you want to work with.
2. Select **Format Paragraph**.
3. In the *keep follow* field, select **Yes**.
4. Press **Enter** or click the command.

During printing, Word checks to make sure the first paragraph and the first two lines of the second paragraph fit at the end of the page. If they do not, Word prints the last two lines of the first paragraph on the next page, followed by the second paragraph. If you select two paragraphs, Word keeps the selected two paragraphs and the following paragraph (a total of three) together.

Aligning Paragraphs Side by Side

Word's column feature wraps text from one column to the next in newspaper style. For some applications, you may want to "tie" the text in the left column to that in the right. To do this, you can use Word's side-by-side paragraph feature.

Figure 6-27 shows an example of side-by-side paragraphs in text-entry mode. The paragraphs appear one after another and align when printed. Notice the positioning of the paragraph symbols. The para-

```
1 L[···L·····1··········2··········]···L···4·········5·········6·········7·····]
   Zoom·in·for·close·up·head·shot·
   of·the·narrator.··Add·the·name·
   key.¶
                                  Welcome·to·today's·issue·of·
                                  Our·City·Close·Up.··Today,·we·
                                  will·be·talking·with·the·chief·
                                  of·police·about·the·
                                  effectiveness·of·neighborhood·
                                  watch·programs.¶
                                  ¶
                                  ¶
   Cut·to·graphic·of·crime·
   statistics·(graphic·#1).··¶
                                  Crime·in·our·city·is·rising·at·
                                  a·rapid·rate.··However,·in·
                                  neighborhood·watch·areas,·
                                  crime·is·at·an·average·of·ten·
                                  percent·lower·than·comparable·
                                  areas.·¶
                                  ¶
                                  ¶
                                  ¶
                                                          CH6.DOC
   Microsoft Word Version 5.0
```

Figure 6-27. Side-by-side paragraphs in text-entry mode

graph symbols trailing the paragraphs cause blank lines to appear. Figure 6-28 shows the same paragraphs in show-layout mode. Notice the blank lines surrounding the paragraphs. In show-layout mode, the paragraphs appear side by side and can be edited. Figure 6-29 shows

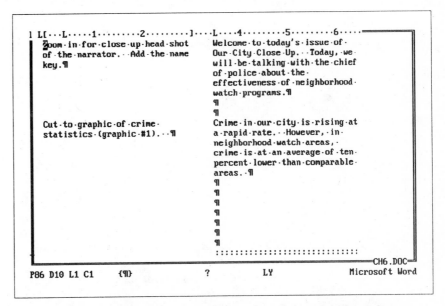

Figure 6-28. Side-by-side paragraphs in show-layout mode

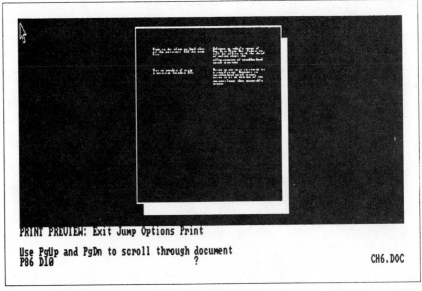

Figure 6-29. Side-by-side paragraphs in print-preview mode

the paragraphs in print-preview mode; the paragraphs appear side by side and cannot be edited. Finally, Figure 6-30 shows the final printed appearance.

```
Zoom in for close up head shot        Welcome to today's issue of
of the narrator.   Add the name       Our City Close Up.   Today, we
key.                                  will be talking with the chief
                                      of police about the
                                      effectiveness of neighborhood
                                      watch programs.


Cut to graphic of crime              Crime in our city is rising at
statistics (graphic #1).             a rapid rate.   However, in
                                     neighborhood watch areas,
                                     crime is at an average of ten
                                     percent lower than comparable
                                     areas.
```

Figure 6-30. Side-by-side paragraphs when printed

Word breaks between side-by-side paragraphs. Therefore, if a set of side-by-side paragraphs are too long to fit on a page, they are placed on the next page. Up to 32 paragraphs (16 pairs) can be aligned side by side.

If you want more than 32 paragraphs, enter the 33rd paragraph as a blank line (without side-by-side formatting). If you don't want to see the blank line, format it as hidden text by highlighting it and pressing Alt-E twice. Then select No in the Options *show hidden text* field. To avoid printing the blank line once it is formatted as hidden text, select No in the Print Options *hidden text* field.

You cannot include side-by-side paragraphs in footnotes or running heads, but you can add footnote references to side-by-side paragraphs.

There are two ways to align paragraphs side by side: with styles and without styles.

Aligning Side-by-Side Paragraphs with Styles

Chapter 9, "Style Sheets," goes into detail about how to set up custom style sheets. In this section, Word's default styles for creating side-by-side paragraphs are covered. Once you learn more about style sheets in Chapter 9, you will be able to create a custom style sheet if Word's default styles don't provide what you need.

Word's default styles accommodate two or three paragraphs of equal width with 0.5-inch space between them. Word assumes you are using 8.5-inch wide paper with left and right margins of 1.25 inches.

Follow these steps to create side-by-side paragraphs using one of Word's default styles:

1. Make sure the SIDEBY.STY style sheet is on your document disk or on your hard disk in the document directory.
2. Select **F**ormat **S**tylesheet **A**ttach.
3. Press **F1** to select SIDEBY.STY from the list.
4. Press **Enter** or click the command name. Word attaches SIDEBY.STY to your document.
5. Press **Alt-F4** to turn on show layout. The prompt LY appears in the status line.
6. Enter the first paragraph (which will be on the left side of the page). You do not need to put a paragraph mark at the end of the paragraph; Word adds it.
7. Press **Alt-2L** to apply the left-hand paragraph style. (If you want three paragraphs across, press **Alt-3L**.) You may notice that if you press Alt-2 and pause, Word displays this message:

   ```
   Enter second character of key code. For speedkey, start
   over with Alt+X
   ```

   Go ahead and press the **L** at this point. Word formats the paragraph on the left side of the screen.
8. Move the highlight after the left-hand paragraph mark. Type in the right-hand paragraph. It will appear directly below the left paragraph.
9. Press **Alt-2R** to apply the right-hand paragraph style. Word aligns the paragraph across from the left-hand paragraph. (If you want three paragraphs across, press **Alt-3C** for center, enter another paragraph, and press **Alt-3R** for the right-hand formatting).
10. Continue with steps 6 through 9 until all paragraphs are entered.

If you want more than one paragraph on the left, you can format two paragraphs in a row with Alt-2L as shown in Figure 6-31. The two paragraphs on the left were formatted with Alt-2L. The next paragraph which appears on the right was formatted with Alt-2R. The process was repeated with the following three paragraphs. Figure 6-32 shows the paragraphs in show-layout mode.

The same procedure can be performed with three columns.
You can modify the style sheet to allow for paragraphs of unequal width or different margins. (See Chapter 9, "Style Sheets," for details on modifying style sheet files.)

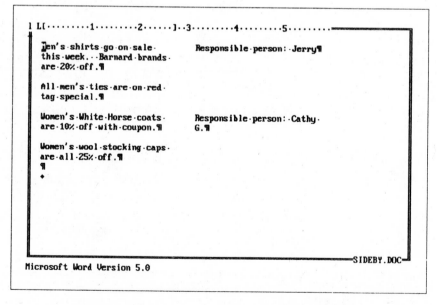

```
1 L[·········1·········2······]·3·········4·········5·········6·········7·····
      ]en's·shirts·go·on·sale·
      this·week.··Barnard·brands·
      are·20%·off.¶

      All·men's·ties·are·on·red·
      tag·special.¶

                              Responsible·person:·Jerry¶

      Women's·White·Horse·coats·
      are·10%·off·with·coupon.¶

      Women's·wool·stocking·caps·
      are·all·25%·off.¶

                              Responsible·person:·Cathy·
                              G.¶

      ¶
      ◆

                                                        ═SIDEBY.DOC═
  261 characters
```

Figure 6-31. Two left-hand paragraphs and one right-hand paragraph

```
1 L[·········1·········2······]·3·········4·········5·········
      ]en's·shirts·go·on·sale·    Responsible·person:·Jerry¶
      this·week.··Barnard·brands·
      are·20%·off.¶

      All·men's·ties·are·on·red·
      tag·special.¶

      Women's·White·Horse·coats·   Responsible·person:·Cathy·
      are·10%·off·with·coupon.¶    G.¶

      Women's·wool·stocking·caps·
      are·all·25%·off.¶
      ¶
      ◆

                                                        ═SIDEBY.DOC═
  Microsoft Word Version 5.0
```

Figure 6-32. The paragraphs in show-layout mode

Aligning Side-by-Side Paragraphs Without Styles

Aligning side-by-side paragraphs without styles is more difficult than using a style sheet. When you align paragraphs without styles, you need to know these sizes:

- The width of the paper minus the left and right margins; this is the area where text will print.
- The width of each paragraph and the space between each paragraph; this should be equal to the area the text will print.
- The indents from the margins for each paragraph; you will set the left indent for the right paragraph and the right indent for the left paragraph.

Figure 6-33 shows the calculations made to set up two side-by-side paragraphs of unequal size. Pay special attention to how the left indent (for the right paragraph) is measured from the left margin to the left side of the right paragraph. The right indent (for the left paragraph) is measured from the right margin to the right side of the left paragraph.

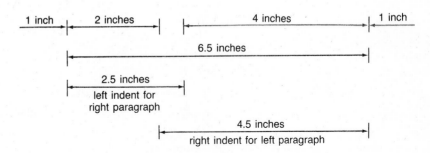

Figure 6-33. Layout of two different side-by-side paragraphs

Figure 6-34 shows the appearance of the paragraphs in show-layout mode. Notice that the highlight is in the lower-right paragraph. In the Format Paragraph settings for this paragraph, the *left indent* field is set at 2.5 inches. The *right indent* field is set at 0. Yes is selected in the *side by side* field.

To format paragraphs without a style sheet, follow these steps:

1. You need to calculate the following measurements:
   - The width of each paragraph
   - The space between paragraphs

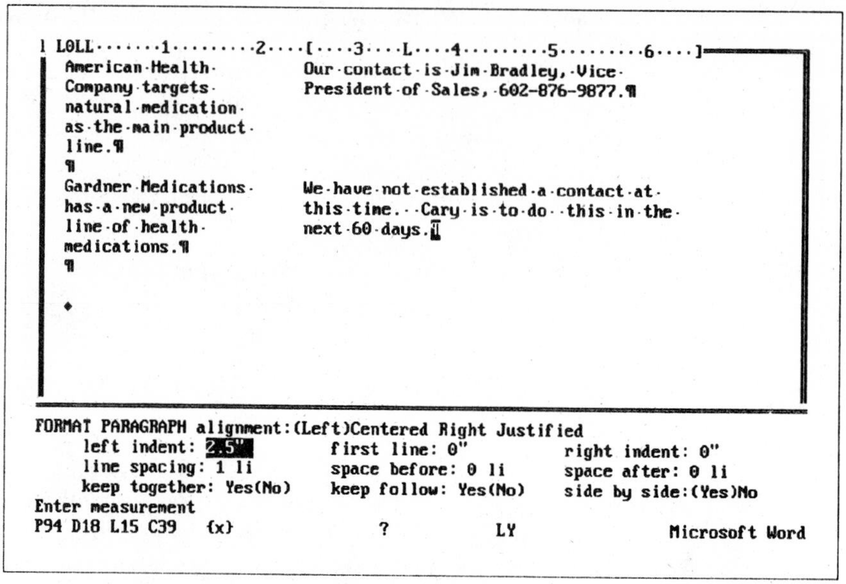

```
1 L0LL·······1·········2····[····3···L····4·······5·········6····]═══
       American·Health·           Our·contact·is·Jim·Bradley,·Vice·
       Company·targets·           President·of·Sales,·602-876-9877.¶
       natural·medication·
       as·the·main·product·
       line.¶
       ¶
       Gardner·Medications·       We·have·not·established·a·contact·at·
       has·a·new·product·         this·time.··Cary·is·to·do··this·in·the·
       line·of·health·            next·60·days.▯
       medications.¶
       ¶


       ◆



FORMAT PARAGRAPH alignment:(Left)Centered Right Justified
      left indent: 2.5"          first line: 0"          right indent: 0"
      line spacing: 1 li         space before: 0 li      space after: 0 li
      keep together: Yes(No)     keep follow: Yes(No)    side by side:(Yes)No
Enter measurement
P94 D18 L15 C39    {x}                   ?           LY           Microsoft Word
```

Figure 6-34. The screen appearance of two side-by-side paragraphs

- The left indent for the right paragraph
- The right indent for the left paragraph

2. Turn on show layout by pressing **Alt-F4**. The LY prompt appears in the status line.

3. Type in the left-hand paragraph.

4. With the highlight in the paragraph, select **F**ormat **P**aragraph.

5. In the *right indent* field, type in a measurement for the right indent and check to make sure zero is entered in the *left indent* field. Select **Y**es in the *side by side* field and type in a value in the *space before* field if you want to leave one or more lines before the paragraph.

6. Press **Enter** or click the command name.

7. Type in the right-hand paragraph.

8. With the highlight in the paragraph, select **F**ormat **P**aragraph.

9. In the *left indent* field, type in the measurement for the left indent. Check to make sure the *right indent* is 0. Select **Y**es in the *side by side* field (Word returns the last setting, so you will have to manually enter 0.)

10. Press **Enter** or click the command name.

11. Repeat steps 3 through 10 until all paragraphs are entered.

You can use the Format Stylesheet Record command to record the formatting. This will speed the process. Or, you can repeat and copy the formatting by selecting text and pressing F4 to repeat the last edit. (For more information, see "Repeating a Command" in Chapter 2, "Starting Microsoft Word.")

Exercise: Using Format Paragraph

A fourth way to quickly format paragraphs: Select the paragraph you want to format. Using a mouse, point in the selection bar next to the paragraph with the formatting you want to copy, hold down Alt, and click the right button. The format is immediately effective.

This exercise gives you practice with common paragraph formats: first-line indent, hanging indent, and left and right indents. Clear your screen with Transfer Clear. Then type in this text:

```
This is a text paragraph to begin learning about Paragraph
Formatting. It will be formatted several ways.
```

Make sure you press Enter to end the paragraph. Press Enter again to add a blank line.

Select Format Paragraph. Set the line spacing to double-space by typing a 2 in the *line spacing* field. Make two copies of the paragraph. Move your highlight to the paragraph and press F10. Select Copy and then press Enter. Move your highlight and press Ins. A copy of the text appears. Press Ins two more times to make a third and fourth copy of the paragraph.

To make a hanging indent, place your highlight in the first paragraph. Select Format Paragraph. Type 1 as the left indent and -1 as the first-line setting. Press Enter. The text has a hanging indent like this:

```
This is a text paragraph to begin learning about Paragraph
          Formatting. It will be formatted several ways.
```

To make a first-line indent, move your highlight to the second paragraph. Select Format Paragraph. Type .5 as the first-line setting and then press Enter. The text looks like this:

```
     This is a text paragraph to begin learning about Paragraph
Formatting. It will be formatted several ways.
```

To use both left and right indents, put the highlight in the third paragraph. Select Format Paragraph. Type 1 as the left indent and 1 as the right indent. Press Enter. Do not press another key.

Complete this portion of the example by moving to the next paragraph, positioning your highlight in it, and then pressing F4, the repeat-command key. Both paragraphs look like this:

```
This is a text paragraph to begin learning
about Paragraph Formatting. It will be
formatted several ways.
```

Now try aligning side-by-side paragraphs without styles. Type in this paragraph:

```
Reorganize the files for the officers.
```

Select Format Paragraph. Because this will be the left paragraph, type in a *right indent* of 4.5 inches. In the *side by side* field, select Yes. Press Enter. The text is aligned on the left side of the screen. Now type in this text:

```
Officer files are found in blue case in the workroom. Organize
them by color.
```

Select Format Paragraph. This is the right paragraph. Enter a left indent of 2.5 inches. In the *side by side* field, select Yes. Press Enter. The text moves to the right of the screen. To see the layout, select Options. In the *show layout* field, select Yes and then press Enter. The paragraphs appear side by side (see Figure 6-35). Press Alt-F4 to turn off show-layout mode. Print the paragraphs and then save the file under the name PARFORM.

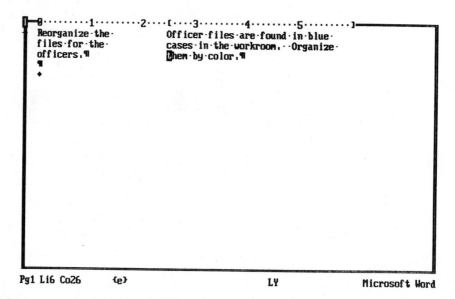

Figure 6-35. Two side-by-side paragraphs

Formatting Characters

The Format characters command controls the appearance of characters on your screen as well as the printed result. The screen appearance is governed by your monitor and whether you are in text-entry or graphics mode. Some monitors do not support all of Word's character options (such as small caps and italics).

You can use graphics mode only if you have a video adapter with graphics capabilities installed. If you have graphics capability, make sure Graphics is selected in the Options *display mode* field. (See Chapter 2, "Starting Microsoft Word," for more information about setting up Word for graphics and switching between graphics and text mode.)

If you can work in graphics mode, Word displays the various character formats on the screen as shown in Figure 6-36.

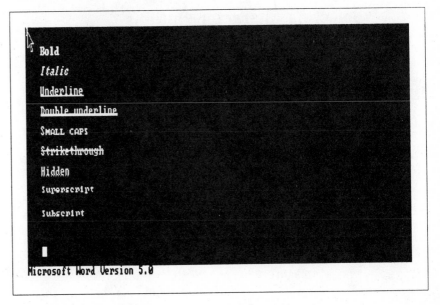

Figure 6-36. Character formats in graphics mode

In text mode, the characters appear as regular text or in different colors (if you have color capability). Some Word users like to set different colors for different character formats. This can be done through the Options *colors* field (see "Screen Colors" in Chapter 2, "Starting Microsoft Word").

Another factor governing the character formats you can successfully use is the printer. If your printer does not handle italics, no amount of work in Word will change that factor. You may want to create and print a document using all the formats on the Format Character menu to determine what formats are supported by your printer.

You can format characters using the Format Character command or speed formatting keys. Using the Format Character command can be tedious if you are repeating the same formatting often in a document. You can use several options to speed up the process. The Format Stylesheet Record command can record formatting for future applications (see Chapter 9, "Style Sheets"). Another alternative is to repeat and copy the character formatting by selecting the options and then pressing F4 to repeat the last edit. (For more information, see "Repeating a Command" in Chapter 2, "Starting Microsoft Word.") Finally, if you have a mouse, you can copy character formatting. Select the characters to format, point to a character with the format you want, hold down Alt, and click the left button.

Selecting Character Options

Word offers these character options:

Bold

Italic

Underline

Double underline

Small caps

Strikethrough

Hidden

Superscript

Subscript

Figure 6-37 shows the printed results of several options. You may want to create a document like that shown in the figure and print it on your printer to determine what options your printer supports.

Displaying Hidden Text

The hidden text option is useful for text that you want to include in a document (comments, reminders, and special information, for example) but that you do not necessarily want to appear when the document is printed. You can choose whether or not to display hidden text on your screen through the Options *show hidden text* field and *show non-printing symbols* fields. You can also choose whether or

Bold

<u>Underline</u>

<u>Double underline</u>

~~Strikethrough~~

This is ^Superscript^

This is ~Subscript~

Figure 6-37. The printed results of several character options

not to print the hidden text through the Print Options *hidden text* field. See "Non-Printing Symbols" and "Hidden Text" in Chapter 3, "Creating Documents." Also see "Hidden Text" in Chapter 5, "Printing Documents."

Selecting Character Options with the Format Character Command

Many Word users like to use the Format Character command to select multiple character options at once. To apply character formatting, you can choose the format first and then type in the text or vice-versa. In either case, here is the process to follow:

1. Select the text you want to format or position the highlight where you want to begin typing text in a new format.
2. Select **F**ormat **C**haracter.
3. Select **Y**es in the appropriate fields.
4. Press **Enter** or click the command.
5. If you chose to type in text after selecting a format, begin typing at the highlight. The text will be formatted according to the options selected.
6. If you are typing text and want to apply other formatting, select **F**ormat **C**haracter. Select **N**o in the fields you want to disable. Press **Enter** or click the command.

Selecting Character Options with Speed Formatting Keys

Using the Format Character menu for applying formats works best if you want to change multiple character options at once, set fonts, or set hidden text. The speed formatting keys are useful for applying character formats one at a time. You can use more than one speed

Word's speed-formatting keys offer beginners the quickest and easiest way to produce polished documents. The character speed-formatting keys are described in this section. For information about the paragraph speed-formatting keys, see "Summary of Paragraph Speed Formatting Keys" earlier in this chapter.

formatting key on text (such as bold and underline). You cannot use speed formatting keys to change fonts.

To use the speed formatting keys, follow these steps:

1. Place the highlight where you want to begin typing.

2. Hold down the **Alt** key and press the speed key for the format. (If you have a style sheet attached, press **Alt-X** then the format key.) These are the format options and speed keys:

Format	Press Alt (or Alt-X) and
Bold	B
Italic	I
Underline	U
Double underline	D
Small caps	K
Strikethrough	S
Hidden	E
Superscript	+ or =
Subscript	- (hyphen)
Normal character	spacebar

3. Type in the text.

4. To go back to "normal" characters, hold down **Alt** and press the **Spacebar.**

You can also use speed keys to format existing text. Simply select the text, hold down the Alt key and press the format key.

Fonts

The Format Character command allows you to identify fonts. Fonts are identified by typeface (such as Helvetica), pitch and point, and character weight (such as bold). Figure 6-38 shows several fonts. Your printer may or may not handle different fonts. Laser printers have the most font options.

Internal fonts are built into the hardware and software of the machine. Some fonts reside on hardware cartridges. Downloadable fonts are software that is loaded from a disk with your machine into the memory of the printer.

Word allows you to have up to 64 fonts in a document. Each font type can have normal, bold, italic, and sub-types of bold and italic for a total of 256 type styles.

Helvetica Bold 14.4 point

Times Roman Medium 10 point

Times Roman Bold 10 point

Times Roman Medium Italic 10 point

Times Roman Light 8 point

Line Printer Light 8.5 point

PRESENTATION BOLD 18 POINT

PRESENTATION BOLD 16 POINT

PRESENTATION BOLD 14 POINT

Letter Gothic Medium 14 point

Courier 10 point

Courier Bold 10 point

Figure 6-38. Font examples

When you use Word's Setup utility, you can identify the fonts you want to use. Use the Setup utility as often as you like to change fonts. (See Chapter 2, "Starting Microsoft Word," for more information about using Setup.)

Understanding Fonts

The Format Character command has three font-related fields:

- **Font name:** The *font name* identifies the type style for the characters. The fonts available when pressing F1 while in the *font name* field are based on the printer you selected in the Print Options *printer* field. (See Chapter 5, "Printing Documents," for more information about this field.)

- **Font size:** The *font size* identifies the height and width of characters (measured in points). The selections available when you press F1 are based on the *font name* you identified previously.

- **Font color:** The *font color* is useful only if you have a printer that prints in color. If you do, *font color* identifies the color of the characters that will print (not as they appear on the screen). If you do not have a printer that prints in color, Black is the only color option displayed when you press F1 in this field.

Selecting Fonts

To use a font, it must be available and valid for your printer type. For example, the Hewlett-Packard LaserJet series has a variety of font cartridges that you can use with Word. The cartridge must be installed in the printer prior to starting Word.

You can select a font for existing text or you can select a font and then type in text. To select a font, follow these steps:

1. Make sure the fonts are available.

2. Select the text you want to work with. (**Shift-F10** selects the entire document.) Or, place the highlight where you want a new font to take effect.

3. Select **F**ormat **C**haracter or press **Alt-F8**.

4. With the highlight in the *font name* field, type in a font name that is valid for your printer selection and printer setup. (Press **F1** in this field to select from a list.)

5. Once you have identified the *font name*, place the highlight in the *font size* field. Enter a valid size for the *font name* or press F1 to select from the list.

6. If you have a color printer, place the highlight in *font color* and enter a color. (Or, press **F1** to select from a list of font colors.)

7. Press **Enter** or click the command name. If you positioned the highlight to enter text, begin typing. The text you type in will be in the font selected. To change to a different font, repeat the process.

Exercise: Using Format Character

You cannot see the fonts you select on screen. To check the font used for a given piece of text, highlight the text and select Format Character or press Alt-F8. The font name and related settings appear.

Take some time to find out what characters your printer will handle. On a clear screen, type in the following:

Bold

Italic

Underline

Double underline

Small caps

Strikethrough

```
Hidden
```

```
Superscript
```

```
Subscript
```

Apply each format using the appropriate speed key. (Refer to the previous section for detailed information.) Save the file under the name CHAR. Then, select Print Printer to see what character styles print. If your printer allows for different font selections in the Format Character font name field, you may want to try several font settings for printing the file.

Changing the Case of Letters

It is easy to change the case of letters with Word. For example, you can have a document typed in upper and lowercase then realize that it should be in uppercase only. With the Format Character command, you can make this change without retyping the entire document.

These are the case options for character formatting:

Option	Example
Uppercase	THE TIME IS NOW
Lowercase	the time is now
First letter uppercase	The Time Is Now

The Format Character menu has an *uppercase* field option. When you set uppercase through this menu, the letters are marked with a format. If you save a document without Word formats, the uppercase is lost. When you use the following method of changing case instead of the Format Character *uppercase* field, the text is treated as though it were typed in the case.

To switch case, follow these steps:

Because Word regards case changes made with Ctrl-F4 the same as if you had typed them in that way originally, you cannot use the Format Search command to find capital letters created by this method.

1. Select the characters whose case you want to change. (You cannot choose the case first and then type in the characters.)

2. Press **Ctrl-F4**. The characters are formatted in the next case in this order: lowercase, uppercase, and first letter uppercase.

3. Move the highlight off the selection when the case is defined.

This command is most useful for correcting typing errors. It is also useful if you prefer to quickly type in text and worry about case afterwards. If you use this command to change the case of large chunks of type, take care. If you change your mind, changing the text back to the way it was may be time-consuming.

Tabs

As with a typewriter, you can press the Tab key and move to the next tab stop, but Word's tab capabilities go far beyond those of a typewriter. Tab stops can be set and changed as you like, and you can set up to 19 tabs in a paragraph.

Unlike a typewriter, Word lets you set five types of tabs:

Tab type	Action
Left	Aligns characters on the left
Right	Aligns characters on the right
Center	Centers characters under the tab stop
Decimal-point alignment	Centers characters at the decimal point
Vertical alignment	Draws a vertical line (the vertical line is not associated with a tab character inserted in the document, as the other tabs are)

Figure 6-39 shows an example of each type of tab.

The tab settings described in this chapter are associated with paragraphs. You can identify the paragraph to affect by placing the highlight in the paragraph. Or, you can select several paragraphs. When you select several paragraphs, the tabs common to all paragraphs are displayed in the ruler for editing. Because tabs are associated with paragraphs, when you delete a paragraph mark, you will also delete the tab settings associated with the paragraph mark.

Remember to use the newline character (Shift-Enter) in place of Enter to treat a block of text as one paragraph.

Setting Tabs

Once you get your tab settings correct, save them as part of a paragraph style. That way, you'll never have to repeat the process. (See Chapter 9, "Style Sheets," for more information.)

Press the Tab key to go to the first tab stop. If the Options *show non-printing symbols* field is set to Partial or All, a tab character (→) fills the space to the tab. You can control the visibility of the tab character through the Options *show non-printing symbols* field. Select All for the tab character to appear on your screen. (See Chapter 3, "Creating Documents," for more information about setting this option.)

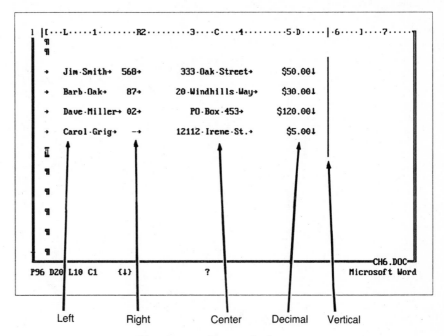

Figure 6-39. Types of tabs

Displaying Tab Stops on the Ruler

Tab stops appear on the ruler, as shown in Figure 6-40.

These tab stops are displayed:

- Left tab stops with L
- Right tab stops with R
- Center tab stops with C
- Decimal tab stops with D
- Ruler measurements with 1, 2, 3, and so forth
- Column indents with [and]
- The tab options to be used with the mouse
- Vertical line stop with a ¦

You can display or hide the ruler. The tabs you set are the new default for the next Word session and are applied to all windows.

To display or hide the ruler using the keyboard, follow these steps:

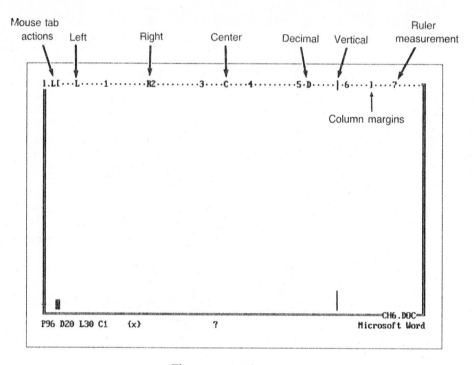

Figure 6-40. The ruler

1. Select **O**ptions.
2. In the *show ruler* field, select **Yes** to display the ruler or **No** to hide the ruler.
3. Press **Enter**.

To display or hide the ruler using a mouse, follow these steps:

1. Point to the upper-right corner of the border.
2. Click the left button to show the ruler or click both buttons to hide the ruler.

Changing Default Tab Stops and Decimal Character

Word sets default tab stops and a default decimal character. When you look at the ruler, the default tab stops are not displayed. However, if you have not set any manual tab stops, when you press Tab, your highlight goes to each default tab stop one at a time.

You can change the default tab stops to new tab stops at regular intervals. Or, you can set custom tab stops at any location between the indent marks ([ ]) which identify the boundaries of the column. The decimal character default is a period (.). You can switch it to a comma (,).

Here is the process for entering tab stops at regular intervals and identifying the decimal character. The current settings become the new defaults for your documents:

1. Select **O**ptions.

2. Select the period or the comma in *decimal character* field.

3. In the *default tab width* field, type in a measurement for the tab stops you desire. You can enter the measurement in inches or another form. (See "Units of Measurement" in this chapter for more information on measurement options.)

4. Press **Enter** or click the command.

Unless a style sheet specifying tab settings is attached to your document, Word immediately implements the new settings.

Adding and Deleting Custom Tab Stops

You can set or delete tab stops between the indent marks ([ ]) marking the column boundaries. When you enter new tab stops, Word automatically deletes default tab stops on the left of the custom tab (unless the custom tab is a vertical tab). Default tab stops to the right of the last custom tab are left in place. Custom tabs you have set earlier are left in place.

You can use the keyboard or the mouse to add or delete tab stops. Instructions for both follow.

Adding or Deleting Tab Stops with the Keyboard

To set or delete tab stops with the keyboard, follow these steps:

1. Select the paragraph, multiple paragraphs, or the entire document (**Shift-F10**).

2. Select **F**ormat **T**ab **S**et and press **F1** to activate the ruler. Or use the speed key (**Alt-F1**).

3. Press these keys as needed to position the highlight (on a new tab stop location or over an existing tab stop to delete it):

Right or **Left Arrow**   to move one space at a time

PgDn or **PgUp**   to move 1 inch at a time

Home or **End**   to move between indent marks ([ ])

Your highlight position is shown in the *position* field. This field helps you align tabs according to precise measurements.

4. With the highlight positioned where you want to enter a tab stop, type in the first letter of the type of tab stop:

L   for left

C   for center

R   for right

D   for decimal

V   for vertical

Or, if you are deleting a tab stop, press **Del** to delete the tab stop marked by the highlight. The letter disappears. Or, press **Ctrl-Del** to delete the highlighted tab stop and all the tab stops to the right.

5. Repeat steps 3 and 4 to set or delete additional tab stops.

6. Press **Enter** to complete setting tab stops.

 Instead of moving the highlight to set a tab stop, you can enter a value in the Format Tab Set *position* field. Simply type in a measurement. For example, a tab stop at one-half inch would be entered as 0.5. (You must enter a zero for settings less than an inch). Then, press the letter of the alignment (L, R, C, D, or V). The tab setting appears in the ruler. Press Enter or click the command name.

Adding or Deleting Tab Stops with the Mouse

To add or delete tab stops with a mouse, follow these steps:

1. Activate the ruler through the Options *show ruler* field.

2. Select the paragraph(s) you want to work with.

3. To delete a tab stop, simply place the mouse pointer on the tab stop and click both buttons.

4. To add a tab stop, place the mouse pointer on the character (L, R, C, D, or ¦) to the left of the ruler and to the right of the window number.

5. Click the left mouse button until the first letter of the desired alignment appears:

L	for left
R	for right
C	for center
D	for decimal
¦	for vertical

6. Point to the location for the tab stop and press the left mouse button. The letter or symbol for the tab stop appears.

7. Repeat steps 3 through 6 to delete or add tab stops as desired.

Clearing Tab Stops

If you want to check measurements as you enter tab stops, select Format Tab Set to see the position field. This field indicates each tab measurement as it is set.

As described earlier, you can delete tabs in the same process as adding other tabs. You can also use the Format Tab Clear command to delete tabs, however, you cannot add tabs while you work with Format Tab Clear.

To delete tab stops using the Format Tab Clear command, follow these steps:

1. Select the paragraph(s) you want to work with.

2. Select **Format Tab Clear**.

3. Press **F1** to activate the ruler.

4. Press the **Down** or **Up Arrow** key to highlight the tab stop you want to delete.

5. Press the , (comma) key—or the ; (semicolon) key if you use the comma as the decimal symbol. A list of positions for tab-stop deletion results.

6. Repeat steps 4 and 5 to identify all tab stops to delete.

7. Press **Enter**.

Word deletes the tab stops.

Moving Tab Stops

You can move a custom tab stop with the keyboard or a mouse. To use the keyboard, follow these steps:

1. Select the paragraph(s) you want to work with.

2. Select **Format Tab Set** and press **F1** to activate the ruler. Or press **Alt-F1**.

3. Press the **Down** or **Up Arrow** key to highlight the tab stop you want to move.

4. Press **Ctrl-Left Arrow** to move the tab stop left or **Ctrl-Right Arrow** to move the tab stop right. If you pass an existing custom tab stop, that tab stop is deleted.

5. Repeat steps 3 and 4 to move all tab stops desired.

6. Press **Enter** to set the tab stops.

To move tab stops using the mouse, follow these steps:

1. Activate the ruler. (Select **Y**es in the **O**ptions *show ruler* field.)

2. Select the paragraph(s) you want to work with.

3. Point to the tab stop you want to move and hold down the right mouse button.

4. Move the pointer to the desired position and release the right button.

5. Repeat steps 3 and 4 as often as necessary.

 If you want to see the location of the new tab stop, you can press Alt-F1 and check the measurement entered in the Format Tab Set *position* field. To save the tab settings you have moved, you must press Enter to leave the Format Tab Set menu. If you press Esc to leave the menu, the tab settings you have moved are restored to the original positions.

Resetting Default Tab Stops

You can use Format Tab Reset-all to reinstate the default tab stop positions. For example, if you have changed tabs but don't like the result, you can restore the original tab stops with this command.

To reset the default tabs, follow these steps:

1. Select the paragraph(s) you want to work with.

2. Select **F**ormat **T**ab **R**eset-all.

Entering Leader Characters

Leader characters fill the space between columns to help draw the reader's eye across a line, as in a table of contents. Leader characters can be hyphens (-), dots (.), or underscores (_).

An example of each leader character is shown in Figure 6-41. Notice that the ruler contains the leader character symbol before the letter identifying the tab stop. Tab stops without a leader character symbol are considered blank. When you press Tab, Word displays the leader characters from your current position to the tab stop identified with a leader character.

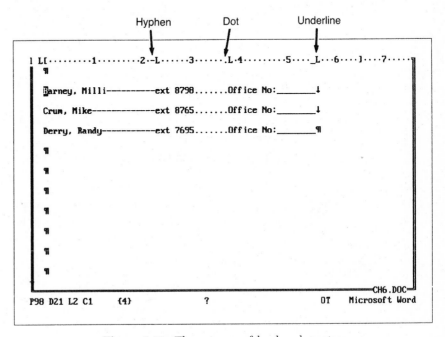

Figure 6-41. Three types of leader characters

The Options show non-printing symbols field must be set to None or Partial for Word to display the leader characters. If the field is set to All, a tab character (->) is displayed instead of the leader characters.

Leader characters are associated with paragraph symbols. You can specify leader characters for a single paragraph or a group of selected paragraphs, and you can set a different leader character for each type of tab stop (L, R, C, and D) except the vertical (V) tab stop.

Adding and Deleting Leader Characters with the Keyboard

You can use the keyboard to add and delete leader character symbols in the ruler. These symbols allow you to select the type of leader character for each tab stop.

To add or delete leader characters, follow these steps:

1. Make sure the **O**ptions *show non-printing symbols* field is set to **N**one or **P**artial. If it is set to **A**ll, the leader characters will not appear.

2. Select the paragraph(s) you want to work with.

3. Select **F**ormat **T**ab **S**et and press **F1**. Or press **Alt-F1**.

4. Move the highlight to an existing tab stop or to the location where you want to enter a new tab stop.

5. To add a leader character, type in a period, hyphen, or underline. The *leader char* field reflects the choice. If you are adding a tab stop, enter the first letter (**L**, **C**, **R**, or **D**). Word displays the leader character before the tab stop letter in the ruler.

6. To delete a leader character, highlight the letter of the tab stop and press **B** (for blank). The leader character symbol disappears. When you reenter the document, the leader characters for the paragraph(s) will be removed.

7. Repeat steps 3 and 5 to set all tab stops with leader characters.

8. Press **Enter** when you are done.

9. Type in the text and press **Tab** to the tab stop with the leader character.

There is an alternative to typing in the leader character symbol or B for blank. You can press Tab to move to the *leader char* field on the menu and then press Spacebar to select Blank, period, hyphen, or underline.

Adding and Deleting Leader Characters with a Mouse

To add or delete leader character symbols using a mouse, follow these steps:

1. Select **N**one or **P**artial in the **O**ptions *show non-printing symbols* field.

2. Select **Y**es in the **O**ptions *show ruler* field.

3. Select the paragraph(s) you want to work with.

4. In the ruler, point to the space after the window number and before the alignment letter. Click the left button until the leader character you want is displayed. The characters are:

. period
- hyphen
_ underscore
blank (no leader character)

Use the blank character if you want to delete an existing leader character symbol.

5. In the next space to the right, the alignment letter appears. Click the left mouse button to display the letter corresponding to the tab stop you want to add or delete.

6. To change or add a leader character, point to the existing or new tab stop position. Click the left mouse button.

7. To delete a leader character, make sure the leader character space at the far left is blank and the appropriate type of alignment letter is displayed. Point to the alignment letter you wish to change and click the left mouse button.

8. Repeat steps 4 through 7 as often as necessary.

9. Type in the text and press **Tab** to move to the tab stop with the leader character. If **N**one or **P**artial is selected in the **O**ptions *show non-printing symbols* field, the leader characters will be displayed on your screen.

Using the Show Line Breaks Option

With Word you can set indents ([ ]) beyond what is displayed on your screen. You can choose whether to extend the lines beyond the right screen boundary, or to have the text wrap around so the line breaks appear on-screen as they will print.

To specify whether or not to show line breaks on your screen, follow these steps:

1. Select **O**ptions.

2. In the *show line breaks* field, select **Y**es to show the line breaks or **N**o to hide line breaks.

3. Press **Enter** or click the command.

The value you enter in the *show line breaks* field is retained after you leave Word.

When you repaginate a document and confirm the page breaks, Word displays the breaks regardless of the setting in the *show line breaks* field.

Tables

Tabs are often used to create tables. Once you create a table with tabs, you can select, delete, move, or copy text in the table.

Tables can be used in conjunction with other Word functions. You can select a column to sort (see Chapter 13, "Sorting Text") or perform math on the columns in a table (see Chapter 19, "Using Math Functions and Importing Files"). For more information on tables, see Chapter 20, "Electronic Publishing and Graphics." Tables can be automatically numbered throughout a document (see Chapter 10, "Revision Marks, Bookmarks, Cross-Referencing, and Hyphenation").

Considerations for Creating Tables

Because tab stops are set for a paragraph, it is easiest to format an entire table as a paragraph. That way, if you change the tab stops, the change immediately affects the entire table. If, on the other hand, you create a table and press Enter at the end of each line, changing tab stops is more complicated. You would have to select all the paragraphs or copy the edited paragraph symbol to the end of each line of the table.

To create a table as a paragraph, you will press Shift-Enter to put a newline character at the end of the lines in the table. If the Options *show non-printing symbols* field is set to Partial or All, Word displays a Down Arrow symbol when you press Shift-Enter. Press Enter at the end of the table row.

Figure 6-42 shows an example of the newline characters in relation to the paragraph symbols. The tab formatting for this table can be handled with one setting.

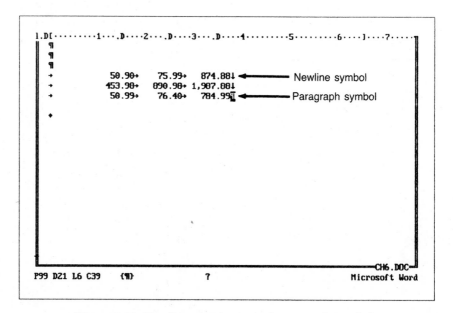

Figure 6-42. Newline characters and paragraph symbol

When you develop tables, consistently use tab stops versus combining spaces and tab stops. Otherwise, your printed result will be different from what you see on the screen. This is especially important if you are using fonts of different sizes. Word can display the equivalent of 12-pitch, 10-point characters in fixed spacing. If you use another font size or a proportional font (where each character is not the same size), the alignment may be different from what you expect.

If you select Yes in the Options *show line breaks* field, Word shows where the line will break at the right margin when printed. The ruler will reflect the size of the font with which you are working. This can help you get a better feel for the printed result.

Deleting, Moving, Copying, and Inserting Columns

Once you have developed a table as a paragraph, you can delete, move, copy, and insert columns. You can also perform math or sort columns. (See Chapter 19, "Using Math Functions and Importing Files," as well as Chapter 13, "Sorting Text.")

When you manipulate a column, always consider the outcome of your work before beginning the delete, move, or copy process. Consider where the resulting columns will fall and what you may need to do to the ruler to make the new table readable. If you are unsure about the manipulation, make a copy of the table in another place in your document. That way, if you destroy the table, you can always copy the original and try again.

Selecting Columns

Before you can edit a column, you must select it. Columns with even edges are easy to select since they easily fit in the "selection" rectangle as shown in Figure 6-43.

Columns with ragged edges can be a bit tricky. Figure 6-44 shows the result when you try to select a column with ragged edges. The left characters can be lopped off.

To select a ragged-edge column, you can select the tab character before the column (see Figure 6-45). This means the tab characters will be manipulated along with the column. If you don't want to manipulate the tab characters, you can temporarily change the type of tab stop used.

Selecting the last column of a table poses some special considerations because you will often want to select trailing tab characters. As shown in Figure 6-46, some last columns don't have trailing tab characters and may not even have a straight margin.

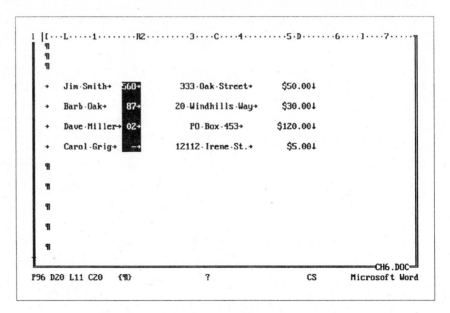

Figure 6-43. A column with even edges selected

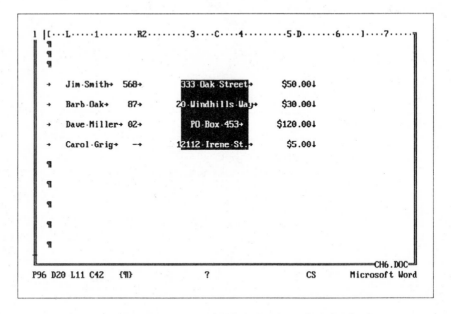

Figure 6-44. Trying to select a column with ragged edges

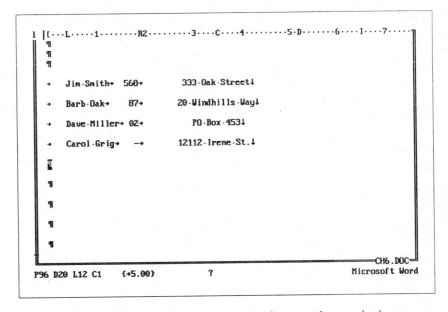

Figure 6-45. A tab character selected

```
1 |[···L·····1········R2·········3···C···4········5·D·····6···]····7·····]
  ¶
  ¶
  ¶
    →   Jim·Smith→  568→        333·Oak·Street↓
    →   Barb·Oak→    87→        20·Windhills·Way↓
    →   Dave·Miller→ 02→        PO·Box·453↓
    →   Carol·Grig→   →         12112·Irene·St.↓
  ¶
  ¶
  𝕀
  ¶
  ¶
  ¶
                                                              CH6.DOC
  P96 D20 L12 C1    {→5.00}           ?                    Microsoft Word
```

Figure 6-46. A decimal-aligned last column with ragged edge

There are several approaches for adding trailing tab characters. You can press Shift-F6, select all the newline characters, and then press Tab. For center, decimal, or uneven edges, follow these steps:

1. Select the table using extend select (**F6**) or the paragraph selection keys (**F9** or **F10**). Do not select the text using column select (**Shift-F6**).

2. Select **R**eplace.

3. In the *text* field, type in the following newline character:

4. In the *with text* field, type in the following tab and newline characters:

   ^t^n

5. Press **Enter** or click the command. The tab characters are inserted after the paragraph mark.

6. To insert a tab character before the paragraph mark, select the paragraph mark and then press **Tab**.

To select a column, follow these steps:

1. Identify the rectangle area you will select. This can include one or more columns. Temporarily change any tab stop characters, if necessary, to fit the column into a rectangle area.

2. Place the highlight in the upper-left corner of the column. Include the trailing tab character (→) if it is important to the function. For example, if you are moving the column, you will want to move the tab character along with the column. Otherwise, the column characters will not align as expected.

3. Press **Shift-F6**. CS for column select appears in your status line.

4. Use the arrow keys or the mouse to extend the selection to the opposite corner of the column. (If you want to quit the function, press **Shift-F6** again.)

Deleting or Moving Columns

Moving a column involves deleting it then inserting it at another location. Before deleting a column, consider where the remaining elements of the table will fall and which tab characters you wish to delete along with the column text.

To delete and insert one or more columns, follow these steps:

1. Select the column with **Shift-F6**. Pay attention to the tab characters you wish to delete or move. Typically, trailing tab characters should be included in the selection.

2. Press **Del**.

3. The column is deleted to the scrap and the remaining text realigns in the table. If you wanted to delete the column, quit now. To move the column, continue with the remaining steps.

4. Assuming you highlighted trailing tab characters, highlight the first character of the column that will be to the right of the column you will insert. Or, if the column will be the last column in the table, highlight the first newline character after the last column.

5. Press **Ins**.

Word moves the columns to the right of the inserted column to the right.

Copying Columns

To copy one or more columns, follow these steps:

1. Select the column with **Shift-F6**. Pay attention to the tab characters you wish to copy. Usually, trailing tab characters should be highlighted.

2. Select **C**opy or press **Alt-F3**. The column is placed in the scrap area.

3. Assuming you selected the trailing tab characters, highlight the first character of the column that will be to the right of the column you are inserting. Or, if the column will be the last column, select the first newline character.

4. Press **Ins**.

Word moves the columns to the right of the inserted column to the right.

Adding Columns

You can add a new, blank column to a table. This opens up space for you to enter new text. Figure 6-47 shows a table prior to adding a column. Figure 6-48 shows the table after adding a column. This table is ready for text to be added.

When you add a new column, make sure there are enough tab stops in the ruler to allow for one more column.

To add a new column, follow these steps:

1. Select the column you want to move to the right with **Shift-F6** and the **Arrow** keys. Include trailing tabs.

2. Press **Tab**.

3. Type in the text in the new column.

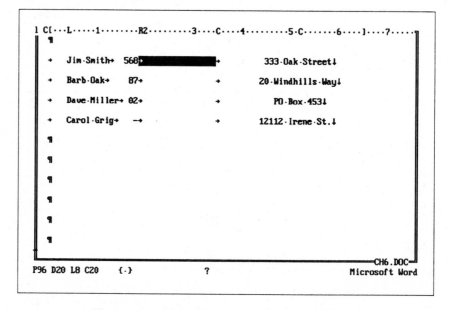

Figure 6-47. The table before adding a column

Figure 6-48. The table after adding a column

Exercise: Using Format Tab

Clear your screen with Transfer Clear All before beginning. In this exercise, you will practice setting tabs and using leader characters.

Set a left tab at 1″ in the ruler, a decimal tab at 3″, and a right tab with a dot leader at 5″. Select Format Tab Set. Move the highlight to the correct number in the ruler. Set the alignment and leader characters as needed. (Or use other methods, such as the mouse.) Select Partial in the Options *show non-printing symbols* field. Press Tab and then type in this text:

`AAA Jacket`

Press Tab and type in this text:

`175.00`

Press Tab and type in this text:

`Overstocked`

Your screen should show the first line as it appears here. Type in the second line.

```
AAA Jacket         175.00          Overstocked
WW Suit            325.00          Out of stock
```

Now save the document as TABLE. You may want to print it with Print Printer.

You have seen how easy it is to manipulate tables. If you needed to refer back to other sections during this exercise, don't worry; with time, the functions will become second nature.

Running Heads, Footnotes, and Annotations

You can give a document a more polished appearance and make it easier to find your way around the document by adding running heads. You can also make it easier to understand a document by using footnotes and annotations.

Word's running-head feature allows you to print the same information at the top or bottom of every page in a document, even though you have to type in the information only once. The footnote feature allows you to provide additional information, cross referenced to a particular spot in your document. The annotation feature works similarly to the footnote feature, but the purpose of annotations is to allow other readers to comment on the document.

Figure 7-1 shows a running head, a footnote, and an annotation as they appear on the screen. Notice the symbols denoting each of them. Figure 7-2 shows how the running head, footnote, and annotation look when the document is printed.

Running Heads

Word treats running heads as paragraphs. You can have any number of running heads in your document. For example, one running head might appear only on right-hand pages and a different running head might appear only on left-hand pages.

Running heads can be any number of paragraphs long and each paragraph can have any number of lines. You can format running-head paragraphs independently of the document and of each other.

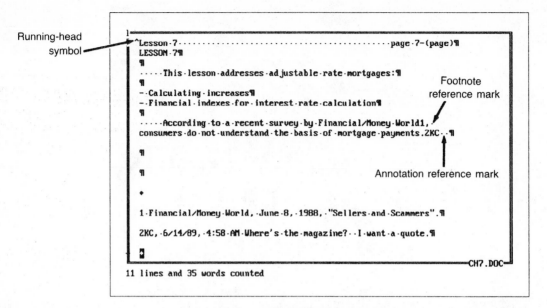

Figure 7-1. A running head, footnote, and annotation
as they appear on the screen

Typically, you use running heads to print the following kinds of
information on each page of a document:

- The title of a report
- The section or chapter number or title
- The date
- The page number
- The names of the author(s)

Because running heads can be any length, you can also use them
to repeat boilerplate text on every page. For example, you could print
the following legal disclaimer on each page of a document by formatting the disclaimer as a running head:

```
This product is sold "as is" without warranty to its use,
reliability, or workmanship. When you are using the product,
your use is at your own risk.
```

Or, you could add elements such as this contract signature line:

```
Sign each page of this contract:
```

_____

```
Lesson 7                                    page 7-1



LESSON 7

    This lesson addresses adjustable rate mortgages:

- Calculating increases
- Financial indexes for interest rate calculation

    According to a recent survey by Financial/Money World[1]
consumers do not understand the basis of mortgage payments.[2KC]
```

```
_____


1 Financial/Money World, June 8, 1988, "Sellers and Scammers".

2KC, 6/14/89, 4:58 AM Where's the magazine?  I want a quote.
```

Figure 7-2. The same running head, footnote,
and annotation when printed

Adding Running Heads

Adding a running head to your document is a simple task. First, you enter the running-head paragraph (ending with a paragraph mark). Then, you format the paragraph to mark it as a running head, by using the Format Running-head command. When you select this command, you identify:

- **The position of the running head on the page:** You use the Top, Bottom, or None settings in the *position* field. Top prints the running head as a "header" (at the top of the page), Bottom prints it as a "footer" (at the bottom of the page), and None, as we'll see later, is used to reformat an existing running head as a regular paragraph.

- **The pages on which the running head prints:** You use the *odd pages*, *even pages*, and *first page* fields. *Odd pages* or *even pages* cause Word to print the head only on a page that has an odd or even number. *First page* causes Word to print the head on the first page. Otherwise, the first page is printed without a running head. The *first page* field temporarily overrides the other two fields. For example, in Figure 7-3, the *odd pages* selection was set at No and the *first page* selection was set at Yes. Word has printed the head on the first (odd) page and the second (even) page but has skipped the third (odd) page.

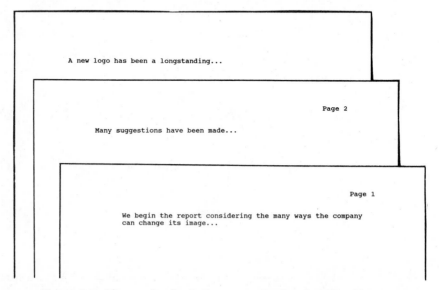

Figure 7-3. The result of printing a running head with *odd pages* set at No and *first page* set at Yes

In contrast, Figure 7-4 shows the result when *odd pages* is set at No and *first page* is set at No. Word has printed the head only on the second page.

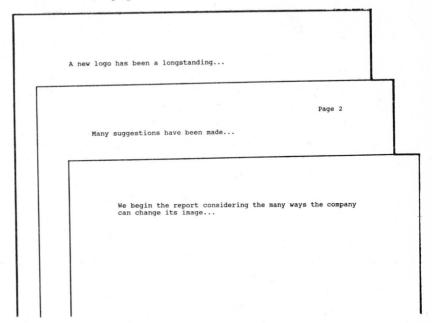

Figure 7-4. The result of printing a running head with *odd pages* set at No and *first page* set at No

The "pages" referred to are the pages designated by the page numbers in Word's status line. You don't have to have a page number in the running head to use the *odd pages*, *even pages*, and *first page* fields. You can change the page that starts printing in the running head by setting the Format Division Page-numbers command's *numbering* field to Starting and entering a value in the *at* field. The page-number change is reflected in the status line.

- **The alignment on the page:** You use the Left-margin or Edge-of-paper settings of the *alignment* field. Some printers (such as certain laser printers) prevent you from printing right up to the left edge of the paper. When you use Edge-of-paper alignment, take the capabilities of your printer into account. Figure 7-5 shows a head where the Format Paragraph *alignment* field was set at Right, and then the Format Running-head *alignment* field was set at Left-margin. In contrast, Figure 7-6 shows a head where the Format Paragraph *alignment* field is set at Right and the Format Running-head *alignment* field is set at Edge-of-paper.

Notice that the Edge-of-paper setting causes Word to print the page number past the document's right margin.

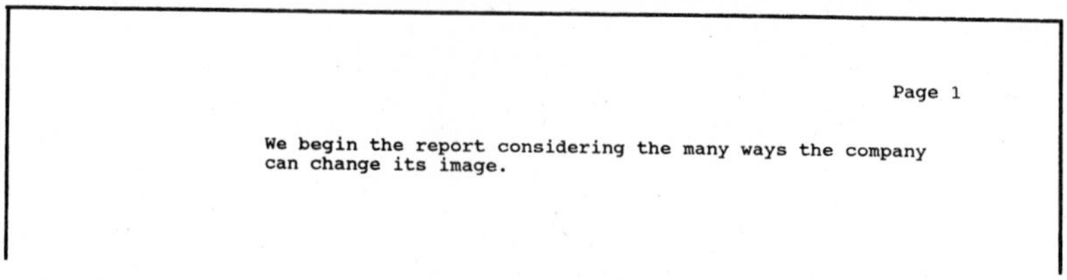

```
                                                    Page 1

       We begin the report considering the many ways the company
       can change its image.
```

Figure 7-5. The result of printing a running head with Right paragraph alignment and Left-margin running-head alignment

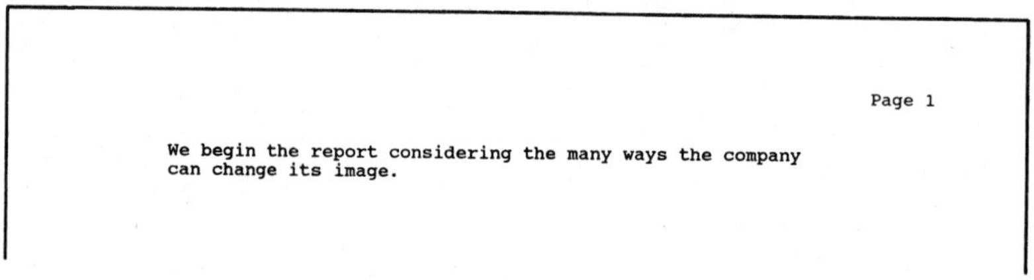

```
                                                    Page 1

     We begin the report considering the many ways the company
     can change its image.
```

Figure 7-6. The result of printing a running head with Right paragraph alignment and Edge-of-paper running-head alignment

Using the Format Running-head Command

To create a running head, follow these steps:

1. Enter the running-head text as one or more paragraphs. The running head for the first page of a document is typically entered at the top of the document. If you want a different running head on subsequent pages, enter a new running head before the page break between the first and second pages. If your document has more than one division, enter a running head on the first page of each new division.

Set margins large enough to hold running heads.

2. For each running-head paragraph, select **Format Division Mar**gins to ensure that the top and bottom margins are the appropriate size for the running head:

   - If your running head is very long, increase the size of the margin in which it will be printed.

   - If you want to print the running head at a measure other than 0.5" from the top or bottom of the page, enter a different value in the *running head position from top* or *from bottom* fields.

   Remember that margins are set by division. If you have more than one running head in a division, the margin settings for the division will affect all running heads in the division.

3. Select the paragraph(s) you want to format as a running head.

4. Select **F**ormat **R**unning-head. The Format Running-head menu appears.

5. In the *position* field, enter:

Top   to print the running head in the top margin

Bottom   to print the running head in the bottom margin

None   if you have highlighted an existing head and want to redefine it as a regular paragraph

6. In the *odd pages* field, enter **Y**es if you want the running head to print on odd-numbered pages. Enter **N**o if you do not want the running head to print on these pages.

7. In the *even pages* field, enter **Y**es if you want the running head to print on even-numbered pages. Enter **N**o to prevent the running head from printing on even pages.

8. In the *first page* field, enter **Y**es to have the running head print on the first page (which is the first page occurring after the running head; see note). Or, enter **N**o for the running head to skip the first page.

The "first page" referred to by the *first page* field is not necessarily the first page of the document. Rather, it refers to the first page on which Word will print the running head. If you have entered the running head at the top of a document, this field affects the first page of the document. If you have entered the running head before a page break, the first page is the page after the page break. This field overrides any No settings in the *odd pages* or *even pages* field.

9. In the *alignment* field, select:

Left-margin   to line up the left margin of the running head with the left margin of the body text

Edge-of-paper   to line up the left margin of the running head with the left edge of the paper

10. Press **Enter** or click the command name to return to your document.

Word formats the running head and displays a caret (ˆ) to the left of each line in the running head.

Using Speed Keys

Rather than use the Format Running-head command, you can use a speed key to format a paragraph as a running-head. When you use the speed key, all the current settings on the Format Running-head menu are used. You cannot change any of the settings when you use the speed key.

To use a speed key to format a running head:

1. Enter the paragraph(s) to format as a running head, as described above.

2. Select **Format Division Margins** for each paragraph to ensure that the top and bottom margins are the appropriate size for the running head, also as described above.

3. Select the paragraphs(s) you want to format as either a header or footer.

4. Use one of the following speed keys:

   Ctrl-F2   to format the paragraph(s) as a header
   Alt-F2   to format the paragraph(s) as a footer

Word formats the running head and displays a caret (^) to the left of each line in the running head.

Placing Running Heads

When you enter a paragraph to be formatted as a running head, pay special attention to where you place the paragraph in the document.

First and Subsequent Running Heads in Documents or Divisions

You should enter the first running head in a document as the first paragraph in the document. Place subsequent running heads before the page breaks of the first pages on which you want them to appear. Figure 7-7 illustrates where to place a running head that you want to appear on the second page of a document. Figure 7-8 shows the printed result. Even though the second running head has been placed before the first page break, it prints on the second page.

Once you enter a running head, Word prints the running head according to your specifications until it reaches the end of the division. Or, Word prints that running head until it encounters a new running head that has been formatted for the same position (top or bottom) and the same pages (odd, even, or first page).

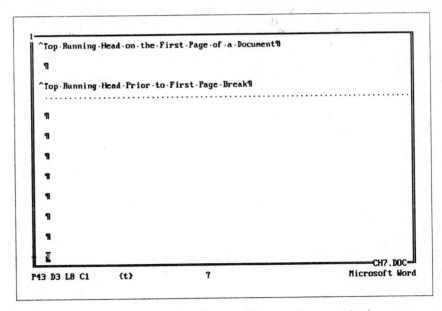

Figure 7-7. Running heads for the first and second pages of a document

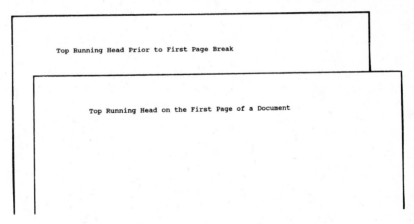

Figure 7-8. The printed result of the running heads in Figure 7-7

Running Heads in New Divisions

Enter a running head on the first page of each division

When you start a new division, the running head from the previous division is not carried over into the new division. To use the same running head, you must enter it again, on the first page of the new division. If you want to use a different running head for the new division, you must also enter the running head on the first page of the new division (not on the page before the division).

Affect on Margins

Word prints running heads in the top and bottom margins of your document. By default, Word prints them one-half inch from the top or bottom of the page. You can change this setting by using the Format Division Margins command. When you select this command, the 0.5″ default appears in the *running-head position from top* and *from bottom* fields. You can enter a new value.

When adusting a running head's print position, make sure you consider the length of the running head and the space that will remain between the running head and the body text. If you create a running head that is larger than the margin, Word calculates the space requirements and allocates less space to the body text.

Sometimes you may actually want the running head to spill over into the body of the document. Normally, Word would adjust the margin to accommodate the size of the running head. However, if you enter a minus sign (−) in the Format Division Margins *top* field, Word leaves the margin as is and allows the running-head text and the body text to overlap.

The Format Position command can be used to format graphics in running heads. See Chapter 19, "Electronic Publishing and Graphics," for more information about using this command.

Controlling Where Running Heads Are Printed

When you enter a running head, you specify whether the running head is to be printed on odd or even pages. But what if you want the running head to print for several pages, then stop for several pages, and then begin again? For example, you may want to insert some illustrations on blank pages rather than on pages with running heads.

To stop printing a running head in a document:

1. Enter the running head on the first page of the document or division.

2. Enter a null running head on the page prior to the page on which you do not want a running head. A null running head is a paragraph mark with no text, formatted as a regular running head.

3. Enter the running head from the first page on the page prior to the page on which you want the running head to begin again

Inserting Page Numbers in Running Heads

You can print consecutive page numbers in running heads, and you can format page numbers just like any other text. To enter a page number, type in the following either at the beginning of a line or with a space prior to the word, and then press F3:

page

Word encloses the word "page" in parentheses. When the pages are printed, (page) is replaced with consecutive page numbers.

To control the format of the page number, use the Format Division Page-numbers *number format* field to specify one of these possible options:

Options	Example	Format
1	1, 2, 3	Arabic
I	I, II, III	Roman uppercase
i	i, ii, iii	Roman lowercase
A	A, B, C	Alphabetic uppercase
a	a, b, c	Alphabetic lowercase

Using different formats and layouts, you can create some interesting page-number variations.

Checking and Changing Formatting

Once you have formatted your running head, you will want to check the formatting. There are two ways to check formatting.

To perform a thorough check, display the Format Running-head menu. While the menu is displayed, you can also make any necessary changes. Follow these steps:

1. Position the highlight in the running head you want to check. If you have more than one running head in a row, you cannot check the formatting of all the running heads at once, unless the formatting is the same for all the running heads. You can set the formatting of all running heads at once, however, as long as you want them all to have the same format. If you used newline characters to end one line in a running head and start another, you can place the highlight anywhere in the paragraph for which you want to check or change the formatting.

2. Select **F**ormat **R**unning-head.

3. Assuming you have highlighted only one paragraph, the current settings appear on the Format Running-head menu. Make any necessary changes. If you highlighted more than one paragraph,

the fields in the menu may be blank. Make any changes that you want to be applied to all the highlighted running-head paragraphs.

4. Press **Enter** or click the command name.

The positioning of the running head may change to reflect the new settings.

You can also get some indication of the current running-head settings by displaying the style bar. When the style bar is turned on, it appears on your screen at the far left of your document. The style codes in the style bar provide information about the format of the adjacent paragraph. (Styles and their codes are discussed in detail in Chapter 9, "Style Sheets.") The style code next to each running head reflects the position and page setting on the Format Running-head menu for that running head. These are the possible combinations:

Style code	*position* setting	Page setting
tf	Top	*first page*: Yes; *odd pages* and *even pages*: No
to	Top	*first page*: Yes or No; *odd pages*: Yes
te	Top	*first page*: Yes or No; *even pages*: Yes
t	Top	*first page*: Yes or No; *odd pages* and *even pages*: Yes
bf	Bottom	*first page*: Yes; *odd pages* and *even pages*: No
bo	Bottom	*first page*: Yes or No; *odd pages*: Yes
be	Bottom	*first page*: Yes or No; *even pages*: Yes
b	Bottom	*first page* Yes or No; *odd pages* and *even pages* Yes

Figure 7-9 shows how your screen looks when you display the style bar. In this figure, the running head is set to print at the top of each odd-numbered page. In the style bar, this style code appears (for top of the page on odd pages):

to

Here's how to turn the style bar on and off:

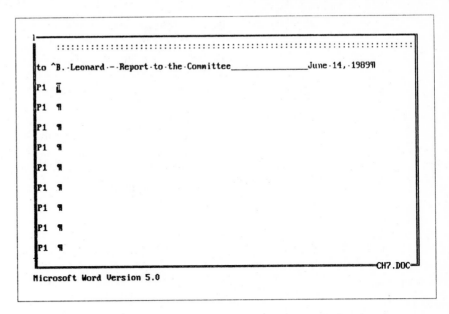

Figure 7-9. The style code to the right of the running head indicates that this running head will be printed at the top of odd-numbered pages

1. Select **O**ptions.
2. In the *show style bar* field, select **Y**es to make the style codes appear.
3. Press **Enter**.

To learn more about the style bar, read Chapter 9, "Style Sheets."

Deleting Running Heads

You can delete an entire running head or you can delete just the running-head formatting and keep the text.

To delete a running head (both text and formatting):

1. Select the running-head paragraph(s) you want to delete, including the paragraph mark. Note that you cannot highlight the caret (^) symbol.
2. Press **Del**.

The running-head paragraphs you selected are deleted and placed in the scrap area. If deleting the running head was a mistake, you can use Undo to put the running-head paragraph(s) back in the document.

To remove running-head formatting but keep the text, you use the Format Running-head command. Follow these steps:

1. If you are removing the running-head formatting for just one paragraph, place your highlight anywhere in the paragraph. If you are removing the formatting for several consecutive paragraphs, select at least a portion of all the paragraphs.

2. Select **F**ormat **R**unning-head. The Format Running-head menu appears.

3. In the *position* field, select **N**one.

4. Press **Enter** or click the command name.

The caret (ˆ) designating the running head disappears. The text is now regular Word text.

Creating Odd/Even Heads with Gutter and Mirror Margins

You can use odd and even running heads with gutter and mirror margins to produce a sophisticated "book-like" document. By using odd and even running heads, you can place a different running head on the left and right sides of pages that are to be printed on both sides. By using gutter margins, you can set a large margin that allows space for binding documents. By using mirror margins you can create margins on left-hand pages that are mirror images of those on right-hand pages, for a balanced appearance.

In this section, we will "build" a document by setting odd and even running heads, adding gutter margins, and then adding mirror margins. Because each setting affects a division, if you have more than one division in a document, you will need to set up the running heads and margins for each division.

Setting Odd and Even Running Heads

Figure 7-10 shows the screen with running heads set up for printing on odd and even pages. Notice that in the style bar, the style code *to* appears to the left of the running head that is formatted to print at the top of odd-numbered pages. Next, a few words represent the text of the document that will be entered. Then the style code *te* appears to the left of the running head that is formatted to print at the top of even-numbered pages. The second running head is positioned prior to the page break. Though you cannot tell it from the style codes, both running heads have the Format Running-head *first page* field set to Yes, in case we change our minds about which page (odd or even) is the first page.

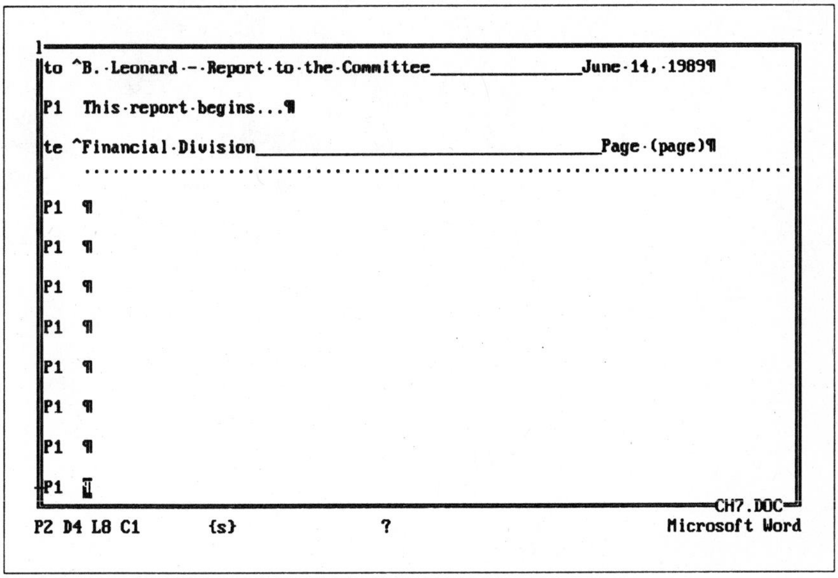

Figure 7-10. Running heads set for printing on odd and even pages

Use Print Preview to see your running heads

The Print Preview screen for the "document" in Figure 7-10 is shown in Figure 7-11. The odd-page running head appears on the right (page 1). The even-page running head appears on the left (page 2). The default Word margins are being used. If we print this document so that page 2 is printed on the back of page 1, page 4 is printed on the back of page 3, and so on, and then we bind the pages (or punch them for a three-ring binder), the center margin would appear smaller than the outside margins because a good portion of the center margin would be taken up by the binding. To even out these margins, we need to use gutter margins.

Adding Gutter Margins

Figure 7-12 shows the Print Preview screen after we have used the Format Division Margins *gutter margin* field to add a gutter margin of 0.5″. We have shortened each running head so that it fits into the smaller area now available for the text. The Print Preview screen

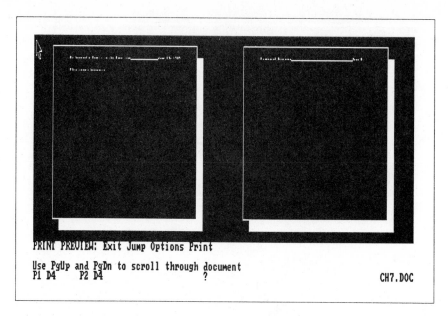

Figure 7-11. Print Preview of the odd and even running heads
from Figure 7-10

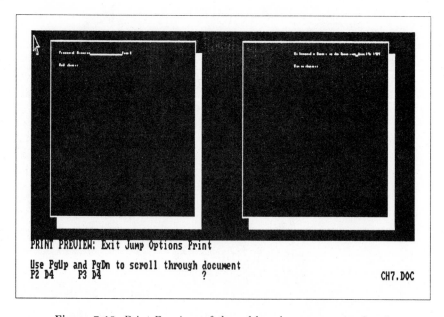

Figure 7-12. Print Preview of the odd and even running heads
with a gutter margin

shows page 2 and page 3 of the document (additional pages and text have been added for illustration). Notice that the gutter-margin measurement has been added to the right margin on the even-numbered page and to the left margin on the odd-numbered page. The result is a wide margin that allows for binding or three-hole punching.

Adding Mirror Margins

Mirror margins add another level of sophistication to your documents. They allow you to have unequal right and left margins, as shown in Figure 7-13. In this case, we used the Format Division Margins command and set the fields to the following values:

left margin	2.0"
right margin	0.5"
gutter margin	1.0"
mirror margins	Yes

We then shortened the running heads to fit within the 5-inch column now available.

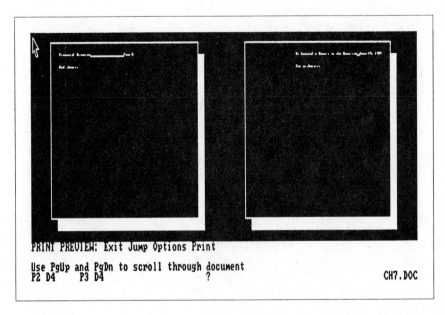

Figure 7-13. Print Preview of the odd and even running heads with mirror margins

Notice that the Format Division Margins settings were applied to the right-hand, odd-numbered page and were then "flipped" to create a "mirror image" on the left-hand, even-numbered page. As you can see, mirror margins combined with gutter margins allow you to create sophisticated layouts.

Exercise: Creating Running Heads

Follow these instructions to create a document with a simple header. You can practice using various settings with this header to develop a better understanding of how to produce documents with a more sophisticated look.

From a clear document screen, enter this line (substituting your name):

`Employee Report of (Your Name)                                    Page page`

With your cursor immediately after the second *page*, press F3. The text now looks like this:

`Employee Report of (Your Name)                                    Page (page)`

On a new line, enter the following to represent the text of your document:

`This report...`

On the next line, enter the following word and press F3:

`date`

The date appears. Press the Spacebar until your highlight is under the *P* of the word *Page* in the first line you typed and then type in:

`Page page`

Press F3 after the second word so that the page number will be substituted when you print the document. The paragraph looks like this:

`June 14, 1989                                              Page (page)`

Next, insert a manual page break by pressing Ctrl-Shift-Enter (press all three keys at once). A dotted line appears. Move your highlight below the line and enter the following to represent the body text on page 2:

And further...

Now you need to format the two headers you've created. With your highlight in the first header paragraph, select Format Running head. Enter these values:

position	Top
odd pages	Yes
even pages	No
first page	Yes
alignment	Left-margin

Press Enter. A caret (^) appears to the left of the running head.

Place your highlight in the second header paragraph. Select Format Running-head. Enter these values:

position	Top
odd pages	No
even pages	Yes
first page	Yes
alignment	Left-margin

Press Enter. A second caret appears.

When creating running heads in a document with more than one division, always remember when you enter page numbers in a running head to suppress any page numbers that might be set by the division. Select Format Division Page-numbers, enter No for the page numbers, and press Enter.

Print the document by selecting Print Printer. The headers will appear on the appropriate pages. Before you quit Word, save the document as HEAD.DOC.

Footnotes

A footnote is text that is tied to a reference mark in your document. You can enter as many footnotes in your document as you want. Typically, footnotes include information about source documents and clarifications or additional information. A reference mark is a symbol (typically a number or asterisk) inserted in the body of the text to indicate the availability of more information in the form of a footnote.

Formatting footnotes

Footnotes can be printed at the bottom of the page or at the end of a division. See Figure 7-14 for an example of reference marks with

```
     According to the President of our firm, John
Williams,  there are three ways to approach the problem[1]:

     1 Ignore it and hope it goes away
     2 Committee it to death
     3 Give it to our competitors  to fix

The third approach seems to be what is happening but with a
twist.  Our competitors  are turning the problem into a
strength.  Business Report[2] suggests that the market is
stronger than ever.
```

———————

```
1 Address at June 1, 1990 Directors Forum.
2 Business Report, "Where Did the Large Retailers Go?", June
30, 1990.
```

Figure 7-14. An example of reference marks in the text and footnotes at the bottom of the page

corresponding footnotes at the bottom of the page. Here, the reference marks have been superscripted with the Format Character command. As you can see, Word has printed a line and then printed the footnotes below the line. See Figure 7-15 for an example of reference marks with corresponding footnotes at the end of a division. Here, the "division" is only one page, but the footnotes still appear at the end of the division, just as they would if the division were multiple pages.

```
According to the President of our firm, John Williams,
there are three ways to approach the problem¹:

        1 Ignore it and hope it goes away
        2 Committee it to death
        3 Give it to our competitors to fix

The third approach seems to be what is happening but with a
twist.  Our competitors are turning the problem into a
strength.  Business Report² suggests that the market is
stronger than ever.

1 Address at June 1, 1990 Directors Forum.
2 Business Report, "Where Did the Large Retailers Go?", June
30, 1990.
```

Figure 7-15. An example of reference marks in the text and footnotes at the end of a division

More About Reference Marks

When you enter a footnote, you can identify what reference mark Word should use in the body of the document. You can have Word number the footnotes automatically, or you can use an asterisk or other symbol. Typically, reference marks are one or two characters. However, you can use up to 28 characters. (If you enter a multiple-character reference mark, keep in mind that the reference mark might wrap around at the end of the line.) For example, you can use these symbols as reference marks:

1, 2, 3, etc.

*

NOTE

(See below.)

(See notes at section end.)

If you use automatic numbering, Word updates the numbers throughout the document as you add new footnotes. If you assign a sequence of reference symbols yourself and then add a footnote, you will also need to update the sequence yourself.

If you use some automatic numbers and some manually entered reference marks, Word "counts" the manually entered reference marks in its numbering sequence. For example, suppose you have created three footnotes. The first is automatically numbered by Word, the second has an asterisk reference mark that you entered manually, and the third is automatically numbered by Word. These are the reference marks in your text (note that the manually entered * is counted in the automatic numbering scheme):

1

*

3

If you are using automatic numbering and you merge other documents with footnotes into your current document, Word renumbers all the footnotes across all the documents.

Creating Footnotes

Follow these steps to enter a footnote:

1. Place the highlight in the body of the text where you want to place the footnote reference mark.
2. Select **Format Footnote**.
3. In the *reference mark* field, carry out one of the following steps:
   - Leave the field blank to have Word automatically number the footnotes in the document (across divisions).
   - Enter the character(s) Word should use for the reference mark (such as an asterisk).
4. Press **Enter** or click the command name.

   The reference mark is inserted at the location of your highlight. You are taken to the end of the document, where the reference mark is displayed.

    If you set the Options *show layout* field to Yes, the footnote appears in a window instead of at the end of the division.
5. Enter the text of the footnote exactly as you want it to appear. The text can be several paragraphs and can include Word formatting.

After you have entered the text, the footnote is complete. You can now move back to the text of your document.

Jumping Between Reference Marks and Footnotes

Move between footnotes and reference marks with the Jump Footnote command

You use the Jump Footnote command to quickly move between footnotes and their reference marks. As the following table shows, Jump Footnote takes you to different places in your document depending on the position of the highlight when you select the command:

Highlight position	Jump Footnote goes to
Document text	Next reference mark
Reference mark	Footnote for that reference mark
Footnote	Reference mark for that footnote

Editing, Moving, and Deleting Footnotes

It is easy to edit, move, or delete a footnote. You can edit the footnote text or its reference mark. To edit a footnote, handle it like any other Word text:

1. To move to the footnote, carry out one of the following steps:
    *   Scroll to the end of the division to find the footnote you want.
    *   Highlight the footnote reference mark and select **Jump Footnote**.
2. Change the footnote text as desired.

    To edit the reference mark:

1. Highlight the reference mark you want to change.
2. Select **Format Footnote**.
    In the *reference mark* field, the symbol (footnote) appears.
3. Replace (footnote) with the characters you want to use for the reference mark.
4. Press **Enter** or click the command name.

Word immediately changes the reference mark in the text of your document and in the footnote area. If you are using automatic numbering, Word renumbers all the footnotes, if necessary.

To delete a footnote:

1. Highlight the reference mark.
2. Press **Del**.

The reference mark, along with the corresponding footnote, is deleted to the scrap area. If you are using automatic numbering, Word renumbers all the reference marks and reorders the footnotes, if necessary.

You cannot simply delete the footnote itself. Deleting the footnote text does not delete the reference mark, which will remain in your document.

If you accidentally delete a reference mark with the Del key, you can use the Undo command (or press Shift-F1) to restore both the reference mark and the footnote text. If the reference mark and footnote are no longer in the scrap area because you deleted something else before discovering your error, you will have to reenter the reference mark and footnote. In either case, if you are letting Word consecutively number footnotes, the numbering will be automatically updated.

To move a footnote reference mark:

1. Highlight the reference mark.
2. Press **Del** to delete the reference mark to the scrap area.
3. Place your highlight in the position where you want the reference mark to appear.
4. Press **Ins**.

The reference mark appears. If you are using automatic numbering, Word renumbers all the reference marks and reorders the footnotes, if necessary.

Exercise: Creating Footnotes

To practice creating footnotes, enter this text in a clear window:

The Product Report published earlier this year indicated
that we are far ahead of our competitors in terms of product
quality and delivery to the market place.

Place your highlight in the space following *Report*. Select Format Footnote. In the *reference mark* field, press Enter. Complete your footnote so that it looks like this:

1 The Product Report was published on July 6, 1990 by J.
Smith and the Product Research Department.

Select Jump Footnote to move back to the footnote reference mark. Select Format Character and then select Superscript in the *position* field. You can also press Alt-+ (Alt-X-+ if you have a style sheet attached to the document) to superscript the reference mark.

Print the document by selecting Print Printer. The location in which the footnote will be printed depends on the setting in the Format Division Layout *footnotes* field. (This field is covered in this chapter after the discussion of annotations.)

Keep the document on your screen so that you can add annotations (covered next).

Annotations

Annotations are a form of footnote that you use to store comments about a document. There is no limit to the number of annotations that you can make in a document. Like footnotes, annotations typically are numbered, but annotation reference marks usually also include the name or initials of the person making the comment.

Figure 7-16 shows an annotated page and its annotations. Footnotes are also included on this page to show how Word numbers annotations and footnotes. Notice that annotations and footnotes are numbered in sequence, but that annotations have names beside the numbers.

Use annotations for reviewer comments

Here's a situation in which annotations are typically used. Suppose you have written a document that you want Jan, Bill, and Fred to review and comment on. You pass a printed copy of the document to Jan for her comments; she passes it to Bill; and Bill passes it to Fred. Each person adds their comments, and you wind up with handwritten notes all over the document.

Now imagine the same scenario, but this time you pass a disk containing a copy of the document to Jan, another disk to Bill, and another disk to Fred, all at the same time. When they have finished their review and you receive their disks back, you can use a macro supplied with Word to combine all the annotations.

A macro is an automated way to perform a function. In this case, Microsoft has developed a macro to automate the process of combining annotations. Word's macros are held in files called glossaries. You do not have to be well-versed in the use of macros or glossaries to combine annotations. This chapter covers the function in detail.

For successful results, it is important to keep the annotations separated by reviewer. Make sure each reviewer consistently uses a unique identifier. That way, you will be able to trace comments back to the original source.

As you saw in Figure 7-16, Word always numbers annotations consecutively throughout the document (across divisions). You can-

According to the President of our firm, John Williams,[1joe2kim] there are three ways to approach the problem[3]:
[4dave5kim]

   1 Ignore it and hope it goes away
   2 Committee it to death
   3 Give it to our competitors[6joe] to fix

The third approach seems to be what is happening but with a twist. Our competitors[7joe] are turning the problem into a strength. Business Report[8] suggests that the market is stronger than ever.

1joe, 6/14/89, 10:56 AM Ask Williams for permission to use his name.
2kim, 6/15/89, 11:10 AM Joe, I asked him last week. It's okay.
3 Address at June 1, 1990 Directors Forum.
4dave, 6/14/89, 11:11 AM About naming the competitors. I don't like it. Too mud slingy.
5kim, 6/15/89, 11:12 AM I disagree with Dave. "Naming names" gets attention. This is a private document.
6joe, 6/14/89, 10:56 AM Should we name names here? Better effect?
7joe, 6/14/89, 10:57 AM Same comment as earlier. Search out this word if we "name names".
8 Business Report, "Where Did the Large Retailers Go?", June 30, 1990.

Figure 7-16. A printed document with both annotations and footnotes

not opt to mark annotations another way. Figure 7-16 also shows how Word can automatically add the date and time to annotations. You can choose to have the current system date and/or time entered after the annotation reference mark or you can omit the date and/or time.

Creating Annotations

Entering an annotation involves using the Format Annotation command. Here are the steps to follow:

1. Place the highlight in the location in which you want the annotation reference mark to appear.

2. Select **F**ormat **A**nnotation.

3. In the *mark* field, enter the unique characters that will be used in the annotation reference mark to identify your comments. Initials are typically used, but you can enter up to 28 characters. The more characters you enter, the more space is taken up by the annotation reference mark.

   If you have used Format Annotation before in this document, the last annotation reference mark you used appears in the *mark* field. Any characters you enter become the new default.

4. In the *insert date* field, select **Y**es if you want the date to be entered after the annotation reference mark in the annotation text. It will look like this:

   1KB, 6/5/89 Why not repeat this section at the end?

   The date is not included after the annotation reference mark that is embedded in the text of the document. Select **N**o if you don't want the system date to appear.

5. In the *insert time* field, select **Y**es if you want the time (with AM or PM) to be entered after the annotation reference mark in the annotation text. It will look like this:

   1KB, 6/5/89, 7:55 PM Why not repeat this section at the end?

   Select **N**o if you don't want the time to appear.

6. Press **Enter** or click the command name. The annotation reference mark is placed in the text of your document.

7. Your highlight appears at the end of the division, after a duplicate of the annotation mark. Enter the comment you want to make.

8. When you are done, you can scroll back up through the document or select **J**ump **A**nnotation to return to your annotation mark.

Editing, Moving, and Deleting Annotations

As with a footnote, you can edit, move, or delete an annotation. You edit the text of an annotation like any other Word text:

1. Move to the annotation using one of these methods:
   - Scroll to the end of the division.
   - Highlight the annotation reference mark and select Jump Annotation.
2. Change the text of the comment as desired.

To edit the reference mark:

1. Highlight the reference mark you want to change.
2. Select **Format Annotation**. In the *mark* field, the characters that identify your comments are displayed.
3. Enter the new characters to use for the annotation reference mark.
4. Press **Enter** or click the command name.

The annotation reference mark is changed both in the text and in the annotation area.

Use a Word macro to remove annotations

You can delete annotations one by one. Or, you can use a Word macro to automatically remove all annotations. To remove all annotations, see "Removing All Annotations" in this chapter. To delete annotations one at a time:

1. Highlight the annotation reference mark.
2. Press **Del**.

The reference mark, along with the corresponding annotation, is deleted to the scrap area. If necessary, Word updates the numbering sequence.

You cannot simply delete the annotation text at the end of the document. If you do, the annotation reference mark stays in place with no corresponding annotation text.

If you accidentally delete a reference mark with Del, use Undo (or press Shift-F1) to restore both the reference mark and the annotation text.

To move an annotation reference mark:

1. Highlight the entire annotation reference mark.

2. Press **Del** to delete the reference mark and the associated annotation to the scrap area.

3. Place your highlight in the position where you want the reference mark to appear.

4. Press **Ins**.

The annotation reference mark appears in its new position. If necessary, Word automatically renumbers and reorders the annotations.

Jumping Between Reference Marks and Annotations

The Jump Annotation command allows you to move quickly between annotation reference marks and annotation text. As the following table shows, Jump Annotation takes you to different places in your document depending on the position of the highlight when you select the command:

Highlight position	Jump Annotation goes to
Document text	Next annotation reference mark
Reference mark	Annotated text for that reference mark
Annotated text	Reference mark for that annotated text

Exercise: Creating Annotations

For an earlier exercise, you entered this text and created a footnote after the word *Report*:

The Product Report[1] published earlier this year indicated that we are far ahead of our competitors in terms of product quality and delivery to the market place.

1 The Product Report was published on July 6, 1990 by J. Smith and the Product Research Department.

Now you will add an annotation. Place your highlight after the period following *market place*. Select Format Annotation. Enter your initials as the annotation reference mark and press Enter. Type in the annotation text like this (your date and time will be different):

2kb, 6/14/89, 10:50 AM Find more facts on this.

Select Jump Annotation to go back to your annotation reference mark. Select Format Character and then select Superscript in the *position* field.

To print the footnotes and annotations at the end of the division, select Format Division Layout. In the *footnotes* field, select End.

Select the Print Printer command to print the document. Save the document as FOOTANN.DOC.

Consolidating and Removing Annotations

As already mentioned, if Jan, Bill, and Fred all enter annotations about your document in separate files, you will probably want to consolidate their comments onto one copy of the document. Word supplies macros to help you with this consolidation task. These particular macros do not remove the annotations. They simply copy them to another location. As you'll learn later, Word supplies another macro to remove annotations.

These are the macros supplied by Word:

- **ANNOT_MERGE.MAC:** Merges annotations from several files into one document. These files must contain documents that are identical except for unique annotation reference marks. This macro is in the MACRO.GLY file and is invoked by pressing Ctrl-A and then M.

- **ANNOT_COLLECT.MAC:** Puts together a list of annotations from several documents. The annotations from one document are listed, followed by the annotations from the next document, and so on. This macro is in the MACRO.GLY file and is invoked by pressing Ctrl-A and then M.

- **ANNOT_REMOVE.MAC:** Removes annotations from a file. This macro is in the MACRO.GLY file and is invoked by pressing Ctrl-A and then R.

These macros are described in detail in the following sections.

Consolidating Annotations

When you consolidate annotated documents, you merge several documents into one document. This is referred to as merging one or more "source" documents into a single "destination" document. Because the annotation marks are copied, you can use one annotated document as the destination document and then merge each individual source document into that destination document.

To use ANNOT_MERGE.MAC to merge annotations, follow these steps:

Save documents before merging annotations

1. Save any documents you want to keep. The merge process changes the document you use as a destination document. You may want to make a copy of the document under another name for future reference.

2. Clear all windows. If you have multiple windows open, select **Transfer Clear All**. If you are working with only one window, select **Transfer Clear**.

3. Load the glossary file MACRO.GLY. This glossary contains the ANNOT_MERGE.MAC macro. To load the glossary file:

    a. Select **Transfer Glossary Load**.

    b. Enter the drive and path (if necessary) and the file name MACRO.GLY, or press **F1** and select the file name from a list.

    c. Press **Enter**.

4. To run the ANNOT_MERGE.MAC macro, hold down **Ctrl** and press the **A** key. Release both keys and press **M**.

5. In the *filename* field, enter the name of the destination document (the document into which you will merge the source documents) and press **Enter**.

    It can't be stressed enough that all the documents whose annotations you want to merge must be EXACTLY alike. Otherwise, the merge process can't be carried out automatically.

6. This message appears:

    Do you want to be prompted for each source file (y/n)?

    Press **Y** and then **Enter**, to tell Word you want to be prompted for each source file name. The window splits (see Figure 7-17).

7. In the *filename* field, enter the name of the first source document (the document you are merging into the destination document). Press **Enter** to begin the merge.

    Word's macro finds the first annotation mark in the source document. It reads the sentence before the annotation mark and searches out that sentence in the destination document. When Word finds the sentence, it copies the annotation to the destination document. If it doesn't find an identical sentence, it gives you the opportunity to place your highlight in the destination document at the correct location for copying the annotation. You can see how keeping the documents identical except for annotation marks is important for speeding the merging process.

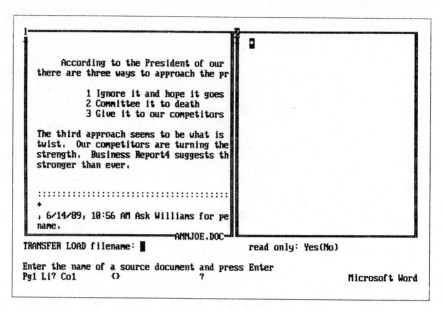

Figure 7-17. Entering the source file name during the annotation merging process

8. When Word has copied the annotations from the source document to the destination document, it automatically saves the destination document to protect the work done thus far.

9. After saving the destination document, Word prompts you to enter the name of another source document for merging into the destination document. Enter the name and press **Enter** or press **N** to end the merging process.

Listing Annotations

Instead of merging all annotations into one document, you may find it more helpful to have Word make a list of the annotations in each annotated document. Word lists the annotations by page. That way, the reviewer can see where most comments occur and can skim comments easily.

For the listing process, documents that have been individually annotated are called source documents. The document that will contain the list is called the destination document. You can create a new destination document during the process. In effect, the annotations from each source document are copied to the destination document. The original source documents are left unchanged.

There are two ways to enter the names of source documents from which you want to list the annotations:

- Enter the name of each source document while the macro is running. If you are compiling a list from several long documents, with this method you will find yourself spending some time in front of your computer waiting for the copying of annotations to be complete so that you can enter a new document name.

- Use the Library Document-retrieval Query command to create a list of documents. This allows you to select documents for the annotation list based on certain criteria. (See Chapter 14, "File Handling and Running Operating System Commands," for details on using the Library Document-retrieval Query command.)

To use ANNOT_COLLECT.MAC to make a list of the annotations by document, follow these steps:

1. Save any currently displayed documents that you want to keep.

2. Clear all the windows. If you have multiple windows open, select **Transfer Clear All**. If you are working with only one window, select **Transfer Clear**.

3. Load MACRO.GLY. The ANNOT_COLLECT.MAC macro is contained in this glossary. To load the MACRO.GLY file:

   a. Select **Transfer Glossary Load**.

   b. Enter the drive and path (if necessary) along with the file name MACRO.GLY.

   c. Press **Enter**.

4. To run the ANNOT_COLLECT.MAC macro, hold down **Ctrl** and press the **A** key. Release both keys and press **C**.

5. In the *filename* field, enter the name of the destination document. This is the file where the list of annotations will be stored. You can enter the name of a new or an existing document. Then press **Enter**. If the file does not exist, this message appears:

   `File does not exist. Enter Y to create or Esc to cancel.`

   Press **Y** to create the new file.

6. Word asks whether you want to enter the name of each source document (the alternative is to use the Library Document-retrieval Query command). Here are your options and the actions required:

   - Press **Y** to enter the name of each source document as the macro runs. You are then prompted for the name of the first source document. Enter the name and press **Enter**.

Word copies annotations from the source document to the destination document. Once that process is complete, you are asked to enter the name of the next source document. You can enter another name or press **N** to quit the process. Figure 7-18 shows the screen after a list has been created.

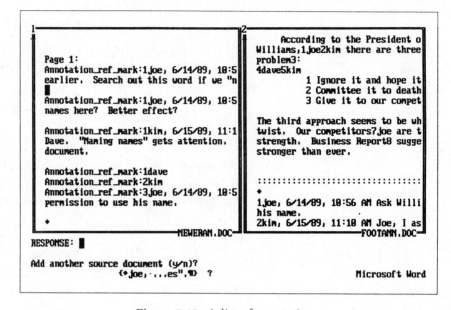

Figure 7-18. A list of annotations

- Press **N** to not enter source document names one by one. You are taken to the Library Document-retrieval Query screen (see Figure 7-19). Enter the criteria on the basis of which documents should be selected. (See Chapter 14, "Handling Files and Running DOS Commands," for details on how to enter criteria to get the result you want.) The documents are listed and then their annotations are collected together.

Once the annotations have been collected together, the destination document appears on your screen (see Figure 7-20).

Removing All Annotations

You may decide that you want to remove all annotations from a document. Perhaps you have reviewed all the comments and no longer require them. Or, perhaps the annotations are your own comments and you want to strip them out of the document. With the Word pro-

```
Path: C:\WORDB\BBDOC
 C:\WORDB\BBDOC\6STUFF.DOC            C:\WORDB\BBDOC\EX6-1.DOC
 C:\WORDB\BBDOC\ANNDAVE.DOC           C:\WORDB\BBDOC\EXPENSE.DOC
 C:\WORDB\BBDOC\ANNJOE.DOC            C:\WORDB\BBDOC\FOOTANN.DOC
 C:\WORDB\BBDOC\ANNKIM.DOC            C:\WORDB\BBDOC\FORM.DOC
 C:\WORDB\BBDOC\APPA.DOC              C:\WORDB\BBDOC\FUN.DOC
 C:\WORDB\BBDOC\APPB.DOC              C:\WORDB\BBDOC\HEAD.DOC
 C:\WORDB\BBDOC\APPC.DOC              C:\WORDB\BBDOC\JUNK.DOC
 C:\WORDB\BBDOC\BBOOKOUT.DOC          C:\WORDB\BBDOC\LASTANN.DOC
 C:\WORDB\BBDOC\BBTODO.DOC            C:\WORDB\BBDOC\LES7.DOC
 C:\WORDB\BBDOC\CH1.DOC               C:\WORDB\BBDOC\OLET.DOC
 C:\WORDB\BBDOC\CH2.DOC               C:\WORDB\BBDOC\PARAFORM.DOC
 C:\WORDB\BBDOC\CH3.DOC               C:\WORDB\BBDOC\PDREORG.DOC
 C:\WORDB\BBDOC\CH4.DOC               C:\WORDB\BBDOC\SAVETO.DOC
 C:\WORDB\BBDOC\CH5.DOC               C:\WORDB\BBDOC\SIDEBY.DOC

QUERY path: C:\WORDB\BBDOC
  author:
  operator:
  keywords:
  creation date:                     revision date:
  document text:
  case: Yes(No)                      marked files only: Yes(No)
Enter search information for source files; Press Enter when done
                                    ?                  Microsoft Word
```

Figure 7-19. The Library Document-retrieval Query screen

```
│
 Page 1:
     joe, 6/14/89, 10:57 AM Same comment as earlier.  Search
     out this word if we "name names".

     joe, 6/14/89, 10:56 AM Should we name names here?
     Better effect?

     kim, 6/15/89, 11:12 AM I disagree with Dave.  "Naming
     names" gets attention.  This is a private document.

     dave, 6/14/89, 11:11 AM About naming the competitors.
     I don't like it.  To mud slingy.

     kim, 6/15/89, 11:12 AM Joe, I asked him last week.
     It's okay.

     joe, 6/14/89, 10:56 AM Ask Williams for permission to
     use his name.

  ◆
                                              ═NEWERAN.DOC═
 Pg1 Li13 Co6      {m}           ?            Microsoft Word
```

Figure 7-20. The completed list of annotations

gram, Microsoft supplies the ANNOT_REMOVE.MAC macro to automate the process for you.

To remove annotations from a document:

1. If you are working on one or more documents, save them.

2. Clear all the windows. Select **Transfer Clear All** if you have multiple windows open. Select **Transfer Clear** if you are working with only one window.

3. The ANNOT_REMOVE.MAC macro is contained in the MACRO.GLY glossary. You must load this file before you can use the macro. To load the MACRO.GLY file:

   a. Select **Transfer Glossary Load**.

   b. Enter the drive and path (if necessary) along with the file name MACRO.GLY.

   c. Press **Enter**.

4. To run the ANNOT_REMOVE.MAC macro, hold down **Ctrl** and press the **A** key. Release both keys and press **R**.

5. The process of removing annotations begins. When the process is done, you are prompted to save the file under a new name. That way, if you want to refer back to the annotated version, you can. Enter the name under which you want to save the document and press **Enter**. The document is saved.

More About Footnotes and Annotations

Because footnotes and annotations are very similar, you carry out several procedures the same way for both of them. The following discussion applies equally to footnotes and annotations.

Formatting Footnotes and Annotations

*Superscript footnote
and annotation
reference marks*

Once you have created footnotes and annotations, you can format them any way you want them. Typically, you will want footnote and annotation reference marks to be superscripted. The formatting process is the same whether the reference mark is for a footnote or an annotation.

To superscript a reference mark:

1. Highlight the reference mark.

2. Select **Format Character**.

3. In the *position* field, select Superscript.

4. Press **Enter**.

How superscripted characters appear on your screen is a function of your monitor and your selection of graphics or text mode. For example, on a color monitor, superscripted characters usually appear in a different color.

To assign other formatting to the reference mark (such as a different font or size), use the process just described to set different options on the Format Character menu.

Word has two styles called Footnote and Annotation that you can use to automatically assign formatting to reference marks. See Chapter 9, "Style Sheets," for more information.

The formatting of footnote and annotation text is up to you and your imagination. You can format the text just as you would any other Word paragraph. Footnotes and annotations can be formatted using any of Word's formatting options, such as bold and italic type or different fonts. You can also include graphics.

Printing Footnotes and Annotations

Before printing footnotes or annotations, you need to identify where in the document you want them to be printed. You have two choices:

- At the end of a division (or at the end of the document if there is only one division in the document).
- On the same page as the footnote or annotation reference mark. If the footnote or annotation is too long to fit on that page, the text of the footnote or annotation is carried over to the next page.

Word's default is to place the footnotes or annotations on the same page as their reference marks.

To check or change the setting:

1. Select **Format Division Layout**.

2. Select one of these options in the *footnotes* field:

Same-page   to print the footnotes and annotations on the same page as the reference mark. If the footnote or annotation is too long, it is carried over to the next page.

End   to print the footnotes and annotations at the end of the division (or at the end of the document if there is only one division).

3. Press **Enter**.

Using the Footnote/Annotation Window

We've already discussed two ways to view a footnote or annotation:

- Scroll through your text until you reach the end of the division.
- Use Jump Footnote or Jump Annotation to go directly from a reference mark to its footnote or annotation.

View footnotes and annotations in a window of their own

A third way to see a footnote or annotation is through the footnote/annotation window. (You can have up to eight windows visible on your screen at once; see Chapter 11, "Windows.") The obvious benefit of using this window is that you do not have to go to the end of the division to see the footnote or annotation. You can "bring up" a footnote or annotation immediately from the page in the document where the reference mark resides.

Figure 7-21 shows an example of a footnote/annotation window (at the bottom of the screen). Notice that the window is separated from the text window by a dotted line. Further, the footnote and annotation displayed correspond to the reference mark visible in the document window.

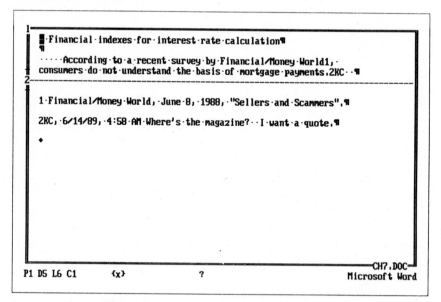

Figure 7-21. A footnote/annotation window

You can edit a footnote or annotation through the footnote/annotation window. If you have more footnotes or annotations than can be displayed in the window at one time, you can scroll the footnote/annotation window just like any other window.

You may use the Next Window (F1) key to move the highlight between the document window and the footnote/annotation window. Once a footnote/annotation window is open, you cannot split the document window until you close the footnote/annotation window. Footnote/annotation windows cannot be split. For more information about windows, see Chapter 11, "Windows."

Accessing the Footnote/Annotation Window with the Keyboard

Follow these steps to display the footnote/annotation window with the keyboard:

1. If you want to immediately view a specific footnote or annotation, make sure the reference mark for the footnote or annotation is on the screen.

2. Select **Window Split Footnote**.

3. Carry out one of these steps in the *at line* field:
   - Press **F1**. A highlight appears in the selection bar. Press the **Up Arrow** or **Down Arrow** key to place the highlight where you want the top of the footnote/annotation window to appear on your screen. The corresponding line number appears in the *at line* field.
   - Enter a line number in the *at line* field.

4. Press **Enter** or click the command name.

The footnote/annotation window opens. You can view and/or edit the text in the footnote/annotation window.

To close the window:

1. Make sure the footnote/annotation window is active. Press **F1** to move the highlight between the document and footnote/annotation windows. The window number in the upper-left corner of the screen is highlighted when that window is active.

2. Select **Window Close**.

3. Press **Enter** to close the footnote/annotation window.

You are returned to your document.

Accessing the Footnote/Annotation Window with a Mouse

To open the footnote/annotation window using a mouse, follow these steps:

1. Place the mouse highlight on the right border of the window at the position where you want the footnote/annotation window to appear.
2. Hold down the **Shift** key and press either mouse button.

The footnote/annotation window opens. You can now view and/or edit the text in the footnote/annotation window.

To close the window:

1. Place the mouse pointer on the right border of the footnote/annotation window.
2. Click both buttons.

Checking Your Spelling and Using the Thesaurus

When you use Word, a spelling checker and a thesaurus are literally at your finger tips. With Word's Spell program, you can look up the spelling of a single word, check the spelling of all the words in a selected part of a document, or check the entire document. With Word's Thesaurus program, you can make your writing more accurate and more interesting by choosing exactly the right words from lists of synonyms.

For those of you who enjoy statistics, the Spell program has 130,000 words in its main dictionary. The Thesaurus program has 15,000 root words and 220,000 synonyms. These comprehensive programs nearly eliminate the need to ever look up a spelling in a printed dictionary or a synonym in a printed thesaurus. Of course, the Spell dictionary is only for checking spelling. You cannot look up the meaning or pronunciation of words. And Word does not have a program that checks sentence structure and grammar. These functions are not typically part of any word-processing package. However, you can buy stand-alone products that perform these functions. See your computer dealer or a software store for more information.

Checking Your Spelling

Word's concept of spell checking can be a little confusing for the beginner. Word identifies words that are "misspelled" by checking each word in a document against the words in a built-in dictionary. Any word that is not in the dictionary is considered to be misspelled, including proper names and professional jargon, as well as actual misspellings. Word also identifies some plural words, words with unusual capitalization, and words with unusual punctuation (such as ;hi) as misspelled. In addition, Word points out strings of characters that are repeated. For example, it is not uncommon to accidentally repeat a word like *a* when you are writing, especially if you pause at the end of a line. The result is something like this:

I went to a a town in Maine.

Word notices this error and brings it to your attention.
When using Word's Spell program, you can:

- Check a single word at a time. You can select a word for checking whenever you think you may have misspelled it.
- Check a portion of a document. This is especially helpful when you add a new section to or edit a section in a document that you have already spell checked. Rather than spell check the entire document again, save yourself some time by selecting just the portion of the document that has changed and checking it for misspellings.
- Check an entire document. Word starts at the location of your highlight and moves through to the end of the document. Spell checking an entire document is typically the last task you perform before printing the document. It doesn't usually make sense to spell check the document before you edit it because you may introduce errors while editing. The best strategy is to finish developing the document and then spell check it.

Dictionaries

In one spell-check operation, Word may consult the main dictionary, a dictionary you have created for this type of document (called a user dictionary), and a dictionary you have created specifically for this document (called a document dictionary). You can change the contents of all these dictionaries at any time.

The spell-check process goes like this:

- Word always checks the main dictionary first.
- If Word can't find the word in the main dictionary, it consults the user and document dictionaries.
- If Word still can't find the word, it identifies the word as misspelled.

You do not have to create user and document dictionaries. However, if you do create them, you should be careful which types of words you add to each dictionary:

Dictionary	Add words used in
Main dictionary	All or most documents
User dictionary	Certain types of documents
Document dictionary	A single document only

The Main Dictionary

The main-dictionary file is called SPELL_AM.LEX. Some Word users always check their spelling with the main dictionary and because they do not create documents that contain special strings of characters, proper names, places, or jargon, they do not need to add words to this dictionary. If your documents contain any of these elements, you will probably want to add words to the main dictionary. These added words are stored, not in SPELL_AM.LEX, but in a separate file called UPDAT_AM.CMP. The UPDAT_AM.CMP file is stored in the WORD directory or on the Word program disk. If you are using a network, each workstation has its own UPDAT_AM.CMP file. The amount of storage space you have available on your system is the only limit on the number of words you can add to this file.

You add words during the regular spell-checking process. See "Spell Checking a Document" for information on how to add words to the main dictionary.

The User Dictionary

The user dictionary stores words that are common to a particular type of document. For example, suppose you are writing a series of proposals that include unusual acronyms and jargon. You don't want to enter the acronyms and jargon into the main dictionary because you will use them only in these proposals. Entering these words in the main dictionary could disrupt it by introducing terms that might cause Word to miss incorrect spellings. In addition, the larger the main dictionary, the longer the spell-checking process takes. You do not want to add a large number of words that will not be used in most documents. The solution here is to create a user dictionary.

Create a different user dictionary for each directory

You can add as many words as you like to a user dictionary, and the dictionary can be accessed by more than one document. You can have as many user dictionaries as you need, but you can use only one user dictionary at a time.

You can create a user dictionary during the spell-checking process and assign it any name. Word adds the extension .CMP to the name. See "Spell-Checking Options" in this chapter for information on creating and naming the user dictionary during a Word session. Once you have created the dictionary, you can add words to it during the spell-checking process. See "Spell Checking a Document" for information on how to add words to the user dictionary.

The Document Dictionary

You can also create a document dictionary during the spell-checking process. This dictionary is associated with the specific document you are spell checking. You cannot use this dictionary with other documents.

Create document dictionaries for special words

Under what circumstances would you want to create a document dictionary? Suppose, for example, that you have created a document in which you have used a special letter notation (such as :A:) that Word will identify as improper punctuation during the spell-checking process. Or, suppose you have used a proper name in this document that you are very unlikely to use in other documents—the proper name *Continu* is a good example. If you have used either the letter notation or the proper name often, you will want Word to skip it while spell checking the document. However, you won't want to add either to the main or user dictionary. The proper name, especially, could create problems because it could cause Word to miss an improper spelling of the word *Continue*.

When you create a document dictionary during the spell-checking process, Word names the dictionary with the same name as the document and adds the .CMP extension. The document dictionary is stored with the document. See "Spell Checking a Document" in this chapter for information on how to create and add words to a document dictionary.

Spell-Checking Options

You spell check your documents using the Library Spell command. Selecting this command brings up the menu shown in Figure 8-1.

As you can see, the Library Spell menu has an Options selection. Like the Options command on the main command menu and the Options selection on the Print menu, the Library Spell Options command is used to control how the function in question works. In this case, you use Options to control certain aspects of the spell-checking operation. Typically, you will want to set the Options fields before beginning a spell-checking session. The Library Spell Options menu is shown in Figure 8-2.

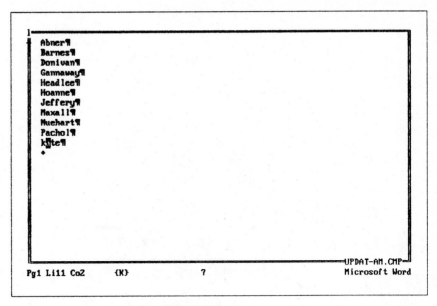

Figure 8-1. The Library Spell menu

The following table briefly describes the fields you can set:

Field	Use to
user dictionary	Create a user dictionary or enter the name of an existing user dictionary
lookup	Tell Word to perform a quick lookup by assuming that the first two letters of a word are correct or tell Word to check all letters
ignore all caps	Tell Word whether you want words in all capital letters to be spell checked
alternatives	Tell Word when you want it to suggest alternative spellings
check punctuation	Tell Word to examine punctuation or tell Word to ignore punctuation

Here is the procedure for setting the Options fields:

1. Make sure you are in a document containing at least one word that is not contained in the active dictionaries.

2. Select **Library Spell** or press **Alt-F6**. Word searches for an unrecognized word. When it finds one, the Library Spell menu appears.

3. Select **Options**.

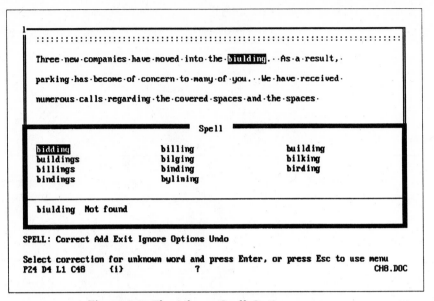

Figure 8-2. The Library Spell Options menu

4. Go to the *user dictionary* field to tell Word the name of the user dictionary you want to use. If you enter the name of a user dictionary that does not exist, Word creates a new user dictionary with that name. The name should comprise a maximum of eight characters. Word will add the .CMP extension.

   If you enter the name of a user dictionary that does exist, Word will use that dictionary in the spell-checking process. You can press **F1** from this field to see and select from a list of existing user dictionaries. If you want, you can switch user dictionaries in the middle of a spell-checking session.

5. Go to the *lookup* field and select one of the following:

   Quick   to speed the spell-checking process but decrease accuracy. Word will assume that the first two letters of each word are accurate. When Word suggests alternative word options, they will all begin with the first two letters of the selected word.

   Complete   to do a slower but more thorough spell check. Word will check every letter and may suggest alternate words. For example, Word will suggest *phone* as an alternative for *fone*. The Complete selection is the default.

6. Use the *ignore all caps* field to tell Word to ignore words that are all capital letters. You might want to use this option when you are spell checking a document that has a lot of acronyms, such as RSL, CTG, TGIF-CO., and others. Enter **Yes** to ignore all words that are all capital letters. Enter **No** to spell check them. No is the default.

7. Go to the *alternatives* field to identify when you want Word to suggest alternative words. Select one of these options:

   Automatic to have Word display the list of alternative spellings whenever it encounters a word that is not in a dictionary. This setting is the default.

   Manual to have Word display the alternative-spellings list only when you select the Correct option to correct the word identified as unknown. If your document includes many proper names or a lot of jargon that is not included in a dictionary, this setting can speed up the spell-checking process.

8. In the *check punctuation* field, identify whether or not you want Word to pay attention to the punctuation. Your options are **Yes** or **No**:

Word can find double periods and commas hidden in a document.

   - If you select **Yes**, Word will identify out-of-the-ordinary uses of punctuation. Word will bring to your attention any string of characters that contains these symbols:

     . , ; : ! ? @ # % & * + = _ 0-9

     Words like these are identified for you to correct or ignore:

     nine%
     myfile.doc
     :okay.
     no*
     one + one = two
     H2O
     house&lawn

   When Word encounters a string of characters like these, it displays one of the following two messages:

   `Improper punctuation`
   `Invalid character`

   Word's default is to check for punctuation.

- Select **No** if you don't want Word to check for instances of out-of-the-ordinary punctuation, such as those just described.

9. When you have set all the Library Spell Options fields the way you want them, press **Enter** or click the command name. If you are spell checking a document, you can then continue with the process.

Word saves the settings you make in this menu from session to session, until you change them.

Spell Checking a Document

As already mentioned, Word simply identifies the words in your document that are not in a dictionary. It is up to you to decide what you want to do with words that Word brings to your attention. These are your options:

- Select a spelling from a list of alternatives. This approach is popular with people who can't remember how to spell a word but can recognize the right spelling when they see it.
- Correct the spelling yourself. You can type in a new spelling (or a new word, for that matter). Word will immediately check the spelling of the new word you enter. You can tell Word to remember the correction and change all other occurrences of this word in this spell-checking session.
- Ignore the word (for example, you would ignore a proper name that is correctly spelled).
- Add the word to the main dictionary, to a user dictionary, or to the document dictionary. By using this option, you give Word the power to correctly identify often-used proper names, professional jargon, or other unusual character combinations. (You use this option to create document dictionaries.)

Word remembers your spelling corrections.

Word learns. Once you have corrected a word, Word automatically makes the same correction for that identical character string throughout the document. If you quit the spell-checking session (by using the Exit command on the Library Spell menu), Word maintains the word correction.

To spell check a document, follow these steps:

1. First you need to check that the path for the Spell-program files is correct. Select **Options** from the main command menu. In the

speller path field, if necessary enter the path and name of the main dictionary (SPELL_AM.LEX). Word will maintain this path until you change it. For example, this is the typical path for a hard-disk system:

```
C:\WORD\SPELL_AM.LEX
```

If the correct path is not entered in the *speller path* field, a message like this one is displayed when you try to use the Spell program:

```
Cannot find standard dictionary. Update speller path field
in Options menu
```

2. Make sure the document you want to spell check is in the active window. Press **F1** until the window number in the upper-left corner of the window you want is highlighted.

3. Save your document. Some users like to create an additional backup of the file under another name. You might want to take this precaution if you think you might want the original document at a later time.

4. If you want to spell check only a portion of the document, select the text before beginning the spell-checking process. You can select a single word or a block of text of any size. If you do not make a selection, Word will spell check the entire document from the location of your highlight to the end. To position your highlight at the beginning of the document, press **Ctrl-PgUp**.

5. To begin the spell-checking process, select Library **S**pell or press **Alt-F6**. If you have a two-floppy-disk system, you may be prompted to remove the Word Program disk and insert the Word Spell disk in its place.

   First, Word loads the dictionaries. If you specified a user dictionary through the Library Spell Options command, the dictionary is loaded, along with any document dictionary that you have created for the document and any custom word file you have added to the main dictionary. Word displays a message like this one as the dictionaries are loaded:

```
Loading dictionaries...
```

Once Word has loaded the dictionaries, it begins the spell-checking session. If you have set the Library Spell Options *check punctuation* field to **Y**es, Word checks punctuation as well.

You will see a message like this one:

Checking document...

Word displays the first word it doesn't recognize in the Spell window. Figure 8-3 shows an example of the Spell window.

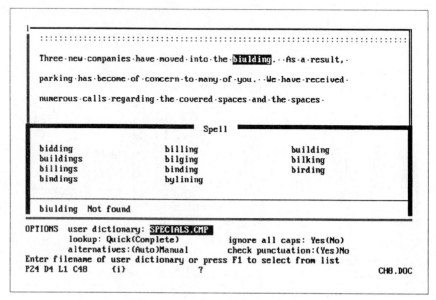

Figure 8-3. The Spell window

If you have set the Library Spell Options *alternatives* field to Auto, Word will suggest alternative spellings, if they are available. If they are not available, Word displays a message like this one:

No alternative words found

followed by this message:

Select correction for unknown word and press Enter,
or press Esc to use menu

6. You now have four choices: Select one of the suggested alternative words, correct the word, ignore the word and go on, or add the word to a dictionary and then proceed:

- To select an alternative spelling, highlight the spelling and press **Enter**. Or, you can point to the spelling and press the right mouse button. Word changes the spelling.

  You can use the Format revision-Marks command to mark each correction while spell checking. Just set the Format revision-Marks Options *add revision marks* field to Yes. When you complete spell checking, the misspelled words are marked with strike-through formatting. The corrections are underlined (unless you have specified another format in the *inserted text* field of Format revision-Marks Options). If you later decide to undo your corrections, you can select Format revision-Marks Undo-revisions to automatically remove strike-throughs and delete inserted text and restore the original spellings. To keep all the changes, you can select Format revision-Marks Remove-marks to implement the changes. For more information on using revision marks, see Chapter 10, "Revision Marks, Bookmarks, Cross-Referencing, and Hyphenation."

- To enter your own correction, select **C**orrect and enter the word. You can press **F1** to see alternative spellings of the word you have entered. To have Word correct future occurrences of the misspelling during this spell-checking session, select **Yes** in the *remember correction* field. Press **Enter** or point to the command name and click the left button. Word makes the correction. If Word doesn't recognize your entry, it displays a message like this one:

  `Word not in dictionary. Enter Y to confirm or N to retype`

  Enter **Y** to keep your spelling or **N** to reenter the word. You can also press **Esc** to leave the process and return to the Library Spell menu.

You can tell Word which words to ignore.

- Select **I**gnore to leave the word as it is and go on. Word skips the word and will ignore future occurrences of that exact string of characters during this spell-checking session. If you later return to this document and spell check it again, Word will once again identify this string of characters.

- Select **A**dd to add the word to a dictionary. Word displays the Add menu.

Select one of these options:

Standard   to add the word to the UPDAT_AM.CMP file associated with the main dictionary.

User   to add the word to the user dictionary identified in the Library Spell Options *user dictionary* field. If no user dictionary is identified, Word creates or adds to a user dictionary file called SPECIALS.CMP.

Document   to add the word to the document dictionary. The dictionary is created if it does not already exist. Word gives the dictionary the same name as the document and adds the extension .CMP.

To quickly add words to a dictionary, create a document containing nothing but a list of the words and then spell check that document, adding each word as Word identifies it.

7. Select **Undo** when you want to go back to the last word identified and have Word suggest alternative spellings. You can change the spelling or leave it as it is.

8. Select **Exit** to stop the spell-checking process and return to your document. Your highlight appears at the location of the last word checked so that you can see the word in context.

If you checked only a part of the document, you are returned to the document when that selection has been completely examined.

If you checked the entire document, Word asks whether you want to check the spelling again because you may have started the spell-checking process in the middle of a document. If you answer **Yes**, Word starts at the top of the document. If you answer **No**, the spell-checking process stops and you return to your document.

Once you return to your document, Word displays a message like the following one:

`24 words checked, 24 unknown`

summarizing the number of words checked and the number of unknown words identified.

You can undo all the changes made during a spell-checking session by using the Undo command from Word's main command menu immediately after exiting the spell-checking process. Just press Shift-F1—the speed key for the Undo command.

Editing or Deleting Words from a Dictionary

Delete unwanted words from your dictionaries

As you have seen, you add words to a dictionary through the regular spell-checking process. You can modify the dictionary by calling up the appropriate .CMP file and editing or deleting the words in the file. You should not use this method to add words to the file, or you might affect Word's ability to correctly process the spell check. Figure 8-4 shows an example of the main-dictionary's UPDAT-AM.CMP file. Notice that the words are in alphabetical order with capitalized words first. Each line ends with the paragraph mark.

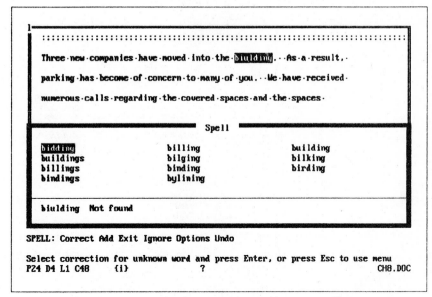

Figure 8-4. An UPDAT-AM.CMP dictionary file

To edit or delete words from a dictionary .CMP file, follow these steps:

1. Identify the .CMP file you want to change. A file of words you have added to the main dictionary is named UPDAT_AM.CMP. A document dictionary has the same name as the document but with the .CMP extension. A user dictionary has any name you have assigned with the .CMP extension.

2. Load the file by selecting **T**ransfer **L**oad. Enter the path if necessary, the file name, and the .CMP extension.

3. The file contents appear in your window. Press **Del** to delete text. Or, edit the file as necessary. If you don't know how to spell a word, there is no point in putting it in a dictionary. Consult a printed dictionary to make sure the words in your dictionaries are spelled correctly.

4. Once you have made all the necessary changes to the dictionary file, save the document. Select **T**ransfer **S**ave and press **Enter**.

You can create a new user dictionary from an old dictionary. This technique can be useful if you have already entered in one user dictionary many words that you need in another dictionary. Just load the dictionary, edit it, and save it under a new name with the .CMP extension.

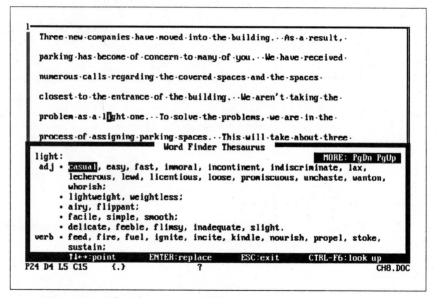

Figure 8-5. The Thesaurus window, showing synonyms for the word *light*

Using the Thesaurus

While writing a document, have you ever found yourself thinking "Now what's the word I need here?" or "I already used that word; is there another word I could use instead?" If you have, then Word's Thesaurus program will come in handy. With the Thesaurus, you can ask Word to display a list of words with similar meanings (synonyms) for the word you have selected. Once you start the process, you can continue to ask for synonyms for the words that Word suggests or for any word you enter.

Using the Thesaurus is easy. Once you try it, you will find many opportunities to put it to good use. The result is documents that are more interesting to read and that communicate more precisely.

When you use the Thesaurus, Word displays your Word document in one half of your screen and the Thesaurus suggestions in the other half. Figure 8-5 shows a typical Thesaurus window. Notice that in this window Word is suggesting synonyms for *light* used as a noun and as an adjective. Also notice that your options appear in the Thesaurus window and in the upper-right corner of the screen. The only option that is not displayed is the option to enter a new word.

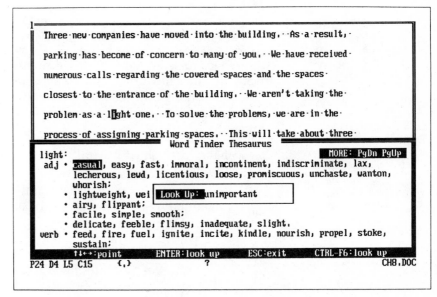

Figure 8-6. The screen displayed when Word does not recognize the word you have highlighted

From the Thesaurus window, you have these options:

- Scroll through the synonym list
- Use a synonym to look up another synonym
- Look at earlier lists
- Enter a word to look up
- Replace a word
- Exit the Thesaurus program

To use the Thesaurus, follow these steps.

1. Place the highlight anywhere in the word you want to look up in the Thesaurus. If you accidentally highlight more than one word, Word uses the first word in the look-up process. If you inadvertently highlight a space, Word looks up the word before the space.

2. Select **Library thEsaurus** or press **Ctrl-F6**. (If you are using a two-floppy-disk system, you may be prompted to remove the Word Program or document disk and insert the Thesaurus disk.)

   Word splits the screen and displays your document in half of the screen with the word you want looked up highlighted. The Thesaurus window with suggested words appears in the other half of the screen.

   If you have highlighted a word that Word does not recognize, you see a screen like the one shown in Figure 8-6.

   As you can see, Word presents a number of similarly spelled words in the Thesaurus window for your selection. If you have misspelled the word, select the correct spelling by highlighting it and pressing **Enter**. Or you can type in a new word and press **Enter**.

3. If you have highlighted a word that Word recognizes, you can carry out one of the following actions:

   How to navigate around the thesaurus

   - Scroll through the synonym list. If the word *MORE* appears in the upper-right corner of the screen, press **PgUp** or **PgDn** to scroll through the list. A new "page" of words appears. Or, if you have a mouse, point to the left border of the Thesaurus window and click the left button to scroll up or the right button to scroll down.

   - Use a synonym to look up another synonym. Use the **Arrow** keys to highlight the synonym and press **Ctrl-F6**. If you have a mouse, point to the synonym and click the left button and then point to *look up* and press the left button again. Word displays the Thesaurus window for the synonym.

   - Look at earlier lists. If you looked up synonyms for a new word by typing it in or selecting it from a list, you can go back to the original word by pressing **Ctrl-PgUp**. With a mouse, point to *last word* in the Thesaurus window and click the left button. Word displays the original list of synonyms. You can walk back through several layers of lists in this way.

- Enter a word to look up. To enter a word, simply type it in. A window like the one shown in Figure 8-7 appears. Press **Enter**, and Word looks up the word.

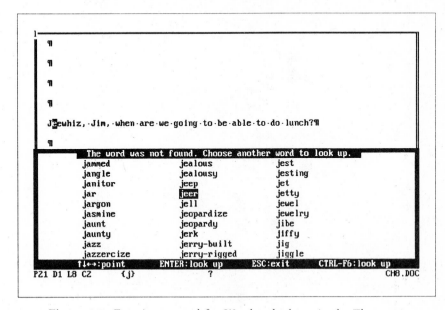

Figure 8-7. Entering a word for Word to look up in the Thesaurus

- Replace a word. From the list of synonyms in the Thesaurus window, highlight the synonym you want to use in your document. Press **Enter** or click the right mouse button. Word replaces the word you originally highlighted in your document with the synonym you have selected. The capitalization and punctuation used in the original word is used with the new word. Word returns you to your document.

- Exit the Thesaurus session. To leave the Thesaurus window without selecting a synonym, press **Esc** or click in the document window with any mouse button. Word returns you to your document. The word you highlighted before starting the Thesaurus session is still highlighted.

Exercise: Using the Spell and Thesaurus Programs

To try out Word's Spell and Thesaurus programs, enter the following paragraph in a clear window (be sure to type in the misspellings):

It takes one ounce of sunscreen to cover your body. If
you are in a higher alltitude, you woll need mure. Appli
sunscreen often and use a high SPF on the arees that need
extra protection.

Select Library Spell to spell check the document. Try selecting
words from those listed and also try typing in correct spellings for
practice.

Place your highlight on the word *cover*. Press Ctrl-F6 to use the
Theasurus. Press PgDn to go to the list of verbs Word displays. Make
a selection.

Style Sheets

Style sheets give you a way of capturing formatting for reuse. Any of Word's character, paragraph, or division formats can be stored in a style sheet as a "style." One style sheet can hold many styles. You give each style in the style sheet a unique key code that enables you to implement that style whenever you need it.

The advantages of using style sheets are many. First and foremost, style sheets can save keystrokes. If you frequently create the same kind of documents (such as memos or reports) and you want them all to look similar, you can store all the formatting that is common to that kind of document (such as margins and tab settings) in a style sheet. Then, you can call up the style sheet each time you create that particular type of document, instead of reentering all the formatting. Attaching a style sheet to a document and applying styles is a matter of a few keystrokes, whereas repeatedly setting up formatting —tabs, margins, page numbers, and the like—can take many keystrokes and consume much time. And entering the same formatting for every document can get tedious and frustrating.

Another important benefit of using style sheets is that you can then change the formatting easily. For example, suppose you have a report with Helvetica headings and Times Roman body text. You can change all the headings or all the body text to another font by simply editing the style in the style sheet. By using style sheets, you can "try out" different appearances without making manual changes because Word finds each occurrence of the style and changes it for you.

Word has a default style sheet, called NORMAL.STY, that is automatically attached to the documents you create. NORMAL.STY contains all of Word's default formatting settings. To use another style sheet, you simply attach it to the document. The formatting defined in the style sheet becomes available immediately. Then you can apply individual styles to different elements in your document by pressing Alt followed by the style's unique key code.

For example, Figure 9-1 shows the result of applying the paragraph styles defined in the attached style sheet to a document. The style sheet in question, called RESUME.STY, comes in the Word package. This style sheet allows you to format side-by-side paragraphs, which are quite time-consuming to set up manually. The fastest manual technique is to format one side-by-side paragraph and then copy the formatting by copying the paragraph mark to each desired location. This approach is cumbersome, however, and if you ever want to change the formatting, you have to recopy each paragraph mark. By using a style sheet that contains a side-by-side style, you can format a side-by-side paragraph with three keystrokes. If you want to change the formatting, you can change it once in the style sheet and Word will change all paragraphs to which that style has been applied. Take a look at Figure 9-1, which shows the formatted document in show-layout mode. Figure 9-2 shows the same document in regular mode.

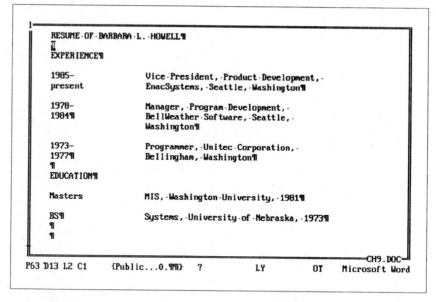

Figure 9-1. A document that has been formatted with styles from the RESUME.STY style sheet, shown in show-layout mode

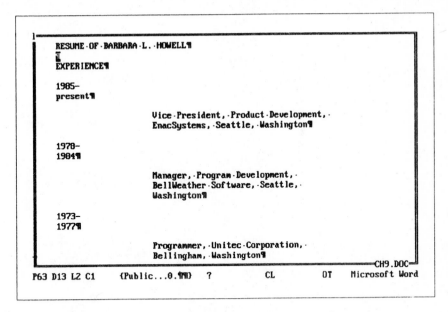

Figure 9-2. The same document shown in regular mode

Styles Versus Direct Formatting

You can override style-sheet formats by entering your own formatting directly in the document. For example, if the tab settings of a paragraph have been placed according to the formatting specified in the attached style sheet, you can override the tab settings by simply using the Format Tab Set command to specify new tab settings for the paragraph. You can later override the direct formatting by reapplying the style. The rule is: Word implements the formatting you applied most recently, whether you applied that formatting with a style or directly.

The Style Bar

When viewing your document, you can turn on the style bar to see the key codes of the styles in use. Figure 9-3 shows the document window with the style bar turned on. The key codes corresponding to particular styles appear in the left column. In this example, the key code 2L stands for two side-by-side left-aligned paragraphs. The key code 2R stands for two side-by-side right-aligned paragraphs. When you create styles, you should be careful to assign key codes that remind you of the function of the style.

When using style sheets, it's a good idea to keep the style bar turned on at all times. That way, you can see at a glance the styles for every paragraph in the document.

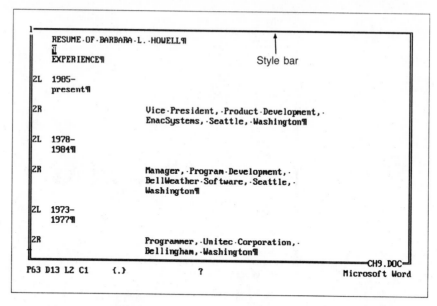

Figure 9-3. The document window with the style bar turned on

To turn the style bar on or off, follow these steps:

1. Select **O**ptions.
2. In the *show style bar* field, select **Y**es to display the style bar. Select **N**o to hide the style bar.

If you select Yes, Word displays the key codes for the styles applied to your document in style bar in the left column.

The Style Sheets Provided with Word

Word comes with a variety of style sheets already assembled for you. To decide which style sheet you want to use, all you need to do is view the style sheets to see the styles available and the key codes that will apply them. Then, you simply attach the selected style sheet and apply the styles to meet your requirements.

Word gives style sheets the extension .STY. To see the style sheets provided by Word, you use an operating-system command that displays a directory of the files on your disk. For example, from the DOS prompt, you would enter DIR, the path for the Word program files, and *.STY to see all the files that have .STY as their extension. Here is typical command entered at the DOS prompt:

```
DIR \WORD\*.STY
```

After you press Enter, a list like this one will appear:

```
SEMI.STY
FULL.STY
ACADEMIC.STY
APPEALS.STY
OUTLINE.STY
RESUME.STY
SAMPLE.STY
SIDEBY.STY
STATE.STY
```

This is a list of the style sheets Word gives you. You can see the contents of these style sheets by starting Word and using the Gallery commands.

Entering and Exiting the Gallery

When you select the Gallery command from the command menu, Word displays the styles in the currently attached style sheet. If you have not explicitly attached a different style sheet, Word displays the styles in its default style sheet, NORMAL.STY. However, NORMAL.STY is blank until you change a format or add one or more styles.

To look at the styles contained in the attached style sheet, follow these steps:

1. Select **G**allery. Word displays the contents of the attached style sheet. Figure 9-4 shows the Gallery window with the RESUME.STY style sheet displayed. (See the following section, "Reading Style Sheets," to learn how to decipher the style descriptions displayed in the Gallery window.)

2. You can scroll through the style sheet like any other document. One style is always highlighted to indicate that it is selected.

3. To view the contents of another style sheet from the Gallery menu, select **T**ransfer **L**oad. Enter the path and name of the style sheet or press **F1** to select from a list. Word displays the contents of the new style sheet, which is not attached to your document at this time.

```
 1    2L  Paragraph 1                            LEFT
          Courier (modern a) 12. Flush left, right indent 5.25", space before
          1 li. Place side by side.
 2    2R  Paragraph 2                            RIGHT
          Courier (modern a) 12. Flush left, Left indent 2", space before 1
          li. Place side by side.

                                                         ┌RESUME.STY┐
GALLERY: Copy Delete Exit Format Help
         Insert Name Print Transfer Undo
Select style or press Esc to use menu
                     {}                  ?               Microsoft Word
```

Figure 9-4. The RESUME.STY style sheet displayed
in the Gallery window

You can scroll through the contents of the new style sheet or load yet another style sheet for viewing. If you load another style sheet, again, the contents of that style sheet replace those of the previous one on your screen.

4. When you are done viewing the contents of a style sheet and want to return to your document, select **Exit**. If the style sheet in the window is different from the one attached to your document, Word displays this message:

   Enter Y to attach new style sheet, N to keep old one, or Esc to cancel

5. Press **Y** to attach the style sheet to your document, press **N** to keep the existing style sheet, or press **Esc** to go back to the Gallery window with the latest style sheet displayed.

Reading Style Sheets

Style sheets may seem confusing at first. In reality, style sheets are both easy to read and very informative. To read a style sheet, you need to know that a style consists of these primary components:

- The style name, which includes the number, key code, usage, variant, and a remark
- Formatting instructions that define the style

As an example, Figure 9-5 shows the styles contained in Word's RESUME.STY style sheet. Here, the key codes are 2L and 2R. Both styles are paragraph usages, with the variants distinguishing between the usages. The remarks describe the styles. The instructions that follow the style names include all formatting that is different from Word's default formatting.

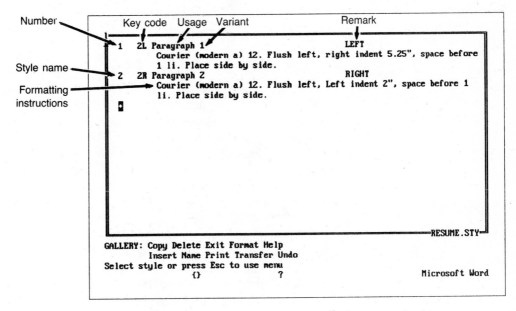

Figure 9-5. The styles in the RESUME.STY style sheet

The Style Number

Each style is assigned a consecutive number (1, 2, 3, and so on) to help you identify the various styles and to reflect the order in which the styles are listed in the style sheet. If you delete a style or add a style, all the subsequent styles in the style sheet are renumbered to reflect the new order.

The Key Code

After the number, Word displays the key code, which represents the keys you press in conjunction with the Alt key to apply the style to a character, paragraph, or division. If you have used the Options command to turn on the style bar, the key code appears in the style bar to remind you which style has been applied to which elements. However, Word does not use the key code to actually identify the style. Instead, Word uses the usage and variant to identify the style.

The Usage

For quick reference, print out your style sheet and keep it by your side. You can also use the Gallery command to view your styles, but sometimes it's easier to read a hard copy.

The usage identifies the kind of formatting that the style uses. These are the options:

- **Character:** Character styles can be applied to a single character or any amount of text. Formats for character styles are those controlled through the Format Character menu (such as bold, italics, and so forth).

- **Paragraph:** Paragraph styles control formats set through the Format Paragraph command and the font (such as Courier) defined for that element. Because Word includes font specifications in paragraph styles, you can set the font by paragraph. That way, it is easy to set different fonts for headings and body text, for example. Paragraph styles affect all the text from one paragraph mark up to and including the next paragraph mark. You can define a Standard Paragraph style to act as the default style when no other style is applied.

- **Division:** Division styles control the margins, page size, page-number position, type of page numbering, columns, position of running heads and footnotes, display of line numbers, and line-number position. You can enter different division styles for each new division and you can define a Standard Division to govern the division formatting when no other division style is applied. Word assigns the key code S/ for Standard Division (/ is the mathematical symbol for division).

The Variant

The variant appears after the usage. When you create a style, you select the variant. Figures 9-6 through 9-8 show the screen that appears when you press F1 to select from a list of the variants available for each of the three usages. Notice that some variant numbers are followed by key codes in parentheses. These variants are being used for the styles with those codes in the style sheet. If you use the variant without assigning a key code, the parentheses are still dis-

```
┌─────────────────────────────────────────────────────────────────────────┐
│  Page number          Line Number       Footnote ref       Summary Info  │
│  Line draw            Annotation ref     1  (ZZ)            2             │
│  3                    4                  5                  6             │
│  7                    8                  9                  10            │
│  11                   12                 13                 14            │
│  15                   16                 17                 18            │
│  19                   20                 21                 22            │
│  23                                                                       │
│                                                                           │
│                                                                           │
│                                                                           │
│                                                                           │
│                                                                           │
│                                                                           │
│                                                                           │
│                                                                           │
│  NAME key code: ZZ                  variant: Page number                  │
│       remark: test                                                        │
│  Enter variant or press F1 to select from list                           │
│              {}                        ?                  Microsoft Word   │
└─────────────────────────────────────────────────────────────────────────┘
```

Figure 9-6. The variant screen for character usage

```
┌─────────────────────────────────────────────────────────────────────────┐
│  Standard (P1)        Footnote          Running Head       Heading level 1│
│  Heading level 2      Heading level 3   Heading level 4    Heading level 5│
│  Heading level 6      Heading level 7   Index level 1      Index level 2  │
│  Index level 3        Index level 4     Table level 1      Table level 2  │
│  Table level 3        Table level 4     Annotation         1  (PR)        │
│  2  (PL)              3  (DD)           4  (P3)            5  (KN)         │
│  6                    7                 8  (31)            9              │
│  10 (ZL)              11                12                 13             │
│  14 (ZR)              15                16                 17             │
│  18                   19                20                 21             │
│  22                   23                24                 25             │
│  26                   27                28                 29             │
│  30                   31                32                 33             │
│  34                   35                36                 37             │
│  38                   39                40                 41             │
│  42                   43                44                 45             │
│  46                   47                48                 49             │
│  50                   51                52                 53             │
│  54                   55                                                  │
│                                                                           │
│  NAME key code: PL                  variant: Standard                     │
│       remark: formats left Para (SBS)                                     │
│  Enter variant or press F1 to select from list                           │
│              {}                        ?                  Microsoft Word   │
└─────────────────────────────────────────────────────────────────────────┘
```

Figure 9-7. The variant screen for paragraph usage

played but they are empty, to alert you to the fact that the variant has been used.

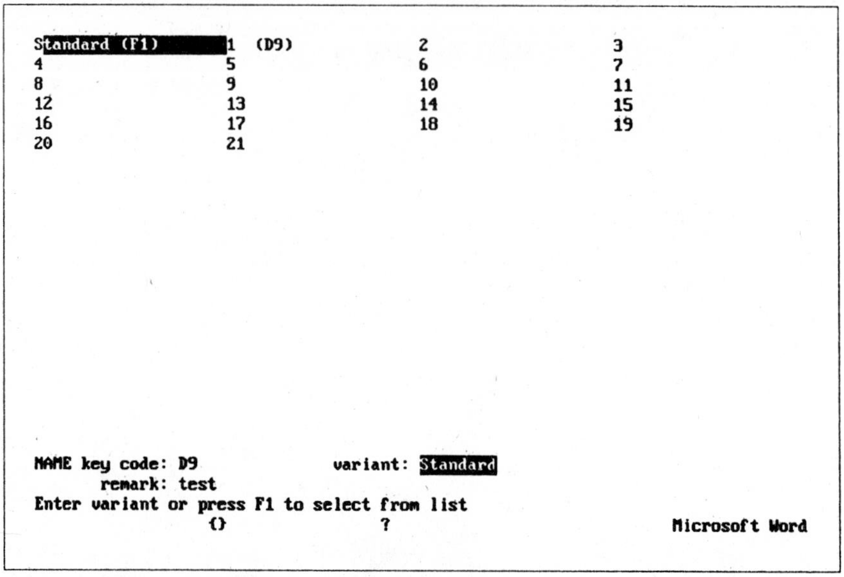

```
Standard (F1)        1   (D9)            2                3
4                    5                   6                7
8                    9                   10               11
12                   13                  14               15
16                   17                  18               19
20                   21




















NAME key code: D9            variant: Standard
     remark: test
Enter variant or press F1 to select from list
                 {}                      ?
                                                  Microsoft Word
```

Figure 9-8. The variant screen for division usage

As you can see from Figures 9-6 through 9-8, you can select from the variants shown in the following table when you create a style for a style sheet:

Usage	Variants
Character	Page number (font and size default)
	Footnote ref (reference number formatting default)
	Annotation ref (reference number formatting default)
	Line number (number formatting default)
	Summary Info (Library Document-retrieval summaries default)
	Line draw (character default)
	1 through 23 (not used as defaults; must be assigned to a style)
Paragraph	Standard (paragraph default)
	Footnote (text of footnote default)
	Annotation (text of annotation default)
	Running head (text of running head default)
	Heading levels 1 through 7 (default)
	Index levels 1 through 4 (default)
	Table levels 1 through 4 (default)

	1 through 55 (not used as defaults; must be assigned to a style)
Division	Standard (division default)
	1 through 21 (not used as defaults; must be assigned to a style)

Many of these styles have default definitions, and Word uses the default formatting unless you either change the formatting or apply a different style. If you change the defaults in the NORMAL.STY style sheet and retain the name NORMAL.STY, Word uses your specifications as the new defaults every time you create a new document.

Together, the usage and variant make up the usage-variant pair that Word stores along with your document to identify the style. It is important to bear in mind how Word uses these two elements of the style name, especially if you want to:

- Change the usage or variant of the style in use
- Switch style sheets
- Merge style sheets

The Remark

If you enter REMARKS in all capital letters, you can scan them quickly when looking for particular styles.

The remark, which is the final component of the style name, is a comment that identifies the use or content of the style. You should use this area to enter a remark that will be useful to you and others who may need to apply the style. You can enter up to 28 characters, or you can leave the remark area blank.

Formatting Instructions

Formatting instructions are sometimes called style descriptions. The description is entered in the style sheet by Word according to the formatting you define for the style. For example, if you look back at Figure 9-5, you'll notice that the formatting instructions for the first style indicate that the font is Courier (modern a) and that the type size is 12 points. (A point is a typographic measurement of character size; 1 inch equals 72 points.) The paragraph alignment is flush left. The right indent is 5.25 inches. The space before the paragraph is 1 line. The paragraph is a side-by-side paragraph. In all other respects, Word is to use the default paragraph formats.

Attaching Style Sheets

As already mentioned, when you attach a style sheet to a document, the default settings for paragraphs and divisions take affect unless you have applied another style to the elements of the document. If you have applied a style, Word matches the usage-variant information that is stored in the document with the usage-variant pair in the attached style sheet and formats the text according to the instructions for the style.

To attach an existing style sheet:

1. From the command menu, select **F**ormat **S**tylesheet **A**ttach.

2. Word displays the path and name of the currently attached style sheet. If you have not attached a different style sheet, Word's default style sheet, NORMAL.STY, is named.

3. Type in the path and name of the desired style sheet. Or, press **F1** to see a list of available style sheets and highlight the style sheet you want to attach.

4. Press **Enter** or click the command name to select the style sheet. The usage-variant pairs in the new style sheet are matched with those in the document. In cases where no match is found, Word applies the default style to the document.

When you save the document, Word remembers which style sheet was attached. When you later load the document, Word also loads the appropriate style sheet.

Exercise: Attaching and Viewing a Style Sheet

In this exercise, you will have an opportunity to attach and view a style sheet and then turn on the style bar.

Start with a blank document screen. You are going to attach the SEMI.STY style sheet provided with Word. Select Format Stylesheet Attach. In the Format Stylesheet Attach menu's only field, enter the path to SEMI.STY. (Unless you did something unusual when you set up Word, SEMI.STY should be on your Word program disk or in your WORD directory.) Press Enter.

To view the contents of the style sheet, select Gallery. Word displays the contents of SEMI.STY in the Gallery window. Scroll through the style sheet to see the various styles available. Locate the SP style, which is for standard paragraphs (see Figure 9-9).

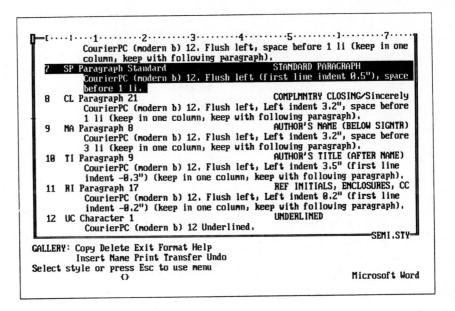

Figure 9-9. The SEMI.STY style sheet with the style for standard paragraphs highlighted

The number 7 is Word's number for this style (which is reassigned if you add, delete, or move styles). The letters SP are the style's key code. *Paragraph* is the usage and *Standard* is the variant. This style will be used as the default for all paragraphs to which you do not apply another style or formatting. The remark STANDARD PARAGRAPH completes the style name by describing the use of the style. The formatting instructions identify the font and the type size (12 points). The paragraph alignment is flush left with the first line indented one-half inch. There is a space before each paragraph that is the equivalent of one line.

Leave the Gallery menu now by selecting Exit. You are returned to your document window.

To turn on the style bar, select Options and in the *show style bar* field under Window Options, select Yes. Press Enter. Word displays the style bar to the left of your document. The letters SP appears in the style bar next to the diamond mark because Word applies the default standard paragraph style to every unformatted element in the document. Press Ctrl-Enter to enter a division break. The S/ style appears in the style bar next to the division mark to indicate that Word has applied the standard division style.

To try out the style sheet, enter the following text:

Thank you for taking the time to speak with me about our upcoming training program. I hope several of your staff will be able to attend.

To recap, we will be offering the training the week of June 30. There are only eight spaces available at this time. Please contact me as soon as possible to arrange your reservations.

Thank you again. I look forward to a profitable session with you and your staff.

Because the first line is automatically indented according to the style-sheet formatting instructions, you don't need to use the Tab key to create the indent. Word also inserts the blank line before each paragraph automatically.

Applying Styles

Once you have attached a style sheet to a document, you can apply the styles to the various elements. There are two ways to apply a style:

- Use the key code
- Use Format commands

If you know the key code, you can simply press Alt and the key code to apply a style. If you do not know the key code, you can use Format commands to select the key code from a list.

Applying Styles Using Key Codes

To apply a style using a key code:

Whenever possible, use key codes to apply styles. The Format Stylesheet command does the job, but more slowly.

1. Select the text you want to format. If you are using a division key code, place the highlight anywhere in the division. If you are using a paragraph key code, place the highlight anywhere in the paragraph. And if you are using a character key code, select all the characters you want to format.

2. Hold down **Alt** and press the key code. If you are setting the style for a single character, you will need to press the key code twice (for example, you might press **Alt-AA** and then **AA** again).

If you press a key code that does not exist, you see the following message:

`Key code does not exist. See style sheet for valid key codes`

Try pressing the key code again or select **G**allery to identify the correct key code.

When you have applied the style, Word immediately formats the text according to the style you have indicated and stores the appropriate usage-variant pair in the document. If you have turned on the style bar, the style's key code appears in the left column.

Applying Styles with Format Commands

To apply a style with Format commands:

1. Select the text you want to format. To format a division, place the highlight anywhere in the division. To format a paragraph, place the highlight anywhere in the paragraph. To format a character or string of characters, highlight the single character or select the string of characters you want to format.
2. Select **F**ormat **S**tylesheet.
3. Select **C**haracter, **P**aragraph, or **D**ivision depending on the usage of style you want to apply.
4. Word suggests the usage and variant you might want to use. Press **Enter** to select this usage and variant or press **F1** to see a list of styles. Word displays the available key codes with their usage, variants, and the beginning of their remarks (in parentheses). Figure 9-10 shows an example list. Select the style you want to apply by highlighting it and then pressing **Enter** or clicking the command name.

Word immediately applies the format defined for the style to the selected text and attaches the usage-variant pair to the document. If you have turned on the style bar, Word also displays the key code of the style.

Turning Off Styles

Occasionally, you may enter the wrong style. Don't panic: Styles are easy to change. Simply position your highlight or select the text you

```
P1 Paragraph Standard (manuscript form) 2L Paragraph 10 (LEFT)
2R Paragraph 14 (RIGHT)                  PR Paragraph 1 (formats right para (SB)
PL Paragraph 2 (formats left Para (SBS) KM Paragraph 5
DD Paragraph 3                           P3 Paragraph 4
31 Paragraph 8




FORMAT STYLESHEET PARAGRAPH: Paragraph Standard

Enter paragraph style variant or press F1 to select from list
P17 D3 L18 C12    {x}              ?                Microsoft Word
```

Figure 9-10. A list of styles that have been defined for the paragraph usage

want to reformat and apply another style.

Alternatively, you can change the text back to the standard (default) format. Follow these steps:

If you have defined a Standard Paragraph style, it becomes the default to which other paragraph styles revert when you press Alt-X-P.

1. Place the highlight anywhere in a division or paragraph, or select the character or characters whose format you want to change.

2. To remove a paragraph style, press **Alt-X-P**. To remove a character style that has been applied to more than one character, press **Alt-X-Spacebar**. To remove a character style that has been applied to one character only, press **Alt-X-Spacebar-Spacebar**.

The text reverts to the style identified as "standard."

Exercise: Working with Styles

In this example, you will apply several styles and then turn off a style. Your document has the SEMI.STY style sheet attached. The text looks like this:

```
Thank you for taking the time to speak with me about
our upcoming training program. I hope several of your staff
will be able to attend.
```

To recap, we will be offering the training the week of June 30. There are only eight spaces available at this time. Please contact me as soon as possible to arrange your reservations.

Thank you again. I look forward to a profitable session with you and your staff.

With your highlight on the *T* of *Thank you*, press Enter to create a new paragraph at the beginning of the document. Apply the RA style to the new paragraph by pressing Alt-RA. Your highlight moves to a left indent of 3.2". Type in the following return address. Because the style is formatted with a space before paragraphs, end each line of the address except the last with a newline character (press Shift-Enter). Complete the last line by pressing Enter. (If you press Enter to end each line, Word will put a blank line before each line of the return address.)

Ms. Carolyn Johnson
Elite Press
430 33rd Avenue
Pittsburgh, PA 15222

You may notice that when you end the return address with a paragraph mark, Word uses the RA paragraph style (not the default SP style) for the next paragraph. Now, enter the salutation with the SA style applied. Press Alt-SA. Word replaces the RA key code in the style bar with SA. Enter:

Dear Carolyn:

Go to the end of the document and press Enter to create a new paragraph for the closing. Press Alt-CL and then type in:

Sincerely,

Word displays the CL key code in the style bar. Try turning off the style. With your highlight in the *Sincerely,* paragraph, press Alt-X-P. Word displays the SP key code (for Standard Paragraph) and applies standard-paragraph formatting. Restore the closing formatting by pressing Alt-CL.

Your document now looks like this:

```
                                        Ms. Carolyn Johnson
                                        Elite Press
                                        430 33rd Avenue
                                        Pittsburgh, PA 15222

        Dear Carolyn:

              Thank you for taking the time to speak with me about
        our upcoming training program. I hope several of your staff
        will be able to attend.

              To recap, we will be offering the training the week of
        June 30. There are only eight spaces available at this time.
        Please contact me as soon as possible to arrange your
        reservations.

              Thank you again. I look forward to a profitable session
        with you and your staff.

        Sincerely,
```

Saving Style Sheets

It is important to save the changes you make to your style sheets. Even though changes and additions you have made to a style sheet may be reflected in the formatting of the document currently on your screen, the style sheet stored on your disk does not include those changes until you use the Gallery Transfer Save command to save the style sheet. If you have changed but not saved the style sheet when you use Transfer Clear All or Quit, this message appears:

```
Enter Y to save changes to style sheet, N to lose changes, or Esc
to cancel
```

Enter Y to save the changes. If you select N, the changes you have made since you last used Gallery Transfer Save are lost. Pressing Esc allows you to go back to the document.

To create a new style sheet quickly, simply edit the current one and save it under a new name.

When you use Gallery Transfer Save, you can save the style sheet under the same name or under a new name. Use the same name when you want to change an existing style sheet. Use a new name when you want to create a new style sheet or when you want to replace the contents of an existing style sheet with that name.

To use Gallery Transfer Save, follow these steps:

1. Make sure the style sheet you want to save is displayed in the Gallery window.

2. Select **Transfer S**ave from the Gallery menu.

3. In the *style sheet name* field, enter the path and name of the style sheet you want to save. These are the options:

   - If you accept the name Word displays in the field, any changes you have made to the style sheet will be saved in the current style sheet.

   - If you enter the path and name of a style sheet stored on disk, Word displays this message:

     `File already exists. Enter Y to replace or Esc to cancel`

     Press **Y** to replace the style sheet.

   - If you enter the name of a style sheet that does not exist, Word creates a new style sheet.

4. After you have entered a name, press **Enter** or click the command name to save the style sheet.

 In network environments, style sheets may be read only, meaning that you cannot save changes under the original style-sheet name. Because style sheets can be shared on a network, the read-only status is often used to prevent anyone from changing the style sheet and making it produce unexpected results for other users. If you are working on a network and the *style sheet name* field is blank when you select Transfer Save from the Gallery menu, the style sheet is probably read only. If you don't want to lose your changes, you will have to save the edited style sheet under a new name.

Loading Style Sheets

You can load a style sheet without attaching it to your document. This allows you to edit the style sheet and save the changes even when you have another style sheet attached to the document. This feature is especially useful when you want to copy or move styles from one style sheet to another.

To load a style sheet:

1. Select **Gallery Transfer Load**.

2. Enter the path and name of the style sheet in the *style sheet name* field or press **F1** to select a style sheet from a list.

3. Press **Enter** or click the command name.

4. If the document you are working on has a style sheet and you have made changes to that style sheet, Word displays this message before loading the new style sheet:

   ```
   Enter Y to save changes to style sheet, N to lose changes, or
   Esc to cancel
   ```

   Press **Y** to save the existing style sheet, **N** to lose the changes you have made, or **Esc** to return to the Gallery window.

5. Once you've taken care of any existing style sheet, Word loads the new style sheet into the window. When you want to leave the Gallery Window, select **Exit**. This message appears:

   ```
   Enter Y to attach new style sheet, N to keep old one, or Esc
   to cancel
   ```

   Press **Y** to attach the style sheet in the Gallery window to your document, **N** to keep the style sheet that is already attached to the document, or **Esc** to cancel the Exit command.

 If you are working on a network and try to load a style sheet, Word may display an *in use* message and prevent you from loading the style sheet. This happens if a style sheet with read/write access is already being used by another person. (If shared style sheets are made read only, this situation does not arise.) Many network users like to keep their style sheets on their own workstations to avoid the possibility that they may not be able to access a style sheet when they need it and so that they can edit style sheets to meet the requirements of their documents.

Creating New Style Sheets

The easiest way to create a new style sheet is to modify a style sheet that already exists. You modify the style sheet by deleting, moving, or copying existing styles. Or, you can create new styles. Then you simply save the style sheet under the new name.

Here are the steps:

1. Start by identifying the existing style sheet that is closest to the style sheet you want to create. This will reduce the amount of editing you will have to do to the styles in the style sheet. If you are unsure which style sheet to use, load various style-sheet files and view their contents by using the Gallery commands (see "Entering and Exiting Gallery" in this chapter).

2. Attach the style sheet you want to use to your document by selecting **F**ormat **S**tylesheet **A**ttach. (See "Attaching a Style Sheet" in this chapter for more information.) Or, use **G**allery **T**ransfer **L**oad to load a new style sheet without attaching it to the current document.

3. Delete, move, or copy existing styles or create new styles. (See the appropriate sections in this chapter for details on how to perform these tasks.)

4. To save the style sheet under the new name, select **T**ransfer **S**ave.

5. The path and name of the style sheet you have edited appears. Since you are creating a new style sheet, enter the path and the new style sheet name in the *style sheet name* field. Do not save the style sheet under its old name or the contents of the new style sheet will replace those of the old.

6. Press **Enter** or click the command area.

Word creates the new style sheet.

Editing Styles

Editing styles lets you change the format of a document without actually touching the document itself. When you edit a style, the formatting in the document changes automatically wherever that style occurs.

Deleting Styles

You might want to delete a style to return all the text to which the style has been applied to standard (default) formatting. Or, you might want to delete a style that is no longer used, simply to "clean up" the style sheet.

You can delete a style to the scrap area just as you can delete text. When you delete a style that has been used in a document, Word displays an asterisk in the style bar in place of the key code and replaces the style with standard formatting.

Before you delete a style, make sure you no longer need it for any of your documents, not just the document on your screen. Just in case you change your mind about the deletion, it is always a good idea to make a backup copy of the style sheet before you delete styles. Rename the style sheet to avoid confusion. That way, if you decide later that you want to use the style after all, you save time and effort by copying it to a new style sheet, instead of having to re-create it.

To delete a style:

If you delete a style and then realize you have made a mistake, check the scrap area to see if your style is still stored there. If it is, redisplay the style sheet, position your highlight, and press Ins to restore the style.

1. Make sure the style sheet from which you want to delete the style is available.

2. Display the style sheet in the Gallery window by selecting **Gallery**.

3. Highlight the style you want to delete.

4. Press **Del** or select **Delete** from the Gallery menu.

5. The style is immediately deleted. Select **Transfer Save** from the Gallery menu to save the changes to the style sheet.

If the deleted style was used in the current document, when you return to the document window, you will notice that Word has replaced the style's key code with an asterisk and has returned the text to which the style was formerly applied to standard formatting.

Moving Styles

You can move a style to a different spot on the style sheet. Or, you can move a style to a different style sheet (in effect, deleting it from one style sheet and inserting it in another). You can use the keyboard to move a style both within and between style sheets. You can use a mouse to move a style within but not between style sheets.

Moving Styles with the Keyboard

To move a style with the keyboard:

1. Make sure the style sheet you want to modify is available.

2. Display the style sheet in the Gallery window by selecting **Gallery**.

3. Highlight the style you want to move.

4. To remove the style from the style sheet and place it in the scrap area, press **Del** or select **Delete** from the Gallery menu.

5. (Complete this step if you want to move the style to another style sheet. To move the style elsewhere within the same style sheet, continue with the next step.) Select **Transfer Load**. Enter the path and name of the style sheet to which you want to move the style. Press **Enter**. Because you deleted a style from the first style sheet, this message appears:

> Enter Y to save changes to style sheet, N to lose changes, or Esc to cancel

Press **Y** to save the change (the deletion). The first style sheet is saved and then Word displays the style sheet you requested in the Transfer Load *style sheet name* field.

6. Place your highlight on the style above which you want the style inserted.

7. Press **Ins**.

8. Word inserts the style above the style that was highlighted. Use **T**ransfer **S**ave from the Gallery menu to save the changes to the style sheet.

Moving Styles with a Mouse

You can use a mouse to move a style within a style sheet without using the scrap area. (To move a style between two style sheets, follow the instructions in "Moving Styles with the Keyboard," earlier in this chapter.)

Here are the steps for moving a style with a mouse:

1. Make sure the style sheet you want to modify is available.

2. Display the style sheet in the Gallery window by selecting **G**allery.

3. Scroll through the style sheet using the scroll bar. Point to the style you want to move and click to highlight the style.

4. Point to the style above which you want to position the highlighted style.

5. Hold down **Ctrl** and click the left button.

6. The style is inserted above the style where the pointer rested. Use **T**ransfer **S**ave from the Gallery menu to save the changes to the style sheet.

Copying Styles

If you want to create a new style that is similar to an existing style, save time by copying the style and editing it. When you copy a style, you must change it before leaving the style sheet because Word does not allow you to have two identical styles in a style sheet.

You can copy a style within a style sheet using either the keyboard or a mouse. You can copy a style between two style sheets only with the keyboard.

Copying Styles with the Keyboard

To copy a style with the keyboard:

1. Make sure the style sheet you want to modify is available.
2. Display the style sheet in the Gallery window by selecting Gallery.
3. Highlight the style you want to copy.
4. Select **C**opy or press **Alt-F3**. The style is copied to scrap. You can see the usage and variant in the scrap area.
5. (Skip this step if you are copying within a style sheet. Complete this step only if you want to copy the style to another style sheet.) Select **T**ransfer **L**oad. Enter the path and name of the style sheet to which you want to copy the style. Press **Enter**.
6. Place your highlight on the style above which you want Word to copy the style.
7. Press **Ins**.
8. The copied style is inserted above the style you highlighted. Use **T**ransfer **S**ave from the Gallery menu to save the changes to the style sheet.

Copying Styles with a Mouse

You can use a mouse to copy a style within a style sheet without using the scrap area. (To copy a style between two style sheets, follow the instructions in "Copying Styles with the Keyboard," earlier in this chapter.)

Here are the steps for copying a style:

1. Make sure the style sheet you want to modify is available.
2. Display the style sheet in the Gallery window by selecting Gallery.
3. Scroll through the style sheet using the scroll bar. Point to the style you want to move and click to highlight the style.
4. Point on the style above which you want the copied style to be placed.
5. Hold down **Shift** and click the left button.
6. The style is inserted above the style where the pointer rested. Use **T**ransfer **S**ave from the Gallery menu to save the changes to the style sheet.

Exercise: Deleting, Moving, and Copying Styles

Try deleting, moving, and copying styles, using the SEMI.STY style sheet and the document you created earlier.

Select Gallery. The SEMI.STY style sheet appears on your screen. Highlight the LH style. Notice the contents of your scrap area and then copy the LH style by selecting Copy. The style's usage and variant (Paragraph 10) appears in the scrap area. Move to the end of the style sheet and highlight the last style. Complete the copy by pressing Ins. The LH style is copied above the last style.

Now move the last style (UC) before the LH style. First, highlight the UC style and select Delete. The UC style appears in the scrap area. Then highlight the LH style (which is now the last style in the style sheet) and press Ins. The UC style is inserted before the LH style.

You cannot leave the Gallery while the style sheet has two identical styles. Delete the last LH style by highlighting it and pressing Del. You can now leave the Gallery by selecting Exit.

Creating Styles in a Style Sheet

Although many users begin to experience the power of styles by using those supplied by Word, it isn't long before most users want to create new styles. Before you try your hand at developing styles, it is important that you think about key-code assignment.

Key-Code Assignment

As you know, when you create a style, you assign it a key code. A key code can be a single character (letter or number) or two characters. If you make it a habit to use two-character key codes, you can have up to 125 styles in a style sheet. Always use a letter or number for the first character. The second character can be a letter, a number, or any printable symbol.

When assigning key codes to styles, try to pick ones that suggest the styles to which they apply.

When you assign a key code, do not start it with an X. Remember that Word's speed formatting keys use Alt combined with X and a letter, such as U for underline, if a style sheet is attached. You do not want to disable the functions Word has already assigned to Alt-X followed by another character.

Sometimes you may forget to enter the X when you use a speed formatting key in a document with a style sheet attached. If you have assigned a two-character key code that begins with the same letter as a speed formatting key, Word displays this message:

Enter a second character of key code. For speed key, start over
with Alt+X

For example, suppose you have assigned the key code B1 to a
style in your style sheet. When you want to apply the style, you press
Alt-B and then 1. To use the speed key for bold in a document to
which you have attached this style sheet, you must enter Alt-X-B. If
you forget the X and just press Alt-B, Word asks whether you want to
enter the second key-code character or start over and enter the speed
key. If you have assigned a key code with the same single letter that is
used by a speed formatting key (such as B), the style is applied rather
than the format.

Ways of Creating Styles

When you create a new style, the style is always added to the style
sheet that is attached to document in the active window. There are
several ways to create a style:

- By example: Simply record an existing format
- By using the Gallery commands to build a style

As you have seen, another way to create a style is to copy an
existing style and then edit it. See "Copying Styles" in this chapter
for more information.

Creating Styles by Example

When you create a style by example, you first format the text the way
you want it. Then you "record" the style.

Creating styles by example is an easy way to apply complex formatting while you work. For example, suppose you have formatted a
hanging paragraph and you know you will use this format often in the
document you are creating. One way to reuse the formatting is to
copy the paragraph mark to other locations; another way is to create a
style by example.

Here are the steps for creating a style by example:

1. Make sure the style sheet to which you want to add the style is
   attached to your document.

2. Format the text with the formatting you want to include in the
   style.

3. Select the formatted text. If you select several characters, Word
   will use the format of the first character in the style. If you select

more than one paragraph, Word will use the format of the first paragraph. If you select multiple divisions, Word will use the format of the first division.

4. Select **F**ormat **S**tylesheet **R**ecord or press **Alt-F10**.

5. Word displays the Format Stylesheet Record menu (see Figure 9-11).

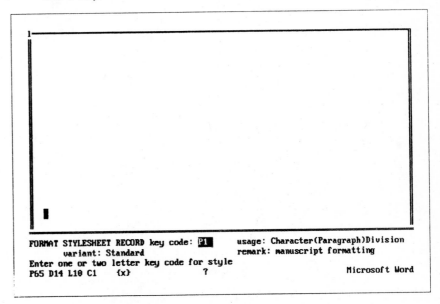

Figure 9-11. The Format Stylesheet Record menu

6. In the *key code* field, enter a one- or two-character code. If you enter just one character, it should be a letter or number. If you enter two characters, use a letter or number followed by a letter, number, or printable symbol. Don't start the key code with an X or you may disable a speed key. Don't use an existing key code; Word will not allow you to create two styles with the same code.

7. In the *usage* field, select the type of usage:

Character	to record the character styles in the selected text that can be set with the Format Character menu.
Paragraph	to record the paragraph styles in the selected text that can be set with the Format Paragraph menu, along with the type style (set through Format Character).
Division	to record the division formats that can be set with the Format Division submenus.

8. Next, move to the *variant* field, where a variant has been entered by Word. This variant may be the "next available" variant in Word's hierarchy or if you entered an existing key code, it may be that variant's key code. You can use the suggested variant, enter a new variant, or press **F1** and select one of the variants listed.

   Remember, Word attaches the style's usage-variant pair to any text to which you apply the style. Make sure you don't try to enter identical usage-variant pairs in one style sheet.

9. In the *remark* field, enter any information about the style that will help you remember what the style is for. You should type in the remark in capital letters. That way, the remark will stand out from the rest of the style information when you view the style in the Gallery window.

10. When all the fields on the Format Stylesheet Record menu are completed the way you want them, press **Enter** or click the command name to create the style.

11. Assuming you entered acceptable values in each field, Word applies the style to the selected text and attaches the usage-variant pair to the appropriate location in the document. The style is added to the attached style sheet. Select **G**allery **T**ransfer **S**ave to save the change you just made to the style sheet (see "Saving Style Sheets" in this chapter for more information).

You should always check the message line to make sure your style was accepted. If this message appears, the style was accepted:

```
Edit document or press Esc to use menu
```

If you have turned on the style bar, you can check there to make sure the appropriate key code appears.

If you attempted to enter a key code and variant that is already in use, this message appears:

```
Style already exists. Enter Y to replace or Esc to cancel
```

Press Y to replace the style or Esc to keep the existing style.

If you entered a key code that is already in use but with a different variant, Word will not accept the new style and displays the following message:

```
Key code already defined. Enter a different key code
```

If you entered a key code that is not already in use with a variant that is already in use, the following message appears:

`Style already defined`

If you entered more than two characters for the key code or entered a symbol as the first character (Word won't accept symbols as the first character of a key code), this message appears:

`Not a valid key code; must be 1 or 2 characters`

Creating Styles with the Gallery Insert Command

When you create a style with Gallery Insert, you identify the style name (key code, usage, variant, and remark). Then you use the Gallery Format command to specify the formatting. The menus you see when you specify the formatting are identical to those accessed by choosing the Format command from the main command menu.

In a multiuser environment where stylistic standards are essential, creating styles on the fly can lead to confusion and inconsistency. Instead, use the Gallery Insert command to plan and implement a comprehensive stylesheet from the ground up.

To create a style from scratch, follow these steps:

1. Make sure the style sheet to which you want to add the style is available.

2. Select **G**allery to display the style sheet.

3. Position your highlight. Where you put your highlight determines the options available on the Format submenus you will later use to specify the style's formatting. Carefully selecting your location now can reduce the number of settings you have to change in the Format submenus. The location also determines where the style appears among other styles. Choose one of these two locations:

On the end mark	to create a style for which you will start with the defaults on the Format submenus.
On an existing character, paragraph, or division style	to start with that style's defaults on the Format submenus. Make sure you select a style with the usage you want to create. (For example, if you want to create a paragraph style, select the existing paragraph style with formatting that is closest to the style you want to create.)

4. Select **I**nsert. Word displays the *key code, usage, variant,* and *remark* fields.

5. Enter a one- or two-character code in the *key code* field.

6. Enter the type of usage in the *usage* field. Select one of these:

Character	to control the formatting that appears on the Format Character menu
Paragraph	to control the formatting that appears on the Format Paragraph menu, along with the type style (set through Format Character)
Division	to record the settings controlled through the Format Division submenus

7. In the *variant* field, Word suggests the next available variant. Use the suggested variant, enter a new one, or press **F1** to select a variant from the list of those available for that usage.

8. In the *remark* field, enter any information about the style that will be helpful later on. Entering the remark in capital letters will help your note about the style's use or contents stand out from the other elements of the style definition.

9. When you are done, press **Enter** or click the command name.

   If you placed your highlight on an existing style with the same usage as the usage you just entered, Word inserts the new style directly above that style and copies that style's formatting instructions to the new style. The styles are renumbered, if necessary. If you placed your highlight on the style sheet's end mark, the new style is added at the end of the styles. Only the font style (such as Courier) appears in the new style's formatting-instruction area. The style is not applied to your text.

   Always check the message line to make sure that Word accepted your style. If Word displays this message, the style was accepted:

   ```
   Select style or press Esc to use menu
   ```

   If you entered a key code and variant that is already in use, this message appears:

   ```
   Key code already defined. Enter a different key code
   ```

   If you entered a key code that is not already in use but a variant that is already in use, the following message appears:

   ```
   Style already defined
   ```

If you entered more than two characters for the key code or entered a symbol as the first character (Word won't accept symbols as the first character of a key code), this message appears:

`Not a valid key code; must be 1 or 2 characters`

10. Assuming you have entered a valid style name, you can now select **F**ormat to add to or change the style's formatting instructions.

11. Specify the formatting on the appropriate character, paragraph, or division submenu.

12. Press **Enter** or click the command name to complete the formatting. Word adds the style to the attached style sheet.

13. Use the **T**ransfer **S**ave command from the Gallery menu to save the style sheet with the new style. (See "Saving Style Sheets" in this chapter for more information.)

14. From the Gallery menu, select **E**xit to return to your document.

Word does not automatically apply the style to the text in which your highlight is positioned. You will have to apply the style manually.

Exercise: Creating Styles

In this exercise, you will create a style in two ways: by example and with the Gallery Insert command. Then you will save the styles in a new style sheet called SEMI2.STY.

Load the TRAINPGM.DOC document, place your highlight after the period that ends the first paragraph. Type in the following text (end the first line and the next paragraph with paragraph marks):

`As Jim Bellows, President of our organization,`
`remarked:`

`"It is the responsibility of all professionals to`
`regularly update their skills. This sales skills seminar is`
`the best I've ever attended."`

The paragraph that begins *It is the responsibility* is indented and follows the formatting of the SP style. You are going to change the formatting of the paragraph and add a new style to the style sheet. With your highlight in this paragraph, select Format Paragraph. Change the *left indent* field to 0.5″, the *first line* field to 0″, and the *right indent* field to 0.5″. Press Enter. The quotation is now indented one-half inch from the right and left margins.

Create the style by example. With your highlight in the quotation paragraph, press Alt-F10. Word displays the Format Stylesheet Record menu. In the *key code* field, enter Q1 for *quote number 1*. In the *usage* field, select Paragraph. In the *variant* field, keep the suggested variant number of 1. In the *remark* field, enter *QUOTE 1-0.5″*. Press Enter. Word adds the style to the style sheet.

To see the style in the style sheet, select Gallery and scroll to the end of the file. The QU key code and style information appears. Notice what information has been included in the formatting instructions.

Next, you will create a style using the Gallery Insert command. Place your highlight on the diamond symbol at the end of the document. From the Gallery menu, select Insert. In the *key code* field, enter Q2 for *quote number 2*. In the *usage* field, select Paragraph. In the *variant* field, keep the suggested variant of 2. In the *remark* field, enter *QUOTE 2-0.75″*. Press Enter. Word adds the style to the style sheet with the default formatting instructions. Now specify the formatting by selecting Format Paragraph. Change the *left indent* to 0.75″, the *first line* to 0″, and the *right indent* to 0.75″. Press Enter. Word changes the style's formatting instructions.

Next you're going to create a new style sheet by saving this style sheet with the name SEMI2.STY. From the Gallery menu, select Transfer Save. In the *style sheet name* field, enter the path, if necessary, and SEMI2 as the style-sheet name (Word adds the .STY extension). Press Enter. When Word has saved the style sheet, it displays the new name in the lower-right corner of the Gallery Window. Select Exit to leave the Gallery window.

Try out the new style. With your highlight in the quotation paragraph, press Alt-Q2. The quotation now has left and right margins of 0.75 inch. The Q2 key code appears in the style bar. Your document looks like this:

```
                              Ms. Carolyn Johnson
                              Elite Press
                              430 33rd Avenue
                              Pittsburgh, PA 15222


        Dear Carolyn:

            Thank you for taking the time to speak with me about
        our upcoming training program. I hope several of your staff
        will be able to attend. As Jim Bellows, President of our
        organization, remarked:
```

```
        "It is the responsibility of all
        professionals to regularly update their
        skills. This sales skills seminar is the best
        I've ever attended."

     To recap, we will be offering the training the week of
June 30. There are only eight spaces available at this time.
Please contact me as soon as possible to arrange your
reservations.

     Thank you again. I look forward to a profitable session
with you and your staff.

Sincerely,
```

Save the TRAINPGM document with Transfer Save.

Changing Key Codes, Variants, and Remarks

You can change every component of entry in the style name except the usage. Figure 9-12 indicates the entries that can be changed: key code, variant, and remark can be changed.

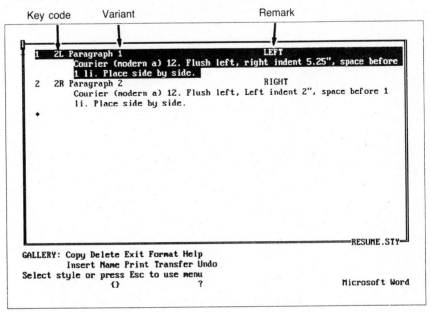

Figure 9-12. The style-name components that can be changed

If you keep forgetting a key code, you should probably change it.

You may want to change the key code of a style if you think of a more descriptive key code to use. Or, you may want to use an existing key code for a new style and give the existing style a new key code. You may want to change the variant so that you can use the existing variant for another style. And you may want to change a remark so that it better describes the style.

To change the key code, variant, or remark with a Gallery command:

1. Make the style sheet which contains the style to rename available.
2. Select **G**allery to display the style sheet.
3. Select the style whose name you want to change.
4. On the Gallery menu, select **N**ame.
5. In the *key code* field, enter the new key code. Make sure the key code is unique in the style sheet.
6. In the *variant* field, enter a variant that you have not yet used or press **F1** to select from a list of available variants. Variants followed by key codes in parentheses are currently in use. Variants followed by empty parentheses are currently in use but no key code has been assigned.
7. In the *remark* field, enter any remark that will help describe the function of the style. Use capital letters to make the remark stand out.
8. Press **Enter** or click the command name. Word immediately changes the style name in the style sheet.
9. To save your changes, select **T**ransfer **S**ave from the Gallery menu (see "Saving Style Sheets" in this chapter for more information).

Change Formatting Instructions

You can change the formatting instructions for a style at any time. Figure 9-13 identifies the formatting instructions.

There are two ways to change formatting instructions. You can:

- Edit the style by using the Gallery Format menus
- Change the instructions by example

When you change a style's formatting instructions, Word changes all the text in the open document to which the style has been applied.

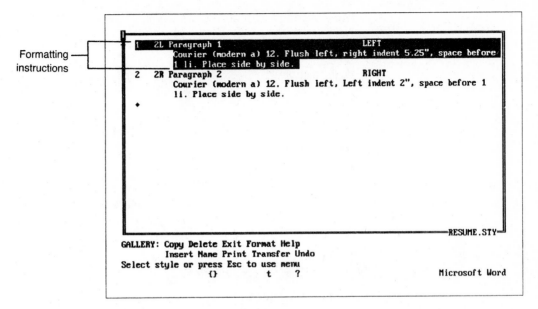

Formatting instructions

```
1    2L Paragraph 1                                   LEFT
        Courier (modern a) 12. Flush left, right indent 5.25", space before
        1 li. Place side by side.
2    2R Paragraph 2                                   RIGHT
        Courier (modern a) 12. Flush left, Left indent 2", space before 1
        li. Place side by side.
    ◆




                                                       ═RESUME.STY═
GALLERY: Copy Delete Exit Format Help
         Insert Name Print Transfer Undo
Select style or press Esc to use menu
                {}            t      ?                 Microsoft Word
```

Figure 9-13. The style's formatting instructions

Assuming that you save the style sheet with the new formatting instructions, when you load documents to which the style sheet has been attached in the future, Word changes the formatting of any text with the style's usage-variant pair.

Changing Formatting with the Gallery Format Commands

These are the steps for changing the formatting instructions through the Gallery format menus:

1. Ensure that the style sheet which contains the style is available.

2. Select **G**allery to display the style sheet.

3. Select the style whose formatting instructions you wish to change.

4. Select **F**ormat. If you are changing the formatting instructions for a style with character usage, you are taken to the character menu. If you are changing the formatting instructions for a style with paragraph usage, select from these options:

   Character

   Paragraph

   Tab

   Border

   p**O**sition

369

If you are changing a style with division usage, select from these options:

Margins

Page-numbers

Layout

line-**N**umbers

5. Complete the Format submenus to edit the formatting instructions.

6. Press **Enter** or click the command name. Word immediately changes the formatting instructions.

7. To save your changes, use **Transfer S**ave from the Gallery menu (see "Saving Style Sheets" in this chapter for more information).

Changing Formatting by Example

Here are the steps to change style formatting by example:

1. Make sure the style sheet you want the style added to is attached.

2. Select **G**allery to view the style you want to change. Jot down the key code, the usage, and the variant, if necessary.

3. Format the text with the formatting you want to include in the style.

4. Select the text with the format. If you select several characters, Word will use the format of the first character in the style. If you select more than one paragraph, Word will use the format of the first paragraph. If you select multiple divisions, Word will use the format of the first division.

5. Select **F**ormat **S**tylesheet **R**ecord or press **Alt-F10**.

6. The Format Stylesheet Record menu appears. The *key code* field is blank. Enter the key code in that field.

7. The *usage* field is already set. Leave the *usage* field as is.

8. In the *variant* field, Word has entered the next available variant, but when you highlight the field, Word displays the variant for the key code you entered. Make sure it is the variant number for the style you want to change.

9. Change the contents of the *remark* field if you want to make the description reflect the new formatting.

10. When all the fields on the Format Stylesheet Record menu are completed the way you want them, press **Enter** or click the command name to change the style.

11. This message appears:

    ```
    Style already exists. Enter Y to replace or Esc to cancel
    ```

    Press **Y** to replace the formatting instructions for the key code and usage-variant pair. Word changes the formatting for all occurrences of the usage-variant pair throughout the document. When you load other documents to which this style sheet is attached, Word will change the formatting of all usage-variant pairs in those documents.

12. To see the new formatting instructions, use the **G**allery command.

13. You may want to use **T**ransfer **S**ave from the Gallery menu to save the change you just made to the style sheet (see "Saving Style Sheets" in this chapter for more information).

Exercise: Changing Styles

In the SEMI2.STY style sheet, you are going to change the name of a style and then change the formatting both with the Gallery Format commands and by example. Make sure the TRAINPGM.DOC document is on your screen. Select Gallery to make sure SEMI2.STY is available. If it is not, use Format Stylesheet Attach or Gallery Transfer Load to view SEMI2.STY.

First, we will change the key code and remark in the names of the quote styles to better describe the styles. Highlight the Q1 style. From the Gallery menu, select Name. In the *key code* field, type in I5 (for *Indent 0.5"*). Leave the variant as it is. In the *remark* field, type in:

```
LEFT/RIGHT INDENT 0.5"
```

Press Enter. Notice that the style name has changed. Now change the next quote style. Select Name. In the *key code* field, enter I7 and in the *remark* field, enter:

```
LEFT/RIGHT INDENT 0.75"
```

Press Enter. Again, notice the style name change.

From the Gallery menu, select Exit to return to the TRAINPGM document. Notice that Word has changed the key code adjacent to the quotation from Q2 to I7, because the style is linked to the document by the usage-variant pair. Since the usage-variant pair did not change, the key code for the pair was updated by Word. Had you changed the variant, you would have had to either reapply the style to the quotation or use the Gallery Name command again to restore the variant to 2.

Next, we will use the Gallery Format command to change the division margins from 1.25 to 1 inch. From the document, select Gallery. Highlight the Division Standard (S/) style. From the Gallery menu, select Format. Because your highlight is on a division style, the Format Division menu appears. Select Margins. In the *left* field, enter 1". In the *right* field, enter 1". Press Enter. Notice that Word has changed the style formatting instructions to include 1-inch margins. Select Exit. Now notice that Word has changed the margins in your document to 1 inch. (You can verify this change by selecting the Format Division Margins command.)

Now change the salutation style by example. We'll place two lines before the salutation instead of one. Place your highlight in the salutation paragraph. Select Format Paragraph. In the *space before* field, enter 2. Press Enter. Notice that Word moves the salutation down one line. Your document looks like this:

```
                              Ms. Carolyn Johnson
                              Elite Press
                              430 33rd Avenue
                              Pittsburgh, PA 15222


Dear Carolyn:

     Thank you for taking the time to speak with me about our
upcoming training program. I hope several of your staff will be
able to attend. As Jim Bellows, President of our organization,
remarked:

     "It is the responsibility of all professionals to
     regularly update their skills. This sales skills
     seminar is the best I've ever attended."

     To recap, we will be offering the training the week of June
30. There are only eight spaces available at this time. Please
contact me as soon as possible to arrange your reservations.

     Thank you again. I look forward to a profitable session with
you and your staff.

Sincerely,
```

With the highlight in the salutation paragraph, press Alt-F10. The Format Stylesheet Record menu appears. In the *key code* field, enter the same key code: SA. Leave the *usage* field as it is. Place your highlight in the *variant* field. Notice that Word changes the variant to correspond with the key code. Leave the *variant* and *remarks* fields as they are and press Enter. This message appears:

`Style already exists. Enter Y to replace or Esc to cancel`

Press Y to replace the formatting instructions. Select Gallery. Notice that Word has changed the formatting instructions for the style.

Save the changes made to the style sheet using Transfer Save from the Gallery menu. Keep the SEMI2.STY name. Word replaces the "old" style sheet with the modified style sheet. Save the document with Transfer Save from the main command menu.

Undoing Style Changes

You can undo some style edits, including:

- Styles you have changed with the Gallery Format commands
- Styles you have inserted, deleted, or copied in a style sheet

You cannot undo:

- Styles you have changed by example
- Styles you have copied or moved between style sheets (only the last insert in the final style sheet is reversed when you use Undo)

If you try to undo a process that cannot be undone, Word displays this message:

`No edit to undo`

To undo a style change:

1. Select **Undo**. Word undoes the change.
2. You can select **Undo** again to restore the edit.

Printing Style Sheets

You can print a paper record of the style sheet displayed in the Gallery window. Follow these steps:

1. Check that your printer is connected to your computer, turned on, on-line, and ready to print.
2. Make sure the style sheet you want to print is attached to the active document.
3. To print the style sheet in the Gallery window, select **P**rint from the Gallery menu.

Word prints the complete style sheet.

Clearing Style Sheets from the Gallery Window

If you want to start with a "clean slate" when developing a style sheet, you can clear the style sheet from the Gallery window. Follow these steps:

1. When you use the Clear command, Word will clear the window without stopping to prompt you to save existing edits, so save any changes you have made to the style sheet currently in the Gallery window by using **T**ransfer **S**ave from the Gallery menu. (The Clear command also clears the window regardless of what style sheet is loaded or attached.)
2. From the Gallery menu, select **T**ransfer **C**lear.
3. Word clears the Gallery window of all styles and removes the style-sheet name from the lower-right corner of the window. You can now create a new set of styles.
4. Select **E**xit from the Gallery menu. This message appears:

   ```
   Enter Y to attach new style sheet, N to keep old one, or
   Esc to cancel
   ```

   Press **Y** or **N** as desired, or press **Esc** to cancel the command.

   If you do not attach the style sheet by selecting N, Word gives you the option of saving the style sheet you have developed in the cleared window:

```
Enter Y to save changes to style sheet, N to lose changes,
Esc to cancel
```

Press **Y** to save the style sheet or **N** to lose it, or press **Esc** to cancel the command.

If you entered Y to save the style sheet, Word displays the Transfer Save menu. Enter a name for the style sheet in the *style sheet name* field and press **Enter**. Word adds the .STY extension. You will see the *Saving* message and then be returned to your document.

Renaming Style Sheets

If you think of a more descriptive name for a style sheet, you can rename it.

When you rename a style sheet, the documents to which the style sheet was previously attached will not recognize the new name when you load them. You will have to reattach the style sheet with the new name when you load each affected document. Otherwise, all the formatting in the document that was formerly implemented with the style sheet will be lost. (Word will implement the default formatting instead.) If you display the Gallery window, the window will be blank.

To strip a style sheet from a document, quit Word, rename the style sheet in DOS, then load the document in Word. Its formatting will have reverted to Word's defaults.

To rename a style sheet:

1. Select **G**allery.

2. Make sure the style sheet you want to rename is displayed in the Gallery window. If it is not, use **T**ransfer **L**oad to display the style sheet.

3. Select **T**ransfer **R**ename.

4. In the *style sheet name* field, enter the new style-sheet name. (You do not have to enter the .STY extension.)

5. Press **Enter** or click the command name. Word immediately renames the style sheet.

As already mentioned, you will need to attach the renamed style sheet to the appropriate documents when they are loaded. Otherwise, Word will not find the "old" style-sheet name and will remove all the formatting applied by the styles in the old style sheet.

Deleting Style Sheets

You can delete any style sheets that you no longer need. Just to be safe, many users like to keep backup copies of style sheets in case a document requires them. Before you delete a style sheet, make sure you have a backup copy or that you will never need the style sheet again in the future.

To delete a style sheet, follow these steps:

1. Regardless of which style sheet is attached to the active document, select **G**allery **T**ransfer **D**elete.

2. You can enter the name of the style sheet you want to delete or press **F1** to select the name of the style sheet from a list. If you press F1, Word displays all the style sheets in the WORD directory. Highlight the style sheet you want to delete. (Actually, you can use this screen to delete any files, not just the .STY files.)

3. Press **Enter** or click the command name to delete the file.

4. Word gives you a chance to change your mind by displaying this message:

   `Enter Y to confirm deletion of the file`

   Enter **Y** to complete the deletion.

Setting the Storage Location

You can set the default storage location from within the Gallery. Whatever drive and directory you specify will become the default setting in the Transfer Options *setup* field as well. Word will use the new setting when saving and loading files, unless you specify a different path for the Transfer Save and Transfer Load commands.

The advantage of setting the default storage location through the Gallery menu is that if you are manipulating several style sheets, you can set the default drive and directory for the whole Word session and avoid having to repeatedly enter the path.

To set the default drive and directory:

1. Select **G**allery **T**ransfer **O**ptions.

2. In the *setup* field, enter the drive and path you want. Or, you can press **F1** to select from a list.

3. In the *save between sessions* field, select **Yes** to keep the drive and directory as the default when you leave Word. Or, select **No** to use the drive and directory for this session of Word only. (When you leave Word, the previous default drive and directory will be restored.)

4. Press **Enter** or click the command name.

Merging Style Sheets

You can merge the contents of two style sheets to add to an existing style sheet or create a new style sheet. For example, the style sheet in Figure 9-14 was merged with the style sheet in Figure 9-15 to create the new style sheet in Figure 9-16. Notice that when Word merged the two style sheets, it merged all the styles, including the identical AA styles. When two style sheets with identical key codes or variants are merged, Word asks you to change one of the key codes or variants before saving the style sheet.

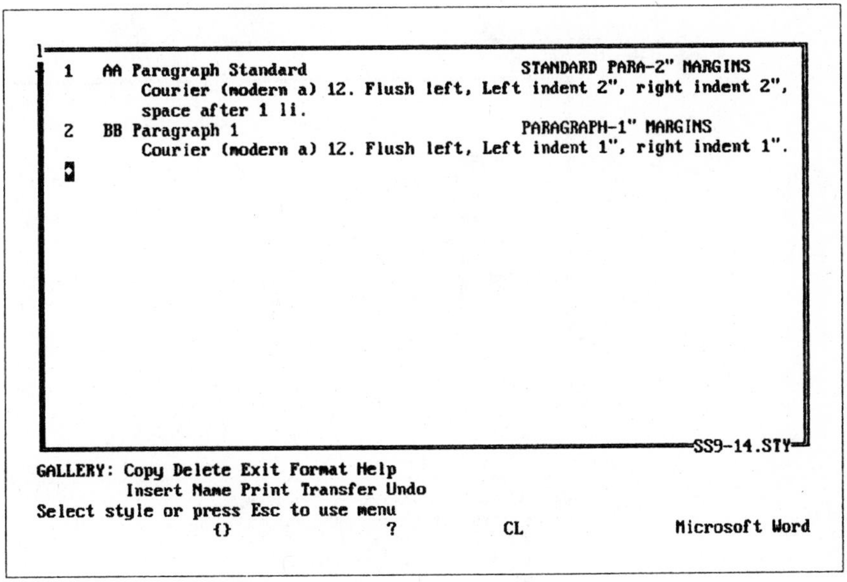

```
1
   1    AA Paragraph Standard                        STANDARD PARA-2" MARGINS
            Courier (modern a) 12. Flush left, Left indent 2", right indent 2",
            space after 1 li.
   2    BB Paragraph 1                               PARAGRAPH-1" MARGINS
            Courier (modern a) 12. Flush left, Left indent 1", right indent 1".




                                                                    SS9-14.STY
GALLERY: Copy Delete Exit Format Help
         Insert Name Print Transfer Undo
Select style or press Esc to use menu
                 {}                    ?          CL           Microsoft Word
```

Figure 9-14. The first style sheet

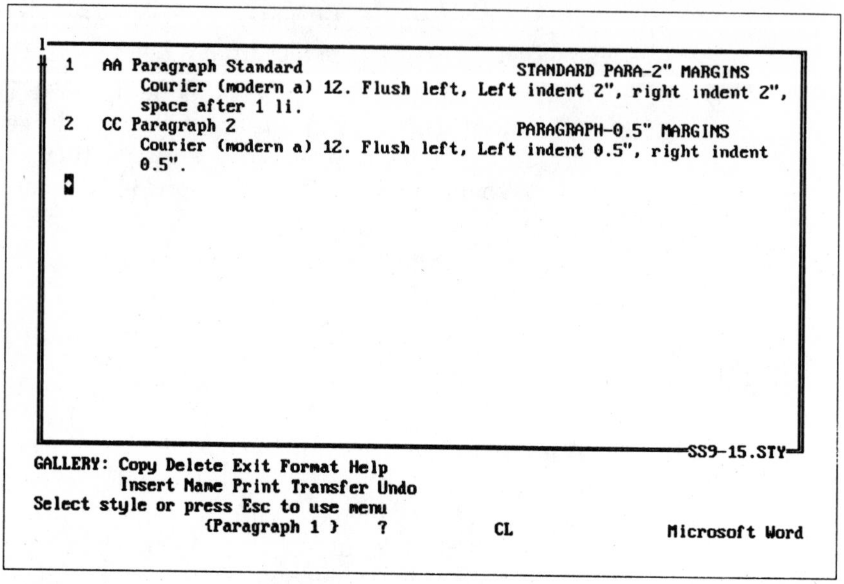

```
1
  1    AA Paragraph Standard                      STANDARD PARA-2" MARGINS
           Courier (modern a) 12. Flush left, Left indent 2", right indent 2",
           space after 1 li.
  2    CC Paragraph 2                             PARAGRAPH-0.5" MARGINS
           Courier (modern a) 12. Flush left, Left indent 0.5", right indent
           0.5".
       █




                                                              SS9-15.STY
GALLERY: Copy Delete Exit Format Help
         Insert Name Print Transfer Undo
Select style or press Esc to use menu
              {Paragraph 1 }      ?              CL              Microsoft Word
```

Figure 9-15. The second style sheet

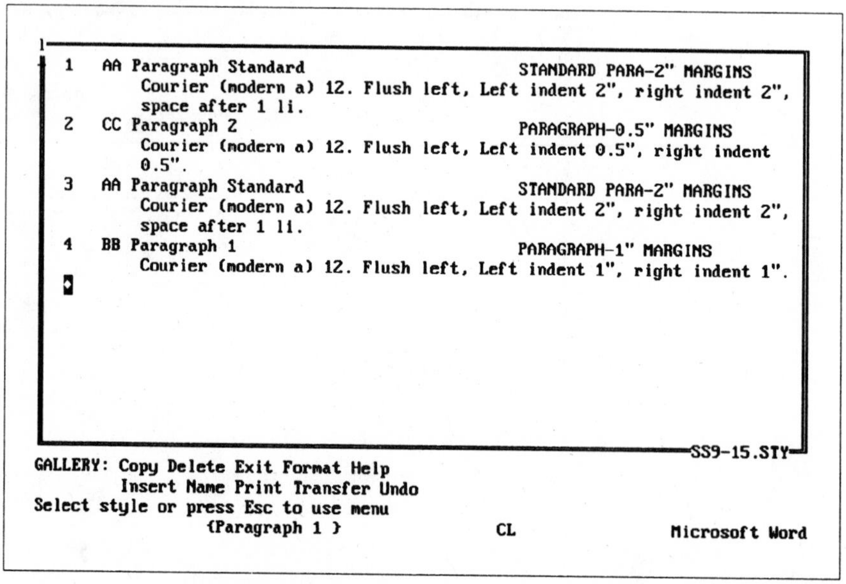

```
1
  1    AA Paragraph Standard                      STANDARD PARA-2" MARGINS
           Courier (modern a) 12. Flush left, Left indent 2", right indent 2",
           space after 1 li.
  2    CC Paragraph 2                             PARAGRAPH-0.5" MARGINS
           Courier (modern a) 12. Flush left, Left indent 0.5", right indent
           0.5".
  3    AA Paragraph Standard                      STANDARD PARA-2" MARGINS
           Courier (modern a) 12. Flush left, Left indent 2", right indent 2",
           space after 1 li.
  4    BB Paragraph 1                             PARAGRAPH-1" MARGINS
           Courier (modern a) 12. Flush left, Left indent 1", right indent 1".
       █




                                                              SS9-15.STY
GALLERY: Copy Delete Exit Format Help
         Insert Name Print Transfer Undo
Select style or press Esc to use menu
              {Paragraph 1 }                     CL              Microsoft Word
```

Figure 9-16. The merged style sheet

This is the process for merging style sheets:

1. Select **G**allery.
2. Make sure the style sheet you want to merge to is in the Gallery window. If it is not, use **Transfer Load** to load the style sheet.
3. Position your highlight, bearing in mind that the merged styles will be placed above the position of your highlight in the Gallery window.
4. Select **Transfer Merge**.
5. In the *style sheet name* field, enter the name of the style sheet you want to merge into the style sheet currently in the Gallery window. Or, press **F1** to select the style sheet from a list.
6. Press **Enter** or click the command name to merge the style sheets. The styles from the style sheet you are merging from are inserted above the styles in the Gallery window. (If you change your mind about the merge, you can use **Gallery Undo** at this point to start again.)
7. If the style sheet now contains styles with identical key codes or usage-variant pairs, use the **Gallery Name** command or **Gallery Delete** command to resolve the duplicates. Word will not let you save the style sheet with conflicting key codes or variants. If you select Exit from the Gallery menu without resolving the duplicates, Word displays this message, forcing you to edit the conflicting style, which is highlighted:

    ```
    Style already defined
    ```

8. Once you have resolved the conflicting styles, you can use **Transfer Save** from the Gallery menu to save the style sheet. If you save it under the name of an existing style sheet, Word will replace that style sheet with the active one. If you enter a new name, Word will create a new style sheet.
9. If you select **Exit** from the Gallery menu without saving the merged style sheet, Word displays this message, asking whether you want to save the style sheet and providing attachment options:

    ```
    Enter Y to attach new style sheet, N to keep old one, or Esc
    to cancel
    ```

    Press **Y** to attach the style sheet or **N** to keep the existing style sheet attached. This message appears:

```
Enter Y to save changes to style sheet, N to lose changes, or
Esc to cancel
```

Press **N** to lose the merged style sheet or **Y** to save the changes. If you have not yet resolved all the conflicting key codes and variants, Word displays the message:

```
Style already defined
```

Otherwise, Word allows you to specify either an existing name or a new name for the style sheet. Press **Enter** and the merged style sheet is saved.

Exercise: Printing and Merging Style Sheets

In this example, you will print a style sheet and merge it with another Word style sheet.

Select Gallery. Make sure the SEMI2.STY style sheet appears. Make sure your printer is connected to your computer, on-line, and ready to print. Select Print. Word prints the style sheet.

Word's ACADEMIC style sheet contains several footnote styles. Suppose you want to use the SEMI2.STY style sheet and the ACADEMIC.STY style sheet with one document. To do this, you can merge the style sheets into one and give the merged style sheet a new name.

Make sure SEMI2.STY is displayed on your screen. You will merge into this style sheet. Place your highlight on the diamond symbol at the end of the style sheet. The merged styles will be placed above this spot.

From the Gallery menu, select Transfer Merge. Enter the drive, the path, and the style-sheet name (ACADEMIC) and press Enter or select the style sheet from a list by pressing F1. The styles from ACADEMIC are inserted above the highlight. Check to see if there are any identical key codes or usage-variant pairs. If there are any duplicates, use Gallery Name or Gallery Delete to resolve the styles. These are duplicates:

Key Code, Usage, Variant	Duplicates
T1 Paragraph 7	DA Paragraph 7
DP Paragraph 1	I5 Paragraph 1
QT Paragraph 2	I7 Paragraph 2

In each case, the usage-variant pairs match. Use Gallery Name to change the variants in the first column to the following:

Key Code, Usage, Variant

T1 Paragraph 3

DP Paragraph 12

QT Paragraph 15

To ensure that these variants are available, press F1 in the *variant* field and select the variant from the list Word displays, making sure that no parentheses are associated with the variant you select.

Check the style in the Gallery window to make sure the variant has been changed.

Now use Gallery Transfer Save to save the style sheet. Enter the drive, the path, and the name SEMI3.STY. Word creates the SEMI3.STY style sheet from the merged style sheets.

Revision Marks, Bookmarks, Cross-Referencing, and Hyphenation

When you get to know Word, you will want to take advantage of its more sophisticated formatting features. This chapter covers four of these features:

- Revision marks
- Bookmarks
- Cross-referencing
- Hyphenation

Revision marks enable you to edit text and, by marking it with special formatting, show what has been inserted, deleted, moved, or replaced. You may later undo or accept the edits, and remove the revision marks.

Bookmarks enable you to mark your place in a document by assigning a name to selected text. You can then quickly move to that text by using the Jump bookmarK command.

The cross-referencing feature uses bookmarks to create automatic cross-references to pages, paragraphs, footnotes, or items in a series. When you edit the document, the cross-references (such as "see page 5") are automatically updated.

Word allows you to hyphenate documents manually or automatically. Several types of hyphens are available.

Revision Marks

Most documents go through several drafts, or revisions, before reaching final form. And often, as when a writer and editor, or supervisor and assistant, work together, more than one person may be involved in the development of a document. In such situations, it is usually desirable for changes made by one party to be visible to others who are involved in preparation of the document or have an interest in its final form. On hard copy, of course, pencil edits are clearly visible, but on word-processed copy, deleted text normally disappears, and inserted text looks just like the rest.

Use Format Annotations to comment on the revisions you make with Format revision-Marks. The annotations can appear on the same pages as the revisions to which they apply or all together at the end of a document.

Word's Format revision-Marks command lets you leave an editing trail, just as you can when working with hard copy. (What Word calls "revision marks" sometimes goes by the name "redlining.") When you select Format revision-Marks, Word strikes through deleted text but leaves it on screen and displays inserted text in a format of your choosing—underlined, double-underlined, boldface, uppercase, or normal. (Except where otherwise specified, the rest of this chapter assumes that you have elected to display inserted text underlined, the default choice.)

When you replace text, the old text is struck through and the new text is underlined. Because moving text consists of deleting the text from one place and inserting it in another, Word's revision-marks feature shows the text struck through in its place of origin and underlined in its new location. Similarly, when you copy text, the program underlines the text in its new location but leaves it untouched in its original spot.

In Figure 10-1, deleted text appears struck through and inserted text is underlined. Unchanged text appears normal. Line 1 shows normal text that has not been revised. Line 2 shows text that has been inserted. This text is underlined. Line 3 illustrates deleted text that is struck through. Line 4 displays text that has been deleted and inserted as line 6. Line 5 shows the word *something* replaced by *a new end*. *Something* appears as deleted text and *a new end* appears as inserted text. Line 7 shows the results of copying the word *again*. The original *again* appears as normal text; the copied *again* text appears as an insert.

When revision marks are turned on, changes made with Library Spell and Library Thesaurus are marked. Changes to text with other Library commands are not. Nor are changes made with Format commands.

Revision marks can be displayed on screen or printed. They can be accepted or undone for a part of a document, a whole document, or individually. A search feature helps you handle revisions individually.

If you have a color monitor, you can make deleted and inserted text appear in different colors instead of being struck through or underlined. Simply start Word in text mode and then set colors through the *colors* field of Word's Options command. (See Chapter 2, "Starting Microsoft Word," for information on setting the strike-through color option.)

You can also cause Word to display and/or print revision bars to identify the text that you have changed. Revision bars are optional. Some Word users feel they make the revised text easier to pick out; others prefer a clean display without the bars.

Word's revision-marks feature should not be confused with annotations. Revision marks show where text has been changed by an author or editor. Annotations are special footnotes used by reviewers and editors of a document for jotting down comments and queries. Annotations do not change the actual text of the document.

Line 1: This text is normal.

Line 2: This text is inserted.

Line 3: ~~This text was deleted.~~

Line 4: ~~This text was moved.~~

Line 5: This text was replaced with something a new end.

Line 6: This text was moved.

Line 7: The last word is copied twice: again again again

Figure 10-1. The result of using revision marks

Turning Revision Marks On and Off

To use revision marks, you must first turn them on. Then, if you want to change Word's default settings, you can do so.

To turn on revision marks:

1. Select **F**ormat revision-**M**arks **O**ptions.

2. In the *add revision marks* field, select **Y**es.

Sometimes you want to temporarily turn off revision marks in order to edit original text without inserting additional revision marks. To speed up the process of turning marks on and off, record a separate macro for each operation (see Chapter 21, "Macros").

When you select Yes, MR appears in the status line. While revision marks are on, text that is inserted or deleted in any way will be marked, and you cannot use the overtype mode or delete text with the Backspace key. (You can, however, use the Backspace key to delete text you have inserted while revision marks are on.) You can press Del to delete any text.

To turn off revision marks:

1. Select **F**ormat revision-**M**arks **O**ptions.

2. In the *add revision marks* field, select **N**o.

If you leave a document without turning off revision marks, the setting remains with the document. When you load the document at a later date, the revision marks will appear and revision marks will be turned on. If you enter text with revision marks and then turn revision marks off, the revision marks already entered will stay in the document until you remove them.

Setting Revision-Marks Options

For most users most of the time, Word's default settings for revision marks (deleted text struck through, inserted text underlined, no revision bar) will do just fine. If the settings are unsatisfactory, however, they are easy enough to change—with the exception of deleted text, which always appears struck through.

To set revision-marks options:

1. Select **F**ormat revision-**M**arks **O**ptions.

2. In the *inserted text* field, enter the format in which you want inserted text to appear. The options are:

Normal

Bold

Underline

Uppercase

Double-underlined

If you select **N**ormal, inserted text will look just like any other text, and you will not be able to distinguish it when you want to accept, undo, or search out revisions. If you change the *inserted text* setting, the format of already existing inserts also changes.

The insert display option you should use depends in part on the capabilities of your video display and, of course, your own visual preference. Try out each option to see which looks best to you.

3. In the *revision bar position* field, select one of the following options:

None: A revision bar does not appear on screen or when the document is printed (see Figure 10-2).

Left: A revision bar appears to the left of the text on screen and when the document is printed (see Figure 10-3).

Right: On screen, the revision bar appears to the left of the text. When the document is printed, the revision bar appears to the right of the text (see Figure 10-4).

Outside: On screen, the revision bar appears to the left of the text. When the document is printed, the revision bar appears in the outside margins; that is, the left one on even pages, the right one on odd pages (see Figure 10-5).

If you select a revision bar option other than None, the revision bar always appears to the left of the text on the screen and appears in the designated position when printed.

```
     Under the agreement, Wessle Corporation will provide up
front funding for the effort.  This funding is estimated to be
one-halfthree quarter million dollars.  An analysis is currently
underway to firm up that estimate and provide complete budget
details.  Until that-analysisit is complete, we will continue our
usual operations.
```

Figure 10-2. No revision bar

```
     Under the agreement, Wessle Corporation will provide up
front funding for the effort.  This funding is estimated to be
one-halfthree quarter million dollars.  An analysis is currently
underway to firm up that estimate and provide complete budget
details.  Until that-analysisit is complete, we will continue our
usual operations.
```

Figure 10-3. Printed result of revision bar on the left

Under the agreement, Wessle Corporation will provide up
front funding for the effort. This funding is estimated to be
~~one-half~~three quarter million dollars. An analysis is currently
underway to firm up that estimate and provide complete budget
details. Until ~~that analysis~~it is complete, we will continue our
usual operations.

Figure 10-4. Printed result of revision bar on the right

2

Under the agreement, Wessle Corporation will provide up
front funding for the effort. This funding is estimated to be
~~one-half~~three quarter million dollars. An analysis is currently
underway to firm up that estimate and provide complete budget
details. Until ~~that analysis~~it is complete, we will continue our
usual operations.

3

The budget report will be complete in late ~~June~~May. This
will give us ample opportunity to respond to all questions posed
by Directors and Stockholders. We anticipate that all related
issues will be resolved by late ~~September~~October. This gives us
two months to complete the contract details ~~by the~~no later than
the end of the year.

Figure 10-5. Printed result of revision bar outside

If you have multiple columns, the revision bar appears in the margin between columns according to your settings.

4. Once you have selected all the options, press **Enter** or click the command area.

If you turned revision marks on, text you insert, delete, or replace is marked according to the options you have set. When you quit Word, the revision marks entered are saved with the document along with the setting in the *add revision marks* field.

Removing Revision Marks

You can easily remove revision marks from part or all of a document. When you do so, you have two choices. You can:

- Accept the revisions and remove the marks.
- Undo (remove) both the revisions and the marks.

You don't need to have *add revision marks* set to Yes to accept or undo revisions.

Before removing revision marks, make a backup copy of the marked document. For added safety, save the document with removed revision marks under a new name. That way, you will have both versions in case you change your mind later.

Accepting Revisions

When you accept revisions, revision-marks formatting (but no other) is removed from inserted text, and deleted text and revision bars are truly deleted. For example, insertions can include underlined text even if underline is the setting for the Format revision-Marks Options *inserted text* field. If you format text by using either the Format Character *underline* field or the Alt-U speed-formatting key, the underline will remain even after you remove the revision marks.

When you accept revisions, struck-through text, including any that may have been formatted with the Alt-S speed-formatting key or the Format Character *strikethrough* field, is deleted.

To accept revision marks:

1. Highlight the revision or revisions you want to accept (to accept all revisions in a document press **Shift-F10**).

2. Select **F**ormat revision-**M**arks accept-**R**evisions.

   Word implements the revisions immediately and then displays the Format revision-Marks menu with the Search option highlighted.

3. Select **S**earch to go to the next revision or **Esc** to return to your text.

You can also choose Options or Undo-revisions. For information on the former, see "Setting Revision-Marks Options," earlier in this chapter. For information on the latter, see the next section.

Undoing Revisions

When you undo the revisions, Word deletes any text marked as inserted and returns to normal format any text marked as deleted.

Text with strikethrough marks is left in place when you undo revisions, but the marks themselves are removed. This is true even if you formatted the text as struck through intentionally, by using the Format Character *strikethrough* field or the Alt-S speed-formatting key.

Because all the methods of entering strikethrough formatting are treated the same when you undo revisions, you can add "deleted" text to your document with any method that produces strikethrough format. For example, you may want to enter alternative text but show it as deleted to suggest different wording in that passage. Instead of entering the text, turning on revision marks, and deleting the text, just enter the text in strikethrough format.

To undo revisions:

1. Highlight the revision or revisions you want to undo (to undo all revisions in a document, press **Shift-F10**).

2. Select **F**ormat revision-**M**arks **U**ndo-revisions.

   Word undoes the revisions immediately and displays the Format revision-Marks menu with the Search option highlighted.

3. Select **S**earch to go to the next revision or press **Esc** to return to your text.

   You can also choose Options or accept-Revisions, both of which are discussed earlier in this chapter.

Searching for Revisions

Instead of accepting or undoing revisions for an entire document or section of a document, you can handle each revision separately. The Format revision-Marks Search command enables you to go to each revision and decide whether to accept or undo it. Or you can leave the text with the revision marks intact.

In most cases, you will need to search for and either accept or reject revisions one at a time. Fortunately, Word makes the process quick and easy.

To search for revisions:

1. Place your highlight in the document before the first revision you want to accept or undo. (Do not highlight the revision itself or the search will begin after the selection.)

2. Select **F**ormat revision-**M**arks **S**earch.

   Word highlights the first revision and displays the Format revision-Marks menu.

3. Select one of the following alternatives:

Options	to change a revision-marks option (see "Setting Revision-Marks Options," earlier in this chapter)
accept-**R**evisions	to accept the revision
Undo-revisions	to undo the revision
Search	to leave revision marks intact and move to the next revision
Esc	to return to your text

If you continue searching, the highlight will stop at each revision until you reach the end of the document.

If you want to accept or undo most—but not all—of the revisions without searching each one out individually, turn off revision marks, fix the exceptions, turn revision marks back on, highlight the entire document, and accept or undo all the remaining revisions all at once.

Exercise: Using Revision Marks

Start with a blank Word screen. Enter this paragraph:

Environmental support products are required in every
workplace. The requirement for these products is certainly
growing every year. In the next five years, the growth is
projected at 25%.

Turn on revision marks by selecting Format revision-Marks Options. In the *add revision marks* field, select Yes. In the *inserted text* field, select Underlined. In the *revision bar position* field, select Left.

Enter these revisions:

Environmental support products are ~~required~~necessary in
every workplace. The requirement for these products is
~~certainly~~ growing every year. In the next five years, the
growth is projected at <u>a minimum of</u> 25%.

Insert the underlined text. Delete the text with strikethrough formatting. Then check the appearance of the text on your screen.

Turn off revision marks by selecting Format revision-Marks Options. In the *add revision marks* field, select No.

Save the document under the name PRODUCT. Print the document to see the printed result of the revision-marked text.

To accept all the revisions, press Shift-F10 to select the entire document. Select Format revision-Marks accept-Revisions. Word removes underlines and struck-through text and highlights the Search option. Press Esc to return to your text. The text should now read as follows:

Environmental support products are necessary in every
workplace. The requirement for these products is growing
every year. In the next five years, the growth is projected
at a minimum of 25%.

Save the document under the name PRODUCT1.

Bookmarks

Bookmarks are placed in books to mark important spots. In Word, bookmarks serve as place holders in a document. If you want to work on another part of a document, you can mark your current place with a bookmark and easily return to it later. You can also use them to identify text you would like to reread, places where you plan to add more information, and/or passages you want to correct. You can enter as many bookmarks in a document as you want.

Naming Bookmarks

To create a bookmark, you select text and assign it a name. A bookmark name can be up to 31 characters long and can incorporate letters or numbers. Underlines, periods, and hyphens can be included but not at the beginning or end of the name. You can't use colons or spaces in a bookmark name and you can't have two bookmarks with the same name in the same document. If you do enter a duplicate name, Word deletes the existing bookmark when it adds the new bookmark.

Don't be shy about assigning bookmarks. The more you create, the easier it is to navigate quickly through a document.

Some Word users devise a list of bookmark names that they use in all documents so that they can easily remember what bookmark to search for no matter what document they are working in. The following list of bookmark names might be useful for you. You can adopt these names or think up ones of your own.

Bookmark name	Bookmark meaning
reread	Reread this section for style and accuracy
addinfo	Add text after more thought or research
correct	Correct an error in this passage after research
stophere	Location you stopped working in the document
question	Answer this question
spell	Correct the spelling of this proper name

These and other bookmark names can be used to jump quickly to the location you want. These particular names also suggest the next task you need to perform. To use the same basic name more than once in a document, add a number at the end. For example, if you have more than one section you would like to reread later, name the bookmarks *reread1*, *reread2*, and so on.

Bookmark Selection Anchors

As already mentioned, you create bookmarks by first selecting the bookmark text and then naming it. When named, the first and last characters of the selection become the *anchors* for the bookmark. If you accidentally delete the first or last character of a bookmark selection, Word makes the new first or last character the anchor. If you type over an anchor, the anchor moves to the first or last character of the selection that was not overtyped.

Once a bookmark is in place, you can delete characters in it. As long as the anchors are not deleted, the start and end of the bookmark remain the same.

If you move a bookmark, the anchors also move. You can even safely move a bookmark to a different document as long as the new document does not have a bookmark of the same name. If a bookmark of the same name does exist in the new document, Word deletes the old bookmark when it inserts the new one.

When you copy a bookmark, Word copies the text but not the anchors. To make the copied text into a bookmark, you must select and name the bookmark text all over again.

Entering Bookmarks

To enter a bookmark:

1. Highlight the bookmark text.
2. Select **F**ormat bookmar**K**.
3. In the *name* field, enter the bookmark name.
4. Press **Enter** or click the command name.

If you make a mistake and want to get rid of the bookmark name, select Undo immediately.

To move a bookmark name:

1. Highlight the text to which you want to move an existing bookmark.
2. Select **F**ormat bookmar**K**. Word displays this message at the bottom of the screen:

```
Enter bookmark name or press F1 to select from list
```

3. Enter the name of the existing bookmark or press **F1** and select the name from the list of your existing bookmarks. Word displays The following message:

```
Enter Y to confirm overwriting bookmark
```

4. Press **Y** to move the existing bookmark to the new location.

To review a list of your existing bookmarks, repeat steps 1 through 3.
If there are no bookmarks in the document, the following message appears:

```
List is empty
```

If there are bookmarks in the document, your screen should look like Figure 10-6. Bookmarks are listed in the order in which they appear in the document from left to right, line by line. For example, in Figure 10-6, correct1 is the first bookmark in the document, reread1 is the second, and reread2 is the third.

When column select (Ctrl-F6) is turned on, bookmarks cannot be assigned to column text.

Jumping to a Bookmark

To jump to a bookmark:

1. Select Jump bookmar**K**.
2. Enter the bookmark name or press **F1** to select the name from a list.
3. Press **Enter** or click the command name.

Word takes you to the bookmark and highlights the bookmark text.

Deleting Bookmarks

To delete a bookmark:

1. Select Jump bookmar**K**.
2. Enter the bookmark name you want to delete.
3. Press **Enter** or click the command area. Word takes you to the bookmark and highlights the bookmark text.
4. Select **F**ormat bookmar**K**.
5. Do not enter a name in the *name* field; instead, press **Enter** or click the command name. Word displays this message:

```
Enter Y to confirm deletion of bookmark(s)
```

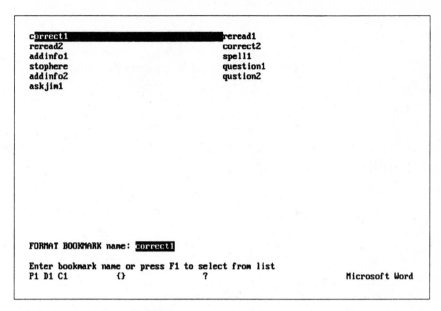

Figure 10-6. Existing bookmarks

6. Press **Y** to delete the bookmark (the text will remain in place). If
   you decide not to delete the bookmark, press **N** or **Esc**.

If you remove the bookmark and then change your mind, select
Undo immediately to restore the bookmark format.

Exercise: Creating Bookmarks

Load PRODUCT1.DOC. If this document is not available, type the following text:

Environmental support products are necessary in every
workplace. The requirement for these products is growing
every year. In the next five years, the growth is projected
at a minimum of 25%.

Highlight the text *Environmental support products*. Select Format bookmarK. In the *name* field, enter *ESP* and press Enter.

Highlight *growth is projected at a minimum of 25%*. Select
Format bookmarK. In the *name* field, enter *ESPgrowth*.

To see the list of bookmarks you've entered, select Format bookmarK. Word lists the names ESP and ESPgrowth. Press Esc to return
to the Word document screen.

Place your cursor at the beginning of the paragraph. Select Jump bookmarK. Enter *ESP* in the *name* field and press Enter. Word highlights the first bookmark. Select Jump bookmarK again. This time enter *espgrowth* in the *name* field and press Enter. Although the new name is all lower case, Word takes you to the same place. To Word, bookmark names like HEIGHT and height are identical.

To finish this exercise, save PRODUCT1.DOC.

Cross References

Cross references make it easy for readers to find information in your documents. Using bookmarks, you can insert cross references to pages, figures, charts, tables, sections, chapters or any other text. Such cross references might take the following forms:

(See page 22.)

Figure 2-7 illustrates this concept.

The detail in chart 7 on page 32 is summarized here.

Table 4 shows the result.

Section 7 goes into more depth on this issue.

Consult Chapter 4, page 20, for a detailed description.

You can insert cross references without knowing the page numbers to which they refer; Word will supply the page numbers when the document is printed. Word also automatically updates cross references when a change in pagination occurs.

It's a good idea to decide what sort of cross references you want to use before you begin a document, not half-way through. That way, your cross references will be complete and consistent.

Cross references consist of two elements: the text you want to reference and the reference itself. Creating a cross reference in Word accordingly consists of two operations. First, you assign a bookmark to the text you want to reference. Second, you insert in your cross reference a code word, followed immediately by the appropriate bookmark name, and press F3. Word encloses the code:bookmark combination in parentheses. When the program encounters this parenthetical phrase during printing, it substitutes the appropriate page number.

For example, suppose you want to cross reference the phrase *Personnel Report* in the sentence *The Personnel Report describes three issues.* On the screen, your cross reference might look like this:

See page (page:per_rept) for more information.

In this example, *page:* is the cross reference code and *per_rept* is the bookmark. When you print the document, the same sentence would look something like this:

See page 16 for more information.

Word provides four kinds of cross references:

- Page numbers (code word *page:*)
- Paragraphs that have been numbered (code word *para-num:*)
- Footnotes (code word *footnote:*)
- Items in a series (code word of your own choosing, such as *table:* or *illustration:*)

The colons are an integral part of cross-reference code words and must always be included.

To create a cross reference:

1. Highlight text you want to cross reference. The text can be anything from a single letter to one or more paragraphs.

2. Assign a bookmark to the highlighted text (for instructions, see "Bookmarks," earlier in this chapter).

3. To insert a cross reference, type it as you would normally but in place of a page number, paragraph number, footnote number, or series number, type the appropriate code word, followed by the bookmark name you assigned to the text you want to cross reference. Here are some examples:

Bookmark name	Code word:bookmark
time1	page:time1
costpar	para-num:costpar
timefoot	footnote:timefoot
janmeals	chart:janmeals

4. Immediately after entering the bookmark name press **F3**.

Word surrounds the code-word:bookmark with parentheses. For example, the above cross references would appear as:

(page:time1)

(para-num:costpar)

(footnote:timefoot)

(chart:janmeals)

Cross-Referencing to Pages

In cross references, page numbers appear in the format you selected using the Format Division Page-numbers command. Figures 10-7 through Figure 10-9 show three page-number formats: arabic, alphabetic, and roman. Figure 10-10 shows how these formats appear in cross references.

Cross
reference

See the Detail Test Specifications on page 3 in this report for more information.

Figure 10-7. Arabic page number

Cross
reference

See the Detail Test Specifications on page C in this report for more information.

Figure 10-8. Alphabetic page number

Cross
reference

See the Detail Test Specifications on page III in this report for more information.

Figure 10-9. Roman-numeral page number

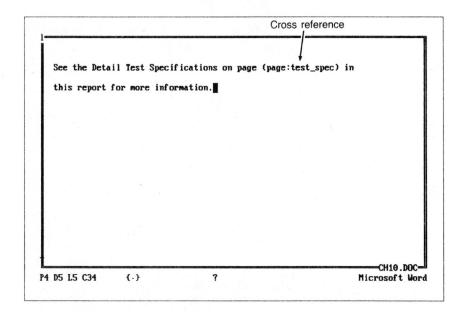

Figure 10-10. The screen appearance of a page cross reference

If a page number is embedded in a header that includes a chapter number, (page 2-5, for example), only the page number appears in the cross reference; the chapter number does not. For example, the printed result of cross referencing to page 2-5 is:

See page 5.

If several chapters have a page 5, however, the chapter number is obviously critical to the reference. To make the reference as clear as possible, you must enter the chapter number in the text before the cross reference. Use one of these options:

Cross reference	Printed result
See page 2-(page:ref1).	See page 2-5.
See Chapter 2, page (page:ref1).	See Chapter 2, page 5.

Cross-Referencing to Paragraphs

You can cross reference numbered paragraphs. Figure 10-11 shows a contract with numbered paragraphs. Figure 10-12 shows the on-screen appearance of a cross reference developed for the contract. The bookmark name *parastart* was assigned to the paragraph in Figure 10-11 that begins *III. Contract Start Date.* Figure 10-13 shows how the cross reference looks when printed.

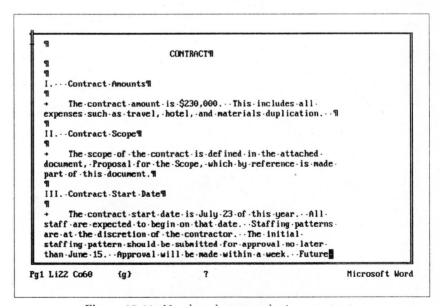

Figure 10-11. Numbered paragraphs in a contract

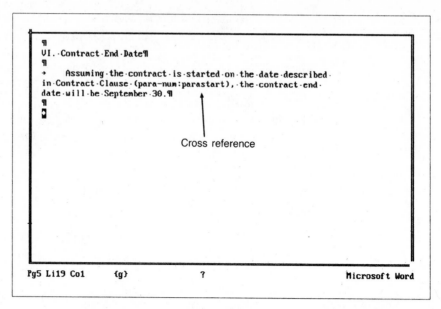

Figure 10-12. Cross reference for a paragraph

VI. Contract End Date

    Assuming the contract is started on the date described
in Contract Clause III, the contract end date will be
September 30.

Cross reference ——————————

Figure 10-13. The paragraph cross reference when printed

Before entering cross references, you must number the paragraphs in the document. You can either manually number paragraphs or use Word's paragraph-numbering feature. For more information on paragraph numbering, see Chapter 18, "Indexes, Outlines, and Tables of Contents."

Cross-Referencing to Footnotes

In addition to pages and paragraphs, you can cross reference footnotes. Figure 10-14 illustrates the screen appearance of a footnote reference mark and the corresponding footnote. In this example, the text marked for the reference is the period following the footnote reference number (1). Figure 10-15 shows the appearance of a footnote cross reference on-screen. Figure 10-16 shows the printed result of the footnote cross reference.

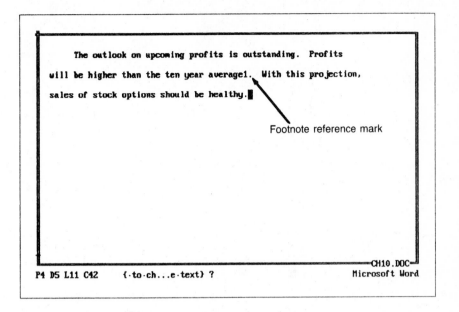

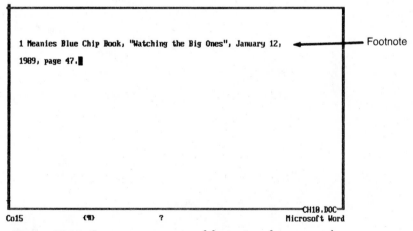

Figure 10-14. Screen appearance of footnote reference mark and footnote

Cross-Referencing a Series

Word also lets you cross reference items in a series. The series might comprise figures, illustrations, charts, tables, sections, or other items that can be sequentially numbered. When you cross reference items in a series, you must number the series before marking the references. Word then refers to the items by number.

Figure 10-17 illustrates two charts and the accompanying cross reference. Figure 10-18 shows the printed result.

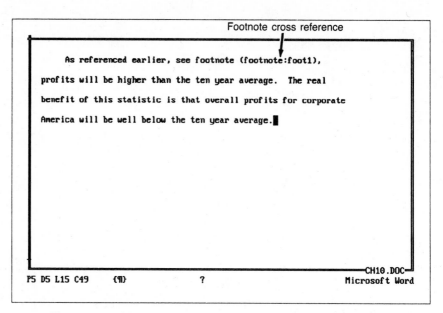

Figure 10-15. Screen appearance of footnote cross reference

Footnote cross reference

As referenced earlier, see footnote 1, profits will be higher than the ten year average. The real benefit of this statistic is that overall profits for corporate America will be well below the ten year average.

Figure 10-16. Printed result of footnote cross reference

Automatically Numbering Items in a Series

Word can automatically number items in a series, and you can number as many series as you like in a single document. For example, you could have Word number tables Table 1, Table 2, Table 3, and so on, and in the same document, have Word number graphics Illustration 1, Illustration 2, Illustration 3, and so on.

To automatically number items in a series:

Many Word users like to automatically number items in a series even if they do not plan to cross reference. This way, the numbers are automatically updated whenever an item is added or deleted.

1. Highlight the first character of the first item of the series.

2. Enter a series label (such as *Chart*), followed by a space.

3. Type a code name for the series (such as *chart*) followed by a colon. The name can be up to 31 characters with letters or numbers. You can include underlines, periods, and hyphens, but not at the beginning or end. Don't enter spaces.

```
1 L[·······D·······D······D···L····4·······5·······6···]···7····]
    ······Jim·····Kitty····Barny¶
    Week·1→ 34.78→   43.56→   53.99↓
    Week·2→ 32.90→   43.95→   54.90↓
    Week·3→ 32.22→   10.09→   89.00¶
    ¶
    Chart·(chart:)·—·January·Meals¶

    ¶

    ······Jim·····Kitty····Barny¶
    Week·1→ 34.78→   43.56→   53.99↓
    Week·2→ 32.90→   43.95→   54.90↓
    Week·3→ 32.22→   10.09→   89.00I
    ¶
    Chart·(chart:)·—·February·Meals¶

    ¶
    Chart·(chart:janmeals)·illustrates·the·averages·for·each·person·
    in·January.··The·next·chart,·Chart·(chart:febneals),·shows·those·
    averages·for·February.¶

    ¶
                                                        CH10.DOC
P3 D6 L12 C34      {}              ?              Microsoft Word
```

Figure 10-17. Screen appearance of two charts and cross references
to them

```
           Jim       Kitty      Barny
Week 1    34.78     43.56      53.99
Week 2    32.90     43.95      54.90
Week 3    32.22     10.09      89.00

Chart 1 - January Meals


           Jim       Kitty      Barny
Week 1    34.78     43.56      53.99
Week 2    32.90     43.95      54.90
Week 3    32.22     10.09      89.00

Chart 2 - February Meals


Chart 1 illustrates the averages for each person in January.   The
next chart, Chart 2, shows those averages for February.
```

Figure 10-18. Printed result of cross references to the charts

4. Press **F3**. The code name is placed in parentheses.

5. Continue entering code names for all the items in the series. Word displays the code names on-screen but will substitute numbers in numeric order when you print the document.

To have Word count an item in the numbering sequence but not print its number, follow the name with two colons (for example, chart::).

To assign a specific starting number, enter the code name, two colons, and the number that precedes the number you want to print. For example:

```
See Chart (chart::4) for details
```

looks like this when printed:

```
See Chart 5 for details
```

Numbers assigned after this point will be in consecutive order. This feature is useful for numbering items throughout a document.

After setting up the series, you can mark the series items for cross referencing. The process is identical to that used for marking page, paragraph, or footnote references. Just be sure to highlight the text *after* the code name, not the code name itself. For example, in the caption:

```
Chart (chart:): January Meals
```

you would highlight *January Meals*.

Exercise: Using Cross References

To try your hand at creating a cross reference, enter cross references in PRODUCT1.DOC. After the last paragraph, enter a new page by pressing Ctrl-Shift-Enter. Then, enter the following paragraph below the page break:

```
Products are being manufactured at a rate never seen in
the history of this country. Future growth in manufacturing
environmental support products is projected at 10% over the
next five years. This is less than half of the growth in the
requirements for the products (see page).
```

Use the bookmark name ESPgrowth for the cross reference. If the reference is not already marked, highlight *growth is projected at a minimum of 25%*. Select Format bookmarK. In the *name* field, enter *ESPgrowth* and press Enter.

Now place the highlight on the parenthesis following *page*, the last word on the screen. Press the Spacebar and then type in:

```
page:ESPgrowth
```

Press F3. Word encloses the cross reference with parentheses, like this:

`(see page (page:ESPgrowth))`

To see the printed result, print the document. The cross reference will look like this:

`...requirements for the products (see page 1).`

Save the document as PRODUCT1.

Hyphenation

You can hyphenate text to even out ragged right margins or to cause justified text to space in a more pleasing fashion. You can enter hyphens manually or have Word automatically enter hyphens for you.

Manual Hyphenation

When you insert a hyphen manually, you can select from three types: normal, optional, and nonbreaking. The following sentences illustrate the three types of hyphens:

- **Normal:** I enjoy out-of-the-way restaurants.
- **Optional:** I looked at the politician and considered his over-statement.
- **Nonbreaking:** Barbara Miller-Smith is the chairperson.

To insert a hyphen manually:

1. Place the highlight where you want the hyphen.
2. Use one of these hyphen types by pressing the key indicated:

Hyphen type	Description	Key
Normal	Breaks at end of line; hyphen always appears	Hyphen
Optional	Breaks at end of line; appears at line end only	Ctrl-Hyphen
Nonbreaking	Breaks before word with hyphen at end of line; hyphen always appears	Ctrl-Shift-Hyphen

To delete a hyphen, highlight it and select Delete or press Del. If a hyphen is not visible (an optional hyphen), set the Options *show non-printing symbols* field to Partial or All. The hyphen can then be deleted.

Automatic Hyphenation

You can automatically hyphenate a document or selected text in a document. Word will select the location of the hyphen at the end of a line. Or, you choose the location as Word hyphenates.

Automatic hyphenation only inserts optional hyphens. You still must enter normal hyphens or nonbreaking hyphens manually (see "Manual Hyphenation," earlier in this chapter).

Because Word looks at the words that can be split at the end of each line, use automatic hyphenation *after* editing and spell-checking a document. Otherwise, if your edits move the lines, you will need to repeat the automatic-hyphenation process.

To automatically hyphenate a document:

Automatic hyphenation is most useful for adjusting word spacing in justified paragraphs. Hyphens are rarely needed in paragraphs with ragged right margins, such as letters, memos, and manuscripts.

1. Select the text to be hyphenated (you can select the entire document by pressing **Shift-F10**).

2. Select **Library Hyphenate**.

3. In the *confirm* field, select one of the following:

   Yes to confirm each suggested optional hyphen

   No to let Word enter the optional hyphens without your input

4. In the *hyphenate caps* field, select:

   Yes to hyphenate words that begin with capital letters

   No to skip words that begin with capital letters (such as proper names)

5. Press **Enter** or click the command name. Word begins automatic hyphenation.

6. If you selected Yes in the *confirm* field, Word highlights the suggested spot for the first potential hyphenation and displays this message:

```
Enter Y to insert hyphen, N to skip word, or use direction
keys to reposition.
```

Press **N** to go on to the next word. Or, reposition the highlight by pressing:

Up Arrow   to move one hyphen position to the left
Down Arrow   to move one hyphen position to the right
Left Arrow   to move character by character left
Right Arrow   to move character by character right

Once you have positioned the highlight, press **Y** to insert a hyphen. Word immediately puts the hyphen in the text and finds the next potential hyphenation.

If you reposition the highlight too far to the right of the spot Word originally suggested, the word may not fit on the line, even when hyphenated.

Once Word has hyphenated the document, it displays a message like this one, indicating the number of words hyphenated:

`Twelve words hyphenated`

You can stop hyphenation at any time during the process by pressing Esc, in which case, Word displays this message:

`Enter Y to continue or Escape to cancel`

You can then press Y to go on hyphenating or Esc to stop the process.

If you have long documents, manually entering optional hyphens can be time consuming. A quick way to handle the problem is to scan the left margin for words you don't want hyphenated. Enter an optional hyphen after the words that you don't want Word to hyphenate (such as proper names). Then use automatic hyphenation with the *confirm* field set to No. The words followed by the optional hyphens will not be hyphenated.

Exercise: Hyphenating a Document

To hyphenate the PRODUCT1.DOC automatically, highlight the entire document by pressing Shift-F10. Select Library Hyphenate. In the *confirm* field, select Yes to review each suggested hyphenation. In the *hyphenate caps* field, select Yes to hyphenate words that begin with capital letters. (This is appropriate for this document because the text contains no proper names.) Press Enter. When Word highlights *workplace*, press Y to insert the hyphen as Word suggests. When Word highlights *environmental*, select N to leave the word alone and continue. Only one word—*workplace*—will be hyphenated in your document.

Windows

Word can display up to eight windows on the screen at one time. Each window is like a separate document screen. Although only one window can be active at a time, moving among windows is easy. There are many benefits of using windows. You can:

- View one or more documents at the same time
- View two or more parts of a single document at the same time
- Move or copy text between documents that appear
- Use a second window to make notes
- Use a second window to see the outline or table of contents of the document on which you are working
- See footnotes or annotated text while you work on the document
- Use a window to show the document with different modes (such as the Options *show hidden text* or *show non-printing symbols* fields set differently)
- View a document in different modes (such as document and outline view) at the same time

You can perform any typical Word editing activity in a window. You can open, close, clear, move, and zoom windows. This chapter covers each window activity in detail.

Some Word settings control all the windows on the screen. For example, if you are in text mode, every window appears in text mode. You cannot use text and graphics modes at the same time.

Window Elements

You size windows by specifying how many lines deep or columns wide they should be. Chapter 2, "Starting Microsoft Word," covers window elements in detail. To review, windows have the elements shown in Figure 11-1:

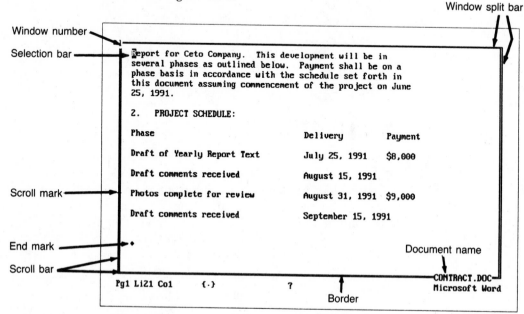

Figure 11-1. Window elements

- **Border:** The borders of a window are the four bars surrounding it. When working with a single window, you can choose to display the borders or not. When working with two or more windows, you must display the borders. Normally, you will want to show the borders to display the scroll mark or to use the mouse to scroll or select text. For more information on borders see Chapter 2, "Starting Microsoft Word."

- **Window number:** Word assigns each window a number in the order of creation. The number of each window appears in the upper left corner. The active window is the one where your highlight happens to rest. The number of the active window is highlighted.

- **Document name:** Once you have assigned a name to a document (usually by saving it), the document name appears in the lower right corner of the window. If an asterisk is before the name, the document is "read only."

- **End mark:** The end mark signifies the end of the document.

Use the scroll bar to get around.

- **Scroll bars and scroll mark:** The left and bottom borders serve as "scroll bars," along which you can move the mouse highlight to scroll vertically or horizontally through a document. The scroll mark is a small horizontal tick mark on the left scroll bar. It shows where you are in a document relative to the document as a whole. For example, if the mark is near the top of the window, you are near the top of the document. See Chapter 3, "Creating Documents," for more detailed information on scrolling.

- **Window split bars:** The top and right screen borders double as window split bars. By clicking on these bars with a mouse, you can split the screen into as many as eight windows. For details, see "Opening Windows" in this chapter.

- **Selection bar:** The far left column of the editing screen is the selection bar. To select a single line, point to the selection bar and click the left button. Press the right button to select a paragraph, or both buttons to select the entire document (see Chapter 4, "Editing Documents," for more information).

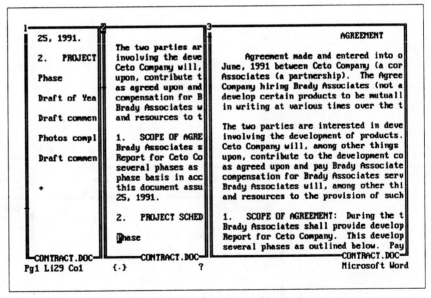

Figure 11-2. Three vertical windows

Opening Windows

Word can display up to eight windows at once and as many as three vertically or six horizontally. Figure 11-2 shows three vertical windows. Figure 11-3 shows seven horizontal windows. Figure 11-4 shows eight windows divided both horizontally and vertically.

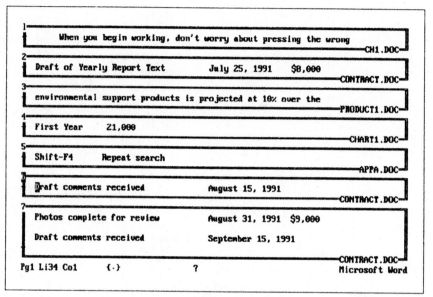

Figure 11-3. Seven horizontal windows

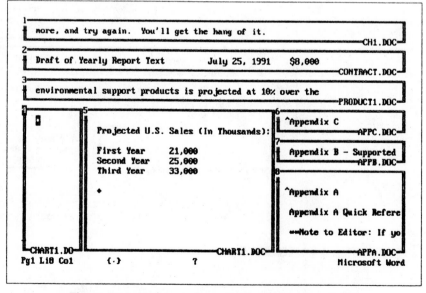

Figure 11-4. Eight windows (horizontal and vertical)

The layout of open windows depends on the order in which they are created. For example, to create the layout in Figure 11-5 you would first split the window vertically at column 30, then horizontally at row 8. In contrast, to create the layout in Figure 11-6 you would first split the window horizontally at row 8, then vertically at column 30. Same splits, different order.

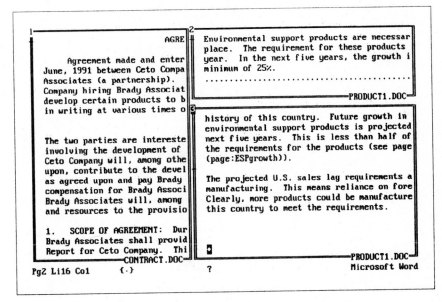

Figure 11-5. Vertical split then horizontal split

If you try to open too many windows, this message appears:

`Cannot open more than 8 windows`

or

`Not a valid window split`

Opening Windows with the Keyboard

To open a window with the keyboard:

1. Select **W**indow and **S**plit.
2. Choose **H**orizontal: Splits the screen left to right. Choose **V**ertical: Splits the screen top to bottom. (For information on opening

footnote windows, see Chapter 7, "Running Heads, Footnotes, and Annotations.")

3. In the *clear new window* field, select **No** to have the document that appears in the active window also appear in the new window. Select **Yes** to clear the new window in preparation for loading or entering a second document.

4. In the *at line* field (for a horizontal split) or *at column* field (for a vertical split), a number appears. This is where Word proposes to split the window. You have three options:

   • Press **Enter** to accept the proposed line or column.

   • Enter the line or column number desired.

   • Press **F1** to cause a highlight to appear on the left border for a horizontal split or the top border for a vertical split. Use the arrow keys to move the highlight to the row or column where you want the split to occur.

5. Press **Enter** to open the window.

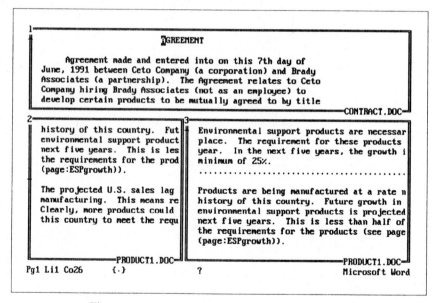

Figure 11-6. Horizontal split then vertical split

The new window will be active, meaning that your highlight will be in that window and any new text you enter will appear there. The new window's number will appear in the upper left corner.

If the current window is filled with text, before splitting the window you can move your highlight to the row or column where you would like the split to occur. Then, when you select the Window

Split command, the number to appear in the *at line* or *at column* fields will be the position of your highlight. This shortcut does not work if the current window is blank or if there are too few lines of text to allow you to move far enough down the screen.

Opening Windows with a Mouse

To open a window with a mouse:

Speed up window management with a mouse.

1. Point to the spot on the right or top border where you want the window to split.

2. Click the **left** button if you want the current document to appear in the new window. Click the **right** button to clear the new window. If the ruler is displayed along the top border and you are pointing to the top border, hold down **Alt** before clicking the button of your choice.

3. As in the keyboard example, the new window will be active and the new window's number will appear in the upper-left corner.

Activating a Window

To make a window active, you must move the highlight to that window. You can use either the keyboard or mouse for this purpose.

Press F1 to move among open windows.

To move to another window with the keyboard, press F1 until you have moved to the window of your choice. The window becomes active and the window number will be highlighted. The highlight moves to and from whatever was last highlighted in each window, or to the first character of a newly loaded document.

To move to a window with a mouse either point to the window number and click the *left* button, or click either button anywhere inside the window borders. The first option selects the text last selected in the window. The second option selects the highlighted text.

Exercise: Opening a Window

In this example, you will open a window. Begin with a single, blank window. Enter this text:

```
Projected U.S. Sales (In Thousands):

First Year    21,000
```

Second Year   25,000
Third Year   33,000

Open a second, cleared window to view the document PRODUCT1.DOC (created in the last chapter). Select Window Split Horizontal. In the *clear new window* field, enter Yes. With your highlight in the *at line* field, press F1. Position the highlight in the middle of the screen (approximately line 12). Press Enter. The window is split. Your highlight is in the newly created, clear window.
Select Transfer Load to load PRODUCT1.DOC into the new window. Your screen should look like Figure 11-7.

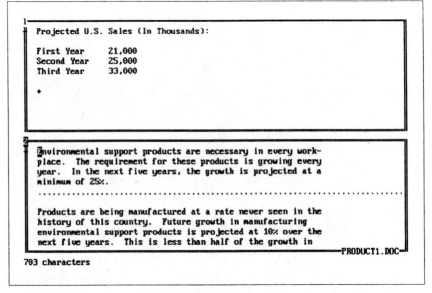

Figure 11-7. Your screen should look like this after completing the window-opening exercise

With your highlight in the PRODUCT1.DOC window, press F1 to move from window to window. Notice how the F1 key returns your highlight to whatever position it last occupied in each window.

Saving the Contents of All Windows

If you often use several windows, you will want to periodically save the contents of them all. You could activate each window one by one and save the contents, but Word provides an easier way.

To save the contents of every window:

1. Select **T**ransfer and **A**llsave. The following message appears:

`Saving all files...`

The name of the first file being saved then appears in a message like this:

`Saving C:\WORD\DOC\MYDOC.DOC`

2. If the document has not been saved, the Transfer Save *filename* field appears. Enter a file name and press **Enter**.

Once each document is saved, you are returned to the regular editing mode. The windows and the text within them appear as they were when you selected Transfer Allsave.

Exercise: Using Transfer Allsave

Select Transfer Allsave. The following message appears:

`Saving all files...`

Use the Transfer Allsave command to speed up closing windows.

Because the chart has not been saved, you are asked to enter a name in the *filename* field. Enter CHART1 as the name of the file and press Enter. If the *summary sheet* field of the Options command is set to Yes, complete summary information and press Enter.

As the next document, PRODUCT1, is saved, the following message appears:

`Saving C:\WORD\DOC\PRODUCT1.DOC`

When both documents are saved, the filename CHART1.DOC appears in the lower right border of window 1 and you are returned to the regular editing mode.

Clearing a Window

You can clear the contents of one window without affecting the contents of the others. If the document has unsaved changes, you are first given an opportunity to save them. Once a window is clear, the original Word defaults are in place in the document.

To clear a window:

1. Move to the window you want to clear.
2. Select **T**ransfer **C**lear **W**indow.
3. If all changes are saved, the window is cleared. If there are unsaved changes, this message appears:

   ```
   Enter Y to save changes to document, N to lose changes, or
   Esc to cancel
   ```

   - Press **Y** to save the changes. If you select **Y**, the document is saved under the document name that appears in the lower-right corner of the window. If the document has not been named, the TRANSFER SAVE *filename* field appears. Enter a file name and press **Enter**. The document is saved and the window is cleared.
   - Press **N** to lose the changes made since the last full save.
   - Press **Esc** to stop the process.

Exercise: Clearing Windows

Your screen should look like Figure 11-8. Clear the PRODUCT1 window. Press F1, if necessary, to move to the window containing PRODUCT1.DOC. Select Transfer Clear Window. Assuming you have not made changes since the last full save, the window is cleared. If you made changes of any kind (even an insertion or deletion), you will need to respond to prompts asking whether you want to save the changes before clearing the window. Your screen should look like Figure 11-9.

Closing a Window

Close as many windows as you like.

You can close a single window or all windows. If you have unsaved changes in a document and start to close the window, Word lets you save the changes.

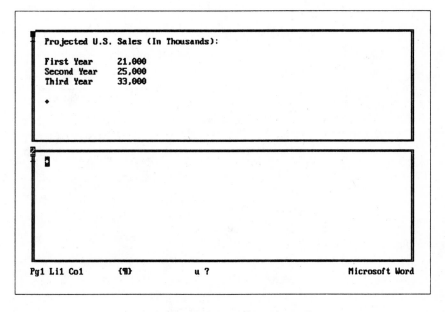

```
1
   Projected U.S. Sales (In Thousands):

   First Year      21,000
   Second Year     25,000
   Third Year      33,000

     ◆


2
   Environmental support products are necessary in every work-
   place.  The requirement for these products is growing every
   year.  In the next five years, the growth is projected at a
   minimum of 25%.
   ......................................................................

   Products are being manufactured at a rate never seen in the
   history of this country.  Future growth in manufacturing
   environmental support products is projected at 10% over the
   next five years.  This is less than half of the growth in
                                                      PRODUCT1.DOC
703 characters
```

Figure 11-8. Two windows with documents

```
   Projected U.S. Sales (In Thousands):

   First Year      21,000
   Second Year     25,000
   Third Year      33,000

     ◆


2


Pg1 Li1 Co1      {¶}          u ?              Microsoft Word
```

Figure 11-9. Cleared window

Closing a Single Window

Select the window you want to close. Figure 11-10 shows several windows. Figure 11-11 shows the result when the bottom horizontal window (window 2) is closed. Notice that the borders realign to take up the former space of window 2.

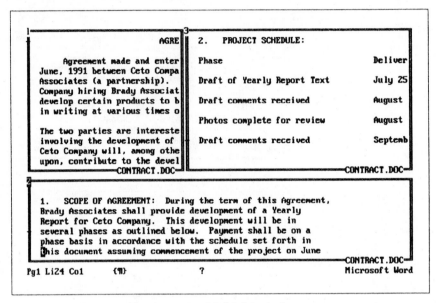

Figure 11-10. Multiple windows

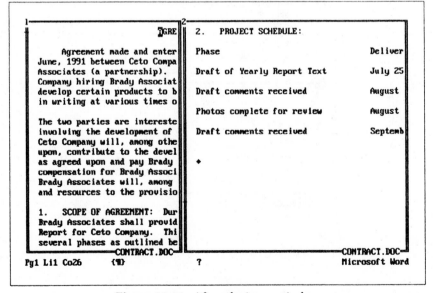

Figure 11-11. After closing a window

You can close a window with the keyboard or a mouse. To use the keyboard:

1. Activate the window you want to close. (Or, you can enter the window number later.)
2. Select **W**indow and **C**lose.
3. The active window's number appears in the *window number* field. Use this number or enter the number of the window you want to close.
4. Press **Enter**.
5. If the window has unsaved changes, the following message appears:

   `Enter Y to save changes to the document, N to lose changes, or Esc to cancel`

   Press one of these options:

Y	to save the changes. The *filename* field appears to enable you to name the document, if necessary.
N	to lose any changes made since the last full save.
Esc	to stop the window-closing process.

When you close a widow, the remaining windows reposition themselves to fill up the screen.

To close a window with a mouse:

1. Point to the top or right border of the window you want to close.
2. Click both buttons.
3. If there are unsaved changes, this message appears:

   `Enter Y to save changes to the document, N to lose changes, or Esc to cancel`

   Press one of these options:

Y	to save changes. The *filename* field appears to enable you to name the document, if necessary.
N	to lose the changes since the last full save.
Esc	to stop the process.

Closing All but One Window

When you close all windows, you are given the opportunity to save any unsaved changes for each document. All but one window is cleared; all scrap and scratch files are cleared; default glossaries and styles are restored. Word's default settings are restored.

To close all but one window:

1. Select Transfer Clear All.

2. For each document with unsaved changes, this message appears:

   Enter Y to save changes to document, N to lose changes, or
   Esc to cancel

   Respond to this message each time it appears. Once you have handled all unsaved changes, all windows are cleared and closed. Window number 1 stays on your screen, but its contents have been cleared. The window is set to Word's defaults.

Exercise: Closing a Window

To start, you should have the window with CHART1.DOC on the screen along with a cleared, horizontal window (see Figure 11-12).

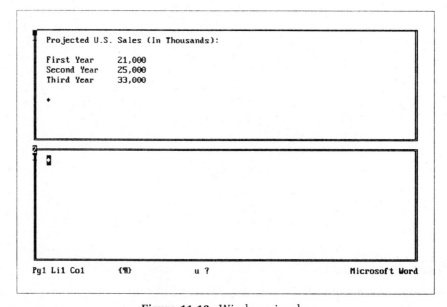

Figure 11-12. Windows in place

In this exercise, you will close the top window with the chart. Select Window Close. Make sure the *window number* field contains the number 1. If you have unsaved changes, you will need to respond to the prompts to save the changes before Word will close the window. Press Enter. Assuming there are no unsaved changes to the window, the window closes immediately leaving you with a single, blank window (see Figure 11-13).

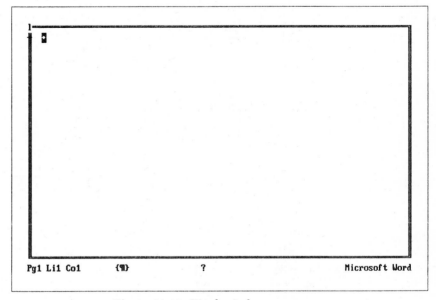

Figure 11-13. Final window appearance

Resizing a Window

You resize a window by moving its borders. Resizing is useful if you and want to see more of a particular window. It is also useful if you create a window and then decide it should be a different size.

Resize windows to fit your needs.

You can resize a window by using either the keyboard or the mouse. In each case, it is the lower-right corner of a window that moves. Keep this in mind as you decide which window you want to move. For example, assume that you want to enlarge the bottom window shown in Figure 11-14. Instead of moving the top border of the bottom window up, you would move the bottom right corner of the top window higher. Figure 11-15 shows the result. The same principle holds true for vertical windows. Figure 11-16 shows two vertical windows split in column 40. To make the right vertical window larger, you would move the lower-right corner of the left vertical window farther to the left. Figure 11-17 shows the result of moving the corner to column 20.

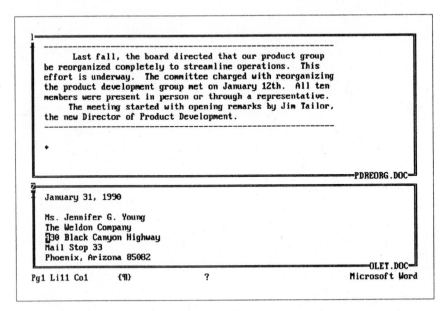

Figure 11-14. Horizontal windows before the move

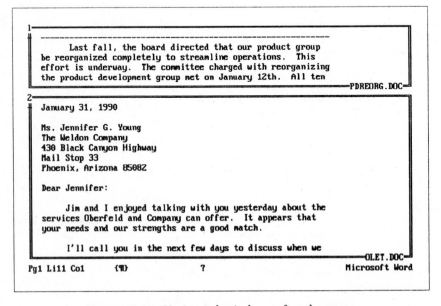

Figure 11-15. Horizontal windows after the move

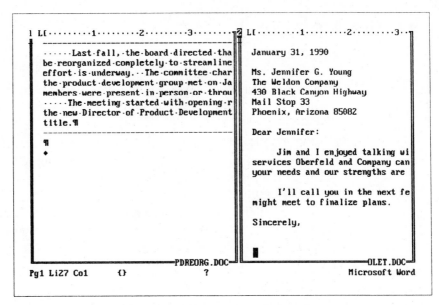

Figure 11-16. Vertical windows before the move

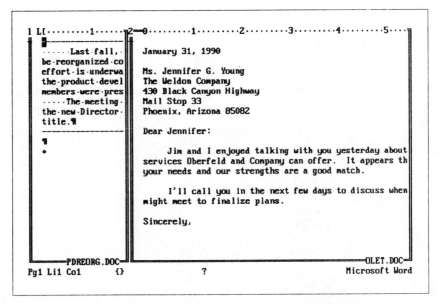

Figure 11-17. Vertical windows after the move

Resizing a Window by Using the Keyboard

To resize a window with the keyboard:

1. Move the highlight to the window you want to resize. Or, stay where you are and enter the number of the target window later in this process.
2. Select **Window Move**.
3. The number that appears in the *lower right corner of window #* field is the number of the active window. Keep this number or enter the number of the window you want to resize.
4. Move the highlight to either the *to row* or *column* fields. If you are resizing a horizontal window, use the *to row* field. If you are resizing a vertical window, use the *column* field.
5. Enter a number or press **F1** to position the highlight on the border with the arrow keys.
6. Press **Enter** when the number in the *to row* or *column* field is what you want.

Resizing a Window by Using a Mouse

Resizing windows is a snap with a mouse.

To move a window by using a mouse:

1. Point to the lower right corner of the window border you want to move.
2. Press and hold down either the **right** or **left** button.
3. Drag the mouse pointer to the new location for the window. (Move the pointer up or down for a vertical window. Move it left or right for a horizontal window.)
4. Release the button.

Exercise: Resizing a Window

Use Transfer Load to load PRODUCT1.DOC into a single, clear window. To create a vertical window, select Window Split Vertical. In the *clear new window* field, select Yes. With your highlight in the *at column* field, press F1. Position your highlight near the halfway mark and press Enter. A new, clear window appears. Figure 11-18 shows the result.

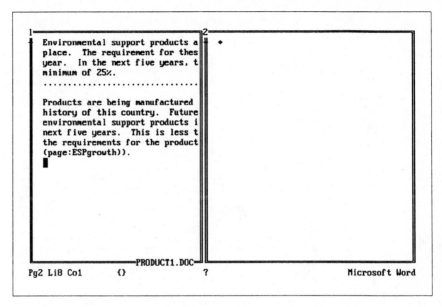

Figure 11-18. PRODUCT1.DOC in a vertical window

Select Transfer Load to load the CHART1.DOC in the new window. The screen shown in Figure 11-19 should appear.

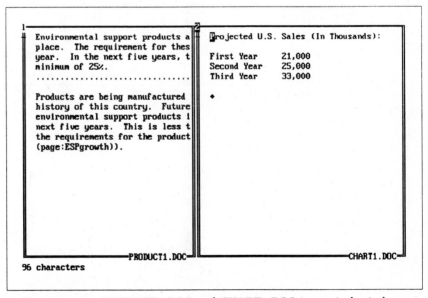

Figure 11-19. PRODUCT1.DOC and CHART1.DOC in vertical windows

Suppose you want to see more of the PRODUCT1.DOC window. If necessary, press F1 to activate the PRODUCT1.DOC window. Select Window Move. The number that appears in the *lower right corner of window #* field is the number of the active window. Keep this number. In the *column* field, enter the number 50. Press Enter. The right border of the PRODUCT1 window should extend to column 50, as shown in Figure 11-20.

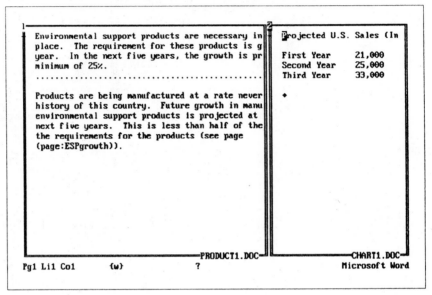

Figure 11-20. The result of moving the PRODUCT1.DOC window

Zooming Windows

You may think that using multiple windows would be confusing or leave little room for work—and it would be if you had to keep them all on screen at once. Fortunately, Word lets you zoom in on any window so that it occupies the full screen.

The phrase *zooming a window* means that one window is expanded to fill the entire window area of the screen. By using multiple windows and zooming the one you want to work in, you can comfortably manage several documents at once. All other windows stay open, you just don't see them.

When a window is zoomed, you can edit its contents as usual. You can also move or copy its contents (see "Copying and Moving Between Windows" later in this chapter). You can also press F1 to move from zoomed window to zoomed window. The reminder ZM appears in the status line when a window is zoomed.

Zoom your windows for full-screen display.

Figure 11-21 shows five windows. Without zoom, this display could be difficult to work within because no one document appears in full view. Figure 11-22 shows the affect of zooming in on window 4. Notice the ZM in the status line. This reminds you that the window is zoomed.

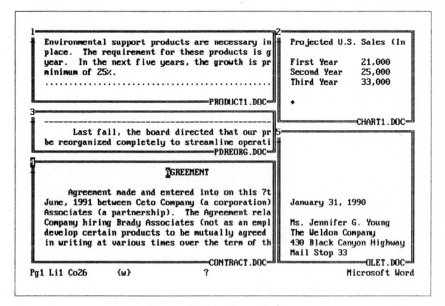

Figure 11-21. Five windows

When one window is zoomed, you cannot open a new one. If you try, the following message appears:

`Cannot split a zoomed window`

You can, however, open a footnote window from a zoomed window so long as seven or fewer windows are already opened. If you zoom a window with an open footnote window, the two are zoomed together.

If you select Quit when working in a zoomed window, all the windows appear. You must then respond to prompts to save unsaved changes in each window.

Zooming with the Keyboard

To zoom in on a particular window with the keyboard:

1. Press **F1** to highlight the number of the window you want to zoom.

2. Press **Ctrl-F1** to zoom the window.

   The window appears on the full screen, and ZM appears on the status line.

3. Press **F1** to move to the next window; it too appears zoomed.

4. When you are done looking at the zoomed documents, press **Ctrl-F1** to unzoom all the windows.

Zooming with a Mouse

To zoom with a mouse:

1. Point to the window number of the window you want to zoom and click the right button. The window does not have to be active.

2. Move to the next zoomed window by pointing to the window number on your screen and clicking the left button. The next consecutively numbered window fills the screen.

3. Once you are done looking at zoomed windows, point to the window number and click the right button to unzoom all the windows.

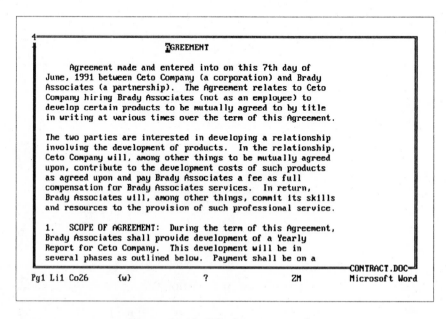

Figure 11-22. Window 4 zoomed

Exercise: Zooming a Window

You still may not be satisfied with your ability to see the documents PRODUCT1 and CHART1 in the vertically split screen (see Figure 11-23). You can zoom each window to see full-screen displays.

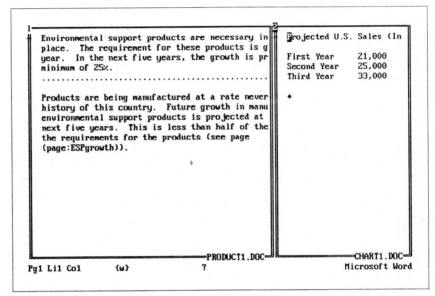

Figure 11-23. Vertical windows displaying PRODUCT1.DOC and CHART1.DOC

Activate the PRODUCT1.DOC window using either the mouse or keyboard. To zoom the window, press Ctrl-F1. The window appears on the full screen and ZM appears on the status line. You can now edit the document as desired.

To see the CHART1.DOC window, press F1. The window appears full-screen. Unzoom the windows by pressing Ctrl-F1. Both now appear on the screen.

Copying and Moving Between Windows

Use windows to move or copy text between two documents. The process is essentially the same as that used to move or copy text within a single document.

Windows simplify moving text between documents.

You can also use windows to view several parts of a document at once. This is useful for moving or copying text within a single document because you can see the text to be moved or copied and the place to which you want to move or copy it on screen at the same time.

To copy an entire document into another document, use the Transfer Merge command described in Chapter 14, "Handling Files and Running DOS Commands."

Copying or Moving Text Between Two Documents

To view two documents at once and copy or move between them, follow these steps:

1. Scroll the window to which text is to be copied or moved and highlight the location to which you want to copy or move it.
2. Press **F1** to move to the window containing the text to be copied or moved.
3. Scroll the window until you find the text to be copied or moved. Highlight it.
4. If you want to move the text, press **Del** to delete it to scrap. If you want to copy the text, select **Copy** and press **Enter** to copy the text to scrap.
5. Press **F1** to move to the target window.
6. Press **Ins** (or select Insert and press **Enter**) to copy the text from scrap to the target location.

Using the keyboard, you can copy or move text between zoomed documents. Just delete or copy the text to scrap, press F1 to move to the target window in zoomed state, move the highlight to the place you want to insert the text, and press Ins.

Copying or Moving Text Within a Single Document

You do not have to use windows to copy or move text within a single document. However, if the text and its proposed new location are more than one screen apart and you want to view both at the same time, windows are essential.

To use windows for copying or moving text within a single document:

1. Open a second window so that both windows contain the same document (see "Opening Windows" in this chapter if you need instructions).

2. Scroll the window to which text is to be copied or moved and highlight the location to which you want to copy or move it.

3. Press **F1** to move to the window containing the text to be copied or moved.

4. Scroll the window until you find the text to be copied or moved. Highlight it.

5. If you want to move the text, press **Del** to delete it to scrap. If you want to copy the text, select **C**opy and press **Enter** to copy the text to scrap.

6. Press **F1** to move to the target window.

7. Press **Ins** (or select Insert and press **Enter**) to copy the text from scrap to the target location.

Exercise: Copying Between Documents

With PRODUCT1.DOC and CHART1.DOC loaded in a vertically split screen (see Figure 11-24), you will copy CHART1.DOC into the PRODUCT1.DOC document.

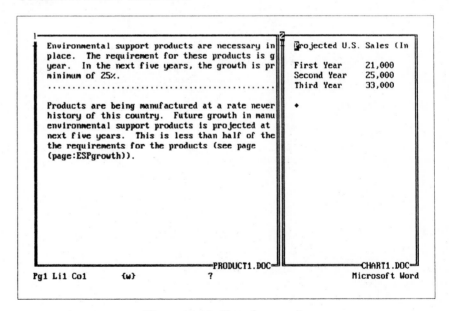

Figure 11-24. Two documents

Place your highlight in CHART1.DOC. Press Shift-F10 to select the entire document. Select Copy and press Enter. The text is copied to the scrap area.

Activate the PRODUCT1.DOC by pressing F1. Place your cursor after the last paragraph in the document and press Ins. The chart is inserted. To complete the document, add this paragraph above the chart:

```
The projected U.S. sales lag behind requirements and exceed
U.S. manufacturing. This means reliance on foreign imports.
Clearly, more products could be manufactured and sold in
this country to meet the requirements.
```

Zoom the PRODUCT1 document by pressing Ctrl-F1. The document should look like Figure 11-25.

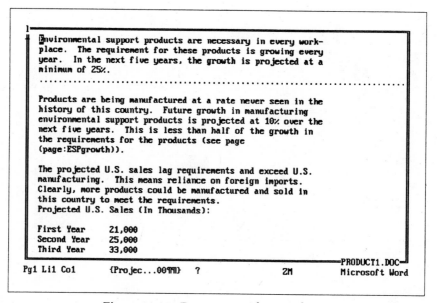

Figure 11-25. Document with copied text

Select Transfer Allsave to save all documents. Then, select Transfer Clear All to clear all windows and return to the single, default Word window.

Search and Replace

Word's search and replace functions have many uses. For example, you can search for specific text, such as a passage you want to review. You can replace a misspelled name with the correct spelling. Or you can search for a symbol that you've used to enter casual notes, such as double asterisks (**), and simply remove it. Replacing text is especially useful if you have entered a recurring error. For example, you may have entered the word *affect* instead of *effect*. Checking your spelling won't reveal this error but searching for *affect* and selectively replacing it with *effect* will quickly correct the document.

Word also allows you to search for and/or replace formats or styles. For example, suppose you want to search for text that is underlined in the document and change its format to bold. You don't remember the text, but you do know that very little other text is underlined. You can search for all instances of the underline format and replace it selectively with bold text. Then you can print a sample of the document using bold text and compare the appearance of the second document to the original.

Searching for Text

When searching for or replacing text, you can specify:

- Letters
- Numbers
- Symbols
- Special characters (such as ^, ?, tabs, spaces, and newline characters)

- Hidden text (as long as Yes is selected in the Options *show hidden text* field)

You can enter up to 250 characters as your search text. Longer search-text entries are more precise and, therefore, increase Word's chances of locating the exact text immediately. However, very long entries slow down the search because they take longer to process. Also, many users are more likely to enter a typographical error or incorrect text in a longer entry.

It is a good practice to keep your search text short and unique. For example, suppose you want to find this sentence in a long report:

`The methods used by the Bander Group seemed amateurish and futile.`

You could search for the *Bander Group* name, but if it appears often in the report, you will spend a good deal of time reviewing each of those occurrences before you find the one you want. If, however, you remember that the word *futile* appears in the passage you want but is rare elsewhere in the report, the fastest approach may be to search only for *futile*.

To search for text:

1. Select **S**earch.

2. In the *text* field, enter the text you want to search for.

   When you search for text, you must enter the exact characters or spaces you want to locate. You can enter up to 250 characters including spaces, numbers, letters, symbols, wildcards, or codes. (See "Wildcards" and "Special Characters," later in this chapter.) Figure 12-1 shows an example of a long *text* field entry. Notice how the text wraps to the next line and how the other fields have moved to accommodate it.

   As you can see in the figure, if you enter more than 250 characters, Word displays this message:

   `Response too long`

Once you enter the search text and select settings for the appropriate fields, those settings remain in effect until you change them. You can do so either by entering new text or specifying new settings in either the Search or Replace commands.

3. In the *direction* field, select **U**p to search from the left of the highlight to the beginning of the document. Or, select **D**own to search from the right of the highlight to the end of the document.

   For example, in Figure 12-2, a search up will start to the left of the *p* in *pilot* in the second line and move to the document's beginning. A search down will start to the right of the selected character and continue to the end of the document. The highlighted character is not included in either search.

```
1 L[····L····1·········2·········3·········4·········5·········6····]···7·····┐
   ▌
       →    The·way·to·find·out·whether·we·want·to·proceed·with·the·
   project·is·to·start·a·pilot·project.···This·way·we·will·gain·the·
   experience·without·the·investment.¶
       →    This·concept·has·the·support·of·upper·management·including·
   the·President·of·the·firm.···The·funding·is·currently·being·
   reviewed·by·the·Executive·Committee.¶
       →    An·outside·consulting·company·could·proceed·with·the·pilot.···
```
```
SEARCH text: We regard the method to complete the project to be the soundest way
 to proceed.  Without further direction, the process will begin as stated on Jan
uary 5.  The project will be directed internally by Jim Jones.  Jim has worked w
ith this type of project in █ direction: Up(Down) case: Yes(No) whole word: Yes(
No)
Response too long
P22 D3 L1 C1      {?}              ?                         Microsoft Word
```

Figure 12-1. Search text field entry

```
1 L[····L····1·········2·········3·········4·········5·········6····]···7·····┐
   →    The·way·to·find·out·whether·we·want·to·proceed·with·the·
   project·is·to·start·a·▒ilot·project.···This·way·we·will·gain·the·
   experience·without·the·investment.¶
   →    This·concept·has·the·support·of·upper·management·including·
   the·President·of·the·firm.···The·funding·is·currently·being·
   reviewed·by·the·Executive·Committee.¶
   →    An·outside·consulting·company·could·proceed·with·the·pilot.···
   This·approach·brings·in·needed·expertise·on·a·temporary·basis.···
   Three·firms·with·appropriate·experience·have·been·identified.¶
   ¶
   ¶
                                                           CH12.DOC
P22 D3 L3 C23    {x}              ?                         Microsoft Word
```

Figure 12-2. Searching with a single character highlighted

In Figure 12-3, a search up will begin with the space immediately to the left of the beginning of the selected text. A search down will begin immediately following the selection, with the word *investment*.

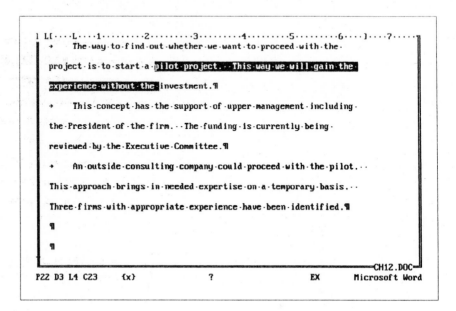

Figure 12-3. Searching with a larger selection highlighted

If you want to search down through a document (the usual direction), place your highlight on the first character of the document or the character immediately preceding the section of the document you want to search and select Down in the *direction* field. If you want to search up through a document, place your highlight on the last character of the document or the character immediately following that section of the document you want to search.

4. In the *case* field, select **Yes** to match exactly the case of the entered text or **No** to ignore it. Case refers to whether letters are capitalized (uppercase) or not (lowercase).

   For example, if you enter the word:

   will

   in the *text* field and select **Yes** in the *case* field, Word finds the second and third occurrences of the word *will* in the following sentence but not the first:

```
Will made the comment that he will go to the dinner before
he will go to the dance.
```

By contrast if you search for the word *five* in the following sentence and select **No** in the *case* field, Word will find every instance of the word *five* (including the typographical error):

```
Give me five reasons why Five and Dimes are no longer a
fixture on the five o'clock news.
```

5. In the *whole word* field, select **Yes** if you want the entry treated as a separate word surrounded by spaces, punctuation, or tabs. Select **No** if the characters entered may be part of a larger word or string of characters.

   For example, if you search for the text *time* and you select **Yes** in the *whole word* field, Word will not find the text in words such as the following:

```
timeliness
overtime
timer
```

   but it will find every instance of *time* in the following sentences:

```
Call me next time.
   Time and time again we have made the same mistake.
Since last time, we have researched further.
Consider the "time" spent killing time.
```

   If you select **No**, Word will find *all* occurrences of the character string you enter, regardless of the context in which it occurs. In the case of *time*, Word will find all the following instances:

```
timeliness
timer
time.
"time"
   time
timeliness
```

6. Press **Enter** or click the command name to begin the search. Word displays the first occurrence of the text. If it finds no occurrence, Word displays this message:

```
Search text not found
```

7. To find the next occurrence of the text, press **Shift-F4** or select Search and press **Enter**. If you are using a mouse, you can select Search again, though this is slower than using the keyboard. Repeat the search as many times as necessary.

Exercise: Searching for Text

Enter the following text in a blank window. (After the numbers 1, 2, and 3, enter a period and a space.)

There are dozens of reasons the real estate business has been in a slump in this area. Many businesspersons have agreed that the business will get tougher before it gets better. Here are three steps every agent can take to protect the investment in his or her career:

1. Make more contacts

2. Qualify buyers more closely

3. Look harder for better deals

To many in real estate, these seem like simple steps. However, when applied by the Whishmail program, these results can be expected:

Higher sales and higher commissions.

Try a search. Suppose you want to move quickly to the name of the program. Place your highlight on the first line and column of the window and then select Search. Enter this text in the *text* field:

Whish?

In the *direction* field, select Down. In the *case* field, enter No, and in the *whole word* field, select No. Press Enter. Your highlight moves to the occurrence of *Whishmail*. Change the spelling to:

Whihmail

Save the document under the name WLET.

Replacing Text

When you replace text, Word searches for the characters you identify and then replaces them with your entry. You can replace letters, numbers, symbols, spaces, tabs, paragraph marks, newline characters, and division marks. (To learn how to replace formats, see "Replacing Formats," later in this chapter.) Unlike the Search command, the Replace command allows you to select only a section of the document in which to replace text.

Before replacing text, you must specify the following:

- The original characters you want to replace
- The substitute text
- Whether you want to confirm each replacement
- How to handle upper and lowercase letters
- How to handle whole words

To replace text:

1. Select the text you want Word to search. The selection must be more than one character because if you select only a single character, Word replaces from that character to the end of the document.

2. Select **R**eplace.

3. In the *text* field, enter the text you want to replace. Make sure your entry is exact. You can enter up to 250 characters, including special character codes, letters, symbols, spaces, or numbers. If you attempt to enter more than 250 characters, Word displays a message indicating that the text is too long. The more characters you enter, the longer the time Word takes to replace it.

4. In the *with text* field, enter the text that is to be substituted for the original. The guidelines for entering text are identical to those given above for the *text* field.

5. In the *confirm* field, select **Y**es for Word to confirm each replacement. Select **N**o to allow Word to make replacements without your review.

When using the Replace command, you cannot search up (to the left of the highlight). Always place your highlight at the beginning of the section in which replacements are to be made.

The smallest inexactitude in entering text in the *text* and *with text* fields can be disastrous. If there is any doubt whatsoever about the results of a replacement instruction, set the *confirm* field to Yes to make sure that only the text you want to be replaced is in fact replaced. You can also choose to confirm only as many replacements as you deem necessary to make sure that the instruction is working properly. When you are satisfied, press Esc to return to the editing screen, select Replace again, and set the *confirm* field to No.

6. In the *case* field, select **Yes** if you want Word to match the upper and lowercase characters entered in the *text* field. Select **No** to ignore case.

If you select **Yes** in the *case* field, Word will find only exact case matches. For example, *Dog* will match with *Dog* but not with *dog* or *dOg*. The replacement text is entered by Word in the exact case.

If you select **No** in the *case* field, Word ignores capitalization in the text to be searched. For example, if you search for *CaT*, Word will find *Cat*, *CaT*, *CAT*, *CAt*, *cat*, *caT*, *cAt*, and *cAT*. If the replacement text consists entirely of lowercase letters, Word will capitalize the replacement depending on the case of the first letter in the word to be replaced. For example, if you want to replace all instances of *Cat* with *dog*, the results will be as follows:

Original word	Replacement word
Cat	Dog
CaT	
CAT	
CAt	
cat	dog
caT	
cAt	
cAT	

If the replacement text contains one or more capital letters, however, Word assumes you want them to appear in the text and includes them in the replacement even if you have set the *case* field to **No**. For example, if you want to replace all instances of *Cat* with *Dog*, the results will be as follows:

Original word	Replacement
Cat	Dog
CaT	
CAT	
CAt	
cat	
caT	
cAt	
cAT	

The following examples illustrate how Word treats uppercase letters depending on what you have selected in the *case* field. (Note that in some cases, no replacement is made.)

Settings	Before replace	After replace
case: Yes	Light	Dark
replace text: Light	light	light
with text: Dark	liGHt	liGHt
case: No	Light	Dark
replace text: Light	light	Dark
with text: Dark	liGHt	Dark
case: Yes	Light	Light
replace text: light	light	Dark
with text: Dark	liGHt	liGHt
case: No	Light	Dark
replace text: light	light	Dark
with text: Dark	liGHt	Dark
case: Yes	Light	dark
replace text: Light	light	light
with text: dark	liGHt	liGHt
case: No	Light	Dark
replace text: Light	light	dark
with text: dark	liGHt	dark
case: Yes	Light	Light
replace text: light	light	dark
with text: dark	liGHt	liGHt
case: No	Light	Dark
replace text: light	light	dark
with text: dark	liGHt	dark

7. In the *whole word* field, select **Yes** to match whole words only. The whole word can be surrounded by spaces, tabs, or punctuation but not by letters, numbers, or symbols.

You can specify whole words when you search text with the Replace command. Whole words, however, can be surrounded by spaces, tabs, or punctuation. For example, select **Yes** in the *whole words* field if you want to select the word *state* in these instances:

```
I'll state for the record.
Iowa is a beautiful state.
State's rights are important.
State it again.
Using only gestures, he tried to "state" his reaction.
```

Select **No** in the *whole word* field if you want to select any occurrence of a string of characters regardless of the spaces, characters, punctuation, or tabs surrounding the characters.

For example, select **No** for *whole words* to select the character string *state* in the following examples:

```
It's a misstatement.
He stated it again and again.
Why not restate it in a kinder fashion.
```

When searching for whole words, use the whole word *option rather than typing in a search word with a space at each end. Since Word doesn't distinguish between spaces and tabs, Word will not find your word if it is preceded or followed by a tab.*

8. Press **Enter** or click the command name to start the replace process.

9. If you selected **Yes** in the *confirm* field, Word finds the first occurrence of the text and displays this message:

```
Enter Y to replace, N to skip and continue, or Esc to cancel
```

Press one of the following:

Y	to replace the original text with the specified substitute text
N	to leave the original text in place
Esc	to stop the replace process

Continue choosing **Yes** or **No** until all instances of the text to be replaced have been found. Once the replacement process is complete, Word displays a message indicating the number of replacements made. Your highlight returns to its original location.

If you have ended the process by pressing Esc, you can begin it again either by selecting Replace again (your previous settings will still be in place) or by pressing Shift-F4 to repeat the previous search and F4 to repeat the previous replacement.

If you need to undo one or more replacements, use the Undo command immediately after completing the replacement process. For example, if you accidently set the *confirm* field to No, you could inadvertently replace text you did not mean to affect. If you are concerned about the outcome of a replacement, make a copy of the document under another name before you replace text. Or, save the document with the replacements under a different name to preserve the original, "unreplaced" version.

Refining Searches with Wildcards and Special Characters

You can refine your searches by using wildcards and special characters. Wildcards are useful when you don't know the exact text you are searching for. Special characters are useful for searching for certain non-printing characters or for combinations of those characters and normal text.

Wildcards

If you don't know the complete spelling of a word, or you want Word to allow any character in a particular place, you can enter a question mark in your search text. This question mark is referred to as a *wildcard* because it will match any character. For example, suppose your document contains the following words:

```
correlation
relation
correlate
relate
```

Here are some examples of text Word locates when you use the question-mark wildcard as a placeholder for selected letters:

Search entry	Finds
?elate	correlate, relate
relat?	correlation, relation, correlate, relate
r?late	correlate, relate
r??late	correlate

Unlike some word-processing programs, Word does not allow use of an asterisk (*) to indicate more than one character. When using Word's search-and-replace functions, each question mark stands for one character or space. You have to enter the same number of question marks as unknown characters in the text.

Because Word reserves the question mark for a wildcard, you cannot search for a question mark by entering that character alone. If you try, Word will stop at each character and space. To search for a question mark, type in a caret (^) before the question mark. For example, searching for *line^?* will find *aline?* and *line?.*.

Special Characters

In Word, a question mark does not function as a wildcard in replacement text as it does in DOS. For example, to replace Jim with Jim? simply type in Jim? in the with text field.

You can refine your searches further by using special characters either alone or in combination with one another or with text. These characters are especially helpful when searching for certain non-printing characters or combinations of those characters and normal text. The following table lists the special characters and the characters they stand for:

Select	To find
^w	Any spaces, tabs, newline characters, paragraph or division marks, manual page breaks, and nonbreaking spaces; use as part of the search text in a search or replace process; do not use this character as replacement text.
^s	Nonbreaking space
^t	Tab character
^p	Paragraph mark
^n	Newline character
^-	Optional hyphen; use to search for identical text with or without optional hyphens; any optional hyphens must be in the exact location entered for the search or replace process
^d	Division mark or manual page break

Because the caret (^) is used to search for special characters, you must enter two carets to search for a caret symbol. For example, to find the text *to^night*, you would enter *to^^night*. Carets in replacement text have no special function and are treated like any other character.

You can combine special and normal characters in search or replacement text, and you can use special characters to replace certain types of formatting, as you'll see in the following examples.

Adding Tabs to Paragraphs

The first example illustrates how to use the Replace command to add tab marks to several paragraphs. The paragraphs in Figure 12-4 can be quickly indented by replacing the current paragraph mark with a paragraph mark followed by a tab mark. See Figure 12-5 for the final outcome.

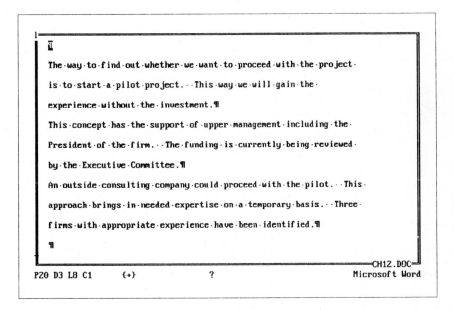

Figure 12-4. Text with paragraph marks

The names in Figure 12-6 are not aligned consistently. You can use the Replace command to swiftly align them. The white space special-character code (^w) was selectively replaced with a paragraph mark and a tab (^p^t). The result is shown in Figure 12-7.

In this example, you have to use paragraph marks *and* tab marks in the *with text* field because Word recognizes all characters except numbers, punctuation, and letters as "white space." As a result, Word highlights the paragraph mark ending one line and the tab(s) or space(s) beginning the next line as a single block of white space to be replaced. If you do not use the paragraph mark in the replace process, Word puts the names on one line, separated by tabs only. In this

¶

→   The·way·to·find·out·whether·we·want·to·proceed·with·the·
project·is·to·start·a·pilot·project.···This·way·we·will·gain·the·
experience·without·the·investment.¶

→   This·concept·has·the·support·of·upper·management·including·
the·President·of·the·firm.···The·funding·is·currently·being·
reviewed·by·the·Executive·Committee.¶

→   An·outside·consulting·company·could·proceed·with·the·pilot.···
This·approach·brings·in·needed·expertise·on·a·temporary·basis.···
Three·firms·with·appropriate·experience·have·been·identified.¶

¶

P2Q D3 L18 C1   {·→·}   ?   CH12.DOC
                                                            Microsoft Word

Figure 12-5. The paragraph marks replaced with paragraph marks and tabs

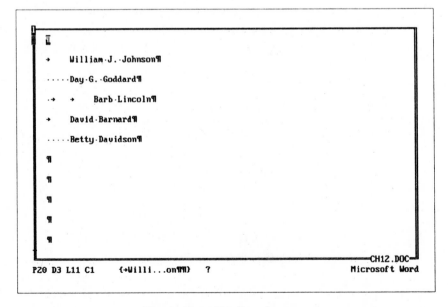

→   William·J.·Johnson¶

·····Day·G.·Goddard¶

·→   →   Barb·Lincoln¶

→   David·Barnard¶

·····Betty·Davidson¶

¶

¶

¶

¶

¶

P2Q D3 L11 C1   {→Willi...on¶¶}   ?   CH12.DOC
                                                            Microsoft Word

Figure 12-6. Unaligned names

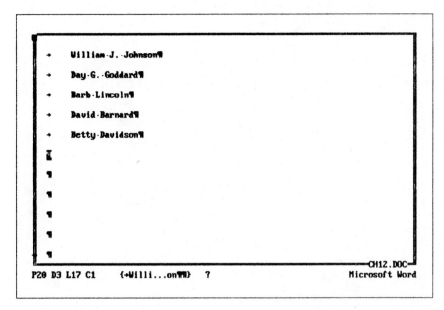

Figure 12-7. The white space replaced with tabs

replace operation, it is also important to confirm each replacement suggested by Word because every space within the names is recognized as "white space." During the replace process, you need to tell Word to leave these spaces as they are.

Replacing Paragraph Marks with Newline Marks

This example illustrates how to fix a problem many Word users face. The table in Figure 12-8 was created with paragraph marks at the end. The decimal tab characters need to be changed so that the columns are spaced farther apart. You could change the decimal tab characters for each paragraph or select the paragraphs and change the tab settings. A faster way to remedy the situation is to replace paragraph symbols with newline characters (see Figure 12-9 for the outcome of the replace). Then, simply change the layout of the decimal tabs in one stroke. Figure 12-10 illustrates the final result.

Removing Manual Page Breaks

You can use the Replace command to quickly remove manual page breaks. Figure 12-11 shows text that was formatted and printed for overhead slides. Once the masters are printed, you need to replace the manual page breaks with nothing. In the replace process, you identify ^d (manual page breaks) as the *replace text* and leave the *with text* field blank. Figure 12-12 shows the result, which can now be printed as a presentation outline or a handout.

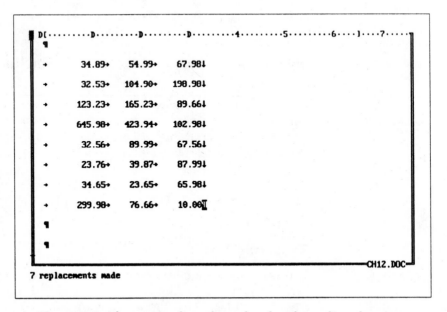

Figure 12-8. A table with paragraph marks

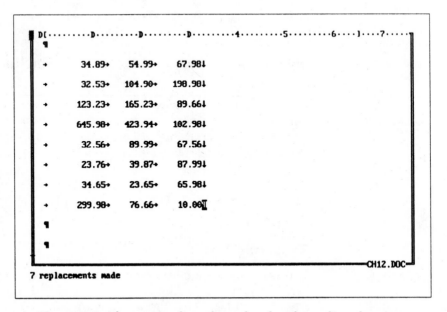

Figure 12-9. The paragraph marks replaced with newline characters

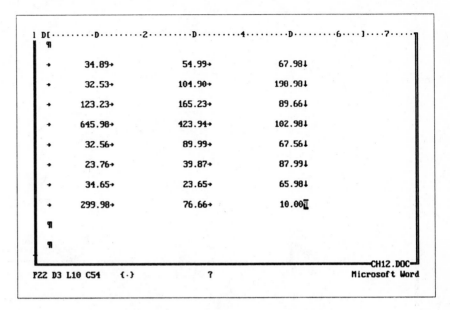

Figure 12-10. The decimal tabs moved

```
T
Steps·to·Get·Published¶
··················································································
1··Identify·a·Concept¶
··················································································
2··Identify·the·Market·and·Audience¶
··················································································
3··Speak·with·a·Publisher·or·Agent¶
··················································································
4··Submit·the·Concept·or·Draft¶
··················································································
5··Negotiate·a·Contract¶
··················································································
6··Complete·the·Work¶
··················································································
7··Review·Editorial·Comments¶
··················································································
8··Incorporate·Editorial·Comments¶
··················································································
9··Deal·with·the·Taxes¶
··················································································
¶
                                                              ═CH12.DOC═
P23 D3 L13 C1     {·}              ?              Microsoft Word
```

Figure 12-11. Masters for overhead slides (with manual page breaks)

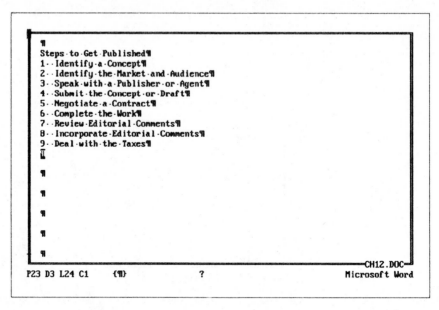

Figure 12-12. The same text without page breaks (can be used as a presentation outline)

Removing Paragraph Marks from ASCII Files

When you replace formats with special character codes, back up your work first, as this process can have unexpected results.

ASCII files can have unwanted paragraph marks at the end of each line. You can use the special characters to replace unneeded paragraph marks from an ASCII file. For example, the ASCII file in Figure 12-13 has a paragraph mark at the end of each line and an extra paragraph mark separating actual paragraphs. Suppose you want to remove the paragraph marks at the end of each line but not the one between each paragraph. You could replace each paragraph mark with a space and use the confirm feature of Word to skip the paragraph marks separating paragraphs. However, because you would have to stop at each occurrence of a paragraph mark, this could be time consuming.

An easier way to remove paragraph marks is to follow these steps:

1. Replace each double paragraph mark (^p^p) with two asterisks (**) or any other series of symbols that does not occur in the text. This "marks" the occurrences of the end of paragraphs. You will later replace the marks with the actual paragraph marks. Figure 12-14 shows the result.

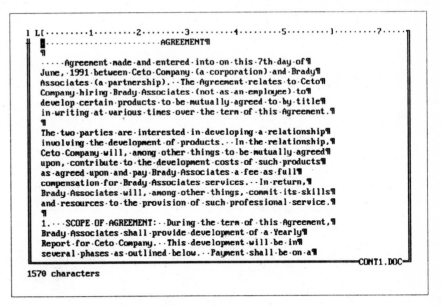

Figure 12-13. An ASCII file with paragraph marks at the end of each line

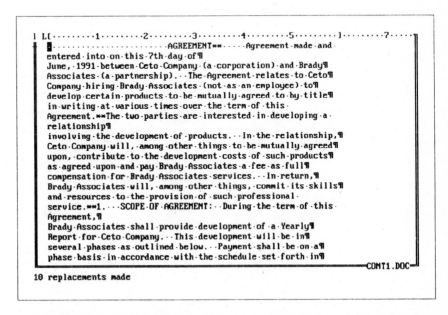

Figure 12-14. The file after double paragraph marks have been replaced

2. Next, remove the paragraph marks at the end of lines. To do this, replace the paragraph mark (^p) with a space, if required, or nothing (leave the *with text* field blank). Figure 12-15 shows the appearance of the document after removing paragraph marks.

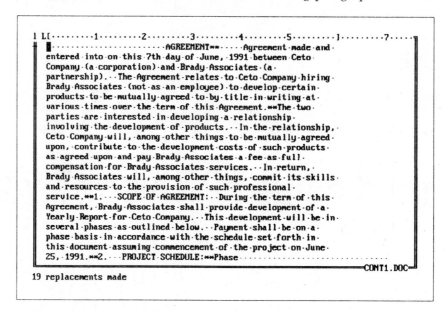

Figure 12-15. The same file after paragraph marks have been removed

3. The last step is to replace the double asterisks (**) with one or more paragraph marks. Figure 12-16 shows the final outcome. Notice that now the only paragraph marks are those that end actual paragraphs.

Exercise: Replacing Text

In this exercise, you will replace a word as well as special characters. Before beginning, set the Options *show non-printing symbols* field to All so you can see tab and paragraph characters. Use the WLET document:

        There are dozens of reasons the real estate business has
    been in a slump in this area. Many businesspersons have
    agreed that the business will get tougher before it gets
    better. Here are three steps every agent can take to protect
    the investment in his or her career:

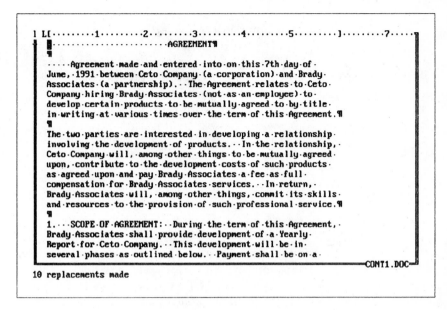

Figure 12-16. Clean ASCII file text

1. Make more contacts

2. Qualify buyers more closely

3. Look harder for better deals

   To many in real estate, these seem like simple steps.
However, when applied by the Whihmail program, these results
can be expected:

   Higher sales and higher commissions.

   Place your highlight on the paragraph mark before *1. Make more
contacts*. Select Replace. In the *text* field, enter a period and a space.
In the *with text* field, enter a period and the tab special character:

   .^t

Leave the default settings in the following fields:

confirm	Yes
case	No
whole word	No

Press Enter. Word displays the first occurrence of the period and space. Press Y to replace the period and tab symbol. Word displays the next occurrence. Press Y again. At the next stop (after 3), press Y again. The highlight moves to the period and space after the word *steps*. Press Esc to stop the process.

Now place your highlight at the beginning of the text. You want to substitute the word *business* for *market* throughout the text. Select Replace. In the *text* field enter:

```
business
```

In the *with text* field enter:

```
market
```

You feel certain about these replacements, so select No in the *confirm* field. Don't search for an exact case match; select No in the *case* field. In the *whole word* field, select Yes to find only the word *business* (not words like *businessperson* or *businesses*). Press Enter to begin the search.

This is the result:

```
    There are dozens of reasons the real estate market has
been in a slump in this area. Many businesspersons have
agreed that the market will get tougher before it gets
better. Here are three steps every agent can take to protect
the investment in his or her career:

1. Make more contacts

2. Qualify buyers more closely

3. Look harder for better deals

    To many in real estate, these seem like simple steps.
However, when applied by the Whihmail program, these results
can be expected:

    Higher sales and higher commissions.
```

Save the document as WLET.

Searching for or Replacing Formats

With Word, you can search for character formats or styles, paragraph formats or styles, or division styles. You can search for tabs, borders, or division formats only if they satisfy the following conditions:

- They are part of a style.
- You are searching for the style.

The Format Search command can be useful in finding categories of text because similar categories usually have similar formats.

Formats can be applied through the Format command or with the speed-formatting keys. The same formats applied through the use of a style sheet must be searched as a style. The style sheet must be attached and must include valid key codes for the styles searched.

Searching for Formats and Styles

To search for character, paragraph, or style formats:

1. Place your highlight where you want the search to begin. (You can search up as well as down through a document.)
2. Select **F**ormat s**E**arch.
3. Select one of the following:

   Character   to search for a character format

   Paragraph   to search for a paragraph format

   Style   to search for a style

4. If you selected **S**tyle, enter the appropriate style code in the *key code* field. Word stops you from searching for invalid key codes. If you enter an invalid key and press Enter, Word displays this message:

   `Key code does not exist. See style sheet for valid key code`

5. In the *direction* field, select **U**p to move from the highlight to the beginning of the document. Select **D**own to move from the highlight to the end of the document.
6. If you selected **C**haracter or **P**aragraph, identify the formats you want to search for.
7. Press **Enter** or click the command name. Word displays the first occurrence of the format or style.
8. If you want to repeat the search, press **Shift-F4** to find the next occurrence of the text. Or, with a mouse, select **S**earch again.

Replacing Formats

To replace a format or style:

1. Select a portion of text for the replace process. Or, place the highlight at the beginning of the text to be searched.

2. Select Format repLace.

3. Select one of the following:

    Character   to search for a character format

    Paragraph   to search for a paragraph format

4. In the *confirm* field, select **Yes** to confirm each replacement individually or **No** to allow Word to automatically replace every occurrence.

5. In the appropriate fields, enter one or more formats for which you want to search. For example, if you want to take all underlined text and make it bold, enter **Yes** in the *underline* field. If you want to search for text that is formatted for both bold *and* underline (but not bold *or* underline), enter a **Yes** in both the *bold* and *underline* fields.

6. Press **Enter** or click the command name. A second formatting screen appears.

7. Enter the formats you wish to use as replacements in the appropriate fields. For example, enter **Yes** in the *italics* field to replace the text that will be identified as italic. Or, enter **Yes** in the *bold* and the *italics* fields to replace bold and italic text.

8. Press **Enter** or click the command name to begin the replacement process.

9. If you have selected **Yes** in the *confirm* field, Word displays the first replacement and this message:

    `Enter Y to replace, N to skip and continue, or Esc to cancel`

    Enter **Y**, **N**, or **Esc**. The original formats are gone. The replacement formats have been substituted.

If you abort the procedure before all replacements have been made, you can restart it by selecting Format repLace Character or Paragraph again or by pressing Shift-F4 to highlight the next occurrence of the text. Press F4 to replace the text. If you use a mouse for this purpose, press Shift-F4 then click COMMAND in the command area.

Replacing Styles

Replacing styles is an easy way to quickly change styles in a document.

To exchange one style for another, select Format rePlace Style. To change the style itself, select Gallery and/or the Name or Format commands.

To replace a style:

1. Select a portion of the text to search. Or, place the highlight at the beginning of the text to be searched.
2. Select **F**ormat rep**L**ace **S**tyle.
3. Enter the key code of the style you want to replace in the *key code* field. Enter the key code of the replacement style in the *with* field. The styles you use must be in the currently attached style sheet.
4. In the *confirm* field, select **Y**es to confirm each of the replacements or **N**o to allow Word to automatically replace every occurrence.
5. Press **Enter** or click the command name to begin the replacement process. If you entered an invalid key code, Word displays this message:

   `Key code does not exist. See style sheet for valid key codes`

6. Assuming the key codes are valid, Word makes the replacements. Or, if you selected Yes in the *confirm* field, Word displays the first suggested replacement and this message:

   `Enter Y to replace, N to skip and continue, or Esc to cancel`

   Enter **Y** to make the replacement, **N** to skip that occurrence and go on to the next one, or **Esc** to stop the process.

If you abort the procedure before all replacements have been made, you can restart it by selecting Format rePlace Style again or by pressing Shift-F4 to highlight the next occurrence of the style and then pressing F4 to replace it. If you have a mouse, click COMMAND in the command area to replace the text after pressing Shift-F4.

Exercise: Replacing Formats

Use the WLET document:

`There are dozens of reasons the real estate market has been in a slump in this area. Many businesspersons have`

agreed that the market will get tougher before it gets
better. Here are three steps every agent can take to protect
the investment in his or her career:

1. Make more contacts

2. Qualify buyers more closely

3. Look harder for better deals

To many in real estate, these seem like simple steps.
However, when applied by the Whihmail program, these results
can be expected:

Higher sales and higher commissions.

Place your highlight above the underlined text. You will change
the underlined text to underlined and bold. Select Format repLace
Character. In the *confirm* field of the Format Replace Character command, select No. In the *underline* field, select Yes to indicate that is
the search text and then press Enter. Select Yes in the *bold* field and
Yes in the *underline* field. Press Enter. Word displays the first occurrence of the text. Press Y to replace the formats. The text is now formatted for bold and underline. If you have a color monitor, check this
setting by placing the highlight on the text and select Format Character. The *bold* and *underline* fields are set to Yes. Save the document.

Sorting Text

You can use Word to sort text, numbers, or symbols. You can also use Word to sort data documents used when merging documents (see Chapter 15, "Merging Documents," for information about data documents).

Word's sorting capability is useful for alphabetizing any list of items (such as telephone lists). It is also convenient to use for organizing lists in numeric order. For example, here is an excerpt of an employee directory before sorting:

Johnson, Julia 349 Westwood Way, Phoenix, Arizona 85082

Hanover, Bill 1243 1st Street, #232, Phoenix, Arizona 85082

Johnson, Kathy 3213 Billings, Tempe, Arizona 85281

Johnson, Kathy 232323 32nd Ave., Phoenix, Arizona 85082

Ivan, Gillian PO Box 432, Phoenix, Arizona 85082

After sorting the list in alphabetic order, this is the result:

Hanover, Bill 1243 1st Street, #232, Phoenix, Arizona 85082

Ivan, Gillian PO Box 432, Phoenix, Arizona 85082

Johnson, Julia 349 Westwood Way, Phoenix, Arizona 85082

Johnson, Kathy 232323 32nd Ave., Phoenix, Arizona 85082

Johnson, Kathy 3213 Billings, Tempe, Arizona 85281

Notice that Word sorted by last name, then by first name, and finally (in the case of the two Kathy Johnsons) by street number to determine the order. Also notice that when sorting, Word uses the first character in each entry. As a result, even though the street number 232323 is larger than 3213, when sorting alphabetically, Word puts 232323 before 3213 because the first character 2 is smaller than the first character 3.

Using Library Sort

Before sorting, save your document to make sure you have a backup in case of error during the sort. It is also important to save the document in case Word runs out of memory before completing the sort. Saving your document also clears those locations in memory where temporary files are held, thereby making it available for sorting. If you are uncertain about the result of a sort and the list of items to be sorted is relatively short, copy a backup version to another location in the document. That way, if the result of the sort is not what you expected, you can use the backup to restore the original version.

To sort a list, follow these steps:

1. Select the paragraphs or columns to sort. To select a column, use **Shift-F6**.

2. Select **Library** and **Autosort**.

3. In the *by* field, select **Alphanumeric** to sort by letters and numbers or **Numeric** to sort by numbers.

4. In the *sequence* field, select **Ascending** (smallest to largest) or **Descending** (largest to smallest).

5. In the *case* field, select **Yes** to sort capital letters before small letters or **No** to ignore the case.

6. In the *column only* field, select **Yes** to sort only the column and leave the surrounding text in place or **No** to sort the entire entry.

7. Press **Enter** or click the command name.

Word sorts the text. If you make a mistake and want to undo the sort, select Undo or press Shift-F1 immediately. Word restores the sorted text to its original order.

If you press Esc during a sort, Word stops sorting and displays this message:

```
Enter Y to continue or Escape to cancel
```

Press Esc to stop the sort. The list remains in the original position. Press Y to continue the sort.

Special Instructions for Sorting Data Records

Data records are documents created for merging (see Chapter 15, "Merging Documents"). They contain the data that is merged into a form letter or other form document. When preparing a mailing, you may want to sort the data records so that the resulting merged documents are organized in a particular order. The procedure for sorting data records is essentially the same as for sorting any other paragraphs, with the following exceptions:

- When selecting text to sort within a data record, do not select the header record; only select data records.
- If you are using records separated by tabs, make sure the margins are wide enough to fit each record on one line. The records cannot wrap. To make more room, use Format Division Margins to increase the text area. Then sort the text. Finally, use Format Division Margins to go back to the original margin settings.

The Order of the Sort

When sorting a list, make sure that each entry ends in a paragraph mark.

Word sorts paragraphs, not lines. If you want to sort lines, you must make each one a paragraph, as shown in Figure 13-1. Note that a paragraph mark ends each line. Figure 13-2 shows the same list when sorted. Word has treated each line as a separate entry and sorted the list by the first character of each line. By contrast, Figure 13-3 shows the same list as in Figure 13-1 but with every other line ending in a newline mark. When Word sorts the list (see Figure 13-4), the lines following the newline symbols are treated as extensions of the lines preceding them. As a result, the lines are sorted on the *E* in *East*, the *G* in *Garden*, and the *S* in *Salads*.

You can specify the precise sort you want by identifying whether the sort is:

- In ascending or descending sequence
- Numeric or alphanumeric
- Sorted by case
- To affect a column only or a complete entry

```
L[LL······1·········2·L······3········4········5········6····]···7····
¶

Area·Restaurants:¶

Salads·and·More→      300·Central·Avenue¶

Club·Morocco·I→       33·East·Village¶

East·India→           456·Central·Avenue¶

Mrs..Whiter→          701·East·Jefferson¶

Garden·Spot→          755·East·Jefferson¶

Club·Morocco·II→      33·South·6th·Avenue¶

¶

¶

¶

                                                        CH13.DOC
P23 D3 L10 C42    {e}              ?                     Microsoft Word
```

Figure 13-1. Lines with paragraph marks before sorting

```
L[LL······1·········2·L······3········4········5········6····]···7····
¶

Area·Restaurants:¶

Club·Morocco·I→       33·East·Village¶

Club·Morocco·II→      33·South·6th·Avenue¶

East·India→           456·Central·Avenue¶

Garden·Spot→          755·East·Jefferson¶

Mrs..Whiter→          701·East·Jefferson¶

Salads·and·More→      300·Central·Avenue¶

¶

¶

¶

                                                        CH13.DOC
P23 D3 L22 C41    {Area·R...¶¶¶}   ?                     Microsoft Word
```

Figure 13-2. Lines with paragraph marks after sorting

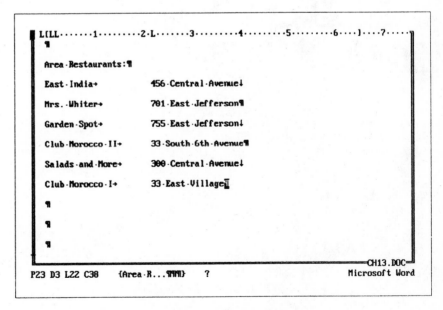

Figure 13-3. Lines with paragraph marks and
newline characters before sorting

Figure 13-4. Lines with paragraph marks and
newline characters after sorting

Ascending or Descending Sorts

You can have Word sort lists in either ascending or descending order. Ascending order is from smallest to largest, such as from A to Z or 0 to 9. Descending order is from largest to smallest, such as from Z to A or 9 to 0. The following lists illustrate how these choices affect alphabetic entries:

Unsorted
Thomas, Shawn

Lee, Johnny

Chan, Sue Ling

Morano, Manuel

Abby, Linn

Ascending order
Abby, Linn

Chan, Sue Ling

Lee, Johnny

Morano, Manuel

Thomas, Shawn

Descending order
Thomas, Shawn

Morano, Manuel

Lee, Johnny

Chan, Sue Ling

Abby, Linn

To ensure that sorted decimal numbers of values less than one (e.g., .3, .76, .9) appear in their proper order (after zero on ascending sorts; before zero on descending sorts), insert a zero before the decimal point (e.g., 0.3, 0.76, 0.9).

The following lists illustrate how the same choices affect numeric entries:

Unsorted
43,909

.34

37

.3

100

42,909

0

34

Ascending Order

.3

.34

0

100

34

37

42,909

43,909

Descending Order

43,909

42,909

37

34

100

0

.34

.3

Notice that Word treats the decimal point as a period and puts the periods before (ascending order) or after (descending order) the 0, giving the impression that it considers decimal numbers to be smaller than 0.

Numeric and Alphanumeric Sorts

You can sort text numerically (numbers only) or alphanumerically (numbers first and then letters). For example, suppose this list of telephone extension numbers needs to be sorted:

56 Bill James

345 Barbara Younger

9-876 Billy Bater

342 Jean Unger

9-87 Jamie Shawer

54 David Hammer

341 Ian Wilson

Here is the same list sorted numerically in ascending order:

9-876 Billy Bater

9-87 Jamie Shawer

54 David Hammer

56 Bill James

341 Ian Wilson

342 Jean Unger

345 Barbara Younger

Notice that all the extension numbers beginning with 9- appear first. That's because for Word, punctuation (in this case, a hyphen) signifies the end of a number. In other words, Word recognizes the 9 but not the numbers following the hyphen. Following 9-, Word sorts the two-digit numbers and, finally, the three-digit numbers.

A very different result occurs when you sort alphanumerically in ascending order:

341 Ian Wilson

342 Jean Unger

345 Barbara Younger

54 David Hammer

56 Bill James

9-87 Jamie Shawer

9-876 Billy Bater

Using the alphanumeric sort causes Word to look at the first character of numbers only. Therefore, Word puts the numbers beginning with 3 first, followed by 5, with 9 at the end of the sort.

Word treats symbols separately, whether it is sorting numerically or alphanumerically. When you perform an alphanumeric sort on text that has symbols, punctuation, numbers, and letters as first characters, the priority of the sort is:

symbols

punctuation

numbers

letters

For example, the first characters of the items in this list are symbols, punctuation, numbers, and letters:

$45.00

#22.00

Overage

12.00

.34

(79)

When Word sorts the list alphanumerically in ascending sequence, the following list is the result:

#22.00

$45.00

(79)

.34

12.00

Overage

Symbols are first, followed by punctuation (the parentheses and the period), numbers, and letters.

When you sort the list numerically in ascending order, the result is a little different:

(79)

.34

12.00

#22.00

$45.00

Overage

Punctuation is first, followed by numbers, then symbols, and, finally, letters.

For reference, the following list shows the result of sorting several symbols in ascending numeric sequence:

!

@

#

$

%

^

&
*
(
)
-
—
+
=
{
}
[
]
:
"
;
'
<
>
?
,
.
/
~
'
¦
\

The following list shows the result of sorting the same symbols in ascending alphanumeric sequence:

!
"
#
$
%
&
'

(

)

*

+

,

-

.

/

:

;

<

=

>

?

@

[

\

]

^

_

'

{

|

}

~

When sorting, Word ignores diacritical marks (accents) and sorts international characters in their order in the alphabet.

Sorting by Case

You can sort alphanumerically by case. If you select Yes in the *case* field of the Library Autosort command, capital letters have priority over small letters. If you select No, Word ignores the case when sorting. The following list contains entries beginning with both uppercase and lowercase letters:

Kaiser Castings	$32.90
three penny bolts	$ .25
cotton batting	$ 1.74
Garden wood set	$54.98
Genuine hammer	$25.90

Sorting alphanumerically by case produces the following list:

Garden wood set	$54.98
Genuine hammer	$25.90
Kaiser Castings	$32.90
cotton batting	$ 1.74
three penny bolts	$ .25

Word sorts lines beginning with capitalized letters first and then sorts lines beginning with small letters.

Sorting alphanumerically without regard to case produces the following list:

cotton batting	$ 1.74
Garden wood set	$54.98
Genuine hammer	$25.90
Kaiser Castings	$32.90
three penny bolts	$ .25

The first letter of the line (regardless of case) determines the order.

Sorting Columns

Word gives you a limited form of spreadsheet capability. You can sort by column only or by row according to the text in a particular column. This feature is very useful when sorting tables.

The following table is an example:

Salesperson	Area code	Phone number	Territory	Start date
Wilton, Jack	202	345-4543	B	05/04/89
Benton, Jim	202	435-8900	C	10/01/89
Ting, Jean	519	768-9000	A	02/09/89

Apple, Kay	519	789-9076	A	01/09/89
Devon, Dean	519	879-0329	B	04/05/89

Suppose you want to sort the table using the letters under *Territory*. First you use column select (Shift-F6) to select the column (see Figure 13-5).

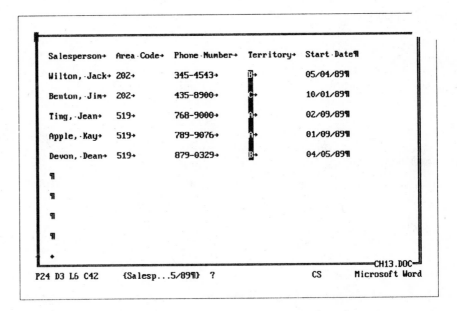

Figure 13-5. The Territory column selected

If you select Library Sort and select No in the *column only* field, Word moves the entire entry for each salesperson during the sort. This is the result:

Salesperson	Area code	Phone number	Territory	Start date
Ting, Jean	519	768-9000	A	02/09/89
Apple, Kay	519	789-9076	A	01/09/89
Wilton, Jack	202	345-4543	B	05/04/89
Devon, Dean	519	879-0329	B	04/05/89
Benton, Jim	202	435-8900	C	10/01/89

If you perform the same sort but with Yes selected in the *column only* field, Word sorts only the selected column. The rest of the row is left in place. The result is shown here:

Salesperson	Area code	Phone number	Territory	Start date
Wilton, Jack	202	345-4543	A	05/04/89
Benton, Jim	202	435-8900	A	10/01/89
Ting, Jean	519	768-9000	B	02/09/89
Apple, Kay	519	789-9076	B	01/09/89
Devon, Dean	519	879-0329	C	04/05/89

When setting up tables that won't be sorted, it is usually a good idea to use the newline character (Shift-Enter), instead of the paragraph mark (Enter), at the end of each line. This way you can easily change the formatting for the paragraph. However, when you will sort the table, it is important to place a paragraph mark at the end of each row. That way, each row is treated as a separate, sortable entity.

When you sort by column, you will want to pay attention to tabs and spaces when selecting text. See "Creating Columns" in Chapter 6, "Formatting Documents," for more information.

In the previous example, sorting by specified column is useful and could be applied to any of the columns. However, setting the *column only* field to Yes yielded a result that is probably not useful because the columns in a row are related. When the columns in a table are not related, however, sorting by column only can be useful. For example, these columns identify the students registered in a class:

Registered	Not coming	Wait list
Miller, Judith	Hiland, Barbara	Delander, Jeff
Hunter, Jilly	Rodine, Michael	Rodine, Brent
Miller, Matthew	Wilson, Brandy	Appleby, Willy
Pander, Kim	Ely, Kitty	Shower, Liddy

If the *column only* field is set to Yes, the names can be sorted individually by column for this result:

Registered	Not coming	Wait list
Hunter, Jilly	Ely, Kitty	Appleby, Willy
Miller, Judith	Hiland, Barbara	Delander, Jeff
Miller, Matthew	Rodine, Michael	Rodine, Brent
Pander, Kim	Wilson, Brandy	Shower, Liddy

Exercise: Sorting a List

In this example, you will enter a list. You will then perform these sorts on the list:

- Alphanumeric in ascending sequence with *case* set to No and *column only* set to No
- Alphanumeric in descending sequence with *case* set to Yes and *column only* set to No
- Alphanumeric in ascending sequence with *case* set to Yes and *column only* set to No

Enter this list of supplies in a blank Word window:

```
Gallenti testers
sleeping bag
bug spray
5 meals (packaged dry food recommended)
tent
Sterni burner
3 gallons of water
toiletries
```

Select Library Autosort. In the *by* field, select Alphanumeric. In the *sequence* field, select Ascending. In the *case* field, select No and in the *column only* field, select No. Press Enter. This is the result:

```
3 gallons of water
5 meals (dry packaged food recommended)
bug spray
Gallenti testers
sleeping bag
Sterni burner
tent
toiletries
```

Now sort the same list alphanumerically in descending sequence. Select Library Autosort. In the *by* field, select Alphanumeric. In the *sequence* field, select Descending. In both the *case* and *column only* fields, select No. Press Enter. Here is the result:

```
toiletries
tent
Sterni burner
sleeping bag
Gallenti testers
bug spray
5 meals (dry packaged food recommended)
3 gallons of water
```

Now try an alphanumeric, ascending sort, taking case into consideration. Select Library Autosort. In the *by* field, select Alphanumeric. In the *sequence* field, select Ascending. In the *case* field, select Yes. In the *column only* field, select No. Press Enter. You will see this outcome:

```
3 gallons of water
5 meals (dry packaged food recommended)
Gallenti testers
Sterni burner
bug spray
sleeping bag
tent
toiletries
```

Go to the end of the window and enter this list of positive and negative numbers to sort:

```
1,200
.80
+90
0
678
.25
(34)
-78
234
```

Sort the list numerically in ascending sequence. Select Library Autosort. In the *by* field, select Numeric. In the *sequence* field, select Ascending. In the *case* field, select No. In the *column only* field, select No. Press Enter. The result is:

```
-78
(34)
0
.25
.80
+90
234
678
1,200
```

Use the same list of numbers to sort in numeric, descending order. Select Library Autosort. In the *by* field, select Numeric. In the *sequence* field, select Descending. In the *case* field, select No. In the *column only* field, select No. Press Enter. The result is:

```
1,200
678
234
+90
.80
.25
0
(34)
-78
```

Save the document under the name SORTTEST.

Exercise: Sorting a Table

Three people's expense reports were combined to make the table that follows. Enter the table in the SORTTEST document.

Date	Initials	Purpose	Expense
100189	KG	Meal	65.99
100689	KG	Meal	34.65
100889	KG	Meal	45.22
100189	BB	Supplies	23.45
100389	BB	Meal	13.89
100589	BB	Supplies	5.33
100189	JT	Meal	45.65
100889	JT	Car Rental	109.89

Sort the table by initials. Press Shift-F6 and select the Initials column (don't include the heading). Select Library Autosort. In the *by* field, select Alphanumeric. In the *sequence* field, select Ascending. Select No in the *case* and *column only* fields. The result is shown here:

Date	Initials	Purpose	Expense
100189	BB	Supplies	23.45
100389	BB	Meal	13.89
100589	BB	Supplies	5.33
100189	JT	Meal	45.65

100889	JT	Car Rental	109.89
100189	KG	Meal	65.99
100689	KG	Meal	34.65
100889	KG	Meal	45.22

Next, sort the table by date. Press Shift-F6 and select the entries in the Date column. Again, only the dates themselves should be highlighted. Select Library Autosort. In the *by* field, select Numeric. In the *sequence* field, select Ascending. Select No in the *case* and *column only* fields. The result is shown here:

Date	Initials	Purpose	Expense
100189	BB	Supplies	23.45
100189	JT	Meal	45.65
100189	KG	Meal	65.99
100389	BB	Meal	13.89
100589	BB	Supplies	5.33
100689	KG	Meal	34.65
100889	JT	Car Rental	109.89
100889	KG	Meal	45.22

Handling Files and Running DOS Commands

As you work, you will want to manage your files to conserve disk space and make the files easy to locate. This chapter contains tips on disk space and memory management. You will also learn how to copy, delete, rename, and merge files.

Chapter 3, "Creating Documents," described how to complete document summary sheets. In this chapter, you will discover how to update summary sheets and how to search document summary sheets and document text to locate the exact document you seek.

Finally, you will learn how to go to the operating system while working in Word, use a command, and then return to your document exactly where you left off.

Disk Space and Computer Memory

It is of the utmost importance that you make sure you have adequate disk space and memory while you work. Disk space refers to the room on your hard or floppy disk for storing documents. Memory (RAM) is the active memory available to hold Word program files, current documents, glossaries, and style sheets. As mentioned in Chapter 2, "Starting Microsoft Word," before starting Word, it's a good idea to double check that your computer has enough memory to run Word efficiently.

Managing Disk Space

Managing your disk space involves five tasks:

- Checking available storage
- Saving documents on backup disks
- Managing storage of temporary files
- Redirecting temporary files
- Deleting .PRD files

Each of these activities is covered in the following sections.

Checking Available Storage

If you periodically check the amount of space available on a disk, you will always be assured of having plenty of room to save documents. A good rule of thumb is to keep at least 10 percent of the total capacity of the disk available. If your disk is more than 90 percent full, remove some files to clear space. You can copy files to a backup disk and then delete them from the original disk. (See "Copying Several Files" and "Deleting Several Files" in this chapter.) Or, if you are certain you will never need the files again, you can just delete them.

To check the available space on a disk follow these steps:

1. Make sure your system prompt designates the drive containing the disk you want to check. If it does not, enter the drive letter designation followed by a colon and press **Enter**. For example, this command will change the operating system prompt to drive A:

   A:

2. If you are checking the space on a hard disk, you must first go to the root directory. At the system prompt type in

   CD

   and press **Enter**.

3. Check the disk to see how much memory is available. On a two-floppy-disk or hard-disk system, enter the CHKDSK command and then press **Enter**. Among other information, Word displays the *bytes total disk space*, which indicates how many bytes of both used and unused space exist. (One byte approximately equals one character.) Compare this figure to the *bytes available*

on disk, which is the amount of storage space you have available. Make sure the amount is 10 percent or more of the *bytes total disk space*.

In addition to storage space, the CHKDSK command shows the *bytes total memory* and the *bytes free*. These numbers indicate how much active memory (RAM) is available for your use. The "Managing Memory" section of this chapter explains why it is important to keep plenty of memory available.

For more information on using the CHKDSK command, see your DOS or OS/2 manual.

Saving Documents to Backup Disks

If you do not regularly check your disk space, you might not find out that your disk is full until you try to save a document. Word stops the save process and displays a *disk full* message. If this occurs, the following methods may enable you to save the document:

- Saving the file to another disk
- Creating space on the current disk for the document

To save the file to another disk, follow these steps:

1. Make sure you have a formatted disk at hand. If you do not have a formatted disk, you can use the **Library Run** command to format a disk without having to quit Word. (See "Entering DOS Commands from Within Word" later in this chapter for instructions on entering an operating system command from within Word.)

2. Place the formatted disk in the drive to which you will save the document.

3. Make sure the window containing the document you want to save is active (press **F1** if necessary).

4. Select **Transfer Save**.

5. If you have previously saved the document, simply enter the name of the drive (probably A:) that contains the formatted disk. If you have not previously saved the document, enter the name of the drive followed by a name for the document you want to save (for example, A:SAMPLE). Press **Enter**. Word saves the document on the disk in the specified drive.

6. If you are using a two-floppy-disk system and have previously saved the document, Word may require access to one or more files on the original document disk. If so, carefully follow

the prompts and switch disks as each part of the document is copied.

Either of the following messages is your signal to place the original document disk back in the drive and press **Y**:

```
Enter Y to retry access to FILENAME.DOC
Enter Y to retry access to FILENAME.BAK
```

When you see the following message, replace the document disk with the new disk and press **Y**:

```
Enter Y to retry access to MWxxxxx.TMP
```

7. Once the document is saved, quit Word and free up storage space on either your hard disk or the original document disk.

Saving the file to another disk is one way to solve a *disk full* problem. Another method is to create space for the document on the current disk by deleting unnecessary files. Many users choose to delete the backup files that are automatically created by Word. (The files with the .BAK extension contain the previous version of the document. The most recent version is identified with a .DOC extension.) For more information on how to delete one or more files, see "Deleting Files" or "Deleting Several Files," later in this chapter.

Managing Temporary Files

When working from a floppy disk, make sure you have planty of extra disk space. Word will need it to save temporary scratch files.

As you work, Word keeps your most recent, unsaved edits in temporary files that are also called *scratch* files. The names of temporary files begin with the letters MW, followed by numbers, and then the extension .TMP. If an accident occurs, such as a power failure, these files can be loaded into Word with the Transfer Load command and used to reconstruct your work.

Because these scratch files are temporary, they remain on the Word program disk or in the WORD directory (unless you specify a different location) only until you save the file. When the file is saved, the temporary files are deleted. However, if you are working from a floppy disk and edit a document for some time without saving it, the contents of temporary files can consume a critical amount of disk space and Word may display the *disk full* message.

To free up disk space used by temporary files, try each of the following options, in the order shown, until the message is no longer displayed.

1. Select **T**ransfer **S**ave to save the document and delete the .TMP files.

   Select **T**ransfer **A**llsave to save all documents if you have multiple windows open. Word completes the save and deletes the .TMP files.

2. Select **T**ransfer **C**lear **A**ll. The .TMP files, together with the scrap, any unsaved glossary entries, and any unsaved styles, are deleted.

3. As a last resort, select **T**ransfer **L**oad to reload the document you are working on. When Word displays the message:

   ```
   Enter Y to save, N to lose edits, or Esc to cancel
   ```

   Press **Y**. If Word does not accept Y you must respond with **N**, and your unsaved edits will be lost. Regardless of whether you enter Y or N, the .TMP files are deleted.

4. When the *disk full* message is no longer displayed, complete the work you are doing and then correct the space problem.

Remember, saving your work often not only protects your work but also keeps ample disk space available.

.TMP files are different from the temporary files that are created when you use the Autosave feature. See Chapter 3, "Creating Documents," for more information about Autosave.

Redirecting Temporary Files

You can also direct .TMP files to a location other than the Word program disk or the WORD directory, by adding one of two possible lines to your AUTOEXEC.BAT file. (For additional information on modifying AUTOEXEC.BAT files, see Appendix D.)

You can add a line to the AUTOEXEC.BAT file to store .TMP files on a disk in a different drive. For example, to store .TMP files on a disk in drive B, you would enter:

```
SET TMP = B:
```

To store the files on a drive other than B, simply change the drive designation in the sample line shown above.

You can also add a statement to the AUTOEXEC.BAT file to assign the .TMP value to a separate directory on a hard disk. Before you do this though, you must first make a directory identified as the storage location of the .TMP files, by using the MKDIR command. For example, if you want to store the files in a directory called TEMP, you will need to create a directory of that name as a subdirectory of the root directory. Adding the statement:

```
SET TMP=C: TEMP
```

to your AUTOEXEC.BAT file causes Word to store .TMP files in a directory called TEMP on drive C.

Never redirect temporary files to a RAM drive. The purpose of temporary files is to protect you in case of power failure. RAM drive contents are lost during a power failure, so the purpose of the temporary file would be negated. (See Appendix D for more information about RAM drives.)

Deleting .PRD Files

When you consider clearing storage space by deleting unnecessary files, don't forget unneeded printer driver (.PRD) files. See Chapter 5, "Printing Documents," for information on how to identify the .PRD files you need.

To delete unnecessary .PRD files, enter this command from the appropriate drive prompt to list all the .PRD files on the disk currently in the drive:

```
DIR *.PRD
```

Identify any .PRD files that will not be used and delete them.

It is assumed that you created backup disks when you initially set up Word. If not, refer to Chapter 2, "Starting Microsoft Word," for information on creating working disks. Delete files only from these working disks. Never delete files from the original Word disks supplied by Microsoft. These disks contain your only copies of all the .PRD files available for use with Word.

Managing Memory

Some Word program files and the files related to the document on which you are working consume memory. As mentioned earlier, saving a file is a good way to free memory.

If you are running low on active memory, Word alerts you by displaying the word *Save* in the status line. The *Save* message is most likely to appear when you use the following commands: Replace, Library Autosort, Library Table, or Library Index. Long or complex operations, such as extensive edits, long macros, or complicated math, can also cause Word to display the message.

When you see the *Save* message, stop what you are doing and save your document immediately. If you fail to save the document and continue working, the word *Save* will eventually begin to blink. At that point, you may not be able to save your document and you risk losing all your unsaved edits.

If you see the *Save* message, use these Word commands in the order shown to try to free enough memory to save your document:

1. Select **Transfer A**llsave. Word saves all documents, style sheets, and glossary entries. Respond to any prompts as each active document is saved.

2. Select **Transfer C**lear **A**ll to clear files related to the documents from memory.

3. Select **Transfer L**oad to reload the document or documents so that you can continue your work.

(See Chapter 3, "Creating Documents," for additional details about using the Transfer Allsave command. See Chapter 4, "Editing Documents," to learn about the Transfer Clear All and Transfer Load commands.)

If you save the document and continue working and Word displays the *Save* message again, save your document and quit Word to clear all related files. Then, restart Word and pick up your work where you left off.

If Word often displays the *Save* message, you may want to use the Autosave feature. This feature periodically saves a record of your edits. (See Chapter 3, "Creating Documents," for information on using Autosave.) If the problem persists, you may want to investigate the possibility and cost of adding more memory to your computer.

File Handling

Word provides file-handling commands that make it easy to organize documents and perform file-management tasks. These include:

- Deleting files
- Merging files
- Renaming files

You can also use Library Document-retrieval options to search for particular files, to update summary sheets, to load a document, to control the appearance of the list of files, to copy or delete several files, and to print one or several summary sheets and/or files. (See "Library Document-Retrieval" later in this chapter for details on these activities.)

Deleting Files

You use the Transfer Delete command to delete a single file. (See "Deleting Several Files" later in this chapter for instructions on deleting more than one file at a time.) Only files that are not active can be deleted. A file in an active window and its related .BAK file cannot be deleted. One caution when deleting: Proceed carefully. Once you delete a file, you cannot recover it through Word.

To delete a file, follow these steps:

1. Select **Transfer Delete**.

   - If you know the name of the file you want to delete, enter the file name (and drive and path if necessary) in the *filename* field and then press **Enter**.

   - If you know part of the file name, enter it in the *filename* field and then press **F1**. For example, you could make the following entry to see all the file names that start with J and end in any extension:

     `J*.*`

     Or, you could type in this entry to see only the files with .BAK as the extension:

     `*.BAK`

     Highlight the file you want to delete and then press **Enter**.

   - If you don't know the name of the file you want to delete, press **F1** in the *filename* field. All the files, regardless of the extension, appear. You can switch to another drive or directory by selecting it. Highlight the name of the file you want to delete and then press **Enter**.

3. The drive, path, and name of the file you have selected to delete appear in the *filename* field. Word displays the following message:

   `Enter Y to confirm deletion of file`

Press **Esc** if you have changed your mind and do not want to delete the file. If you do want to delete the file, press **Y**. After you press Y, Word deletes the file. You cannot undo the deletion.

Do not delete files that you may want in the future. Instead, copy the files to another disk using the operating-system's Copy command or the Library Document-retrieval Copy command. (See "Copying Several Files," later in this chapter.)

To use the operating-system Copy command, go to the system prompt for the drive where the document you want to delete resides and type in this command:

COPY *FILENAME.EXT A*:

substituting the name of the file for *FILENAME* and the extension for *EXT*. In this example, the operating system will copy the specified file to the A drive; you can substitute the drive of your choice. Press Enter after typing in the command. If the copy is successful, the operating system indicates that one file was copied.

Merging Two Documents

You can merge a complete document file on disk into a document that is displayed on your screen. This feature is useful for adding boilerplate text to documents. When you perform the document merge, the entire file you specify is brought into the active document at the location of the highlight. The formatting of the active document is retained unless formatting is specifically attached to a merged character, paragraph, or division.

For information on how to copy or move only a portion of one document file into another document file, see Chapter 11, "Windows." For details on using Word's mail-merge feature to merge a data document with a form letter, see Chapter 15, "Merging Documents."

To merge one complete document file into another, follow these steps:

1. If you are using windows to display more than one document, move the highlight to the document into which you want to merge a document from disk.

2. Position the highlight to identify the location where the second document will be placed. These are the possibilities:

Anywhere in the body of the text	to insert the second document to the left of the highlight
At the start of the current document	to insert the second document at the beginning of the active document
On the file's diamond-shaped end mark	to insert the second document at the end of the document

3. Select **Transfer Merge**.

4. In the *filename* field, enter the file name and then press **Enter**. Or, press **F1**, select a file name, and then press **Enter**.

Word merges the document with the specified name into the active document at the location you specified. You can then edit the document just like any other file. When you save the document, you can save it under the existing name or under a new name. (Save it under a new name if you want to keep the original unmerged document.)

Renaming Documents

To create a copy of the current document, save it under a new name. To rename the current document without creating a copy, select Transfer Rename.

Occasionally, you may want to rename documents. This feature is useful when you have created related documents with unrelated names. Later, you may decide to assign file names that allow Word to display the files together in alphabetized lists (for example, if you press F1 when using Transfer Load or Transfer Save).

To illustrate, here's a list of several files and their uses:

File name	Use
RESJILL.DOC	Jill's first resume
RESJILL1.DOC	Jill's second resume
DOUGRES.DOC	Doug's resume
BURNPROP.DOC	A proposal about the services offered by Jill and Doug, which was sent to the Burns Company
LETBURN.DOC	A letter sent by Jill to the Burns Company
D&JLIT.DOC	Literature Jill and Doug developed about their consulting services

Jill and Doug find it difficult to quickly locate consulting-related documents from among the 60 or so documents Jill has stored on the hard disk of her computer, so they rename the documents as follows:

Old file name	New file name
RESJILL.DOC	DJJRES1.DOC
RESJILL1.DOC	DJJRES2.DOC
DOUGRES.DOC	DJDRES1.DOC
BURNPROP.DOC	DJBURNP.DOC
LETBURN.DOC	DJBURN1.DOC
D&JLIT.DOC	DJLIT1.DOC

The first new name, DJJRES1.DOC, stands for:

D&J Consulting Company, Jill, Resume Number 1

Now the files are easy to distinguish among all the available files and appear in one location in the file name lists.

To rename a document file, follow these steps:

1. Make sure the file you want to rename is in the active window.

2. Select **Transfer Rename**.

3. Word displays the drive, path, and name of the document in the active window in the *filename* field. Enter the drive, path, and new file name in this field. You can press **F1** to see a list of currently assigned file names or to change the name of the file in the active window.

4. Press **Enter** or click the command name.

Word renames the document. Any associated backup document with the .BAK extension is not renamed. When you save the document, Word creates a .BAK file with the new document name.

Word's Transfer Rename command only changes the name of an existing document. It does not create a separate copy of the document.

Exercise: Using Transfer Merge, Transfer Rename, and Transfer Delete

To merge a document, you will use the FORM.DOC created in an earlier chapter. Before merging, enter the following text in a blank Word window:

```
Don't forget about the company picnic on June 21. The time
is 11:00 a.m. in Barker Park. Food, refreshments, and games
will be provided. Bring the family!
```

Place your highlight in the top line and column of the window. Select Transfer Merge. In the *filename* field, enter FORM.DOC and press Enter. Here is the result:

```
Please fill out the form which appears below. It will be
used to compile a company-wide telephone and address
directory. If you have any questions about completing the
form, call Janie at extension 540. Please return the form to
Janie by the last day of this month.

Name: _____

Address: _____

City/State/ZIP: _____

Phone: _____

Don't forget about the company picnic on June 21. The time
is 11:00 a.m. in Barker Park. Food, refreshments, and games
will be provided. Bring the family!
```

Now use Transfer Save to save the document under the name MERGETST.DOC

Next, rename the MERGETST.DOC. Select Transfer Rename. Enter the drive, path, and the name MTST. Press Enter. Word renames the document.

Finally, delete the merged document. Select Transfer Delete. Enter the drive and path and the name MTST.DOC. Press Enter. Press Y when Word asks whether you want to delete the document. The document is deleted.

Library Document-Retrieval

Beginners can really benefit from taking the time to learn Word's Library Document-retrieval feature. It lets you search for, move, copy, and delete documents without having to exit to DOS.

Word's Library Document-retrieval command is useful for manipulating several files at once. These operations include:

- Searching for files
- Updating summary sheets
- Loading documents
- Changing the appearance of the list of file names
- Copying several files at once
- Deleting several files at once
- Printing one or multiple summary sheets and/or files

When you select Library Document-retrieval, a special screen appears (see Figure 14-1). The drive and path of the documents currently displayed appear in the top line, followed by the drive, path, and names of documents which you can manipulate. At the bottom of the screen, the Document-retrieval commands are shown.

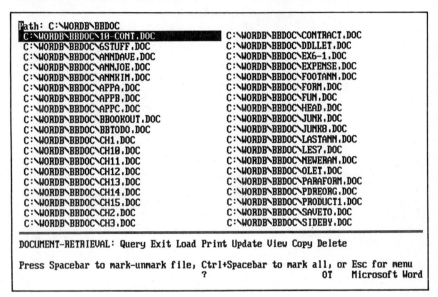

Figure 14-1. Word's document-retrieval screen

The following table summarizes the use of each document-retrieval command:

Command	Use to
Query	Search summary sheets and text
Exit	Go back to the editing screen
Load	Load the highlighted document
Print	Print one or more marked documents
Update	Update the summary sheet for a selected file
View	Display the files in short, long, or full view or sort the document list
Copy	Copy one or more marked documents to a drive or directory
Delete	Delete one or more marked documents

Each command is described in detail in the following sections.

Searching for Files

Using Word's Library Document-retrieval Query command, you can search for any file on any disk drive or in any directory. Mastery of this command is the key to unlocking your drives and directories so that you can quickly find whatever files or group of files you need.

Only documents that have been saved on disk are searched. Documents that you have been working on in one or more windows but have not yet saved will not be included in the search. To search such documents, you must save them first.

To perform a simple file search:

1. Select **Library Document-retrieval**. Word displays the files on the drive or in the directory listed in the Query *path* field.

2. If the file or files you are looking for are not listed, select **Query** and enter, in the *path* field, the directory and/or drive you want to search. You can either type in the search path or press **F1** to select from a list of drives and directories. If you type in the search path, file names can also be included, and you can use wildcard characters to limit the search to certain groups of files.

3. When you have corrected the search path, press **Enter**.

Word lists all files that meet the criteria in the *path* field.

If you are working on a network and see a message indicating that the results of the query may be incomplete, it may be because some documents are in use (locked). Try repeating the search later, when other users are less likely to be working with the documents.

Once you have completed a search, you should delete the search criteria. Otherwise, when you next select Library Document-retrieval, you will automatically initiate the same, perhaps time-consuming search. You may also want to enter a different search path; otherwise, the one you last entered will be maintained even after you leave Word.

You can refine your searches in three ways:

- By marking particular files to be searched
- By filling in one or more of the other fields of the Query command
- By using logical operators, quotation marks, and wildcards

The following sections describe in greater detail how to use the various search techniques.

Specifying the Search Path

When you select Library Document-retrieval Query, a form resembling the document summary sheet appears. You tell Word where to search and what to look for by filling in one or more of the fields on this form. As already discussed, the *path* field tells Word where to search and determines which files are listed on the Library Document-retrieval screen. The first time you select Query, the *path* field lists whatever drive and directory will appear in the *setup* field of Word's Transfer Options command. If you specify a new path, that path remains in effect until you change it, even if you quit the program.

Each path consists of a single drive, directory, and file name—any one of which is optional. If no drive is specified, the search is limited to the current drive. If no directory is specified, the search is limited to the current directory. If no file names are listed, the search includes all the files in the specified directory. When specifying a path, observe the following rules:

- The drive letter, if any, must be followed by a colon and separated from the following directory or file name by a backslash.
- Directories and subdirectories must be separated from one another and from the following file name by a backslash.
- File names can include the DOS wildcards * and y/.

Normally, Word searches only for files ending in the extension .DOC. To have it search for other files—ASCII or binary files, for example—you must enter the appropriate file-name extensions (.ASC, .COM, .EXE, and so forth). To see all files in a directory, enter the following file name in the *path* field:

`*.*`

The first asterisk tells Word to search for files with any name; the second asterisk tells Word to search for files with any extension—in other words, all files.

You can specify more than one path in the *path* field as long as your entry does not exceed 128 characters. Use a comma to separate the paths.

The following Query *path* statement asks Word to search for all files with the .ASC extension in the C:\WORD\DOC directory, for all document files in the C:\WORD\BBDOC directory, and, finally, for all files on the disk in drive A:

`C:\WORD\DOC\*.ASC,C:\WORD\BBDOC,A:*.*`

Word 4 requires you to type out every path. However, Word 5 considerably streamlines the process. To select one or more drives or directories:

1. Select **Library Document-retrieval Query**.

2. Move to the *path* field and press **F1**. A list of drives and directories appears.

3. Highlight the drive or directory you want to search and press **Enter**. The drive or directory you have chosen appears in the *path* field. If the drive or directory you want to search does not appear on the list, do one of the following:

   - Select a subdirectory of one of the directories on the list by highlighting the parent directory and pressing **F1**, and then highlighting the subdirectory and pressing **Enter**.

   - Select a directory or subdirectory that does not appear in the list but does exist on your hard disk by highlighting [..] and pressing **F1**. Word displays the next highest level of directories in the directory tree. If you still do not find the directory you want, repeat this procedure until you do. Then highlight the directory and press **Enter**.

4. To specify additional drives and/or directories, type in a comma after your first selection and repeat steps 1 through 3. Continue until you have specified all the drives and directories you want to search. If you exceed the *path* field's 128-character limit, Word refuses to accept the entry and you will have to backspace to remove the excess characters.

You cannot enter specific file information (such as *.BAK or file names) with this method.

Marking and Unmarking Documents

You can further limit searches by marking only certain documents for consideration. Marking documents is also useful when copying or printing them from the Library Document-retrieval screen. For information on copying or deleting files, see "Copying Several Files," "Deleting Several Files," and "Printing Documents and Summary Sheets," later in this chapter.

To mark one or more files:

1. Highlight the file to be marked.

2. Press the **Spacebar**. An asterisk (*) appears before the file.

3. Repeat steps 1 and 2 to mark additional files.

To unmark a file:

1. Highlight the file to be unmarked.
2. Press the **Spacebar** again.

To mark and unmark all the files on the list, press Ctrl-Spacebar.

Limiting Searches

The remaining fields of the Query command allow you to limit your search—and therefore the amount of time the search will take—by specifying additional criteria that sought-for files must meet. You will notice that all but three of these fields (*document text*, *case*, and *marked files only*) also appear on the summary sheets that Word prompts you to fill out whenever you save a file for the first time. When searching on these fields, Word excludes files for which no summary sheets exist or, if they do exist, for which the fields being searched were not filled in when the files were saved.

Word's summary sheets are the key to unleashing the power of Word's Library Document-retrieval command.

Because summary sheets provide the quickest way for Word to search for documents, being able to conduct fast, comprehensive searches depends on how faithfully you fill out summary sheets for every document you save and how consistent you are in filling out the fields. For example, using John P., johnny, and JP to identify the same author is not a good idea. If you do this, Word has to complete three searches to find all the files with this author's name entered.

The remaining Query command fields are:

- *Author, Operator, and Keywords*:

  Enter one or more authors, operators, or keywords. Up to 80 characters are allowed. Separate multiple entries in one field by the logical operators comma (,), ampersand (&), space, or tilde (~). For information on using logical operators, see the next section, "Searching with Logical Operators, Quotation Marks, and Wildcards."

- *Creation date and Revision date*:

  Enter one or more creation or revision dates. If more than one date is entered in a field, separate them by the logical operators earlier than (<), later than (>), comma (,), ampersand (&), space, or tilde (~). For information on using logical operators, see the next section, "Searching with Logical Operators, Quotation Marks, and Wildcards."

  You must enter the date so that it matches the format specified in the Options *date format* field. These are the alternatives:

MDY   Month/Day/Year   such as 1/4/89

DMY   Day/Month/Year   such as 4/1/89

Word's default is MDY.

Do not use wildcard characters (* or ?) in this field. You must search for specific dates.

- *Document text*:

  Enter the characters that you want Word to search for in the text of the documents. You can enter up to 80 characters. Word assumes that your entries may be part of a larger word or phrase. Use the logical operators comma (,), ampersand (&), space, or tilde (~) to limit your searches. For information on using logical operators, see the next section, "Searching with Logical Operators, Quotation Marks, and Wildcards."

- *Case*:

  Select Yes if you want Word to find an exact match of capital and small letters as entered in the *document text* field. If you enter No, Word will disregard case in the search.

- *Marked files only*:

  Select Yes for Word to search only files you have marked with an asterisk (rather than all the files in the Query *path* field). Select No if you want Word to search all the files specified in the Query *path* field.

Searching with Logical Operators, Quotation Marks, and Wildcards

The more precise your search criteria are, the more complete and accurate the search will be. You can refine your searches by using Word's *logical operators*—special symbols that allow you to indicate precise relationships among the elements making up your criteria. Word recognizes the following logical operators:

Logical operator	Meaning	Example	Explanation
ampersand (&) or (space)	AND	Doug&Bill Doug Bill	Word searches to find both names in a document
comma (,)	OR	Doug,Bill	Word searches for either name in a document

tilde (~)	NOT	Bill~Doug	Word searches for the name Bill but not the name Doug
<(date)	EARLIER THAN	<8/9/89	Word finds dates earlier than April 9, 1989
>(date)	LATER THAN	>8/9/89	Word finds dates later than April 9, 1989

Word processes logical operators in this order:

Tilde (NOT)
Space or & (AND)
Comma (OR)

Placing parts of the search criteria in parentheses can override this order. For example, these search criteria:

```
spring&fall,summer
```

tell Word to choose documents with these occurrences:

spring AND fall OR summer

In contrast, these search criteria:

```
spring&(fall,summer)
```

tell Word to choose documents with these occurrences:

spring AND fall OR spring AND summer

You use quotation marks to specify how to handle logical operators that are actually part of the search text. For example, the following search criteria tell Word to look for the company name *CromCo* and the company name *David & David*:

```
CromCo&"David & David"
```

The quotation marks around *"David & David"* tell Word to treat the spaces and ampersand as part of the phrase that it is searching for. If you leave out the quotation marks, Word treats the ampersand as a logical operator. For example, if you enter:

```
CromCo&David & David
```

Word would be instructed to search for these text strings joined by AND:

CromCo AND David AND & AND David

If you want to specify quotation marks as part of the search text, enter two sets of quotation marks. For example, these search criteria:

`speech,""'kinder and gentler'""`

tell Word to search for documents with the following occurrences:

speech OR "kinder and gentler"

Wildcards can be used to identify one or more unknown characters. Use a question mark as a placeholder for a single unknown character. Use the asterisk (*) as a placeholder for one or more characters. For example, if you enter:

`p?t`

Word locates words like:

pit

pot

put

If you enter:

`p*t`

Word locates words like:

pint

put

peat

To search for an actual question mark or asterisk, place a caret (^) before the character. This entry:

`case^*`

directs Word to search for the characters *case** in a string like:

case*ment

Word will not, however, locate character strings like these:

casement

cased

Do not use wildcards in the *creation date* or *revision date* fields of the summary sheet when you search. You must search for actual dates in these fields.

Logical operators are particularly useful in refining text searches. When searching for a particular word, Word does not distinguish between the word by itself and an identical string of characters embedded within a larger word or string. For example, when you ask Word to search for the word:

pay

Word locates documents that include not only *pay* but such words as:

pay

payee

payment

repayment

Use the tilde (~) to avoid finding undesired occurrences. For example, Word locates documents with the word *pay* but not the word *repayment* if you specify these criteria:

pay~repayment

Here are some more examples using logical operators, quotation marks, and wildcards:

- This entry in the *creation date* field instructs Word to search for documents with creation dates later than 2/3/89 and earlier than 5/6/89 but not the date 4/15/89:

>2/3/89<5/6/89~4/15/89

- This entry in the *document text* field tells Word to search for documents with the word *Davidson* but not *David* in the text:

    `Davidson~David`

- The following entry specifies search text as the name *Green Cap Company* and the word *"buyers"* in quotation marks:

    `"Green Cap Company" """buyers"""`

- The following entry specifies search text as *Go Company* and *kites* or *Go Company* and *string*:

    `"Go Company"&(kites,string)`

- Finally, the following entry specifies search text as any word ending in *ing* or *ed*.

    `*ing,*ed`

Updating Summary Sheets

Unless you set the Options command *summary sheet* field to No, Word automatically gives you the opportunity to fill in a summary sheet the first time you save a document. (For information on filling in summary sheets, see "Summary Information Sheets" in Chapter 3, "Creating Documents.") Figure 14-2 shows an example of how the summary sheet appears on the screen when a new document is created. Figure 14-3 shows a printout of the same summary sheet.

You can use summary sheets to create a simple database. Simply make each summary sheet a single record and use the Query command to select the records you want to view. The documents themselves can be dummy files consisting of only a single character.

Whether you use document summary sheets for the purpose of keeping a record of each document, for searching files, or for both, it is important that you update the summary sheet whenever you make substantial revisions to a document. You can update the summary sheet associated with a document by selecting the Library Document-retrieval Update command. Figure 14-4 shows a summary sheet as it appears on the Library Document-retrieval screen.

To update a summary sheet:

1. Select Library Document-retrieval. Word displays the names of the documents in the drive and path set through the Transfer Options command.

2. Highlight the name of the document with the summary sheet you want to update. If the document is in another drive or direc-

```
¶
Dear·Carolyn,¶
¶
→I·have·been·in·touch·with·the·members·of·the·team.··Each·has·a·
different·opinion·about·the·outcome·of·the·last·meeting.···I·
believe·we·need·to·clarify·several·points.¶
¶
```

```
SUMMARY INFORMATION
    title: Letter to Carolyn Brown          version number: 1
    author: J. Williams                      creation date: 07/10/89
    operator: B. Ian                         revision date: 07/18/89
    keywords: Carolyn Brown team
    comments: The letter clarifies team meeting issues.
Enter text
P20 D1 L18 C1      {¶¶De...oints.}   ?                    Microsoft Word
```

Summary sheet

Figure 14-2. The screen appearance of a summary sheet

```
filename: C:\WORDB\BBDOC\CARLET.DOC
title: Letter to Carolyn Brown
author: J. Williams
operator: B. Ian
keywords: Carolyn Brown team
comments: The letter clarifies team meeting issues.
version number: 1
creation date: 07/10/89
revision date: 07/18/89
char count: 47256
```

Figure 14-3. The summary sheet when printed

tory, follow the procedures described in "Specifying the Search Path," earlier in this chapter.

3. Select **U**pdate. Word displays the summary sheet for the document.

4. Edit the summary sheet as you want. Use the **Arrow** keys and **Tab** key to move from field to field. You can change the dates; however, Word will reassign the actual dates when you leave the screen.

5. When you are done with your edits, press **Enter** or click the command area.

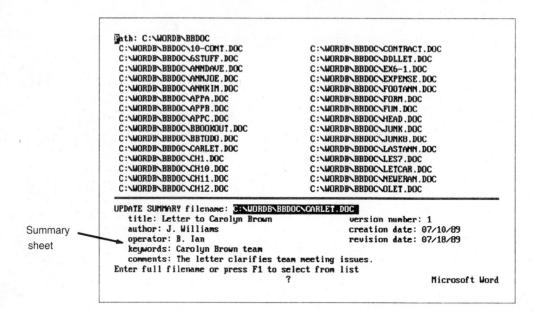

Summary sheet

Figure 14-4. A summary sheet as it appears on the
Library Document-retrieval screen

Loading Documents

If you can't remember the name of a file you want to load, you can
search for it using the Library Document-retrieval Query command.
Once the file is listed, you can load it without having to leave the
Library Document-retrieval screen or use the Transfer Load command. When you choose Library Document-retrieval Load, the specified file is loaded and you are returned at once to Word's document
screen.

To load a file from the Library Document-retrieval screen:

1. Activate the window into which you want to load the document.

2. Select **Library D**ocument-retrieval **L**oad. Word lists the files in
   the current Query path on the screen.

3. You now have three choices:

   - If the file you want is listed, press **F1** and highlight the file
     you want to load. (You can also just type in the file name,
     but this is more work.)

   - If the file you want is not listed but you remember its
     name, type in the appropriate drive, directory, and file
     name.

- If the file you want is not listed and you don't remember its name, press **Esc** to return to the Library Document-retrieval menu and select **Q**uery to initiate a search for the file.

 If you are connected to a network or using Microsoft Windows, when the Library Document-retrieval menu is displayed, update the screen by pressing Ctrl-F4.

4. When the file you want to load is listed in the *filename* field, press **Enter** or click the command name.

5. If there is a document in the active window with unsaved changes, Word warns you with a message. Press **Y** to save the changes or **N** to lose them.

Once you have made your choice, Word loads the specified file into the document window and returns you at once to the document screen.

See Chapter 4, "Editing Documents," for further information on loading files and for notes about loading files on a network.

Altering the Appearance of File Lists

When Word displays files through Library Document-retrieval, directories and files within directories are listed alphabetically. You can change the view of the display and/or the order in which documents are displayed.

Changing Document View

You can display the list in short, long, or full view. Figure 14-5 shows the short view. This view lists each document in the path. Figure 14-6 illustrates the long view, which shows fewer document names than the short view but identifies the author and title of each document. Figure 14-7 displays the full view. The full view is the same as the short view except that the bottom of the screen displays the summary sheet for the highlighted document.

To change the view, follow these steps:

1. Select Library **D**ocument-retrieval **V**iew.

2. In the View menu, select one of the following:

Short

Long

Full

3. Press **Enter** or click the command name.

```
Path: C:\WORDB\BBDOC
C:\WORDB\BBDOC\10-CONT.DOC          C:\WORDB\BBDOC\CONTRACT.DOC
C:\WORDB\BBDOC\6STUFF.DOC           C:\WORDB\BBDOC\DDLLET.DOC
C:\WORDB\BBDOC\ANNDAVE.DOC          C:\WORDB\BBDOC\EX6-1.DOC
C:\WORDB\BBDOC\ANNJOE.DOC           C:\WORDB\BBDOC\EXPENSE.DOC
C:\WORDB\BBDOC\ANNKIM.DOC           C:\WORDB\BBDOC\FOOTANN.DOC
C:\WORDB\BBDOC\APPA.DOC             C:\WORDB\BBDOC\FORM.DOC
C:\WORDB\BBDOC\APPB.DOC             C:\WORDB\BBDOC\FUN.DOC
C:\WORDB\BBDOC\APPC.DOC             C:\WORDB\BBDOC\HEAD.DOC
C:\WORDB\BBDOC\BBOOKOUT.DOC         C:\WORDB\BBDOC\JUNK.DOC
C:\WORDB\BBDOC\BBTODO.DOC           C:\WORDB\BBDOC\JUNK8.DOC
C:\WORDB\BBDOC\CARLET.DOC           C:\WORDB\BBDOC\LASTANN.DOC
C:\WORDB\BBDOC\CH1.DOC              C:\WORDB\BBDOC\LES7.DOC
C:\WORDB\BBDOC\CH10.DOC             C:\WORDB\BBDOC\LETCAR.DOC
C:\WORDB\BBDOC\CH11.DOC             C:\WORDB\BBDOC\NEWERAN.DOC
C:\WORDB\BBDOC\CH12.DOC             C:\WORDB\BBDOC\OLET.DOC
C:\WORDB\BBDOC\CH13.DOC             C:\WORDB\BBDOC\PARAFORM.DOC
C:\WORDB\BBDOC\CH14.DOC             C:\WORDB\BBDOC\PDREORG.DOC
C:\WORDB\BBDOC\CH15.DOC             C:\WORDB\BBDOC\PRODUCT1.DOC
C:\WORDB\BBDOC\CH2.DOC              C:\WORDB\BBDOC\SAVETO.DOC

DOCUMENT-RETRIEVAL: Query Exit Load Print Update View Copy Delete

Press Spacebar to mark-unmark file, Ctrl+Spacebar to mark all, or Esc for menu
                          ?                      OT    Microsoft Word
```

Figure 14-5. Short view

```
Path: C:\WORDB\BBDOC                author        title
C:\WORDB\BBDOC\10-CONT.DOC          K. Barnes     Contract for Chapter 10
C:\WORDB\BBDOC\6STUFF.DOC           K. Barnes     Chapter 6 Misc Materials
C:\WORDB\BBDOC\ANNDAVE.DOC          J. Smith      Proposal from Ann and Dav
C:\WORDB\BBDOC\ANNJOE.DOC           J. Smith      Proposal from Ann and Joe
C:\WORDB\BBDOC\ANNKIM.DOC           J. Smith      Proposal from Ann and Kim
C:\WORDB\BBDOC\APPA.DOC             Y. Randall    Appendix A for End of Yea
C:\WORDB\BBDOC\APPB.DOC             Y. Randall    Appendix B for End of Yea
C:\WORDB\BBDOC\APPC.DOC             Y. Randall    Appendix C for End of Yea
C:\WORDB\BBDOC\BBOOKOUT.DOC         Mary Jon      Broadcast Book Outline
C:\WORDB\BBDOC\BBTODO.DOC           Mary Jon      Broadcast Book To Do List
C:\WORDB\BBDOC\CARLET.DOC           J. Williams   Letter to Carolyn Brown
C:\WORDB\BBDOC\CH1.DOC              P. Fellow     Broadcast Book Chapter 1
C:\WORDB\BBDOC\CH10.DOC             P. Fellow     Broadcast Book Chapter 10
C:\WORDB\BBDOC\CH11.DOC             P. Fellow     Broadcast Book Chapter 11
C:\WORDB\BBDOC\CH12.DOC             P. Fellow     Broadcast Book Chapter 12
C:\WORDB\BBDOC\CH13.DOC             P. Fellow     Broadcast Book Chapter 13
C:\WORDB\BBDOC\CH14.DOC             David D.      Broadcast Book Chapter 14
C:\WORDB\BBDOC\CH15.DOC             P. Fellow     Broadcast Book Chapter 15
C:\WORDB\BBDOC\CH2.DOC              David D.      Broadcast Book Chapter 2

DOCUMENT-RETRIEVAL: Query Exit Load Print Update View Copy Delete

Press Spacebar to mark-unmark file, Ctrl+Spacebar to mark all, or Esc for menu
                          ?                      OT    Microsoft Word
```

Figure 14-6. Long view

```
Path: C:\WORDB\BBDOC
C:\WORDB\BBDOC\10-CONT.DOC         C:\WORDB\BBDOC\CONTRACT.DOC
C:\WORDB\BBDOC\6STUFF.DOC          C:\WORDB\BBDOC\DDLLET.DOC
C:\WORDB\BBDOC\ANNDAVE.DOC         C:\WORDB\BBDOC\EX6-1.DOC
C:\WORDB\BBDOC\ANNJOE.DOC          C:\WORDB\BBDOC\EXPENSE.DOC
C:\WORDB\BBDOC\ANNKIM.DOC          C:\WORDB\BBDOC\FOOTANN.DOC
C:\WORDB\BBDOC\APPA.DOC            C:\WORDB\BBDOC\FORM.DOC
C:\WORDB\BBDOC\APPB.DOC            C:\WORDB\BBDOC\FUN.DOC
C:\WORDB\BBDOC\APPC.DOC            C:\WORDB\BBDOC\HEAD.DOC
C:\WORDB\BBDOC\BBOOKOUT.DOC        C:\WORDB\BBDOC\JUNK.DOC
C:\WORDB\BBDOC\BBTODO.DOC          C:\WORDB\BBDOC\JUNK8.DOC
C:\WORDB\BBDOC\CARLET.DOC          C:\WORDB\BBDOC\LASTANN.DOC
C:\WORDB\BBDOC\CH1.DOC             C:\WORDB\BBDOC\LES7.DOC

filename: C:\WORDB\BBDOC\10-CONT.DOC          char count: 838
title: Contract for Chapter 10                version number: 1
author: K. Barnes                             creation date: 06/30/89
operator: K. Barnes                           revision date: 06/30/89
keywords: contract chapter 10 agreement
comments: This is a document used for figures in chapter 10.

DOCUMENT-RETRIEVAL: Query Exit Load Print Update View Copy Delete

Press Spacebar to mark-unmark file, Ctrl+Spacebar to mark all, or Esc for menu
                              ?                      OT    Microsoft Word
```

Figure 14-7. Full view

Sorting Documents

The documents that Word displays can be sorted by author, operator, revision date, creation date, or size. Figure 14-8 shows the documents sorted by document name (Word's default). The documents starting with numbers appear first, followed by documents starting with A, then B, and so on. Figure 14-9 shows the result of sorting by author. The first letter of each author's name is sorted in alphabetic order (A to Z).

To sort documents, follow these steps:

1. Select Library Document-retrieval View.

2. In the *sort by* field, select one of the following:

   Directory

   Author

   Operator

   Revision date

   Creation date

   Size

3. Press **Enter** or click the command name.

Word reorganizes the documents according to your selection.

```
Path: C:\WORDB\BBDOC                 author          title
 C:\WORDB\BBDOC\10-CONT.DOC          K. Barnes       Contract for Chapter 10
 C:\WORDB\BBDOC\6STUFF.DOC           K. Barnes       Chapter 6 Misc Materials
 C:\WORDB\BBDOC\ANNDAVE.DOC          J. Smith        Proposal from Ann and Dav
 C:\WORDB\BBDOC\ANNJOE.DOC           J. Smith        Proposal from Ann and Joe
 C:\WORDB\BBDOC\ANNKIM.DOC           J. Smith        Proposal from Ann and Kim
 C:\WORDB\BBDOC\APPA.DOC             Y. Randall       Appendix A for End of Yea
 C:\WORDB\BBDOC\APPB.DOC             Y. Randall       Appendix B for End of Yea
 C:\WORDB\BBDOC\APPC.DOC             Y. Randall       Appendix C for End of Yea
 C:\WORDB\BBDOC\BBOOKOUT.DOC         Mary Jon        Broadcast Book Outline
 C:\WORDB\BBDOC\BBTODO.DOC           Mary Jon        Broadcast Book To Do List
 C:\WORDB\BBDOC\CARLET.DOC           J. Williams     Letter to Carolyn Brown
 C:\WORDB\BBDOC\CH1.DOC              P. Fellow       Broadcast Book Chapter 1
 C:\WORDB\BBDOC\CH10.DOC             P. Fellow       Broadcast Book Chapter 10
 C:\WORDB\BBDOC\CH11.DOC             P. Fellow       Broadcast Book Chapter 11
 C:\WORDB\BBDOC\CH12.DOC             P. Fellow       Broadcast Book Chapter 12
 C:\WORDB\BBDOC\CH13.DOC             P. Fellow       Broadcast Book Chapter 13
 C:\WORDB\BBDOC\CH14.DOC             David D.        Broadcast Book Chapter 14
 C:\WORDB\BBDOC\CH15.DOC             P. Fellow       Broadcast Book Chapter 15
 C:\WORDB\BBDOC\CH2.DOC              David D.        Broadcast Book Chapter 2

DOCUMENT-RETRIEVAL: Query Exit Load Print Update View Copy Delete

Press Spacebar to mark-unmark file, Ctrl+Spacebar to mark all, or Esc for menu
                              ?                         Microsoft Word
```

Figure 14-8. Sorted by document name

```
Path: C:\WORDB\BBDOC                 author          title
 C:\WORDB\BBDOC\CH14.DOC             David D.        Broadcast Book Chapter 14
 C:\WORDB\BBDOC\CH2.DOC              David D.        Broadcast Book Chapter 2
 C:\WORDB\BBDOC\ANNDAVE.DOC          J. Smith        Proposal from Ann and Dav
 C:\WORDB\BBDOC\ANNJOE.DOC           J. Smith        Proposal from Ann and Joe
 C:\WORDB\BBDOC\ANNKIM.DOC           J. Smith        Proposal from Ann and Kim
 C:\WORDB\BBDOC\CARLET.DOC           J. Williams     Letter to Carolyn Brown
 C:\WORDB\BBDOC\6STUFF.DOC           K. Barnes       Chapter 6 Misc Materials
 C:\WORDB\BBDOC\10-CONT.DOC          K. Barnes       Contract for Chapter 10
 C:\WORDB\BBDOC\BBOOKOUT.DOC         Mary Jon        Broadcast Book Outline
 C:\WORDB\BBDOC\BBTODO.DOC           Mary Jon        Broadcast Book To Do List
 C:\WORDB\BBDOC\CH1.DOC              P. Fellow       Broadcast Book Chapter 1
 C:\WORDB\BBDOC\CH10.DOC             P. Fellow       Broadcast Book Chapter 10
 C:\WORDB\BBDOC\CH11.DOC             P. Fellow       Broadcast Book Chapter 11
 C:\WORDB\BBDOC\CH12.DOC             P. Fellow       Broadcast Book Chapter 12
 C:\WORDB\BBDOC\CH13.DOC             P. Fellow       Broadcast Book Chapter 13
 C:\WORDB\BBDOC\CH15.DOC             P. Fellow       Broadcast Book Chapter 15
 C:\WORDB\BBDOC\APPA.DOC             Y. Randall       Appendix A for End of Yea
 C:\WORDB\BBDOC\APPB.DOC             Y. Randall       Appendix B for End of Yea
 C:\WORDB\BBDOC\APPC.DOC             Y. Randall       Appendix C for End of Yea

DOCUMENT-RETRIEVAL: Query Exit Load Print Update View Copy Delete

Press Spacebar to mark-unmark file, Ctrl+Spacebar to mark all, or Esc for menu
                              ?                         Microsoft Word
```

Figure 14-9. Sorted by document author

Copying Several Files

Using the Library Document-retrieval Copy command, you can copy one or more files to another directory or drive. For example, you may want to use Library Document-retrieval Query to select certain files by name or date. Then you can mark the files to be copied to an archive disk.

To copy several documents follow these steps:

1. Select **Library Document**-retrieval. Word displays the files in the search path.

   To change the file display, select **Query** and then enter the drive and directory containing the files you want to see. Don't enter selection criteria. Press **Enter**. Word displays all the files for that drive and path.

   If you are connected to a network or using Microsoft Windows, update the screen by pressing **Ctrl-F4**.

2. Mark the file or files you want to copy using one of the following options:

   - To mark or unmark a single file, highlight the file name and press **Spacebar** or **Enter**.

   - To mark all files, press **Ctrl-Spacebar**. (To unmark all files, press **Shift-Ctrl-Spacebar**.)

   Asterisks (*) appear before every marked file.

3. From the Library Document-retrieval menu, select **Copy**.

4. In the *marked files to drive/directory* field, enter the drive and path you want to copy the files to.

5. To delete the files after copying, select **Yes** in the *delete files after copy* field.

6. To copy the style sheets that are related to the documents, select **Yes** in the *copy style sheets* field.

7. Press **Enter** or click the command name.

Word completes the copy according to your instructions. Marked files are unmarked and the names of deleted files are removed from the list. If there is not enough room on the destination disk to copy all the files, those not copied remain marked. (If a file on a network is in use, it is not copied and remains marked.) You can then switch to a disk with space available and select Library Document-retrieval Copy again to copy the remaining files.

Deleting Several Files

You can delete one or more document files using Library Document-retrieval. (To delete one file, you can also use Transfer Delete.) Once you delete a file, you cannot recover it through Word.

To delete several files, follow these steps:

1. Select Library **D**ocument-retrieval. Word displays the files in the search path.

   To change the file display, select **Q**uery and then enter the drive and directory containing the files you want to see. Don't enter selection criteria. Press **Enter**. Word displays all the files for that drive and path.

   If you are connected to a network or using Microsoft Windows, update the screen with **Ctrl-F4**.

2. Mark the files to delete using one of the following options:

   - To mark or unmark a single file, highlight the file name and press **Spacebar** or **Enter**.

   - To mark all files, press **Ctrl-Spacebar**. (To unmark all of them, press **Shift-Ctrl-Spacebar**.)

   Asterisks (*) appear before every marked file.

3. Select **D**elete from the Document-retrieval menu.

4. Press **Enter** or click the command name.

5. Word displays this message:

   `Enter Y to confirm deletion of marked files`

   Press **Y** to delete the marked files.

    Once a file is deleted, you cannot undo the deletion through Word.

   After you press **Y**, Word deletes the files and no longer displays the file names on the screen.

Printing Documents and Summary Sheets

When you want to print several documents in succession, use the Library Document-retrieval Print command.

With Library Document-retrieval, you can print one or more documents at a time. You can also print summary sheets, either by themselves or with the documents. You can use the Library Document-retrieval Print command to print only those documents that have already been saved on disk. To print unsaved documents in current windows, you must use the Print command from the document screen. Whichever method you choose, the settings currently specified in the Print Options command fields will govern the printing.

To print summary sheets and/or documents:

1. Select **Library Document-retrieval**. Word displays the files in the search path. To list files other than the ones you see, select **Query** and then enter the drive and path. Don't enter selection criteria. Press **Enter**.

   If you are connected to a network or using Microsoft Windows, update the screen with Ctrl-F4.

2. Mark the files to print using one of the following options:

   - To mark or unmark a file, highlight the file name and press **Spacebar** or **Enter**.

   - To mark all files, press **Ctrl-Spacebar**. (To unmark all of them, press **Shift-Ctrl-Spacebar**.)

   Asterisks (*) appear before marked files.

3. Select **P**rint from the Document-retrieval menu.

4. Select one of these print options in the *marked files* field:

   Summary   to print summaries only

   Document   to print documents only

   Both   to print both summaries and documents

5. Make sure the printer is ready to print.

6. Press **Enter** or click the command name.

Word prints the marked documents. After they are printed, the documents remain marked.

See Chapter 5, "Printing Documents," for information on using the Print and Print Options commands to control the way documents are printed and the printing of summary sheets for documents in active windows.

Exercise: Using Library Document-Retrieval

In the following exercises, you will change the appearance of the listed documents. First, display the long view by selecting Library Document-retrieval View and then selecting Long and pressing Enter.

To update several summary sheets, select Update from the Library Document-retrieval menu. Select a file of your choice and enter your name in the *author* field and the word *test* in the *keywords* field. Do this for two additional files. Be consistent in how you enter your name. In a fourth file, enter your name as author and the words *test* and *practice*. Leave the *keywords* field blank.

To search the files, select Query from the Library Document-retrieval menu. Enter your name in the *author* field. In the *keywords* field enter:

```
test~practice
```

Press Enter or click the command area. The three files with *test* but not *practice* in their *keywords* field are selected.

To copy the file to a floppy disk, highlight the file and press Enter. Word marks the file. Highlight one more file and press Enter to mark that file. Select Copy. Put the disk in a drive. In the *marked files to drive/directory* field, enter the drive containing the formatted disk. Make sure the *delete files after copy* field and the *copy style sheets* field are set to No. Press Enter. Word copies the file.

To print two files and their summary sheets, first mark both documents. Select Print. In the *marked files* field, select Both. Make sure your printer is ready and then press Enter. The documents and their summary sheets are printed.

From the Library Document-retrieval menu, select Exit to return to your document screen.

Entering DOS Commands from Within Word

The Library Run command lets you enter DOS commands from within Word. For example, you may want to briefly run another application or perform a simple housekeeping chore, such as formatting a disk that you need before you can save the current document. Any command that can be entered at the DOS prompt can also be entered using Library Run.

To enter a DOS command from within Word:

1. Select Library **R**un.
2. You now have two choices:
   - Type in any DOS command you like.

     When Word finishes carrying out the command, it displays the following message:

     ```
     Press a key to resume Word
     ```

Press any key. You return to your current location in the current document.

- Simply press **Enter** to go to the DOS prompt, where you can enter any command in the usual way. Word remains loaded in your computer's memory. When you want to return to Word, type in **Exit**. You return to your current location in the current document.

Exercise: Using Library Run

In this exercise, you will list the files in the current directory without leaving Word. Select Library Run. After the word *COMMAND*, type in the following and then press Enter:

```
dir/p
```

View each screenful of file names. Follow the instructions on the screen. When this message appears:

```
Press a key to resume Word
```

you know that you have viewed the whole directory. Press any key to return to your Word document.

In the next exercise, you will exit to the DOS prompt, carry out a DOS command, and then return to Word. Select Library Run and then press Enter. The DOS system prompt appears on your screen. You can now issue any legal DOS command. You can even load a new application program—if you have enough memory! If you want to see for yourself how this works, try a few commands now. When you are ready to return to Word, type in the following and press Enter:

```
Exit
```

When this message appears:

```
Press a key to resume Word
```

press any key to return to your Word document.

Merging Documents

Merging is the process by which a computer combines data from one file with a document template, such as a form letter, in a second file to automatically produce multiple customized copies of documents. Merging makes it easy to create individualized letters, billings, announcements, mailing labels, and other documents requiring different versions of the same basic form.

Word's powerful merging features enable you to:

- Create virtually any kind of customized document
- Manage mailing lists
- Combine data created in programs other than Word with form documents created in Word
- Combine multiple documents into a single document for purposes of printing
- Fill out forms automatically (see Chapter 16, "Creating and Filling In Forms.")

In Word, the document that is to serve as a template into which specific data will be merged is called the *main document*; the document containing the data to be merged is called the *data document*. The merging process consists of creating separate main and data documents and then merging them with the Print Merge command. Figure 15-1 shows a main document for a form letter. Figure 15-2 shows a data document. Figure 15-3 shows several letters that were produced by the merge process.

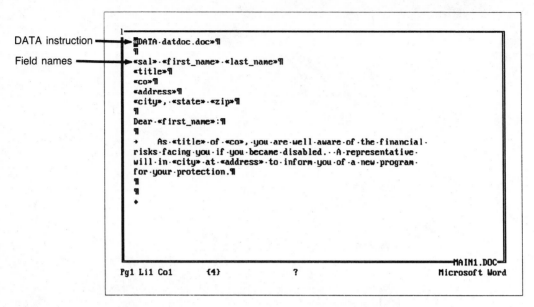

DATA instruction

Field names

Figure 15-1. A main document

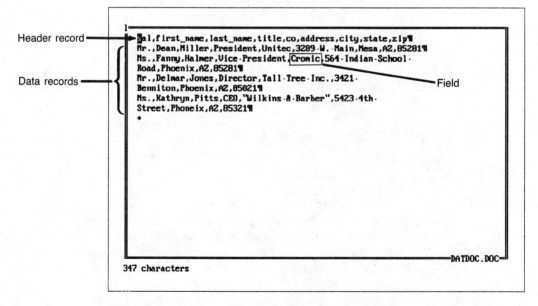

Header record

Data records

Field

Figure 15-2. A data document

```
Mr. Dean Miller
President
Unitec
3289 W. Main
Mesa, AZ 85281

Dear Dean:

    As President of Unitec, you are well aware of the
financial risks facing you if you became disabled.  A
re
a
        Ms. Fanny Halmer
        Vice President
        Cromic
        564 Indian School Road
        Phoenix, AZ 85281

        Dear Fanny:

            As Vice President of Cromic, you are well aware of the
        financial risks facing you if you became disabled.  A
        re
        in
            Mr. Delmar Jones
            Director
            Tall Tree Inc.
            3421 Benniton
            Phoenix, AZ 85021

            Dear Delmar:

                As Director of Tall Tree Inc., you are well aware of
            the financial risks facing you if you became disabled.  A
            re
            yc
                Ms. Kathryn Pitts
                CEO
                Wilkins & Barber
                5423 4th Street
                Phoenix, AZ 85321

                Dear Kathryn:

                    As CEO of Wilkins & Barber, you are well aware of the
                financial risks facing you if you became disabled.  A
                representative will in Phoenix at 5423 4th Street to inform
                you of a new program for your protection.
```

Figure 15-3. Several merged letters

Notice that in Figure 15-1, the main document includes a *DATA instruction* listing the name of the document where Word will find the data to be merged into the letters. The main document also includes the *field names* assigned to each different type of data (such as *first_name*, *last_name*, etc.)

In Figure 15-2, the data document consists of a *header record* followed by four *data records*. The header record is always the first paragraph of a data document. By listing all the field names in order, it tells Word how to interpret the information found in the data records. Each data record contains values that correspond to the fields in the header record and that are substituted for the same field names wherever they occur in the main document.

As you can see from the printed result in Figure 15-3, each data record results in one merged document.

One benefit of merging documents is that you can use a single data document in combination with more than one main document. For example, Figure 15-4 illustrates a mailing-label main document. Figure 15-5 shows the mailing labels produced by merging this main document with the same data document shown in Figure 15-2. In other words, the same data document has been used to produce both form letters and mailing labels.

```
[·········1·········2·········3·········4·········5·········]·········7·····
«DATA·datdoc.doc»¶
¶
«first_name»·«last_name»¶
«title»¶
«company»¶
«address»¶
«city»,·«state»·«zip»¶
¶
«NEXT»«first_name»·«last_name»¶
«title»¶
«company»¶
«address»¶
«city»,·«state»·«zip»¶
¶
«NEXT»«first_name»·«last_name»¶
«title»¶
«company»¶
«address»¶
«city»,·«state»·«zip»¶
¶
«NEXT»«first_name»·«last_name»¶
«title»¶
                                                                   ADDMD.DOC
Pg1 Li1 Co1        {d}                                          Microsoft Word
```

Figure 15-4. A mailing-label main document

In this chapter, you will learn how to develop and merge main and data documents. You will also learn how to handle special cases. For example, by inserting a specific instruction in your main document, you can skip certain fields when the corresponding data are missing in some records. You can also print all or selected data

```
                    Mr. Dean Miller
                    President
                    Unitec
                    3289 W. Main
                    Mesa, AZ 85281


                    Ms. Fanny Halmer
                    Vice President
                    Cromic
                    564 Indian School Road
                    Phoenix, AZ 85281


                    Mr. Delmar Jones
                    Director
                    Tall Tree Inc.
                    3421 Benniton
                    Phoenix, AZ 85021


                    Ms. Kathryn Pitts
                    CEO
                    Wilkins & Barber
                    5423 4th Street
                    Phoneix, AZ 85321
```

Figure 15-5. Several merged mailing labels

records to create one merged document. These are only a few of Word's custom merge features.

Creating Main Documents

The main document is like any other Word document, with two exceptions: The first paragraph of all main documents is a DATA instruction identifying the name of the data document to be used in the merge; and the body of the main document contains field names corresponding to those named in the header record of the data document.

Figure 15-6 shows a sample main document with a DATA instruction and field names. In this sales flyer, the DATA instruction shows that the data document is called SALEDD.DOC. The data field names are surrounded by chevrons. Punctuation and spacing specify how to print the document after the data is merged.

To create a main document:

1. At the top of a regular Word document, type in a DATA instruction identifying the file name of the data document to be used in the merge. Press **Ctrl-[** to enter an opening chevron, type in the

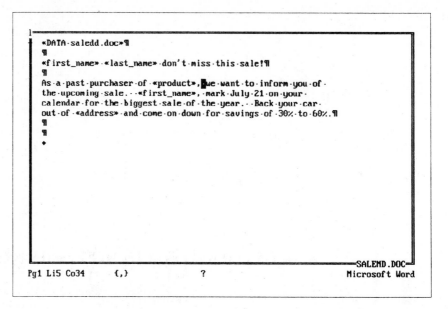

Figure 15-6. The sales-flyer main document

word *DATA* followed by the name of the data document file, and press **Ctrl-]** to enter a closing chevron. Do not use two less-than (<<) or greater-than (>>) symbols. Here is the format to follow:

«DATA *DATA_FILENAME*»

You can include a drive or path in the DATA instruction. The following example tells Word to use the data document called PROSPECT on the disk in drive A:

«DATA A:PROSPECT.DOC»

If the header information is in a separate file and the data document contains data records only, you can type in the DATA instruction in this format:

«DATA *HEADER_FILENAME,DATA_FILENAME*»

The header file name appears first, followed by a comma and then the data document file name. Drives and paths can be included.

2. Once you have entered the DATA instruction, type in the text common to all document versions and enter field names as desired. All field names must be surrounded by chevrons. Press **Ctrl-[** for the left chevron and **Ctrl-]** for the right chevron. For example:

    «firstname»

    Field names can be up to 64 characters in length and can contain letters, numbers, or underscores. They cannot include the following symbols:

    space period + - * / % & # ^ $ @ !

    In the main document, field names can be used as often as you like and in any order. You do not have to use every field available in the data document. If you want to format an entire field—for example, with italics—apply the formatting to at least the first letter of the field name. Word will format the rest of the field when you print it.

3. Carefully proofread the document before saving it. Make sure chevrons surround the DATA instruction and each field name. Check that the spacing and punctuation around each field name will result in the desired appearance. Double-check that the formatting for each field is correct.

4. Save the document with **T**ransfer **S**ave.

Creating Data Documents

To create a data document from a file generated in another program, save the file in ASCII format, load it into Word, and type in a header record.

The data document contains the information Word substitutes for the field names in the main document.

The first paragraph, or header record, lists the field names used in the data document. The subsequent paragraphs, or data records, contain data corresponding to the field names in the header record. Field entries are separated by commas or tabs. (If the decimal character is a comma instead of a period—as it is in some countries—fields can be separated by semicolons.) Entries can contain commas as long as the entire field is enclosed in quotation marks. For example, this sentence in a main document calls for the name of a firm to be merged:

The firm «firm» will be represented by «name».

Suppose the field entry corresponding to *firm* in the data document contains commas. To prevent Word from mistaking each part of the field entry as separate fields, surround the data document field with quotation marks, as shown here:

```
"Janice, Betty, and Miller", Jim Smith
```

The printed result will look like this:

```
The firm Janice, Betty, and Miller will be represented by
Jim Smith.
```

Figure 15-7 shows a sample data document for the sales-flyer main document shown earlier in Figure 15-6. The header record ends in a paragraph mark. The field entries of the data records are in the same order and number as the field names in the header record. If data for any field were missing, a placeholder (double commas or double tabs) would be used to mark the missing data. If commas were part of a field entry, the field contents would be surrounded by quotation marks.

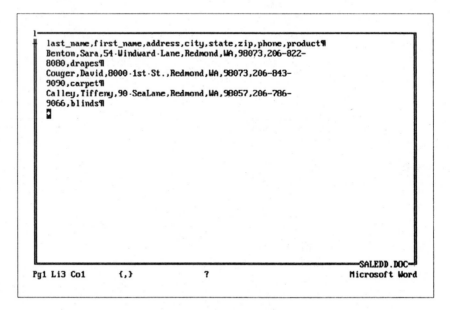

Figure 15-7. The data document for the sales flyer

You can use the files created by other programs (such as database programs) as data documents. Just make sure the program creates ASCII files with commas or tabs between the fields. Also, each record must end with a paragraph mark. For Word to be able to use the file, you must either enter a header record in the file or create a separate header-record file. (See "Creating Main Documents" in this chapter for instructions on how to enter the DATA instruction when you have separate files containing the header record and the data.)

To create a data document:

1. Type in the header record paragraph on the first line of the data document. You can list up to 256 field names, each one containing up to 64 characters. Field names can contain letters, numbers, or underscores. They cannot include the following symbols:

   space period + - * / % & # ^ $ @ !

   Use a comma or a tab to separate field names. The spelling of each field name must be identical to that of corresponding fields in the main document. (Using windows to display both documents is a handy way to verify the spelling). You can have more fields in the data document than are used in the main document. Press **Enter** at the end of the header record.

2. Create each data record by typing in the field entries, separating them with commas or tabs. (If the field entry contains an internal comma, use a semicolon to help you distinguish between punctuation and field separators.) Type in the same number of fields in the order they appear in the header record. If you don't have data for a particular field, just leave the field blank but type in a separator character (comma, tab, or semicolon) for that field. For example, suppose your data document has this header record:

   `name,rank,serial_number`

   To include a record for which you have no *rank* field entry, simply type in:

   `johnson,,898887654`

   Fields can be any length. If a field includes a comma, a tab, or quotation marks, surround the entire field with quotation marks. For example, you would enter this field entry:

   `"Why not ""shoot""" the idea?"`

   to produce this result:

Why not "shoot" the idea?

The outside quotation marks indicate that there are quotation marks within the field. The double set of quotation marks tells Word to treat the quotation marks literally and to print the word *shoot* in quotation marks. Here is another example:

""""Sharkey""""

gives this printed result:

"Sharkey"

Press **Enter** at the end of each data record. Do not leave a blank line between data records. Unless you enter special Word instructions (described later in this chapter), each record will result in a single merged document, with the field entries replacing the field names in the main document during the merge.

Word prints merged documents in the order in which the data records appear. You can sort data records to change the order—for example, to alphabetize a mailing list. (See Chapter 13, "Sorting Text," for more information.)

3. Carefully proofread your data document before saving it. Make sure the header record includes all the field names used in the main document (more field names are allowed). Check each data record to make sure it contains fields for every field name in the header record (or that you have used placeholders to identify missing fields). Finally, make sure you have enclosed fields with internal punctuation in quotation marks.

4. Save the document with **Transfer Save**.

Using the Print Merge Command

Once you have created a main document and data document, use Print Merge to merge them. The main document must be active. Figure 15-8 shows the merged documents printed from the sales-flyer main document (shown earlier in Figure 15-6) and the sales-flyer data document (shown earlier in Figure 15-7).

You can print all the records in the data document or only selected records. You can print directly to the printer or you can "print" to disk (see Chapter 5, "Printing Documents").

Printing to disk can be a time and paper saver because you can check the result before commiting it to paper. If you are using fonts or formatting that do not appear on your screen, print one page to make sure the layout is correct. Once you are satisfied, print that document file or perform the merge and print directly to the printer.

```
Sara Benton don't miss this sale!

As a past purchaser of drapes, we want to inform you of the
upcoming sale.  Sara, mark July 21 on your calendar for the
biggest sale of the year.  Back your car out of 54 Windward
La
```

```
    David Couger don't miss this sale!

    As a past purchaser of carpet, we want to inform you of the
    upcoming sale.  David, mark July 21 on your calendar for the
    biggest sale of the year.  Back your car out of 8000 1st St.
    an
```

```
        Tiffeny Calley don't miss this sale!

        As a past purchaser of blinds, we want to inform you of the
        upcoming sale.  Tiffeny, mark July 21 on your calendar for
        the biggest sale of the year.  Back your car out of 90
        SeaLane and come on down for savings of 30% to 60%.
```

Figure 15-8. Merged sales flyers after printing

If you merge documents as disk files, you can edit them before printing them. If you plan to print the new documents just once, it can be faster to merge them to a file and edit any errors that appear, rather than fixing the errors in the main or data document and merging again.

To merge main and data documents:

1. If you plan to print only selected records from the data document, identify the number of each record you want to print. For example, the first record listed in the data-document file after the header record is record number 1, the second is record number 2, and so on.

2. Select **T**ransfer **L**oad to load the main document in the active window. (The main document is the document with the DATA instruction, field names, and text common to all documents.) Press **F1** to move your highlight to the window, if necessary.

3. Select **P**rint **M**erge.

4. At this point, you have three choices. You can:

    a. Select **O**ptions to enter selected records to print. (Before you can select records, you must first number them. For information on numbering paragraphs, see Chapter 18, "Indexes, Outlines, and Tables of Contents.")

    b. In the *range* field, select **R**ecords.

c. In the *record numbers* field, type in the number of each record. (Before you can select records, you must first number them. For information on numbering paragraphs, see Chapter 18, "Indexes, Outlines, and Tables of Contents.") Use a comma to separate individual records and a colon or hyphen to enter a range of records.

For example, the following entry selects records 3, 9, and 12 through 20, 25 through 28, and 35:

```
3,9,12-20,25:28,35
```

d. Press **Enter** or click the command name. You can select **P**rinter to begin printing or select **D**ocument to "print" to a document file.

Or you can:

a. Select **P**rinter to merge and print the main and data documents. (Make sure the printer is ready to print.)

After you select Printer, these messages appear:

```
Merging...
Formatting a page...
```

If Word can't match the data document identified in the DATA instruction, Word displays a message informing you that the data document is not a valid file.

If Word can't find a field name in the main document with one in the header record, this message is printed in each field:

```
Unknown field name
```

Or you can:

a. Select **D**ocument to "print" to a document file.

b. In the *filename* field, type in a name for the merged document file.

c. Press **Enter** or click the command name to start the merge. Word displays this message for each record as it is merged:

```
Merging record 1
```

The merged document is stored on the disk.

If you select an existing document name for the name of the new, merged document, Word displays this message:

```
File already exists. Enter Y to replace or Esc to cancel
```

If the named document is open, you cannot merge. This message provides a warning prior to canceling the merge:

```
Cannot merge to an open document
```

5. To cancel a merge process, press **Esc**. Word displays a message asking you to press **Y** to continue merging or **Esc** to stop.

Exercise: Merging Documents

In this example, you will create a main document and a data document, then merge them into a single file.

Create a main document by typing in the following text in a blank Word window:

```
«DATA M1DD.DOC»

«first_name»«last_name»
«address»
«suite»
«city», «state» «zip»
Dear «first_name»:

«message» Plan to arrive for the meeting by 10 a.m. on July 21.
The meeting will be over at noon on July 22. Hope this brief
note clears up any miscommunications.
```

Press Ctrl-[for the left chevron and Ctrl-] for the right chevron. Figure 15-9 shows how the document should appear on the screen.

Select Transfer Save to save the document under the name M1MD, which stands for *merge 1 main document*.

In a different Word window, type in the following text for the data document:

```
last_name,first_name,address,suite,city,state,zip,miles,message
Bend,David,43 Oak,Su 230,Oakland,CA,86755,345,"Hello ""Davie""!"
```

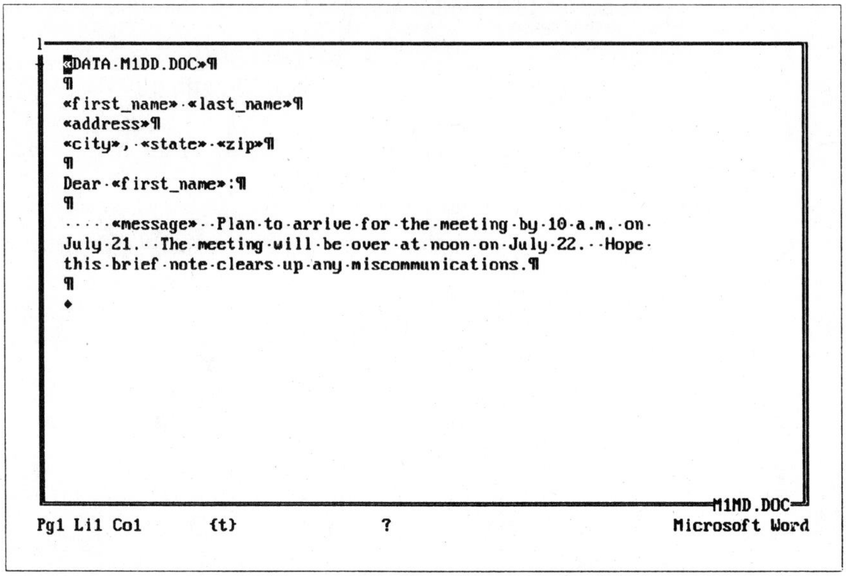

```
1
 ▓DATA·M1DD.DOC»¶
 ¶
 «first_name»·«last_name»¶
 «address»¶
 «city»,·«state»·«zip»¶
 ¶
 Dear·«first_name»:¶
 ¶
 ·····«message»··Plan·to·arrive·for·the·meeting·by·10·a.m.·on·
 July·21.··The·meeting·will·be·over·at·noon·on·July·22.··Hope·
 this·brief·note·clears·up·any·miscommunications.¶
 ¶
 ◆



                                                         ┌M1MD.DOC┐
 Pg1 Li1 Co1        {t}              ?            Microsoft Word
```

Figure 15-9. The screen appearance of the main document

```
Ceal,Barb,21 Waymond,,Culver City,CA,87544,167,"I'm looking
forward to meeting you, Barb."
Dillion,Willy,PO Box 342,,San Diego,CA,83244,25,Look for Jim
at the meeting.
```

Figure 15-10 shows how the document should appear on the screen. Notice that you enter the last name first to make it easy to sort the document later. Pay attention to the treatment of the fields that are missing, as well as to spaces and punctuation. Don't forget to enter a paragraph mark at the end of each record. An extra field, *miles*, is included for use in a later example.

Select Transfer Save to save the document under the name M1DD, which stands for *merge 1 data document*.

Carefully proofread both documents before merging them. Many merging problems can be avoided by identifying incorrect spacing, punctuation, and entries *before* beginning the merge process.

When you are ready to merge, make sure your highlight is in the main document. (The main document must be in the active window.) Press F1, if necessary, to go to the correct window.

Select Print Merge Document. In the *filename* field, enter the path and the file name M1RESULT. Press Enter. Word completes the merge process and stores the resulting document on the disk (not in the main document window).

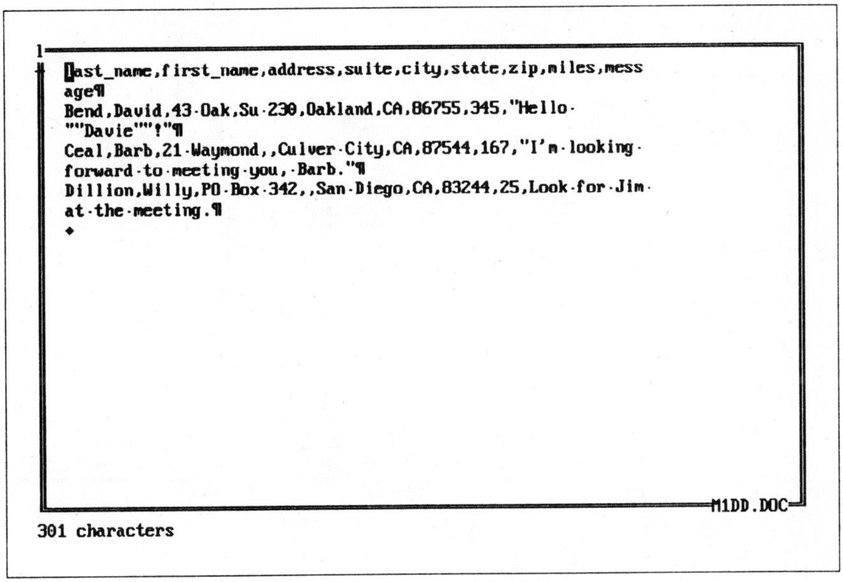

```
1┌─────────────────────────────────────────────────────
 │last_name,first_name,address,suite,city,state,zip,miles,mess
 │age¶
 │Bend,David,43·Oak,Su·230,Oakland,CA,86755,345,"Hello·
 │""Davie""!"¶
 │Ceal,Barb,21·Waymond,,Culver·City,CA,87544,167,"I'm·looking·
 │forward·to·meeting·you,·Barb."¶
 │Dillion,Willy,PO·Box·342,,San·Diego,CA,83244,25,Look·for·Jim·
 │at·the·meeting.¶
 │◆
 │
 │
 │                                                  ─M1DD.DOC─
 │301 characters
```

Figure 15-10. The screen appearance of the data document

Once the merge process is complete, select Transfer Load to look at the M1RESULT document. The printed documents will look like those in Figure 15-11. If there are errors, carefully compare your main and data documents with the examples shown earlier. Correct the mistakes and try again.

Save the M1RESULT document.

Using Math Instructions and Conditional Instructions

You can use math instructions and conditional instructions when merging. These instructions allow you to:

- Perform mathematical calculations on the data in the data document
- Select different print options based on the data in the data document
- Print only those records that meet criteria you specify

Math instructions and conditional instructions are included in the main document to perform operations on the data supplied by the data document.

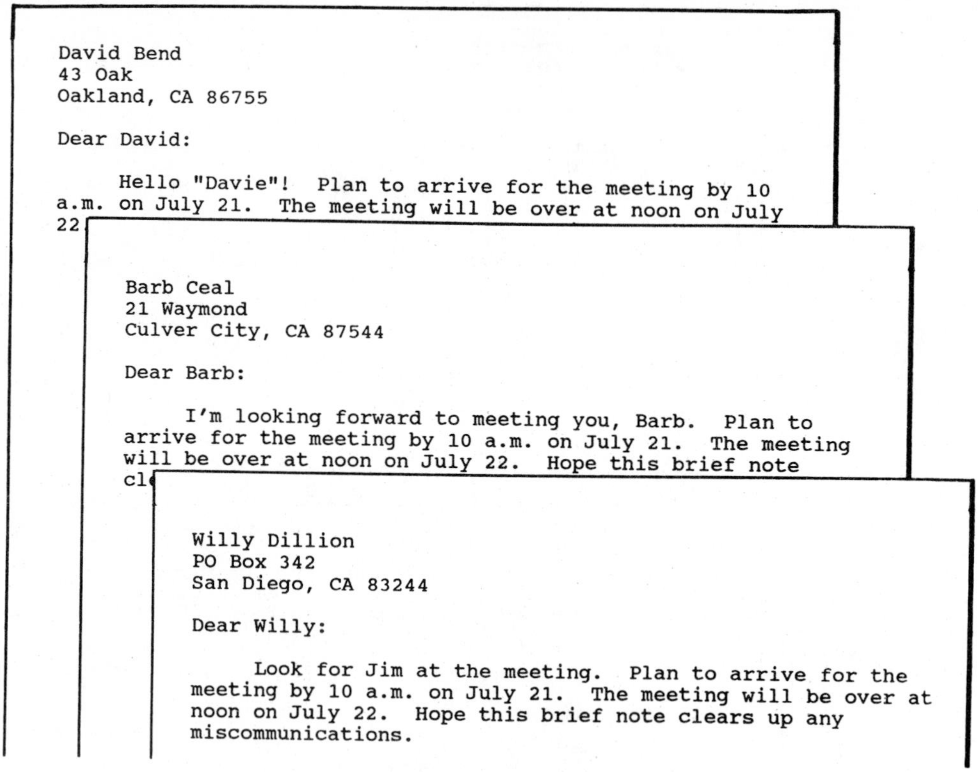

```
David Bend
43 Oak
Oakland, CA 86755

Dear David:

     Hello "Davie"!  Plan to arrive for the meeting by 10
a.m. on July 21.  The meeting will be over at noon on July
22
```

```
Barb Ceal
21 Waymond
Culver City, CA 87544

Dear Barb:

     I'm looking forward to meeting you, Barb.  Plan to
arrive for the meeting by 10 a.m. on July 21.  The meeting
will be over at noon on July 22.  Hope this brief note
cl
```

```
Willy Dillion
PO Box 342
San Diego, CA 83244

Dear Willy:

     Look for Jim at the meeting.  Plan to arrive for the
meeting by 10 a.m. on July 21.  The meeting will be over at
noon on July 22.  Hope this brief note clears up any
miscommunications.
```

Figure 15-11. The M1RESULT document after printing

Math Instructions

To avoid routine hand calculations, set up expense reports as merge documents with embedded math instructions.

You can include math instructions in a main-document field if the contents of the field will be a number. For example, this statement

«miles*.21»

tells Word to multiply the number inserted for *miles* by 21 cents and print the result. If the *miles* field value is 10, the merged result is 2.10.

You can use the following mathematical symbols:

Symbol	Use
. (period)	Decimals
+	Addition
−	Subtraction

*	Multiplication
/	Division
%	Percentages

Conditional Instructions

Conditional instructions allow you to define specific conditions under which operations of your choosing are or are not to be carried out during a merge. Using conditional instructions, you can choose whether or not to print certain text or include certain records depending on whether or not a given condition is true or false. For example, you may want to print this text if a given field entry is *Dallas*:

`Texas is the Lone Star State.`

If the given field entry is *Los Angeles*, you may want this text to print:

`California is truly the home of the stars.`

As another example, you may wish to skip all the records that have *Ohio* for the *state* field. By making it possible for you to draw these and other, more complex, distinctions, conditional instructions provide powerful tools for customizing form letters and other merge documents for particular audiences.

Word recognizes the following conditional instructions:

- IF and ENDIF (may also use ELSE)
- SET
- ASK
- SKIP
- NEXT
- INCLUDE

You embed conditional instructions within the text of your main documents. When the resulting merge documents are printed, Word replaces the instructions with the appropriate data.

All conditional instructions must be surrounded by chevrons. To enter a left chevron, press Ctrl-[. To enter a right chevron, press Ctrl-]. Do not use two less-than (<<) or greater-than (>>) symbols in place of the chevrons.

The sections that follow describe the use of each conditional instruction in detail.

IF, ENDIF, and ELSE Instructions

IF, ENDIF, and ELSE are used in the main document to define the conditions under which designated data or text are or are not to be merged or printed. When you use IF, you must always use ENDIF to end the instruction; ELSE is optional. For example, the following statement identifies the text to print if condition 1 is met.

«IF *condition 1*»*print this*«ENDIF»

Below, the ELSE conditional instruction is used to provide two alternatives:

«IF *condition 2*»*print this text*«ELSE»*print this substitute text*«ENDIF»

IF can be used to identify the following:

* Whether there is data
* Whether data matches a value you enter
* How numeric data compares with a value

As mentioned, you can use IF to identify whether there is data in a given field and, if there is, the text to print. Use this format and substitute the information specific to your situation:

«IF *field name*»*this text prints*«ENDIF»

The following example uses this format:

«IF deadline»The project deadline is critical.«ENDIF»

In this example, if there is a value in the *deadline* field, this text is printed in the location of the IF statement in the main document:

The project deadline is critical.

If there is no data in the *deadline* field, neither text nor spaces are entered.

IF can also be used to identify whether a field name matches a field entry or value you enter. The value can be a number or a text string that can include letters, numbers, symbols, and/or spaces. You must enter the value to be matched in quotation marks. This is the format to use:

«IF *field name* = *"value to match"*»*text to print*«ENDIF»

This example shows a sample use of the format:

«IF time = "3 o'clock p.m."»You will be met at the airport by
Darlene.«ENDIF»

In cases where the *time* field was not *3 o'clock p.m.*, Word would
continue on to the following text or the next main-document instruction (which could be another *IF time=...* statement). No spaces
would be left.

Finally, IF can be used to see how numeric data in a specific
field compares with a value entered in the conditional statement. You
must identify the field name, the operator, and the number. Here is
the format:

«IF *field name operator number*»*text to print*«ENDIF»

This is an example of this format:

«IF discount >= 20»As a result of your loyalty to our company,
you are receiving our highest discount level.«ENDIF»

When Word encounters this statement in the main document, it
prints this text if the *discount* value is greater than or equal to 20:

As a result of your loyalty to our company, you are receiving
our highest discount level.

If the *discount* value is less than 20, Word continues on to the next
statement or text in the main document. No text or space is entered in
place of the conditional statement.

IF statements may or may not include ELSE instructions. When
included, ELSE portions of a statement tell Word what text to print if
the first condition is false. As with all IF statements, when ELSE is
used, end the statement with ENDIF. This is the format:

«IF *condition*»*text to print*«ELSE»*alternative text to print if
condition not met*«ENDIF»

An example follows:

«IF group = "product"»We are proud of the Product Group.«ELSE»
We are proud of the Sales Group.«ENDIF»

In this example, if the field named *group* equals *product*, Word prints this text:

`We are proud of the Product Group.`

If this condition is not met (*group* does not equal *product*), Word prints this text:

`We are proud of the Sales Group.`

When you use IF with ELSE, either the first or second option is entered.

As shown in the previous examples, you can use these logical operators in IF statements:

Operator	Meaning
>	Greater than
<	Less than
=	Equal to
<>	Not equal to
>=	Greater than or equal to
<=	Less than or equal to
AND	Both parts of the statement must be true
OR	Either part of the statement can be true
NOT	The NOT part of the statement is omitted

For example:

`«IF month = "June" AND year = "1989"»June 1989 was a good month.«ENDIF»`

The statement shown here requires that the *month* be *June* and the *year* be *1989* before Word prints this text:

`June 1989 was a good month.`

In all IF statements, you will want to pay special attention to paragraph marks. If you place a paragraph mark after the ENDIF and chevron (»), Word regards the chevron as the end of the statement and the paragraph mark as starting a new line. Figure 15-12 shows a main document that uses this example on the screen, and Figure 15-13 shows how the document looks when printed.

```
│
├─────────────────────────────────────────────────────────────────
│ «DATA·date.doc»¶
│ ¶
│ You·were·responsible·for·performance·in·the·month·of·
│ «month».«IF·month="June"·AND·year="1989"»··June·1989·was·a·
│ good·month.«ENDIF»¶
│ We·need·to·increase·sales·in·the·second·half·of·the·year.¶
│ ⌶
│ ◆
│
│
│
│
│
│
│
│
│
│                                                        ┌─MONMD1.DOC─┐
│ Pg1 Li7 Col        {*}              ?                     Microsoft Word
```

Figure 15-12. The screen appearance of a conditional instruction in
which «ENDIF» is followed by a paragraph mark

You were responsible for performance in the month of June.
June 1989 was a good month.
We need to increase sales in the second half of the year.

You were responsible for performance in the month of July.
We need to increase sales in the second half of the year.

Figure 15-13. The printed result of a conditional instruction in which
«ENDIF» is followed by a paragraph mark

You can avoid starting a new line in two ways:

- Enter text immediately after the final chevron. Figures 15-14 and
  15-15 illustrate the screen and printed appearance of entering
  text immediately after the right chevron of ENDIF.

- Follow the ENDIF with a paragraph mark instead of the closing
  chevron. This alternative is shown in Figures 15-16 and 15-17,
  which illustrate the screen and printed appearance when the
  ENDIF is followed by a paragraph mark instead of the right
  chevron. No space is added after the ENDIF statement. Spaces
  would need to be entered manually.

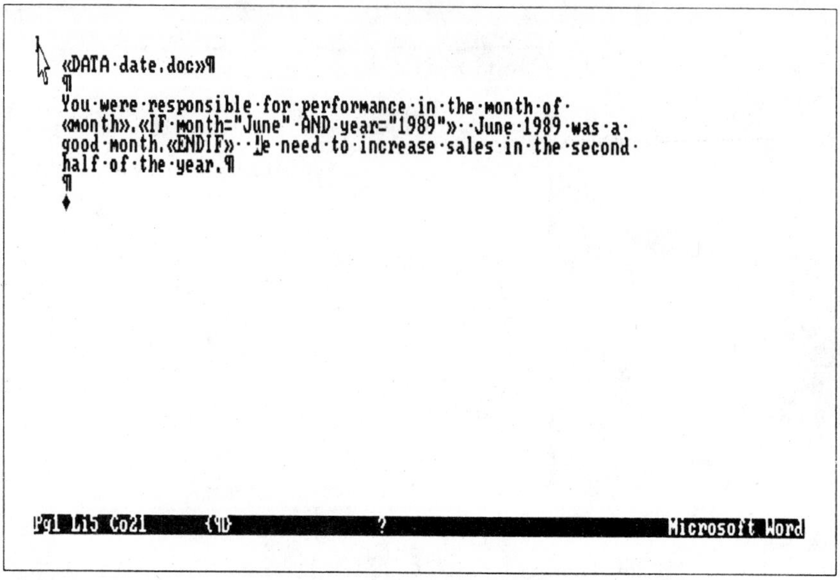

Figure 15-14. The screen appearance of a conditional instruction in which «ENDIF» is followed by text

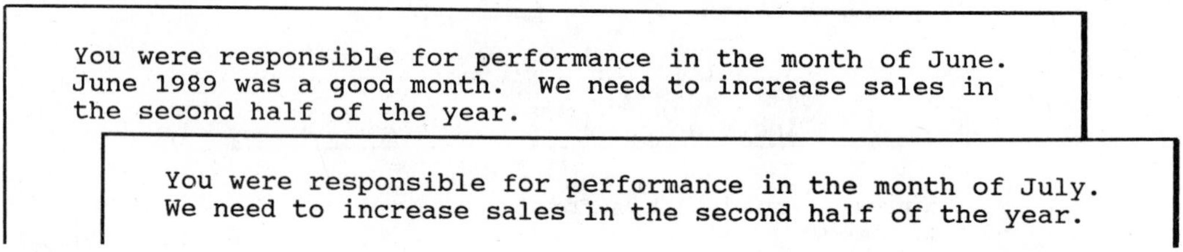

Figure 15-15. The printed result of a conditional instruction in which «ENDIF» is followed by text

You can also nest IF statements; that is, you can place one statement inside another. Nesting IF statements is useful when you have two criteria to meet and don't want to use the AND logical operator. Don't forget to place two ENDIFs at the end of the statement. Here is an example:

```
«IF age > 60»«IF state = IA»Retired Iowans Want«ENDIF»«ENDIF»
```

If you nest IF statements, double check to be sure that every IF has a corresponding ENDIF.

In this example, if the age is greater than 60 and if the state is Iowa, Word prints the text *Retired Iowans Want*. If the age is less than 60, Word stops reading the statement and goes on to the text or statement following the ENDIFs.

```
┌─────────────────────────────────────────────────────────────┐
│ ▌════════════════════════════════════════════════════════    │
│ ║ «DATA·date.doc»¶                                            │
│ ║ ¶                                                           │
│ ║ You·were·responsible·for·performance·in·the·month·of·       │
│ ║ «month».«IF·month="June"·AND·year="1989"»··June·1989·was·a· │
│ ║ good·month.«ENDIF¶                                          │
│ ║ ⌐e·need·to·increase·sales·in·the·second·half·of·the·year.¶  │
│ ║ ¶                                                           │
│ ║ ◆                                                           │
│ ║                                                             │
│ ║                                                             │
│ ║                                                             │
│ ║                                                             │
│ ║                                         ═════════════════   │
│ ║                                          MONMD2.DOC═        │
│ Pg1 Li6 Co1    {¶¶¶Yo...¶¶§¶}     ?        Microsoft Word     │
└─────────────────────────────────────────────────────────────┘
```

Figure 15-16. The screen appearance of a conditional instruction in which «ENDIF is followed by a paragraph mark, instead of a »

```
You were responsible for performance in the month of June.
June 1989 was a good month.We need to increase sales in the
second half of the year.
```

```
You were responsible for performance in the month of July.We
need to increase sales in the second half of the year.
```

Figure 15-17. The printed result of a conditional instruction in which «ENDIF is followed by a paragraph mark, instead of a »

The SET Instruction

With the SET instruction you can type in a field entry once and that field entry or value is used for every occurrence of the field name throughout the main document. (SET does not allow you to enter a different field value for each data record. See "The ASK Instruction" later in this chapter for details about that process.)

SET is especially useful if you don't have the field information available when creating the data document and don't want to take the time later to add the same field value to each record in the data document.

These are three ways you can use SET:

- To enter specified data for every occurrence of a given field name

- To enter the field value from the keyboard at a Word prompt
- To enter the field value from the keyboard at a prompt you have identified

When you use SET, you can:

- Include the field value ahead of time in the main document
- Enter the field value from the keyboard when prompted to do so during the course of merging
- Include both alternatives in the main document, along with merging data from a data document. The field name used with the SET command must not appear in the data document; if it does, the values in the data document are used.

To enter the field value in the main document, place the SET instruction at the beginning of the main document after the DATA instruction. In the SET instruction, identify the field name and field value to enter in all documents for that field name. You can enter up to 256 characters for the field value. This is the format:

«SET *field name* = "*text to print*"»

Consider this example:

«SET state = "AZ"»

Whenever Word encounters the *state* field name in the main document, it prints this state code:

AZ

This particular use of SET assumes that no field name or fields for *state* are in the data document. Notice that the quotation marks in the statement indicate the text Word should print and do not themselves appear in the merged documents.

The SET instruction can also be used to enter data from the keyboard. To use the instruction in this way, replace the field value (AZ in the above example) with a question mark:

«SET *field name* = ?»

When Word encounters the field name in the main document, it displays the following prompt:

```
RESPONSE:_
Enter text. Press Enter when done
```

You can then type in whatever text you wish and press Enter when finished. Word uses this text as the field value for this and every other occurrence of the field name encountered during the merge.

You cannot include Enter as part of a field value. Word assumes Enter completes the field and continues processing.

Specifying your own prompt provides a better reminder of the appropriate type of data to enter from the keyboard. To specify your own prompt, type in a question mark and then the prompt in the format shown below:

«SET *field name* = *?your prompt here*»

Your prompt can be up to 80 characters long. Word displays the prompt when the field name is encountered in the main document. Type in the data and then press Enter. The field entry is used for every occurrence of the field name during the merge.

For example, when Word encounters this SET instruction:

«SET money = ?Enter bonus amount. Press Enter.»

it displays the prompt:

```
RESPONSE:_
Enter bonus amount. Press Enter.
```

You type in the bonus amount and press Enter. The amount you enter becomes the value of the *money* field.

The ASK Instruction

Use ASK to enter a specific field value from the keyboard for every data record. You can enter a different value for each merge record. (To enter a common field value to be used for all occurrences of a specific field name, see the preceding discussion of the SET instruction.) You can use ASK with or without using a data document, as long as the specified ASK field does not appear in the data document. If it does, Word displays a message during the merge like the following:

data_field_name: Field name redefined

In the merged document, Word prints the ASK statement along with the message and abandons the merge.

ASK is useful for occasional use of a data field that is not included in a data document. For example, you might use ASK for addressing form letters that you create only occasionally, rather than as part of a regular bulk mailing. In such instances, entering information from the keyboard in response to prompts during the merge can be faster than positioning your highlight in each record and entering the data before you perform the merge.

To use the ASK statement, simply add it after the DATA instruction in the main document. If you type in:

«ASK *field name* = ?»

Word displays this prompt:

Enter text. Press Enter when done

To display your own prompt of up to 80 characters, use the following format:

«ASK *field name* = ?*your prompt here*»

For example, suppose you want to assign seat numbers to each person who has registered for a tour. Create the data document without the seat-number information. Add this line after the DATA instruction in the main document:

«ASK seat = ?Enter the seat number now and press Enter.»

Then, during the merge process, whenever the field name *seat* is encountered during the merging of each record, Word displays this message:

RESPONSE:_
Enter the seat number now and press Enter.

You can type in each person's seat number and press Enter. Word replaces the field name with the specified seat number and continues the merge process.

The SKIP Instruction

Make ASK messages as specific as possible. Reminding the user to

The SKIP instruction is useful for bypassing a complete record if a condition you entered is true. If the condition is true, the record is

press Enter is also a good idea. More than one user has waited for a few moments after entering data, wondering when the merge would continue. Using prompts can avoid such confusion.

skipped and Word continues to the next record. By using SKIP to select the records to bypass, you are actually selecting the records you want to print.

The SKIP instruction uses the following format:

«IF *condition*»«SKIP»«ENDIF»

In the following example, all the records in which the *name* field equals *Johnson* are skipped:

«IF name = "Johnson"»«SKIP»«ENDIF»

You can use numbers and/or logical operators in the conditional statement. For example, this statement bypasses every record where the *copies* field is a number greater than 12:

«IF copies > 12»«SKIP»«ENDIF»

The NEXT Instruction

During a merge, each record ordinarily creates one merged document. To print more than one record in a single merged document, use NEXT. Word uses the data from one record and when it encounters the NEXT statement, it uses the data from the next record in the same main document, instead of going on to a new document.

An address list is a good illustration of how many records can be printed in a single merged document. Figure 15-18 shows the main document. Notice that the DATA instruction is on the same line as the first and second field names. Also, notice that the NEXT statement, enclosed in chevrons, is included before the field name that begins each new record. The NEXT statement indicates that the record should be included on the same page as the previous record. Figure 15-19 shows the data document and Figure 15-20 shows the printed result of the merge.

The INCLUDE Instruction

INCLUDE prints two or more documents as one. INCLUDE is useful for printing several documents with contents that together form a single document—the chapters of a book, for example. Use INCLUDE, instead of Word's Transfer Merge command, to merge documents during printing rather than in memory. This procedure is often necessary when printing a book manuscript, where the finished document is too long to fit into memory all at once.

```
«DATA·DATDOC.DOC»«first_name»·«last_name»¶
«co»¶
«address»¶
«city»,·«state»·«zip»¶
¶
«NEXT»«first_name»·«last_name»¶
«co»¶
«address»¶
«city»,·«state»·«zip»¶
¶
«NEXT»«first_name»·«last_name»¶
«co»¶
«address»¶
«city»,·«state»·«zip»¶
¶
«NEXT»«first_name»·«last_name»¶
«co»¶
«address»¶
«city»,·«state»·«zip»¶
¶
▯
```
```
                                                       ═MONMD2.DOC═
Pg1 Li21 Col      {y}                 ?                Microsoft Word
```

Figure 15-18. A main document with NEXT statements

```
Sal,first_name,last_name,title,co,address,city,state,zip¶
Mr.,Dean,Miller,President,Unitec,3289·W.·Main,Mesa,AZ,85281¶
Ms.,Fanny,Halmer,Vice·President,Cromic,564·Indian·School·
Road,Phoenix,AZ,85281¶
Mr.,Delmar,Jones,Director,Tall·Tree·Inc.,3421·
Benniton,Phoenix,AZ,85021¶
Ms.,Kathryn,Pitts,CEO,"Wilkins·&·Barber",5423·4th·
Street,Phoneix,AZ,85321¶
♦
```
```
                                                       ═DATDOC.DOC═
Pg1 Li1 Col       {y}                 ?                Microsoft Word
```

Figure 15-19. The data document for merging

You can use INCLUDE in a main document to refer to another Word document or to an ASCII file. The contents of the specified document are placed in the main document at the location of the INCLUDE instruction. Use the following format:

```
Dean Miller
Unitec
3289 W. Main
Mesa, AZ 85281

Fanny Halmer
Cromic
564 Indian School Road
Phoenix, AZ 85281

Delmar Jones
Tall Tree Inc.
3421 Benniton
Phoenix, AZ 85021

Kathryn Pitts
Wilkins & Barber
5423 4th Street
Phoneix, AZ 85321
```

Figure 15-20. The printed outcome of merging with NEXT statements

«INCLUDE *FILENAME*»

Included documents can themselves contain any of Word's merge instructions. If a main document is made up of only INCLUDE statements with no data field names, it does not need a DATA instruction. But if included documents have data field names, each field name must be entered in a DATA instruction in the main document, rather than in each document.

If a style sheet is attached to the main document, Word uses the format defined in that style sheet for all documents, except when direct formatting has been applied. In that case, the formatting in the style sheet is overridden.

INCLUDE statements can refer to a maximum of 64 documents.

Exercise: Using Math Instructions and Conditional Instructions

For this exercise, use the data document created in the exercise earlier in the chapter (see Figure 15-21).

Type in the following text for the main document (Figure 15-22 shows how it looks on the screen):

«DATA M1DD.DOC»
«SET organization="Product Manager's Group"»

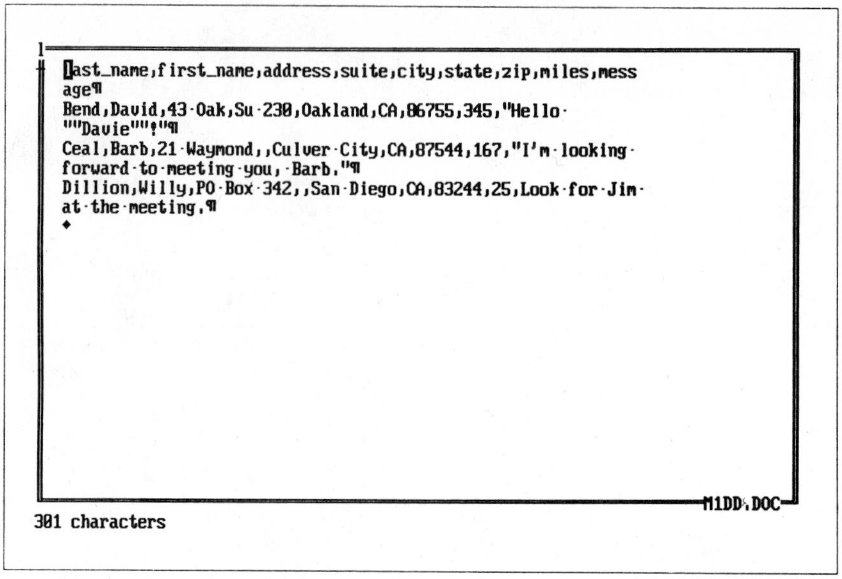

```
┃━━━━━━━━━━━━━━━━━━━━━━━━━━━━━━━━━━━━━━━━━━━━━━━━━━
┃ ▌ast_name,first_name,address,suite,city,state,zip,miles,mess
┃ age¶
┃ Bend,David,43·Oak,Su·230,Oakland,CA,86755,345,"Hello·
┃ ""Davie""!"¶
┃ Ceal,Barb,21·Waymond,,Culver·City,CA,87544,167,"I'm·looking·
┃ forward·to·meeting·you,·Barb."¶
┃ Dillion,Willy,PO·Box·342,,San·Diego,CA,83244,25,Look·for·Jim·
┃ at·the·meeting.¶
┃ ◆
```

301 characters   M1DD·DOC

Figure 15-21. The data document created in the previous exercise

                                  Invoice for
                                «organization»

Mileage Invoice for «first_name» «last_name»:

   Miles: «miles»

   Due: «If miles<100»«miles*«18»«ELSE»«miles*«21»«ENDIF»

The «organization» will pay within 30 days of receipt of
this signed invoice. «organization» is not responsible for
costs not shown on this invoice.

   Select Center in the Format Paragraph *alignment* field to center
the first character of the centered field name (the *o* in the first occurrence of *organization*).
   Check the main document carefully. Select Transfer Save to save
the main document under the name M2MD, which stands for *merge 2
main document*. When you are ready to merge, make sure the main
document is the active document. Select Print Merge Document. In
the *filename* field, enter M2RESULT, which stands for *merge 2 result*.
Press Enter. Once the merge is complete, use Transfer Load and Print
Printer to print the result. It should look like the documents shown in
Figure 15-23.

```
  1
    ¶
    «DATA·M1DD.DOC»¶
    «SET·organization="Product·Manager's·Group"»¶
    ¶
                        Invoice·for¶
                      «organization»¶
    ¶
    Mileage·Invoice·for·«first_name»·«last_name»:¶
    ¶
    ··Miles:··«miles»¶
    ¶
    ··Due:····«If·miles<100»«miles»*.18»«ELSE»«miles»*.21»«ENDIF»¶
    ¶
    The·«organization»·will·pay·within·30·days·of·receipt·of·
    this·signed·invoice.···The·«organization»·is·not·responsible·
    for·costs·not·shown·on·this·invoice.¶
    ¶
    ▯
```

```
 Pg1 Li18 Col      {¶}              ?              Microsoft Word
```
└─M2MD.DOC─┘

Figure 15-22. The screen appearance of the main document

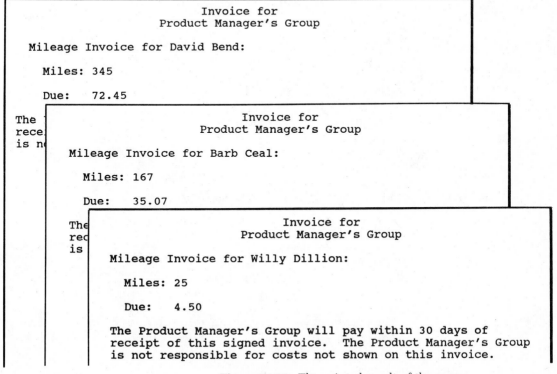

```
                        Invoice for
                  Product Manager's Group

    Mileage Invoice for David Bend:

       Miles: 345

       Due:   72.45
```
```
                        Invoice for
                  Product Manager's Group

    Mileage Invoice for Barb Ceal:

       Miles: 167

       Due:   35.07
```
```
                        Invoice for
                  Product Manager's Group

    Mileage Invoice for Willy Dillion:

       Miles: 25

       Due:   4.50

    The Product Manager's Group will pay within 30 days of
    receipt of this signed invoice.  The Product Manager's Group
    is not responsible for costs not shown on this invoice.
```

Figure 15-23. The printed result of the merge

If your merged document has errors, carefully check your documents against the examples shown in this section of the chapter.

Handling Missing Data Fields

Sometimes data records are missing data fields, such as business titles or ZIP codes. The result can be incorrectly printed documents. For example, this address has five lines:

```
Jay Gerald
President
Corning Inc.
340 East Highway
Denver, CO 45322
```

In contrast, this address has four lines:

```
Stevie Haddon
Treeline Company
PO Box 432
Denver, CO 45322
```

If you enter each line as a separate field, you can end up with incorrect blank spaces. For example, Figure 15-24 shows the main-document layout of the address, Figure 15-25 shows the data-document layout of the records, and Figure 15-26 shows the incorrect printed result. As you can see, when the title or company is missing, Word skips lines, producing results that are unacceptable for letters and mailing labels.

Using the "One Big Field" Approach

There are several ways to avoid the blank-line problem. One way is to enter the lines as one big data field and create a newline character with Shift-Enter at the end of each line in the field. That way, the addresses appear without blank lines. Figures 15-27, 15-28, and 15-29 show the main document, data document, and printed result.

The disadvantage to placing an entire address in one field is that you cannot sort by fields or select just one part of the field. For example, you could not select just the name for a salutation. The main document entry:

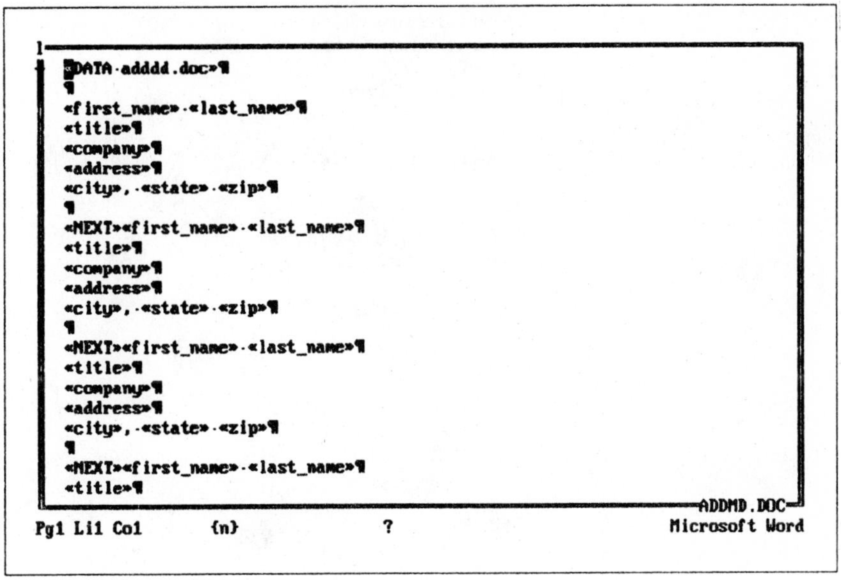

```
|—
 ▌DATA·adddd.doc»¶
 ¶
 «first_name»·«last_name»¶
 «title»¶
 «company»¶
 «address»¶
 «city»,·«state»·«zip»¶
 ¶
 «NEXT»«first_name»·«last_name»¶
 «title»¶
 «company»¶
 «address»¶
 «city»,·«state»·«zip»¶
 ¶
 «NEXT»«first_name»·«last_name»¶
 «title»¶
 «company»¶
 «address»¶
 «city»,·«state»·«zip»¶
 ¶
 «NEXT»«first_name»·«last_name»¶
 «title»¶
                                              ┌ADDMD.DOC┐
 Pg1 Li1 Co1        {n}              ?          Microsoft Word
```

Figure 15-24. The main document for addresses

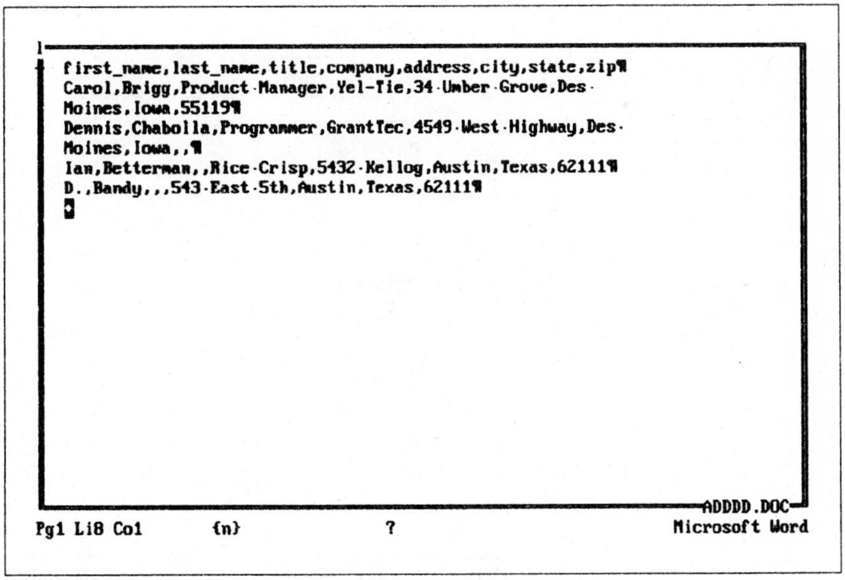

```
|—
 first_name,last_name,title,company,address,city,state,zip¶
 Carol,Brigg,Product·Manager,Yel-Tie,34·Umber·Grove,Des·
 Moines,Iowa,55119¶
 Dennis,Chabolla,Programmer,GrantTec,4549·West·Highway,Des·
 Moines,Iowa,,¶
 Ian,Betterman,,Rice·Crisp,5432·Kellog,Austin,Texas,62111¶
 D.,Bandy,,,543·East·5th,Austin,Texas,62111¶
 ▊




                                              ┌ADDDD.DOC┐
 Pg1 Li8 Co1        {n}              ?          Microsoft Word
```

Figure 15-25. The data document for addresses

```
Carol Brigg
Product Manager
Yel-Tie
34 Umber Grove
Des Moines, Iowa 55119

Dennis Chabolla
Programmer
GrantTec
4549 West Highway
Des Moines, Iowa

Ian Betterman

Rice Crisp
5432 Kellog
Austin, Texas 62111

D. Bandy


543 East 5th
Austin, Texas 62111
```

Figure 15-26. The unacceptable printed result

```
1
 «DATA·add1dd.doc»¶
 ¶
 «address»¶
 ¶
 «NEXT»«address»¶
 ¶
 «NEXT»«address»¶
 ¶
 «NEXT»«address»¶
 ¶
 ¶
 ♦
                                                        ADD1MD.DOC
Pg1 Li1 Co1       {,}          ?                    Microsoft Word
```

Figure 15-27. The main document for "one big field" addresses

```
1
  Address¶
  "Carol·Brigg↓
  Product·Manager↓
  Yel-Tie↓
  34·Umber·Grove↓
  Des·Moines,·Iowa·55119"¶
  "Dennis·Chabolla↓
  Programmer↓
  GrantTec↓
  4549·West·Highway↓
  Des·Moines,·Iowa"¶
  "Ian·Betterman↓
  Rice·Crisp↓
  5432·Kellog↓
  Austin,·Texas·62111"¶
  "D.·Bandy↓
  543·East·5th↓
  Austin,·Texas·62111"¶
  ◆
                                              ADD1DD.DOC
  265 characters
```

Figure 15-28. The data document for "one big field" addresses

```
                        Carol Brigg
                        Product Manager
                        Yel-Tie
                        34 Umber Grove
                        Des Moines, Iowa 55119

                        Dennis Chabolla
                        Programmer
                        GrantTec
                        4549 West Highway
                        Des Moines, Iowa

                        Ian Betterman
                        Rice Crisp
                        5432 Kellog
                        Austin, Texas 62111

                        D. Bandy
                        543 East 5th
                        Austin, Texas 62111
```

Figure 15-29. The printed result of using "one big field" addresses

```
Dear «first_name»:
```

could not pick a first name out of the data document unless you
entered the first name again as another data field.

Using IF to Skip a Field

To keep fields broken into specific data elements, you can combine multiple field names and an IF instruction. Using the IF instruction causes Word to skip a field and not enter a blank line or space if a value for the field is not present in a given record. Figure 15-30 shows the main document with an IF statement designed to skip the company name if it does not exist. The IF statement indicates that if the field named *title* has a value, Word should print the title. Otherwise, Word should go on to the field named *company*. By placing a paragraph mark after the last «title», you cause Word to go to the next line. Leaving off the chevron and placing a paragraph mark after the ENDIF statement tells Word to omit any blank line (which would appear if ENDIF had a closing chevron). Figure 15-31 shows the data document. Its layout is no different from those shown previously. Figure 15-32 shows the printed result. Word prints one line between each address for a pleasing effect.

```
1
  «DATA·adddd.doc»¶
  ¶
  «first_name»·«last_name»¶
  «IF·title»«title»¶
  «ENDIF¶
  «IF·company»«company»¶
  «ENDIF¶
  «address»¶
  «city»,·«state»··«IF·zip»«zip»«ENDIF»¶
  ¶
  «NEXT»«first_name»·«last_name»¶
  «IF·title»«title»¶
  «ENDIF¶
  «IF·company»«company»¶
  «ENDIF¶
  «address»¶
  «city»,·«state»··«IF·zip»«zip»«ENDIF»¶
  ¶
  «NEXT»«first_name»·«last_name»¶
  «IF·title»«title»¶
  «ENDIF¶
  «IF·company»«company»│

                                                  ─ADD2MD.DOC─
  Pg1 Li22 Co22      {¶}              ?            Microsoft Word
```

Figure 15-30. The main document for IF-statement addresses

Skipping a Field and Inserting a Blank Line

Use the IF statement to automatically adjust the number of lines printed on mailing labels.

An especially tricky blank-line problem can be created if you are using sheets of labels or labels in continuous forms. Each label must be a given number of lines long to set up printing of the next label in

```
┃first_name,last_name,title,company,address,city,state,zip¶
Carol,Brigg,Product·Manager,Yel-Tie,34·Umber·Grove,Des·
Moines,Iowa,55119¶
Dennis,Chabolla,Programmer,GrantTec,4549·West·Highway,Des·
Moines,Iowa,,¶
Ian,Betterman,,Rice·Crisp,5432·Kellog,Austin,Texas,62111¶
D.,Bandy,,,543·East·5th,Austin,Texas,62111¶
◆
```
ADDDD.DOC

308 characters

Figure 15-31. The data document for IF-statement addresses

```
Carol Brigg
Product Manager
Yel-Tie
34 Umber Grove
Des Moines, Iowa 55119

Dennis Chabolla
Programmer
GrantTec
4549 West Highway
Des Moines, Iowa

Ian Betterman
Rice Crisp
5432 Kellog
Austin, Texas 62111

D. Bandy
543 East 5th
Austin, Texas 62111
```

Figure 15-32. The printed result of using IF-statement addresses

the correct position. If you skip printing a line, that shortens the total length of the label and throws off the positioning of the next label. The solution is to use an IF statement to skip the field name if a field value is not present and to insert a blank line after the text if the

549

field value was skipped. The effect is that the space for the skipped text is moved to the end of the record, making the overall length identical to records that have values for all fields.

For example, Figure 15-33 shows the IF statement used to skip the field in the main document (see the last section "Using IF to Skip a Field" for more information on setting up this condition). Placed at the end of the field names for the record, the IF statement states, in effect, "if the title is blank, go on." The setup of the paragraph marks (with a chevron after the ENDIF statement) causes an extra blank line to print when the title field is blank. Figure 15-34 illustrates the data document and Figure 15-35 shows the final printed result. The printed page could be used for continuous form labels since there are the equivalent of six lines for each address.

```
1
  «DATA·adddd.doc»¶
  ¶
  «first_name»·«last_name»¶
  «IF·title»«title»¶
  «ENDIF¶
  «IF·company»«company»¶
  «ENDIF¶
  «address»¶
  «city»,·«state»·«IF·zip»«zip»«ENDIF»«IF·title=""»«ENDIF»«IF·
  company=""»¶
  «ENDIF»¶
  ¶
  «NEXT»«first_name»·«last_name»¶
  «IF·title»«title»¶
  «ENDIF¶
  «IF·company»«company»¶
  «ENDIF¶
  «address»¶
  «city»,·«state»·«IF·zip»«zip»«ENDIF»«IF·title=""»«ENDIF»«IF·
  company=""»¶
  «ENDIF»¶
  ¶
Pg1 Li1 Co17        {¶}              ?           ═ADD2MD.DOC═
                                                 Microsoft Word
```

Figure 15-33. The main document for IF-statement addresses that will be printed on labels

Exercise: Handling Missing Data Fields

In this exercise, you will use the M1DD.DOC data document created earlier (see Figure 15-36).

Select Transfer Load to load the M2MD.DOC main document used in the previous example. Add these lines after the SET instruction line and before *Invoice for:*

```
1
   first_name,last_name,title,company,address,city,state,zip¶
   Carol,Brigg,Product·Manager,Yel-Tie,34·Umber·Grove,Des·
   Moines,Iowa,55119¶
   Dennis,Chabolla,Programmer,GrantTec,4549·West·Highway,Des·
   Moines,Iowa,,¶
   Ian,Betterman,,Rice·Crisp,5432·Kellog,Austin,Texas,62111¶
   D.,Bandy,,,543·East·5th,Austin,Texas,62111¶
   ◆
                                                   ADDDD.DOC
308 characters
```

Figure 15-34. The data document for IF-statement addresses that will be printed on labels

```
Carol Brigg
Product Manager
Yel-Tie
34 Umber Grove
Des Moines, Iowa 55119

Dennis Chabolla
Programmer
GrantTec
4549 West Highway
Des Moines, Iowa

Ian Betterman
Rice Crisp
5432 Kellog
Austin, Texas 62111


D. Bandy
543 East 5th
Austin, Texas 62111
```

Figure 15-35. Labels printed with IF-statement addresses

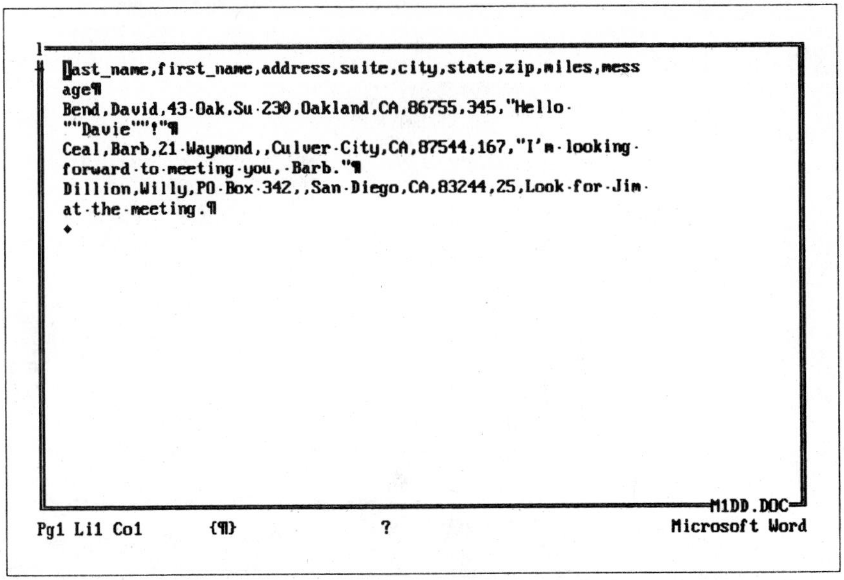

```
1
  ▌ast_name,first_name,address,suite,city,state,zip,miles,mess
  age¶
  Bend,David,43·Oak,Su·230,Oakland,CA,86755,345,"Hello·
  ""Davie""!"¶
  Ceal,Barb,21·Waymond,,Culver·City,CA,87544,167,"I'm·looking·
  forward·to·meeting·you,·Barb."¶
  Dillion,Willy,PO·Box·342,,San·Diego,CA,83244,25,Look·for·Jim·
  at·the·meeting.¶
  ◆

                                                      ═M1DD.DOC═
  Pg1 Li1 Co1        {¶}           ?            Microsoft Word
```

Figure 15-36. The M1DD.DOC data document

```
«first_name» «last_name»
«address»
«IF suite»«suite»
«ENDIF»
«city», «state» «zip»
```

Make sure you omit the chevron after the ENDIF statement (end the line with a paragraph mark). The result is shown in Figure 15-37.

Use Transfer Save to save the document as M3MD, which stands for *merge 3 main document*.

After proofing the main document to ensure it is correct, make the main document the active window. Select Print Merge. Type in M3RESULT as the file name and then press Enter. After the merge is complete, select Transfer Load to view the results. Figure 15-38 shows the outcome. If the *suite* data is missing, Word does not print the line; neither does it insert a blank line.

If your invoices do not match those in Figure 15-38, carefully edit the main and data documents until Word produces the correct result.

```
¶
«DATA·M1DD.DOC»¶
«SET·organization="Product·Manager's·Group"»¶
¶
                        Invoice·for¶
                     «organization»¶
¶
«first_name»·«last_name»¶
«address»¶
«IF·suite»«suite»¶
«ENDIF»¶
«city»,·«state»·«zip»¶
¶
Mileage·Invoice·for·«first_name»·«last_name»:¶
¶
··Miles:·«miles»¶
¶
··Due:····«If·miles<100»«miles»·.18»«ELSE»«miles»·.21»«ENDIF»¶
¶
The·«organization»·will·pay·within·30·days·of·receipt·of·
this·signed·invoice.···The·«organization»·is·not·responsible·
for·costs·not·shown·on·this·invoice.¶
```
```
                                                        M3MD.DOC
Pg1 Li14 Co5      {¶}              ?              Microsoft Word
```

Figure 15-37. The edited M2MD.DOC main document

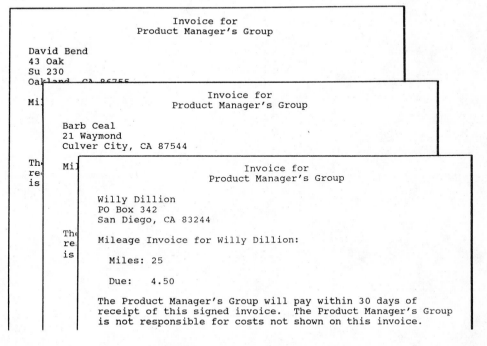

```
                        Invoice for
                   Product Manager's Group

David Bend
43 Oak
Su 230
Oakland, CA 86755
                              Invoice for
                         Product Manager's Group
Mil
          Barb Ceal
          21 Waymond
          Culver City, CA 87544
Th    Mil
re                            Invoice for
is                       Product Manager's Group

              Willy Dillion
              PO Box 342
        Th    San Diego, CA 83244
        re
        is    Mileage Invoice for Willy Dillion:

                  Miles: 25

                  Due:    4.50

              The Product Manager's Group will pay within 30 days of
              receipt of this signed invoice.  The Product Manager's Group
              is not responsible for costs not shown on this invoice.
```

Figure 15-38. The printed invoices

553

Creating and Filling In Forms

Completing forms is something that most word processing programs don't do well. In fact, many people have turned back to the typewriter to create and fill in forms. With Word you can create your own forms, or you can easily jump from blank to blank to fill in the data on pre-printed forms. In addition, you can use the Print Merge command to fill in the form with information from a data document, or you can complete part of the form from the keyboard and part from a data document.

Figure 16-1 shows a preprinted form. Figure 16-2 shows the Word template that is used to complete the form from the keyboard. The category labels are formatted as hidden text so that they will not print on the preprinted form. Figure 16-3 shows the form when completed.

Employment Application

Date:_____

Name:_____

            Last   First   Middle

Employment History:

Company	From Date	To Date	Pay	Title	Supervisor

Figure 16-1. A preprinted form

```
 L[·········1··L····2··L····3·L·····L····L·········L······L]········7···
 
 Employment.Application¶
 ¶
 Date:→ ....»→                                        ¶
 ¶
 Name:→ ....»→              »→              »→   ¶
 ·········Last·············First···············Middle¶
 ¶
 ¶
 ¶
 Employment.History:¶
 ¶
 Company.······From.Date··To.Date.Pay·····Title······Supervisor¶
 »→→       »→      »→     »→   »→      »→      ¶
 ¶
 »→→       »→      »→     »→   »→      »→      ¶
 ¶
 »→→       »→      »→     »→   »→      »→      ¶
 
                                                  20-2.DOC
 Pg1 Li26 Col    {+}            ?              Microsoft Word
```

Figure 16-2. A Word form template with category labels
formatted as hidden text

    Using Word to create forms is easy. For example, you might create an expense-account form that you can use as a template, eliminating the need for a preprinted form.

Employment Application

Date:_____9/22/89_____

Name:_____Barney_____Kathleen_____Susan____
　　　　　　　Last　　　　　　　　　　　First　　　　　　　　Middle

Employment History:

Company	From Date	To Date	Pay	Title	Supervisor
GenTECH	4/88	now	40K	Mgr	J. Smith
J Control	2/86	4/88	35K	Mgr	H. Young
Tie Back	1/84	2/86	32K	Superv	T. Hands

Figure 16-3. A completed form

Designing Forms

Designing forms to work the way you want them to is the most important step in successfully using Word's powerful form-processing features.

Form Elements

Figure 16-4 illustrates the elements that make up Word's forms. Notice the layout of the elements in relation to each other.

As indicated in the following descriptions, not all forms have all of the elements:

- **Merge instructions:** Using Word's merge capability (see Chapter 15, "Merging Documents," for more information), you can create forms that are wholly or partly filled out with data supplied from other, specially created data documents. If you want to merge a form with a data document, type in the DATA instruction specifying the name of the data document at the top of the form. Type in an ASK instruction to manually enter data common to all the forms to be filled out. Type in a SET instruction if you want to manually enter data that is unique for each document.

Figure 16-5 illustrates a form that has been set up to incorporate data from a data document. The DATA instruction identifies the data document to be used for the merge. The ASK instruction allows you to enter individual meeting times directly.

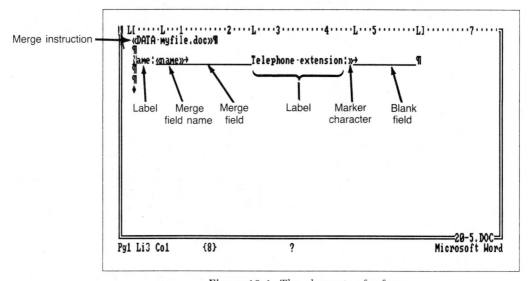

Figure 16-4. The elements of a form

- **Fields:** These are the spaces in a form that are to be filled with data. Use a blank field for data that is to be manually entered.

- **Labels:** Labels specify the kind of data to be entered in each field. Labels can be formatted as regular text or as hidden text. Word always prints regular-text labels. You can choose whether or not to print hidden-text labels. In Figure 16-4, *Name* and *Telephone extension* are labels.

- **Marker characters:** Marker characters (») enable you to move quickly from blank to blank, rather than tediously moving the highlight. You can use marker characters when the form is to be filled in manually. They are not necessary if you are filling in a form automatically with information from a data document.

- **Merge field names:** If you are using the Print Merge command to fill in a form with information from a data document, enter the field name surrounded by chevrons. The field name must match the field name used in the data document. The merge field name in Figure 16-4 is «name». (See Chapter 15, "Merging Documents," for complete merging information.)

If you have a form with merge field names in the blanks, you can still fill in the fields manually. Simply format the data field names as hidden text and enter the data.

```
L[··········1·········2·········3·········4·········5·········]········L7····
«DATA·stlist.doc»¶
«ASK·time=?Enter·meeting·time·and·press·Return»¶
¶
¶
¶
Name:«name»→                                                              ¶
¶
Job·title:«title»→                                                        ¶
¶
Meeting·time:«time»→                                                      ¶
¶
¶
♦
```

Pg1 Li10 Co70   {→}   ?   Microsoft Word

Figure 16-5. A form used with merged data

Creating Forms

To create a form, follow these steps:

1. If you are using a preprinted form, carefully measure the position of each label and response.

2. If you want to use hidden text, select **Y**es in the Options *show hidden text* field. If you want to change tab settings, select **Y**es in the *show ruler* field.

3. If you want to merge the form with a data document, type in a DATA instruction identifying the name of the data document. If you want to manually enter data (such as the date) that applies to all the forms to be merged, type in a SET instruction. If you also want to enter individual data items for each form, type in an ASK instruction.

4. Use the **F**ormat **T**ab **S**et command to enter tab positions for the labels and fields that should appear in the first line (paragraph) of your form (see Chapter 6, "Formatting Documents," for more information about setting tabs).

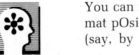

   You can fix the location of each label and fill it in with the For-mat p**O**sition command. The benefit is that if the form is altered (say, by accidentally entering a blank line), the positions are fixed on the page. For each form element, select Format pOsition and enter the appropriate horizontal and vertical page positions. (For a complete description of Format pOsition, see Chapter 20, "Electronic Publishing and Graphics.")

5. Type in the first label. If you want it to print, type it in as regular text. If you're using a preprinted form, format the label as hidden text so that you can see the label on the screen but not print it. To enter the text as hidden text, press **Alt-E** (or **Alt-X-E** if a style sheet is attached). Type in the text. Press **Alt-Spacebar** to regular text.

6. Enter the marker character as hidden text. Place your highlight after the label. Press **Alt-E** (or **Alt-X-E** if you are using a style sheet). To enter the marker character, press **Ctrl-]**. Word displays the marker as a chevron (»). Then type in **Alt-Spacebar** (or **Alt-X-Spacebar**) to turn off hidden-text formatting.

Do not type in two less-than (<<) or greater-than (>>) symbols instead of chevrons. Word will treat them as regular text instead of as marker characters.

7. Press **Tab** to move to the beginning of the first field. If you want the field (and the text entered in it) to appear as an underlined blank, highlight the tab character and press **Alt-U** (or **Alt-X-U**) twice. Word displays an underline to appear in the blank field from one tab setting to the next. When text is entered in the field, it will also be automatically underlined.

8. If you are merging data into the form from a data document, enter the data field name after the label. Field names must be entered between chevrons (« »). Press **Ctrl-[** for the left chevron and **Ctrl-]** for the right chevron. To format the data to be entered, format the first letter of the field name. You can enter any conditional instructions or other information permitted by Word's merge function.

9. Move to the position for the next field label. If the label is on the same line as the previous field, press **Tab**. If it is on the next line, press **Enter**. Repeat steps 4 through 8 as needed to complete the data entry elements of the form.

10. Add any lines, boxes, or common text.

11. Select **Transfer Save** to save the form.

To be safe, save the form under several related names. That way, if you accidentally forget to save the template under a new name when you use it, you will have a backup copy.

Using Forms

The process for using a form differs depending on whether you are filling it in manually, or automatically by merging data.

To manually enter data:

1. Use **Transfer Load** to load the form.

2. To display the markers, make sure **Yes** is selected in the Options *show hidden text* field.

3. Press **Ctrl->** to move to the first marker. Word positions the highlight immediately after the marker. (To move backward through markers, press **Ctrl-<.**)

4. Type in the data.

5. Move to the next field and repeat the process.

6. When you have finished, save the filled-in form under a different name. This allows you to reuse the original.

7. Print the form. If you do not want to print hidden text, make sure that **No** is selected in the Print Options *hidden text* field. Then, select **Print Printer**.

To fill in a form by merging information from a data document:

1. Make sure of the following:

   - The necessary DATA, SET, and ASK instructions are entered at the beginning of the form.
   - The data document specified in the DATA instruction is available.
   - The field names in the form are surrounded by chevrons and match those in the data document.

2. In the Print Options *hidden text* field select **Yes** to print hidden text or **No** to not print it.

3. To print the merged form, select **Print Merge Printer**. To save the merged form to disk, select **Print Merge Document**. The advantage of using Print Merge Document is that you can check the result of the document merge and make small edits before actually printing the document.

4. If you included SET or ASK instructions, respond to the prompts as they appear.

Word merges the data in the data document into the form and either prints the completed form or stores it on disk so that you can view it before printing.

Exercise: Creating and Using a Form

In a blank Word window, select All in the Options command's *show non-printing symbols* field. In the *show ruler* field, select Yes. In the *show hidden text* field, select Yes.

Type in these labels (enter a paragraph mark between each line):

```
Name:
Street:
City:State:Zip:
Home phone:
Date of birth:
Employer:
Work phone:
Doctor:
```

Highlight the paragraph mark following the *Name:* label. Select Format Tab Set. Press F1 in the *position* field to activate the ruler. Move the highlight to the right end of the ruler (5.9" is displayed in the *position* field). Type in a capital L. Word displays an L symbol (for left alignment) at the right end of the ruler line. Press Enter.

Move your highlight to the paragraph mark after the *Street:* label. Press F4 to repeat the previous command. Notice that Word

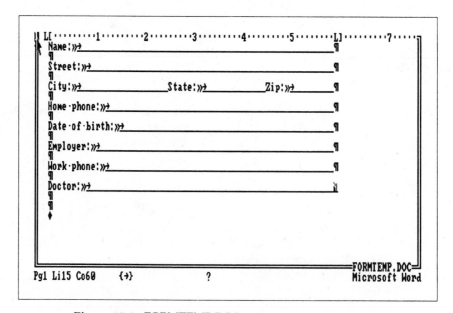

Figure 16-6. FORMTEMP.DOC as it appears on screen

again displays an L symbol in the ruler line. Move to the paragraph mark after the *Zip:* label. Press F4. The L symbol appears. Move to the paragraph mark after each of the remaining labels and press F4.

Place the highlight in the *City:State:Zip:* label. Select Format Tab Set. Press F1. Type in L at 2.5″ and 4.5″.

Next, type in a hidden-text marker (») after each colon. With the highlight on the colon after *Name,* press Alt-E (or Alt-X-E if you have a style sheet attached). Press Ctrl-]. The chevron (») appears as hidden text. Use F4 to insert a chevron after each colon. Then go back and press Tab after each chevron.

Format the first tab symbol with Alt-U (or Alt-X-U if you are using a style sheet). An underline appears from the tab symbol to the next tab stop or paragraph mark. Use F4 to repeat the formatting for each tab stop.

The form you have created so far is shown in Figure 16-6. Use Transfer Save to save the document as FORMTEMP (form template). Make sure No is selected in the Print Options *hidden text* field and then use Print Printer to print the form. Figure 16-7 shows the printed result. Notice that the markers did not print.

```
Name:_____

Street:_____

City:_____State:_____Zip:_____

Home phone:_____

Date of birth:_____

Employer:_____

Work phone:_____

Doctor:_____
```

Figure 16-7. FORMTEMP.DOC as it appears when printed

Place your highlight at the upper-left corner of the screen. Press Ctrl-> to move from field to field, filling in the form with this data:

```
Name: Dick Caterman
Street: 30 45th Street
City: Phoenix
State: Arizona
Zip: 85281
Home phone: 602-786-9785
Date of birth: 9/30/53
```

```
Employer: Winkelsmith Company
Work phone: 602-666-4000
Doctor: Beth Ritter
```

Word automatically underlines the data you enter. Figure 16-8 shows how the completed form looks on the screen. Use Print Printer to print the document. Figure 16-9 shows the printed result. Save the document as FORMDONE.

```
L[·········1·········2····L····3·········4····L····5········L]·········7·····
 Name:»Dick·Caterman→_______________________________________¶
 ¶
 Street:»30·45th·Street→____________________________________¶
 ¶
 City:»Phoenix→__________State:»Arizona→_____Zip:»85281→____¶
 ¶
 Home·phone:»602-786-9785→__________________________________¶
 ¶
 Date·of·birth:»9/30/53→____________________________________¶
 ¶
 Employer:»Winkelsmith·Company→_____________________________¶
 ¶
 Work·phone:»602-666-4000→__________________________________¶
 ¶
 Doctor:»Beth·Ritter→_______________________________________¶
 ¶
 ♦

                                                          FORMDONE.DOC
Pg1 Li5 Co60      {→}            ?                        Microsoft Word
```

Figure 16-8. FORMDONE.DOC as it appears on screen

```
Name:Dick Caterman

Street:30 45th Street

City:Phoenix              State:Arizona         Zip:85281

Home phone:602-786-9785

Date of birth:9/30/53

Employer:Winkelsmith Company

Work phone:602-666-4000

Doctor:Beth Ritter
```

Figure 16-9. FORMDONE.DOC as it appears when printed

Glossaries

Word's glossary feature allows you to save text and then recall it as often as you like. This feature is particularly useful for boilerplate text, such as contract clauses, and for any pieces of text you use frequently in the course of your work, such as:

- Addresses, salutations, and closings in letters
- Fully formatted headers and footers
- Memo templates
- Forms

You can also use the glossary as a holding place for text you want to delete now and use later. The glossary is more permanent than the scrap because you can save it like a document, but it is more convenient than a document because, as you'll learn in this chapter, it is always close at hand.

Glossary entries are text entries that you copy or delete from your document to a *glossary file*. You assign each entry a *glossary name* that you use if you later need to recall the text. You can create any number of glossary files, but only one can be active at a time.

Glossary Entries

Many new Word users think of glossary entries as just a word or two of text, but in fact a glossary entry can contain any amount of text. Its size doesn't matter, as long as the entry has a name so that you can recall it.

In this section, we'll cover creating, using, and deleting (clearing) glossary entries. For information on merging the entries from one glossary file into another, see "Merging Glossary Files" in this chapter.

Creating and Changing Glossary Entries

You can type in the text that you want to be a glossary entry and then delete it to the glossary. Or you can copy existing text from a document to a glossary. Simply select the desired text, copy or delete the text through the menu, and assign the glossary entry a name. If you enter a name that doesn't already exist in the current glossary file, Word creates a new glossary entry. If you enter a name that already exists in the current glossary file, Word asks whether you want to replace the contents of the existing glossary entry with the new contents.

If you think of a more appropriate name for an existing glossary entry, you can change the name by recalling the glossary entry (see "Using Glossary Entries" in this chapter) and then "creating" a new glossary entry with the same text but a new name. You can then delete the old glossary entry. See "Deleting (Clearing) Glossary Entries" in this chapter for details.

To edit the contents of a glossary, recall the entry, change the text, and then recreate the glossary entry using the same name. Word replaces the old contents with the new.

If your document contains text that is almost, but not exactly, what you want in the glossary entry, edit the text, create the glossary entry, and then quit Word, respond N to the prompt to save unsaved edits. That way, the glossary entry is created without your document being changed.

Here are the steps for creating or changing a glossary entry:

1. Enter the text you want to be included in the glossary entry or make sure the existing text that you want to use as a glossary entry is displayed on your screen.

2. Select the text.

3. Select one of the following options:

   Copy   to leave the selected text in the document and copy it to the scrap area

Delete to remove the selected text from the document and place it in the scrap area

4. In the *to* field, enter a glossary name of up to 31 characters. The name must begin with a letter or number and can include any letters, numbers, underscores, periods, and hyphens. The name cannot include colons (:) or spaces.

You can press **F1** to see the glossary names already used or to select the name of an existing entry. Glossary names must be unique. If you enter the name of an existing glossary entry, this message appears when you attempt to complete the entry:

```
Enter Y to replace glossary entry, N to retype name, or Esc
to cancel
```

Press **Y** to use the new glossary text, **N** to enter a new name, or **Esc** to cancel the process.

5. Press **Enter** or click the command name.

The new glossary entry is available for use in this Word session only. To save the glossary entry in the glossary file of your choice, use Transfer Glossary Save (see "Saving Glossary Files" in this chapter). If you try to quit Word without saving the glossary entry, Word asks whether you want to save the glossary changes you have made. If you press Y in response to this prompt, Word saves the glossary entry in the current glossary file.

When editing a document, you may want to delete a block of text and store it in a safe place, rather than risk putting it in the scrap area where it might be overwritten by other deletions. To do this, delete the text as a glossary entry. You can then continue editing your document, recalling the glossary entry at the desired location. If you use this feature often, you may want to give the glossary entries a common name (such as JUNK1, JUNK2, and so on). Adopting a naming convention makes it easy to purge the glossary file occasionally of those entries that you created for temporary use.

Word's Permanent Glossary Entries

Word supplies several ready-made glossaries. They should be located in your Word 5 directory. To see what each glossary contains, use Transfer Glossary Load to load each one individually. Then select Insert and press F1 to see a list of the entries.

Word provides several permanent glossary entries that you can use at any time, regardless of which glossary file is active. The following table lists the permanent entries and how Word responds to them:

Glossary entry	Use
page	Word inserts *(page)* in your document. During printing, Word replaces *(page)* with consecutive page numbers.
footnote	Word inserts consecutive footnote numbers in your document.
date	Word immediately inserts the current system date, formatted according to the Options *date format* setting. You can edit the date. Once entered, it is not automatically updated by Word.
dateprint	Word inserts (dateprint) in your document. During printing, Word replaces (dateprint) with the system date, formatted according to the Options *date format* setting. You cannot edit dateprint.
time	Word immediately inserts the current system time, formatted according to the Options *time format* setting. You can edit the time. Once entered, it is not automatically updated by Word.
timeprint	Word inserts (timeprint) in your document. During printing, Word replaces (timeprint) with the system time, formatted according to the Options *time format* setting. You cannot edit timeprint.
nextpage	Word inserts (nextpage) into your document. During printing, Word replaces (nextpage) with the page number that follows the current page (customary in some legal documents).
clipboard	Word inserts text or graphics or copies or deletes text using the clipboard; Microsoft Windows version 2.0 or greater only.

Using Glossary Entries

You can insert a glossary entry anywhere in a document. These are the steps:

1. Make sure the glossary file you want is available. (See "Loading Glossary Files," later in this chapter.)

2. Position the highlight where you want the glossary-entry text to appear. The highlight must be preceded by a space or punctuation mark.

3. Enter the glossary entry by doing one of the following:

- Type in the glossary name and press **F3** to have Word replace the name with the glossary-entry text. For example you can type in the following and press **F3** to insert Word's permanent page-numbering glossary entry:

page

The glossary feature will not work if you press **F3** after typing the following because the glossary entry is not surrounded by spaces:

thepage

- Select Insert and press **F1** to display a list of the available glossary names. The names of available macros will be included in the list. To make sure you don't accidentally run a macro, use the **Arrow** keys to highlight a name and then type in a caret (^) in the *name* field. Press **Enter** or click the command area. If you do accidentally select a macro, the caret causes Word to insert the text of the macro in your document, instead of running the macro. You will have to delete the text and select Insert again. If you select a glossary entry, Word inserts the glossary text in your document.

Deleting (Clearing) Glossary Entries

If you no longer use a particular glossary entry or if you have stored the same text in the same glossary file under a new name, you can delete obsolete glossary entries and thereby maintain the efficiency of your glossary files.

To delete a glossary entry:

1. Assuming the glossary entry you want to delete is in the active glossary file, select **T**ransfer **G**lossary **C**lear.

2. Press **F1** to display a list of the available glossary names. (Word's permanent glossary entries are not displayed and cannot be cleared.)

3. Identify the glossary entry you want to clear by using one of these methods:

- Use the **Arrow** keys to highlight the glossary name. If you want to clear more than one entry at the same time, type in a comma and then highlight the next name.
- Point to the glossary name and click the left mouse button. If you want to delete more than one glossary entry at a time, type in a comma and select the next name.
- Leave the *names* field blank if you want to clear all glossary entries.

4. When you have entered the names of all the entries you want to clear, press **Enter**.

5. Word displays this message:

```
Enter Y to clear glossary names
```

Press **Y** to clear the glossary entries or press **Esc** to stop the process.

Word deletes the glossary entry for the current Word session but does not actually delete the entry from the glossary file. To permanently delete the entry from the file, save the glossary before leaving Word, by using Transfer Glossary Save or Quit.

Glossary Files

Word's default glossary file is called NORMAL.GLY. If you use only a small number of glossary entries, you may be able to store them all in NORMAL.GLY without it becoming too unwieldy. However, you can create other glossary files. Custom glossary files are useful if you often insert text from the glossary and you want to create different glossaries for different types of documents.

In this section, we cover loading glossary files, merging the contents of glossary files, and printing glossary files, in addition to saving them.

Saving Glossary Files

Reserve NORMAL.GLY for general glossary entries that could apply to any document. Save document-specific entries in glossaries of their own that you load only when you need them.

When you create glossary entries, Word does not immediately save them in the active glossary file. When you save the glossary file, Word stores any entries you have created (and not deleted) during the current Word session in the file.

To create a new glossary file, you simply save the active glossary file under a new name. Then you can add or delete individual entries to customize the file.

If you have more than one glossary file, you can use Transfer Glossary Save to check which glossary file is currently loaded.

To save a glossary file, follow these steps:

1. Select **T**ransfer **G**lossary **S**ave.

2. In the *filename* field, Word displays the current drive, path, and glossary file name. You can:

   - Leave the file name as is. The glossary entries you have created in this Word session will be added to the specified glossary file.

   - Enter a new glossary file name to create a new file containing the glossary entries of the old file and any glossary entries you have created in this Word session. The file name must be unique and can be up to eight characters, including letters, numbers, or an underscore. Word automatically adds the .GLY file name extension. You can enter a different extension; however, Word does not display glossary files with extensions other than .GLY when you press F1 while using the Transfer Glossary commands. For easy management of glossary files, it's best to stick with the .GLY file-name extension.

3. Once you have entered the name of the glossary file, press **Enter** or click the command name.

Word displays a *saving* message as it saves the glossary file.

If you are on a network and the Transfer Glossary Save *filename* field is empty, the active glossary file is read only. You cannot save this glossary file under the same name. However, you can enter a new name to save the contents of the active glossary file plus any glossary entries you have created during the current Word session.

Loading Glossary Files

You can have only one glossary file available at a time. When you start a Word session, Word loads its default glossary file, NORMAL.GLY. If you want to use a different glossary file, you will need to load it.

Regardless of which glossary file you load, Word's permanent glossary entries (such as page, date, and time) are always available.

To load a glossary file, follow these steps:

1. Use **Transfer Glossary Save** if you want to save glossary entries you have created in this Word session in a glossary file other than the current gloassary. Otherwise, when you load a new glossary file, Word asks whether you want to store any unsaved entries in the active file. You can press **Y** to have Word save the entries in the current file, but you don't have the option of saving them in a different file.

2. Select **Transfer Glossary Load**.

3. Regardless of which glossary file is currently loaded, the *file-name* field will be blank. Enter the name of the glossary file you want to load or press **F1** to select from a list (only .GLY files are listed).

4. If you want the glossary file to be read only (that is, to prevent changes from being made to the file), select **Yes** in the *read only* field. If you want to be able to add and delete glossary entries from the file, make sure the *read only* field is set to **No**.

   If you enter a file name that doesn't exist, you will see this message when you try to load the file:

   `File or directory does not exist`

   Enter a new name or press **F1** to select from a list.

5. Press **Enter** or click the command name.

Word loads the glossary files you specified. The previously loaded glossary file is no longer available.

If you use the Transfer Glossary Load command on a network, Word looks for the glossary file you specify first in your workstation directory and then in the Word program directory on the server. If Word displays an *in use* message, someone else is using the specified glossary file with the *read only* field set to No. (Only one network user can open a read/write file at a given time.) When the *read only* field is set to Yes, all network users can access the file at the same time.

Merging Glossary Files

Before merging glossary files, delete all entries you are unlikely to use. That way, the ones you do use will be easier to locate.

If you often use Word's glossary feature and you make extensive use of customized glossary files, you may find that the quickest way to create the file you need is to merge the contents of existing files. Once you have completed the merge, you can add or delete glossary entries to create the exact combination you want.

These are the steps:

1. The active glossary file is the file into which you will merge the entries. Use **T**ransfer **G**lossary **S**ave to check that the correct glossary file is currently loaded. Load a new glossary file, if necessary, with **T**ransfer **G**lossary **L**oad.

2. Save the active glossary file if you have unsaved changes that you want to keep.

3. Select **T**ransfer **G**lossary **M**erge.

4. In the *filename* field, do one of the following:

   - Enter the drive, path, and name of the glossary file you want to merge into the active glossary file.

   - Press **F1** to select from a list of glossary files.

5. Press **Enter** or click the command name.

Word merges the entries from the glossary file specified in the *filename* field into the active glossary file. If two entries have identical names, the entry from the glossary file on disk replaces the entry in the active glossary.

To save the merged glossary file, use Transfer Glossary Save. If you end the Word session without saving the glossary file, the entries that were merged (and any unsaved changes) are lost.

If you are using a network, save the merged glossary file immediately. When you specify the name of the glossary file whose entries you want to merge into the active glossary file, the specified file is temporarily considered to be read/write, and other users are locked out of it. When you save the merged glossary file, the specified glossary file is freed up so that others can use it. Until you save the merged file, Word displays an *in use* message when another user attempts to access the specified glossary file.

Printing Glossary Files

You can print a glossary file to see the glossary entries (name and text) it contains. Figure 17-1 shows the result of printing a glossary file. This particular glossary file contains boilerplate text used for contract agreements. Word prints the glossary names on the left in alphabetical order, with the full text of the glossary entry indented on subsequent lines.

```
address
     Ceto Company
     342 General Street
     Suite 34
     Phoenix, AZ 85281


adhead1
                              AGREEMENT
                   Ceto Company Standard Agreement

aghead

                              AGREEMENT

cont1
          Agreement made and entered into on this 7th day of
     June, 1991 between Ceto Company (a corporation) and
     Brady Associates (a partnership).  The Agreement
     relates to Ceto Company hiring Brady Associates (not as
     an employee) to develop certain products to be mutually
     agreed to by title in writing at various times over the
     term of this Agreement.

cont2
     The two parties are interested in developing a
     relationship involving the development of products.  In
     the relationship, Ceto Company will, among other things
     to be mutually agreed upon, contribute to the
     development costs of such products as agreed upon and
     pay Brady Associates a fee as full compensation for
     Brady Associates services.  In return, Brady Associates
     will, among other things, commit its skills and
     resources to the provision of such professional
     service.

cont3
     1.    SCOPE OF AGREEMENT:  During the term of this
     Agreement, Brady Associates shall provide development
     of a Yearly Report for Ceto Company.  This development
     will be in several phases as outlined below.  Payment
     shall be on a phase basis in accordance with the
     schedule set forth in this document assuming
     commencement of the project on June 25, 1991.

sign
     Signed by:  _____

     Title:      _____

     Date:       _____
```

Figure 17-1. A printout of the contents of a glossary file

Follow these steps to print the contents of a glossary file:

1. Make sure your printer is ready to print.
2. Select **P**rint **G**lossary.

   Word prints the contents of each entry that you have added to the active glossary file. Word's permanent entries (such as date, time, and page) are not printed.

Exercise: Working with the Glossary

In this exercise, you will have the opportunity to perform many glossary-related tasks, including:

- Creating a new glossary file
- Creating and using glossary entries
- Editing a glossary entry, storing it under a new name, and deleting the old entry
- Saving the new glossary entries in the active glossary file
- Printing the glossary file

To create a new glossary file, select Transfer Glossary Save. Word displays the name of the active glossary file in the *filename* field. (The default is NORMAL.GLY.) Enter the drive and path for the glossary file if they are different from the drive and path specified in the Transfer Options *setup* field. Enter the glossary file name MYGLOS and press Enter. Word adds the .GLY extension and displays a message like this one:

```
Saving C:\WORD\DOC\MYGLOS.GLY
```

The MYGLOS.GLY glossary is now the active glossary.

To create several glossary entries, type in the text below in a new Word document. Substitute your name and related information where indicated. Feel free to alter the glossary entries to make them more useful for you.

```
(your name)
(your address)
(your city, state ZIP code)

Dear

To: (enter two tabs)
From: (enter one tab and then your name)
```

```
Re: (enter two tabs)
Date: (enter a tab, type in dateprint, and press F3)
Sincerely,

(your name)
```

To create the first glossary entry, select your name, address, city, state, and ZIP code. Select Copy. In the *to* field, type in *address*. Press Enter. Word creates a glossary entry named *address*. For the next entry, select *Dear*. Select Copy and, in the *to* field, type in *sal* for *salutation* and press Enter. Next, select the *To:* through *Date:* lines. Select Copy and, in the *to* field, type in *memo* and press Enter. Notice that you have included one glossary entry in another glossary entry by using dateprint within the memo. Now select *Sincerely* through your name. Select Copy and, in the *to* field, type in *closesin* and press Enter. You now have four glossary entries:

address

sal

memo

closesin

Test out the entries. Move to the end of the document and use the glossary feature to enter this brief letter:

```
(your name)
(your address)
(your city, state ZIP code)

July 20, 1989

Dear Jean:

The group decided on this format for club
correspondence:

To:      Jean Smith
From:    (your name)
Re:      Club Memo Format
Date:    (dateprint)

Call me if you have questions.

Sincerely,


(your name)
```

To insert a glossary entry, position your highlight, type in the glossary name, and press F3. The glossary text appears. Use Word's permanent *date* entry to insert the current date after the address; simply type in *date* and press F3.

For the closing, change the word *Sincerely* to *Yours truly* and then use the edited text to create a new entry. Select the text. Select Copy and, in the *to* field, enter *closeyt* and press Enter.

Now delete the *closesin* glossary entry. Select Transfer Glossary Clear. Type in the following glossary name and press Enter:

closesin

Press Y at the prompt to delete the glossary entry.

At this point, the glossary entries you have created are useful for this Word session only because you have not saved them. Save the entries now. Select Transfer Glossary Save. Word displays the MYGLOS.GLY file name in the *filename* field. Press Enter. Word displays a *saving* message. Once the modified glossary file is saved, print it by selecting Print Glossary. The printed entries are shown in Figure 17-2. If you created the MYGLOS.GLY file from a glossary file that contains additional entries, your printout will include these other entries as well.

```
address
        Kathy Jones
        453 W. 45th Avenue
        Phoenix, Arizona 85321

closeyt
        Yours truly,


        Kathy Jones

memo
        To:
        From:
        Re:
        Date:      July 20, 1989


sal
        Dear
```

Figure 17-2. Printout of the glossary file created in this exercise

You can keep MYGLOS.GLY to use in the future. Or, you can delete the MYGLOS.GLY and MYGLOS.BAK files just like any other file, by selecting Transfer Delete.

Indexes, Outlines, and Tables of Contents

Long document? Complex structure? With Word, you can create long documents and then use special features to generate an index, an outline, and a table of contents. Word even numbers indexes, paragraphs, and tables of contents—automatically. This means you have the power to create professional-quality documents and easily keep them up to date.

Because indexes, outlines, and tables of contents can be numbered automatically, it is best to complete your document—including editing—before generating the numbers.

Using Hidden Text

To take advantage of the features described in this chapter, you need to be familiar with the hidden text. Among other uses, hidden text identifies entries for indexes and tables of contents.

As you know, hidden text is a character format available through the *hidden* field of the Format Character command. You can also use Alt-E (or Alt-X-E if you have a style sheet attached) to hide text. To turn hidden text on, set the Format Character *hidden* field to Yes. To turn hidden text off, set the *hidden* field to No. Or, press Alt-Spacebar to go back to the normal character format.

You can display hidden text on your screen by setting the Options *show hidden text* field to Yes. It is a good idea to work with this option set at Yes to ensure that hidden text is entered properly. (See Chapter 3, "Editing Documents," for more information on this Options field.)

The appearance of hidden text depends on your monitor. If you have a monochrome monitor or have a color monitor but use Word in the graphics mode, hidden text will appear underlined with small dots. If you have a color monitor and use Word in the text mode, hidden text can be displayed in a different color than the rest of the text. The color is selected through the Options *colors* field. (See Chapter 2, "Starting Microsoft Word," for additional details on setting the *colors* field values.)

Indexes

Before word processors, creating an index meant jotting down index entries on 3-by-5 cards, adding new page numbers to existing entries, alphabetizing the cards, typing the index, and proofreading the result. Word automates the process of creating an index as much as possible, but indexing even a modest-sized document can still be a big chore.

The process of creating an index in Word consists of the following three steps:

- Marking words and phrases (entries) to be contained in the index
- Compiling the index
- Formatting the index

Marking Index Entries

An index entry consists of the word or phrase to be indexed and the page number or numbers on which that text is to be found. Marking an index entry for Word consists of inserting as hidden text the code **.i.** before the word or phrase you want to index and an end mark after it. Word supplies the page numbers automatically.

Figure 18-1 shows two coded index entries. Notice that the codes and end marks are both underlined with dots, indicating that they are formatted in hidden text. The text between the code and end mark will appear in the index as a single entry. The code and end mark do not print (unless you specify otherwise) because they are in hidden text.

In addition to marking already existing text, you can write the text for an index entry. Just format whatever text you add as hidden text and make sure it is preceded by the index code and followed by an end mark. In the second listing in Figure 18-1, for example, the

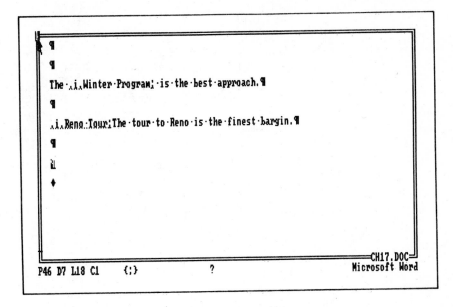

Figure 18-1. Word index entries, showing codes, text, and end marks

order of the text in the document is not appropriate for the index. Therefore, new text has been typed ahead of the sentence in hidden-text format:

`.i.Reno Tour;`

Such text can appear anywhere in a paragraph so long as it is properly coded and formatted as hidden.

A further example should help clarify when it is appropriate simply to mark existing text or write new text:

> The <u>research method</u> we have employed is called the <u>Learner Approach</u>. The <u>Barner School of Medicine</u> has used this method successfully for six years.

In the above paragraph, the underscored phrases would make appropriate index entries just as they are and can be coded directly. But consider the following:

> Police in the United Kingdom are known for their friendly attitude. The training includes methods of self defense, investigation, and public relations.

Because the appropriate index entries *United Kingdom Police* and *Training Methods* do not appear verbatim in the paragraph, they must be inserted.

In summary, if the index text appears in the document as you want it to appear in the index, don't hide the text. Hide the text if you are adding an index entry that does not logically fit in the text.

The endmark for an index entry can be a semicolon (the most usual), paragraph mark, or division mark. If any one of these three marks appear in the text already, there is no need to format them as hidden. If you add an end mark, however, you must format it as hidden text.

Figure 18-2 shows a document with index entries ending with a paragraph mark (*Restaurants*), a semicolon (*Flower Drum* and *Low Price*), and a division mark (*Toorak*). Notice that each starts with the .i. index code. Both existing text (such as *Flower Drum*) and hidden text (*Low Price*) are included.

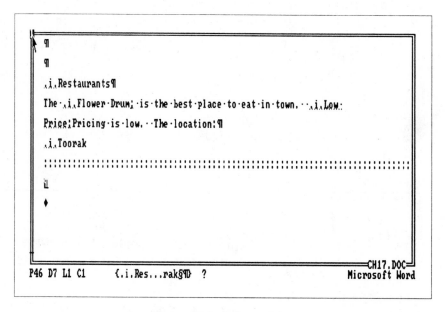

Figure 18-2. Index entries

If you accidentally delete part of an index entry, you can delete all index markings for the entry and begin again. Or, you can copy the index code and/or end mark from another index entry.

Including Punctuation in Index Entries

In some cases, you will need to include colons, semicolons, or quotation marks in an index entry. If you do, some special steps need to be taken.

To include colons or semicolons, place the entry in quotation marks. Format the quotation marks as hidden text. For example, you can include *Build:Rest* in an index entry in this sentence:

The trainer covered the Build:Rest approach.

Figure 18-3 shows the layout of the hidden text. Notice that the index code (.i.), quotation marks (" "), and semicolon (;) are all hidden text.

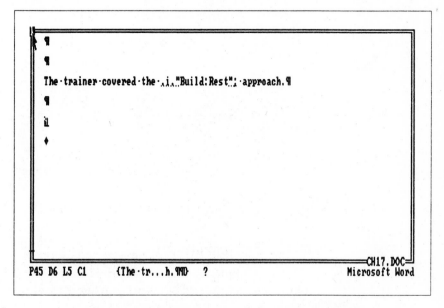

Figure 18-3. Hiding a colon using quotation marks

If the index entry includes quotation marks, enclose the complete entry in quotation marks formatted as hidden text. Use two quotation marks for each quote to appear in the text. For example, you may want this index entry:

"Rivers Of Our Earth"

to print from this text entry:

The book "Rivers Of Our Earth" is available. Don't miss it.

Figure 18-4 shows the index entry to use. Notice that there are two quotation marks for each quote.

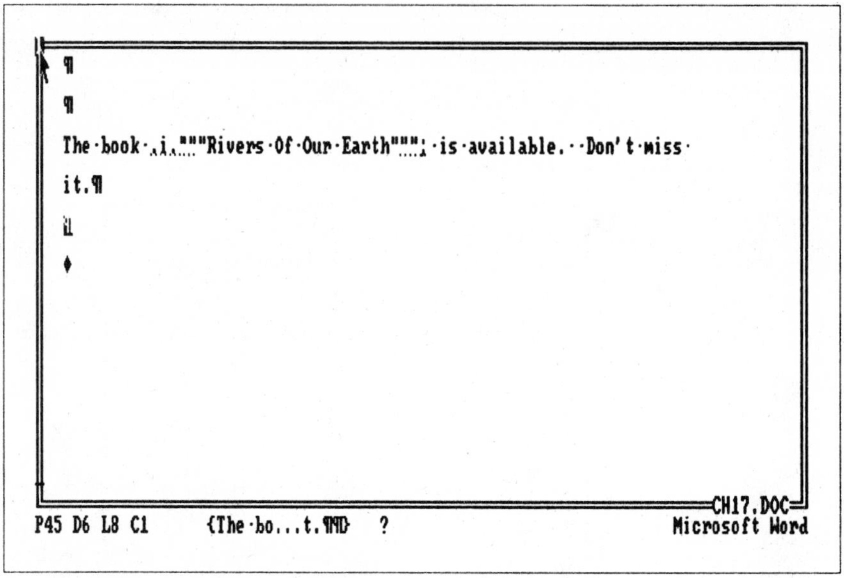

```
 ¶
 ¶
 The·book·ₐiₐ"""Rivers·Of·Our·Earth"""ₗ·is·available.··Don't·miss·
 it.¶
 ╵╵
 ♦
                                                    ═CH17.DOC═
 P45 D6 L8 C1      {The·bo...t.¶¶}   ?              Microsoft Word
```

Figure 18-4. An index entry containing quotation marks

Including Subentries

You can include up to five levels of subentries under a main entry. Here is an example of subentries at the first and second level:

Gears	
Hub	23
Measurement	13
Tires	
Mountain	45
Street	12
Spokes	
Radial	12
Extra Spokes	5, 15–18

The main entries and subentries rarely appear in the text in the proper order. You will usually manually enter the complete index entry. When you enter subentries, place the main entry and subentries on the same line separated by colons. For example, the following entries would be used to mark several of the index entries for the index shown earlier:

.i.Tires:Mountain;

.i.Tires:Spokes:Radial;

Omitting Page Numbers

You may want to omit the page number in an index. This is especially useful when you have main entries and subentries.

To omit a page number when you have subentries, omit the main index entry. That way, the main entry is identified through the subentries only and no page number is printed.

Consider this example:

Tires
    Mountain   45
    Street   12
Spokes
    Radial   12
    Extra Spokes   5, 15–18

The index entries in the text would be:

.i.Tires:Mountain;

.i.Tires:Street;

.i.Tires:Spokes:Radial;

.i.Tires:Spokes:Extra Spokes;

Notice that the following index entries are not included. If they were, page numbers would print for *Tires* and *Spokes*:

.i.Tires;

.i.Spokes;

Another way to omit page numbers is to include the main entry and place a colon, not a semicolon, at the end. Carrying forward the example, you could enter these main entries and no page numbers would print:

.i.Tires:;

.i.Spokes:;

Use colons if you want to note main headings in the context of the document. This can be a useful reminder of the main headings that exist.

Entering Page Ranges

You may want readers to be able to distinguish significant text references from smaller ones by showing page ranges. For example, the *Extra Spokes* entry indicates that there is information on page 5 and on pages 15 through 18. For detailed information, the reader would probably turn to page 15 before page 5.

Tires		
	Mountain	45
	Street	12
Spokes		
	Radial	12
	Extra Spokes	5, 15–18

To create a reference for a range of text, enter the index code, the index text, and a symbol not otherwise used in index entries (such as a plus). At the end of the document text, type in the same entry. Figure 18-5 shows an example of this entry as placed in the document:

.i.Timeshare + ;

Below is the resulting index after compilation:

Timeshare + 2, 5

Use the Replace command to search for each plus symbol, replacing it with nothing. Then, edit the comma and space and replace them with a single hyphen. (Or, on each line with a plus, use selective Replace to replace the comma and space with a hyphen. Then, use Replace to replace the plus with a space.)

Here is the final result:

Timeshare 2–5

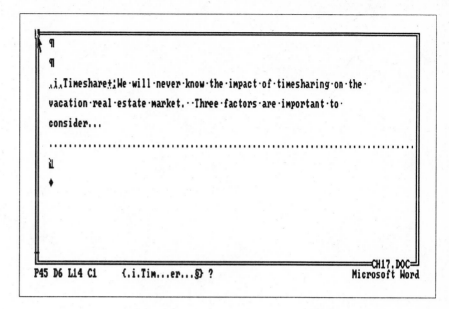

Figure 18-5. A page-range index entry

Using Macros to Mark Existing Text

The fastest way to mark existing text for an index is to use the Word-supplied macro INDEX_ENTRY.MAC. Here is the procedure:

1. Select the text for the index entry.
2. Make sure that the glossary file MACRO.GLY is loaded. (Use **T**ransfer **G**lossary **L**oad.)
3. Press **Ctrl-I E** to run INDEX_ENTRY.MAC.

The hidden index code and end mark are added to the text. The selected text is not hidden.

Manually Marking Existing Text

Because using the macro approach (covered above) is faster for marking existing document text, you will rarely want to manually mark existing text as index entries. The manual approach is useful if, for some reason, the macro will not function appropriately with your text.

To manually mark existing text, follow these steps:

1. Make sure the **O**ptions *show hidden text* field is set to **Yes**.
2. Highlight the first letter of the text to include in the index. Don't include spaces or the index entry will not align properly.
3. Press **Alt-E** (or **Alt-X-E** if you have a style sheet attached).
4. Type in a period, a small letter *i*, and a period:

   `.i.`

   The text is formatted as hidden.
5. Move your highlight to the end of the text to be included in the index. When you move the highlight, the hidden text character format is turned off.
6. If there is not a paragraph mark, division mark, or semicolon at the end of the text, press **Alt-E** (or **Alt-X-E**) to turn on hidden text. Type in a semicolon (;). The semicolon is formatted as hidden text.

Manually Marking Inserted Text

To speed the creation of index entries, use macros, glossaries, or the F4 (repeat command) key.

You can manually mark text you insert specifically as an index entry, not as part of the document text. The entire entry is marked as hidden text so it does not print with the text of your document. These entries are placed just before the text to which they refer. That way, the corresponding page number is the same as the referenced text. Figure 18-6 shows the index entry placed in a paragraph. Notice that the index entry *Communications Planning* is placed immediately before the reference. Also, the spacing is left in place so there are no extra spaces when the text is printed without the hidden text.

To manually mark inserted text, follow these steps:

1. Make sure the **O**ptions *show hidden text* field is set to **Yes**.
2. Place the highlight before the document text to which the index entry will refer. For example, to add the index entry *Start switch* to the following sentence, you would place the highlight on the *T* of *The*.

   `The switch to start the motor is red.`

3. Press **Alt-E** (or **Alt-X-E** if you have a style sheet attached). You will now be entering hidden text.

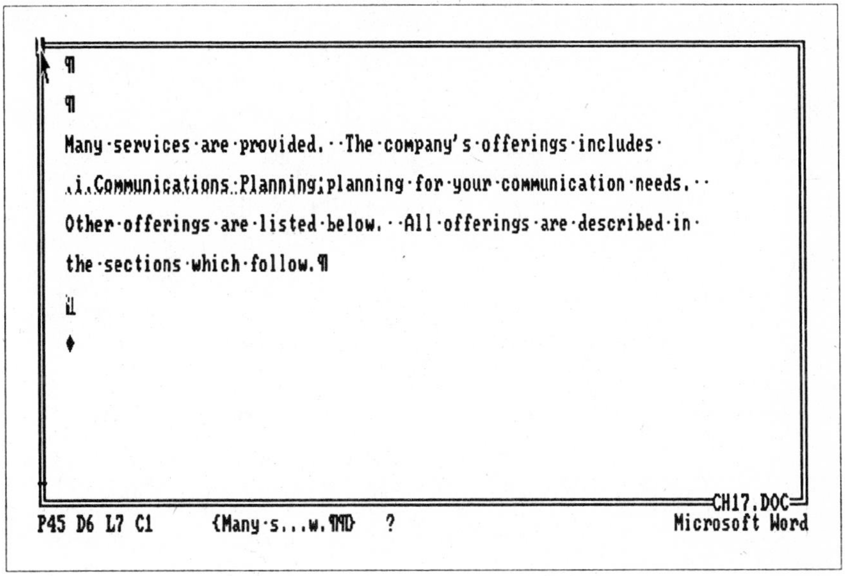

```
¶
¶
Many·services·are·provided.··The·company's·offerings·includes·
.i.Communications.Planning;planning·for·your·communication·needs.··
Other·offerings·are·listed·below.··All·offerings·are·described·in·
the·sections·which·follow.¶
↕
♦
                                                              CH17.DOC
P45 D6 L7 C1        {Many·s...w.¶¶        ?              Microsoft Word
```

Figure 18-6. An index entry with inserted text

4. Type in a period, a small letter *i*, and a period:

   .i.

   The text is formatted as hidden.

5. Type in the index entry text. Enter it exactly as you want it to appear in the index.

6. Follow the text with a semicolon (;) unless there is a paragraph mark, division mark, or semicolon at the end of the text. (If there is, leave the mark or semicolon in regular text format. Do not include a hidden mark or semicolon.) Assuming you've added a semicolon, it is now formatted as hidden text.

7. Press **Alt-Spacebar** to return to normal character formatting. (When you move your highlight, normal character formatting may return without you having to use the speed key.) The index entry remains formatted as hidden text.

Listing and Automatically Marking Entries

To create a list of text and automatically mark each occurrence of the text in the document, you can use the Word-supplied macro INDEX.MAC. This approach saves a great deal of time if you know most of the index entries you want. After completing the process, you can always check the index and delete or add entries as appropriate. (To delete an index entry, just delete the hidden text marks.)

To list and automatically mark entries, follow these steps:

1. Enter the words to be marked as index entries in a separate document. You can enter individual words or phrases. Press **Enter** at the end of each text line to mark it as an index entry. Save the document with the **Transfer Save** command.

2. Place your highlight at the beginning of the document you want to mark with index entries (not the document with the list of words).

3. Make sure that MACRO.GLY is loaded. If necessary, use **Transfer Glossary Load** to load the glossary file.

4. Press **Ctrl-I W** to run INDEX.MAC.

5. Word displays this message:

   ```
   RESPONSE:-
   Enter the filename of the document which contains words to
   be indexed
   ```

   Type in the name of the document containing the list of words and phrases to mark as index entries (created in step 1).

6. Press **Enter**. The macro adds index codes and end marks to the words in the document.

7. Review the index codes and end marks to make sure the macro ran correctly. Add any additional index entries desired using either the macro or manual approaches described earlier in this chapter. Or, delete any index entries you don't want. To delete the entry designation, just delete the index code (.i.) and any end mark that is hidden text.

8. Save the document with **Transfer Save**.

Compiling the Index

Once you have identified all the entries for the index, you can compile the index. This creates the alphabetized list of index entries and corresponding page numbers. Duplicate entries are combined. The same process can be used to recompile the index after making changes in the document. The index is created for the entire document file regardless of division breaks.

Typically, indexes are arranged alphabetically by index entry. However, you may want to organize the index by page number. For example, you may want to check the index entries by page or you may want a draft "outline" of the document by index text. With Word, you can arrange indexes alphabetically or by page number.

During the compilation process you can also identify formatting for the index. You can control the leader character, capitalization of main entries, the indent for subentries, and the use of a style sheet.

To compile the index, follow these steps:

1. Select **O**ptions. In the *show hidden text* field, select **N**o. This is necessary because compiling the index paginates the document. Visible hidden text is considered part of the document and will cause page numbers to be inaccurate.

2. Select **P**rint **O**ptions to make sure a printer is named in the *printer* field. If the field is blank, enter a printer name or press **F1** to select a printer name from the list.

3. Select **L**ibrary **T**able. In the *index code* field, enter a *C* to organize the index by alphabetical order or *i* to organize it by page number.

4. Select **L**ibrary **I**ndex. Change any of these fields:

   - ***entry/page # separated by***: Enter the characters to place between the entry and a page number. For example, a comma and space are often used:

     `Daily Quotes, 6`

   - ***cap main entries***: Select **Y**es to have Word capitalize the first character of each main entry. All other main entries and subentries remain as you entered them. Select **N**o to leave the capitalization as entered.

   - ***indent each level***: Change the 0.2″ indent to any measure. This value indents each subentry to the right of the superior entry.

   - ***use style sheet***: Select **Y**es to ignore the *indent each level* field value and use the formats for the Paragraph Styles, Index Levels 1 through 4, you have entered in a style sheet. If you have not created these styles, the default paragraph format is used. (See Chapter 9, "Style Sheets," for more information on setting up paragraph styles.)

5. Press **Enter** or click the command name. If you are recompiling the index, this message appears:

   `Index already exists. Enter Y to replace or Esc to cancel`

   Press **Y** to replace the index.

The index is compiled and placed at the end of the document.

See Figure 18-7 for a sample index. A division mark is placed after the document and before the index. This ensures that the formatting applied to the index is for the index only. The indicator *.Begin Index.* signals the start of the index and *.End Index.* marks the end. Don't delete these indicators because you will need them when you update the index. Notice that Word prints punctuation first in the index. If you want the entries with punctuation in another place, you can edit the index after compiling. The index entries beginning with numbers appear next (*36 Methods to Reduce Your Paperwork*). Finally, other index entries are organized alphabetically and include subentries. Notice that lowercase letters (*financial/moneyWorld*) are alphabetized along with uppercase letters.

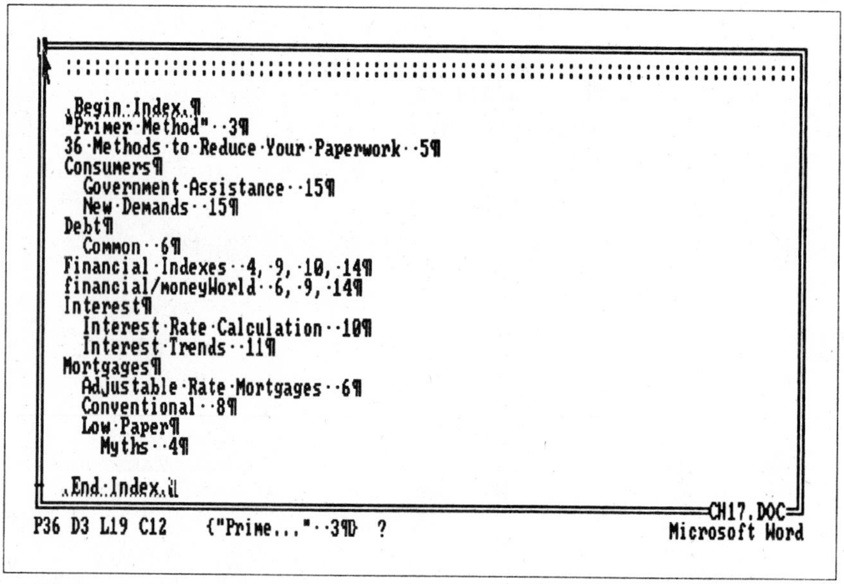

Figure 18-7. A sample index

You can format the index as you would any document text. You can add headings, running heads, and format characters. If an index entry wraps around the end of a line, Word creates a 0.4" hanging indent. You can use Format Paragraph to change the hanging indent or use a style sheet to control all the instances of the runover.

Exercise: Creating an Index

To create an index across several document files, merge the document files before compiling the index.

In this exercise, you will create an index. Select Options. In the *show hidden text* field, select Yes. That way, you can see the index entry markings.

Enter the following text in a clear Word window:

Bank Rate Trends

Bank rates have been fluctuating in a healthy fashion over the past ten years. This trend will continue into the future, making for a healthy, moving economy.

Economists' Predictions

Economists predict that loosening credit will be the response to a slowdown in economic growth and an easing of inflation.

Interest Rates

Interest rates have gone from some of the highest seen in this century to high single digits. Most economists predict that interest rates will continue to decline over five years.

In the first paragraph, make the text *Bank rates* an index entry. Place your highlight on the *B* and press Alt-E to enter hidden text. Type in:

.i.

Move the highlight after the *s*, press Alt-E, and then type in a semicolon.

In the second paragraph, place the highlight on the *E* in *Economists predict. . . .* Then press Alt-E and type in this line:

.i.Economist predictions:Loosening credit;

The entire line just entered should now be hidden text.

In the third paragraph, use a macro to mark the index entry. Make sure that MACRO.GLY is attached. Select Transfer Glossary Load. Enter the drive, path, and MACRO.GLY file name. Press Enter. To make sure the glossary file is loaded, select Transfer Glossary Save to check the name of the current glossary. Highlight *Interest rates* and then press Ctrl-IE. The entry is complete.

In the same paragraph, place the highlight under the *f* in *Five years.* Press Alt-E and then enter this line:

.i.Interest rates:Five years;

The text is displayed as hidden text. Figure 18-8 shows the text marked with index entries. Put each paragraph on a different page using Ctrl-Shift-Enter to separate the pages.

```
┌─[·········1·········2·········3·········4·········5·········]·········7·····
│ :::::::::::::::::::::::::::::::::::::::::::::::::::::::::::::::::::::::::::::
│ ¶
│ Bank·Rate·Trends¶
│ ·····,i,Bank·rates;·have·been·fluctuating·in·a·healthy·
│ fashion·over·the·past·ten·years,··This·trend·will·continue·
│ into·the·future·making·for·a·healthy,·moving·economy,¶
│ ·········································································
│ ¶
│ Economist·Predictions¶
│ ·····,i,Economist·predictions:Loosening·credit;Economists·
│ predict·that·loosening·credit·will·be·the·response·to·a·slow·
│ down·in·economic·growth·and·an·easing·in·inflation,¶
│ ·········································································
│ ¶
│ Interest·Rates¶
│ ·····,i,Interest·rates;·have·gone·from·some·of·the·highest·
│ seen·in·this·century·to·high·single·digits,··Most·economists·
│ predict·that·interest·rates·will·continue·to·decline·over·
│ ,i,Interest·rates:Five·years;five·years,¶
│ ¶
│ ¶
│ ◆
P2 D2 L1 C1        {:}                              Microsoft Word
```

Figure 18-8. Index entries

To compile the index, select Print Options. Complete the *printer* field for your printer and press Enter. Select Options. In the *show hidden text* field, select No and press Enter. The hidden text disappears from view. Select Library Index and use Word's defaults. Press Enter. The index is compiled.

Figure 18-9 illustrates the completed index. There is no page number after *Economists' Predictions* because it was included as a heading only. There is a page number after *Interest Rates* because it is a separate index entry.

Save the document under the name INDEX.

Outlines

Outlines are useful for creating summaries of documents and speech notes, and for examining the overall structure of a document. An outline is a regular Word document with specially marked headings. To see the document in outline form, switch from Word's document view to *outline view*. While in outline view, you can use two modes:

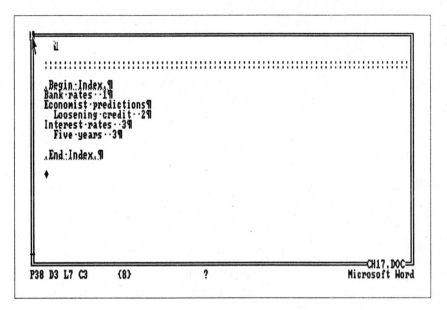

Figure 18-9. The completed index

- **Outline edit:** Use outline edit to edit headings. Outline edit is Word's default mode when you switch from document to outline view. The status line shows the level of the heading on which you are working.

- **Outline organize:** Outline organize mode is used when you move, copy, delete, or sort headings. The status line reflects ORGANIZE.

Figure 18-10 shows text in regular text mode. Figure 18-11 illustrates the text in outline view/outline edit mode. Notice that the prompt in the lower-left corner says *Text.* When the highlight is placed on a heading, Word displays the level of the heading. Figure 18-12 shows the text in outline view/outline organize mode. The appearance is similar to outline edit mode. Notice that the word ORGANIZE is displayed in the lower-left corner.

Headings and subheadings are organized in levels. You can collapse and expand the outline to see major headings, headings and subheadings, or headings, subheadings, and body text. By expanding and collapsing the outline, you can see the global organization of a document as well as the organization of individual sections. Figure 18-13 shows an outline in the fully collapsed view. A plus appears in the left column to indicate that there are subheadings. Figure 18-14 illustrates the outline partially collapsed. The *Acceptance* heading has a plus to the left indicating there are subheadings under the heading. Figure 18-15 shows the fully expanded version. Notice that there are no plus symbols in the left column.

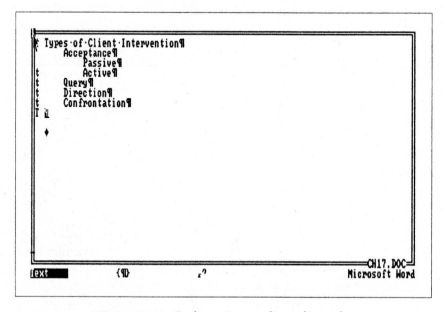

```
►Types·of·Client·Intervention¶
    →    Intervening·in·client·situations·is·a·touchy·issue·for·the·
consultant.··Success·is·all·important.··¶
¶
Acceptance¶
    →    Give·the·client·a·sense·of·acceptance.··This·way,·the·client·
will·open·up.··Acceptance·may·be:¶
Passive¶
Active¶
¶
Query¶
    →    The·query·mode·questions·the·client's·approaches·in·a·
rational·way.··The·desired·is·for·the·client·to·see·a·new·
approach·or·rethink·old·conceptions.¶
¶
Direction¶
    →    Directional·intervention·provides·the·client·with·specific·
instructions.¶
¶
Confrontation¶
    →    The·consultant·must·be·careful·to·delivery·confrontative·
messages·in·private·and·softly.▓
                                                      ═CH17.DOC═
P36 D3 L22 C32    {Confro...rf".··} ?              Microsoft Word
```

Figure 18-10. Regular text mode

```
►Types·of·Client·Intervention¶
        Acceptance¶
            Passive¶
            Active¶
t   Query¶
t   Direction¶
t   Confrontation¶
T ▓

    ◆



                                                      ═CH17.DOC═
Text▬▬▬          {¶}           r²              Microsoft Word
```

Figure 18-11. Outline view, outline edit mode

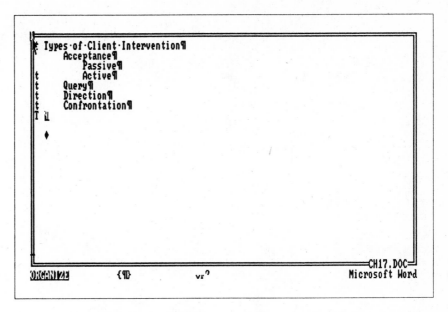

Figure 18-12. Outline view, outline organize mode

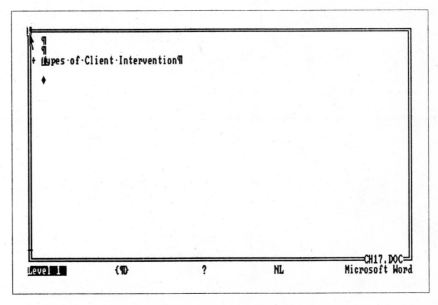

Figure 18-13. A fully collapsed outline

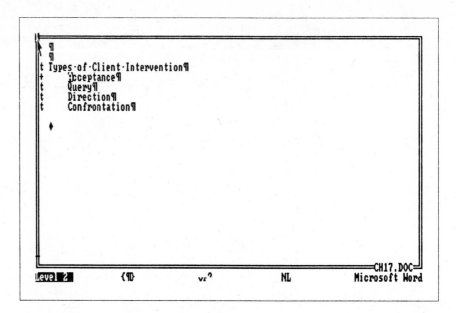

Figure 18-14. A partially collapsed outline

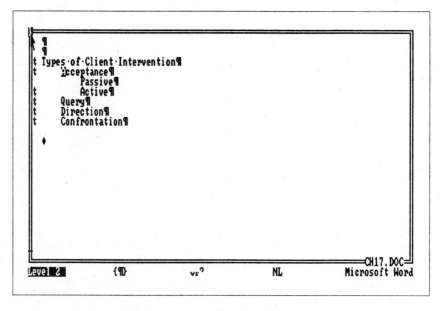

Figure 18-15. A fully expanded outline

Keystrokes for Outlining

There are a variety of key strokes you can use when outlining. Each of these key combinations are described in detail in the examples that follow. Use this chart as a quick reference while you work.

Key press	Purpose
Shift-F2	Switch document view and outline view
Shift-F5	Switch outline edit and outline organize
Alt-0 (to row zero)	Lower heading level
Alt-9 (top row 9)	Raise heading level
Minus (- on numeric keypad or Alt-8)	Collapse heading or body text
Shift-Minus (- on numeric keypad or Shift-Alt-8)	Collapse body text
Plus (+ on numeric keypad or Alt-7)	Expand headings
Shift-Plus (+ on numeric keypad or Shift-Alt-7)	Expand body text
* (asterisk on numeric keypad or PrtSc)	Expand all headings under section
Ctrl-Plus (+ on numeric keypad), number of heading level	Display headings to level

Creating Outlines

The paragraph mark contains information on heading levels. If you accidentally enter a level mark and don't want that level, you can copy a paragraph mark for body text and quickly change the heading to body text. Or, you can use the Alt-P speed formatting key to make the switch.

To create an outline in outline view, you will type in a heading, determine the level, and end the heading with a paragraph mark. When you use Alt-9 or Alt-0, remember to use the 9 and 0 that are on the top row of the keyboard and not the 9 and 0 on the numeric keypad.

Follow these steps to create your outline:

1. Press **Shift-F2** to switch to outline view. Or, set the Options *show outline* field to **Yes**.

2. Enter the first heading and press **Enter**. You may need to press **Alt-9** first; experiment with your computer setup.

3. Enter the next heading. Press **Alt-0** to indent the heading to a lower level. Press **Alt-9** to raise an indented heading one level. Or, leave the level as is. Press **Enter**.

4. To change the level of an existing heading, place the highlight on the heading and press **Alt-0** or **Alt-9**.

5. To add body text while in outline view, place the highlight on the paragraph mark at the end of the heading under which you want to add body text. Press **Enter**. Press **Alt-P** (or **Alt-X-P** if you have a style sheet attached). The highlight returns to the left margin and you can now enter body text.

6. To switch back to document view, press **Shift-F2** again.

You can edit outline text like any other Word text. You may find the Search and Replace commands useful for editing tasks. There are seven reserved styles for outline headings (heading levels 1 through 7) in each Word style sheet. Styles can be used to assign heading levels and formatting. Word's OUTLINE.STY style sheet has formats for headings. (See Chapter 9, "Style Sheets," for information on using style sheets.)

Printing Outlines

To print an outline, go into outline mode. Set up the outline to appear as you want it to print. Select **Print Printer**. The appearance in the window is what prints.

Collapsing and Expanding Outlines

When an outline is created, you can collapse the outline to see less detail. Or, you can expand it to see more detail.

You can also collapse or expand several headings at once. When working with several headings, press Shift-F5 to go to outline organize mode (ORGANIZE should appear in the status line). Select the headings. Then use the collapse or expand process (described in the following section) to get the desired result.

Using a Keyboard

With a keyboard, you can use the following methods to collapse or expand an outline:

- **Collapse all subheadings and body text under a heading:** Place the highlight on the heading and then press the minus key on the numeric keypad or Alt-8.
- **Collapse body text under a heading:** Place the highlight on the heading and then press Shift_ (using the minus key on the numeric keypad) or Shift-Alt-8.
- **Expand the level below the heading:** Place the highlight on the heading and then press plus (+ on the numeric keypad) or Alt-7.
- **Expand levels below a heading:** Place the highlight on the heading and press an asterisk (* on the numeric keypad) or PrtSc.
- **Expand body text under a heading:** Place the highlight on the heading of the body text and then press Shift-+ (using the plus on the numeric keypad) or Shift-Alt-7.
- **Expand all headings to a single level:** Press Ctrl-+ using the plus on the numeric keypad. Type in the heading level.
- **Expand all headings and body text:** Select the outline with Shift-F10. Press * (asterisk on the numeric keypad) to expand all headings and press Shift-+ (using the plus on the numeric keypad) to expand all body text.

Using a Mouse

To go into organize mode with a mouse press Shift-F5. (More alternatives are available with the keyboard than with the mouse.)

- To collapse all subheadings and body text under a heading, point to the heading and click both buttons.
- To expand the next level under a heading, point to the heading and click the right button.

Reorganizing Outlines

You can reorganize outlines by moving, copying, deleting, and sorting headings. In outline organize mode, the body text is collapsed. When you select and manipulate a heading, all the associated body text is manipulated as well.

To reorganize an outline, follow these steps:

1. From document text view, go to outline view by pressing **Shift-F2**.

2. Go to outline organize mode by pressing **Shift-F5**.

3. Select headings using the keyboard or a mouse. These are the keystrokes:

Keystroke	Purpose
Up	Select previous heading at level
Down	Select next heading at level
Left or F9	Select previous heading (any level)
Right or F10	Select next heading (any level)
Home	Select nearest heading, next higher level
End	Select last subheading at next lower level
F6	Select all subheadings and text under current heading
F6, then Down	Select same level headings under current heading

To use the mouse:

Mouse action	Purpose
Point to heading, click left button	Select a heading
Point to first heading, hold down left button, move pointer down, release at end of selection	Select several headings

4. Rearrange the headings as needed, by using the following operations:

   - **Move:** Press **Del**. Insert at new location.
   - **Copy:** Select **Copy** or press **Alt-F3**. Insert at new location.
   - **Delete:** Press **Del**. The paragraph mark remains to keep the outline structure. You can delete it later.
   - **Sort:** Select **Library Autosort**. In the *by* field, select Numeric. Press **Enter** or click the command name.

When you manipulate the headings, the subheadings and body text are manipulated along with the associated heading. When headings are inserted, the highest level equals the level of the heading after the point of insertion.

If you sort the outline in a new numeric order, make sure the numbers are changed to the order you want after the sort. (For information on how to number outline headings, see "Numbering Outline Headings and Paragraphs," later in this chapter.)

Numbering Outline Headings and Paragraphs

You can manually number outline headings in outline view or paragraphs in document view. Word can also number outlines automatically. If you edit outlines or paragraphs, you can use Word to renumber them automatically. You can also remove all the numbers.

You must follow numbers with a period or right parenthesis followed by a tab or space. The number formats you can use are shown in the chart below:

Format	Style
Arabic numerals	1, 2, 3, 4. . .
Uppercase Roman	I, II, III, IV. . .
Lowercase Roman	i, ii, iii, iv. . .
Uppercase letters	A, B, C, D. . .
Lowercase letters	a, b, c, d. . .
Legal numbering	1, 1.1, 1.2, 1.3. . .

Figure 18-16 shows outline headings and Figure 18-17 illustrates the corresponding numbered paragraphs.

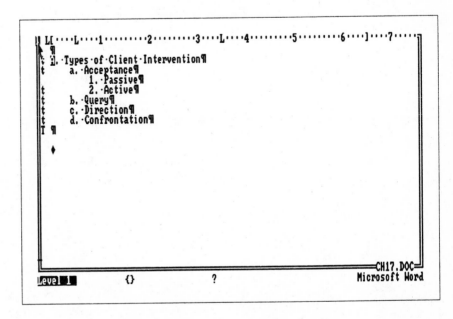

Figure 18-16. Numbered outline headings

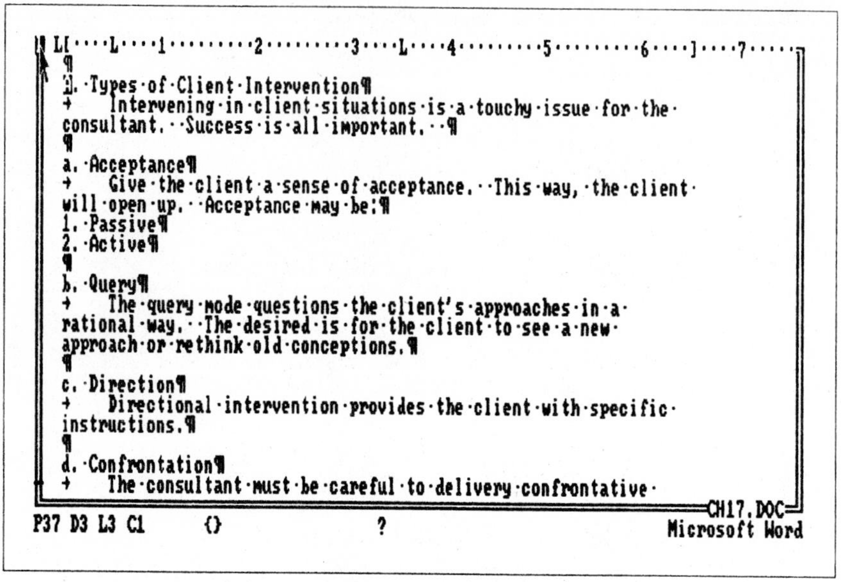

```
L[····L····1·········2·········3···L···4·········5·········6···]···7····
¶
1. Types of Client Intervention¶
→    Intervening in client situations is a touchy issue for the
consultant.  Success is all important.  ¶
¶
a. Acceptance¶
→    Give the client a sense of acceptance.  This way, the client
will open up.  Acceptance may be:¶
1. Passive¶
2. Active¶
¶
b. Query¶
→    The query mode questions the client's approaches in a
rational way.  The desired is for the client to see a new
approach or rethink old conceptions.¶
¶
c. Direction¶
→    Directional intervention provides the client with specific
instructions.¶
¶
d. Confrontation¶
→    The consultant must be careful to delivery confrontative
                                                        ╒CH17.DOC╕
P37 D3 L3 C1        {}              ?              Microsoft Word
```

Figure 18-17. Numbered paragraphs

Numbering Outline Headings

When you number outline headings, Word numbers all headings that
don't start with a hyphen (-), asterisk (*), or bullet (●).

To number, renumber, or remove outline headings, follow these
steps:

1. Press **Shift-F2** to move from document view to outline view.

2. Select the appropriate text:

   - To number the entire outline using Word's default number-
     ing scheme, select the first character in a heading. The
     numbering scheme is:

     I.

     A.

     1.

     a)

   - To affect only the selected text, select several headings.

- To number headings in legal format, type *1.* followed by a space or tab at the outline's beginning. Select the 1. you entered.

3. Select **Library Number**.

4. Select one of the following:

Update   to number or renumber an outline. Select **Yes** in the *restart sequence* field to number from the first number in a sequence (such as 1), or select **No** to number from the current location (such as 3).

Remove   to remove numbers.

5. Press **Enter** or click the command name.

Renumbering Paragraphs

You can manually number paragraphs then use Word to renumber them automatically. You must follow numbers with a period or right parenthesis, and then a tab or space.

To number paragraphs, follow these steps:

1. Press **Shift-F2** to return from outline view to document view.

2. Make sure all paragraphs you want to renumber have a number in a valid Word format followed by a period or right parenthesis, and then a tab or space.

3. Highlight the first character in the document or select the portion of the document to renumber.

4. Select **Library Number**.

5. Select **Update**.

6. Press **Enter** or click the command name.

The paragraphs are renumbered using your format including the character format and the amount of indentation.

Exercise: Outlining

Start with a blank Word window. Go into outline view by pressing Shift-F2. Enter this text and then press Alt-9 to raise the indent level or Alt-0 to lower it.

```
Carpet
   Construction
      Methods
         Tufted
         Woven
         Needle punched
         Hand knotted
      Density of pile
   Fibers
      Man-made
         Nylon
         Acrylic
         Polyester
         Polypropylene
      Natural
         Wool
```

To quickly move through your document, move to outline mode and collapse all text. Then move to the heading nearest the text you want to see and press Shift-F2 to return to document mode.

Switch back to document view (Shift-F2) to see how the text is displayed. Word aligns it on the left margin. Go back to outline view (Shift-F2) and place your highlight on the *C* of *Construction*. Press the minus key (on the numeric keypad) or Alt-8. The body text under the *Construction* heading collapses. Notice the plus (+) symbol in the left column indicating there are additional subheadings. To expand the heading, press the plus (+) symbol (on the numeric keypad) or press Alt-7. The text is restored, and the next subordinate subheadings appear. A plus (+) appears before *Methods*. Place the highlight on the *M* in *Methods* and press plus (on the numeric keypad) or Alt-7. All headings appear.

Number the outline. Press Shift-F2 to go to document view, and then select the *C* in *Carpet*. Select Library Number, and then select Update and Yes in the *restart sequence* field. Press Enter. Press Shift-F2 to see the result in both outline and document view. This is the outcome:

```
I. Carpet
   A. Construction
      1. Methods
         a) Tufted
         b) Woven
         c) Needle punched
         d) Hand knotted
      2. Density of pile
```

```
  B. Fibers
    1. Man-made
      a) Nylon
      b) Acrylic
      c) Polyester
      d) Polypropylene
    2. Natural
      a) Wool
```

Save the document with the name OUTLINE.

Tables of Contents

A table of contents can make your documents impressive and easy to use. To create a table of contents, you:

- Mark headings and subheadings to be included in the table of contents
- Compile the table of contents

To mark a heading or subheading for inclusion in a table of contents, place a *table code* before each heading and an *end mark* after it. The end mark can be a semicolon, paragraph mark, or division mark. Figure 18-18 illustrates several table of contents entries with formatting described in this chapter. Figure 18-19 shows a portion of the resulting table of contents after it has been compiled.

Marking Table of Contents Entries

To mark a table of contents sublevel, just add a colon as hidden text after the .c. table code. Use one colon for each level of indentation. Figure 18-18 shows several headings marked with:

.c.

This marking designates the first level. The same figure shows this marking:

.c.:

The colon tells Word to indent to the second level. You can add additional colons for third and subsequent levels.

```
.C.The·Scriptwriter's·Process¶
→     Being·a·scriptwriter·is·fun·and·hard·work.··It·requires·
skill·and·self·discipline.··Scriptwriters·have·a·process.¶
¶
.C..The·Planning·Meeting¶
→     The·script·must·be·planned.··At·the·planning·meeting,·
the·scriptwriter·meets·with·those·involved.··¶
¶
.C..."Research:·Formal·and·Informal"¶
→     Scriptwriters·typically·have·to·research·the·subject.··
This·may·be·library·or·experience·based·research.¶
¶
.C..."Considering·the·""Concept"""¶
→     All·scripts·must·have·a·basic·concept·or·theme.··This·
guides·the·development·of·the·script.¶
¶
.C..Treatment,·Rough·Script,·and·Script¶
→     The·first,·loose·draft·is·called·the·treatment.··From·
there·the·rough·script·and·final·script·are·developed.¶
¶
.C.Financial·Rewards¶
→     The·financial·rewards·of·scriptwriting·vary.▌
                                                              ═17TC.DOC═
P1 D1 L22 C50     {·from·...writer}·?              Microsoft·Word
```

Figure 18-18. Table of contents entries

```
¶
.C..Treatment,·Rough·Script,·and·Script¶
→     The·first,·loose·draft·is·called·the·treatment.··From·
there·the·rough·script·and·final·script·are·developed.¶
¶
.C.Financial·Rewards¶
→     The·financial·rewards·of·scriptwriting·vary.¶
¶
¶
::::::::::::::::::::::::::::::::::::::::::::::::::::::::::::::::::::::::::
.Begin.:Table.:C.¶
The·Scriptwriter's·Process→                          1¶
    The·Planning·Meeting→                            1¶
    Research:·Formal·and·Informal→                   1¶
    Considering·the·"Concept"→                       1¶
    Treatment,·Rough·Script,·and·Script→             1¶
Financial·Rewards→                                   1¶
.End.:Table.:C.¶
▯
                                                              ═17TC.DOC═
P2 D2 L9 C1       {·from·...writer}·?               Microsoft·Word
```

Figure 18-19. The table of contents after compilation

You can also indent table of contents entries that are entered as
hidden text. The benefit of hidden text entries is that you can be very

specific without worrying about the language in the document text. To indent text, separate the main entry and subentries with colons as shown in the following entries:

```
.c.United States:Alabama;
.c.Europe:France:Paris;
```

result in this indentation when printed:

> United States
>   Alabama
> Europe
>   France
>   Paris

Including Punctuation in Table of Contents Entries

If the table of contents entry includes colons or semicolons, surround the text with hidden quotation marks. For example, this is a table of contents entry (the quotation mark is entered as hidden text).

```
.c."Rivers: Mississippi";
```

The printed result is:

> Rivers: Mississippi

If you want the table of contents entry to include quotation marks, enter two quotation marks for each quotation mark that you want to print. For example, this is a table of contents entry with the "outside" quotation marks in hidden text.

```
.c."Richard ""Slugger""" Jones";
```

Omitting Page Numbers

To omit a page number in a table of contents entry, enter a colon as hidden text at the end of the entry. For example:

```
.c.Window:;
```

will print the word *Window* without a corresponding page number.

Creating Entries Using an Outline

A fast way to create a table of contents is to use outline headings.

1. Create an outline. (See the instructions earlier in this chapter.)
2. Edit the outline so that only table of contents headings are visible. If you have text that you want to keep in place, you can temporarily format it as hidden text.
3. Compile the table of contents by selecting **Library Table**.
4. In the *from* field, select **O**utline. Complete the other fields as appropriate. (See "Compiling the Table of Contents" later in this chapter for details.)
5. Press **Enter**.

All visible outline headings are placed in the table of contents and indented according to the outline level.

Marking Existing Text with a Macro

You can use Word's TOC_ENTRY.MAC macro to mark table of contents entries. Here are the steps:

1. Make sure the MACRO.GLY glossary file is available. Use **Transfer Glossary Save** to see the current glossary. If necessary, use **Transfer Glossary Load** to enter the drive, path, and MACRO.GLY file name.
2. Once MACRO.GLY is available, select the text for the table of contents entry.
3. Press **Ctrl-T E**

The table of contents codes are added as hidden text.

Entering Table Codes

Entering individual table codes to mark table of contents entries is more time consuming than using outline headings or the macro. These are the benefits:

- It is the only method to enter all the table of contents entries as hidden text.
- The entries can be more specific.
- You can easily designate several levels.

  To enter table codes follow these steps:

1. Select **O**ptions.
2. In the *show hidden text* field, select **Y**es to view the hidden codes as you enter them.

3. Position the highlight where you want to type in the table of contents entry.

4. Press **Alt-E** (or **Alt-X-E** if you are using a style sheet). This turns on the hidden text format.

5. Enter:

    .c.

6. Add a colon as hidden text for each level you want to indent. To include the text entry as hidden text, enter it now. The .c. entry, any colons, and text (if entered) appear as hidden text.

7. If the table of contents entry ends in a semicolon, paragraph mark, or division mark, you do not need an end mark. If there is no end mark, position the highlight after the entry and type in a semicolon in hidden text. Remember to press **Alt-E** (or **Alt-X-E**) first to type in hidden text, if necessary.

Use F4 to repeat the hidden text activity. Or save the hidden-text semicolon as a glossary entry. Either method can streamline the creation of table of contents entries.

Compiling Tables of Contents

You use Library Table to paginate the document and create the table of contents complete with page numbers. Make sure the document is finished before generating the table of contents. Otherwise, if you perform additional edits, the page numbers will change.

To compile the table of contents, follow these steps:

1. Select **O**ptions. In the *show hidden text* field, select **No**. This way, the table of contents hidden text will not be counted as regular document text when the document is compiled.

2. Select **P**rint Options. Make sure there is a value in the *printer* field. If not, enter one and press **Enter**. This value is necessary to tell Word how to repaginate the document.

3. If you have an index in the document, compile it first. Add a table of contents entry to cover the index. Then, generate the table of contents which will include the index entry.

4. Select Library **T**able.

5. Complete these fields:

- ***from***:   Select **O**utline to compile an outline. Select **C**odes to compile using the table of contents codes.
- ***index code***:   Enter a *C* for table of contents codes. (These are the other types of codes for other tables: i for index as well as l, d, and g for graphics, spreadsheet data, and other text. Or, you can enter your own code for a table of a special kind. For example, .p. can be your code to make a table of pictures. Use your own code anytime you want to create a list.)
- ***page numbers***:   Select **Y**es to enter page numbers in the table or **N**o for no page numbers.
- ***entry/page number separated by***:   Enter any leader character to appear between the table of contents entry and the page number. For example, ˆt means a right-aligned tab. You can use spaces, periods, underlines, or any other character.
- ***indent each level***:   The indent level for subentries set by Word is 0.4". You can enter any indent.
- ***use style sheet***:   Select **Y**es to use the style sheet for the paragraph styles reserved by Word for table of contents (table levels 1 through 4). The *indent each level* field entry value is ignored. Enter **N**o to use the *indent each* field entry.

6. Press **Enter** or click the command name. If you are recompiling a table, the existing table is highlighted and this message appears:

```
Table already exists. Enter Y to replace, N to append,
or Esc to cancel
```

Press **Y** to replace the table. Press **N** to add the new table after the existing table. Or, press **Esc** to stop the process.

Assuming you continued to create the table and the Library Table *page numbers* field is set to Yes, the document is paginated as the table is developed.

The table of contents is placed at the end of the document preceded by a division mark. You can move the table of contents to the beginning of the document if you like. Formatting changes in the division affect only the table of contents. These identifiers are placed at the beginning and end of the table of contents respectively:

```
.Begin Table C.
.End Table C.
```

Do not remove these identifiers or Word will not know where to place the table of contents if you later recompile the table.

To create a table of contents for several files, place your highlight at the end of the first file and use Transfer Merge to bring the next file into the first. Continue until all file contents are in one document file. Then, use Library Table to compile the large document. If you run out of memory, Word will notify you on the status line.

Exercise: Creating a Table of Contents

You can have table of contents entries that are too long for one line. You can format them with a hanging indent or use new line.

In this exercise, you will gain experience creating a simple table of contents. In a blank Word screen, type in this text:

```
Lighting

Special Effects
    Lighting in your home can be dramatic. Consider all
types of lights: downlights, uplights, and spotlights.

Downlights
    Downlights are typically installed on the ceiling or
wall. They give a spacious, uncluttered look.

Uplights
    Uplights are usually canisters that sit on the floor.
They create dramatic patterns.

Spotlights
    Spots throw light on special objects to create centers
of attention.

Bulbs and Fixtures
    There are two main types of lights. These are
incandescent bulbs and fluorescent lights.
```

You are going to create this table of contents:

```
Lighting   1
    Special Effects          1
        Downlights           1
        Uplights             1
        Spotlights           1
    Bulbs and Fixtures       1
        Incandescent Bulbs   1
        Fluorescent Lights   1
```

To create the table of contents, place the highlight under the *L* in *Lighting*. Press Alt-E (or Alt-X-E if a style sheet is attached) and type in the following code (which appears as hidden text):

`.c.`

The heading ends in a paragraph mark which serves as the end mark for the table of contents entry.

Place your highlight on the *S* in *Special Effects*. Press Alt-E (or Alt-X-E if a style sheet is attached). Type in:

`.c.:`

The colon will indent the heading one level.

Continue this process for *Downlights*, *Uplights*, and *Spotlights*. Enter two colons instead of one so the headings will be indented two levels. When you mark *Bulbs and Fixtures*, use one colon.

The final two entries require you to place hidden text in the entry. Place your highlight on the *i* in *incandescent*. Press Alt-E or Alt-X-E. Type in:

`.c.::Incandescent Bulbs;`

The entire line is in hidden text. Use the same process to enter the *Fluorescent Lights* table of contents entry. Figure 18-20 shows the text complete with the table of contents entries.

Compile the table of contents. Select Library Table. In the *from* field, make sure Codes is selected. Use the other Word defaults:

index code	C to link with the .c. entry for table of contents entries
page numbers	Yes to enter page numbers
entry/page number separated by	^t for tab
indent each level	0.4" for the indent
use style sheet	No for no style sheet

Press Enter. The table of contents is created.

The dot leader characters can be entered now. Select Options and then, in the *show ruler* field, select Yes. In the *show non-printing symbols* field, select Partial. Now select the entire table of contents beginning with *Lighting* and ending with *lights*.

Select Format Tab Set. In the *position* field, press F1. Place the highlight on the tab mark under which the page numbers are aligned.

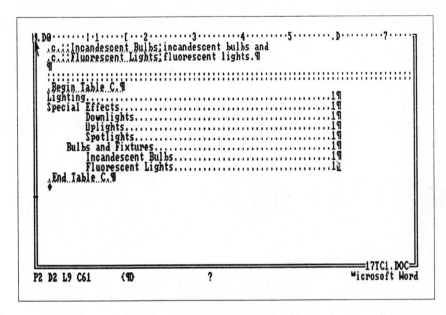

Figure 18-20. The text with table of contents entries

Press a period (.) for the leader character and enter a D for decimal character. Press Enter. The leader characters appear. Figure 18-21 shows the completed table of contents.

```
¶.D0·······|·1·······[···2·······3·······4·······5·······.D·······7····¶
 .C...Incandescent Bulbs:incandescent bulbs and
 .C...Fluorescent Lights:fluorescent lights.¶
¶
 ::::::::::::::::::::::::::::::::::::::::::::::::::::::::::::::::::::::::::
 .Begin Table C.¶
Lighting.............................................................1¶
Special Effects......................................................1¶
        Downlights...................................................1¶
        Uplights.....................................................1¶
        Spotlights...................................................1¶
    Bulbs and Fixtures...............................................1¶
        Incandescent Bulbs...........................................1¶
        Fluorescent Lights...........................................1¶
 .End Table C.¶
 ◆




                                                            ═17TC1.DOC═
P2 D2 L9 C61        {¶}              ?                    Microsoft Word
```

Figure 18-21. The table of contents

Using Math Functions and Importing Files

With Word, manipulating mathematical data in a document is easy, whether it involves performing simple math functions or importing complex spreadsheets. You can also import one Word document into another Word document. Once files have been imported, you can edit them as you would any other Word text and you can have Word automatically update a linked document to reflect changes made in the original document.

Mathematical Functions

Word can add, subtract, multiply, divide, and calculate percentages. These are the math symbols Word recognizes:

To	Enter
Add	+
Subtract	−
Multiply	*
Divide	/
Calculate a percentage	%

Using Math

Using math is easy. You simply enter the appropriate formula or data in the context of a sentence, select the numbers, and then calculate.
Here are the steps:

1. Type the mathematical expression, including the necessary symbols, in the document. (You can enter the symbols as hidden text if you prefer; see the next section, "Math Guidelines," for details.)

2. Select the expression. If you are selecting a vertical column, use **Shift-F6**. Include all necessary mathematical symbols in the selection. Selected characters that are not numbers or mathematical symbols are ignored.

3. With the selection highlighted, press **F2**.

4. Word puts the result of the calculation in the scrap area. To paste the result back into the document, first postion the highlight in the document where you want the result to appear and then press **Ins**.

After performing mathematical calculations, it's a good idea to check that the result is reasonable. You can edit the document as needed or redo the calculation, if necessary.

Math Guidelines

Here are some guidelines to remember when performing math:

Length Limitations

The results of calculations can be up to 14 digits long. For example, the following expression includes a 15-digit number:

```
123456789012345 + 1 =
```

If you enter this expression and calculate the result, Word displays this message:

```
Result has too many digits (over 14)
```

On the other hand, Word can calculate this expression without any problem:

```
12345678901234 + 1 =
```

This is the result:

12345678901235

Positive and Negative Numbers

If you enter a number without a mathematical symbol in front of it, Word assumes it is positive. If you enter a number in parentheses, Word assumes it is negative. If you enclose numbers and mathematical symbols in parentheses, Word assumes they are a mathematical expression that is to be calculated. Here are some examples:

Expression	Calculation performed
5 + 3 = 8	Addition of positive numbers
−5 + 3 = −2	Addition of a negative number and a positive number
(5) + 3 = −2	Addition of a negative number and a positive number
5 + −3 = 2	Addition of a positive number and a negative number
5 + (3) = 2	Addition of a positive number and a negative number
(5 + 3) = 8	Addition of positive numbers
(−5 + −3) = −8	Addition of negative numbers
(5) + (3) = −8	Addition of negative numbers

Selections for calculations may include characters other than numbers. For example, this line includes text and does not include any mathematical symbols. If you select this line and tell Word to perform the calculation, Word assumes that the numbers are positive and that the calculation to be performed is addition:

We need 453 green and 54 red shirts for a total of

Calculation yields a result of 507, and you can complete the sentence by copying the result from the scrap area to the end of the line:

We need 453 green and 54 red shirts for a total of 507 shirts.

Precedence

If you enter an expression that involves several calculations, Word performs the calculations in this order:

- Percentages
- Multiplication or division
- Addition or subtraction

Consider the following example:

```
6 + 4 / 2 = 8
```

Word divides the number 4 by 2 with the result of 2. Then, Word adds 6 to 2 for the total of 8.

If parts of an expression are enclosed in parentheses, the order of calculation changes. Word calculates expressions in parentheses first. For example, in the expression in the following table, Word performs the multiplication first until the subtraction part of the expression is enclosed in parentheses; then Word performs the subtraction first:

Expression	Calculation performed
10 − 8 * 2	8 * 2 = 16; 10 − 16 = −6
10 − (8 * 2)	8 * 2 = 16; 10 − 16 = −6
(10 − 8) * 2	10 − 8 = 2; 2 * 2 = 4

Decimals

Word calculates results up to two decimal places or to the number of decimal places used in the expression. Consider these examples:

Expression	Number of decimals
6 / 5 = 1.2	Only one required to give the exact result
6 / 5.75 = 1.04	Two required to give the exact result
41 / 3 = 13.67	Two; the result is actually 13.6666. . . , but two decimal places are the maximum when none are used in the expression
16.000 / 8.000 = 2.000	Three, because three are used in the expression
7.123456789 / 10 = 0.712345679	Nine, because nine are used in the expression
3 * 67% = 2.01	Two; percents always yield results with two decimal places

Percentages

Percentages should be thought out carefully. Make sure you understand the mathematical calculation necessary to produce the desired result. For example, this expression adds the number 60 and the number .10:

```
60 + 10% = 60.1
```

This expression divides 60 by 10 percent:

```
60 / 10% = 600
```

This expression calculates 10 percent of 60:

```
60 * 10% = 6
```

Symbols and Punctuation

Word does not carry over currency symbols (such as $ or ¢) from the expression to the result. Here is an example:

```
$40 + $50 = 90
```

You will have to add the dollar symbol manually to produce:

```
$40 + $50 = $90
```

In contrast, commas are carried over:

```
60,000 * 2 = 120,000
```

Hidden Math Symbols

You can use a separate window to enter calculations that you then insert into your document.

When calculating expressions that occur in text, you can enter math symbols as hidden text. To enter hidden text, set the Format Character *hidden* field to Yes or press Alt-E (Alt-X-E if you are using a style sheet). Then enter the symbol. If you want to see the symbol you are entering, make sure the Options *show hidden text* field is set to Yes.

In the following sentence, the minus sign (displayed with dots below it) was entered as hidden text. The result, 28, was pasted in from the scrap area after calculation:

```
Of 139 members – 111 won't attend. A total of 28 will attend.
```

In the next example, the multiplication symbol was entered as hidden text. After calculation, the result, 224.64, was enclosed in parentheses for readability. Because you can't have .64 of a person, the result needs to be rounded down to 224.

```
Of 432 people, * 52% (or 224.64) scored in the top range.
```

In the sentence that follows, the division symbol has been formatted as hidden text (the result, 3.17 sandwiches, is probably more precise than you need).

```
We'll have 200 sandwiches for / 63 people. That's 3.17 each.
```

You can also format the entire expression as hidden text. In this example, the calculation is hidden:

```
A trip from the Texas office to the Illinois office costs
1500 * .21 315.00 in mileage expense alone.
```

Horizontal and Vertical Calculations

In addition to setting up mathematical expressions horizontally, you can set them up vertically. The same guidelines apply whether you are calculating horizontally or vertically. The following table shows addition and subtraction performed with different tab layouts. Both horizontal and vertical math totals are shown. In this table, the first column was selected with Shift-F6 and Word calculated the result. Each column was selected and calculated independently of the other columns. Then each row was selected and calculated, also independently.

	Left tab	Decimal tab	Center tab	Right tab	Horizontal totals
	456	65	(232)	521	810
	32	1.23	3	32	68.23
	1.45	3.433	231	−32	203.883
Vertical totals	489.45	69.663	2	521	1082.113

These examples show that multiplication and division can be performed vertically as well as horizontally.

Horizontal:

```
560 * 4 = 2240
300 / 8 = 37.5
```

Vertical:

```
          560    300
          * 4    / 8
Totals    2240   37.5
```

Word calculates regardless of the formatting. Here, the expression is in underlined text:

788 + 800 + 76 = 1664

but the result is formatted as regular text. In the next example, the line was included in the text selected for the calculation:

```
560
431

991
```

but the line has no effect on the result.

Exercise: Using Math

Try out Word's math capabilities for yourself. First, you are going to enter this table:

	Meals	Miles	Misc	Total
1/2	65.33	234*.21	10.22	
1/5	23.00	13*.21		
1/6	9.98		15.76	
Total				

Start by selecting Format Tab Set and setting decimal tabs at 1″, 2″, 3″, and 4″. Enter the headings Meals, Miles, Misc, and Total.

Press Tab before each entry and type in each line. Enter the *.21 under the Miles column as hidden text. First, set Options *show hidden text* to Yes, press Alt-E (Alt-X-E if you are using a spreadsheet), and type in the text. Press Alt-Spacebar to go back to normal text.

Now calculate each vertical and horizontal total. Select the first vertical column using Shift-F6. Press F2. Word puts the result of the calculation in the scrap area. Place the highlight in the appropriate Total column and press Ins to insert the result into the document. Continue this process for each vertical column.

Now for the row totals. To select the first row, press F6 and then press End. Press F2 to have Word calculate the total. Position the highlight and press Ins to insert the result at the appropriate location. Continue this process for each row. This is the result (with the Options *show hidden text* field set to No).

	Meals	Miles	Misc	Total
1/2	65.33	234	10.22	124.69
1/5	23.00	13		25.73
1/6	9.98		15.76	25.74
Total	98.31	51.87	25.98	176.16

Importing Spreadsheets

To import non-Excel-Multiplan-123-compatible spreadsheets, first save them as ASCII files with the extension .DOC, then import them into Word with the Library Link Document command. You will need to reformat them, but they will have retained their essential columnar form.

Word's math capabilities are useful but limited when compared to those of a spreadsheet. The advantage of importing spreadsheets is that you can perform more sophisticated mathematical manipulations and then integrate the data into Word documents. With Word, you can import data from files created with Lotus 1-2-3, Multiplan, or Microsoft Excel for Windows. You can import up to 32 KB (approximately 32,000 characters) at a time. If the spreadsheet data is larger than 32 KB, break it into smaller pieces and import each section individually.

You can import several spreadsheets or portions of spreadsheets into one document. Or, you can import the same spreadsheet data into several documents.

Linking Spreadsheets

To link a spreadsheet and import its data into a Word document, follow these steps:

1. In the spreadsheet program, identify the block of cells whose data you want to import, by naming the block or by using any other mechanism the spreadsheet provides. You can use the row-and-column designations to identify the block, but bear in mind that if you later edit the spreadsheet, the rows and columns may change, requiring that you change the Word document before you can update it.

2. Quit the spreadsheet program, start Word, and load your Word document. Place your highlight where you want Word to insert the spreadsheet data.

3. Select **Library** **Link** **S**preadsheet.

4. In the *filename* field, enter the drive, path, and name of the spreadsheet file.

5. In the *area* field, enter the name of the block of cells whose data you want to import. Here are specific steps for specific spreadsheet programs:

   - **Multiplan or Microsoft Excel for Windows:**

     Press **F1** to select from a list of available range names. Or, enter the upper-left row and column designation and the lower-right row and column designation. For example, this entry will import the block of cells from row 4, column 6 through row 8, column 12:

     R4C6:R8C12

     With Microsoft Excel, you can also use the F4:L8 notation style.

   - **Lotus 1-2-3:**

     Press **F1** to display a list of available range names. Or, enter the upper-left and lower-right corner cells, such as:

     G12..M30

     Leave the *area* field blank if you want to import the entire spreadsheet into the document at the highlighted location.

6. Press **Enter** or click the command name.

If Word cannot find the spreadsheet or if you have entered an invalid name, Word alerts you with a message. If part of the specified area is password protected, you will need to enter the password at the Word prompt. Otherwise, Word imports the data, separating each cell with a tab and ending each row with a newline character.

At the beginning of the data, Word displays this hidden text:

`.L.pathname, area name or range of cells<newline>`

At the end of the data, Word adds this code:

`.L.`

Leave these codes in the Word document if you want to be able to update the data later. The codes enable Word to find the data to be updated.

Updating the Spreadsheet Data

You can update spreadsheet data at any time. The update can involve data from one or from many spreadsheets. As already mentioned, the .L. codes that mark the beginning and ending of each occurrence of spreadsheet data in the Word document must be in place, or Word will not be able to locate the data to update.

To update spreadsheet data in a Word document, follow this procedure:

1. Select the entire Word document with **Shift-F10**. Or, select only the area you want to update. Make sure to include the .L. codes for the data areas in your selection.
2. Select **L**ibrary **L**ink **S**preadsheet. Don't fill in the *filename* and *area* fields.
3. Press **Enter** or click the command name.
4. Word finds the first occurrence of spreadsheet data and displays a message asking whether you want to update the data. Press **Y** to update the data or **N** to skip to the next occurrence.

If you press Y, Word updates the data. If you have added paragraph formatting to the data in the Word document, Word retains the formatting when it updates the data. Character formatting is only retained if it is part of an attached style sheet.

Importing Other Documents

As well as linking spreadsheet files to Word documents, you can also link one Word document to another. Linking documents is different from merging them in that you can update linked documents if you make a change in the original document.

Linking Documents

To link one document to another:

1. Load the document that contains the text you want to import.
2. Select the text to be imported.
3. Select **F**ormat bookmar**K** to name the text selection by placing a bookmark.
4. Type a name for the text in the *name* field.
5. Press **Enter** or click the command name.
6. Continue marking text with bookmarks in this and other documents until all the text you want to import is marked.
7. Load the document into which you want to import the text you have just marked.
8. Position the highlight at the location where you want Word to insert the imported text.
9. Select **L**ibrary **L**ink **D**ocument.
10. In the *filename* field, enter the drive, path, and name of the document that holds the marked text. Press **F1** if you want to select the file from a list.
11. In the *bookmark* field, type in the name of the bookmark. Or, press **F1** to select from a list. Leave the field blank if you want to import the entire document or if the document is in ASCII format.
12. Press **Enter** or click the command name.

Word imports the text, adding this hidden code at the beginning:

`.D.`*pathname;bookmark name*

Word also adds this hidden code at the end of the imported text:

`.D.`

Do not remove these codes if you anticipate updating the text in the future. The codes are used by Word to identify imported text that may need to be updated.

Updating Document Text

You can quickly update imported text by following these steps:

1. Select the entire document to be updated by pressing **Shift-F10**. Or, select just the text to be updated. Make sure to include the beginning and ending .D. codes.

2. Select Library Link **D**ocument.

3. Leave the *filename* and *bookmark* fields blank and press **Enter** or click the command name to begin updating.

4. When Word finds the first block of imported text, it asks if you want to update the text. Press **Y** to update it or **N** to go to the next block.

If you press Y, Word updates the text. If you have added paragraph formatting to the text imported into the Word document, Word retains the formatting. Character formatting is only retained if it is part of an attached style sheet.

Exercise: Linking Documents

Create the following document in a blank Word screen. Use Word's math capabilities to calculate the totals. Simply enter the formula values, select the formula text, and press F2 to have Word calculate the total and place it in the scrap area. Then insert the total, adding dollar signs and commas where necessary.

```
Determining stock gain:
Total gain = Net selling price - Dividends - Net purchase price
Example:
$1,860.00 = ($2,000 - 0.02 * $2,000) - $100

Determining return on investment:
Return on investment = (Net cash inflows) / (Initial cash outlays)
Example (-56%):
-0.56 = ($1,468 - $2,040) / $1,020

Determining total cash outlays:
Total cash outlays = Purchase price + Transaction cost
$2,040.00 = ($20 * 100) + ($20 * 100 * 0.02)
```

Select the first calculation group. Then select Format bookmar**K** and, in the *name* field, enter STOCK and press Enter. Follow the same process for naming the second calculation group ROI and the third calculation group CASH.

Save the document as ACCT.DOC.

Now clear the Word screen. Enter the following text into a new document, leaving two blank lines between each paragraph.

```
Dear Jim:

We have decided to use the standard formula for determining
stock gain. Here is an excerpt from our accounting manual
which details our calculations.

The ROI calculation is the same as your firm uses. To recap:

You will find the cash outlay calculation to be a bit
different. This is the method.

Call me if you have any questions.
```

Place your highlight on the second line after *calculations*, which ends the first paragraph. Select Library Link Document. In the *filename* field, enter:

```
ACCT
```

In the *bookmark* field, enter STOCK. Press Enter. Word imports the text marked with the STOCK bookmark in the original document. Repeat this procedure for the ROI and CASH bookmarks. The completed text will look like this (adjust any incorrect line spacing manually):

```
Dear Jim:

We have decided to use the standard formula for determining
stock gain. Here is an excerpt from our accounting manual
which details our calculations.

Determining stock gain:
Total gain = Net selling price - Dividends - Net purchase price
Example:
$1,860.00 = ($2,000 - 0.02 * $2,000) - $100

The ROI calculation is the same as your firm uses. To recap:

Determining return on investment:
Return on investment = (Net cash inflows) / (Initial cash outlays)
Example (-56%):
-0.56 = ($1,468 - $2,040) / $1,020

You will find the cash outlay calculation to be a bit
different. This is the method.

Determining total cash outlays:
Total cash outlays = Purchase price + Transaction cost
$2,040.00 = ($20 * 100) + ($20 * 100 * 0.02)
Call me if you have any questions.
```

Electronic Publishing and Graphics

Electronic publishing (also widely known as desktop publishing) is the term given to the production of professional-quality documents using personal computers. In addition to a computer, electronic publishing requires:

- Software capable of manipulating and displaying page layouts, fonts, and graphics.
- An output device capable of producing high-resolution text and graphics.

The most common output devices used in electronic publishing are laser printers, whose 300-dot-per-inch resolution represents a minimum for producing near-print-quality text and graphics. Laser printers, however, cannot emulate the high-quality output of traditional phototypesetting and are therefore unsuitable for professional-quality output. For that, you must turn to digital-typesetting equipment such as the Linotronic 300, which provides output at resolutions 2450 dots per inch.

Word 5 provides the page-layout and graphics tools you need to produce a wide variety of published documents, from flyers and leaflets to newsletters, pamphlets, reports, and even short books. For very long documents or those including complicated layouts and extensive use of graphics, you really need dedicated page-layout software. But for the great majority of publications produced on desktop systems, Word 5 is all you need.

The following Word 5 commands, which are essential for electronic publishing, are featured in this chapter:

- Library Link Graphics for importing graphics
- Format pOsition for positioning text and graphics on the page
- Options *show layout* for showing the layout of text and graphics on the screen
- Format Border and Line draw for creating lines, borders, and boxes

The following essential features for electronic publishing are discussed in other chapters:

- Format Stylesheet for maintaining consistency of styles throughout a publication (see Chapter 9, "Style Sheets")
- Print preView for showing text and graphics on scaled-down pages, just as they will appear when printed (see Chapter 5, "Printing Documents")
- Format Footnote, Format Annotation, and Format bookmarK for creating cross-references and documentation (see Chapter 10, "Revision Marks, Bookmarks, Cross-Referencing, and Hyphenation")
- Library Table and Library Index for creating tables of contents and indexes (see Chapter 18, "Indexes, Outlines, and Tables of Contents")

With Word 5, you can import graphic files into documents, position text and graphics precisely on a page, add borders and lines, and position text. Word's line-draw feature allows you to add paragraph borders, shading, and vertical lines as well as draw boxes.

Graphics

Word can import either bit-mapped or Postscript graphic files. Bit-mapped graphics are created pixel by pixel (dot by dot), using graphics software. Postscript graphics are imported as text files containing instructions written in the Postscript page-description language for printing out the graphics.

Word recognizes the following graphics file formats:

- Lotus .PIC
- Microsoft Paintbrush .PCX or .PCC
- PostScript
- Pageview by Microsoft (may require resizing)

- HPGL plotter (Hewlett-Packard)
- TIFF B or TIFF G scanner files
- Windows Clipboard

For the latest list of Word-supported graphics packages, load the README.DOC document located on one of the Word Utilities disks and review the information regarding graphics. If you have graphics from a different software program, try out a test case. If you have trouble using the graphic, contact Microsoft's technical support for assistance.

In addition to graphics created by graphics packages, files created by "printing" to a file can also be imported as graphics; so can files created by Word's CAPTURE.COM utility.

Capturing a Screen Image with CAPTURE.COM

CAPTURE.COM is a memory-resident program that uses approximately 20K of memory. It allows you to capture and save screen images from any DOS program into files that can then be imported into a Word document. If the screen image contains graphic elements, CAPTURE.COM saves it as a graphics file with an .SCR extension. If the screen image consists only of text, you can choose to have CAPTURE.COM save it either as an ASCII text file with the extension .LST or as a graphics file with an .SCR extension. Word treats these two types of files quite differently:

- To import a graphics (.SCR) file, use the Library Link command. Once the file is imported, you can clip or rotate it as needed.

- To import a text (.LST) file, use the Transer Load or Transfer Merge commands. You cannot clip or rotate text files.

As a practical matter, save a screen image as a text file if you want to edit the text and as a graphics file if you want to clip or rotate the image. Text files also print considerably faster than graphics files.

CAPTURE.COM file is located on the Word 5 Program 1 disk. If you used Setup with a hard disk system, CAPTURE.COM should also be on your hard disk. If you are using OS/2, be sure to run CAPTURE.COM only in the DOS compatibility mode.

To capture a DOS program screen image with CAPTURE.COM:

1. From the drive or directory with the CAPTURE.COM file, type in one of the following:

CAPTURE /s   to set up and then run CAPTURE.COM for the first time

CAPTURE   to run CAPTURE.COM

If you are setting up CAPTURE.COM, Word displays these options (press the letter indicated to make each selection):

D   to select display adapter. Type in the number corresponding to your video display. If in doubt, or if you have trouble using another selection, select **0**—Standard IBM PC display.

T   to enable/disable text screens as pictures. If you selected 0 (zero) as the display adapter, you can choose to save screen images either as ASCII text files or as graphics files. Enter your choice here.

V   to enable/disable saving in reverse video CAPTURE.COM can save images in reverse video, that is, whatever appears black on the screen is white in the saved file, and whatever is white on screen is black in the saved file. Press **Y** to save images in reverse video or **D** to save them in normal video.

P   to enable/disable clipping. Clipping allows you to capture only part of the screen. If you are using Microsoft Windows, disable this feature by pressing **N**. Clipping does not work with all applications.

R   to enable/disable 90 degree rotation. Press **Y** to save screens with the image rotated 90 degrees to the right.

N   to enter number of text lines per screen. Depending on your display, you may need to enter the number of lines on the screen. This is not necessary if your display is CGA, MCGA, EGA, or VGA.

Q   to quit and save settings.

When the utility is loaded, Word displays this message:

```
CAPTURE.COM Loaded
```

2. Load the application program and screen you want to capture.

3. Press **Shift-PrtSc**. If you didn't select General IBM as the display adapter and you want a text-mode screen, press **Esc** after pressing **Shift-PrtSc**.

Word displays a prompt like the following:

```
File Name: CAPT0005
```

4. Press **Enter** to accept the proposed file name or enter a new name and then press **Enter**.

CAPTURE.COM will add an .SRC extension for graphics screens or an .LST extension for text screens.

5. If you are using a graphics screen, you can now clip the graphic using these keys:

Arrow keys	to adjust the boundaries
Ins	to move top and bottom lines together
Del	to go to single line control (after using Ins or Tab)
Tab	to move bottom and right lines then top and left lines
Numeric keypad plus (+)	to move lines in larger increments
Numeric keypad minus (−)	to move lines in smaller increments

Then press **Enter** to capture the screen.

For additional information on the CAPTURE.COM utility, see the CAPTURE.DOC document on Word Program 1 disk.

After processing, CAPTURE.COM beeps. The file is created and placed in the directory of the software program you are using. You can capture another screen or go on to other work.

To remove CAPTURE.COM from memory without resetting or turning off your computer, enter:

```
capture /E
```

Word displays this message:

```
Capture program successfully removed from memory
```

Basic Graphics Concepts

To work with Word's graphics capabilities, you will need to be familiar with some new terms. A paragraph *frame* encloses a paragraph, including all text, spaces, and borders. You position graphics (or text) by specifying the position on the page of the frame surrounding each graphic.

When you import a graphic, you can control the width and height of the graphic, the space above and below the graphic, and the horizontal placement of the graphic (left, right, or centered). You can also add borders, shading, or captions.

Importing and Printing Graphics

To import and print a graphic in a Word document:

1. Make sure the graphic file is available. Jot down the drive, path, and file name if necessary. If you are using a Microsoft Excel chart, save it to the Windows Clipboard in bitmap format (see your Excel manual for more information).

2. Load the document to which you want to import graphics.

3. Place the highlight at the position in which you want to load the graphic.

4. Select **Library Link Graphics.**

5. Type in the drive, path, and file name of the graphic. Or, press **F1** to select a graphic file from a list. If you saved the graphic to the Windows Clipboard, you can select Clipboard.

6. The *file format* field will be filled in if Word can determine a suggested file format. For example, Word automatically enters the PCX file format for Microsoft Paintbrush files. If Word does not enter a file format, you can enter one or press **F1** to select from formats such as the following:

   - HPGL
   - Postscript
   - Print file

7. Select one of the following options for the *alignment in frame* field:

Left	to align the left side of the graphic with the left margin of the document. (See Figure 20-1.)
Right	to align the right side of the graphic with the right margin of the document. (See Figure 20-2.)
Centered	to center the graphic between the left and right margins. (See Figure 20-3.)

The *alignment in frame* setting has an effect only if the width of the graphic is larger or smaller than the one-column default width.

This seminar is presented by:

Future Technologies Company is dedicated to bringing the latest in technology updates to you.

Figure 20-1. Left-aligned graphic

This seminar is presented by:

Future Technologies Company is dedicated to bringing the latest in technology updates to you.

Figure 20-2. Right-aligned graphic

This seminar is presented by:

Future Technologies Company is dedicated to bringing the latest in technology updates to you.

Figure 20-3. Centered graphic

Press **F1** and select an option. (If the graphic is as wide as the space between margins, the *alignment in frame* setting will have no effect.)

8. Complete the *graphics width* field. You can accept Word's proposed width (the space between the right and left margins),
press **F1** to see alternative widths, or enter a new width.

In Figure 20-3, the graphic is 3″ wide by 1.5″ high. In Figure
20-4, the graphic is widened to 5″.

This seminar is presented by:

Future Technologies Company is dedicated to bringing the latest
in technology updates to you.

Figure 20-4. A graphic that is 5″ wide and 1.5″ high

9. In the *graphics height* field, a height proportional to the width is
the default. You can accept this height, press **F1** to select from
suggested heights, or enter a desired height.

In Figure 20-5, the width is set at 1.5″ and the height is
expanded to 3″.

This seminar is presented by:

Future Technologies Company is dedicated to bringing the latest
in technology updates to you.

Figure 20-5. A graphic that is 1.5″ wide and 3″ high

10. In the *space before* field, type in a measurement for the white space before the graphic. Notice this is in inches not lines.

11. In the *space after* field, type in the number of inches to leave after the graphic. (Don't enter the number of lines.) Figure 20-6 illustrates the graphic with 1″ as the *space before* and 2″ as the *space after*. The space appears in the document in text mode.

This seminar is presented by:

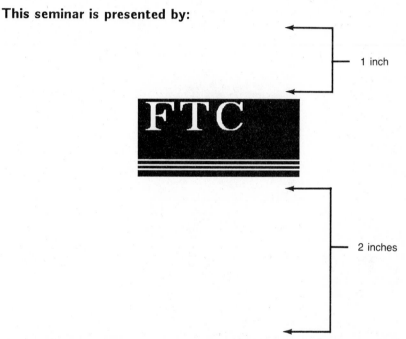

Future Technologies Company is dedicated to bringing the latest in technology updates to you.

Figure 20-6. A graphic with 1″ space before and 2″ space after

12. Press **Enter** or click the command name. The graphic is imported.

To edit a graphic, select the .G. hidden text notation. Use the Library Link Graphics command to change field values.

13. The graphic notation (.G.) is placed in the document in hidden text format to identify the position of the graphic. To see the hidden text, select **Y**es in the Options *show hidden text* field.) This is the identifying information and format for the graphic:

```
.G.drive/path/file name;width;height;file format
```

The .G. symbol is the hidden text notation indicating that the line describes a graphic. The drive, path, and file name follow. Word displays the dimensions of the graphic. Finally, a notation of the file format is in place. Figure 20-7 shows the screen appearance of the graphic paragraph in the text.

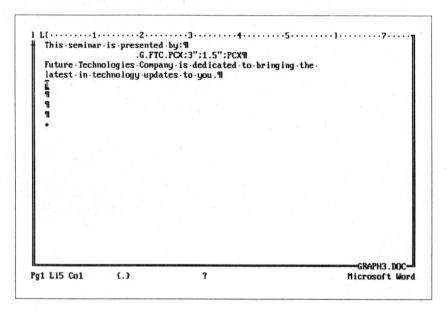

Figure 20-7. The screen appearance of a graphic paragraph

This entry will "move" with the surrounding text when it is edited. (To fix the position of a graphic on a page, see "Fixing the Frame on a Page" in this chapter.)

14. To add a border to the graphic, select **F**ormat **B**order. Complete the fields and then press **Enter**. (See "Developing Paragraph Borders" in this chapter for more information.)

    Figure 20-8 shows a border made up of background shading set at value 40 (Medium).

15. You can add a caption to the graphic in the paragraph following the paragraph marked with the graphic notation (.G.). To place the caption inside a border, press **Shift-Enter** to place a newline character at the end of the graphic notation paragraph. Then, type in the caption. Format the characters in the caption with the **F**ormat **C**haracter command.

    Figure 20-9 shows how the newline character is used to add the caption *A division of MetaDATA, Inc.*

This seminar is presented by:

Future Technologies Company is dedicated to bringing the latest in technology updates to you.

Figure 20-8. Medium background shading

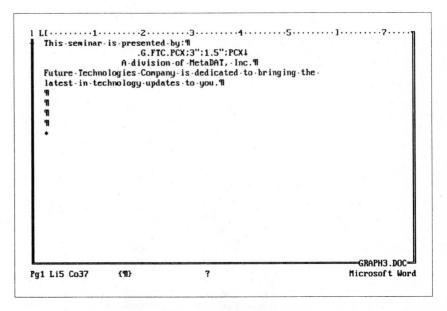

Figure 20-9. The screen appearance of a caption

16. Select **Yes** in the Options *show layout* field to see the layout of the page. You can edit while in *show layout* mode. Figure 20-10 illustrates *show layout* mode. Use **P**rint pre**V**iew to see how the page will look when it is printed. (You cannot edit from the print-preview screen.)

Figure 20-11 gives you a view of the print-preview screen. For more information about the Options *show layout* field, see Chapter 6, "Formatting Documents." See Chapter 5, "Printing Documents," for details about Print pre**V**iew.

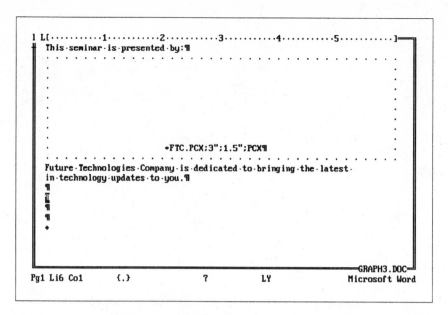

Figure 20-10. The show-layout screen

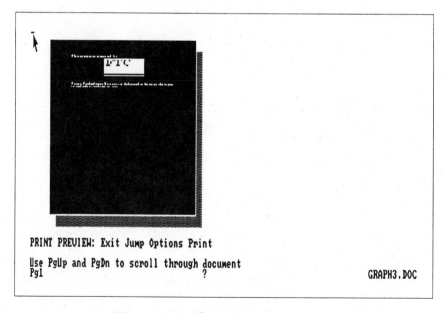

Figure 20-11. The print-preview screen

17. You can control the resolution of the graphic through the Print Options *graphic resolution* field. (For the graphic to print, make

sure to select **No** in the Print Options *draft* field. Otherwise, space will be left in place of the graphic.) Use the **Print Printer** command to print the document with graphics. Printing a page with graphics takes longer than printing the same page without.

18. If you imported a graphic through the Windows Clipboard, the document you named after importing the file is saved. Word places the file in the directory containing the *imported to* document. The file extension indicates the order in which the files were imported: .P01, .P02, and so forth.

To move a graphic, move the .G. hidden text notation for the graphic. When the text is edited, the graphic stays in the same position relative to the text and can move on the page as the text is moved. To secure a graphic to a fixed page position, use Format pOsition command. (See the next section in this chapter, "Fixing the Frame on a Page.")

Fixing the Frame on a Page

When you import a graphic, it is placed in the location of your highlight. When the document is edited, the graphic moves with the text. This approach is fine for most reports, but some documents (like newsletters) require a specific graphic position for a pleasing layout. The solution is to select Format pOsition to fix the position of the graphic on the page. As you edit the document, the text flows around the graphic. Using Format pOsition, you can also fix the position of text-only paragraphs.

Figure 20-12 shows the positioning of a text paragraph with the horizontal position set to the left relative to the margins. The vertical position is set to the top relative to the margins. The frame width is set to 3" and the distance from the text to the frame is .05".

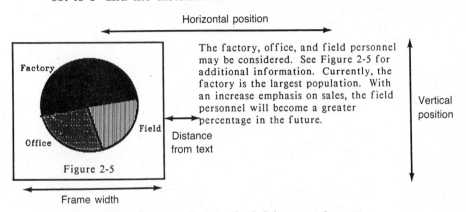

Figure 20-12. Text in the left horizontal position

In Figure 20-13, the horizontal position is set to the right.

The factory, office, and field personnel may be considered. See Figure 2-5 for additional information. Currently, the factory is the largest population. With an increase emphasis on sales, the field personnel will become a greater percentage in the future.

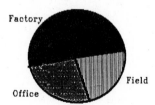

Figure 2-5

Figure 20-13. Text in the right horizontal position

Figure 20-14 shows the screen layout of the text. Notice that the graphic paragraph follows the text. The Format pOsition command determines the position on the screen. Also notice that the caption *Figure 2.5* is included in the graphic paragraph following a newline character. The graphic paragraph is centered with Format Paragraph. As more text is added to the paragraphs, the graphic stays in place relative to the margins.

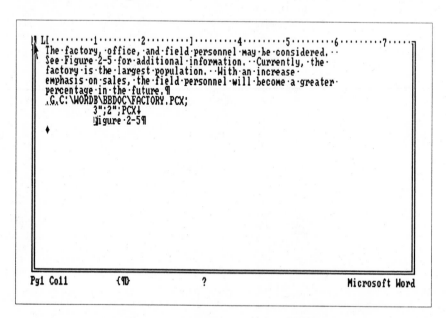

Figure 20-14. The screen layout of the text

To fix the position of one or more paragraphs follow these steps:

1. Place the highlight on the .G. notation to fix a graphic paragraph. To fix the location of one or more paragraphs, select the paragraph(s).

2. Select **F**ormat p**O**sition.

3. In the *horizontal frame position* field of the Format pOsition command, do one of the following:

   - Press **F1** and select **L**eft, **C**entered, **R**ight, **O**utside, or **I**nside to position the frame horizontally according to the setting in the adjacent *relative to* field.

     Outside or Inside are used when pages will be double sided and bound. Text is aligned on the left side of even-numbered pages and on the right side of odd-numbered pages. Outside aligns text on the outer edge of the page; Inside aligns it on the inner edge.

   - Type in a measurement to position the left edge of the frame a precise distance from the left edge of the page, the column edge, or the margin, depending on your selection in the adjacent *relative to* field.

4. In the *relative to* field, enter the edge to which the *horizontal frame position* relates:

   Column

   Margins

   Page

5. In the *vertical frame position* field, do one of the following:

   - Press **F1** and select **I**n line, **T**op, **C**entered, or **B**ottom to position the frame vertically according to the setting in the adjacent *relative to* field. If you select In line, the frame maintains its present vertical position on the page. Adding or deleting text that changes the line position changes the position of the graphic.

   - Type in a measurement to position the top edge of the frame a precise distance from from the top edge of the paper or the top margin, depending on your selection in the adjacent *relative to* field.

6. In the *relative to* field, enter the top edge to which the *vertical frame position* relates:

   Margins   from the top margin

   Page   from the top edge of the page

7. In the *frame width* field, Word displays the default width of a single column. This means that the frame will be one column wide. You can change the default in two ways:

   - Press **F1** to select a width suggested by Word.

   - Type in a measurement for the width of the frame.

   The height of the frame is automatically set based on the width.

8. In the *distance from text* field, type in the measurement for white space to be added between the frame and the text outside the frame (the default is 1/6 inch—0.167"). The space is added to any white space you may have inside the frame.

9. Press **Enter** or click the command name. If you are in the normal editing mode, the frame is formatted for the new position but remains in its original position. No special indicator appears. To see the frame in its actual position on the page, press **Shift-F4** or select **Yes** in the Options *show layout* field to switch to the show-layout mode. (To switch back to the normal editing mode, press **Shift-F4** again or select **No** in the Options *show layout* field. To see the entire printed page, including graphics, select **Print preView.**

10. To remove the Format pOsition placement, select the formatted paragraph or paragraphs and press **Alt-P** (or **Alt-X-P** if a style sheet is attached).

Because PostScript graphics are text files Word's print-preview screen does not display them. To see the frame in which the graphics will appear, use the show layout mode (Alt-F4). To see the graphics themselves, you will have to print them out.

If you want to position a graphic on every page, format the graphic in a running head. After that, use Format pOsition to place the running head in the correct position. The Format pOsition command overrides the value selected in the *running head position* field. You can also set a top and bottom running head. If you do, all heads must be in consecutive paragraphs at the start of the document or division, or before a page break.

Exercise: Importing Graphics

To complete this exercise, you will need to have a graphics file to import. You can use a file from another software program or capture an image using the CAPTURE.COM utility.

Once you have the graphics file to use, begin with a blank Word screen and type in the following information:

```
The expectation of business managers to have the "story
told with pictures" is increasing. A primary drive in this
```

trend is the popularity and cost-effectiveness of personal
computers and laser printers. Many businesses are beginning
to rely on graphics like the one shown in Figure 1.

Add the graphic as Figure 1. Place your highlight on the
line following the paragraph. Select Library Link Graphics. In the
filename field, type in the drive, path, and name of the graphic file.
In the *file format* field, type in a file format if Word has not entered
one for you. In the *alignment in frame* field, enter Centered. In the
graphics width and *graphics height* fields, type in measurements that
reflect an appropriate size and dimension for the graphic you are
using. In both the *space before* and *space after* fields, type in 0.5".
Press Enter. If you accidentally leave the Library Link Graphics menu,
you can reenter it by placing the highlight on the .G..

Add the caption for Figure 1. Place your highlight on the paragraph mark ending the graphic paragraph. Press Shift-Enter. Word
displays a newline character. Type in:

Figure 1

It is centered along with the rest of the paragraph.
Type in this text after the graphic:

Graphics like these are easily developed.

Check the appearance of the graphic. Select Options and Yes in the
show layout field. Set *show layout* back to No when you are finished
viewing the screen. Select Print preView. Press Esc and then select
Exit when you are finished viewing that screen. Figures 20-15, 20-16,
and 20-17 show sample document, show-layout, and print-preview
screen views. Make any adjustments necessary.

Select Print Options. Make sure No is selected in the *draft* field.
Other fields should be completed as usual. Use the Print Printer command to print the document. Figure 20-18 shows the sample printed
version.

Use Format pOsition to anchor the graphic to the left of the
screen and have the paragraph which follows move to the right of the
graphic. Select Library Link Graphics and then enter zero in the *space
before* and *space after* fields. Press Enter. With the highlight on the
.G., select Format pOsition. Enter these values:

horizontal frame position   Left relative to: Margins
vertical frame position   Top relative to: Margins

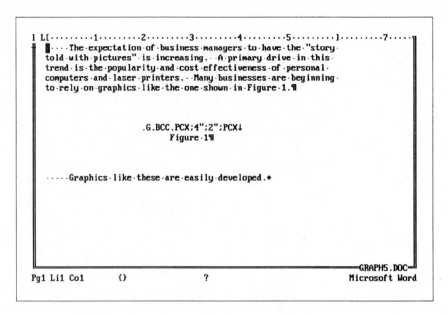

Figure 20-15. Document-screen view

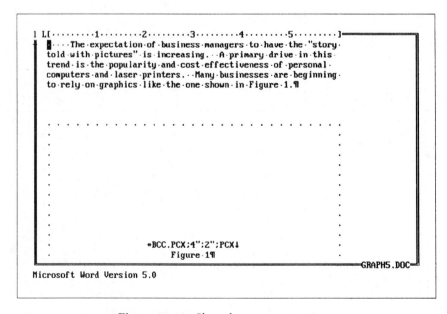

Figure 20-16. Show-layout screen view

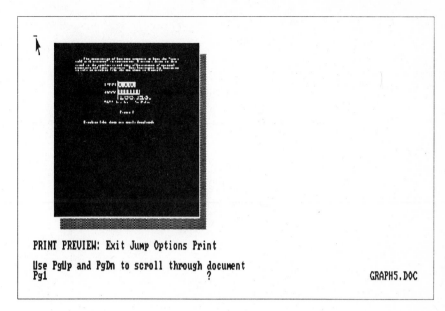

PRINT PREVIEW: Exit Jump Options Print

Use PgUp and PgDn to scroll through document
Pg1   ?   GRAPH5.DOC

Figure 20-17. Print-preview screen view

The expectation of business managers to have the "story told with pictures" is increasing. A primary drive in this trend is the popularity and cost effectiveness of personal computers and laser printers. Many businesses are beginning to rely on graphics like the one shown in Figure 1.

BCC Industries in the Future

Figure 1

Graphics like these are easily developed.

Figure 20-18. Printed version

frame width   3"

distance from text   0.5"

You can use the Options *show layout* field and Print preView to check the layout. Figures 20-19 through 20-22 show the different views.

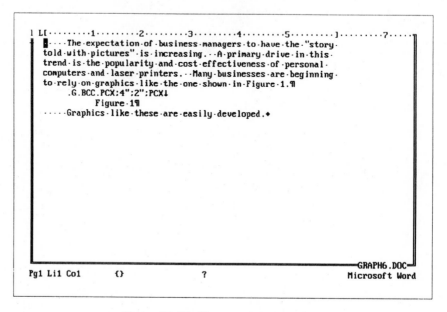

Figure 20-19. Document screen view

Save the document as GRAPHEX.

Bordering, Boxing, and Shading Paragraphs

Using the Format Border command, you can place paragraphs within borders (see Figures 20-23 and 20-24), boxes (see Figure 20-25), or (if you have a laser printer) shaded blocks with or without borders or boxes (see Figure 20-26).

With the line option, you can choose to place a line on any or all sides of a paragraph. This feature is different from line draw in that Word does the drawing for you. When you add or delete material in the paragraph, the borders automatically realign. If you change the width of the box or line, the lines are automatically redrawn.

You can elect to have borders printed in color if your printer supports color.

To add or remove borders or shading:

```
│────────────────────────────────────L[·········1·········2····]─────────
#   ·  ·  ·  ·  ·  ·  ·  ·  ·  ·  ·     █····The·expectation·of·
                                        business·managers·to·have·
                                  ·     the·"story·told·with·
                                  ·     pictures"·is·increasing.··
                                  ·     A·primary·drive·in·this·
                                  ·     trend·is·the·popularity·
                                  ·     and·cost·effectiveness·of·
                                  ·     personal·computers·and·
                                  ·     laser·printers.··Many·
                                  ·     businesses·are·beginning·
                                  ·     to·rely·on·graphics·like·
                                  ·     the·one·shown·in·Figure·
     ·  *BCC.PCX;4";2";PCX↓       ·     1.¶
             Figure·1¶            ·     ····Graphics·like·these·
        ·  ·  ·  ·  ·  ·  ·  ·  ·  ·  · are·easily·developed.◆




                                                           ┌GRAPH6.DOC┐
Microsoft Word Version 5.0
```

Figure 20-20. Show-layout screen view

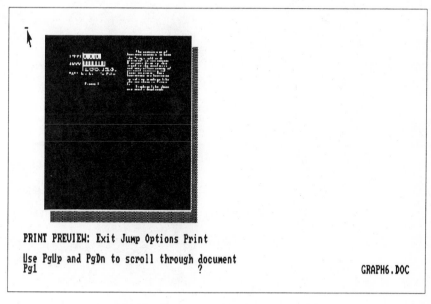

```
PRINT PREVIEW: Exit Jump Options Print

Use PgUp and PgDn to scroll through document
Pg1                                    ?                    GRAPH6.DOC
```

Figure 20-21. Print-preview screen view

BCC Industries in the Future

Figure 1

The expectation of business managers to have the "story told with pictures" is increasing. A primary drive in this trend is the popularity and cost effectiveness of personal computers and laser printers. Many businesses are beginning to rely on graphics like the one shown in Figure 1.

Graphics like these are easily developed.

Figure 20-22. Printed version

The art center CIRCLE ART show will open February 29. All members are invited to a wine and cheese party at 5 p.m.

Figure 20-23. Lines above and below a paragraph

The art center CIRCLE ART show will open February 29. All members are invited to a wine and cheese party at 5 p.m.

Figure 20-24. Lines on each side of a paragraph

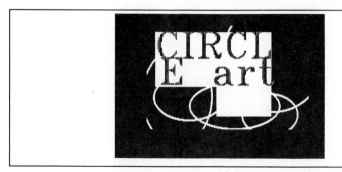

The art center CIRCLE ART show will open February 29. All members are invited to a wine and cheese party at 5 p.m.

Figure 20-25. A boxed paragraph

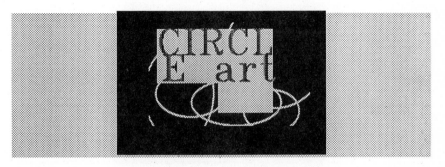

The art center CIRCLE ART show will open February 29. All members are invited to a wine and cheese party at 5 p.m.

Figure 20-26. Background shading

1. Place the highlight in the appropriate paragraph. If you select more than one paragraph, Word draws separate lines or boxes around each one.

To put several paragraphs in a single box or between lines, separate them with newline characters (press Shift-Enter) rather than paragraph marks.

2. Select **F**ormat **B**order.

3. In the *type* field, select one of the following options:

None   to remove border settings

Box   to add a box

Lines   to add lines

4. In the *line style* field, enter one of the following options (press **F1** to select from the list):

Normal   for single lines

Bold   for bold lines—wider than a single line but thinner than a thick line

Double   for double lines

Thick   for thick lines

Figure 20-27 shows normal, bold, double, and thick borders as printed on a Hewlett-Packard LaserJet Series II printer. Your printer may produce a different result.

Figure 20-27. Borders

5. Use the *color* field if you have a color printer. Press **F1** to select from a list of available colors. Otherwise, leave Black as the default.

6. Next, select **Yes** or **No** in the *left*, *right*, *above*, and *below* fields. Use these fields only if you selected **Lines** in the *type* field.

7. If you want to add shading and your printer does not support color, press **F1** in the *background shading* field to select a number representing the percentage of shading you desire (0 represents no shading, 100 is solid black). If your printer supports color, also press **F1** in the *shading color* field to select the color to be used in shading.

8. Press **Enter** or click the command name.

   Boxes or lines will show up on your screen; shading only appears when the document is printed. Bordered or shaded paragraphs that fall at page breaks will be divided between two pages unless you highlight the paragraphs and select **Yes** in the Format Paragraph *keep together* field.

9. Print the document page to see whether your printer supports the graphics used. Many printers will print single lines but not lines that are double, bold, or thick.

10. To change the width of the box or line, change the paragraph indents. The box or line is automatically redrawn to fit the new paragraph size.

11. To remove all border lines, select **None** in the *type* field of the Format Border command. To remove specific lines, edit the *left*, *right*, *above*, and *below* field entries. To get rid of shading, type in 0 in the *background shading* field. Or, delete or copy over the paragraph mark to change the settings.

12. Press **Enter** or click the command area.

To move or copy a paragraph with a box, lines, or shading, select the text in the paragraph and the paragraph mark. Don't worry about selecting the box, lines, or shading itself. The borders are moved or copied along with the paragraph mark.

Exercise: Creating Paragraph Borders

Using the GRAPHEX.DOC document, add a single line border around the graphic. Place your highlight on the paragraph and select Format Border. In the *type* field, select Box. In the line style field, select Normal. Leave the other fields in Word's defaults. Press Enter. The border appears on your screen. View the page with Print preView. Print the page with Print Printer. The result is shown in Figure 20-28.

BCC Industries in the Future

Figure 1

The expectation of business managers to have the "story told with pictures" is increasing. A primary drive in this trend is the popularity and cost effectiveness of personal computers and laser printers. Many businesses are beginning to rely on graphics like the one shown in Figure 1.

Graphics like these are easily developed.

Figure 20-28. GRAPHEX.DOC with a border

Save the GRAPHEX.DOC document.

Drawing Lines

Word's line-draw feature lets you can draw vertical or horizontal lines within paragraphs, a useful feature for creating such devices as flow charts and columnar rules.

Word uses IBM graphics characters for drawing lines. Some printers don't handle these characters. Check your printer manual.

Drawing Vertical Lines

When you draw a vertical line, you can specify where to place it, and Word will draw the line through the entire paragraph. You don't have to do any actual drawing. (For a discussion of vertical lines used with tabs and tables, see Chapter 6, "Formatting Documents.") An example of vertical lines used with a chart follows. Vertical lines are also useful between columns or as text accents.

Costs for July

Barb	Dave	Carol
76.88	34.56	23.44
34.76	321.65	23.67
12.54	23.67	45.77

To insert or remove vertical lines, using the keyboard:

1. Select **Y**es in the Options *show ruler* field to activate the ruler.
2. Select the paragraph(s) to which you want to add or from which you want to remove vertical lines.
3. Select **F**ormat **T**ab **S**et and then press **F1**, or simply press **Alt-F1**.
4. In the *alignment* field, select **V**ertical.
5. In the *position* field, press **F1** to go to the ruler line.
6. Position the highlight where you want to draw the vertical line and follow these steps:
   a. Press **V** to insert a vertical line; Word displays a vertical line (I) in the ruler line and in your text
   b. With the highlight on the vertical line symbol (I), press **Del** to delete a vertical line
7. Press **Enter** when you are finished editing vertical lines.

To add or remove vertical lines, using a mouse:

1. Display the ruler. Point to the upper-right corner of the window border and click either button.
2. Select the paragraph(s) you want to work with.
3. Point to the left of the left bracket ([) in the ruler line. Click the left mouse button to display a vertical bar.
4. Point to the position on the ruler where you want to delete or insert the vertical line symbol (I).
5. To insert the line: click the left button. To delete the line: click the right button.
6. Continue until all vertical lines are edited.

Drawing Horizontal Lines

The tab leader character can be used to create a horizontal line. Leader characters can be entered between tab stops. This example shows underlines of equal lengths created with leader characters.

Name: _____

Address: _____

Phone: _____

To enter a leader character:

1. Select **P**artial in the Options *show non-printing symbols* field. (Selecting All will hide leader characters.)
2. Select **F**ormat **T**ab **S**et.
3. Press **F1** in the *position* field. Press **L** for left tab at the start point for the leader character (or leave the left bracket as the start point). Place the highlight where you want the end point for the leader character to be and then press the underscore (**_**) **and L** for left tab. This appears in the ruler line to indicate the left end of the leader character:

   _L

4. Leader characters will appear between tabs. Enter other leader-character tab stops as appropriate.
5. Press **Enter** when all tab stops have been entered.
6. In the document, press **Tab** to move to a tab stop with the _L character.

Word displays the underline.

Drawing Lines

You can draw boxes freehand using the arrow keys and any character. Figure 20-29 shows a simple organization chart created with line draw.

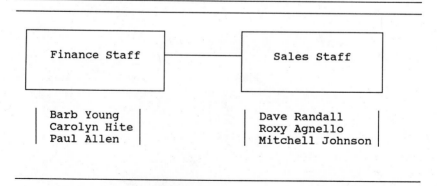

Figure 20-29. An organization chart created with line draw

1. Select the type of line draw character. Select **O**ptions. In the *linedraw character* field, press **F1** and then select a style. Or, enter a character in the field. If the character is not allowed for some reason, Word will let you know. For extended characters, hold down **Alt** and enter the number for the character on the numeric keypad. Press **Enter**. The line draw character is selected for this session of Word or until you change the character.

2. Position your highlight where you want to begin drawing. It is best to draw the lines, then type in the text after you have left line draw. Entering text then line drawing around it can be a problem when it comes to tabs, paragraph marks, and newline characters. Use the overtype, not insert, mode to avoid disturbing the lines. To overtype press **F5**.

3. To turn on line draw, press **Ctrl-F5**. The letters LD appear in the status line.

4. Use these keys to draw lines:

Arrow keys	to draw in the direction indicated on the key
Home	to draw from the highlight to the left indent of the paragraph
End	to draw from the highlight to the right
Esc	to leave line draw and go to the command menu

5. Press **Ctrl-F5** to turn off line draw if you have not already pressed Esc.

6. Delete any lines you don't want after turning off line draw. Use **Del** or **Backspace** to delete the lines.

You can format lines with Format Character and Format Paragraph commands. (If your font is smaller than 12 point, enter *auto* in the Format Paragraph *line spacing* field.) You can also use the automatic style-sheet style called Line Draw to add formatting to lines.

Exercise: Using Line Draw

In this exercise you will create the example shown earlier in Figure 20-29.

Activate the ruler by selecting Yes in the Options *show ruler* field. To create the horizontal lines, select Format Tab Set. Press F1 and place an ⌐L in the far-right position on the ruler. Press Enter. From the document, press the tab key to create a horizontal line.

Press Enter and then press Tab again to create the second line. (To see the horizontal lines, select Partial, not All, in the Options *show non-printing symbols* field.)

To create the boxes, position the highlight where you want to begin drawing. Press Ctrl-F5. The letters LD appear in the status line. Use the arrow keys to enter the boxes. Press Ctrl-F5 when you are done. To enter the text in the boxes, press F5 to overtype (OT appears in the status line). Type in the captions.

To create the name lists below the boxes, type in the names and then press Shift-Enter at the end of each line to place all the names in a single paragraph. To add the vertical lines, place the highlight in the paragraph with the names. Select Format Tab Set. Move your highlight to the appropriate position for the first vertical line and then press V. The vertical line appears. Continue until all lines are entered and then press Enter.

To enter the horizontal lines at the bottom of the page, repeat the process used for the top lines or copy the top lines to the bottom. Save the document under the name LINEEX.

Pulling It All Together: The Restaurant Flyer

This chapter has discussed a variety of procedures useful for electronic publishing. This section shows how these various features were combined to produce the restaurant flyer shown in Figure 20-30

The drawing of the chef was created using Microsoft Paintbrush and was imported into a Word document as a graphic file. A Hewlett-Packard LaserJet Series II printer with cartridge R was used to print the flyer. (All examples in this chapter were created with cartridges R and B on the Hewlett-Packard printer.)

Word's Library Link Graphics command was used to import the chef graphic. The graphic is centered and the height and width are defined with these settings:

filename	john.pcx
file format	PCX
alignment in frame	Centered
graphics width	3″
graphics height	1.779″
space before	0″
space after	0″

Figure 20-30. The restaurant flyer

Word's Format Border command was used to place a double-line border around the graphic and add the shading. These are the settings:

type	box
line style	double
background shading	10 (Light)

To create the vertical lines, the Format Tab Set command was used. Vertical tabs were entered at the appropriate increments.

The Format Character command was used to select the font name (Presentation) and font sizes (14, 16, and 18 point) for the text.

The Format Paragraph command for the graphic paragraph includes these field settings:

alignment	Center
left and right indent	1.5″

For all other paragraphs, that is, text paragraphs, these are the options selected for the Format Paragraph command fields:

alignment	Center
left indent	0"
right indent	0"

Figure 20-31 shows the actual screen appearance of the flyer. The highlight is on the .G. symbol which marks the beginning of the graphic import entry. Figure 20-32 illustrates the view selected in the Options *show layout* field. This view allows you to see the size of the graphic relative to the rest of the flyer. Figure 20-33 shows the print-preview appearance of the flyer. This view gives you a full page view of the flyer including a rough image of the graphic itself.

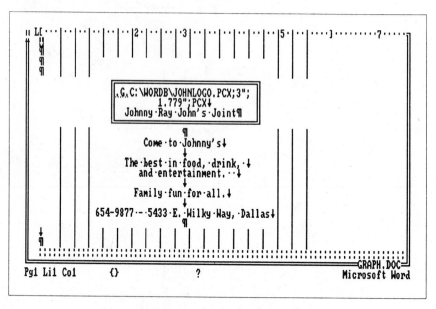

Figure 20-31. The screen appearance of the flyer

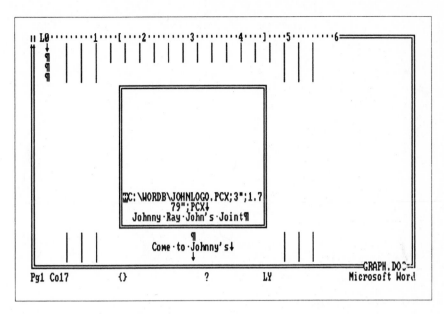

Figure 20-32. The show-layout view of the flyer

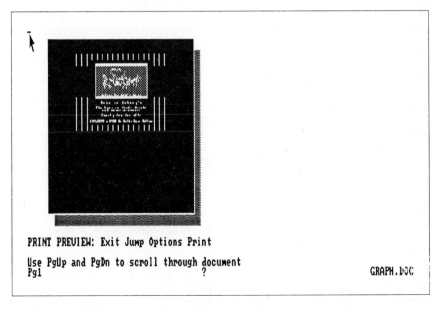

Figure 20-33. The print-preview view of the flyer

Macros

Macros are recorded keystrokes that can be replayed in any document. The beauty of macros is that you can use them to automate repetitive and frequently used functions, thereby saving time and keystrokes. Macros are more powerful than glossary entries because you can record not only text but also keystrokes, commands, and special instructions. On the other hand, glossary entries allow you to store and recall text only.

Macros have names and are stored in glossary files along with glossary entries. To use a macro, the glossary file in which the macro is stored must be active. You can check which glossary file is active by using the Transfer Glossary Save command, and you can load a different glossary file with Transfer Glossary Load.

Let's look at a simple example. Suppose you want to enter this "boilerplate" text for a contract heading (you will use Word's date glossary entry to enter the date):

```
Contracting company:
Contract type:
Contract date: July 30, 1990
```

You consider whether to create a glossary entry or a macro. If you created a glossary, you would enter the text like this:

```
Contracting company:
Contract type:
Contract date: date
```

With a glossary, you would need to press F3 after *date* to enter the date, and you would also need to position your highlight after *Contracting company:* to begin entering the text. (See Chapter 17, "Glossaries," for more information about glossary entries.)

The following macro could do this work for you:

```
Contracting company:<enter>
Contract type:<enter>
Contract date: date<f3><up 2>
```

Here is what the macro would do: In the first line, the macro enters the text *Contracting company:* and presses Enter to start a new line. On the following line, the macro enters *Contract type:* and presses Enter again to start another new line. On the final line, the macro enters *Contract date:* and then types in *date* and presses F3 to insert the date. Then the macro moves the highlight up two lines so that when the macro is finished, the highlight rests at the end of the first line.

The concept behind this contract heading also applies to memo headings, as well as letter salutations or closings.

Here is a somewhat longer macro that involves the use of Word commands to activate the ruler and set decimal tab stops at 2", 3.5", and 5":

```
<esc>O<down>y<enter>
<esc>FTS<f1><right 20>d<right 15>d<right 15>d<enter>
```

The first line of the macro activates the ruler by pressing Esc to activate the command menu, typing in O to select Options, pressing the Down Arrow key (<down>), entering *y* in the *show ruler* field, and pressing Enter to complete the command.

The second line of the macro sets the tab stops. <Esc> activates the command menu, *FTS* selects Format Tab Set and <f1> places the highlight in the ruler line. The macro then moves the highlight 20 spaces to the right and sets a decimal tab stop (*d*) in that location. Then the macro moves the highlight another 15 spaces to the right and enters another decimal tab stop. Finally, the macro moves the highlight 15 additional spaces to the right and enters the final decimal tab stop. <Enter> sets the tabs.

As you can see, macros are powerful tools that can automate time-consuming tasks. With only a little study, you can use macros to save time. As you become more familiar with macro development and use, you can build on the skill you gain at a basic level to create complex macros that take the tedium out of processing.

Merging Glossary Files

Before merging glossary files, you might weed out the entries you don't want.

Word's default glossary file is NORMAL.GLY. The macros supplied with Word are stored in a glossary file called MACRO.GLY. To have these macros available every time you start Word, you may want to merge the contents of MACRO.GLY into NORMAL.GLY. You can merge the MACRO.GLY file into NORMAL.GLY (or into any other glossary file) by following these steps:

1. The contents of MACRO.GLY will be merged into the active glossary file, so select **T**ransfer **G**lossary **S**ave to check the name of the active file. If NORMAL.GLY is active, its name appears in the *filename* field. To merge into a different glossary file, select **T**ransfer **G**lossary **L**oad, enter the drive, path, and file name of the glossary file and press **Enter**.

2. Select **T**ransfer **G**lossary **M**erge.

3. In the *filename* field, type in *MACRO.GLY* preceded if necessary by the drive and path.

4. Press **Enter**.

Word merges the contents of MACRO.GLY into the active glossary file. The merged glossary file is now available for this Word session only. To make the merge permanent, save the glossary file by selecting **T**ransfer **G**lossary **S**ave. You can save the merged glossary file under the same name or a new name. Once saved, the merged glossary file is available for future use.

Word's Macros

The following table lists the macros supplied with Word in the MACRO.GLY glossary file:

Control code	Macro name	Description
Ctrl-A C	ANNOT_COLLECT.MAC	Compiles a formatted list of annotations in a document
Ctrl-A M	ANNOT_MERGE.MAC	Merges reviewer annotations
Ctrl-A R	ANNOT_REMOVE.MAC	Removes annotations from a document

Control code	Macro name	Description
Ctrl-A A	ARCHIVE_AUTHOR.MAC	Copies files by author to the specified subdirectory
Ctrl-A K	ARCHIVE_KEYWORD.MAC	Copies files by keyword to the specified subdirectory
Ctrl-A E	AUTHORITY_ENTRY.MAC	Marks citations for a table of authorities; you highlight the citation and then select the scope from a list; the macro marks the citation for the table of authorities and prompts you to store it as glossary text
Ctrl-A T	AUTHORITY_TABLE.MAC	Generates a table of authorities from marked citations
Ctrl-B L	BULLETED_LIST.MAC	Formats paragraphs as bulleted lists and formats text within the paragraphs as 12-point Helvetica
Ctrl-C P	CHAINPRINT.MAC	Prints a list of documents and numbers pages consecutively; enters the position of the page number
Ctrl-C H	CHARACTER_TEST.MAC	Prints all characters in the selected Format Character *font name* style; use as a test for your printer
Ctrl-C S	CLEAN_SCREEN.MAC	Redraws the Word screen; use to get rid of undesirable graphics characters
Ctrl-C F	COPY_FILE.MAC	Moves a document with graphics from the document window; closes other windows
Ctrl-C T	COPY_TEXT.MAC	Copies selected text to the designated position
Ctrl-D L	DCA_LOAD.MAC	Converts a DCA-RTF document to Word format and

Control code	Macro name	Description
		loads it into Word; prompts for the source-document name; gives the Word document the same name with the .MSW extension
Ctrl-D S	DCA_SAVE.MAC	Converts the current Word document to a DCA-RTF document with the .RTF extension
Ctrl-E N	ENVELOPE.MAC	Prints selected addresses on envelopes; prompts for dimensions
Ctrl-F N	FILENAME.MAC	Places the name of the current document at the highlight position
Ctrl-F S	FREEZE_STYLE.MAC	Converts formatting that has been applied with styles into direct formatting; use to retain formatting with conversion utilities
Ctrl-I W	INDEX.MAC	Places index codes around words in the document based on a list of words in a separate file
Ctrl-I E	INDEX_ENTRY.MAC	Adds hidden index codes at the beginning and end of selected text
Ctrl-M L	MAILING_LABEL.MAC	Prints labels in one, two, or three columns after prompting for the name of the file containing addresses
Ctrl-M H	MEMO_HEADER.MAC	Creates a traditional memo header with *From*, *To*, and *Subject* fields; prompts you to fill in the fields
Ctrl-M T	MOVE_TEXT.MAC	Moves selected text to the designated destination

Control code	Macro name	Description
Ctrl-J N	NEXT_PAGE.MAC	Places the highlight at the beginning of the next page after printing or after Print Repaginate has been used
Ctrl-P L	PRINT_LETTER.MAC	Prints the first page of a document with margins different from the other pages; prompts for margins
Ctrl-J P	PREV_PAGE.MAC	Places the highlight at the beginning of the previous page after printing or after Print Repaginate has been used
Ctrl-R P	REPL_W_GLOSS.MAC	Replaces the specified search text with the specified glossary entry
Ctrl-R P	REPL_W_SCRAP.MAC	Replaces the specified search text with the scrap contents
Ctrl-S S	SAVE_SELECTION.MAC	Saves the selected text to the named file
Ctrl-S B	SIDEBYSIDE.MAC	Prompts for the number of paragraphs to place side by side, the space between them, and their alignment
Ctrl-S L	STOP_LAST_FOOTER.MAC	Use with the nextpage glossary entry to prevent printing of the footer on the last page of the document
Ctrl-T T	TABLE.MAC	Sets tabs for tables; prompts for the first tab position and the space between them
Ctrl-T 1	TABS.MAC	Sets tabs; prompts for the position of the tabs and their alignment
Ctrl-T 2	TABS2.MAC	Sets tabs; prompts for the number of columns in a

Control code	Macro name	Description
		table, the first column position, and column alignment
Ctrl-T 3	TABS3.MAC	Sets tabs; prompts for the number of columns in a table, the alignment on the page, the width and alignment of each column
Ctrl-T E	TOC_ENTRY.MAC	Adds hidden codes for creating a table of contents to selected text
Ctrl-D D	3_DELETE.MAC	Deletes selected text to a glossary entry; saves up to three deletions in one glossary entry
Ctrl-U U	3_UNDELETE.MAC	Recovers up to three previous deletions; use with 3_DELETE.MAC

Notice that a "control code" is listed for each macro. The control code is the keystrokes you use to execute the macro. You can also use the macro name to run a macro.

You can use the macro-editing feature to view the macros supplied with Word (see "Editing Macros" later in this chapter). Studying working macros is a good way to get ideas for setting up your own macros. You can also edit Word-supplied macros to customize them for your own use. Give the edited macro a new name and control code so that you will still have access to the original macro.

Using Macros

There are three ways to run a macro. You can select the macro from a list, enter the macro's name, or use the control code for the macro.

To select the macro from a list, follow these steps:

1. Save your document with **T**ransfer **S**ave. That way, if the macro does not perform as expected, you will be able to return to your original document with no harm done.

2. Place the highlight in the position where you want to execute the macro.

3. Select **Insert**.

4. In the *from* field, press **F1** and then select the macro from the list. Press **Enter**.

The macro executes in the location specified.

To run a macro by entering the macro name, follow these steps:

1. Save your document with **Transfer Save**.

2. Place the highlight in the position where you want to execute the macro and then type in the name.

3. Press **F3**.

The macro name is deleted and the macro runs.

To run a macro with the control code, follow these steps:

You can stop a macro from running by pressing Esc. Word asks whether you want to continue. In response to the message, press Y to restart the macro or press Esc to stop execution of the macro.

1. Save your document with **Transfer Save**.

2. Position your highlight in the location you want the macro to execute.

3. Press the macro control-code keys. Word-supplied macros have control codes that include three keys to press. For example, if you want to run SIDEBYSIDE.MAC (control code: Ctrl-S L), hold down **Ctrl** and press **S**. Then release both keys and press **L**.

The macro executes at the position of the highlight.

Developing Macros

You can create a macro by recording actions as you perform them, or you can type in keystroke symbols. You can use macros to store keyboard actions but not mouse actions.

Recording Macros

You can create a macro by recording a series of actions you perform in any Word document.

Always save the document before recording the actions in case the macro doesn't record or perform as expected. Also, make sure you are familiar with the keystrokes you will use to create the macro. If you need to, run through the keystrokes before recording them and jot down notes.

To record actions as you perform them, follow these steps:

1. Save your document with **T**ransfer **S**ave.

2. Place your highlight in the position where you want to start recording keystrokes.

3. Press **Shift-F3**. Word displays RM for *Record Macro* in the status line. Any keystrokes you enter from now on will be part of the macro.

4. Perform the actions you want to record. You can select commands, move the highlight, and select characters. Make sure you enter any desired formatting.

Do not use Transfer Glossary Clear or Transfer Clear All in a macro because either of these commands will clear the macro from the glossary.

5. When you have completed the actions you want to record, press **Shift-F3** to stop recording. RM disappears from the status line, and the Copy submenu is displayed in the command area.

6. Type in a unique macro name including a control code if you want. The name and control-code string can be up to 31 characters long. You can use letters, numbers, underscores, hyphens, and periods in macro names. Do not use spaces. It is recommended that you use MAC somewhere in the name to differentiate the macro from glossary entries in the glossary file. For example, these names clearly identify the glossary-file entry as a macro:

> LABEL_MAC
>
> LABEL.MAC
>
> MACLABEL

7. To add a control code after the macro name, type in a caret (ˆ) and enter the keystrokes for the control code. For example, if you have entered LABEL_MAC as the macro name, typing a caret and then holding down **Ctrl** and pressing **L** produces the following entry (Word adds the brackets):

`LABEL_MACˆ<ctrl l>`

8. Press **Enter** to store the macro in the current glossary. If you entered a macro name that already exists, Word displays this warning message:

Note: If you prefer, you can type in the control code—including the brackets, Ctrl, and the desired characters—after the caret (ˆ) symbol.

`Enter Y to replace glossary, N to retype name, or Esc to cancel`

Press **Y** to replace the macro in the glossary with the new contents, press **N** to enter a new name, or press **Esc** to start the process again.

If you enter a unique macro name and a macro code that is already used, Word displays this message:

```
Macro code already defined. Enter new code
```

Because the name is different, Word assumes you want a different code as well. Type in a different macro code and press **Enter**.

Be sure to save the glossary file before leaving Word. To permanently store the macro in the glossary file, select Transfer Glossary Save. Make sure the proper glossary file name is entered and then press Enter.

Testing Macros

To check the macro performance, you can run the macro in regular mode and check the result, or you can run it in step mode and observe the effects of each keystroke.

To run the macro in regular mode:

1. Position the highlight where you want the macro to run.
2. Run the macro using one of these methods:
    - Press the control code.
    - Type in the name and then press **F3**.
    - Select Insert, press **F1** to select the macro from a list, and then press **Enter**.

To run the macro in step mode:

1. Position the highlight where you want the macro to run.
2. Press **Ctrl-F3** to turn on step mode. Word displays ST in the status line.
3. Run the macro using any of the methods you would use in regular mode.

    Word carries out the first keystroke and waits for you to press a key to indicate you want the program to move on to the next keystroke.

4. Press a key to have Word carry out the next step. When the macro is finished, Word displays this message:

```
End of macro
```

5. Press **Ctrl-F3** to turn off step mode.

You can press Esc at any time to stop execution of a macro. If the macro doesn't perform as expected, you can record it again or you can edit it (see "Editing Macros" later in this chapter).

Writing Macros

Writing macros is usually more difficult than recording them. When you record a macro, you perform the steps while Word records them, and because you are working in context, it is usually easier to recall the next step to take. When you write a macro, you must be aware of the order of the keystrokes necessary to complete an action without being able to "work through" the task.

The primary reason for writing a macro instead of recording it is so that you can include special macro instructions. For example, when you write a macro, you can include conditional instructions such as IF-ELSE statements (see "Creating Intelligent Macros," later in this chapter).

Keynames

When writing macro instructions, you use symbols called keynames to represent every keystroke in the macro. You can enter keynames with any combination of capital or small letters. Keynames must, however, be enclosed in angle brackets (< >). This table shows the valid keynames to use when writing a macro:

Keyname	Meaning
Starting the macro:	
<ctrl esc>	Starts the macro from the main command menu if you are in the command area; starts the macro from the Gallery command menu if you are in the Gallery when the macro begins running
<ctrl esc><esc>	Starts the macro from the document window if you are in the document; starts the macro from the Gallery window if you are in Gallery when the macro begins running
<shift ctrl esc>	Starts the macro from the main command menu regardless of where you are when the macro begins running

Keyname	Meaning
<shift ctrl esc><esc>	Starts the macro from the document window regardless of where you are when the macro begins running
Specific keystrokes:	
<alt *x*>	Alt followed by any key (substitute the specific key for *x*)
<backspace>	Backspace; use <backspace *n*> where *n* is the number of times to press the Backspace key
<capslock>	Toggles Caps Lock on or off (depending on its current state)
<ctrl *x*>	Ctrl followed by any key (substitute the specific key for *x*)
<del>	Delete; use <del *n*> where *n* is the number of times to press the Del key
<down>	Down Arrow; use <down n> to move the highlight down *n* times (substitute the specific number for *n*)
<end>	End
<enter>	Enter; use <enter *n*> to indicate the number of times to press the Enter key
<esc>	Esc; use <esc *n*> to indicate the number of times to press the Esc key
<home>	Home
<ins>	Ins; use <ins *n*> to indicate the number of times to press the Ins key
<keypad*>	Asterisk on the numeric keypad
<keypad + >	Plus on the numeric keypad
<keypad->	Minus on the numeric keypad
<left>	Left Arrow; use <left *n*> to move the highlight left *n* times (substitute the specific number for *n*)
<numlock>	Toggles Num Lock on or off (depending on its current state)
<pgdn>	Pgdn; use <pgdn *n*> to move the page down *n* times (substitute the specific number for *n*)
<pgup>	Pgup; use <pgup *n*> to move the page up *n* times (substitute the specific number for *n*)

Keyname	Meaning
\<right\>	Right Arrow; use \<right *n*\> to move the highlight right *n* times (substitute the specific number for *n*)
\<scrolllock\>	Toggles Scroll Lock on or off (depending on its current state)
\<shift *x*\>	Shift followed by any key (substitute the specific key for *x*)
\<space\>	Moves from command to command in a command menu or from option to option in a command field
\<tab\>	Tab; use \<tab *n*\> to tab the number of times indicated by *n*
\<up\>	Up Arrow; use \<up *n*\> to move the highlight up *n* times (substitute the specific number for *n*)
Function keys:	
\<f1\>	Moves to next window
\<shift f1\>	Undoes the previous window
\<ctrl f1\>	Zooms the active window
\<alt f1\>	Sets a tab
\<f2\>	Performs a calculation
\<shift f2\>	Switches to outline view
\<ctrl f2\>	Formats a header
\<alt f2\>	Formats a footer
\<f3\>	Replaces a glossary name with its glossary entry
\<shift f3\>	Records a macro
\<ctrl f3\>	Turns on macro step mode
\<alt f3\>	Copies to the scrap
\<f4\>	Repeats the last edit action
\<shift f4\>	Repeats a search
\<ctrl f4\>	Recompiles a list if in document-retrieval mode or toggles between upper and lowercase if in edit mode
\<alt f4\>	Turns on show-layout mode
\<f5\>	Turns on overtype mode
\<shift f5\>	Switches between outline edit and outline

Keyname	Meaning
	organize (outline view must be turned on first)
<ctrl f5>	Toggles line draw on or off
<alt f5>	Selects the Jump Page command
<f6>	Toggles extend select on or off
<shift f6>	Toggles column select on or off
<ctrl f6>	Activates the Thesaurus program
<alt f6>	Activates the Spell program
<f7>	Selects the word to the left
<shift f7>	Selects the previous sentence
<ctrl f7>	Selects the Transfer Load command
<alt f7>	Toggles the Options *show line breaks* field on or off
<f8>	Selects the word to the right
<shift f8>	Selects the next sentence
<ctrl f8>	Prints
<alt f8>	Selects the Format Character command with the *font name* field selected
<f9>	Selects the previous paragraph
<shift f9>	Selects the current line
<ctrl f9>	Activates print-preview mode
<alt f9>	Switches the display mode between the previous two display modes
<f10>	Selects the next paragraph
<shift f10>	Selects the complete document
<ctrl f10>	Selects the Transfer Save command
<alt f10>	Records the current formatting as a style
<f11>	Collapses headings
<shift f11>	Collapses body text
<f12>	Expands headings
<shift f12>	Expands body text
<ctrl f12>	Expands the whole outline

Writing a Macro Step by Step

To write a macro, follow these steps:

1. Identify the tasks you want the macro to perform. If the macro is complex, try out the macro tasks in a document and jot down the keystrokes necessary to accomplish them.

2. Load a document and place the highlight where you want to execute the macro. You can create a new document specifically for storing the macro text.

3. Enter the macro instructions just as you would enter any other text. Enclose the keynames in angle brackets. For example:

   <enter>

   You can repeat keys by entering a number after the keyname. The following entry indicates that the <enter> key should be pressed twice:

   <enter 2>

   Unless the symbol is in a text string, you can enter angle brackets (< >) or chevrons (« ») and they will print as brackets or chevrons, instead of indicating a keyname or an instruction. Just place a caret (^) before the symbol. For example, this entry will cause the left-angle bracket to print:

   ^<

You can press Enter at any point in the macro to improve readability. You might, for example, want to put each discrete action on a line by itself. The Enter keystroke is not included when you run the macro.

4. Once you have entered the macro instructions, select the entire macro text.

5. Select **C**opy to store the macro in the glossary file and leave the instructions in the document. Or, select **D**elete to store the macro and delete the instructions from the document. (Use the Delete command, not the Del key.)

6. In the *to* field, enter a name for the macro. The name can be up to 31 characters long and can include a control code. You can use letters, numbers, underscores, hyphens, and periods in the name. If you use a control code, it must be preceded by a caret (^). For example, if you have named your macro REMOVE_ LINES.MAC and you want to assign the control code **Ctrl-R** and then **L**, this is what you would enter in the Copy or Delete command's *to* field:

   REMOVE_LINES.MAC^<ctrl r>l

   Using the MAC extension in the name allows you to easily distinguish between a macro and a glossary entry.

If you enter a macro name or control code that is already used in the glossary file, Word asks whether you want to "write over" the macro that exists or to change the name or control code to one that is not in use.

7. Press **Enter** to store the macro in the current glossary file.

8. Test the macro by running it in regular mode or in step mode as described in "Testing Macros," earlier in this chapter. If the macro does not execute as you expect, edit the macro instructions (see "Editing Macros," later in this chapter).

To permanently save the macro, you need to save the glossary file before quitting Word. Select Transfer Glossary Save. Enter the glossary file name, if necessary, and press Enter.

Troubleshooting

When you first test a macro you may see a message like this:

```
Unknown key; macro aborted after text
```

This message indicates that a keyname, instruction, date, or use is invalid. Check the accuracy of the macro instruction and the formatting of brackets at the point where the execution failed.

If you hear a beep while the macro is executing, the data you have entered into a command field may be invalid. The macro will continue running, but it may not perform as you expect. To stop the macro, press Esc and respond to Word's prompt. Then check the macro instructions for errors.

If Word displays this message:

```
Macro too large
```

the macro exceeds the size limits imposed by Word. Macros should be less than 32 KB. If your macro has more than 80 characters in a line and more than 400 lines, it will probably be too large to run.

Editing Macros

Macros can be edited just like regular text. The text of any macro can be inserted into a document, changed, and copied or deleted to the glossary. If you copy or save the macro to the glossary under its "old" name, Word replaces the old macro with the new, edited version. If you copy or save the macro under a new name, Word preserves the old macro and creates a new one. Sometimes, the fastest way to create a new macro is to start with an existing macro that is similar to the one you want, edit that macro, and save it under a new name.

To edit an existing macro, follow these steps:

1. Position your highlight in a convenient location for editing the macro.

2. Insert the macro text into the document using one of these methods:
   - Select **Insert** and type in the macro name followed by a caret (^). Press **Enter**.
   - Select **Insert** and then press **F1**. Select the macro name from the displayed list and enter a caret (^). Press **Enter**.
   - Type in the macro name followed by a caret (^) and then press **F3**.

3. Edit the macro.

4. When you have finished editing, select the macro text.

5. Select **C**opy or **D**elete. (Do not press the Del key.)

6. In the *to* field, type in the name of the macro with the control code, if desired. Enter the same name and control code if you want to replace the contents of the old macro. Enter a new name and control code if you want to create a new macro.

7. Press **Enter**.

8. If you used the same name, press **Y** at the prompt to overwrite the earlier macro version.

Word creates the macro under the name specified.

Exercise: Creating Macros

The first macro you will create formats headings. Enter the following heading in a blank Word document and then press Enter:

```
Sample Heading 1
```

Place your highlight anywhere in the heading and then press Shift-F3 to start recording a macro. Word displays RM in the status line. Now all the keystrokes you enter will be recorded in the macro.

Press Home to move to the first character of the heading. Press F6 and then press End to select the heading. To enter the formatting, press Esc and then select Format Character. In the *bold* field, select Yes. Press the Down Arrow key and then the Left Arrow key to move the highlight to the *uppercase* field. Select Yes and then press Enter.

Press Shift-F3 to turn off macro recording. In the Copy command's *to* field, enter this macro name (don't press Enter yet):

`HEADBOLDCAP.MAC`

Enter a caret (^), press Ctrl-H, and then press C. Press Enter. The sample heading is formatted as bold and uppercase text.

To test the macro, enter the following heading and then press Enter:

`Sample Heading 2`

Place your highlight anywhere in the heading. Run the macro by pressing Ctrl-H and then C. The heading is formatted with bold uppercase letters. If you get a different result, reenter the macro and assign the same name so that the new version replaces the old.

Next, edit the macro to create a second macro that formats with bold text only. To insert a copy of the macro text in the document, place your highlight at the end of the document, type in the name of the macro followed by a caret (^), and press F3. The following macro text is displayed:

`<home><f6><down><left><esc>FCy<down><right>y<enter>`

To remove the uppercase formatting, delete these entries:

`<down><right>y`

Now, select the remaining macro contents:

`<home><f6><down><left><esc>FCy<enter>`

Press Esc and then Copy. Enter the following macro name and control code:

`HEADBOLD.MAC^<ctrl h>b`

Finally, save the document as MACROTEST.DOC.

To test the result, type in the following heading and press Enter:

`Sample Heading 3`

Place the highlight anywhere in the heading, press Ctrl-H, and then press B. The heading is formatted as bold text. If your result is different, correct the macro by following the steps described above. In the

Copy command's *to* field, enter the same macro name and control code.

You will create the next macro by writing the macro and copying it to the glossary file. This macro automates the opening of a blank, horizontal window at line 12. At the bottom of your document, type in these instructions:

```
<esc>WSH12<right>y<enter>
```

Select the text, press Esc, and then select Copy. In the Copy command's *to* field, enter this macro name and control code:

```
WINDOWH.MAC^<ctrl w>h
```

Press Enter and save the document.

To test the macro with the step mode, press Ctrl-F3. Word displays ST on the status line. Press Ctrl-W and H. Then press any key to begin execution of the macro and continue pressing a key after each step until the horizontal window is created and you see this message:

```
End of macro
```

Turn off step mode by pressing Ctrl-F3. Close the window by using the Window Close command.

Though you have created three macros, they are not saved in the glossary file until the file itself is saved. To save the glossary information in the current glossary file, select Transfer Glossary Save and then press Enter.

Save the MACROTEST.DOC document and then clear the document screen with Transfer Clear Window.

Nesting Macros

You can create macros that execute other macros. The second macro is said to be *nested* within the first. You can even nest a macro within a nested macro. In fact, you can use up to 16 levels of nested macros.

You use one of three macro instructions to have one macro excute another. Suppose the macro you are writing needs to execute a macro called MACRONAME.MAC that has the control-code Ctrl-M. Here are the three methods of accomplishing this task:

- Use the Insert command. Include this statement in your macro:

```
<ctrl esc>IMACRONAME.MAC<enter>
```

- Enter the name of the macro to be executed and press F3. Include this statement in your macro:

```
MACRONAME.MAC<f3>
```

- Enter the control code of the macro to be executed. Include this statement in your macro:

```
<ctrl m>
```

Exercise: Nesting Macros

Give it a shot. In this macro, you will:

- Create a macro that sets decimal tab stops (the one shown at the beginning of the chapter)
- Enter a table heading
- Nest the decimal-tab macro
- Enter column headings

First you will create a macro that activates the ruler and sets decimal tab stops at 2″, 3.5″, and 5″. Enter these macro lines in a blank Word window:

```
<esc>0<down>y<enter>
<esc>FTS<f1><right 20>d<right 15>d<right 15>d<enter>
```

Select the macro lines. Press Esc and then select Copy. Enter the following macro name and control code and then press Enter:

```
DECTAB.MAC^<ctrl d>t
```

Now enter the following macro lines. Make sure to include the I (for Insert) in the second line to insert the macro just created:

```
Sales by Salesperson<enter>
<ctrl esc>IDECTAB.MAC<enter>
<tab>Jan.1989<tab>Feb.1989<tab>Mar.1989<enter>
```

Select the macro lines. Select Copy. Enter the following macro name and control code and then press Enter:

```
SALESPERSON.MAC^<ctrl s>p
```

Save the macro document as SALESPMAC.DOC and then test the macro by running it. If the macro is not correct, edit it. When the macro works perfectly, use Transfer Glossary Save to save it in the active glossary file. Save the SALESPMAC.DOC document as well, if necessary. Use Transfer Clear Window to clear the window.

Creating "Intelligent" Macros

With macro instructions you can add intelligence to your macros. These "intelligent" macros can accept input from the keyboard, evaluate two tasks for the appropriate steps to take, pause, quit, repeat keystrokes, use reserved variables, and display messages.

The following macro illustrates a simple example of the decision-making capabilities you can build into Word macros:

```
<esc>S.begin table c.<enter>
«IF found»<esc>LTC<enter>y
«ENDIF»
```

This particular macro searches for an existing table of contents and updates it.

<Esc> activates the command menu and S selects the Search command. The text to find is *.begin table c.*, which indicates the beginning of an existing table of contents. <Enter> begins the search.

The second line is an IF decision-making instruction. If the text is found, the macro updates the table using the Library Table Codes command. «ENDIF» ends the IF instruction.

This macro uses the IF and ENDIF instruction keywords. Notice that they are enclosed by chevrons (« »). Here, they are typed in capital letters for readability. Also notice that the macro uses one of Word's reserved variables, *found*, to identify the result of the search.

Without the IF and ENDIF instructions and the reserved variable, two macros and human intervention would have been required to perform the task this single macro performs. The first macro would search out the table of contents. Then, if the macro found the table, you would need to run a second macro to update the table. With the IF and ENDIF instructions and reserved variable, no intervention on your part is necessary.

Macro instructions are always surrounded by chevrons (« »). To enter a chevron, press Ctrl-[and Ctrl-]. Do not use double less-than (<<) or greater-than (>>) symbols.

Variables

A variable is a name assigned as a placeholder for a value that can change. Sometimes, the value stays the same while the macro is running but can vary from one macro run to the next, and sometimes the value changes during the actual processing of the macro. For example, this instruction sets the variable called *milemoney* equal to 21 cents and the value will be 21 cents until the variable is changed.

«SET milemoney = .21»

You can create tables of related variables (arrays) for use in any or all your macros. See the Microsoft Word manual for more information on how to use this advanced function.

On the other hand, this instruction increments the value of *milemoney* by 1 every time the macro executes the instruction:

«SET milemoney = milemoney + 1»

You can assign any name you want to a variable. Under some circumstances, though, you will want to make use of Word's reserved variables, which are discussed in more detail later in the chapter.

Macro Keywords

Macro instructions can include the keywords shown in the following table. In addition to keywords, this table shows the following:

- The use of each keyword
- The way the keyword is used in an instruction (the way the keyword is used is called the *syntax*)
- An example (with sample operators identifying the action to take)

Notice that in the examples:

- Text is enclosed in double quotation marks (unless it is a prompt to be used with the ASK or SET keyword) and may include:

  ^w   for white space
  ^s   for nonbreaking space
  ^t   for tab character
  ^p   for paragraph mark
  ^n   for newline character

^-   for optional hyphen

^d   for division mark

?   for any character

- Numbers can include mathematical operators.
- Dates can be entered as mm/dd/yy or mm/dd/yyyy with a slash, hyphen, or period between the month, day, and year.

Keyword	Purpose	Syntax	Example
ASK	Stops the macro for a moment and prompts the user to enter a response. The response is used as the value of the variable in the instruction. It can be text, a number, or a date. If you don't specify a prompt when using the ASK statement, Word displays this prompt: *Enter text, press Enter when done.*	«ASK *variable*=?*prompt*»	«ASK name=?Enter your name and press Enter»
COMMENT. . . ENDCOMMENT	Encloses comments embedded in the macro without affecting how it runs.	«COMMENT text» or «COMMENT» text «ENDCOMMENT»	«COMMENT Age is calculated by the years of service.»
IF. . . ELSE. . . ENDIF	Adds a conditional statement to the macro. If the following IF condition is true, a specified action is taken. If this condition is not true, no action is taken unless the statement includes an optional ELSE component, in which case the action following ELSE is taken.	«IF *condition 1*» *do this* «ENDIF» or «IF *condition 1*» *do this* «ELSE» *do this* «ENDIF»	«IF age < 18» "You're at home." «ELSE» "You're on your own." «ENDIF»
MESSAGE	Displays a specified message when the macro processes to that point.	«MESSAGE *text*»	«MESSAGE "Wait while the work is saved."»
PAUSE	Stops the macro to allow you to perform Word operations. You can include a prompt of up to 80 characters with the pause. Press Enter to continue the execution of the macro.	«PAUSE» or «PAUSE *prompt*»	«PAUSE "Select the text to copy and press Enter."»

Keyword	Purpose	Syntax	Example
QUIT	Stops the macro. Often used with an IF or WHILE statement to stop the macro when a given condition is not true.	《QUIT》	《IF 45 < age》《QUIT》
REPEAT... ENDREPEAT	Repeats all the macro instructions enclosed within the REPEAT and ENDREPEAT statements. These macro instructions are repeated as many times as indicated in the REPEAT statement.	《REPEAT n》 statements to repeat 《ENDREPEAT》	《REPEAT 3》 "Materials are complete." <home><f6> <end><esc>c<enter> <own><esc>I<enter> 《ENDREPEAT》
SET	Assigns a value to a specific variable. That value can be a constant, an expression, or another variable. It can also be decreased or increased by a certain amount, or entered by you.	《SET variable = expression》 or 《SET variable = ?》 or 《SET variable = ?prompt》	《SET score = oldscore + 1》
WHILE... ENDWHILE	Carries out the macro instructions between WHILE and ENDWHILE if a specific condition is true. If the condition is not true, the instructions aren't carried out.	《WHILE condition》 task 《ENDWHILE》	《WHILE months < 5》 《SET day = day + 1》 《SET months = months − 1》 《ENDWHILE》

Macro Operators

As shown in the examples for the keywords, macros can include operators. Valid operators are:

Operator	Meaning
=	Equal to
<>	Not equal to
<	Less than
<=	Less than or equal to
>	Greater than
>=	Greater than or equal to
*	Multiply

/	Divide
+	Add
−	Subtract
AND	Both parts of the statement must be true
OR	One part of the statement may be true
NOT	Not the value
( )	Multiply; also specifies the order in which other operators should be evaluated, as in 6(4 + 9) − 9

Word's Reserved Variables

Word assigns specific uses to several variables. Including instructions that use these reserved variables can add an extra dimension of power to your macros.

Activewindow

You can use the *activewindow* reserved variable with the SET keyword to set the active window to the value of the current window. This is the syntax:

`«SET activewindow = window#»`

Selection

The *selection* reserved variable has the value of the current selection, whether it is text, numbers, or a date. If the *selection* variable has no value, the document's diamond-shaped end mark is currently selected. In the following example, if the selected text is *Downer Company*, the macro will continue execution:

`«IF selection = "Downer Company"»`

Scrap

You can use the *scrap* reserved variable to refer to text, numbers, or a date that is currently in the scrap area. For example, after a mathematical calculation, if the scrap contains the value 8, a macro containing this statement will continue execution:

`«IF scrap = 8»`

Field

The *field* reserved variable is assigned the value in the active command field. The value in the command field can be text, numbers, or a date. In the following example, assume you have moved to a field in a command menu. If the field is set to Yes, the macro continues processing:

```
«IF field = "Yes"»
```

Found and Notfound

The *found* and *notfound* reserved variables are used with IF instructions to identify the result of a search. If Word found the search text, the value of *found* is true and the value of *notfound* is false. If Word did not find the search text, the value of *found* is false and the value of *notfound* is true. After a search, you can use this statement:

```
«IF found»
```

and then identify what you want Word to do if the search text is found. Notice that you don't need to say:

```
«IF found = true»
```

The = *true* part of the statement is assumed.

Save

You use the *save* reserved variable to carry out an action if the *Save* message begins to flash in the status line. For example, you could have a macro select the Transfer Allsave command if the *save* variable is true. You might want to include the following instruction in any macro that uses a good deal of memory, such as autosorting or replacing, or any activity that requires Word to manipulate a lot of information:

```
«IF save»<esc>TA«ENDIF»
```

Window

You can use *window* to activate a specific window. This instruction makes window 1 the active window:

```
«SET window = 1»
```

The next instruction checks to see whether window 1 is the active window (that is, whether *window* has the value 1):

«IF window = 1»

If window 1 is the active window, the remainder of the statement is executed.

Echo

The *echo* reserved variable determines whether the screen display is active during macro execution. Setting *echo* to off makes macros run faster but no macro activity is displayed on the screen. Setting *echo* to on displays macro activity on screen. Here are two examples:

«SET echo = "off"»
«IF echo = "on"»

Promptmode

The *promptmode* reserved variable stores the origin of a response to a Word prompt. The value of *promptmode* can be:

user
macro
ignore

For example, when you have been working on an active document with unsaved changes and you select Quit, Word displays this prompt:

Enter Y to save changes to document, N to lose changes, or Esc to cancel

If you select Quit from within a macro, Word displays the same prompt. There are three ways to respond to the prompt:

- The macro can respond (you will need to include Q for Quit and Y for Yes as part of the macro).
- The macro can ignore the prompt (the document is not saved when Word quits).

If you decide that you want the user to respond to the prompt, you will need to include this instruction to set *promptmode* for user input in your macro:

```
«SET promptmode = "user"»
```

Wordversion

The *wordversion* reserved variable stores the Word version number. For example, you might want your macro to carry out certain instructions based on identification of a certain version number, as in the following example:

```
«IF wordversion = 5.0»
```

Math and String Functions

Word macros have the capability of manipulating numbers and strings of characters. The following table lists Word's math and string functions:

Function	Purpose	Syntax	Example
INT	Truncates the number resulting from the expression to the next smallest integer	INT(*expression*)	INT(5 / 3) The five-decimal-point result of 5 divided by 3 is 1.66667 which Word will round off to 2.
LEN	Identifies the number of characters in a string of characters	LEN(*expression*)	
MID	Identifies the value of a segment of a character string. Identifies the character where the segment starts as well as the segment length. The syntax includes the *variable* (it can be the string name which can be a variable or a constant), *x* (the start), and *y* (the length)	MID(*variable,x,y*)	SET initial = MID(name,1,1)

You can also join (concatenate) multiple strings together with the SET keyword. When combined, the strings must be 255 characters or less. This is the syntax:

```
SET variable = string1 string2 string3 . . .
```

Macro Samples

This section contains several macro examples with instructions.

Adding Columns

With this macro, you can add up the numbers in three-line columns with five characters in each number. You can also identify the number of columns to add. Before using the macro, you must set up the numbers in each column as well as insert tabs for the totals at the bottom of each column. The highlight must be at the left of the first column. Figure 21-1 shows a sample layout.

```
«COMMENT This macro adds columns of numbers»
«ASK columns = ?Type in the number of columns to add then
     press Enter»
«REPEAT columns»
<right><shift f6><right><right><right><right><down><down><f2>
<down><down><down><right><esc>I<enter><up><up><up>
«ENDREPEAT»
```

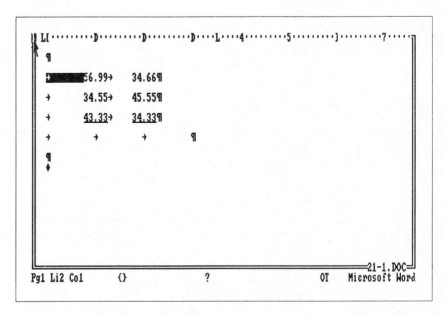

Figure 21-1. A sample column layout for use with the addition macro

The first line is a command that describes the macro. The ASK instruction causes this prompt to be displayed:

```
Type in the number of columns to add then press Enter
```

The user must type in the number of columns and press Enter to continue. The number of columns entered becomes the *columns* variable.

In the «REPEAT columns» instruction, the text between REPEAT and ENDREPEAT is repeated according to the number of columns entered by the user. The macro text between REPEAT and ENDREPEAT moves the highlight, turns on column select, adds the numbers in the column, inserts the total, and positions the highlight for calculating the next column.

Resetting Fields

You can use Word's macro capabilities to reset fields. In the following example, the ruler is toggled on or off, depending on the setting in the *show ruler* field.

```
<esc>O<down>
«IF field="Yes"»n
«ELSE»y
«ENDIF»<enter>
```

First, the Options *show ruler* field is accessed. If the field is set to Yes, the macro sets it to No. If it is set to No, the macro sets it to Yes.

Selecting .PRD Files

You may want to select different .PRD files for different documents. For example, if you are using a certain font, such as Times-Roman, you may need a different .PRD file than if you are using Courier. You can automate the selection of the .PRD file based on hidden text that you enter at the beginning of the document. Using this method not only saves you keystrokes but also relieves you of the task of remembering which .PRD file goes with each of the fonts you use. Here is a sample macro:

```
<esc>Stimes-roman<enter>
«IF found»<esc>POhplaser1<enter>
«ELSE»<esc>POhplaser3<enter>
«ENDIF»
<esc>
```

The macro searches for the words *times-roman*. If the words are found, Print Options is selected and the HPLASER1.PRD file is entered in the *printer* field. If *times-roman* is not found, Print Options is selected and the HPLASER3.PRD file is entered. <Esc> brings you back to the document.

Exercise: Using Macro Instructions

In this macro, you will open a second window and copy text to it. First, you will nest in the new macro, the WINDOWH.MAC macro created earlier, to open a horizontal window (window 2). Then the macro will take you to the original window and pause to allow you to select text. Once you have manually selected the text, the macro will copy the text to the scrap, move the highlight to window 2, and copy the text into that window.

Start with a single, blank Word window. Enter this text:

```
Ms. Judith Curry
45 Winslow Way
Topeka, Kansas 60333
```

Next, enter these macro instructions:

```
<ctrl esc>IWINDOWH.MAC<enter>
<f1>
«PAUSE Select the text to copy and press Enter»
<esc>C<enter>
<f1>
<esc>I<enter>
```

Select the macro text. Press Esc and then select Copy. In the Copy command's *to* field, enter this macro name and control code and then press Enter:

```
WINDOWCOPY.MAC^<ctrl w>c
```

Use the Transfer Save command to save the document with the name WINDOWCOPY.DOC. Test the macro. Edit the macro if it doesn't perform as planned. Once the macro is working correctly, save it in the active glossary file with Transfer Glossary Save.

A Quick Reference to Keyboard and Mouse Functions

Keyboard Functions

These keyboard functions may be used instead of menu selections or highlight scrolling.

Deleting and Inserting

Task	Press
Delete, not to scrap	Shift-Del
Delete to scrap	Del
Insert contents of scrap	Ins
Insert contents of scrap, replacing selection	Shift-Ins

Display

Task	Press
Show line breaks	Alt-F7
Switch text/graphics mode	Alt-F9

Editing

Task	Press
Copy to scrap	Alt-F3
Create footer	Alt-F2
Create header	Ctrl-F2
Go to designated page	Alt-F5
Insert nonbreaking space	Ctrl-Spacebar
Repeat last edit	F4
Repeat search	Shift-F4
Set tab	Alt-F1
Switch uppercase/lowercase	Ctrl-F4
Turn overtype mode on/off	F5
Turn show-layout mode on/off	Alt-F4
Undo	Shift-F1

Formatting

Format	Press Alt or Alt-X and
Bold	B
Double underline	D
Hidden	E
Italic	I
Normal character	Spacebar
Small caps	K
Strikethrough	S
Superscript	+ or =
Subscript	-
Underline	U
Center	C
Create hanging indent	T
Double space	2
Increase left indent	N
Indent first line to next tab	F
Indent from left and right	Q
Justify	J

Format	Press Alt or Alt-X and
Left flush	L
Open space above paragraph	O
Reduce left indent to previous tab	M
Return to normal paragraph	P
Right flush	R

Highlight Movement

Task	Press
Create new column	Ctrl-Alt-Enter
Create new division	Ctrl-Enter
Create new line	Shift-Enter
Create new page	Ctrl-Shift-Enter
Create new paragraph	Enter
Extend down one line	Shift-Down
Extend left one character	Shift-Left
Extend up one line	Shift-Up
Move between document and menu	Esc
Move to bottom of window	Ctrl-End
Move down one line	Down
Move down one windowful	PgDn
Move to end of document	Ctrl-PgDn
Move to end of line	End
Move to first character of next paragraph	Ctrl-Down
Move to first character of next word	Ctrl-Right
Move to first character of previous paragraph	Ctrl-Up
Move to first character of previous word	Ctrl-Left
Move left one character	Left
Move left one third window	Scroll Lock-Left
Move to next field in form	Ctrl->

Task	Press
Move to next show-layout object	Ctrl-Keypad 5-Right
Move to previous field in form	Ctrl-<
Move to previous show-layout object	Ctrl-Keypad 5-Left
Move right one character	Right
Move right one third window	Scroll Lock-Right
Move to start of document	Ctrl-PgUp
Move to start of line	Home
Move to top of window	Ctrl-Home
Move up one line	Up
Move up one windowful	PgUp
Scroll up one line	Scroll Lock-Up
Scroll down one line	Scroll Lock-Down

Hyphenating

Task	Press
Insert nonbreaking hyphen	Ctrl-Shift--
Insert optional hyphen	Ctrl--

Loading and Saving

Task	Press
Load	Ctrl-F7
Save	Ctrl-F10

Macros and Glossaries

Task	Press
Expand glossary name	F3
Step through macro	Ctrl-F3
Turn macro record on/off	Shift-F3

Mathematics

Task	Press
Calculate	F2

Outlines

Task	Press
Collapse body text	Shift-F11
Collapse heading	F11
Expand all	Ctrl-F12
Expand body text	Shift-F12
Expand heading	F12
Turn outline organize on/off	Shift-F5
Turn outline view on/off	Shift-F2

Printing

Task	Press
Change font name	Alt-F8
Print document	Ctrl-F8
Turn print-preview mode on/off	Ctrl-F9

Selecting

Task	Press
Turn column select on/off	Shift-F6
Select current line	Shift-F9
Extend selection down one windowful	Shift-PgDn
Extend selection right one character	Shift-Right
Turn extend select on/off	F6
Extend selection to end of line	Shift-End
Extend selection to start of line	Shift-Home
Extend selection up one window	Shift-PgUp
Select next word	F8
Select next sentence	Shift-F8
Select next paragraph	F10
Select previous paragraph	F9
Select previous sentence	Shift-F7
Select previous word	F7
Select whole document	Shift-F10

Special Tools

Task	Press
Get help	Alt-H
Mark all document-retrieval files	Ctrl-Spacebar
Mark/unmark document-retrieval file	Spacebar
Spell	Alt-F6
Thesaurus	Ctrl-F6
Turn line draw on/off	Ctrl-F5

Style Sheets

Task	Press
Record style	Alt-F10

Windows

Task	Press
Move to next window	F1
Zoom window in/out	Ctrl-F1

Mouse Functions

If you have a mouse, use this section to remind you of mouse operations.

Commands

Task	Procedure
Cancel command	Point in command area; click both buttons
Carry out command	Point to command name; click left button
Confirm command	Point in command area; click left button
See choices in command field	Point to command field; click right button

Task	Procedure
Select command, field, or option	Point to choice in command area; click left button
Select option and carry out command	Point to option in command field; click right button

Editing

Task	Procedure
Copy character format to selected text	Point to character in format; hold down Alt; click left button
Copy paragraph format to selected text	Point to selection bar to left of paragraph with format; hold down Alt; click right button
Copy selected text	Point to new location; hold down Shift; click left button
Move selected text	Point to new location; hold down Ctrl; click left button

Ruler

Task	Procedure
Move paragraph indents	Choose Format Paragraph; point to indent mark on ruler; hold down right button; move to new ruler position; release button
Turn ruler off	Point to upper-right corner of window; click both buttons
Turn ruler on	Point to upper-right corner of window; click left button

Scrolling

Location	Procedure
Down	Point to left window border; click right button
End of document	Point to bottom of left window border; click both buttons
Left	Point to bottom window border; click left button

Location	Procedure
Relative horizontal position	Point to bottom window border; click both buttons
Relative vertical position	Point to left window border; click both buttons
Right	Point to bottom window border; click right button
Start of document	Point to upper-left window border; click both buttons
Up	Point to left window border; click left button

Selecting

Selection desired	Procedure
Character	Point to character; click left button
Line	Point to selection bar to left of line; click left button
Paragraph	Point to selection bar to left of paragraph; click right button
Sentence	Point to sentence; click both buttons
Whole document	Point to selection bar; click both buttons
Word	Point to word; click right button

Tabs

Task	Procedure
Clear tab stops	Display ruler; point to tab marker on ruler; click both buttons
Move tab stops	Display ruler; point to tab marker on ruler; hold down right button; move to new position; release button
Set alignment or leader character	Display ruler; click on alignment letter at left of ruler or on leader character to left of alignment letter; point to desired ruler position and click left button
Set tab stops	Display ruler; point to desired ruler position; click left button to insert tab

Windows

Task	Procedure
Close window	Point to top or right border; click both buttons
Move border	Point to lower-right corner of window; hold down left button; move pointer to new spot; release button
Open empty window	Point to top or right border; click right button
Open footnote/ annotation window	Point to right border; hold down Shift; click left button
Return to window; show previous selection	Point to window number; click left button
Split horizontally	Point to right border; click left button
Split vertically	Point to top border; click left button
Zoom next window	Point to window number of zoomed window; click left button
Zoom/unzoom window	Point to window number; click right button

Supported Printers

This appendix presents a partial list of the printers supported by Word and their corresponding printer-driver (.PRD) files. If you can't find the file for your printer in the list, try using a generic printer driver. Word offers these four generic .PRD files:

Generic .PRD file	Type of printer
TTY.PRD	Dot matrix or teletype-like
TTYBS.PRD	Dot matrix or teletype-like with backspace
TTYFF.PRD	Dot matrix or teletype-like recognizing form-feed character at page end instead of carriage return
TTYWHEEL.PRD	Daisywheel printer

If the generic printer driver for your type of printer does not enable you to print your Word documents:

- Read the PRINTERS.DOC file to see what .PRD files have been recently added to the list.
- Contact the dealer from whom you bought your printer or the printer manufacturer.
- Contact the dealer or manufacturer of your printer.
- Call Microsoft Product Support.
- Create a printer driver using the MakePRD utility supplied with Word (see Chapter 5, "Printing Documents," for more information).

The list of supported printers and their drivers follows, together with notes about switch and Control-Panel settings.

Printer	Printer driver	Notes
ALPS ALQ 200/300	ALQ20018.PRD ALQ20024.PRD	18-pin print head 24-pin print head
ALPS P2000	ALPS2000.PRD	
ANADEX DP-6500	ANDX6500.PRD	
ANADEX DP-9625	ANDX9625.PRD	Switches SW1 and SW3 should be off
ANADEX DP-9725 and PRINTRONIX DP-9725 COLOR SCRIBE	ANDX9725.PRD	
ANADEX WP-6000	ANDX60CS.PRD ANDX60LT.PRD ANDX60DP.PRD	Correspondence quality Letter quality Draft quality
APPLE LASERWRITER	POSTSCRP.PRD PSDOWN.PRD	Built-in fonts Downloadable Adobe fonts The MODE command should be: MODE COM1:9600,N,8,1,P or MODE COM2:9600,N,8,1,P
AST TURBOLASER	ASTTURBO.PRD	
AST TURBOLASER/PS	POSTSCRP.PRD	
BROTHER BPI 5420AI	BPI5420.PRD	
BROTHER HR-15/25/35	BROTHER.PRD	
BROTHER M-1509/1709	BROM1509.PRD	
BROTHER M-1724L	BROM1724.PRD	
BROTHER SP-1000	BROM1509.PRD	

Printer	Printer driver	Notes
BROTHER TWINRITER 5	TWIN5DM.PRD BROTWIN5.PRD	Dot-matrix print head Daisywheel print head
BUSINESSLAND 45LQ	BL45LQ.PRD	
C.ITOH C-310/15 XP and CXP menu	CITOH310.PRD	Use the front panel to select IBM Proprinter emulation mode
C.ITOH C715A RELIANT	CITOH715.PRD	Typically, set middle alignment through the control panel
C.ITOH CIE LIPS 10 PLUS	LIPS10-1.PRD LIPS 10-2.PRD	Cartridges B, D, E, G, H, J
	LIPS 10-2.PRD	Cartridges 6-F, 11-K
	LIPS 10-3.PRD	
	LIPS 10-L.PRD	
C.ITOH F10-40/55	CITOHF10.PRD	
C.ITOH JET-SETTER	CITOHJS1.PRD	Portrait fonts on B, C, D, H, J, K, L cartridges
	CITOHJS2.PRD	Portrait fonts on F, K cartridges
	CITOHJS3.PRD	Portrait fonts on T cartridge
	CITOHJSL.PRD	Landscape fonts for internal fonts and G cartridge
C.ITOH PROWRITER 815 SUPRA	CITOH815.PRD	
C.ITOH PROWRITER JUNIOR	CITOHPJR.PRD	
C.ITOH STARWRITER FP-1500-45P	CITOHSTR.PRD	
CANON BJ-130 BUBBLE JET	CANONBJ.PRD	
CANON LBP-8A1/A2	CANON.PRD CANON-L.PRD	Portrait mode Landscape mode

Printer	Printer driver	Notes
CANON LBP-8II, LBP-8IIR and LBP-8IIT	CANON8II.PRD CANON8-L.PRD	Portrait mode Landscape mode If serial interface, set mode to 9600,N,8,1,P
CITIZEN MSP-10/15	CITMSP10.PRD	
CITIZEN MSP-50/55	CITMSP50.PRD	
CORDATA LP300/CORONA LP300	CORDATA.PRD	
DEC LN03 LASER PRINTER	DECLN03.PRD DECLN03L.PRD	Portrait mode Landscape mode
DIABLO 620	D620.PRD	
DIABLO 630/630 API/630 ECS	D630.PRD D630A.PRD D630ECS.PRD	DIABLO 630 DIABLO 630 API DIABLO 630 ECS
DIABLO P32	DP32.PRD	
EPSON EX-800/1000	EPSONEX.PRD	
EPSON FX PRINTERS	EPSONFX.PRD EPSONFXQ.PRD	Microspace justification No microspace justification
EPSON GQ-3500	GQ3500P.PRD GQ3500L.PRD	Portrait mode Landscape mode
EPSON JX-80	EPSONJX.PRD	
EPSON LQ-500	EPSONLQ3.PRD	
EPSON LQ-800/1000	EPSONLQ1.PRD	
EPSON LQ-850/1050	EPSONLQ2.PRD	
EPSON LQ-1500	EPSONLQ.PRD	
EPSON LQ-2500	LQ2500.PRD	
EPSON LX-80/86	EPSONLX.PRD	
EPSON LX-800	EPLX800.PRD	
EPSON	EPSONMX.PRD	Without GRAFTRAX

Printer	Printer driver	Notes
MX-80/100 and MX-80/100 with GRAFTRAX/ GRAFTRAX PLUS	GRAFTRAX.PRD EPSONMXG.PRD	With GRAFTRAX With GRAFTRAX PLUS
EPSON RX-80/100	EPSONRX.PRD	
EPSON SQ-2000	EPSONSQ.PRD	
FUJITSU DL2400	FDL2400.PRD	
FUJITSU DL2600/5600	FDL2600.PRD	
FUJITSU DX-2300/2400	FDX2000F.PRD	EPSON and DX 2300F emulation
	FDX2000I.PRD	IBM emulation
		For EPSON emulation, put inside toggle switch at F position
		For IBM emulation, put inside toggle switch at I position
HEWLETT-PACKARD 2934A	HP2934A.PRD	
HEWLETT-PACKARD DESKJET 2276A	HPDESK1.PRD	Internal fonts and A, B, C cartridges
	HPDESK2.PRD	Internal fonts and D, E, F cartridges
	HPDESK3.PRD	Internal fonts and G, H, J cartridges
	HPDESK4.PRD	Internal fonts and M, P, Q cartridges
HEWLETT-PACKARD LASERJET	HPLASER.PRD HPLASER1.PRD	Internal fonts Portrait cartridges A, B, C, D, E, G, H, J, L, Q, W, X
	HPLASER2.PRD	Portrait cartridges F, K, P, R, U
	HPLASER3.PRD	Portrait cartridges J, R, Z

Printer	Printer driver	Notes
	HPLASPS.PRD	Portrait cartidge B US ASCII symbol set
	HPLASRMN.PRD	Potrait cartidge F ROMAN 8 symbol set
	HPLAS2S1.PRD	Portrait cartridge S1 PC-8 symbol set
	HPLAS2S2.PRD	Portrait cartridge S2 PC-8 symbol set
	HPLASTAX.PRD	Portrait cartridge T ASCII and LINEDRAW symbol sets
	HPPCCOUR.PRD	Portrait cartridge Y PC SET 1 symbol set
	HPLASMS.PRD	Portrait cartridge Z MICROSOFT 1 ECMA symbol set
	HPLASMS2.PRD	Portrait cartridge Z MICROSOFT 1 ROMAN 8 symbol set
	HPLASMSA.PRD	Portrait cartridge Z MICROSOFT 1A ASCII symbol set
	HPLASLAN.PRD	Landscape cartridges A, B, C, G, H, L, M, N, P, Q, R, U, V
	HPLASMSL.PRD	Landscape cartridge Z ROMAN 8 symbol set
	HPDWNACP.PRD	Portrait AC font set TMSRMN/HELV base font ASCII symbol set
	HPDWNACL.PRD	Landscape AC font set TMSRMN/HELV base font ASCII symbol set
	HPDWNADP.PRD	Portrait AD font set TMSRMN/HELV base font ROMAN 8 symbol set

Printer	Printer driver	Notes
	HPDWNADL.PRD	Landscape AD font set
		TMSRMN/HELV base font
		ROMAN 8 symbol set
	HPDWNSFL.PRD	Landscape AC and AE font sets
		ASCII symbol set
	HPDWNSFP.PRD	Portrait AC and AE font sets
		ASCII symbol set
	HPDWNR8L.PRD	Landscape AD and AF font sets
		TMSRMN/HELV base and supplemental fonts
		ROMAN 8 symbol set
	HPDWNR8P.PRD	Portrait AD and AF font sets
		ROMAN 8 symbol set
	HPDWNHHP.PRD	Portrait AG font set
		HELVE HEADLINE base font
		ROMAN 8 symbol set
	HPDWNLGL.PRD	Landscape DA font set
		LETTER GOTHIC base font
		Several symbol sets
	HPDWNLGP.PRD	Portrait DA font set
		Several symbol sets
	HPDWNPRL.PRD	Landscape EA font set
		PRESTIGE ELITE family
		Several symbol sets
	HPDWNPRP.PRD	EA Portrait font set
		PRESTIGE ELITE family
	HPDWNGAP.PRD	Portrait RA font set
		ITC GARAMOND ASCII symbol set
	HPDWNA8.PRD	Portrait RB font set
		ITC GARAMOND ROMAN 8 symbol set

Printer	Printer driver	Notes
	HPDWNCNP.PRD	Portrait SA font set
		CENTURY SCHOOLBOOK ASCII symbol set
	HPDWNCN8.PRD	Portrait RB font set
		ITC GARAMOND ROMAN 8 symbol set
	HPDWNCNP.PRD	Portrait SA font set
		CENTURY SCHOOLBOOK ASCII symbol set
	HPDWNCN8.PRD	Portrait SB font set
		CENTURY SCHOOLBOOK ROMAN 8 symbol set
	HPDWNZHP.PRD	Portrait TA font set
		ZAPFT HUMANIST ASCII symbol set
	HPDWNZH8.PRD	Portrait TB font set
		ZAPFT HUMANIST ROMAN 8 symbol set
	HPDWNHLP.PRD	Portrait UA font set
		HEADLINE TYPEFACE COLLECTION ASCII symbol set
	HPDWNHL8.PRD	Portrait UB font set
		HEADLINE TYPEFACE COLLECTION ROMAN 8 symbol set
HEWLETT-PACKARD PAINTJET	HPPAINT.PRD	PC-8ROM8 dip switch should be set to PC-8 for graphics
HEWLETT-PACKARD QUIETJET PLUS	HPQUIET.PRD	
HEWLETT-PACKARD THINKJET	HPTHINK.PRD	
IBM COLOR INKJET	IBMCOLOR.PRD	Draft quality
	IBMCLRLQ.PRD	Near letter quality
IBM GRAPHICS PRINTER	IBMGRAPH.PRD	

Printer	Printer driver	Notes
IBM PAGEPRINTER 3812	PRGEDL.PRD	All fonts for these PRD files: PAGEMDRN.PRD PAGEMN.PRD PAGEPS.PRD PAGESNRN.PRD
IBM PERSONAL PAGEPRINTER 4216	IBMLASER.PRD	
IBM PROPRINTER SERIES	IBMPRO.PRD IBMPROXL.PRD IBMPRO3.PRD IBMXL24.PRD IBMXL24D.PRD	Proprinter PROPRINTER II and XL PROPRINTER III/IIIXL PROPRINTER X24/XL24 PROPRINTER X24 and XL24
IBM QUICKWRITER	IBMQUICK.PRD	
IBM QUIETWRITER I and II	IBMQUIET.PRD	
IBM QUIETWRITER III	IBMQWTR3.PRD	
IBM WHEEL PRINTER	IBMWHEEL.PRD	
KYOCERA F-1010	KYOCERAP.PRD KYOCERAL.PRD	Portrait mode Landscape mode
MANNESMANN TALLY 1X	MT1X.PRD	
MANNESMANN TALLY 80	MT80.PRD	
MANNESMANN TALLY 330	MT330.PRD	
MANNESMANN TALLY 910	MT910.PRD MT910BS.PRD MT910IS.PRD	Internal cartridge fonts BUSINESS style Downloadable font sets INDUSTRY style Downloadable font sets

Printer	Printer driver	Notes
	MT910SF.PRD	SPECIALTY fonts Downloadable font sets
	MT910DP.PRD	DATA PROCESSING Downloadable font sets
NCR-6416 LASER PRINTER	NCR6416.PRD	
NEC LC860+	NEC860_1.PRD	Portrait fonts on B, C, D, H, J, K, L cartridges
	NEC860_2.PRD	Portrait fonts on F and K cartridges
	NEC860_3.PRD	Portrait fonts on T cartridge
	NEC860_L.PRD	Internal and cartridge landscape fonts
NEC P6/P7 AND NEC P5 XL/P9 XL	NEC.PRD	
NEC P560/P565	NECP5.PRD	
NEC PINWRITER P2/P3	NECP2.PRD	
NEC PINWRITER P2200	NECP2200.PRD	
NEC SILENTWRITER 890	POSTSCRP.PRD	
NEC SPINWRITER 3550	NEC3550.PRD	
NEC SPINWRITER 7710	NEC7710.PRD	
OKIDATA 192	OKI192.PRD	No microspace justification or proportional fonts
	OKI192PS.PRD	Microspace justification and proportional fonts
	OKI92.PRD	For OKI model
OKIDATA 292/293	OKI292.PRD	

Printer	Printer driver	Notes
OKIDATA LASERLINE 6/8	OKILASER.PRD OKISLAN.PRD	Portrait mode Landscape mode
OKIDATA MICROLINE 92/93	OKI92.PRD	
OKIDATA MICROLINE 393/393C	OKI393.PRD	
OKIDATA PACEMARK 2410	OKI2410.PRD	
PANASONIC KX-1092I/1091I and KX-P1080I/ P1592	PANA1092.PRD PANA1080.PRD	For KX-1092I/1091I For DX-P1080I/P1592)
PANASONIC KX-P1524	PANA1524.PRD	
PANASONIC KX-P4450 LASER	PANA4450.PRD	
POSTSCRIPT PRINTERS	POSTSCRP.PRD PSDOWN.PRD	Supports most fonts Supports ADOBE POSTSCRIPT fonts
QMS KISS/KISS PLUS	QMSKISS.PRD QMSPOR.PRD	Built-in fonts Downloadable fonts in portrait mode
	QMSLAN.PRD	Downloadable fonts in landscape mode
	QMSSMART.PRD	Cartridge fonts KISS PLUS only
QMS PS 800/800 PS II	POSTSCRP.PRD	
QMS SMARTWRITER	QMSSMART.PRD	SMARTWRITER cartridges
	QMSPOR.PRD	Downloadable fonts in portrait mode
	QMSLAN.PRD	Downloadable fonts in landscape mode
QUADRAM QUADLASER	QUADLASR.PRD	

Printer	Printer driver	Notes
QUME SPRINT 11	QUME11.PRD	
RICOH LP4080	RICOHLP.PRD	Portrait mode
	RICHOLPL.PRD	Landscape mode
RICHO PC LASER 6000	RICOHPC.PRD	Portrait mode
	RICOHPCL.PRD	Landscape mode
SEIKOSHA BPI-5420AI	BPI5420.PRD	
SEIKOSHA SP-1000	SP1000.PRD	
SILVER REED EXP 400	SREXP.PRD	
STAR MICRONICS DELTA	DELTA.PRD	
STAR MICRONICS NB 24-15	STARNB24.PRD	
STAR MICRONICS NX-10/15	STARNX15.PRD	
STAR MICRONICS RADIX	RADIX.PRD	
TANDY DMP 106	DMP106.PRD	
TANDY DMP 130	DMP130.PRD	If the computer is not TANDY, set the dip switches for IBM mode emulation (see printer manual)
TANDY DMP 200	DMP200.PRD	
TANDY DMP 400	DMP400.PRD	
TANDY DMP 430	DMP430.PRD	
TANDY DMP 2100	DMP2100.PRD	Print in standard mode
	CMP2100.PRD	Print in condensed mode

Printer	Printer driver	Notes
TANDY DMP 2100P	DMP2100P.PRD	
TANDY DMP 2110/2120	DMP2110.PRD DMP2120.PRD	TANDY DMP 2110 TANDY DMP 2120
TANDY DMP 2200	DMP2200.PRD	
TANDY DW II/ DW IIB	DWII.PRD DWIIB.PRD	DW II model DW IIB model
TANDY DWP 220/230	DWP220.PRD DWP230.PRD	DWP 220 model DWP 230 model
TANDY DWP 510/520	DWP510.PRD DWP520.PRD	DWP 510 model DWP 520 model
TANDY LP 1000	LP1000.PRD	
TEXAS INSTRUMENTS 850	TI850.PRD	
TEXAS INSTRUMENTS 855/857	TI855.PRD	
TEXAS INSTRUMENTS OMNILASER1 and OMNILASER 2108/2115	POSTSCRP.PRD	
TOSHIBA P321, P321SL/341SL	TOSHP321.PRD	
TOSHIBA P351/ P351C	TOSHP351.PRD	
TOSHIBA P351 SX/P351 SXC	P351SX.PRD	
TOSHIBA P1340	TOSH1340.PRD	
TOSHIBA P1350/ P1351	TOSH1351.PRD	
TOSHIBA PAGELASER	TOSHLAS1.PRD	Cartridges with ROMAN 8 symbol set
	TOSHLAS2.PRD	Cartridges with US ASCII symbol set
XEROX 2700 LASER PRINTER	X2700.PRD	

Printer	Printer driver	Notes
XEROX 4020	X4020.PRD	
XEROX 4045	X4045PSP.PRD	Portrait mode
	X4045PSL.PRD	Landscape mode
	X4045.PRD	Cartridges or self downloading
	X4045DLP.PRD	Portrait mode automatic downloading
	X4045DLL.PRD	Landscape mode automatic downloading

Extended Character Set Codes

The display characters assigned to the 256 codes in the extended character set are shown below. To enter characters in your document:

1. Hold down the **Alt** key.
2. Enter the character code on the numeric keypad. Do not use the numbers across the top of your keyboard.
3. Release the **Alt** key.

The character shown in the Character column of the following table appears on your screen.

For codes below 33 and above 126, the character that appears on your screen is not necessarily the character that your printer will print. See Chapter 5, "Printing Documents," for instructions on how to use the CHARACTER_TEST.MAC macro to find out which characters your printer assigns to the extended-character-set codes. Your printer may not assign a character to every code.

Code	Character	Code	Character	Code	Character
0	(null)	10	■	20	¶
1	☺	11	♂	21	§
2	●	12	♀	22	▬
3	♥	13	♪	23	↨
4	♦	14	♫	24	↑
5	♣	15	☼	25	↓
6	♠	16	▶	26	→
7	●	17	◀	27	←
8	▪	18	↕	28	∟
9	○	19	‼	29	↔

Code	Character	Code	Character	Code	Character
30	▲	82	R	134	à
31	▼	83	S	135	ç
32		84	T	136	ê
33	!	85	U	137	ë
34	"	86	V	138	è
35	#	87	W	139	ï
36	$	88	X	140	î
37	%	89	Y	141	ì
38	&	90	Z	142	Ä
39	'	91	[	143	Å
40	(	92	\	144	É
41	)	93	]	145	æ
42	*	94	^	146	Æ
43	+	95	—	147	ô
44	,	96	`	148	ö
45	-	97	a	149	ò
46	.	98	b	150	û
47	/	99	c	151	ù
48	0	100	d	152	ÿ
49	1	101	e	153	Ö
50	2	102	f	154	Ü
51	3	103	g	155	¢
52	4	104	h	156	£
53	5	105	i	157	¥
54	6	106	j	158	P_t
55	7	107	k	159	ƒ
56	8	108	l	160	á
57	9	109	m	161	í
58	:	110	n	162	ó
59	;	111	o	163	ú
60	<	112	p	164	ñ
61	=	113	q	165	Ñ
62	>	114	r	166	ª
63	?	115	s	167	º
64	@	116	t	168	¿
65	A	117	u	169	⌐
66	B	118	v	170	¬
67	C	119	w	171	½
68	D	120	x	172	¼
69	E	121	y	173	¡
70	F	122	z	174	«
71	G	123	{	175	»
72	H	124	¦	176	░
73	I	125	}	177	▒
74	J	126	~	178	▓
75	K	127	DEL	179	│
76	L	128	Ç	180	┤
77	M	129	ü	181	╡
78	N	130	é	182	╢
79	O	131	â	183	╖
80	P	132	ä	184	╕
81	Q	133	à	185	╣

Code	Character	Code	Character	Code	Character
186	‖	210	╥	234	Ω
187	╗	211	╙	235	δ
188	╝	212	╘	236	∞
189	╜	213	╒	237	φ
190	╛	214	╓	238	ε
191	┐	215	╫	239	∩
192	└	216	╪	240	≡
193	┴	217	┘	241	±
194	┬	218	┌	242	≥
195	├	219	█	243	≤
196	─	220	▄	244	⌠
197	┼	221	▌	245	⌡
198	╞	222	▐	246	÷
199	╟	223	▀	247	≈
200	╚	224	α	248	°
201	╔	225	β	249	•
202	╩	226	Γ	250	·
203	╦	227	π	251	√
204	╠	228	Σ	252	η
205	═	229	σ	253	²
206	╬	230	μ	254	■
207	╧	231	τ	255	(blank)
208	╨	232	Φ		
209	╤	233	Θ		

Advanced Setup Procedures

Modifying CONFIG.SYS and AUTOEXEC.BAT

Before you install Word, you need to make some decisions about two important files: CONFIG.SYS and AUTOEXEC.BAT.

The CONFIG.SYS file gives your operating system information about your computer system. If you do not have a CONFIG.SYS file, the operating system uses default settings. AUTOEXEC.BAT is a batch file that runs a specific set of DOS commands every time you start up your computer, saving you the trouble of typing in the commands one by one. The AUTOEXEC.BAT file is optional. If it exists, you will find it in your root directory or on your operating-system working disk.

CONFIG.SYS Commands Needed by Word

When you use Word's Setup utility to install Word, Setup automatically changes your CONFIG.SYS file to meet Word's requirements. Some people do not want Setup to change their CONFIG.SYS file because Word's requirements may not be the same as those of other programs they use. If you are one of these people, just make sure your CONFIG.SYS file includes the following commands and skip Setup's offer to change the file for you.

If you are using DOS, your CONFIG.SYS should contain these two commands:

- On a hard-disk system or a network workstation:

    FILES = 20 (or more)
    DEVICE = *MOUSE_PATH*\MOUSE.SYS

If you are using OS/2, your CONFIG.SYS should contain these commands:

- On a hard-disk system or a network workstation:

    IOPL = Yes (or add Word to the path)

- On a hard-disk system:

    SET PATH = *WORD_DIRECTORY*

- On a network workstation:

    SETPATH = *SERVER_DIRECTORY*
    SET MSWNET = *LOCAL_WORD_DIRECTORY*

For dual boot systems (DOS and OS/2), change the CONFIG.SYS file manually. Instructions for changing the CONFIG.SYS file on DOS two-floppy-disk and hard-disk systems follow. These instructions assume that you are using DOS 2.0 or a later version. (For OS/2 instructions, see the OS/2 manual.)

Changing CONFIG.SYS on a DOS Two-Floppy-Disk System

If you have a two-floppy-disk system and you want to change the CONFIG.SYS file yourself (instead of letting Word's Setup utility do it for you), follow these instructions:

1. Insert your working DOS disk in drive A.
2. At the A> prompt, type in:

    COPY CON:A:CONFIG.SYS

3. Press **Enter**.
4. Type in the changes and press **Enter**.
5. Hold down **Ctrl** and press the **Z** key. This message appears on your monitor:

```
^Z
1 File(s) copied
```

Word can now use the updated CONFIG.SYS file. Restart your system, using the disk on which you altered the CONFIG.SYS file.

Changing CONFIG.SYS on a DOS Hard-Disk System

If you have a hard-disk system you can also change the CONFIG.SYS file yourself (instead of using Setup). Follow these instructions:

1. At the C> prompt, type in the following to go to the proper directory:

```
CD\
```

2. Press **Enter**.
3. Type in:

```
DIR CONFIG.SYS
```

4. If DOS displays the message *File not found*, follow these instructions:

   a. Type in:

   ```
   COPY CON CONFIG.SYS
   ```

   b. Press **Enter**.
   c. Type in the following line (using the number 20 or larger):

   ```
   FILES = 20
   ```

   d. Press **Enter**.
   e. If you are using a mouse, type in:

   ```
   DEVICE = MOUSEPATH\MOUSE.SYS
   ```

   f. Press **Enter**.
   g. Hold down the **Ctrl** key and press the **Z** key. This message appears on your screen:

   ```
   ^Z
   1 File(s) copied
   ```

5. If you see *config.sys* after entering *DIR CONFIG.SYS*, follow these instructions:

   a. Type in:

   ```
   TYPE CONFIG.SYS
   ```

   b. Press **Enter**.

   c. DOS displays the commands in your CONFIG.SYS file on the screen. If FILES equals less than 20, type in the following line (using the number 20 or larger) then press **Enter**:

   ```
   FILES = 20
   ```

   d. If you are using a mouse, type in the following and press **Enter**:

   ```
   DEVICE = MOUSEPATH\MOUSE.SYS
   ```

   e. Hold down the **Ctrl** key and press the **Z** key. This message appears on your screen:

   ```
   ^Z1 File(s) copied
   ```

Restart your computer so the new CONFIG.SYS file is used.

Useful AUTOEXEC.BAT Commands

Any command can be placed in an AUTOEXEC.BAT file. You might find it useful to enter a PATH command that will tell DOS where to find the directory that contains your Word program files. Here is an example using a directory called WORD:

```
PATH = c:\WORD
```

If you are working on a network, the AUTOEXEC.BAT file must contain the identification of the workstation Word directory, and this directory or drive must be read/write. Word writes the MW.INI file to this directory. The MW.INI file contains the changes you have made to Word's default settings. Here is an example of a command that identifies the workstation Word directory in the AUTOEXEC.BAT file:

```
SET MSWNET=LOCAL_WORD_DIRECTORY
```

If you are using DOS or OS/2, your AUTOEXEC.BAT file should contain the information below.

- On a hard disk or workstation:

```
PATH = WORD_DIRECTORY
```

- On a network workstation:

```
PATH = SERVER_DIRECTORY
SET MSWNET = LOCAL_WORD_DIRECTORY
```

If you are using DOS, you can alter your AUTOEXEC.BAT file with the following steps (see your OS/2 manual for instructions specific to that operating system):

1. At the system prompt, enter:

```
COPY CON AUTOEXEC.BAT
```

2. Press **Enter**.
3. Enter the commands you want stored in the file.
4. Press **F6**. This message appears on your screen:

```
^Z
```

5. Press **Enter**.

Using Word to Edit CONFIG.SYS or AUTOEXEC.BAT

You can use Word to edit your CONFIG.SYS file, AUTOEXEC.BAT file, or other similar files. Here is the procedure to follow:

1. From within Word, select **Transfer L**oad or press **Ctrl-F7**.
2. Enter the path of the file you want (such as C:\CONFIG.SYS).
3. Edit the file as desired.
4. Select **Transfer S**ave or press **Ctrl-F10** to save the document. Do not change the file name. Press **Enter** or, if you are using a mouse, click the command name.
5. Select **Q**uit.
8. Restart your computer.

Using Word with a RAM Drive

A RAM drive turns a portion of your computer's memory into an electronic disk drive. If you have expanded memory (more than 640 KB), processing can be noticeably faster when you work with a RAM drive.

Saving work to a RAM drive means that the work is still in temporary memory (not on permanent disk storage). Periodically save your work to permanent storage because work saved to the RAM drive is still vulnerable to loss due to power failure.

You can purchase an electronic RAM drive or create one with your operating system. To create a RAM drive in DOS, follow these steps:

1. Insert the DOS disk in drive A.
2. Type in:

   `COPY CON A:CONFIG.SYS`

3. Press **Enter**.
4. Type in this line (using the number 20 or larger):

   `FILES = 20`

5. Press **Enter**.
6. Type in this line:

   `DEVICE = RAMDRIVE.SYS`

7. Press **Enter**.
8. Press **Ctrl-Z**. This message appears:

   `File(s) copied`

To use Word with the RAM drive, follow these steps:

1. From the Word disk, use your operating system Copy command to copy these files to the RAM drive:
   - *.PGM (all files with the .PGM extension)
   - MW.INI (option settings)
   - WORD.EXE (the file that starts Word)
   - HYPH.DAT

- MW.HLP (optional help files)
- The .PRD files for the printers you'll use
- SCREEN.VID (the video driver)

For example, in DOS you would enter the following after the system prompt to copy the .PGM files to a RAM drive designated as drive D:

```
COPY *.PGM D:
```

2. Make the RAM drive the active drive by entering its letter identifier. For example, to go to a RAM drive designated as drive D, enter:

```
D:
```

3. Start Word from the RAM drive.

Your work can be saved to the RAM drive but always copy your work from the RAM drive to permanent storage before turning off your computer.

Creating Read-Only Files on a Network

Most files are read/write. This means that you can look at the file (read it), edit it, and save (write) it back on disk. If you do not want anyone to be able to change a file, you might want to make the file read only. You cannot enter edits in a read-only file and save it with the original file name; you can edit a read-only file only if you intend to save it under a new name.

Use the read-only option any time you want people to be able to use a file but not make changes to the *original* file. For example, NORMAL.STY, the default style sheet, can be shared by many users on a network. It is a good idea to keep this style sheet intact to avoid creating formatting problems in the documents of other users on the network. A read-only file is also handy when you want people to be able to view, but not change, a file. For example, you might want to circulate personnel rules on a disk. You would want employees to be able to read the document but not change the policies.

On a network, you can identify a file as read only either permanently or temporarily. Word has two utilities that Setup places in the Word program directory to allow you to create permanent read-only files on a network:

Utility	Purpose
RDONLY	To make files read only
RDWRITE	To change a read-only file back to a read/write file

Once you have identified a file as permanently read only with the RDONLY utility, you must use the RDWRITE utility to change its status back to read/write.

You identify a file as temporarily read only when you load the file with Transfer Load. The file retains its read-only status for the period of time you are accessing it. This allows other users on a network to view the file at the same time.

When you load a read-only file, a message appears indicating its read-only status. Word places an asterisk (*) before the file name that appears on your screen.

Using the RDONLY Utility

Use the RDONLY utility to change a file's status from read/write to read only. Enter the name of the file you want to change. You can use wildcards to change more than one file at a time. For example, the following file name uses an asterisk (*) as a wildcard to change all the files with the name beginning with LET and ending with .DOC:

LET*.DOC

Follow these steps to use RDONLY:

1. From the system prompt, move to the directory where the RDONLY utility is stored. For example, typing in this command after the system prompt and pressing **Enter** places you in the WORD directory:

```
CD \WORD
```

2. From the system prompt, type in RDONLY, the path, and the name of the file you want to identify as read only. Press **Enter**. In this example, the status of the file named CALENDAR.DOC, which is stored in the DOC directory, will be changed to read only:

```
RDONLY DOC\CALENDAR.DOC
```

Make sure you have entered the path and file name correctly.

There are no special prompts or messages to let you know when the procedure is complete. When your computer has finished processing, the file's status will be read only.

Once the status is changed, the file can be read but not overwritten with an edited version. If you attempt to save an edited version of the file with Transfer Save, Word prevents the save and responds with this message:

`Read-only file must be saved with a different name`

To save an edited version of a read-only file, enter a new file name when you select the Transfer Save command. Files that you make read only by this method remain read only until you use the RDWRITE utility.

Using the RDWRITE Utility

The RDWRITE utility allows you to change a read-only file back to a read/write file. When you specify the file name, you can use wildcards (*) to change more than one file at a time.

Follow these steps:

1. From the system prompt, move to the directory where the RDWRITE utility is stored. For example, typing in this command after the system prompt and pressing **Enter** places you in the WORD directory:

   `CD WORD`

2. From the system prompt, type in RDWRITE, the path, and the name of the file whose status you want to change to read/write. Press **Enter**. In this example, the file named CALENDAR.DOC will become a read/write file:

   `RDWRITE DOC\CALENDAR.DOC`

Be sure you enter the file name correctly. If you enter the name of a file that does not exist, no message appears to indicate your error. It is possible to overlook the incorrect entry and proceed as if the file has been made read/write when, in fact, it has not.

Once the process is complete, you can read, edit, and overwrite the file with its original name.

Temporarily Changing a File to Read Only

You can temporarily change a file to read-only status by loading it as a read-only file. When you clear the file from your screen, the file's status reverts to read/write.

To temporarily change a file's status to read only, follow these steps:

1. Select **T**ransfer **L**oad.
2. Enter the file name.
3. In the read-only field, select **Y**es.
4. Press **Enter**. Word loads the document with an asterisk (*) before the name (shown in the lower-right corner of the screen) to indicate that it is a read-only file.

If you load a file as read-only and then edit it, Word will refuse to save any changes to the file. If you attempt to save the changes, you will see a message like:

```
Read-only file must be saved with a different name
```

Index

D